SHEFFIELD ENVIRONMENTAL AND ARCHAEOLOGICAL
RESEARCH CAMPAIGN IN THE HEBRIDES

VOLUME 6

FROM CLAN TO CLEARANCE

*History and Archaeology on the Isle of Barra
c. 850–1850 AD*

KEITH BRANIGAN

with

J. M. Bumsted, D. Barker, P. Foster and C. Merrony

and contributions from

E. Campbell, L. Cihakova, R. Craigie, C. Cumberpatch, S. Davis, M. J. Dearne, M. Edmonds,
C. Frederick, J. Heron, J. Swann and C. R. Wickham-Jones

Oxbow Books

Published by
Oxbow Books, Park End Place, Oxford OX1 1HN

ISBN 1 84217 160 7

A CIP record for this book is available from The British Library

This book is available direct from
Oxbow Books, Park End Place, Oxford OX1 1HN
(Phone: 01865-241249; Fax: 01865-794449)

and

The David Brown Book Company
PO Box 511, Oakville, CT 06779, USA
(Phone: 860-945-9329; Fax: 860-945-9468)

and

our website
ww.oxbowbooks.com

*The author is pleased to acknowledge the generous support
of the Leverhulme Trust during the documentary research
and the preparation of this volume for publication*

Printed in Great Britain at
The Short Run Press, Exeter

Contents

SCROLL OF SUBSCRIBERS

We are pleased to record the support of the following subscribers who helped ensure the publication of this volume:

Alfred Adams, St Louis, Missouri
Peggy Bennett, Kippens, Newfoundland
Jane Brooks, Newburyport, Massachusetts
Bernadine Campbell, Richmond Hill, Ontario
Mary Currie, Sydney, Nova Scotia
Don Duffy, Palgrave, Ontario
Norma Duffy, Palgrave, Ontario
Carol Ewald, Portland, Maine
Debbie Fazekas-Maclean, Baddeck, Nova Scotia
Ruth French, Glasgow, Scotland
Stephen French, Glasgow, Scotland
Veronica Girdwood, Thursby, Cumbria
Mary Gumlak, Marion, Massachusetts
Sarah Christine Gumlak, Marion , Massachusetts
Michael.R.Hall,Stockton on Tees, Durham
Elizabeth Hamilton, Nanaimo, British Columbia
Wyn M.Hamilton, Calgary, Alberta
Highland Village Museum, Iona, Nova Scotia
John Hoetker, Schenectady, New York
Margaret Karrer, Windsor, Ontario
Oighrig Keogh, Aurora, Ontario
Valerie Levesque, Sydney, Nova Scotia
Mary Jane McCool, Bridgewater, Massachusetts
Juanita MacDonald, Whycocomagh, Nova Scotia
Lawrence B.McGurk, Natick, Massachusetts
Russell F.McGurk, Washington, DC
William McGurk, Vernon River, P.E.I.
William McGurk III, Lakeville, Massachustts
Kathy McHale, Needham, Massachusetts
Lorna McIlroy, Grand Prairie, Alberta
Penelope MacKinnon, Northbay, Barra
Virginia MacKinnon, Whangerei, NZ
Catherine MacLean, Northbay, Barra
Donald E.McNeal, Aurora, Colorado
Macneil and Mrs Macneil of Barra
Allan MacNeill, Vancouver, British Columbia
Alene McNeill, Newmarket, Ontario
Barbara McNeil, Buzzards Bay, Massachusetts
Bruce MacNeil, Lincolm,, Massachusetts
Calum MacNeil, Nask, Barra
Calum MacNeil, Selkirk, Ontario
Daniel S.MacNeil, Aurora, Ontario
David M.MacNeil, Lakehead, California
Dian MacNeil, Selkirk, Ontario
Don MacNeill, Halifax, Nova Scotia

Doreen MacNeil, Glen, Barra
Elizabeth McNeill, Lauderhill, Florida
H.J.McNeil, Modesto, California
Heather MacNeil, Glen, Barra
Helen McNeil, Ottawa, Ontario
Jon McNeil, Linden Park, South Australia
John Macneil, Cambridge, Ontario
Leslie MacNeil, Bow, New Hampshire
Malcolm McNeil, Linden Park, South Australia
Mary MacNeill, Brampton, Ontario
Neil MacNeil, Aurora, Ontario
Neil M.McNeil, Calgary, Alberta
Paul J.McNeil II, Lakewood, Washington
Phyllis MacNeil, Woods Hole, Massachusetts
Rhoda MacNeil, Nask, Barra
Rod MacNeil, Oshawa, Ontario
Rod C.MacNeil, Barra Glen, Nova Scotia
Teresa Macneil, Bruernish, Barra
Tony McNeil, Ottawa, Ontario
Vincent MacNeil, Bedford, Nova Scotia
William J.McNeil, Buzzards Bay, Massachusetts
William M.MacNeil, Los Angeles, California
Chrissie MacPherson, Balnabodach, Barra
Murdock MacPherson, Creignish, Nova Scotia
Niall MacPherson*, Balnabodach, Barra
Yvette S.Moon, Wyongah, New South Wales
Barra Myllynen, Inverness, Florida
Elizabeth Noonan, Naples, Florida
Barbara Reid, Saint-Lazare, Quebec
Brian Roberts, Lakewood, Washington State
David Savory, Bogach, Barra
Diana Savory, Bogach, Barra
Darlene Soligo, Trail, British Columbia
Alec Stansell, Wellfleet, Massachusetts
Carol Stansell, Freedom, Massachusetts
Pamela J.Stewart, Pittsburgh, USA
Andrew Strahern, Pittsburgh, USA
Georgiana Welch, Georgiana, Florida

1

Introduction

This book is about the island of Barra and the islands immediately south of it which together form the parish of Barra and once formed the estate of Macneil of Barra, ancestral chief of the Clan Macneil.

The islands are both the southernmost and westernmost in the Outer Hebrides, 130kms west of Oban, and 180kms south of the Butt of Lewis (Fig. 1.1). They are also the smallest. Barra itself is a roughly square island (14,500 acres), about 8kms wide and long, but for the Eoligarry peninsula which juts northwards a further 4kms. Eoligarry and small areas of the west coast have developed the sand-based machair pastures seen more extensively in the islands north of Barra, but the centre of Barra is dominated by a series of high hills and peatlands, the highest of which is Heaval, peaking at 383m OD. Vatersay (2,400 acres) separated from Barra by 200m of water but now joined to it by a causeway, is almost split in two by sweeping back-to-back beaches. The northern half of the island is mostly rugged, the southern is mostly rolling machair. At its greatest extent, Vatersay is less than 6kms long and little more than 4kms wide. South of Vatersay lies Sandray (950 acres), a roughly circular island little more than 2kms in diameter, dominated by a high rocky centre and famous east coast dunes up to 50m high. Below Sandray is the island of Pabbay (600 acres), just 3kms long and 1km wide, a rather bleak place, with its only small area of machair found (unusually) on its east coast. South of Pabbay lies Mingulay (1,600 acres), perhaps the best known of these islands not only for the 'Mingulay Boat Song' (which was actually composed on the mainland in 1938!) but for the more authentic grandeur of its western cliffs which plunge almost vertically over 200m into the Atlantic. The island is a little more than 4kms long and just over 2kms at its widest, dominated by the high ground rising to 274m on the west, and like Pabbay boasting a small area of machair only on the east coast. The southernmost of the Barra islands is Berneray (500 acres), on the south-west tip of which stands the Barra Head lighthouse, perched atop a near vertical cliff of 190m. The rest of the wedge-shaped island, which is only 3kms long and little more than 1km wide, slopes down north-eastwards from this high point, supporting a rich growth of grass and preventing the development of the peatlands so characteristic of much of the Hebrides.

All of these islands were probably first permanently occupied by human populations in the fourth millennium BC, and since then occupation has been continuous to the present day – excepting that the four southern islands were abandoned by their last occupants during the twentieth century; Sandray in 1911, Mingulay and Pabbay in 1912, and Berneray by its lighthouse keepers in 1980 (its last crofters had left in 1910).

It was to try and trace the story of human occupation of the islands that in 1988 a group of archaeologists at the University of Sheffield decided to launch a programme of archaeological research on South Uist, Barra and adjacent islands. The programme was to be called SEARCH (Sheffield Environmental and Archaeological Research Campaign in the Hebrides) and after a preliminary 'pilot' year was to run for five years. The Barra part of the project finally finished its fieldwork in 2000, and its documentary research in 2004; the Uist campaign continues. Our research programme has continued far beyond its allotted six-year span simply because so many ancient sites and monuments were found and so much excavation was needed to even begin to understand them. On the islands that make up the parish of Barra, we recorded 1,967 sites and monuments, which in fact amounts to well over 2,000 structures.

Seventy of these structures were sampled by excavations, although many of these were small-scale, investigating kelp ovens, clearance cairns, shepherds shelters, and similar monuments occupying only a couple of square metres of land. But whilst such structures may be insignificant in some respects, they are also the most common man-made features in the landscape and for this reason they deserve attention and examination. At the same time, we also carried out two more intensive explorations of specific areas of landscape. One was the area around the little burn of Alt Chrisal on the south coast of the Tangaval peninsula, and the other was in the township of Balnabodach on the south side of Loch Obe.

The initial excavations at Alt Chrisal were published by us in *Barra: Archaeological Research on Ben Tangaval* (Branigan and Foster 1995). Meanwhile, our colleague Prof. David Gilbertson had led a team researching the environmental history of the islands and they published their findings in *The Outer Hebrides: The Last 14,000 Years* (Gilbertson and Grattan 1996) the following year. A third book, *From Barra to Berneray* (Branigan and Foster 2000), was published in 2000, and this volume included the catalogue of sites from our survey of all the islands from Barra southwards, and excavations on some fourteen prehistoric sites. The volume concluded with three chapters which attempted to provide an overview of the prehistory of Barra to the 6th century AD, and to set prehistoric Barra in its wider context. Having published three volumes of academic reports on our work we took the opportunity to write an overview of the archaeology of Barra from 4000 BC to AD 1850 for a wider audience, which was published as *Barra and the Bishop's Isles* (Branigan and Foster 2002). Meanwhile, in preparing to publish the final reports on the excavation of post-prehistoric sites, we had inevitably become interested in, and involved with, both the later history of Barra and the documents which threw light on that history. Following our last fieldwork season in Barra in 2000 we undertook documentary research, mainly in Scotland and Canada, over a four year period.

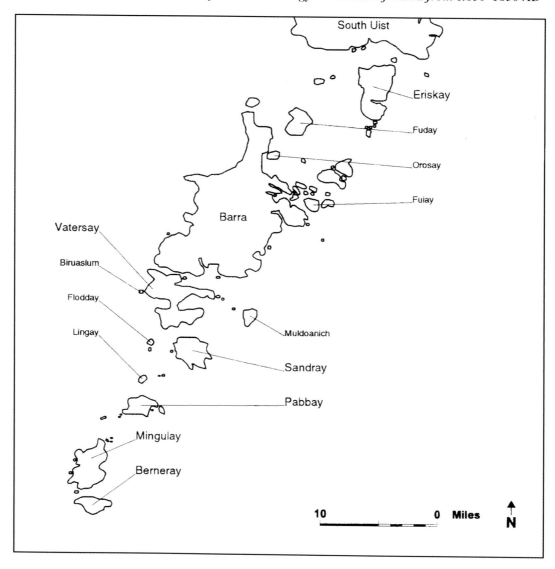

Figure 1.1 Barra and its neighbours

This volume now brings together the results of field survey, excavation and documentary research which have explored, and we hope illuminated, the history and archaeology of Barra from c. AD 850 to AD 1850. In chapter two we attempt to provide an overview of the history of Barra from the arrival of the Norsemen to the end of the Napoleonic Wars, both of which events, as it happens, had significant effects on the human settlement of the island. Documentary sources for most of this period are scarce, but the archaeological evidence left by this millennium of human activity is relatively rich and we describe and discuss the historical archaeology of Barra and its islands in the third chapter. In trying to understand the history and function of these monuments, we excavated a variety of sites – ranging from blackhouses to shieling huts and shepherds shelters – and the results of these excavations are described in chapter four. We took one township, Balnabodach, and undertook a programme of work which involved survey, excavation and documentary research, to try and bring history and archaeology together. The results of that study are presented in chapter five. The excavation of four blackhouses at Balnabodach produced four groups of 18th–19th century ceramics which for the first time allows us to investigate the types and sources of

pottery which the crofters acquired, and Dr David Barker presents an overview of this material in chapter six. The last thirty years of the period covered by this book, from 1822 to 1851, were particularly traumatic ones for the people of the islands, due to a number of intertwined processes. One of these was the collapse of the market for kelp, an alkaline ash extracted from seaweed, the manufacture of which had come to be the prime (in some cases the only) source of cash to pay rents. In chapter seven Professor J Bumsted describes and discusses the rise and fall of the kelp industry. This sets the scene for chapter eight which, using documentary and archaeological evidence traces the collapse of the ancestral estate of Macneil of Barra, its purchase by Gordon of Cluny, and the calamitous events of 1848–1851 which culminated in the 'clearance' of over half the population of the island. Some of those cleared by Gordon were sent to Canada, representing not the first but the last group emigration from Barra to British North America. Chapter nine traces the history of emigration to Canada from Barra between 1772 and 1851 and explores the changing roles of laird, tacksmen, tenants, agents, priest, church, and government in this exodus which saw perhaps 3,500 people leave the island. The chapter concludes by briefly examining the ways in which the emigrant families kept alive their Gaelic culture and traditions, and their memories of the homeland. A short epilogue takes the history of Barra from 1851 to the beginning of the present century. To assist those who wish to trace their ancestors who migrated, an appendix provides details of over 1000 identified emigrants from Barra to British North America from 1771 to 1851.

We hope that not just the appendix but much else in the book will provide a basis and an encouragement for others to continue to research the history and archaeology of Barra.

Acknowledgements

A project running for seventeen years inevitably involves a huge number of people, all of whom in some way contributed to such success as the project achieved. It is impossible to do them all justice, but the following is an honest attempt to say a genuine and heartful thank you to all those who in any way contributed to the SEARCH project as it was played out on Barra and its islands.

Without the willing and generous co-operation of those who own and those who occupy the islands the project could never have even begun. We are indebted to Macneil of Barra, the Department of Agriculture and Fisheries, and the Barra Head Sheepstock Co. for permission to work on the land under their ownership, and to the other owners, crofters and tenants on Barra and Vatersay, and to their township Grazing Committees, for permission to walk their crofts and grazing, and to excavate in these same places.

Equally essential for the project was provision of funding, primarily to enable fieldwork to be undertaken, but also for documentary research and post-excavation analysis. The entire project on Barra and its islands cost around £300,000 – a modest sum these days for a project run over seventeen years, involving about 250 people in the field over that period of time, and 30 post-excavation specialists. Such a sum, however, could only be raised by the generous support of many institutions, grant awarding bodies, charitable trusts and individuals. Though their contributions inevitably varied from a few hundreds of pounds to many thousands, everyone of them was important and much appreciated, and we are pleased to have this opportunity to thank them:

Buaile-nam-Bodach Preservation Society
British Academy
Historic Scotland
The Hunter Trust
The Leverhulme Trust
Loganair
Macneil of Barra Trust
Ian and Nancy Macneil of Barra
The Pilgrim Trust
The Robert Kiln Trust
St Mary's University, Halifax, NS
The Scouloudi Foundation
Society of Antiquaries of London
Society of Antiquaries of Scotland
University of Sheffield
Western Isles Council/LEADER Programme

The support of Historic Scotland extended to far more than financial assistance, and we were encouraged by the interest and advice of Patrick Ashmore, Noel Fojut, and Olwyn Owen. We were also grateful to the Royal Commission staff.

Working in the field on an archaeological project may be exciting and exhilarating, but it is also physically and mentally tiring. The task is made so much easier, and so much more enjoyable, by being able to share it with supportive colleagues. In that respect, SEARCH has been exceptionally fortunate. It is a pleasure to have the opportunity to record how much the project in the field owed in particular to Patrick Foster, David Gilbertson, and Colin Merrony over many years, and over shorter periods to Kevin Edwards and Andrew Fleming. Others who took on supervisory roles at particular sites included Linda Cihakova, Steve Davis, Andy Hammon, Jo Heron, Steve Marsden, John Pouncett, and Keith Scherewode. But that so much ground was covered, and in some places uncovered, was of course due also to the efforts of over 200 students who were the 'foot soldiers' of the field survey and excavations. They performed valiantly in some times difficult and unpleasant conditions and we are indebted to them. All who worked on the project in turn owe much to the efforts of our successive project officers, Cathy Coutts, Sarah Darnborough and Angie Foster, who took much of the organisational burden off our shoulders and also did their best to ensure that facilities for the team were as good as possible.

Particularly important was the provision of accommodation facilities for a team of 20–25 persons most years, and we are grateful to those who provided it through the years and were generous both in their discounted rents and in their tolerance of their student tenants. We are particularly grateful for being allowed to use the Fishermens Rest for many years, and on another occasion the Vatersay community hall, to house some of the student team. We must also record our gratitude to David and Diana Savory for their hospitality at Northbay House during the Balnabodach project, and most of all our debt to Mrs Flora Morrison for making Horveside available to us for so many years (and Fiona Brown for ensuring it was always ready to receive us).

There were others on Barra who made our fieldwork possible and successful. Our work on the further islands in the group would not have been possible without the generosity and seamanship of John Allen Macneil, and some of the nearer islands were made accessible by the willing support and skills of Calum Macneil and Alistair Macneil. Accessing facilities on Barra was made possible by the help of Jessie Macneil in the Social Services offices, and Rhoda Macneil in the Heritage Centre.

The Balnabodach project owes much to the enthusiasm and support of Niall and Chrissie Macpherson. There are many others who have helped our project in various ways. At one time or another we have been grateful for the assistance of the Reverend Canon Macqueen, Mary Kate Mackinnon, Peter Nicholson, and Donald Ferguson, and we hope they will 'stand proxy' for all those others which it is impossible to name here.

Documentary research involved a different set of skills and of course a different group of people. On Barra itself we have been reliant on the remarkable knowledge of island genealogy which hides behind the modesty of Calum Macneil. In Edinburgh we have worked in the National Archives of Scotland, the National Library of Scotland, and the Edinburgh City Library, and are grateful to their staff for helping us access a wealth of material. The Scottish Catholic Archives were also a source of important information and we are grateful to them, and particularly the Keeper, Dr Christine Johnson, for their help. We are also indebted to John MacInnes for his generous sharing of knowledge of the National Archives. At Fort George, we received the hospitality of Colonel Fairrie and his staff when we examined the records of General Roderick Macneil's last command. In London, Dr Martin Dearne has pursued sources in the Public Record Office, the British Library, the National Army Museum, and Lloyds Register, with his customary diligence and persistence and we are deeply indebted to him. We are also grateful to the Staffordshire Record Office for their assistance, and to Geoffrey Watts of Southampton whose research into the General Cemetery there (where General Macneil is buried) has led us to new sources of information. We have also benefited from many discussions about the historical archaeology of the Hebrides, emigration, and Nova Scotia with our colleague Jim Symonds.

Four visits to the wonderful Public Archives of Nova Scotia were initiated by the invitation from Dr Steven Davis to visit St Mary's University in Halifax, and we owe much to Steve for his hospitality and for that invitation. At the PANS we have received superb support from the staff, and especially Barry Cahill, and it is a pleasure to have this opportunity to acknowledge both his generous help and his professionalism.

We received great support too from the staff of the Public Archives of Prince Edward Island, and from Dr Michael Kennedy and Ed Macdonald on PEI. To Bill and Ann McGurk Macneil we are grateful not only for hospitality there, but also for documentary help and introducing us to Meacham's wonderful Atlas of PEI. In Cape Breton we were given much help at both the Beaton Institute at the University College, and at the Highland Village, Iona, where Rodney Chaisson and his staff provided us with documentary sources available nowhere else.

The staff at Louisburg were generous with their time and their information, and we must particularly mention Charles Burke.

We are also pleased to record the assistance of Jocelyn Gillis at the Antigonish Heritage Centre, Dr Terence Punch of the Nova Scotia Genealogical Society, and the staff of the Archives of Ontario in Toronto. More recently we have carried on a mutually productive long-distance collaboration with Vincent Macneil at Bedford, NS, to whom we are much indebted. Our mentor, however, in our work on emigration to British North America has been Prof. Jack Bumsted and we benefited enormously from having the opportunity to work alongside him in the Scottish archives over a period of several weeks. Finally, overseas, we needed to see the letters written to Angus Macdonald, former parish priest of Barra, when he was Rector at the Scots College in Rome. We were warmly welcomed and given every facility by the present Rector, Dr Christopher McElroy, to whom we are very grateful.

All this research activity would have been wasted however if a report on it was not completed and published. The production of this report owes much to the graphic skills of Colin Merrony, Jo Mincher, Martin Dearne and Andrea Vianello and to the painstaking integration of texts and illustrations by Jenny Moore. The complex task of ordering, presenting and cross-referencing the database of Barra emigrants was brilliantly resolved and managed by Stuart Boutell, to whom we are immensely grateful.

We are also greatly indebted of course to all those who have provided specialist reports or co-authored sections of the book, whose names are recorded on the title page. The principal author will always be deeply grateful to Nong Branigan for her support over so many years, and for understanding this new 'passion' in her husband's life.

Finally, we could not have published this volume without the support of our subscribers, whether members of the Clan Macneil or others who, like us, have come to know and love the Isle of Barra. It is with pleasure and gratitude that we record their names on the scroll of subscribers.

Barra from the Norsemen to Napoleon
(AD 871–AD 1820)

The historical sources for Barra between the arrival of the Norse invaders and the end of the Napoleonic Wars (both of which were seminal events in the history of the island) are at best patchy, of variable quality and reliability, and open to many different interpretations. This is neither the place nor the author to undertake a detailed review of these sources, to produce an authoritative history of Barra from the 9th to the early 19th century. Our objective here is much less ambitious, namely to provide a historical context for the archaeology which is described in the following chapters. This chapter attempts to sketch the outlines of some of the key episodes and developments in this period which are particularly pertinent to either the archaeology of the islands or to the traumatic events of the years from 1820 to 1851, which are examined in detail in chapter eight. These episodes include the Norse colonisation, the development of Clan society, the struggle between Catholicism and Presbyterianism, and the Jacobite rebellion. The chapter concludes by using the documentary sources to paint a picture of the economy of the island at the beginning of the 19th century.

Norse colonisation

The Norsemen arrived in the Hebrides in the last decade of the 8th century, the raid on Iona in 794 being followed first by further raids and then by settlement. Initially the settlement may have been short-lived overwintering by raiding parties, but permanent settlement followed, and the Norse origin of the great majority of Hebridean place-names suggests that it was dominant and probably extensive. The physical traces of the settlements have proved elusive however until the extensive surveys and excavations of our colleague Dr Parker Pearson in South Uist (Sharples and Parker Pearson 1999). These have revealed that there were Norse settlements at frequent intervals along the machair of the west coast. Excavations at Kilpheder revealed a long sequence of successive houses occupied from the end of the 10th century to the mid-13th. They were mostly oblong buildings, with two opposed entrances in the long walls, and a central oblong hearth. They followed the tradition on the machair of being constructed by digging a flat-bottomed pit in the sand and lining the sides with a stone wall; the superstructure was probably of turf. The discoveries on South Uist are important in two respects in particular. They confirm that Norse settlement, at least on South Uist, was quite intensive, and they reveal that its architectural expression was not the classic Norse long boat-shaped house but a local form suited to local conditions and materials.

The historical record certainly puts Uist and Barra within the Norse Kingdom of the Isles which embraced the Inner and Outer Hebrides and the Isle of Man. Although the Norse grip on the region weakened from the mid-12th century as a Gaelic dynasty under Somerled MacGillibride carved out a kingdom which included the Uists and Barra, allegiance was still notionally owed to the King of Norway (Duncan 1975). That remained the case until the Treaty of Perth in 1266, in which the King of Norway ceded the Isle of Man and the Hebrides to Scotland. They were subsequently held by Somerled's successors, under allegiance to the King of Scotland, who eventually took the title Lords of the Isles.

The extent to which the Norse settled Barra, however, is still a matter for debate. According to the Grettir Saga, Onund Woodenleg reached Barra in 871 and defeated a king called Kjarval. Kjarval (Celtic Cerball?) may have been an Irish ruler who was himself no more than a visitor to Barra. Onund over-wintered in the island for three years, using it as a base for summer raids in both Ireland and mainland Scotland. After a brief return to Norway, he came back to Barra in 875 and continued to use it as a base for raids further afield. Although he later moved on to Iceland, he remained involved in Barra affairs, arranging the marriage of a kinsman to Alfidis 'the Barra-woman', the daughter of Konal (Anderson 1922, i , 319–21, 326–8, 385–7). Two further Norse occupants of the island are identified by the inscribed memorial stone found at Kilbarr (Fig. 2.1), set up for 'Thorgerth, Steiner's daughter' (RCHM 1928, 124–5). Otherwise, the only Norse settlers discovered in Barra are those found in a handful of poorly documented 'Norse' burials. The best known and published is that excavated by Commander Edge in the 1860's, probably on Borve headland, containing the remains of a woman buried with two Scandinavian oval brooches, and her personal equipment including a comb, whetstone, shears, heckles, and a weaving sword (Graham-Campbell and Batey 1998, 82–3).

Whether these scarce burials and brief glimpses in the sagas reflect substantial settlement in the island is unclear. It can be fairly argued that until the SEARCH discoveries on South Uist, there was no more there than there is on Barra to document extensive settlement. It is certainly possible, perhaps even probable, that Norse occupation sites remain to be found beneath the machair on Barra (Branigan and Foster 2002, 105). Indeed, since the publication of *From Barra to Berneray* (Branigan and Foster 2000), the five small friable sherds found in the midden at site E4 on the islet of Orosay at the north end of Traigh Mhor have been re-examined by Dr Parker Pearson, who suggests they are from a Norse platter (rather than of Beaker date as previously thought). But there are two reasons for suggesting that Norse settlement in Barra was on a lesser scale than further north in the island chain. The first is that the Norse place-names of Barra are notably lacking in those which refer to human settlements (Borgstrom 1998), with the exception of shielings (e.g. Skallary, Earsary). The second is that, following the

Figure 2.1 A 10th-century Cross-slab found at Cille Bharra. It has an Old Norse Runic memorial inscription on the reverse (ht. 1.36m)

discoveries on South Uist, we undertook further survey on the largest area of machair on Barra (Eoligarry) including a 'walkover' survey with Parker Pearson but found no sites which demonstrated the presence of buried Norse remains. There are certainly buried middens in the machair, but such pottery as they yield appears to be either LIA or later medieval/early modern. At present any extensive Norse settlement of Barra needs to be demonstrated rather than assumed (MacLeod 2003, 346).

Whatever the extent and nature of Norse occupation of Barra and its islands, there is little doubt that it will have incorporated the existing population and culture rather than extinguished it. Although that population and culture had its roots deep in prehistory it had no doubt been refreshed by a slow but steady flow of incomers from other islands and coastlines along the western seaboard, including Ireland.

Clan society and the Clan MacNeil

Amongst the Irish peoples who arrived in Barra in the early second millennium AD were those who would become known as the Clan Macneil. The Macneils trace their ancestry back to the fourth century Irish king Niall of the Nine Hostages, and believe that the first Macneil to establish himself in Barra was Neil of the Castle who landed there in c. AD 1030. This was said to be recorded in the *Barra Register*, a manuscript chronicle of the Macneils and Barra allegedly begun in 1049 and last seen in the 1880's in the hands of the sisters of the last of the direct

line of chieftains, General Roderick Macneil (Macneil 1964, 54). Others argue for a much later date for the arrival of the Macneils. Maclean Sinclair (1907) believed the first chief to possess Barra was Roderick Macneil (born c.1380), whilst others assume that Macneil ownership began with the charter given at Finlagan in 1427 by Alexander, Lord of the Isles, to Gilleonan Macneil, son of Roderick. There is clearly much confusion and disagreement between the documentary sources, Clan tradition, and oral histories, which can only be resolved by dismissing one or the other. The sources are not necessarily incompatible, however, (any more than they are necessarily correct). In particular we should not assume that the grant of a charter to a Macneil in 1427 meant that the Macneils had only recently arrived in the islands.

If there were an agreed date for the construction of Kisimul Castle (Fig.2.2) then of course it might throw much needed light on the problem, but this too is an area of dispute. Received wisdom is that the castle was built in the 15th century (RCAHM 1928, 45; Dunbar 1978; Pringle 1994, 36-8). Ian Macneil (forthcoming) rightly questions the validity of a 15th century date based on two pieces of inconclusive documentary evidence and an uncritical assumption. The documentary evidence is the absence of Kisimul Castle from both Fordun's description of Scottish islands, written c.1370, and the charter of 1427. The assumption is that any early architectural features in Kisimul must be, by definition, 'outlandish survivals' in some remote backwater. This author believes that the architectural history of Kisimul appears to be long and complex, and it is likely to stretch back beyond the mid 15th century. We must hope that some further, artefactual, evidence might emerge when the 2001 excavations in the castle are published. For example, the interim report mentions a gold tag, 'provisionally dated' to the 12th century, which was incorporated into the material making up the original floor of the tower.

The date at which the Macneils arrived in Barra, and at which they began the construction of Kisimul Castle, (which are not of course necessarily the same thing) are clearly still open to debate at the time of writing. In any event, the Macneils were firmly installed in Barra by 1427, and the charter was renewed by James IV at Stirling in 1495. They were now part of the Clan system which had developed in the highlands and islands in the preceding two centuries. In his recent study of the Clans and the transformation of their leaders from chiefs to landlords, R. A. Dodgshon (1998) has highlighted some of the characteristic features of clan society and its 'ideology of behaviour'. The strength of the clan was underpinned by kinship on the one hand and territory on the other. Devine (1994, 4–6) has rightly warned that we should not over-emphasise the importance of kinship in the clan system, and that feudal legal structures still exerted powerful influences on clan society. But kinship laid obligations on both the chief and his people, even if many of 'his' people were not, strictly, kin. The clans, and their chiefs, were driven by the need to expand their territory, of which the chief was seen as the guardian rather than the proprietor. The chiefs maintained their status by a rich mixture of feasting and feuding, and sought to increase their wealth and power by making both marriage and political alliances. Feasting in particular was the driving force behind the chiefs' preference for rents and other dues to be paid in

Figure 2.2 Kisimul Castle, ancestral home of the Macneil of Barra, after restoration by the 45th chief

kind, although the chief was also the source of relief in times of hardship.

Although our glimpses of the Macneils are few and far between over the next two centuries, the fragmentary sources that survive document activities which reveal that the Macneils conformed almost entirely to this established pattern of clan behaviour. The importance of kinship is emphasised in Martin Martin's account of Barra c.1690, where he describes how the Macneil takes responsibility for widowers and widows alike, and takes into his own household old people who can no longer till their own land. Similarly, says Martin, if anyone loses milk-cows, Macneil replaces them from his own herd. But the chief also exacted rent in kind from his people. Macfarlane's account of Barra in 1620 claims that he took 'for his dewtie, the half of their cornes, butter, cheese, and all other commodities'. The claim is repeated by Martin Martin, who adds that each family paid Macneil an 'Omer' (two pecks) of barley a year. Although there are no direct references to the Macneil using these perquisites to provision great feasts, Martin Martin noted in 1695 that Macneil maintained a herd of 70–80 deer on the island of Muldonich on the approach into Castlebay and these must surely have been kept to provide hospitality in Kisimul Castle. There may also be echoes of the importance of the feast in the Clan Macneil way of life in the tradition that dictated that after the Macneil had dined each evening, a steward would proclaim from Kisimul's tower, that 'the great Macneil having finished his meal, the princes of the earth may dine'.

There can be no doubt however that the Macneils resorted to other traditional methods – feuding and political and marriage alliances – to enhance their prestige and power. It is said that in 1589, a large force of Barramen raided Erris in Co. Mayo, killing 600 cattle and carrying off 500 hides (Thompson 1974, 137), but raids on this scale may have been exceptional. Based on a small island at the southern end of the island chain, opportunities for raiding other chiefdoms and carrying off animals and stores must have been somewhat limited. However, the Macneils made up for this by piracy and Kisimul Castle had a galley house and a crew house immediately outside its gateway (Fig. 2.3). In a notorious episode at the end of the 16th century, Roderick the Turbulent seized an English ship, which brought down the wrath of Queen Elizabeth, as a result of which James VI ordered that Macneil should be seized and put on trial. He was granted a pardon, and although he forfeited his estate to Mackenzie of Kintail, it was restored on payment of an annual feu-duty of 60 merks. It was said that Roderick's cellar at Kisimul was stocked with fine French and Spanish wines which he had seized during the course of his piratical raids.

Feuding was not confined to raids on other clans, however, and there were probably dynastic struggles and competition for the chieftainship within the clan. One episode is recorded in the *Register of the Privy Council* (X, 6–7), involving Roderick the Turbulent. In 1613 he and his son and heir, Gilleonan Og Macneil, were seized and imprisoned in Kisimul Castle by two of Roderick's natural sons, Neil Og Macneil and Gilleonan Macneil. The Council declared them rebels and commissioned Clanranald to arrest them but there is no evidence that the ageing Clanranald did so. Neil Og appears to have succeeded Roderick, according to Macfarlane after disposing of other claimants (Campbell 2000, 94), in c.1620.

The acquisition of the southern islands was achieved soon after in 1623, when the lease of the teinds of the Bishop's Isles was given to Neil Og. This may have ultimately been the outcome of a marriage alliance which Roderick had contracted with Mary Macleod, widow of Duncan Campbell of Aucinbreck, and in all probability the mother

Figure 2.3 A galley seen on a late medieval grave-slab from Cille Barra

of Neil Og (Campbell 2000, 93). Mary's son by her first marriage, Dougall, held the lease on the southern islands but had failed to pay his tack duty for many years (*Register of the Privy Council* XI, 244), and thus the lease was given to his step-brother Neil Og. Neil's successor as chief, Gilleonan, contracted a marriage with Katherine, sister of Donald Macdonald of Moydart (NAS GD/201/1/93). A receipt of 1680 (NAS GD/201/1/122) reveals that Macdonald subsequently entered into a leasing arrangement, probably for the island of Eriskay, which involved an annual rental to Macneil of 2,000 merks.

The Macneil's feudal allegiance was itself subsequently moved by a marriage alliance, in which the Macneils had no part, between a daughter of Mackenzie of Kintail and Sir James Macdonald of Sleit, which resulted in the superiority of Barra being made over to Macdonald of Sleit in 1695.

Political alliances were more dangerous affairs than marriages, but the Macneils sporadically became involved in them. During the hostilities between the English and Scottish crowns in 1545, Gilleonan Macneil of Barra joined with the Macleods of Lewis and Harris, the Macleans of Duart, Clanranald and others in a 'rebel council' which allied itself with the English king (Donaldson 1978, 72). But in 1689 Roderick Dhu Macneil fought alongside Dundee at the Battle of Killiecrankie in support of the deposed King James, and he was again in the field against the English to support James Stuart in 1715.

Interestingly, Roderick Dhu's kinsman and the tacksman of Vatersay, Donald Macneil, was the one Macneil to benefit from the events of 1715. A decree issued in Edinburgh on September 25th 1723 (NAS GD/201/5/15) recognised him as a lawful creditor on the estate of Ronald Macdonald of Moydart. Macdonald had been identified as

one of 'certain traitors and Popish recusants' whose estates were to be forfeited and sold for the benefit of the public and to give 'relief to lawful creditors'. Macdonald, who would have been a distant relative by marriage of Macneil of Vatersay, apparently owed him 2,000 merks – which by coincidence is the amount of rental payable by the Macdonalds of Moidart to Macneil of Barra (see above).

The Macneils and the '45

Donald Macneil of Vatersay was himself identified as a Catholic in a list of 'children under popish parents' in South Uist and Barra which was drawn up in 1703 (Campbell 2000, 96), but by the mid 1720s was involved with the rabidly anti-Catholic Society for the Propagation of Christian Knowledge, which he urged to establish a school on Barra to combat popery. Campbell suggests that he had converted on his second marriage, to a daughter of the protestant Macleod of Greshornish. Yet, come the Jacobite rebellion of 1745, the position of Macneil of Vatersay was as ambivalent, at least as far as the documentary evidence goes, as was that of Macneil of Barra. That evidence has been gathered by J L Campbell and what follows is based on his accounts (1998; 2000).

Prince Charles Stuart arrived off the coast of Barra on July 22nd 1745 with a small retinue which included some 'relations' of the Macneil. Macneil's piper was taken on board as a pilot, and he conducted them safely into Eriskay on the following day. A message was sent to Macneil suggesting that he meet the Prince and his party in Eriskay but 'he happened to be from home'. Although Campbell suggests (1998, 49) that this may have been a diplomatic absence, Macneil having been aware both that the Prince came in a single ship with no supporting French troops and that Macdonald of Boisdale had refused to get involved, subsequent events suggest that Macneil was committed to the Prince's cause. The Prince and his supporters sailed on, but a Spanish ship under the command of Don Kindelan landed 2,500 stands of arms and $4000 on Barra in October. This fact apparently became widely known, and Macneil's feudal superior, Macdonald of Sleat, wrote to Forbes of Culloden on November 30th informing him that the arms had been taken from Barra to Arisaig. In fact, Don Kindelan sent orders to his lieutenant, Don Macmahon in Barra, the very next day (December 1st) to deliver the arms and cash to the Prince's director of supplies.

This letter is of particular interest as it reveals that the Royalists were already doubting Macneil's commitment to the cause. 'If the Laird of Barra does not come out with you with all his kinsmen...' writes Don Kindelan; but he also asks Macmahon to 'give my service to Macneil of Vatersay and apply to him for his assistance'. A postscript urges Macmahon to let Barra know that a French army of 6,000 men has arrived in the South, presumably in the hope that this would encourage him to commit to the cause.

It may indeed be that Macneil was influenced by this news, for early in January 1746 he issued a receipt to Lieut. Macmahon, for £10 'to bring up my men for his Royal Highness' service' and also a promissory note to the Lieutenant 'to be out with my men to convey Pastich of war for his Royal Highness'. But Barra's involvement was an open secret. On January 20th Forbes of Culloden received an anonymous note that Macneil had 120 men ready to act as escort to arms and money for Prince Charles, and at the end of the month, Macdonald of Sleat confirmed to Forbes that Macneil had been ready for some weeks to go south.

Macdonald himself acted honourably throughout this episode, never betraying the trust the government had in him, but equally doing all in his power to save Macneil from self-imposed disaster. On January 25th he had written to Clanranald urging him to use his influence to persuade Macneil to hand over the remaining arms that were stored in Barra to him (Macdonald), which would give him a 'pretext of keeping Barra free from any molestation'. There is no evidence that Clanranald intervened, or that Barra took the opportunity to extricate himself - rather the opposite.

In April, shortly before Culloden, the Prince's aides collected £380 from Barra which had been left there for safe-keeping. They were apparently almost intercepted by Captain Ferguson on their return voyage, in which case he may well have been on his way to arrest Macneil, for he reported to the Duke of Cumberland in May that he had taken Macneil on April 8th, in a pre-emptive strike to prevent him joining the Royalist forces. He further informed Cumberland that in Macneil's possession he found hidden 'three chests of arms, one and a half barrels of gunpowder, two boxes of ball and some flints and $160'. A further 115 stands of arms were recovered from tenants to whom Macneil had distributed them, whilst $500 had been sent to Boisdale just two days earlier. This evidence, together with that provided by the documents which Macneil had signed in January and which fell into government hands in June, were more than enough to identify Macneil as a supporter of the Jacobite cause.

He was first questioned by General Campbell and then taken to Inverness. Meanwhile, with Prince Charles Stuart in hiding in the Western Isles, Captain Ferguson returned to Barra with several hundred redcoats in an attempt to either discover or isolate the Prince. Captain Scott landed on Mingulay and arrested the Catholic priest, James Grant, and executed a local man who had allegedly fought for the Jacobite cause. The same officer is said to have hanged a man on Barra for the same offence, although the man loudly protested his innocence - and probably rightly too, since he proved to be one of only eight or nine protestants who were living in Barra at the time.

Macneil was taken from Inverness to London on the prison ship *Pamela*, which anchored off Tilbury on August 27th. They remained on the ship, sustained by a daily allowance of 1/2lb bread and 1/4lb of cheese a day, until November 1st when they were removed to a private house in London. On May 29th 1747, an order was made for Macneil's discharge. Given the strength of the evidence against him, there is no reason to discount the record in *The Prisoners of the Forty-Five* that he turned King's Evidence.

Macneil of Barra's involvement in the '45 nevertheless seems to have been essentially peripheral, albeit perhaps less by design than circumstance. He offered support, harboured weapons and money, gave commitments, but never took his men into battle, or indeed anywhere, between July 1745 and April 1746. Remarkably perhaps, in view of Donald Macneil of Vatersay's anti-Catholic activities in the 1720's, the Macneil's of Vatersay seem to have been more actively involved in the '45. The only Barramen to appear in the muster at Culloden are John Macneil and Roger Macneil, both from Vatersay and serving in Clanranald's regiment, whilst Donald's son Hector was arrested and imprisoned in June. It may be that Don Kindelan's suggestion back in December 1745 that

Don Macmahon should ask for assistance from Vatersay elicited a positive response.

Whilst Roger Macneil of Vatersay was subsequently transported to the Americas as a rebel, Macneil of Barra returned to the island and retained his estate, perhaps through the continuing good offices of his superior, Macdonald of Sleit. In a remarkable turn of events, just twelve years later his son and heir, Roderick the Resolute, wore the king's uniform as a lieutenant in Frasers Highlanders at the battle for Quebec. In fact he laid down his life for King George on the Heights of Abraham on September 13th 1759. His father died in 1763 and the chieftainship passed to Roderick the Resolute's son, Roderick the Gentle, who at this time was still a minor. In yet another twist of fate, he was brought up by his uncle, Angus Macneil, who was not only the surviving son and heir of Donald Macneil of Vatersay, but a protestant minister to boot!

Catholic and Protestant

The history of the Christian church in the Western Isles goes back to the sixth century. Following St Columba's foundation of a monastery on Iona in the mid-sixth century, Columban monks introduced Christianity to the islands. If, as is widely (though not universally) agreed, the Norse named Barra after St Barr, then it suggests there was a church dedicated to the saint at Cille Bharra when the Norsemen arrived in Barra in the later 9th century. Similarly the Norse assignation of the name Pabbay, 'Priest's Island' to the small island south of Vatersay is thought to indicate that a priest or hermit was already in residence there in the 9th century, and Fisher (2001, 11) believes that cross-marked slabs found there are of pre-Norse origin (2001,106). It may be at this time that Pabbay's Pictish symbol-stone (Fig. 2.4) was adapted for use as a Christian burial marker. Subsequent adoption of Christianity by some of the Norse settlers is attested by the cross slab of c. AD 1100 with an added runic inscription found in the cemetery at Cille Bharra (above Fig. 2.1)

Figure 2.4 Pictish symbol stone from Pabbay with a 'flower' symbol surmounted by a crescent-and-V-rod symbol. The stone was turned into a Christian grave-marker by the addition of a Latin cross (HT 1.2m)

The surviving remains of the church at Cille Bharra (Fig. 2.5) probably date to the 12th century, and its architecture betrays the influence of early medieval Ireland. Other chapels were said by Donald Munro in 1549, to have been built on each of the southern islands, but the only surviving visible remains are on Mingulay and at Cille Bhrianain on the eastern tip of Vatersay. Whether they first began to fall into decay in the aftermath of the Reformation is unknown, but perhaps suggested by the description of Cille Bharra as roofless in 1625 (Macquarrie 1989, 25).

The Reformation probably had far less immediate impact in Barra than it had on the mainland or even in the Inner Hebrides, although in the longer term religious preference and prejudice were to play important roles in Barra's history. However, the Statutes of Iona which were adopted by some island chiefs in 1609 may have encouraged at least the toleration of the Protestant religion by the Catholics of Barra. The slaying of John Macneil, the Protestant parson of Barra, in 1609 by Macneil's brother-in-law, Macdonald of Benbecula, may have had little or nothing to do with rivalry between the two religious factions. In fact neither the Catholic nor the reformed church seem to have made any strenuous efforts to minister to, let alone convert, the people of Barra in the late 16th-early 17th century. But from 1625, Irish Franciscan missionaries set out to reclaim the Western Isles for the Catholic church. Cornelius Ward, who went to Barra in November 1625, was the first Catholic priest to visit the island since the Reformation, and he records baptising two sons of the laird in 1625, and in 1626 he solemnised the marriage of the lawful, but usurped, heir to the chieftainship. The usurper, Neil Og Macneil, 'refused the faith' and in 1629 accepted a commission to apprehend priests. However, in 1633 Father Patrick Heggarty reported that he had reconciled over 2,000 souls, and baptised 1,200. Amongst these was, Macneil of Barra

(Macquarrie 1989, 25), that is, Neil Og who had apparently repented, and was subsequently denounced in 1643 by the minister of South Uist for having a statue of Our Lady in his chapel. In 1652 he invited Father Dermot Duggan, an Irish Lazarist priest, to minister to the people of Barra. Duggan records that in 1654 he received into the church 'the young laird with his brothers and sisters', but noted that he had hopes of 'getting the old laird' on his next visit, suggesting that Neil Og, despite his invitation, had perhaps himself lapsed (Mackenzie 1998, 9).

Whatever the inconsistency in the laird's devotion at this time, the island as a whole was clearly committed to the Catholic faith by the mid 17th century. Despite the Cromwellian laws that forbade the practice of the Catholic faith, 'in the remote islands these laws are not carried into execution' wrote the Prefect of the Scottish Missions in 1669, concluding that 'the Catholics live in peace ...in Uist and Barra' (Mackenzie 1998, 211). By 1671 Father Macdonnel was able to report to the Propaganda 'there are 1000 Catholics in the island' (Blundell 1917, 8–9). The zeal for the church was so great that in 1675 a Catholic school was established on the island, only the second such school in the whole of Scotland. The enthusiasm of the islanders for the faith was such that four years later two visiting priests (Fathers Leslie and Munro) had to plead with them to be allowed to leave. By now Gilleonan, who had become a Catholic in 1654, had succeeded to the chieftainship and both he and his successor, Roderick Dhu, were firm adherents to the cause of both the church and the deposed House of Stuart as we have seen above.

Even before the '45, however, the Protestants had begun to fight back against the surge of Catholicism in Barra. We noted earlier Donald Macneil of Vatersay's campaign to establish a Protestant school on Barra, which came to fruition in 1729 with the appointment of a teacher for the

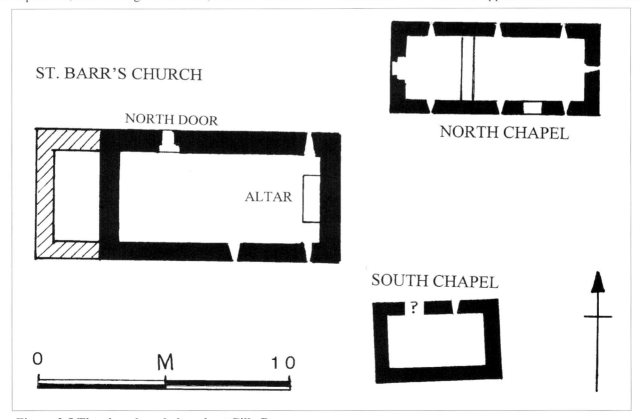

Figure 2.5 The church and chapels at Cille Barra

new school, though an appointee did not take up post until 1732. Progress, however, was slow. In 1746 the Presbyterian minister at Fort William was able to speak of only 'seven or eight common people' on Barra that were Protestants.

Nevertheless, the outcome of the '45 had now swung the balance in favour of the Protestant cause. Punitive legislation was enacted to crush the Catholic religion, particularly amongst the lairds. Mackenzie quotes a summary of some of the measures which were introduced: 'Children under the care of Catholic parents were to be taken from them and entrusted to a "well-affected friend", the means for their support being provided out of the property of their parents....Catholics were incapable of acquiring real property either by purchase or by deed of gift....They were also incapable after the age of fifteen of inheriting estates....Catholics could be neither governors, schoolmasters, nor factors....Protestants were forbidden from employing Catholic servants....'

In the face of such punishments, it is amazing to find that the Reverend John Walker in visiting Barra in 1764 still found only 50 Protestants in a population of 1,285 people (Walker 1980, 85). Thirty years later, the Reverend Edward MacQueen reported only 80 Protestants in a population now grown to over 1,600 souls (MacQueen, E. in Campbell 1998, 59). But the hardest hit by the legislation were the Catholic lairds, and it is hardly surprising that every island laird apostatised in the years following the '45. In the case of Macneil of Barra, the conversion to the Protestant cause was made the more certain by the early death at Quebec of Roderick, Dove of the West, which left his son in the hands of his uncle, the Protestant minister of Vatersay.

Barra under the chieftainship of Roderick the Gentle

When Roderick the Gentle succeeded his grandfather as chief of the Clan Macneil in 1763 the position and circumstances of the chiefs of the highland clans had changed dramatically over the past century and a half. Under James VI the crown had gradually re-asserted its control over the highlands and islands by a combination of shows of force and setting new obligations on the clan chieftains. These were embodied in the Statutes of Iona of 1609 and Devine (1994, 13) has identified their purpose as 'a comprehensive attempt to impose lowland values on Gaeldom'. In particular the requirements for highland chiefs to send their heirs to the lowlands for their education and for themselves to appear personally before the Privy Council in Edinburgh (from 1616 on an annual basis) in time began the process of turning highland chiefs into landlords and city-dwelling gentlemen. The process was accelerated after the '45 by the various Acts of Parliament which denied the clansmen the right to wear their kilts, play their pipes, and carry their weapons, and denied many highland chiefs their estates. Dr Johnson, touring the region in 1773, noted that by then clanship was in terminal decline.

Roderick the Gentle reflects this process of transformation. He was educated initially by his uncle (under whose guidance he converted to the Protestant religion) and then in Aberdeen, before attending Glasgow University to which he matriculated in 1769. He followed his father's example, joining the army and serving in North America, this time in the American War of Independence. His grandfather had lived in Borve, but the new chief established a large farm on the Eoligarry peninsula at the north end of the island, existing tenants being moved to other parts of the island. It was probably Roderick the Gentle who built the mill near Northbay (Fig. 2.6), for it first appears in a document of 1776, and then again is mentioned in Roderick's contract of marriage in 1788 (NAS TD 85/63 (A8), Roll 2). He was therefore responsible for both the first 'clearance' in Barra and for introducing the requirement that tenants should pay to have their grain processed in the chief's mill.

Despite this he appears to have been generally well-regarded in most respects by his tenants, and there are several small pointers to his maintaining at least some semblance of the chief of the clan's traditional care for his people. Buchanan in 1790 praised him for his 'humanity and prudence' and his efforts to protect his tenants from oppression. MacQueen in 1794 recorded that when a group of Barra families who had left the island, some to emigrate and others to seek work in Glasgow, were left marooned and destitute, Macneil provided them not only with land but also with money to purchase cattle and farming equipment. A letter from Macneil to his father-in-law, dated September 1800, reveals that he had arranged for a doctor to come and inoculate the people, as smallpox had reared its head in the islands (NAS GD202/70/8). An incomplete account to March 1818 reveals that in 1816 he had allowed a reduction in rents totalling £10 for the tenants of Gortein, a settlement

Figure 2.6 The remains of Macneil's mill at Northbay

on the Sound of Vatersay (NAS CS/44/446), and in 1819 he contributed to a fund established to provide gratuities for the relief of the poor, though he only provided £17-15-4 to top the fund up to £400 (NAS GD/244/34). On such acts, presumably, was Roderick the Gentle's reputation and title built.

Roderick and his wife, Jean Cameron, daughter of Ewen Cameron of Fassifern, lived in his new house at Eoligarry, a really quite impressive Georgian three-storey mansion, described elsewhere in this volume. There they raised their two sons and five daughters in the Protestant faith. But Macneil acquired a house in Liverpool, possibly the result of business trips concerned with the marketing of kelp to Liverpool soap and glass manufacturers. At least in his later years, he seems to have spent much of his time there.

There is no doubt, however, that he also took an active interest in the economic development of both his estate and his Eoligarry farm. After returning from America he apparently travelled in Europe and was inspired to set about improving his estate. The Rev. John Buchanan who visited Barra in the 1780s noted that Macneil 'encourages all kind of improvement' (Buchanan 1997, 11). MacQueen in the *Old Statistical Account* of 1794 was more explicit: 'within these last five years Macneil, returned from visiting foreign countries, has begun to introduce the method used in the low country'. He further comments on Macneil's introduction of the plough to plant potatoes ('and everyone begins to follow the example') and that Macneil has invested in buying good quality animals so that he 'can now produce a fold of his own rearing equal to any of them'. He also seems to have invested in road building on the island, an account for the period 1810 to 1818 revealing an expenditure of £124-15-6 on 'making roads on Barra' (NAS CS44/446). In a letter to the parish priest, Angus Macdonald, in September 1818 he expresses a wish to create larger, more viable, holdings and to offer permanent leases to anyone who cleared and enclosed land (Campbell 1998, 127). He may have met resistance to this scheme from his tenants, to judge by a further letter in December of the same year, when he says he 'will use every exertion, that the land, and hay, are permanently divided; those for and against it will show me who I must look to and who not' (Campbell 1998, 129). Further references in Nicolson's *Statistical Account* of 1840 to improvements by 'Colonel Macneil, the late proprietor' (a term he reserves for Roderick the Gentle) include tree-planting on the east coast of the island, and draining and enclosing the Eoligarry farm. There is therefore sufficient evidence to suggest that from the 1770s onwards, Macneil encouraged improvements which should have made the economic basis of the estate more sustainable.

From three sources we can gain insights into that economy , and its development from c.1770 to 1815, a period which covers most of the chieftainship of Roderick the Gentle. These sources are John Walker's account of Barra in 1774, MacQueen's report for the *Statistical Account* of 1794, and Macculloch's account of Barra in 1816.

Pride of place in Walker's list of Barra's exports in 1764 goes to Black Cattle, of which about 300 were sent to the Clyde each year, half as salted carcases the rest on the hoof. By 1794 whilst the quantity of cattle sold was much the same, the price they fetched had increased significantly. MacQueen reports the sale of between 200 and 250 head a year, plus an additional 100 carcases, at a price which he said had risen by 30–40% in the last eighteen years. Although the number of sheep kept on the island was double that of cattle (2,216 to 1,170), in terms of cash value cattle were clearly the more important. Macculloch (in Campbell 1998, 95) confirms the continuing importance of Black Cattle in 1816, noting that they 'form the chief agricultural wealth of the island'. Large scale sheep-farming came late to Barra.

Next to cattle-raising, fishing was regarded by early visitors to the island as the other food-producing activity which paid rents and yielded a profit. Walker reported 6,000 ling caught and cured in 1764 and sold on to Glasgow at £4–£5 a hundred. This was the haul of just eight boats operating over a three month period on the nearer banks, just a mile offshore. But he notes that fishing activity was limited by the small boats which were poorly equipped to fish on the further and richer banks, and in the less clement weather of spring and autumn.

By 1794, the price of ling had risen by 20% (to £5–£6 a 100) and the quantity of fish caught had risen dramatically. MacQueen records 30,000 ling sent to Glasgow in 1787, and notes that 20–30 boats were now employed in the activity. But the fishing is still restricted to a three month period, and the boats are still small, manned by only five men. By 1816 this situation had been changed, for Macculloch reports that their boats are 'large and well found' and 'of considerable size, so as easily to carry ten or twelve men'. Who had taken the initiative in developing bigger and better boats is not clear and one is tempted to assume that it was part of Macneil's improvements strategy. But the Barra fishermen must have played an important role in this significant development for they built the boats themselves, and Macculloch notes that their construction is 'very peculiar', implying it was not simply a design by boat-builders brought in from elsewhere by the landlord. One of the boat-building communities of this period was probably located at Crubisdale, near Nask (Fig. 2.7).

Both MacQueen and Macculloch note that Macneil allowed the fishermen to take their catch direct to Glasgow and sell it themselves, making no claim on the proceeds, whereas he purchased cattle from his tenants and took on their exportation himself. This appears to have been a genuinely philanthropic policy on Macneil's part, though not without benefit to himself since his tenants were therefore able to pay increased rents. Macculloch specifically links higher rentals to the success of the fisheries, and also comments that the fisheries have also allowed the creation of what he calls 'small farms' on the seashore otherwise 'nearly incapable of paying [rents] from any of their surplus produce'.

Arable crops were certainly never a source of income in Barra and they rarely produced any surplus over subsistence needs; indeed they seem often to have fallen short of what was needed to feed a growing population. All three sources comment on the difficulties of crop-growing on Barra, a result of the climate, soils and topography, but exacerbated by the small size of the tenancies. Walker (1980, 85) records that in 1764 a great part of the arable land was cultivated with the spade, which in the Western Isles meant the *caschrom*. This was laborious back-breaking work. Grant (1961, 104) says that a man would work from January to April to turn over 5 acres of land with a *caschrom*. But its great merits were that it could cultivate

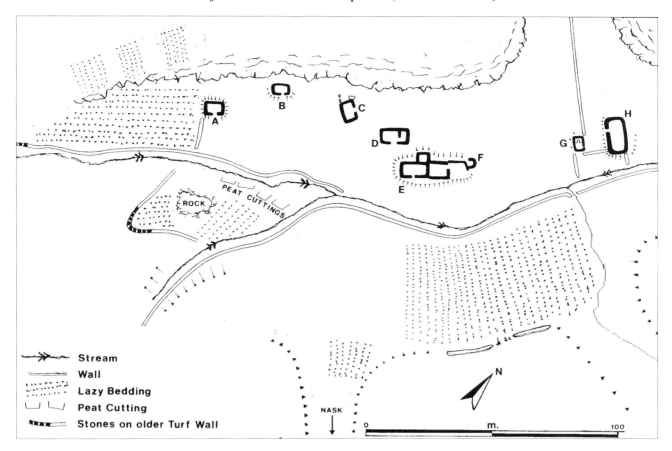

Figure 2.7 The abandoned settlement of Crubisdale, Nask where, according to oral tradition, Barramen built their fishing boats

small rock-strewn plots of soil on steep slopes which could never be tackled by a plough, and Barra and its islands were so short of arable land that such plots were cultivated throughout the islands. Furthermore, the *caschrom* created a better dug soil than the primitive light ploughs which were the only alternative known in the islands at this time, and it produced a significantly higher crop yield than ploughed land. The *caschrom* could also be used to create 'lazy-beds' (*fiannagan*) , where soil was taken from a two feet wide strip and piled up on an adjacent strip, thus creating both a deeper soil and much-needed drainage. Relict lazy-beds are widely spread over Barra, and small lazy-bed plots can still be seen in use today in some parts of the island (Fig. 2.8). According to Walker seaweed (ware) was placed on the old ground surface during the winter to fertilize the soil before the lazy-beds were dug in February and left to drain. Bere (barley) was then sown thinly on the lazy-beds in April or May, and by careful maintenance with a wooden hand harrow through the summer, yielded a good crop. But Walker also noted that already bere had to share the lazy-beds with potatoes, a crop introduced to Barra only in the 1750s.

By the time MacQueen wrote the *Statistical Account* in 1794, there seem to have been some significant developments in agriculture on Barra, perhaps stimulated by Macneil's enthusiasm for improvements. MacQueen reports that although the *caschrom* is used on rocky ground, 'people here for the most part use the plough', and that where seaweed manure is laid thickly, the fields can produce successive crops – of potatoes, black oats and a second crop of oats. Barley is still the principal cereal crop,

but is now sown in fields, lazy-beds being used for potatoes. The precarious nature of arable farming on Barra is underlined however when MacQueen notes that 'in good seasons they can raise as much crop as will be sufficient for their subsistence, otherwise there is a scarcity; but the proprietor supplies the country with low-country meal at market prices'. There were of course many seasons in Barra which were not 'good'. Macculloch puts a gloss on MacQueen's description, by noting that although the plough is indeed employed, it is the ristle plough 'an ancient instrument' which was light and carried only a coulter. 'The small farms' says Maculloch 'are mostly cultivated by the spade'. He notes the 'superior cultivation of the farms' held by Catholics and puts it down to the

Fig 2.8 Potatoes growing in lazy-beds at Eoligarry 1995

13

influence of the priest. Interestingly, Macneil himself in a letter to Father Angus Macdonald, the parish priest, in 1816 writes of his *Glebe* that it is 'the least portion but the best cultivated' (Campbell 1998, 123). Nevertheless Macculloch recognised both the chronic over-population of Barra and the chronic over-exploitation of the land for arable farming, a purpose for which very little of it was suited. Strangely, he makes no mention of the potato, but that may be because by 1816 the overwhelming importance of the potato in the subsistence regime was simply an accepted fact of life.

The potato had been introduced to Barra in 1752 according to Walker, and as elsewhere in the highlands and islands it was adopted with enthusiasm. Devine (1988) has set out clearly and at length in his brilliant book on *The Great Highland Famine* the reasons why the potato was so widely and quickly adopted. In summary, it was suited to the Hebridean climate, it was easy to grow and process, it provided better yields and more calories than cereals, and it could be grown on small plots on almost any soil. It has been estimated that an acre of potatoes could support four times as many people as an acre of oats. By 1811 up to 80% of islanders' nourishment came from the potato! (Devine 1988, 12). On Barra the multitude of relict tiny lazy-bedded plots testify to the importance of the potato in the local subsistence economy, for these miniscule plots are too small to have ever been used for growing cereals. As noted above, the lazy-beds were normally fertilised with seaweed, but as early as 1794 MacQueen reported that 'since kelp became valuable, proprietors everywhere restricted people cutting it for manure, to the prejudice of agriculture', and he confirmed that on Barra tenants were not allowed to cut shore kelp for manuring. Paradoxically therefore kelp and potatoes, which had become the two main props of the island economy, were to some extent in competition.

Walker (1980, 87) records that kelp production began on Barra in 1763, just nine years after the introduction of the potato. In that first year the island produced 40 tons of kelp, and the following year, 60 tons. Kelp was used as a source for alkali (used in the manufacture of soap, glass and other products) as well as lesser quantities of iodine and muriate of potash, and was exported to lowland Scotland and industrial centres in England. The industry blossomed, and by 1794 200 tons of kelp were being sent annually to Liverpool and Leith (MacQueen E. in Campbell 1998, 66). By this time kelp had already become a significant factor in the crofters' ability to pay their rents. Macneil offered tenants from £1-10-0 to £2-2-0 a ton for making kelp on his Eoligarry farm, and for those with crofts by the shore he paid them £2-12-6 per ton for kelp made from ware gathered locally. The commercial price for kelp at this time was around £4-10-0 per ton, so that although the rate paid to the tenants was said to be the best anywhere in the highlands, even after shipping costs, Macneil made a decent profit.

Kelping was extremely hard and unpleasant work and during the summer months it dominated the working day of the crofters to the extent that they found it difficult to look after crops and animals. Together with the restrictions placed on using seaweed for manuring the land, kelping thus had a significant and increasingly malign influence on food production in Barra. But because it paid rents, and even allowed for the purchase of a few luxuries (tobacco and whiskey were allegedly the most popular), its advance was inexorable. During the Napoleonic Wars, when Spanish barilla was unavailable, the price of kelp rose to an all time high of about £20 per ton, and the Hebridean landlords produced ever-larger amounts of kelp to meet the demand. With the defeat of Napoleon and the coming of peace, Spanish barilla returned to the market-place and the demand for Hebridean kelp began to decline. But the decline was not as abrupt nor as steep as is sometimes supposed. An account prepared for the estate's trustees following Macneil's death in 1822 provides details of kelp sales in the years from 1817 to 1821. At a price averaging around £8–£10 per ton, Macneil was exporting about 300 tons of kelp to Liverpool and Greenock in each of those years. Although the 'cost of manufacture' rose sharply during this period (presumably not through increased payments to his kelpers, but perhaps due to shipping costs) Macneil still managed to show kelp profits over the five year period of over £6,300. Only in 1821 did profits dip below a £1,000 for the year.

It is often emphasised how the highland landlords obtained a double benefit from kelp, taking not only the considerable profits of the kelp making but also raising rents because kelping enabled their tenants to pay more. What evidence is there that Roderick the Gentle followed this path ? It is difficult to answer this question in detail because rental records for Barra are rare. In general terms we can say that whereas Walker records the total rental income of Barra and its islands in 1764 as around £300, in 1817 it was just over £1,400, according to Roderick the Gentle's trustees. Even allowing for the inflation in the period of the Napoleonic Wars, this suggests a substantial increase, in real terms, in the rental income Macneil received from his tenants over a period of about fifty years. MacQueen unfortunately does not provide a total rental figure for 1794 in the *Old Statistical Account*, so it is impossible to tell at what point in this fifty year period rental income rose fastest. Both Walker and a sole surviving rental list for 1811 do, however, give rental totals for the individual islands south of Barra. These figures (table 2.1) confirm a significant increase in the rental value of these small islands, but also suggest that the rental increases on Barra were proportionally even greater. Rental income in the southern isles tripled, whereas on Barra itself it rose by almost 600%.

Vatersay was of course held by Macneil's cousin as tacksman which presumably explains its preferential treatment. The discrepancy between the scale of increase on Barra itself, and that in the southern islands is important, and in seeking its explanation we may also avoid falling into the trap of assuming that the rents of individual tenants

Table 2.1 Rentals for the southern islands 1764 and 1811

	Walker 1764	Rental List 1811	% Increase
Barra	£200-00	£1173-05	600%
Vatersay	£35-00	£60-00	170%
Sandray	£12-00	£42-00	350%
Pabbay	£5-00	£16-10	330%
Mingulay	£12-00	£40-00	330%
Berneray	£6-00	£21-00	350%

on Barra were all raised by Roderick the Gentle by 600%. The population of the four southernmost islands appears to have remained more or less static between 1764 (128 inhabitants) and 1794 (23 families), and indeed up until 1811 (25 tenants / families). These are small islands which already in 1764 were almost 'full' (though Mingulay could and later did take significantly more people). The number of tenants in 1764 is therefore probably very similar to that in 1794 and 1811, and we may reasonably assume that the total rental increase of 330–350% represents the likely increase in individual rents. On Barra the situation was very different. Its population almost doubled between 1764 and 1811 to over 2,100 people. Although the number of cottars was to become a significant problem on Barra in time, at this period it was probably still relatively low. Equally on Barra itself in 1811, apart from Macneil's Eoligarry farm there appears to have been only one other small farm at Northbay to employ labourers. It is likely therefore that much of the increased population became small tenants, crofters, and that Macneil created new crofts to accommodate them. Indeed MacQueen confirms this saying that 'the proprietor was obliged to divide the lands into smaller portions', and also implying that previously unoccupied land had been turned into new crofts. A significant part of the increased rental income would probably have come therefore from new rents rather than higher ones. There is no reason why the tenants on the southern islands should have been treated differently to those on Barra itself and we might therefore suggest that rent increases on Barra between 1764 and 1811 were perhaps of the order of 350%.

This seems to be broadly confirmed by the details of the 1811 rental. The 1811 rental provides a list of tenants and their rents but does not record the size of their tenancies. MacQueen however noted in 1794 that 'no tenant here possesses more than a halfpenny, for which he pays £3–£4 for single lands and £6 for the halfpenny of double lands...and many have but 1/4 and 1/8 of a penny'. Bearing this in mind we can make some sense of the 1811 rental in terms of croft sizes.

In Northend for example 3 tenants pay rents of £8-8-0, 21 pay £5-12-0 and 27 pay £2-16-0. We can suggest that the lowest figure is for 1/8d of land, and this is apparently confirmed by the single rental entry that actually says how much land is rented. Lachlan Mclean of Northend rents a plot for £5-12-0 (1/4d?) but also has the tenancy of '1/8 without kelp or grass' at £1-5-0. A 1/8d of land *with* rights to kelp and grass would therefore presumably be the next highest sum - £2-16-0. Northend is some of the best land on the island, and rents elsewhere appear somewhat lower, but the general pattern holds. On this basis the rents rose by about 320% between 1794 and 1811.

The figures from Northend, and indeed other parts of Barra, in the 1811 rental seem to underline MacQueen's comment in 1794 that many tenants held only 1/4d and 1/8d lands, tiny plots incapable of supporting a family without recourse to fishing and kelping. There is little doubt that landlords encouraged this pattern at this time, to ensure that their tenants spent time kelping, although in fairness to Roderick the Gentle it must be recognised that with Barra's burgeoning population and limited (even marginally) arable land crofts were necessarily going to be small if the demand for them were to be

met. Barra's population growth during the lifetime of Roderick the Gentle is remarkable. The available figures from 1755 to 1821 are in table 2.2.

Table 2.2 Population figures for Barra parish

1755 (Webster)	1,150
1764 (Walker)	1,285
1794 (MacQueen)	1,604
1801 (Census)	1,925
1811 (Census)	2,114
1821 (Census)	2,303

In 66 years the population doubled! In fact, however, the figures underestimate the demographic dynamic for between 1772 and 1821 Barra saw a series of significant emigrations. We discuss and document these in detail in the final chapter of this volume, but here we may note just some of the more significant episodes (table 2.3).

Table 2.3 Some emigrations from Barra to Canada 1772–1817

1772	8 families to Island of St John (PEI) on the *Alexander*
1790	28 families on the *Queen* (of Greenock) to Cape Breton
1801	c.80? on the *Sarah* and the *Dove* to Cape Breton
1802	c.370? on the *Hector* to Cape Breton
1817	c.300 on the *William Tell* and *Hope* to Cape Breton

These seven ships alone probably carried over 900 people to British North America in this period, and there were certainly many other emigrants from the island who crossed the Atlantic during this time. There were also others who drifted to the mainland, and in particular the newly industrialised lowlands. MacQueen describes one such group from Barra in the early 1790s, who went to work in the cotton mills in Glasgow. Between 1770 and 1820 Barra must have lost at least 1,500 inhabitants to emigration. This figure emphasises just how dramatic the increase in population over this 50 year period was, how catastrophic it might have been but for emigration, and how many Barramen were anxious to leave the island.

The reasons for emigration were several, and they are discussed in the final chapter, but we may note that the two earliest 'group migrations' in the *Alexander* in 1772 and in the *Queen* in 1790 seem to have been motivated in part by religious considerations. The *Alexander*'s passengers received financial support from the Catholic church, who were using the emigration to pressure Protestant landlords to treat their Catholic tenants with more humanity and tolerance. Burke, in his *Mission of St Patrick*, claims that the much bigger emigration in 1790 was sparked by Macneil's attempts to prevent his Catholic tenants rebuilding a church. Although we have no evidence from Barra to support this assertion, there is a little evidence from the end of the century to suggest that Roderick the Gentle was not above discrimination. Bishop Chisholm received two letters in 1799 from the parish priest of Barra

(James Macdonnel) 'which gives some light on 'Barra's' persecution. Barra's conduct from first to last has been of a more black complexion than I at first imagined' (Blundell 1917, 202). No further details are provided, but it seems that Macneil was in dispute with the priest and the church. With an even bigger emigration following in 1801/2 there is the possibility that this too was at least partly inspired by religious intolerance on Macneil's part. Before he died in 1822, Roderick the Gentle, who had expressed his sadness at the departure of his people on the *William Tell* in 1817, had to wave farewell to another ship-load of Barra emigrants – perhaps as many as 350 – on the *Harmony* in 1821, though both these emigrations were probably driven by economics more than religion.

Roderick the Gentle has generally had a 'good press' both from contemporary recorders (e.g. MacQueen and Buchanan) and from modern commentators (e.g. J L Campbell). Whether he deserved such accolades is perhaps debateable. We noted earlier some of the evidence that he perhaps still retained some sense of a chieftain's responsibility to his people, and equally that he tried to improve the island's economy. His letters certainly convey the impression of a patient and generally humane landlord. Yet we must recall too that he was responsible for the first 'clearance' in Barra, to create his Eoligarry farm, and that he built the mill to which his tenants were forced to take their grain. He too prevented crofters taking seaweed to manure their land, and he both divided crofts and raised their rents. As we have seen there is reason to think he practised a degree of discrimination, though that may have been against the Catholic church rather than against his Catholic tenants. He also accumulated debts that allowed his son and heir little room for manoeuvre if the island's economy took a down turn.

And Barra at the time of Roderick's death was in a potentially perilous position. It had become overpopulated, although many of its most active and ambitious families had emigrated to British North America. Its tenants were living on tiny plots, their subsistence heavily dependent on a single crop – the potato. Their rents bore little relation to the size of their croft, but much to the price of kelp, which was now declining sharply. Barra in 1822 was a disaster waiting to happen.

3

The Historical Archaeology of Barra

The historical archaeology of the Western Isles has not received much attention either in the field or in print. It may be that much of it is too 'recent' to be thought worthy of recording and research, and that some elements of it, such as the blackhouse, are so ubiquitous and so well documented that there is little point to, and not much scope for, original research on these monuments. Yet they constitute not only a very large, rich and diverse body of evidence for the way the islands were inhabited and used over the millennium, but even the briefest acquaintance with them reveals how little we really know about them, and how wrong is most of what we think we 'know'. The purpose of this chapter is to draw attention to these neglected monuments, to show how much potential they have for further study, and thereby to stimulate future programmes of research.

Our survey has revealed perhaps 1,500 post-prehistoric monuments, which can be classified into about two dozen main groups. Excavations have examined examples of some of these groups, most notably blackhouses, and thrown light on their structure, function, and the material culture which was associated with them. In this chapter we want to discuss each of these groups of monuments with a view to establishing a better understanding of them, in terms of their chronology, purpose and function. It is not the intention to describe either the groups or any individual monuments in great detail. We shall give most consideration to those monuments which were

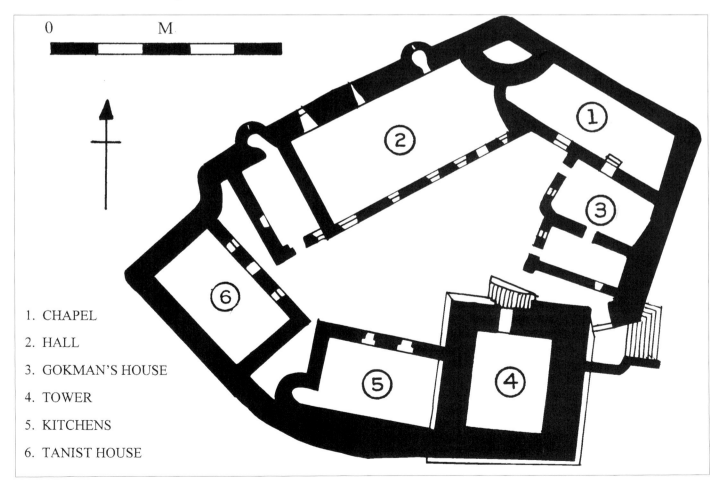

1. CHAPEL

2. HALL

3. GOKMAN'S HOUSE

4. TOWER

5. KITCHENS

6. TANIST HOUSE

Figure 3.1 Plan of Kisimul Castle as restored by Robert Lister Mcneil. The castle originally consisted of the tower and curtain wall, to which the hall and chapel were first added, followed by the other buildings

particularly ubiquitous but have until now been least studied and recorded. Having discussed each group in isolation, we shall then try to examine some areas of landscape where their inter-relationships can be appreciated.

We shall begin with the monumental structures, castles, towers, and estate houses, followed by churches and chapels, before moving to more common vernacular architecture, including blackhouses and their associated ancillary buildings. We shall then consider other structures concerned with agricultural activity, before moving on to monuments built principally for control of animals, including not only pens and enclosures but also shielings and shelters. Finally we examine structures concerned with the exploitation of marine resources.

Castles and towers

There are only two such structures on the Barra islands, and they stand within 3kms of each other on the south side of Barra. Kisimul Castle is known world-wide as the 'Castle in the Sea', whereas Castle Sinclair is barely known outside the island. They share a common location – on islets surrounded by water, albeit one in the sea and the other in a freshwater loch. Kisimul Castle is one of a small group of curtain-wall castles of irregular plan found on the western seaboard of Scotland (Fig. 3.1). A tall keep stands on the south side and within the curtain wall are other buildings, some substantially restored by the 45th chief in the mid-twentieth century and others represented by no more than footings. Further description of the castle and debate about its date is not pursued here (see p. 6). The castle is described and its date discussed by Cruden (1960), Macneil (1964), Dunbar (1978) and RCHM (1928) among others. The present Macneil discusses the premises on which the date of the castle may be established elsewhere (Macneil forthcoming), whilst we await the published report on excavations undertaken in the castle on behalf of Historic Scotland in 2001.

Castle Sinclair was a three-storey tower, about 6m square, built on an islet in Loch Tangasdale. It is now reduced to two storeys and its wooden floors have long since disappeared (Fig. 3.2). Given that its principal chambers, on the first and second floors, were less than 3m square and had no fireplaces, it is doubtful if it ever held a household. It is presumed to be of medieval date, and traditionally was built for the Chief's half-brother, Iain Garbh c. AD 1430.

Estate houses

The successors to the Castles were the estate houses of the Chiefs in the 18th and 19th centuries. There were two in the Barra islands, that occupied by Macneil at Eoligarry and the estate house on Vatersay. Both stand in the middle of good machair pastures and arable which formed the nucleus of the farms they supported. Vatersay still stands as a ruin, but Eoligarry was demolished in the 1970s, although its garden wall and outbuildings partly survive. Photos of Eoligarry House show an imposing Georgian mansion, which was built by Colonel Roderick Macneil, 40th Chief of the clan (Fig. 3.3). The ground floor had a spacious entrance hall flanked by drawing and dining rooms, and there were four bedrooms

Figure 3.2 The remains of 'Castle Sinclair', a simple tower on an islet in Loch Tangasdale. Originally three stories high, it is now reduced to two

on the first floor, approached by an impressive staircase. In addition there was an attic which ran the length of the building, and a large basement. A two-storey wing attached to the rear of the house contained four servants' bedrooms, the housekeeper's room, a milk house and stores. Further outbuildings included a ten-stalled stable, a mill house, two loose boxes, a nine-stalled byre, two stirk houses and a bull house. A high wall enclosed about an acre of garden. It was really quite an impressive country seat for a somewhat impoverished highland chief.

The house on Vatersay, was probably built about the same time although an article in the *Inverness Courier* (Dec 3rd 1845) describes it as 'a two-storied house – long the residence of cadets of the ancient family of Macneil'. It was occupied in the late 18th/early 19th century by the Chief's cousin, Donald Macneil, and seems to have been a scaled-down version of Eoligarry. Its ruins reveal two storeys and an attic but no basement, and only a single one-storey annexe attached to the rear. A modest garden plot nearby was surrounded by a low wall.

Churches, chapels and cemeteries

The most significant Christian building in the Barra Isles is the church of St Barr, Cille Bharra, near the north end of Barra. The surviving structure is much damaged, but its north door with tapering jambs and a false arch of two inclined lintels (Fig. 3.4), is thought to indicate a twelfth century date for the church, which was 13m long and 5.5m wide, with an altar against the east wall.

Figure 3.3 Eoligarry House, built by Roderick the Gentle in the late 18th century as the centre of his Eoligarry farm (Crown Copyright: RCAHMS)

A small free-standing south chapel, 5m long, is almost entirely destroyed above ground level, whilst the north chapel has been substantially re-built and re-roofed and is in any case a late structure, probably of the later 16th century. There was almost certainly an earlier church on the site, since it is thought that the Norse named the island Barray after St Barr when they arrived in the late ninth century. Furthermore a tenth or eleventh century Norse memorial stone found in the churchyard is decorated with an elaborate Celtic cross (Fig. 3.5).

Martin Martin mentioned (c.1695) a chapel 'about half a mile on the south side of the hill near St Barr's church', and Walter Macfarlane (1620) also refers to a chapel, 'Kilmoir', on the south side of the hill from the church, and that the seas almost meet where the chapel stands. Clearly this refers to the neck of machair which separates Traigh Mhor from Traigh Eias. This area was subjected to considerable sand blows, most notably in the 18th century (e.g. Walker 1989, 88), and the chapel subsequently disappeared. In 1988 we discovered a much robbed structure built of large blocks (site E19) in the sand dunes at NF 697 067, and this was partly excavated in 1990 (below p. 59). It had been used as a rabbit catcher's hut in the later 19th century, but the size of the remaining stone blocks suggest that originally it was a more significant building than this, and it may have been the lost chapel. The only other early chapel on Barra was that of St Brendan, situated on the mound in Borve headland cemetery (site B163). Only a fragment of wall and a pile of stones marks its location, but it was clearly a very small structure.

Both Dean Munro (1549) and Bishop Nicholson (c.1697) report chapels on all the larger islands south of Barra. That of Cille Bhrianain (site VN133) at the north-east tip of Vatersay is still just visible (Fig. 3.5). In size it is not much smaller than Cille Bharra at 11 x 5m, but its walls appear much narrower. There are traces of an enclosure around it, and it

Figure 3.4 The north door of Cille Bharra with its false arch, thought to date from the 12th century

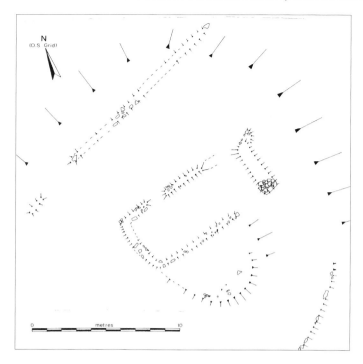

Figure 3.5 A surveyed plan of the remains of Cille Bhrianain on the north-east tip of Vatersay

stands on a low mound from which handmade sherds have been thrown up by rabbits. The chapels on Sandray (Cille Bhride), and Pabbay (site PY55) cannot be traced today, although both were reputedly seen as fragmentary wall foundations by the RCHM. The alleged dimensions of the Pabbay chapel (9.5 x 4.5m) could not be fitted onto the mound on which it is said to have stood. St Columba's chapel on Mingulay was recorded by the OS in 1973 as the remains of a building 3m wide, and our survey saw fragments of walling in 1991 (site MY88). Finally, neither RCHM or OS found any trace of the chapel on Berneray, although the site (BY55) has a complicated sequence of structures on it amongst which the remains of a chapel could be hidden.

Despite the dubious or non-existent traces of these chapels there is no reason to doubt that they once existed, not least because all of these sites except perhaps Sandray, appear to be associated with early cemeteries. The best documented is that on Pabbay from which comes the well-known Pictish symbol-stone apparently re-used as a Christian grave-marker. The cemetery consists of a mound of sand 15m in diameter and up to 3m high, covered with a layer of stone cobbles. Apart from the Pictish stone with its added cross, three other simple cross-marked slabs are recorded from the site (Fisher 2001, 106). On Mingulay the site of the chapel is on a mound inside a circular enclosure wall, which was used for burials up until 1910. The Berneray cemetery is a sub-circular enclosure 40 x 25m, at the centre of which is a cobble-clad mound about 10m in diameter. Two grave markers hidden in the vegetation on this mound included one with a simple pecked cross and the other with a cup mark. Of the cemetery sites on Barra, we might note that St Brendan's chapel on Borve headland stood on the stony mound created

by the ruins of the former Iron Age broch. As for Cille Bharra itself, its early use as a cemetery is presumably indicated by the Norse memorial stone, and perhaps by three small grave-markers with simple incised crosses which still sit on the site (Fig. 3.6). By the early 16th century the Macneils themselves may have been buried here, and three fine decorated grave-slabs now lying in the restored north chapel may have covered 16th-century chiefs or their nearest kin.

Figure 3.5 A simple grave marker with an incised Latin cross at Cille Bharra

Blackhouses

The Hebridean blackhouses have been a source of interest and comment since the first visitors wrote accounts of them in the 18th century. Most surviving descriptions of blackhouses, however, refer to buildings of the second half of the nineteenth century and much of what has been written about blackhouse architecture is based on descriptions and examples of that period. Our concern in this volume is essentially with buildings erected before 1850, although inevitably our survey data will include some which were probably built after that date.

A description of blackhouses which would find general acceptance would say they were low, thick-walled rectangular buildings with rounded external corners, varying from 10m to 20m in length. They had one, or quite often two opposing, doors found towards one end of the long walls. Inside was a central hearth, with an area for human occupation to one side, and another (sometimes with rough cobbling, and usually a drain) for animals on the other.

Whilst the blackhouses we found on Barra and the other southern islands fit this description in a general sense, they also vary from it in some significant ways, and in 2000 we published a paper (Branigan and Merrony 2000) which drew attention to these differences. The main structural differences pertain to size, shape, and entrances and may be summarised in the following table which compares information from our Barra blackhouse database (comprising a total of 190 blackhouses) with information on a group of 18 blackhouses from South Uist (surveyed by colleagues of the SEARCH team) and 15 on North Uist (recorded in the archives of the School of Scottish Studies, University of Edinburgh). We also include a group (of 18) blackhouses recorded by us on Vatersay.

Table 3.1 Size and proportions of Hebridean blackhouses

	BARRA	VATERSAY	S.UIST	N.UIST
Length under 12m	83%	83%	33%	13%
Length over 12m	17%	17%	67%	87%
Length/Width ratio above 2	15%	11%	78%	73%
Door central*	75%	94%	33%	47%

(* the great majority, but not all, blackhouses recorded in survey revealed the location of the door with certainty)

The obvious conclusions to draw from this table are that the great majority of blackhouses on Barra and Vatersay were shorter than those on South and North Uist, and they were also *relatively* wider. They might be said to be short and fat in contrast to the more northern blackhouses which could be described as long and thin. The central door is found on most of the Barra and Vatersay blackhouses, but is much less common further north. The use of two, opposed doorways, often found in the northern blackhouses (nearly half of the South Uist group have them) is found in just two cases (1%) on Barra, and none on Vatersay.

As might be expected from the above observations, the Barra and Vatersay houses have considerably less floor space than the houses on South Uist. In the South Uist sample 60% of houses have a floor space in excess of 40m² and only one (6%) falls below 20m²; in North Uist 93% have more than 40m² of floor space. This is in very sharp contrast with Barra where only 12% of the blackhouses offer over 40m² of space, and as many as 25% have less than 20m².

Excavations on Barra and South Uist blackhouses point to further differences inside the houses. The presence of a partition wall is obviously of considerable interest in view of the stalling of animals in one end of the blackhouse. But we know that some of these partitions were entirely of wood or turf, so they may not leave any remains which might be visible on unexcavated sites. Our excavations on Barra however suggest that the visible remains of stone partitions must also be interpreted with care on unexcavated sites. We have excavated four blackhouses on Barra which had stone-founded partition walls visible before excavation. These were Alt Chrisal (site T26), and Balnabodach L8A, L8C, and L9F. In all four cases the partition wall proved to be a secondary structure and not an original, integral part of the house.

Evidence for animal occupation at one end of these buildings is at best dubious. In the Alt Chrisal house (Fig. 3.7) there was a drain at the east end of the house in its first phase, but there was no metalling of any kind, and the excavator specifically noted there was no trace of any disturbance or churning of the floor material by animals (Branigan and Foster 1995, 71. Furthermore there was a free-standing byre built alongside the house, and churning of the floor material there, which included a 'gravel' metalling, was clearly distinguished (Branigan and Foster 1990, 93). In the case of Balnabodach L9F the insertion of the partition wall was part of a major remodelling of the building which appears to have changed it from a house into a barn / byre with further partitions / pens and cobbling. The small room created by the secondary partition in house L8C was itself sub-divided by a narrow wall and the smaller of the two spaces, 2.7 x 1.3m, was provided with light and patchy cobbling but no drain. If an animal was housed here it would have been small, cramped, and have reached its accommodation only by walking through the main 'living' space of the house. Finally, house L8A was not partitioned so much as extended. Its additional room was entered through a narrow gap just 0.25m wide. Near the centre of the room was a small fireplace, with a pot-stand next to it. There was no cobbling or drain in the room. We are convinced this room was for human rather than animal occupation.

These excavations tend to support the conclusion which common sense, and ethnographic data, suggest must be drawn from considering the size of the Barra blackhouses alone. The vast majority were simply too small to house animals and humans under the same roof. Most peasant families provide around 10m² of space per occupant in the family home (Naroll 1962, Caselbury 1974, Summer 1979, Hassan 1981). The average amount of floor space in a Barra blackhouse was 28m², and the average Barra household in 1840 consisted of 5.7 persons (Nicholson 1840). Without any space given over to animals at all, the average Barra household was grossly overcrowded, with less than 5.0m² of space per inhabitant. Many families of course were considerably larger than 'average'; families of eight to ten were quite common in these Catholic islands.

We are convinced, therefore, that the vast majority of blackhouses on Barra and its neighbouring islands did not accommodate cattle. Furthermore this view is supported by the testimony of a contemporary eye-witness. In the *Inverness Courier* of December 10th 1845, a lengthy article by 'a late resident of the island' makes this point very forcibly: 'In one respect the Barra cottars are considerably in advance of their more northerly neighbours as they have outhouses for their cattle and horses, though these may still be seen in one end of the dwelling in a very few instances'. The exceptions are presumably to be found amongst the handful of blackhouses of 15m and upwards in length. The out-houses include both free-standing examples, which we shall briefly discuss below, and annexes built either onto one end or onto the back of the blackhouse. These have their own independent access, and have no doorway into the house itself. We have noted at least fourteen examples of annexed outhouses of this kind in field survey.

Figure 3.7 The blackhouse at Alt Chrisal (site T26) in its final form, as it was abandoned c. 1830

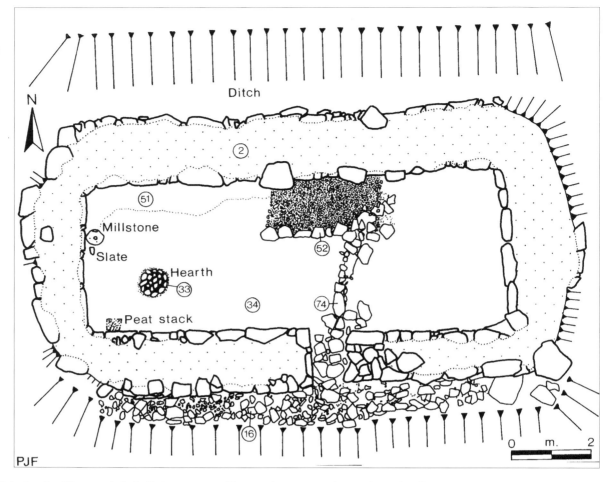

The way in which the families used their living space will not be discussed in any detail here, partly because it is also discussed in the study of the blackhouse settlement at Balnabodach, and partly because the evidence is still very sparse. Few of the early travellers who describe Hebridean blackhouses have much to say about their interior, and the excavation of six blackhouses on Barra (T26, T30, L8A, L8C, L8D, and L9F) has yielded little direct evidence. The archaeological evidence suggests that hearths were for the most part surprisingly small, usually towards one end of the room. Some houses had emplacements for a dresser, usually against a rear wall and facing the door. Floors were bare trampled earth, sometimes sprinkled with sand. We found no evidence, in the form of differential wear or spread of debris on the floor, for built bed-boxes against the walls. Equally, there were no metal pieces which may have come from substantial pieces of furniture or trunks; the largest such items could only have come from small boxes.

Three contemporary accounts of the interior of island homes certainly suggest that they were sparsely furnished. George Buchanan, in 1582 says that the islanders 'lie upon the ground; strewing fern or heath on the floor' to form a bed (Campbell 1998, 33). No suggestion of a bed-box here, but at this date he may be describing the interior of a house other than a blackhouse. The Reverend John Buchanan who visited the islands two centuries later, however, paints a fuller picture. The houses are described as 'quite destitute of furniture, except logs of timber collected from the wrecks of

the sea, to sit on about the fire...or seats made of straw, like foot hassocks, stuffed with straw or stubble. All persons must have their own blankets to sleep in, they make their beds in whatever corner takes their fancy'. He repeats that the houses are 'without furniture except a loom, or old chest to hold their eatables and a few plates, or sacks made of benty grass' (Buchanan 1793, 39–40). Even as late as 1840 we find the Rev. Nicholson repeating this picture: 'they have seldom much furniture to boast of; sometimes not a chair to sit on; a bed to sleep-on, or bed-clothes to cover them'. The archaeological evidence suggests that most furnishings were removed when the house was abandoned, and the historical sources suggest that furnishings were very sparse in the first place.

The distribution of the blackhouses on Barra and Vatersay (Fig. 3.8) is potentially of great interest, since it should obviously reflect where the concentrations of the tenant and cottar populations were. We have to bear in mind, however, that the distribution map, like most of its kind, is incomplete and therefore to be used with care. Some blackhouses may have been totally destroyed by demolition and re-use of the building materials. But many more will have been modified, first by the addition of chimneys and additional windows (so that they became white houses), and later by adaptation for non-occupational use (barns, byres, sheds etc). Only a close and detailed inspection of the ruins of such buildings might reveal their original character, and this has often been precluded by the fact that such structures are still in use

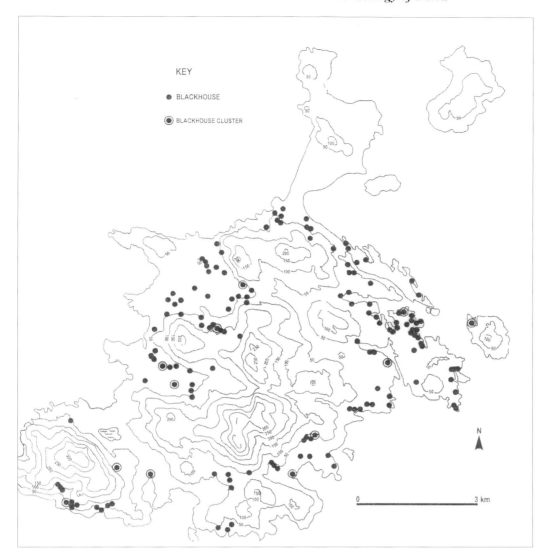

Figure 3.8 The distribution of identified blackhouses on Barra

today and lie immediately adjacent to present day homes. In trying not to intrude on the privacy of the crofters, some former blackhouses will therefore almost certainly have avoided recognition and record. This might apply particularly in the denser areas of modern settlement (notably the lower Borve valley, Castlebay, and Vatersay township).

Nevertheless, there are some valid points to be made on the basis of the distribution of recorded blackhouses. First we might note that taking their relative size into consideration, Barra has about twice the density of blackhouses as Vatersay. On Vatersay itself, all but two of the recorded blackhouses are found on the northern half of the island. These two observations may be explained by the fact that Vatersay was run as a farm estate up until the early 20th century, and that the 'home farm' of the estate was centred on the house above Vatersay township. The southern half of Vatersay therefore saw neither crofters nor cottars in the heyday of the blackhouse.

On Barra itself, a similar phenomenon is to be noted by the absence of blackhouses in Eoligarry, which was of course the home farm of Macneil (centred on Eoligarry House). As for the rest of the island, the blackhouses are found distributed almost equally between the eastern and western sides.

However this statement obscures some real differences between the distribution pattern in east and west Barra. The eastern blackhouses are mostly close to the sea (83% within 250m of the sea, 93% within 500m), whilst the western houses are more frequently found 'inland' (only 26% within 250m of the sea, and 35% within 500m). This is undoubtedly partly a function of the topography, with the valleys and dales of Borve/Craigston, Allasdale/Cuier, and Grean/Cleat, providing crofting lands which stretch back towards the centre of the island. There are no comparable areas on the east, except for Glen (facing onto the south coast) and a very limited area around Brevig, and it is in these areas that the only 'eastern' blackhouses more than 500m from the sea are to be found.

Not surprisingly the pattern of blackhouse settlement is therefore different on the two sides of the island. On the west, blackhouses are found in loose 'clusters' around the valleys and vales. This applies even in the remote and rugged south-western corner of the island (Tangaval) at Gortein, Alt Chrisal, and Crubisdale. On the east coast, the pattern is a linear one for the most part with blackhouses strung out along the coastal margin. There is a particular concentration of blackhouses around the coast of Bruernish, and here many of the blackhouses stand within a few metres of the waters edge. Apart from their close proximity to each other and the sea, some of the blackhouses around the south-east coast of Bruernish are surrounded only by barren peat bog and moor. The households in these homes must have depended heavily on the sea for a significant part of their livelihood, and there is good reason to think that the concentration of blackhouses around the coast of Bruernish may relate to managerial strategies of the 1830s or 1840s, discussed elsewhere in this volume.

We had hoped that our excavations might help to throw light on the origins of the blackhouse, at least in Barra, and the excavation of site A128 in particular was undertaken with this aim in view. A128 was barely visible on the surface, does not appear even as a ruined building on the 1878 OS map, and (sitting within the grounds of Northbay School erected c.1880) was unlikely to have been built after that date. We surmised therefore that this building must have been abandoned and reduced to near invisibility long before 1878. Excavation however provided little evidence to date the structure and nothing to suggest it was of 18th century or earlier date (see below, p. 73). None of the other excavated blackhouses produced more than a handful of even late 18th century pottery.

Byres, drying sheds and other outbuldings

A variety of free-standing thick-walled, usually round-cornered, buildings were recorded in our surveys, which for various reasons we believe were not blackhouses. Some were simply too small ever to have been occupied as homes, but most were different from the blackhouses in two other respects – they were nearer to square than oblong, and their doors were almost always in or at one corner. The excavated sites T25 and T27 at Alt Chrisal provide ideal 'type-sites' for some of these structures. Building T25 measured 7 x 5.5m externally and had a door at its south-east corner (Fig. 3.9).

Inside, one end of the building had a raised platform, up the centre of which ran a narrow flue. This is identified as a drying shed in which crops could be dried or parched before threshing. Building T27 was very similar in size (7 x 5m) and it too had a door in the corner, though here the doorway was across the corner itself, rather than in the end of a long wall. The rough metalling and churned floor material, and the capped drain which ran down the slope of the building and out of through the doorway, allow the building to be identified as a byre (Fig. 3.10).

We believe we can identify drying sheds with confidence because the raised platform is clearly visible even in long abandoned and ruined buildings. Byres are more difficult to be certain about without excavation because the drains are not usually visible, but thick-walled near-square buildings with a door at, or most commonly actually across, the corner and with no trace of a raised drying platform we think are probably byres. The remaining free-standing structures we can only collectively call 'outbuildings', although we make some suggestions about their usage below.

We identify at least 33 buildings on Barra and a further 4 on Vatersay as free-standing byres. They range in length from 4m to 9m, but they average just below 6m, and the commonest examples are 5–6m in length and 4–5m wide. Only two do not have a door in the corner. The majority stand immediately adjacent or close to one or more blackhouses, and they are found on both the east and west sides of the island.

The drying sheds tend to be larger than the byres (with an average length of over 7.5m). There are far fewer of them than there are byres, just 10 on Barra and 1 on Vatersay. It seems likely that these sheds were used by groups of families, and we shall mention one or two examples where this seems to be the case below. There was no need for each croft to have its own shed, given the small areas of arable land for crop production, and in some parts of the island, no

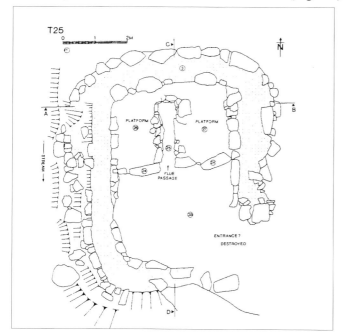

Figure 3.9 An excavated drying shed (site T25) with its raised platform and central flue

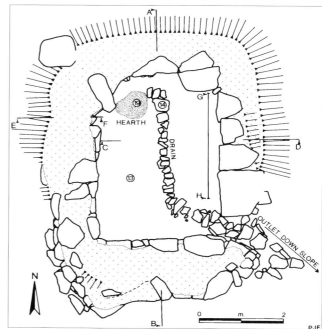

Figure 3.10 An excavated byre (site T27) with its door in one corner and a central drain

suitable land at all. It is notable for example than none are found in Bruernish, despite the heavy concentration of blackhouses there, and the only two on the east side of the island at all are at Brevig (S29 and S34). The two Brevig examples are unusual in having flues running diagonally into the platform, which might have warmed a greater part of the platform floor than the shorter central flue.

The remaining 30 or so thick-walled, round-cornered buildings are mostly small buildings, averaging only a little above 5m in overall length. Many have their door in the centre of either a long or short wall. Some are built against rock faces, although it would be misleading to call them 'lean-to's'. Some stand very close to (within a few metres of) the high water mark. Their functions were probably varied, and of course may well have changed through time as well. One example was excavated, L10, and proved to have a mixture of paving on one side of the door and cobbling on the other (see below, chapter four). This building appears to have been a well-constructed store with its differential flooring. Other examples were probably stores or barns, and some may have been byres of course. The small examples found close to the water's edge on the other hand are more likely to have been fishermens' stores or botheys.

Finally, we must mention the mill-buildings. There are in fact only two such structures in the survey, both on Barra (a third on Mingulay, MY132, was built in 1892). That at the east end of Loch an Duin (site L26) stands by the road, is well known, and might even be called notorious. This is Macneil's mill, to which, according to local oral tradition, crofters were obliged to bring their crops for processing, for which a charge was made, their traditional hand-querns having been confiscated by Macneil. The mill-building itself stands by two boulder-built conduits which brought water from the loch to drive its machinery. Behind it stands a two-roomed building, presumably the miller's house, and a small square structure most likely to have been a store. These remains may belong mostly to the reconstruction of the original mill in the 1830s (Nicholson in Campbell 1998, 158). The second structure (site G23) is something of a mystery. It stands on a flat shelf, at about 70m OD, on the northern slopes of Ben Erival and is invisible from Vaslain below. A substantial stone revetted platform has been constructed and two streams diverted around it to pass between two parallel strongly built walls, 0.7m apart. At one point a large capping stone bridges the gap between the walls. Downstream of this structure, a built conduit takes the water into a natural ravine. The structure has the appearance of a small 'mill race' but there is no remaining structural evidence of how a millstone and its drive may have been mounted over the water channel.

Haystack bases, clearance cairns and cultivation plots

Hay is a scarce commodity in the Western Isles, and after drying it was traditionally piled into high, narrow hay cocks supported by a tripod of sticks and stood on a platform of stone. We occasionally noted small platforms presumably used as stack bases, but not very often. The biggest group were six circular platforms, varying between 2m and 2.5m in diameter, at site A36 in Bruernish. Near the settlement of Balnabodach a pair of rectangular platforms each 2m square were recorded (site L28). The stone paving of these platforms is comprised of small stones and many stack bases may well have become completely overgrown.

Clearance cairns are far more ubiquitous. We recorded the location of all clearance cairns we saw and distinguished three types. Primary cairns were comprised more or less entirely of large blocks of stone such as one might expect to be removed during initial clearance of a piece of land. Secondary cairns were made up of small 'field stones', the sort of stones one would expect to be removed during the digging over and cultivation of a cleared plot. Mixed cairns were usually those where a heap of large stone from primary clearance was covered by smaller field stones from subsequent cultivation activity. All three types in Barra and the other southern islands are round or oval. Secondary cairns predominate, probably because many stones from primary clearance were taken away for use in constructing field walls and buildings. The value of the clearance cairns of course is that they indicate both specific plots and general areas of land which have at some time been cleared for cultivation, even though it may have long since reverted to pasture or moorland. Excavation of two clearance cairns near the blackhouse at Alt Chrisal (Branigan and Foster 1995, 163) confirmed that they have little structure apart from an occasional very rough 'kerb' of larger blocks, and that artefactual material is scarce and provides only a terminus post quem for the creation of the cairn. We found no examples of 'linear' clearance cairns forming banks such as are associated with rig-systems, and it may be that the clearance cairns of Barra reflect the nature of the cultivation systems that were in use on the island.

Cultivation plots are most commonly marked by the appearance of relict lazy-beds (Fig. 3.11). These again are a ubiquitous feature of the Hebridean landscape, but one which has been taken very much for granted and has not been studied in any detail. We were unable to plot all relict lazy-beds in Barra and the adjacent islands – that would be a massive undertaking although appropriate low-angle aerial photographs could certainly be used to plot the major concentrations. We did however plot the lazy-bed cultivation of the settlements at Crubisdale, Gortein and Balnabodach and comment further on these below. These lazy-beds are seen today as low parallel mounds, rarely as much as 3m wide. Originally the ridges were narrower and straight-sided with the soil between removed to the subsoil or even to the rock and mounded up on the ridge. This obviously produces both a well-drained and a deep soil in which to sow crops. Although wheat or barley could be grown on lazy-beds, they were mostly used from the later 18th century onwards for potatoes. They can occasionally still be seen being used for this crop in Eoligarry, Borve and Tangasdale. They occur in plots as small as 3 x 5m, and on steep slopes, because they were dug with either the spade or the *caschrom*. Small plots like these occur mostly close to the blackhouses where their cultivators lived and are often unenclosed, but sometimes they are protected by a walled or embanked enclosure.

We found a small number of cultivation or garden plots which showed no signs of lazy-beds but were apparently raised above the surrounding ground level, enclosed by a low

Figure 3.11 Relict lazy-beds at Caolis, Vatersay. The beds clearly pre-date the sheep wall which runs across the middle of the picture

bank or wall, and carefully cleared of stones. All five examples that we recorded on Barra were in the area of Grean and Cuier; another example was noted on Vatersay and there are other less certain examples found elsewhere. They varied in size from 7 x 8m up to 10 x 21m, and in each case were very close to blackhouses. Whether they were simply alternatives to lazy-beds or were used for different crops is unknown, although the care with which they were constructed perhaps suggests the latter.

Land boundaries

Field systems are of great interest to students of agrarian history and landscape archaeologists alike, and there has been considerable research on highland and island field systems in recent decades (e.g. Dodgshon 1980; 1992; Foster and Smout 1994). When we began work on Barra, in the Borve Valley, in 1988 we were both impressed and stimulated by the plethora of relict land boundaries. Soon, however, we were overwhelmed by them and rather than record every such structure we found in our surveys we had to opt for a more selective strategy. We therefore carried out a detailed study of boundaries at the top end of Craigston township (in the Borve valley), and also recorded boundaries in detail in our survey of Gortein and two areas on Mingulay. Apart from recording what we found in the landscape, we also talked extensively to some of the older crofters of Borve and Craigston. However, they knew little about the pre-crofting boundaries and so we were dependent on our own observations in the field. Apart from the sheer quantity of boundaries, we were also surprised by their remarkable variety. Excluding post and wire fences which now mark out most of the croft boundaries, we identified eight principal types of boundary (Fig.3.12). These were variations and combinations of earth banks, built stone walls, and spaced boulders or blocks of stone. All eight types were found somewhere in the Borve valley. Most confusing, but also perhaps most enlightening of all, was the way in which an apparently continuous boundary would change its construction at several points along its length. Whether this indicated repairs and replacements at different periods in the boundary's history, or adapting the construction to the most convenient supply of materials at a particular point in the landscape is uncertain, but probably it was a mixture of both. The detailed study of the walls at the top end of Craigston did not produce any clear chronological sequence of boundary types, but does allow some suggestions to be made about the purpose of some boundaries. The stone revetted turf walls (type 7) are of a type which is well-known and is essentially designed to keep sheep out of cultivated areas or winter grazings. The vertical stone face prevents sheep getting into the protected area, whilst the rounded bank behind allows any strays to be easily driven out again. A major boundary of this sort runs around most of the Borve valley, and might be called a head dyke. It presumably marks out what was once regarded as the summer high pastures and runs at around the 100m contour. Other examples of this type of boundary are found inside this major boundary however and presumably mark fluctuations in the designation of summer pasture. It is perhaps significant that some shielings which excavation has revealed to be used initially in the medieval period and re-used in the early modern era (see below, p. 52) stand inside the major sheep-wall. Since the condition and preservation of the sheep-wall is generally quite good, it is unlikely to be pre-medieval; the location of the medieval and early modern shielings inside the wall suggest that it is not contemporary with them, and is

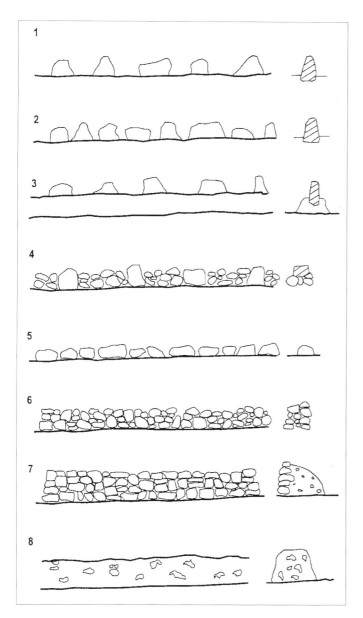

Fig 3.12 Stylised diagram of the principal types of land boundaries on Barra

physical barrier, nor are there any traces of turf or earthen banks which might have followed the lines of these stone boundaries. That is, these boundaries must have been essentially markers rather than barriers. Some of these boundaries are linear and run for 50m–200m, but many run for shorter distances and often seem to mark out irregular areas which, were the boundaries more substantial, one might describe as enclosures. At Craigston one such 'enclosure' appears to be crossed by the major sheep wall, and another by a stone croft wall. These two examples of 'orthostat' boundaries therefore may be pre-crofting (18th century or earlier). Further support for a pre-crofting date for some of these boundaries may come from one section of the sheep wall at Craigston which appears to have been constructed by in-filling the gaps in a spaced orthostat boundary of large blocks (type 4). However, we would certainly not claim that all 'orthostat' boundaries are pre-crofting, and we would be particularly hesitant about placing a relatively early date on the continuous boundaries of small blocks. These may be variants of the type 5 boundary, where stones are laid lengthwise to form a continuous kerb, again usually marking some sort of 'enclosure'. The one example where we examined these by excavation, at site B54 (Branigan and Foster 2000, 217) suggested they were associated with lazy-bed cultivation at a relatively recent date and that one of the inner of the two 'kerbs' may have marked the line of a fence.

Boundaries of type 8, simple banks of mostly earth mixed with some stone, are common, rarely more than 30–40cms high, and mostly degraded, eroded and apparently long-since ignored. One group are found following the sinuous courses of streams down the slopes, but others run along the contours, and can sometimes be traced for hundreds of metres. Even allowing for erosion and degradation they seem unlikely ever to have been major barriers, but the distances over which they run suggest that they were meaningful boundary markers. There is no direct evidence for their date, although the major sheep wall runs across or cuts straight through them in places. It is likely they are pre-crofting but how much earlier is impossible to say.

This leaves boundaries of type 3. These are what we call 'orthostat on bank', where a spaced series of large stones is set on top of an earth or turf bank. They are not common, and we found only one very battered example in the Borve valley. Other examples were found near Dun Scurrival and Dun Caolis on Vatersay, and on Borve headland, west of the broch that is incorporated into one corner of Borve cemetery. That is, three of the four examples we found of this type of boundary are close to Iron Age brochs. The boundary on Borve headland forms what appears to be a triangular enclosure (site B85), two sides being banks with spaced stones on top and the third today being the sea. Given the marine ingressions on the west coast of Barra, a third banked side may well have been eroded. A bank without spaced othostats then runs from the apex of the triangular enclosure back across the headlands and can be seen passing beneath the cemetery wall, heading directly towards the broch. At Dun Caolis a type 3 boundary runs in an arc around the broch, about 60–70m distant from it but with at least three radial banks 'tying' the arc to the base of the prominent little

therefore probably of relatively recent (late 18th/19th century?) date.

Stone built walls (type 6) mostly run in straight lines and are often found in very reduced conditions running alongside modern croft fences. That is, the croft fences appear to often replace stone walls, which previously marked out the boundaries of the croft and which therefore themselves belong to the period of the crofting era, and particularly that of the later 19th/early 20th century.

Boundaries comprised simply of alignments of blocks of stone or boulders, either more or less continuously or spaced, (types 1 and 2) are particularly difficult to interpret. Some such boundaries are made of large boulders and, where continuous, would form some sort of barrier. Others are constructed of small blocks, perhaps 50–70cms in length, and these may be spaced out. They can never have formed a

hill on which the broch stands. In two places the encircling bank disappears into peat bog and re-emerges again further on. Probing revealed that it ran continuously beneath the bog. On the basis of this evidence we think there is a case for suggesting that the 'orthostat-on-bank' boundaries of type 3 *may* have originated in the Iron Age. The battered example found in the Borve valley was apparently relict when a thick-walled D-shaped hut (site B60, see below p. 56) was built against it and probably utilised some of its stones. The hut was probably constructed in the earlier 18th century.

There is one other land boundary, on Vatersay, which deserves special mention. This is an earth bank which runs from north to south across the saddle of south Vatersay, east of Ben Cuier. Strictly this is two banks. The southern end is a very broad bank, about 5m wide, and preserved to a height of about 2m. It runs from a rock formation northwards for about 400m, where it appears to terminate. After a gap of 15m another bank, narrower (1–1.5m wide) and steep-sided, continues northwards, swings north-westwards, and runs downslope towards the sea for about 150m. In the gap in between the two sections of bank lies an impressive monolith 2.15m long and 1 x 0.4m in section. This bank, or banks, appears to be a significant boundary marker between Am Meall and Eorisdale and the rest of southern Vatersay, and would have involved considerable expenditure of effort to build. It is undated.

Clearly, study of the relict land boundaries on Barra and the southern islands is scarcely in its infancy. The evidence that we gathered for the boundaries and their chronological sequence and dating is at best flimsy, and there is no doubt that there are no easy options for pursuing the matter much further. Aerial photography may provide some help in plotting at least the better preserved boundaries but will reveal little or nothing of the character of their construction. That can only be done by painstaking survey on the ground. Some progress might be made by careful inspection of the junctions and relationships between boundaries in establishing a relative chronological sequence of boundary types. The loss of the early estate maps of Barra, however,

are a serious bar to progress on sorting out even modern from pre-18th century boundaries. Discussion of surviving traces of early field systems is reserved for the later part of this chapter, where we examine a number of landscapes.

Pens and enclosures

The distinction between pens and enclosures (and indeed between them and enclosed cultivation plots and small fields) is not an easy one to define. We certainly envisage pens and enclosures are structures related to pastoral rather than arable activities, and our distinction between them is essentially on the basis of size. Our pen is for a handful of animals, and our enclosure is for a flock or a herd. The smaller structures, enclosing between $20m^2$ and $100m^2$, we certainly regard as pens, whilst those structures which enclose $500m^2$ or more we confidently call enclosures. If we make the division line between pens and enclosures $200m^2$ then about 60% of the 80 structures we recorded in all of the islands we surveyed are pens, and the rest are enclosures. We recognise this is an arbitrary distinction but that it has some significance, since pens and enclosures relate to different scales of animal management.

Size is not the only distinction that can be drawn between the various structures we recorded. Another difference is obviously in construction. There are examples of pens and enclosures with substantial stone walls, and others with earth and stone banks. Amongst the pens in particular there are a good many with a stone wall or earth bank which encloses a space in front of a rock face or large boulder which forms the rear side of the pen. About one in three pens are enclosed by a spaced setting of boulders or large stones. We can only suggest that bundles of heather or possibly turves were stuffed into the gaps between the stones to form a temporary 'wall'.

Shape is another variable (Fig. 3.13). Almost 50% of the pens and enclosures we recorded were rectangular or sub-rectangular, about 25% were D-shaped (almost always the result of utilising either a rock face or existing boundary as a rear wall), and about 25% were oval or circular. There were

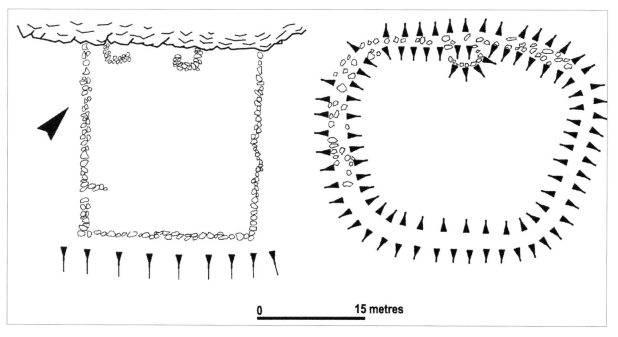

Figure 3.13 Examples of enclosures, one built of boulders and the other with an earth and stone bank. Both enclosures have shepherds' shelters attached

0   15 metres

a small number of irregularly shaped structures. There was no obvious correlation between shape and method of construction, except that many D-shaped pens were built with spaced boulders or large stones. The size, location and construction of these pens suggest they were for very temporary usage.

We were perhaps surprised not to have found more enclosures and pens than we did, and there are certainly some areas where they are almost non-existent. Eoligarry has no examples at all, and Ardveenish and Bruernish have only a handful of small pens. Only three pens are found further south down the east coast. There are a scatter of pens on Ben Erival and Ben Vaslain, and on the high ground around the Borve valley, and half a dozen pens are located on the Tangaval peninsular, though they are notably nearer the sea rather than the centre of this bleak, rocky landscape. The pens are for the most part located on or near high, waterlogged moorlands and areas with only scrub vegetation at best, and were presumably used by shepherds. The relatively flimsy construction of most pens supports their use for the temporary shelter of small numbers of sheep.

Eighteen enclosures (of over $200m^2$) were recorded on Barra, and they were concentrated in three locations, with three on the west facing slopes of Ben Cliad, nine in the Borve valley (mostly on upper slopes), and six on the Tangaval peninsular, all but one in the Gortein valley. Borve and Ben Cliad overlook areas of good cattle pasture and some of the enclosures might well relate to summer grazing of cattle. The cluster around Gortein is more likely to include enclosures for folding sheep which may well have been brought here from almost the entire Tangaval peninsular.

There are interesting variations in the frequency of pens and enclosures on the islands south of Barra. For its size,

Vatersay has about the same density of these structures as Barra, but here the majority are enclosures rather than pens. Four of the seven enclosures are found on the much smaller southern part of the island, an area of noted cattle grazing.

One circular enclosure above Eorisdale (site VS36) is notable for its regularity and its very substantial stone and earth bank with near vertical sides and one metre wide. The interior has relict lazy-beds but one suspects this is a late re-use of manure-enriched soils within the enclosure and that it was originally used for the cattle which grazed the pastures in this corner of the island. Sandray has only one small enclosure, and seven or eight pens, which contrasts with its near neighbour, Pabbay, where there are eight enclosures but only one recorded pen. Whereas Sandray was cleared and turned over to sheep grazing around 1835 (Buxton 1995, 162), Pabbay was occupied as crofting land through to 1911. Some of its enclosures, which cluster close to the only area of modern settlement at Bagh Ban, may well belong to post-1911 use of the island as a sheep run and saw the adaptation of existing buildings and structures as pens and dipping tanks. Three conjoined curvilinear enclosures south of the settlement are reputed, in oral tradition, to have been used for breeding pit-ponies, but we have not found documentary confirmation of this. Mingulay, despite being a much larger island than any of its neighbours, has only half a dozen pens and one enclosure, but the apparent dearth of enclosures may be explained by the many small 'fields' in the surviving field systems which could have fulfilled the function of cattle enclosures. In the later 19th century there were between 80 and 100 cattle on Mingulay, (Buxton 1995, 66–7) so in terms of meat and dairy products they formed a more important part of the pastoral economy than the 140–150 sheep. Cattle

Table 3.2 Shape, size and date of huts on Barra and Vatersay

Excavated sites				
Site Number	**Site Type**	**External Dimensions**	**Dating**	**Comment**
T19	Round hut	5m diameter	'Beaker'	Occupation hut
T18	Round hut	3m diameter	?'Beaker'	Store?
T54	Round hut	5.6m diameter	LBA / EIA	Occupation hut
A127B	Round hut	3.5m diameter	Pictish ?	Temporary hut
T17(V)	Rectangular	3.8 x 2.3m	Norse ?	Temporary hut
L15(I)	Oval hut	7.5 x 6.75m	Norse ?	Shieling hut
L15(II)	Oval hut	3.5 x 2.9m	Medieval	Shieling hut
L15(II)	Oval hut	5 x 2.5m	Medieval	Shieling hut
B58(I)	Tent setting?	4m	Medieval	Shieling site
B88	Tent setting?	4.5m	Medieval	Shieling site
T211(1)	Sub-rectangular	2.7 x 2m	? C16th	Temporary hut
T211(2)	Sub-rectangular	3.3 x 2.3m	? C16th	Temporary hut
T211(3)	Oval hut	2.4 x 1.8m	? C16th	Temporary hut
B60(I)	Square hut	$5.7m^2$	? C17th	Shieling hut?
Survey Sites				
VN32	Oval hut	6 x 4.5m	? MIA	Flint, Sherds

Figure 3.14 The distribution of shielings and small round and oval huts on Barra

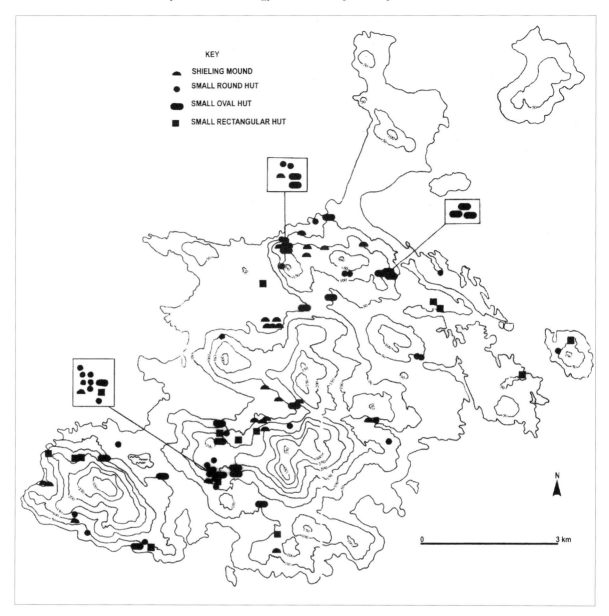

also became important on the smallest of the southern islands, Berneray, where 40 cattle are recorded in 1883 (Buxton 1995, 142) and the three significant enclosures recorded there may relate to this late flourish of cattle production.

Shielings and huts

The difficulty in the Outer Hebrides of ascribing small circular, oval and rectangular buildings to even a broad chronological period has been outlined by Branigan and Foster (2000, 327–8, 334–6). The evidence provided by excavations, and in one case by unexcavated but disturbed sites which have produced a little material culture, has to be the starting point for ascribing dates to certain types of structure. Such evidence from Barra and Vatersay is tabulated in table 3.2.

Although the dates given to these various structures are in varying degrees open to argument, we are happy that the table of excavated sites represents a broadly correct sequence

of structures. On the basis of this we might suggest that roundhuts are essentially prehistoric, whilst oval huts and rectangular huts are Norse to early Modern. But this would of course be too simplistic. We have excavated or sampled Iron Age sites with oval houses (Branigan and Foster 2000, 334–6), though all of these are larger structures (8m or more in diameter). Only VN32, with a handful of surface finds, suggests that small oval huts were used in the Iron Age. Equally not only are some of the Norse huts only marginally oval (as opposed to round), but the hut emplacements excavated at B58 and B88 confirm that round shieling shelters of at least one type were used in the medieval period. As we noted in discussing the possible prehistoric date of some of these various small huts, we have to take into account the degree of embedding that we see in the survey examples, and also of course any observed structural relationships which suggest the precedence of one type over another. We also have to bear in mind that what we see in survey does not always correspond to what we find when the

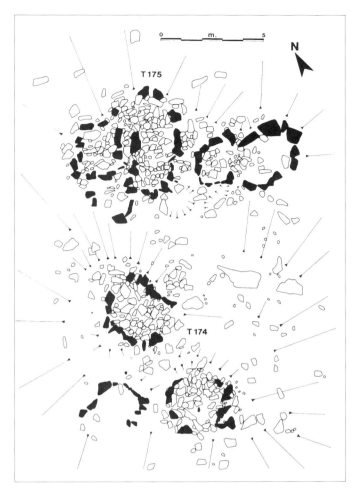

Figure 3.15 The collapsed remains of shieling huts at Bretadale near the remote south west corner of Ben Tangaval

topsoil is removed. Good examples of this, directly relevant to our discussion here, are sites B60 (recorded as a round house in survey but proving on excavation to be a D-shaped building) and sites B58 and B88 (recorded in survey as probably roundhouses but proving on excavation to be circular 'tent' emplacements). In drawing up our list of 75 potential medieval and early historic small huts we have born all these factors in mind, but as with the Bronze Age huts and smaller Round/Oval huts of the Iron Age, (listed in Branigan and Foster 2000, 328, 336) we have to emphasise that our identifications are tentative and some would probably prove wrong on excavation.

We distinguish in our discussion, and on the distribution map, between round and oval huts on the one hand and 'shielings' on the other. The distinction is not in the form/shape of the huts, but between mounded, probably multi-phase sites and huts which lie on level ground with little evidence of repeated use of the site. Some of the round and oval huts in the latter category may well have been used as shielings, indeed given their relatively small size they were probably not used as permanent homes. But the distinction is made here so that we can pick out for discussion those sites and areas which saw repeated use as shieling locations, very often in two or three different chronological periods.

Our excavated examples of shielings reveal a multiplicity of types which should not surprise us, not least because they span (we believe) at least seven or eight centuries. The oval Norse hut at L15 was a substantial structure, probably with two rooms, a bedbox, and fireplace and was used for a considerable period of time. It was rebuilt in a modified form with a second smaller hut alongside probably some centuries later. Sites B55 and B88 produced evidence which suggested that in the Borve valley at least, some of the medieval shielings were the site of tent-like structures the annual re-use / modification of which cannot easily be recognised. But the notable mounding of these and other nearby sites suggests repeated re-use of the same locations. B58 was certainly re-modified after a period of disuse. Finally site B60, probably built as a substantial rectangular structure in the earlier 18th century, saw abandonment before re-use and modification in the earlier 19th century.

To the evidence of these excavated sites we should certainly add that of Balnacraig (B3) on the north side of the Borve valley. The site was originally occupied by a round cairn in the Neolithic period. Stone from the cairn was used to build a substantial roundhouse, perhaps as much as 12m in diameter, most probably in the MIA. Both this structure and the remains of the cairn, have small oval, square and sub-rectangular cabins built over and around them. Some of the cabins are heavily embedded, and in at least one place one two-roomed structure can be seen to overlie an earlier cabin of similar plan. These two structures appear to be about 6m long and a little over 2m wide. One of the least embedded huts is an oval one, about 3 x 2m, west of the MIA roundhouse. All of these structures appear to be post-MIA, and to judge from their embedding are probably pre-modern. We believe they represent a lengthy sequence of occupation of the site as a shieling, probably in the medieval period.

The distribution of the sites we confidently identify as shielings is seen on the map in Fig. 3.14. The shielings can be seen to cluster in three principal groups. One is on the north-facing high ground of Ben Erival between the 50m and 150m contours. This location would logically serve the machair pastures of the Eoligarry peninsula. A second group is tightly clustered on the gentle lower slopes west of Ben Verrisey, and would serve the machair pastures of Cleat, Grean and Allasdale. The shieling locations, however, are not far removed from the machair and lie at only 30m - 40m OD, at the lower edge of the rough pasture which stretches up to the edge of the natural catchment between Beinn Mhartainn and Grianan. The third group is spread around the east end of the Borve valley, mostly between 80m and 150m OD, and would serve the machair of Borve headland and the pastures of the lower Borve valley. A rather dispersed final group might be identified serving the Tangasdale-Kinloch machair, with one example identified on the steep ground north of Kinloch, and three others in the south-west corner of Tangaval. The two adjacent shieling mounds at Bretadale (Fig. 3.15) are perhaps the most remote on the island.

The two examples on the east side of the island, including the excavated Norse? example L15 presumably reflects the absence of related areas of low pasture. Yet paradoxically it is along the east coast that we find a series of place names –

Ben Gunnary, Earsary, and Skallary – that incorporate the Gaelic element 'airigh' (shieling).

The distribution map also shows the location of the small round and oval huts. To a considerable extent these follow the same pattern as the shielings, concentrated on high ground on the west side of the island. In several cases shielings and round or oval huts are close to one another. This may support the suggestion made above that some of these huts were also shielings, but as they did not develop into mounded sites they presumably had a relatively short life. Their overlapping distribution might also suggest they belong to a different era to the mounded shieling sites. In that case, taking into account the evidence of the excavated shieling sites, we would place the small round and oval huts in the late medieval/early modern period.

The picture may be more complex than this, however. Some round and oval huts are on low ground, on or near the coast, and are more likely to have been fishermen's 'bothies' or huts than shielings. There is also the remarkable cluster of round and oval huts north of Kinloch, where eleven of them lie immediately above the lone shieling mound in this area. This cluster is by far the largest on the island and is hard to explain unless it is related to an even more remarkable cluster of 'shelters' at the same altitude, but just to the east of the huts (discussed below).

Finally there are the small rectangular huts. The excavated examples, T211 and B60, probably in use in the 17th and 18th centuries respectively, were both probably intended for repeated use but their specific locations prevented the build-up of a mounded site. That is, they were probably the site of shielings. B60 appears to have replaced the medieval shielings just to the north, and T211 and its unexcavated neighbour T210 may have replaced the shielings in Bretadale. Other rectangular huts on the south side of the Borve valley, above Kinloch and on the eastern side of Ben Orosay stand close to shielings which they could have replaced. On the other hand two examples on the coast of Tangaval and two at Northbay remind us that, as with small oval and round huts, some rectangular ones may have served the needs of fishermen.

Shelters

The sites we designate 'shelters' are the most numerous type of site recorded in our survey of Barra and the southern islands. On Barra our catalogue of sites includes 371 'shelters' and in the islands a further 311, which represents about 35% of all recorded sites. The number of actual structures is in fact somewhat greater, since it is not uncommon to find shelters built over the ruins of shielings and oval and round huts, which though they are noted and recorded do not appear with a separate site entry from the structure they overlie.

Since they turned up in large numbers from the first year we began work in Barra, we quickly constructed and adopted a six-type classification for them. That classification, seen in Fig. 3.16, seems to be adequate and satisfactory; it is important to note that though the figure shows the types as circular, they can be circular, oval or rectangular. With such small structures, which because of their ephemeral nature are often collapsed and/or overgrown, distinguishing the original

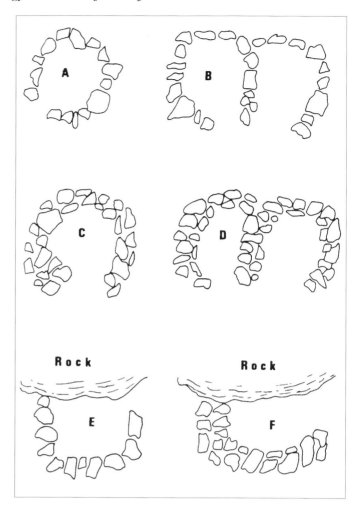

Figure 3.16 Stylised diagram of shelter types found on Barra and Vatersay

shape purely from surface indications is not always easy. There is no reason to think that shape has any great significance in terms of either function or date.

We have no doubt that these structures fulfilled several different functions, including temporary shelter for those attending or seeking animals on high pastures, (and on Mingulay for those cutting and drying peat on Carnan, MacPhee's hill and the ridge in between). Some others on high ground were probably used as temporary shelters/pens for lambs or calves. Others may have been used as store-places (though most are not as substantial as the cleitean of St.Kilda). Others on lower ground or sometimes on the coast may have been used by fishermen as shelters or stores, as well as for shelter by herders. The majority, however, are on high ground and probably therefore to be associated with providing temporary or short-term shelter for those looking after animals. In some cases a connection with animal management is clear because the shelters are attached to pens and enclosures.

The structures of types A, B and E are comprised of settings of single stones, usually 1.5m–3m across. The stones are mostly small blocks (c.30–60cms long) which may form a continuous alignment or be slightly spaced. They could never have been built into even a low wall (nor would they serve as stable base for a turf superstructure). We believe, therefore, that they must be no more than the stones placed around the edge of a blanket or cover of some sort to keep it in place and to provide just enough sheltered space in which to curl up and sleep. A rod or staff could easily have been used to raise the centre a couple of metres from the ground. There is often a gap in the setting suggestive of an 'entry' to the sleeping area. These settings, as found, must therefore represent a single episode of use; but the specific site, and the same stone blocks, may have been visited and used many times over.

The shelters of type C, D and F, with built structures usually two stone blocks wide and sometimes a surviving height of two or even three 'courses' obviously required more effort to construct and seem to imply a greater degree of permanence. They are unlikely to have been for seasonal occupation - the largest of them is little more than 2m across internally and many are smaller – but they may have served as sleeping places either for a few nights at a time or for occasional visits through a season. We may assume that they were probably used for many seasons, and quite possibly repaired and re-used after years of neglect, but it would be difficult to detect such activity in such unsophisticated structures.

Occasionally, some shelters of types C, D and F are so upstanding and unembedded that they probably represent relatively recent (20th century) usage. The majority however appear to be long since abandoned and our *impression* is that they are more likely to be 18th/19th-century, but the excavation of two such sites, as expected, yielded no cultural material at all. As represented by types B and D, the shelters are sometimes built in conjoined pairs. Where this is not the case it is quite common to find two shelters of the same type only a few metres apart, and very probably in contemporary use. We wonder if this may reflect the same behaviour as is recorded by several sources as being followed in the shielings, with separate huts being constructed for the young men and the young women in the group. If that were so, then it might suggest that these paired shelters were in fact associated with the seasonal use of the high pastures and are perhaps the latest and last of the shielings.

One group of shelters, of type A, need special consideration. This is a group of 70 small oval or circular stone settings clustered around the head of the valley north of Ben Leribreck and east of The Croig. This is a rather boggy area and the shelters are either at the edge of the area, or else on small hillocks. They are between 2m and 3m in diameter, and many are complete circuits with no obvious 'entry' point. There are so many in such a small area, and the area itself is so unlikely a spot to want to site a shelter, that we believe these cannot be used as 'shepherds'' shelters but must be associated with animal management activity, possibly involving a substantial number of animals at a particular time of year. It has been suggested to us by a local shepherd that they may have been used to separate lambs from their mothers, but unless the stone rings were the base for turf walls it is unclear how they would work in this way.

Peat cutting and peat dryers

Peat has been a source of fuel for fires in the islands from at least the Bronze Age, when slabs of peat were already being systematically cut and stacked to dry (Branigan, Edwards and Merrony 2002). In historical times peat cutting, drying and stacking was a major activity in which the whole family engaged in the summer months. It is still practised today, but only by a small and declining number of families.

Areas of former peat extraction abound in most parts of Barra and are represented by regular sunken areas in the peat beds. Ponies were used to carry peat from the beds to the crofts in baskets or creels. Partly paved or cobbled roads running up to the high ground from Cleat and Brevig, and a surfaced road along the slope of MacPhee's hill on Mingulay, were almost certainly made for the use of pack ponies.

Apart from the sunken areas of former peat-cuts, the only other trace that peat-cutting has left in the landscape may be a group of monuments we found on Mingulay. The 120 structures we identify as 'peat dryers' are found exclusively on that island (but for a single example on Pabbay). Mingulay has good sources of peat which supplied not only its own inhabitants but those of Berneray, Pabbay and Sandray. Areas from which peat was extracted are still easily visible, and it is near these that the peat dryers are found, almost always on high ground, presumably to catch the wind. They are usually oval or oblong in shape, or something in between, and mostly between 4m and 7m long (Fig. 3.17). They stand either on natural hillocks or prominences or on low man-made mounds, apparently to raise them above the surrounding wet land. On the mound are scattered stone blocks, usually still retaining some semblance of shape. The stones seem to have been built around the peat stack to stop it blowing over.

It should be emphasised that there is no direct evidence to confirm our interpretation of these monuments. Indeed, a photo of Malcolm Macphee building a peat stack on the slopes of Carnan, taken in 1905 (Buxton 1995, pl.8), shows a mounded stack with no trace of stones around its base. It may be that our structures belong to an earlier era and tradition (though traditions were long-lived on Mingulay), or it may be that they served a different purpose altogether. But it is difficult to think what other function they may have served, unless they were in some way involved in the summer management of animals (as pens for individual lambs or calves).

Kelp ovens and Macneil's chemical factory

Like peat, kelp was a major resource and kept the people of the islands occupied for many months each year. Its economic importance in the early 19th century cannot be over-estimated and the history of kelping between c.1750 and 1850 is explored by Jack Bumsted elsewhere in this volume. Equally the part which both the boom and decline of the kelp industry played in the emigrations from Barra are explored in a later chapter. Bearing in mind the dominant part that kelping played in the crofting calendar, it is amazing that there is so little trace of it left in the landscape. This is largely because the only structure associated with the normal pattern of kelp production was the so-called 'kelp oven', which needed to be little more than a hollow in the ground. The Rev. John Buchanan described the kelp ovens that he saw in the Outer Hebrides in the 1780s (Buchanan 1997, 68):

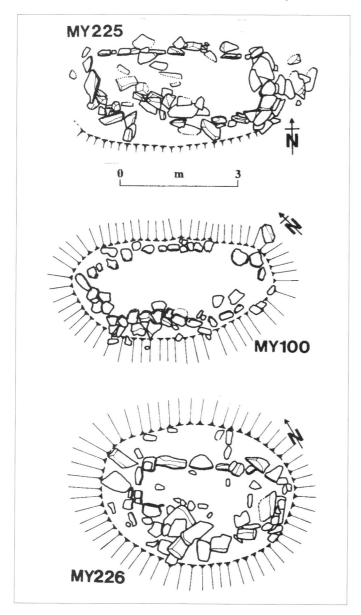

Figure 3.17 Stone settings on low platforms, identified as 'peat dryers', on Mingulay

'The kelp kilns are from eight to twelve feet long, and three feet broad. After one floor full is burnt...they burn another stratum above...and so on from one stratum to another. And then it is well covered with turfs to keep out the rain'

The glassy residue of the burnt kelp was of course removed in due course and the turf cast aside. All that remained was the hollow and the ashes, and the latter were presumably washed away by the winter rains. John Macculloch's description of kelp production, specifically on Barra, in 1816 suggests however that the hollow was surrounded 'by a coffer of stones, a construction which, however rude it may appear, seems fully adequate to the purpose'. He notes that attempts to introduce 'kilns of a more refined construction' have failed.

We identified twelve probable kelp ovens on Barra, all in coastal locations, and five of them within 5m of the water's edge. Several had been disturbed and truncated but those which appeared to be complete, ranged from 2m to 3.7m in length, apart from one exceptional example 9m long in Grean. Widths ranged from 0.5m to 1.8m. All the ovens were marked by embedded stones outlining a roughly oblong area which was sometimes, but not always, slightly sunken. At Alt Chrisal we excavated two of the 'ovens' but there was no visible trace of burning on the stones or of ash residues (although the grass inside the oven area grew lush and green). One of the sites discovered in survey, A73, showed signs of burning on the stone blocks which lined it. It is remarkable that such a large-scale activity, albeit operating almost as a cottage industry at the basic production end, should leave so little trace in the landscape. Interestingly, even at the late 19th century kelp-working site at Rubha Ardvule on South Uist, it is the kelp workers' bothies which provide the visible surviving monuments, not the ovens or kilns (Symonds, 201, 279–80).

In the case of Barra, however, there is one other monument which attests to the importance of the industry on the island in the earlier 19th century. In the late 1820s Macneil of Barra began the construction of a factory at Northbay. In island lore it is still remembered as Macneil's glass factory, but contemporary sources all refer to it as Macneil's chemical, soda or alkali factory, and there are financial documents which confirm that he was buying raw kelp or seaweed in large quantities from the Clanranald estate on Uist to process there. The history and significance of the factory is explored in a later chapter; here we are concerned with its physical remains.

All that survives as an upstanding monument today is the outside wall of the factory, some attached sheds, and two quays (Fig. 3.18). The factory was about 40 x 35m square, its outside wall about 3m high, with an entrance on the west side. Along the south and west walls sheds were attached to the outside face of the wall. Since the site was subsequently (from 1873) the residence of the estate factor and then the parish priest, these buildings are likely to be residual from the factory. The north side of the factory fronts immediately onto the waters of Northbay; at either end of the front (north wall) is a quayside. That at the east end is built to the high water level, and was made simply by constructing a solid masonry wall in front of the natural bank. The western quay is quite different. It juts out about 15m from the line of the factory wall, and is an artificial platform 20m x 10m, filled with small boulders which appear to have been deliberately covered with a layer of sand. The present level of the quay is well below the high water mark and there is nothing to suggest it has ever been higher. It appears to have been built specifically so that boats could load or unload at times other than high water. The sand deposited over the boulder fill was presumably to ensure that there was a flat but well-drained surface on which goods could be stacked.

The north wall of the factory, between the two quays, was pierced by eight large (double-door) entrance ports, the thresholds of which were set just above high water level. The building of so many large ports, designed for loading/unloading bulky cargoes, suggests that a high level of

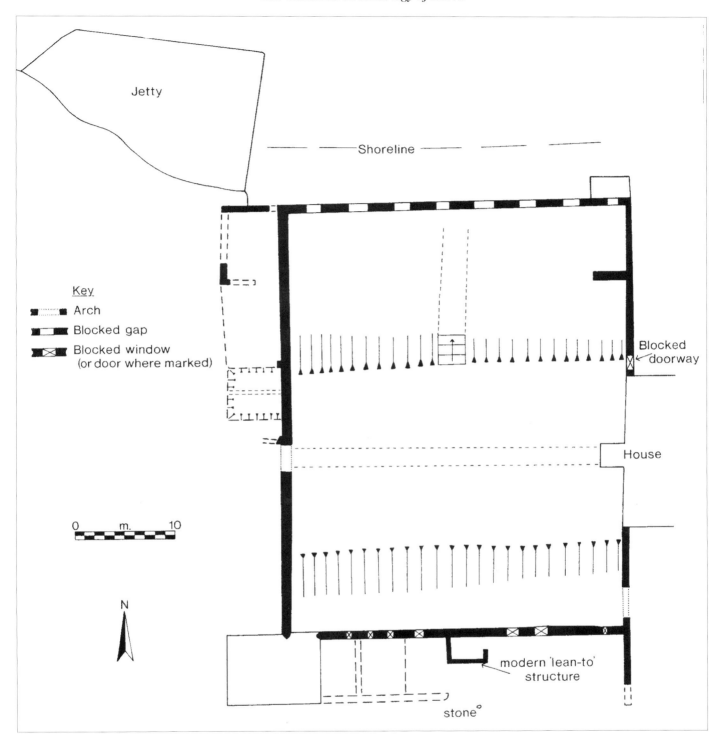

Figure 3.18 The plan of the surviving remains of Macneil's 'chemical' factory at Northbay

activity was anticipated. Documentary evidence discussed in chapter 8 confirms this; the factory was a truly industrial establishment. Inside the walls, the interior of the factory has been entirely removed to make a pleasant walled garden. However, the garden has three levels which ascend from the north to the south, and we believe it likely that these represent three original levels to the factory. The lowest level, immediately inside the eight bay-side ports was

presumably mostly kept clear of buildings so that incoming and outgoing commodities could be piled here. This included not only the imported 'made' kelp, but also peat which was the principal fuel used in the factory (NAS CS96/4274).

For the rest of the interior, including presumably the sheds attached to the south wall, we have only documentary evidence in the form of an inventory of the factory drawn up in November 1836, and some brief references in the South

Uist estate books of 1873 during the factory's demolition. The 1836 inventory mentions workshops for a smith, a joiner and a cooper. The latter would have been particularly busy as 'made' kelp was shipped out in barrels. The 'business' area of the factory included a mixing house, a carbonating furnace room and a crystallising house. One of these (presumably the furnace room) had a brick chimney, which was demolished for its bricks in 1873. There was also a kelp store and a packing room, as well as a low shed and a middle shed (which might be the buildings attached to the south wall). Exactly what went on in the various processing rooms was a much-discussed mystery in the 1830s and it remains veiled in mystery today – the terms used here are those given in the 1836 inventory.

There remains one further room which, if we read the hand-writing correctly is described as the 'barrack room'. At the time of the inventory it seems to have been used as a general store, but the name applied to it suggests it might have been something more interesting. Macneil's factory is said in one contemporary document to have employed hundreds of people, although that might well include those crofters and cottars who cut kelp to send to the factory. There is also a record that the people of Mingulay were removed by Macneil and sent to work in his chemical factory at Northbay, only returning when Macneil went bankrupt and the factory closed down (Stevenson 1838) Was the 'barrack room' their temporary home on Barra? This is speculation, but the reference to the Mingulay temporary clearance of the 1830s comes from a disinterested and reliable source.

Boat-noosts, fish-traps, shell-middens and quaysides

Alongside kelp, fish were one of the principal 'cash-crops' of the islands, generating income which helped the tenants pay their rent and made a contribution to the laird's income. In 1816 Macculloch described the men of Barra as 'amongst the most active and industrious fishermen in Scotland'. Apart from their boats and their nets, the early 19th century industry presumably required little equipment and material infra-structure. This may help to explain why it has left little trace in the landscape.

Only three boat-noosts have been recorded, all within 10m of the waters edge, and taking the form of a boat-shaped hollow edged with stones. Shelters, stores and botheys close to the water's edge are more numerous and are probably to be related to fishing activities. Small circular huts built of beach-cobbles and standing on storm beaches west of Halaman Bay, Barra (T191) and at Tresivick, north Vatersay (VN96) surely fall into this category and are recent structures. Such huts would be frequently destroyed by winter storms and would leave no trace.

More substantial buildings associated with fishing once stood on the south side of Vatersay bay, and at least a dozen building platforms can still be traced here, especially when the sun is low in the sky. They range in length from 4m to 25m, and they were the site of rectangular timber huts and storehouses which served the herring industry. They can be seen on postcards of the Edwardian era (and probably do not date back more than a few decades before that) forming quite an impressive settlement. Contemporary with them were the piers and jetties which today are crumbling relics lining the

margins of Castlebay, and which were also backed by timber buildings no longer standing. But these remains, of course, are beyond the chronological range of this book.

Probably of greater antiquity, but quite possibly still used in the twentieth century, was the tidal fish-trap across Cornaig Bay on north Vatersay (VN154). A crudely built wall about 1.5m wide was constructed in an arc running from one side of the bay to other, about 100m from its head. The other traces of exploitation of marine food resources are the shell-middens around Traigh Mhor. Some of these were of prehistoric date (Branigan and Foster 2000, 322, 343) and one which was sampled by excavation might be of the late 1st millennium AD (below p. 62) but others yielded 18th/19th century ceramics, and E9 revealed five or six episodes of use ending in the 19th century. There is no doubt that the cockles here were exploited continuously from the earliest occupation of the island, and still are today. At times in the 19th century they were a crucial source of food (below p. 140).

Finally we should mention the Barra Head lighthouse on the southern cliffs of Berneray, designed by Robert Stephenson and built 1830–1833.

Boat-shaped stone settings

We have left these enigmatic structures until last. All of these structures consist of a setting of small stone blocks or boulders arranged in the shape of a boat, though some have a pointed prow and flat stern and others are pointed at both ends (Fig. 3.20). The interior is usually flat, never hollowed and only rarely slightly mounded. They range in size from 2.5m to 11m in length, but 75% of them are between 4m and 8m. We originally recorded 44 structures within this category, but were dubious about several of them. These doubtful examples included elongated oval examples scattered amongst the dozens of 'peat driers' on the high land of Mingulay, and some of the similar but less well-defined examples on Berneray. We now retain 33 of the sites in this category.

Barra itself has but one example (T188), Sandray and Mingulay each have two (SY18, SY147; MY97, MY293) and Pabbay and Berneray have three (PY30, PY93, PY106; BY37, BY45, BY49). The remaining twenty two examples are all found on Vatersay, six on north Vatersay and sixteen on south Vatersay. All but one of the latter are concentrated in one area, over the slopes west of Am Meall at the extreme eastern tip of the island.

The function, significance and date of these monuments remains a mystery. One example (VS42) was excavated in 1995 and the report on that excavation appears in this volume (p. 50). The excavation, however, produced no material culture and there was no trace of anything having been deposited inside the boat outline.

Several of the examples below Am Meall stand close to, or are incorporated into, a relict land boundary consisting of a stone alignment which runs across the saddle from Eorisdale to the north coast. The excavated example (VS42) appears to have had its west side incorporated into this boundary, and VS47 may have been similarly treated. In the case of VS51 the east side of the 'boat' has completely disappeared, and one suspects that its stones were removed to be used in the boundary which runs just a metre further to the east. Finally, outlying example on south Vatersay (VS35) also stands alongside a very relict boundary (here a low earthen bank). On careful inspection the bank appears to curve around the outline of the 'boat', which is itself very embedded and has probably had many of its stones removed. These various observations lead us to think that these boat-settings on south Vatersay pre-date the stone alignment boundary and the earth bank, which are themselves undated but unlikely to be later than 19th century to judge from their relict embedded condition. The Am Meall boat-settings are both smaller and more upstanding than VS35 (just as the stone boundary is more upstanding than the earth bank), and they may be more recent than VS35.

As to their function, we can at least dismiss the suggestion that they might be boat-noosts. In the Am Meall group several of the settings are up to 300m from the sea. The other boat-settings also include examples up to 500m from the sea, and several are also at a considerable height above sea level. It should also be noted that not a single example has a sunken or hollowed interior that might take a boat's keel. We have obviously considered the possibility that these monuments might be Norse 'boat-burials'. The example excavated at Scar, Sanday, Orkney (Owen and Dalland 2000) is similar in shape and size to some of the Vatersay settings, but is significantly different in being essentially a sunken hollow in which the boat was set. We must also remember that nothing was found in VS42 – not even a small fragment of an iron nail – to suggest that the setting ever contained a boat.

The variation in orientation and location of our boat-shaped settings is also marked enough to throw doubts on any interpretation involving an established pattern of funerary (or any other ritual) beliefs and behaviour. If we look at the alignment of the 22 Vatersay settings we find there are seven aligned north-south and seven aligned east-west, three each aligned north-north-east/south-south-west and north-north-west/south-south-east, and one each aligned north-east/south-west and north-west/south-east. These are the basic alignments of the monument, ignoring those which have a clear prow which provides an orientation. If we exclude the two settings with two pointed ends whose orientation is uncertain, there are six settings oriented north and five oriented east; five more are oriented north-north-west or north-north-east. The remaining four are oriented north-east, west, south and south-south-east. There is perhaps a clear preference for a northerly orientation, but not to the exclusion of east, west or south.

None of the south Vatersay settings occupy dominant or prominent positions, though most of them look to the sea either on the north or south coast of south-east Vatersay. Of the north Vatersay settings one is in a hollow from which the sea is not visible, whilst two at 180m and 100m OD are oriented not onto the nearest bay (Cornaig Bay and Bagh Siar respectively) but one on the broch at Caolis and the other onto Vatersay township. Even more unexpected is the orientation of the sole example on Barra, in remote Bretadale. It sits only 50m from a 30m high west-facing cliff, but is oriented to the south – looking into the rising slopes on the south side of Glen Bretadale. There is clearly not only no over-riding tradition of orientation but also no noticeable interest in relating the 'boat-settings' to the sea.

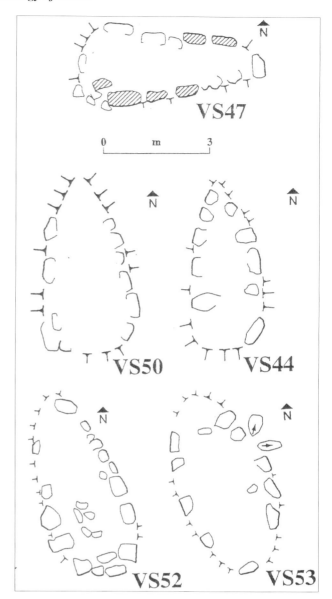

Figure 3.19 A selection of 'boat-shaped settings' from the Eorisdale area of southern Vatersay

Nevertheless, the fact remains that these monuments are 'boat-shaped', in several cases with a clear prow and stern, and equally with dimensions that cannot be confused with an oval shelter. The concentration of them on Vatersay and particularly below Am Meall is also fascinating and recalls the similar concentration of Bronze Age kerbed cairns on Vatersay, in that case with a remarkable cluster just west of Tresivick (Branigan and Foster 2000, 330–2). Beyond this we can only speculate. Given their shape we believe that, in the minds of those who erected them, they must have been associated with the idea of a boat or ship and that they represent that idea. On the evidence of VS42 they contained neither boat, nor burial, nor any inorganic products – they were, apparently, empty. We speculate that the settings below Am Meall represent a sequence of ritual events that took place over decades or centuries. Such rituals might have been concerned, for example, with the erection of memorials for those who died at sea.

Monuments in the landscape

It is axiomatic that none of the monuments we have discussed above stood in splendid isolation – not even Kisimul Castle. All were involved in social and economic relationships with other structures and their builders and users, and those relationships changed through time. Even more fundamentally, all were related to the natural landscape around them both by the original decisions to construct them where they stood, and by the roles they played in the exploitation and utilisation of the landscape. Although we do not yet have anything like enough information about the functions and dates of all these monuments, it seems worthwhile trying to explore their relationships with each other and with their setting, by examining two or three different areas of the island in some detail. One of these, around Loch Obe, is discussed in the special study of Balnabodach (chapter 5). Three other, very different, areas are considered here.

GORTEIN

The first area chosen is focussed on the abandoned settlement of Gortein on the southern edge of the Tangaval peninsula. This is a narrow valley flanked by steep rocky slopes, which runs back north-eastwards from the coast. On all but the south side the ground rises to over 150m OD, so the valley is relatively protected from most directions. The valley stretches back for almost a kilometre, its middle section about 200m wide and filled with soil washed down from the upper reaches, rather damp and vegetated with coarse grass. At the south end the valley broadens to about 500m, with a low hill with generally thin soils, situated east of the stream which runs down the west side of the valley.

Although this is quite a remote area with difficult access except by boat, there is some evidence that it attracted permanent settlement in the Iron Age if not before. There are half a dozen thick-walled round or oval huts around 5m –7m diameter in the valley and traces of a larger example beneath the later settlement at T118/119. Two further examples are on the coast just to the west, whilst the excavated wheelhouse of Alt Chrisal is 800m to the east.

Monuments of the historical period are shown in Fig. 3.20, and include blackhouses, small round/oval huts, shelters, enclosures, clearance cairns, boundary walls, and single examples of other structures. The only documentary sources we have to throw any light on these structures are the births and marriages entered in the Barra Parish Register which begins in 1805 but is very patchy until the end of 1812. Gortein was never a township, so it does not appear in

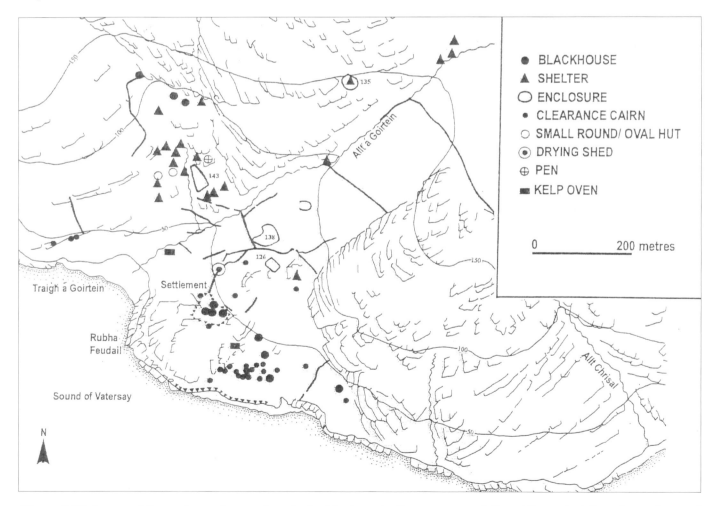

Figure 3.20 A map of the early modern archaeological features in the area around the settlement at Gortein on the south coast of Barra

surviving rental lists, nor does it appear in the census records.

Between 1814 and 1830 twenty-three children are recorded in the BPR as born to eleven families in Gortein. That is a very neat fit with the eleven blackhouses recorded at Gortein, but almost certainly the equation is not so simple. Four of the couples were only married in 1824 or later and would not have been 'households' before that date; equally four other families with between two and four children each (small families by Barra standards) have no children born at Gortein after 1822 and might therefore have left the settlement in the early to mid 1820s. In fact, we know at least two of these families emigrated to Canada in 1821. Even without knowing anything of the history of the blackhouse settlement before 1814, therefore, there is reason to think that not all the blackhouses were ever in contemporaneous occupation.

The blackhouses occur in three groups. The eastern group comprises three in a line up-slope from a large cairnfield, and an outlier beyond a boundary wall to the east. The central group is a tight cluster comprised of four blackhouses and associated outbuildings and possibly earlier structures on the crest of the low hill, with a view over the whole valley. The third group are three houses across the river and at 80m to 100m above datum, tucked into a shallow side-valley. The location of this third group is very different to that of the others – almost hidden away compared to their exposed position, and also with no cultivable land close by even for small vegetable/potato plots. It seems likely that they are a discreet chronological as well as a spatial group. The other two groups are also very different one from the other. The central group forms a complex which has the appearance of growth and development over a lengthy period of time, whereas the three adjacent houses of the eastern group reveal no traces of alteration or modification. They are also the least embedded of the houses. We think it is likely that these houses were the last built and occupied here, perhaps the homes of James Campbell, Duncan Campbell and Donald Macsween, the last three families recorded in Gortein in the parish register. The four blackhouses in the central group form the natural focus of the whole settlement complex and were probably occupied and the land around them cultivated for decades (Fig. 3.21). It was probably from here that the

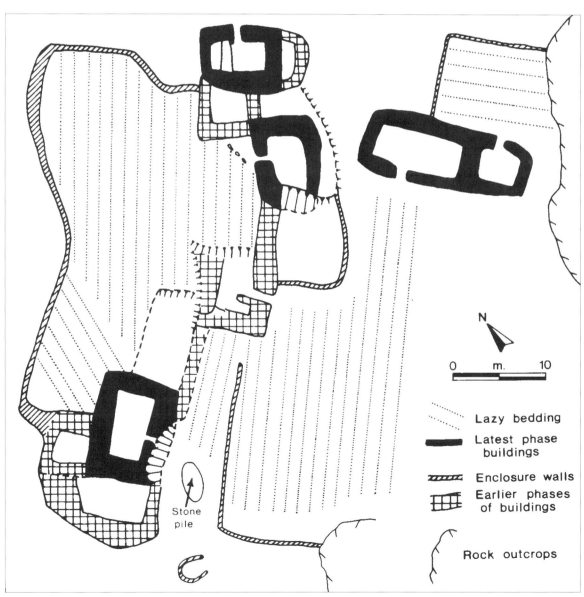

Lazy bedding

Latest phase buildings

Enclosure walls

Earlier phases of buildings

Rock outcrops

Stone pile

Figure 3.21 The central settlement cluster at Gortein

Mackinnons and Macleans emigrated in 1821. Three other Gortein families left the island, and the remaining families moved to less remote locations (Glen, Kentangaval, Borve and Caolis) in the years around 1830. By 1835 Gortein was deserted.

During the decades of its occupation, its occupants had left their mark on the landscape however. Lazy-beds are found around the central group of blackhouses, and on the south-facing slope of the low hill on which the central and eastern house groups are found. There are also clearance cairns scattered throughout this area, with a particular concentration on the south-east slopes of the hill. Within this cluster of cairns there are both primary and secondary cairns, the latter outnumbering the former two to one, confirming that this land was probably cultivated and continuously 'improved' by clearing over a considerable period of time. Two outlying cairns to the east, however, are primary cairns and the absence of evidence for secondary clearance suggests that perhaps this area (which is quite boggy) proved unsuitable for cultivation. Although there are fewer cairns around the central group of blackhouses there are substantial areas of lazy-bedded land reaching from the houses down the slope almost to the sea. It may well be that stones removed from here were used in the building of houses and walls; smaller stones from secondary clearance were probably utilised in building the low revetment that encloses and supports the platform on which the houses and vegetable/potato plots are located. The area behind the houses also carries two secondary cairns and one primary and has been cultivated, though less intensively. A wall runs from the edge of the settlement enclosure in an arc to meet the steep rock face north-east of the houses, and thus enclosed the entire area of cultivated land. Situated along this wall was a well-built drying shed with a raised flue-heated platform at one end. It was presumably a communal facility.

Beyond the cultivated area the valley is effectively divided into three blocks of coarse pasture by four earth and stone walls which run across the valley to meet the stream, and a fifth wall which runs alongside the stream. The central 'field' contains two enclosures. The larger, T138, is built of boulders and encloses about 1,400m^2; it abuts one of the cross walls and was clearly constructed after the wall, but may well have been in contemporary use with it. The smaller, oval enclosure (T137), is one of those enigmatic enclosures, made with spaced boulders, so that strictly speaking it demarcates an area rather than encloses it. Whether it is part of the 18th-19th century landscape is unknown. Across the river, on the east facing slope is a third, trapezoidal, enclosure (T143) enclosing about 1,100m^2. Like T138 it is built of boulders and we believe they are probably contemporaries. Much further up the valley on the east-facing slope is another enclosure (T135) with an earth and stone bank enclosing about 850m^2. An enclosure of similar size and construction (T126) is found within the cultivation area north of the settlement. Its position here is surely anomalous and it must either pre- or post-date the cultivation area and its enclosing wall. Given the low-level of post-1835 exploitation of the whole of the south-west corner of Tangaval, we think it likely that these two enclosures pre-date the blackhouse settlement.

The other resources and structures associated with the blackhouse settlement can be briefly mentioned. Two small kelp ovens demonstrate that even in this remote spot, the opportunity to boost the cash income of the tenants was not missed, presumably in the period c.1795–1820. The natural food resources of the Sound of Vatersay were presumably exploited, with boats launched from the small beach of Traigh Gortein. As for peat, the only suitable peat for cutting and drying for fuel lay far up on the higher ground of Ben Tangaval. There are traces of old peat cuttings here, from which the settlement was probably supplied.

The other monuments recorded in the Gortein valley, all to the west of the stream, are unlikely to be associated with the 18th/19th century occupation of the settlement. There are two small round/oval huts, each overlain by a smaller, later shelter. Further up the valley (T132, T134) two more shelters overlie oval huts, but in this case rather larger ones which we have previously suggested might be of Iron Age date (Branigan and Foster 1995, 167–8). Our inclination at present (as discussed above) is to place the majority of small round/oval huts in the medieval and early modern periods and to see them as more permanent shelters used sporadically if not regularly over a period of years. In the Gortein valley they would represent the occasional visits of shepherds who lived perhaps at Kentangaval or Tangasdale. The more ubiquitous shelters, also found concentrated west of the stream, might represent a much longer episode of intermittent usage of the area which could have been both before and after the settlement of Gortein was occupied. Certainly the shelters in this valley appear, on the basis of the four examples overlying round/oval huts, to belong to a later era than the huts.

In summary the history of settlement at Gortein probably begins with a substantial roundhouse on the low hill, occupied in the MIA and with other, perhaps rather smaller, round/oval houses further up the valley or along the coast which are broadly contemporary. A late medieval or early modern phase of occasional usage by shepherds is marked initially by small round/oval huts and then by the building of temporary shelters. It is possible that the two smaller enclosures with earth and stone banks are associated with this phase of use (a shelter is actually built inside enclosure T135 and another close to T126). The blackhouse settlement perhaps began with the three houses tucked away on the west side of the stream, but its focus became the hill near the beach. Intensive cultivation of small plots for vegetables and potatoes, and (to judge from the drying shed) the growing of cereals on the southern slopes of the hill, was accompanied by sheep-rearing, and supplemented by cutting kelp and fishing the Sound of Vatersay. After the settlement was abandoned in the early 1830s the valley only saw intermittent usage by shepherds living on the other side of Ben Tangaval.

BORVE AND CRAIGSTON

The crofting townships of Borve and Craigston occupy the south and north sides of the valley that, for convenience, we call the Borve valley. This is a much larger, and very different, area to that occupied by Gortein. It is much more accessible, and has a substantial area of machair on Borve headland and at the foot of the valley, behind which is moderately good and tolerably well-drained land in the floor of the valley. Only at the head of the valley does it become wet and boggy. Although open to the winds and weather from the west, the steep slopes of Beinn Mhartainn (230m) to the north and Beinn na Moine (210m) to the south provide protection from those directions. To the rear of the valley, the rugged slopes give way and broaden into gentler slopes with rough pasture, though much of this is boggy, especially on the southern side. The back of the valley is dominated by the western slopes of the peaks of Heaval, Hartaval, and Grianan (all around 300m) but there is a pass through to the east side of the island, albeit a particularly boggy passage.

Early prehistoric occupation is well attested in the upper reaches of the valley by the chambered cairns of Dun Bharpa and Balnacraig, by further smaller cairns, two standing stones, a stone ring, and two possibly early hut circles. Two further standing stones once stood on Borve headland. Iron Age occupation appears to have been even more intense, with a broch on Borve headland, a second Atlantic Round House of less regular shape in the valley, possibly as many as three wheelhouses, and half a dozen round houses or huts. Some of the latter are found at relatively high altitudes (150m) and seem to represent an episode of permanent settlement of high pastures evidenced elsewhere on Barra too.

The burial of a wealthy woman of the Norse period was excavated by the standing stones on the headland in the 1860s, accompanied amongst other things by two oval Scandinavian brooches made in the later 8th century AD.

Medieval occupation is attested by the shielings (one of which was excavated) on a plateau in the south east corner of the valley. Pollen recovered from a 12th century soil beneath a clearance cairn on the north side of the valley confirms pastoral activity, but also indicates agriculture (Edwards and Brayshay 2000, 317). Some of the round and oval huts on the map in Fig. 3.14 may also belong in the Medieval era. Early post-medieval structures include the D-shaped stone hut at B60 (below p. 56) and the re-occupation of shieling B58. The remaining structures recorded on the map are mostly of later eighteenth or nineteenth century date, though some are probably earlier.

We have earlier discussed the various types of land boundaries that we recorded in the Borve valley, and particularly in a pilot project in Craigston. In so far as we can put dates to these boundaries most appear to belong to the eighteenth - nineteenth century, and so they provide some sort of framework within which the other elements of the man-made landscape of this period can be placed (Fig. 3.22). One group of boundaries may be slightly earlier than the rest. These are the field boundaries surviving towards the top end

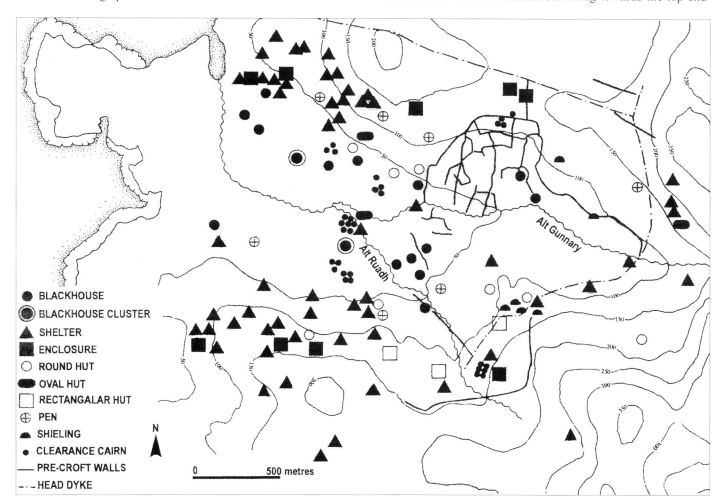

Figure 3.22 A map of the Borve valley showing the early modern archaeology of the area

of Craigston (downslope from Dun Bharpa). They are fragmentary and the fields they enclose are irregular in shape and size. They are mostly stone revetted turf walls, but also include earth and stone banks and spaced boulders. They are separated from the rough pasture by a boundary of our type 7 (above p. 26), a sheep-wall, which sweeps in a arc around them and runs down to meet Alt Gunnary in the valley bottom. Croft boundaries cut across them in many places but sometimes incorporate them in others. They are clearly not croft boundaries, neither are they the remains of a runrig system. It seems likely therefore that they belong to a period perhaps no later than the mid-eighteenth century. Whether more of Craigston, and indeed Borve, was once enclosed in a similar way we cannot say. There are scattered fragments of pre-croft boundaries elsewhere in the valley but nothing at all coherent.

Although two blackhouses are located within this field system there is no evidence to link them to the use of the system. These two blackhouses are the only two in the valley which lie above the 50m contour; the rest are found on the low ground, mostly towards the sides of the valley. There are clusters of blackhouses in both Craigston and Borve which formed the focus of the townships, but there are also three locations where a pair of blackhouses stand adjacent to each other. Whether these represent a crofter and a relative who was a cottar, or whether they might represent the sub-division of an existing croft is unknown. None of the houses have an attached byre, but three have free-standing byres close by, and a fourth has a drying-shed.

Clearance cairns are mostly located in the valley, but some are upslope in the field system we have just described. A group on the opposite side of the valley at almost 150m OD could possibly relate to the Iron Age occupation sites in this high location. Lazy-beds can be traced on many locations along the lower slopes, and again in the field system at the top end of Craigston. In places, they can be seen to be overlain and crossed by croft boundaries. Traces of an extensive rectilinear field system on Borve headland are probably related to arable agriculture at some time in the historic period.

The headland is today used for grazing cattle, and the importance of animal husbandry in the Borve valley is clearly demonstrated by several monuments. The shielings, used in medieval and early modern times on the evidence of excavated site B58, and the small round, oval and rectangular huts spread along the south side of the valley, mostly at 100m OD or higher, demonstrate seasonal use of these high pastures in the 12th–17th century. Two D-shaped enclosures near Dun Bharpa appear to relate to a boundary wall which runs up-slope from the enclosed field system described above and eventually runs beneath the main 'head-dyke' sheep wall which runs along the water shed. That is, they were probably part of the pre-crofting landscape and were broadly contemporary with the irregular field system, perhaps in the 18th century. Other large enclosures, with either earth and stone banks or boulder walls, are strung along the north and south sides of the valley, in the rough pastures mostly between 50m and 150m OD. Their size (four of them are in excess of

1,500m^2) and the effort taken to build them, suggest the management of large flocks or herds over many years. The largest enclosures all have shelters built against or within them. The clusters of other shelters in the vicinity of these enclosures seem unlikely therefore to be used in conjunction with them, but to represent a different (probably more recent) phase of exploitation of the rough pastures.

Peat was cut in some of these upland areas at the head of the valley, though the relict peat cuttings noted seem too limited to have supplied the whole valley for long. Oral tradition tells of peat being brought to Borve and other west coast townships from the east side of the island. There are no surviving traces of either fishing or kelp production around the Borve headland, although the appearance of two men described as fishermen in the 1841 census, one in each township, suggest that the resources of the sea were not entirely ignored.

The 1841 census records 39 households in Borve and 22 in Craigston, and a total population of 372 souls. These figures emphasise how incomplete is the archaeology even of a recent period like the 19th century, for we have only two dozen blackhouses recorded in the valley. Well over half of the houses of 1841 appear to have vanished without trace, although detailed study of some of the relict 'outbuildings' adjacent to whitehouses and early-mid 20th century homes might well reveal the remains of modified blackhouses. Equally the archaeology does not yield any obvious clues to the dichotomy that split the valley literally down the middle by 1841. The census details make it clear that Craigston had become a single farm by 1841, with a Ground Officer and 17 heads of family described as agricultural labourers; not a single crofter remains. But in Borve, there were 31 crofters amongst the 39 households, as well as a publican, a shoemaker, and a blacksmith.

The Borve valley has probably been a focus of settlement on Barra since the Neolithic, and in recent centuries has carried a particularly heavy population. In 1841 it housed almost a fifth of the entire population of the island. The man-made elements of the landscape have been constantly and endlessly re-worked, particularly in the lower part of the valley, so that rich though the historical archaeology might be, it is fragmentary and, of course, still evolving.

BRUERNISH

The Bruernish peninsula, on the east coast of Barra, is in some respects like the Tangaval peninsula in which Gortein is located, having a rugged coastline, and an interior which is mostly boggy rough grazing. But it does not rise as high as Tangaval (its highest point is only 94m OD) and it is much less isolated, not least because it is flanked by two important inlets – Northbay and Loch Obe.

There is at present no evidence for early prehistoric occupation or use of the peninsula, although a stone ring stands on the Ardveenish side of Northbay, and a Neolithic site is known on the south shore of Loch Obe. Even in the Iron Age, when settlement of Barra appears to have been relatively dense, there is only a broch, built on a small islet in Northbay, and a suspected roundhouse, almost in the centre of the peninsula. Bruernish does not appear to have been an attractive place to settle.

All the more surprising then to see on our map of the historical archaeology of the peninsula so many blackhouses (Fig. 3.23). With two exceptions, they cling to the coastline, particularly thick around Northbay, but seven examples strung down the remotest part of the peninsula. The latter are located on small inlets or bays. There are traces around several of them of small areas of lazy-bedding, and in one place a couple of clearance cairns, but the plots were only large enough to make potatoes a worth-while crop. Otherwise they were clearly dependent on the sea. The blackhouses clustered along the approach to Northbay, and around the indented shore of Northbay itself, are in places packed so closely together that they too had only room for small cultivation plots. The almost total absence of clearance cairns again emphasises how little cultivation went on in Bruernish.

Some of the Bruernish households raised cattle to judge from half a dozen byres, all standing near blackhouses, and they presumably exploited the rough pastures of the peninsula. Hay was cut and stacked to feed overwintered animals, half a dozen haystack bases surviving at site A36. But the lack of enclosures and pens, and the scarcity of even the ubiquitous 'shelter', suggests that the number of animals raised on the Bruernish peninsula was small.

The census of 1841 reveals that of the 26 heads of Bruernish households for whom an occupation is given, eight are crofters, but nine are fishermen, one is a boat-builder and five more are cottars. This may well help to explain how so many households could be clustered together. A further six men in the township are described as fishermen, and we think the 'bothies' shown on the map, all built close to the water's edge, are probably fishermen's stores and sheds.

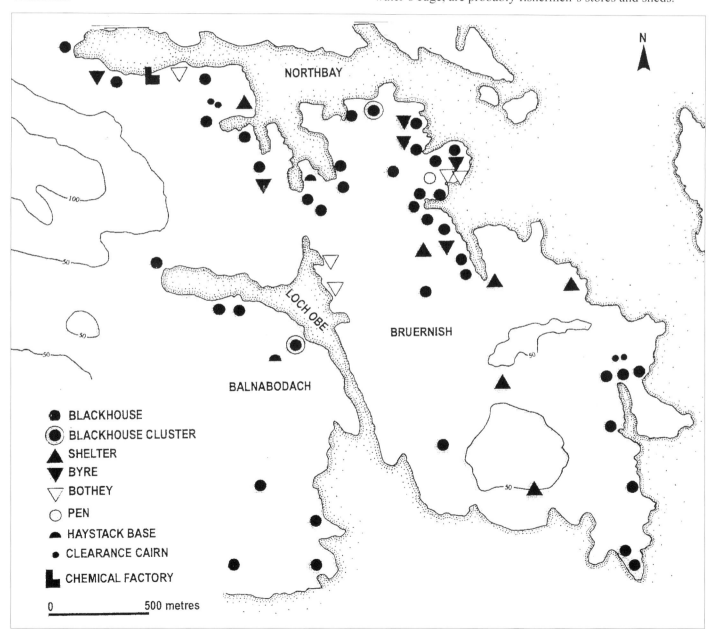

Figure 3.23 A map of early modern archaeology of the Bruernish peninsula and Northbay

Life on the Bruernish peninsula must always have been particularly difficult for crofters and intermittently dangerous for fishermen. We suspect that most of the blackhouses on Bruernish date from the 1830s or 1840s when families were cleared from some of the western townships (Craigston, Cleat and Green). General Macneil certainly intended to move people from the west coast to the east, and to encourage crofters to become fishermen, and similar advice was offered to Gordon of Cluny.

Some evidence for the movement of families from the west coast townships to Bruernish can be found by tracking down some of the 1841 residents of Bruernish in earlier entries in the Parish Register. We have not done this systematically, but we have found the following information:

	Parish Register	1841 Occupation
Norman Macleod*	Bruernish (1820)	Crofter
Alex Macmillan	Craigston (1821) Northbay (1834)	Cottar
John Macnais	Green (1815)	Cottar
Eoin Maclean	Cleat (1835) Bruernish (1836)	Fisherman
Eoin Gillies	Cleat (1834) Glen (1836)	Fisherman

(* described as a native of South Uist)

What this information suggests is that crofters who had occupied crofts in Bruernish for some time retained their crofts through the events of the mid-late 1830s. Those crofters who had originally held tenancies in Craigston, Cleat and Green were probably cleared in 1834 and 1835 to Bruernish where they were either given tenancies as fishermen or became cottars. On this evidence, the clearance of the west coast townships may have been begun whilst the estate was still notionally in the hands of General Macneil (he was formally declared bankrupt in 1836).

For a brief period c.1833–1836 Macneil's chemical factory at Northbay, attempting to enhance the quality of 'made' kelp, provided work for dozens (one report even mentioned 'hundreds') of workers. This may have brought temporary relief, if only by paying the rent, from the grinding poverty of the Bruernish families. But Macneil's bankruptcy, and the factory's inability to pay for itself, led to its closure in 1836. The potato famine which began in Barra in 1846 must have hit communities like Bruernish particularly hard, and one imagines that many of the families 'cleared' to Canada in 1850/51 would have come from Bruernish and other east coast communities.

There were certainly some crofts here before 1830, and we must assume the safe harbourage of Northbay would always have encouraged fishing activities. But for the most part, the historical archaeology of Bruernish, may well represent the activities of a very limited period of time from c.1830 to 1850, when people were first being pushed into the area, and then were subsequently pushed out of it. The historical landscape of Bruernish may, above all others in Barra, reflect the turmoil that surrounded the collapse of the Macneil estate.

4

Excavation of Historical Sites on Barra, Vatersay and Sandray

Our archaeological survey of Barra and its neighbouring islands to the south recorded almost two thousand sites and monuments. Whilst structures like passage graves, brochs and blackhouses can be assigned with confidence to their respective periods of construction and use, the great majority of sites held no intrinsic clue to their date. We therefore undertook a programme of excavation to examine a wide selection of different types of site. The purpose of the excavations was not just to establish, if possible, their date, but also to understand how they were used. In *Barra to Berneray* we described the results of excavations of prehistoric sites. In this chapter we report on the excavations we conducted on sites of the medieval and modern periods. None of the sites is architecturally large or impressive, but they are representative of many hundreds of similar sites found throughout the islands. They are presented here in what we judge to be their probable chronological order.

Excavation of L15 (multi-period shieling near Earsary)

Site L15 was found in survey in 1996. It was recorded as a two-phase monument. The later was a loosely built shepherd's shelter, whilst the earlier was a circular hut and an oval hut with a rectangular annexe. These earlier structures were thought to be of later prehistoric or medieval date. The site lies on a raised shelf at the foot of the steep slope of Ben Gunnary (Gunnary – Gunnar's shieling). Excavation was undertaken because small oval and circular stone-founded huts are types which are relatively common on Barra but have not yet been sampled by excavation. The excavation revealed at least three phases of occupation, each with its own structural remains.

Phase 3

The uppermost structure (D) was a very simple shepherd's shelter represented by a loosely piled circle of medium-sized stones 2 x 1.5m in size. This had been constructed over the embedded remains of a rather larger circular structure and utilised the hollow depression inside it to provide a sunken, sheltered area. Just outside the shelter, to the east, a small fire area was found below the turf, which may be associated with the use of the shelter. Four coarse hand-made sherds were found in topsoil and amongst the stones of the structure (contexts 2 and 3), but none were clearly associated with this shelter, and they were probably residual material from earlier occupation. To judge from its relatively unembedded condition, this simple shelter is of modern date.

Phase 2 (Fig. 4.1)

Beneath the shelter, a more substantial structure (B) was found. This was an oval hut, 2.3 x 1.7m internally, with a

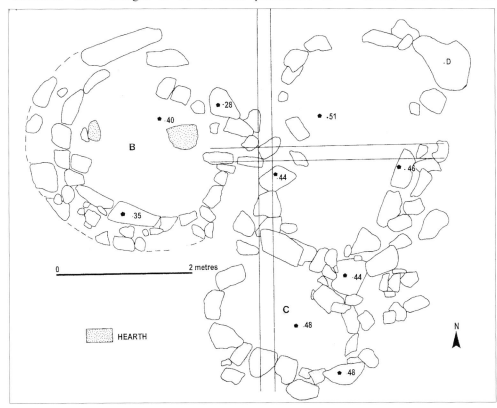

Figure 4.1 The shieling huts at site L15 in phase 2 (medieval) (spot heights are in cm below datum D)

stone-faced earth/turf wall 0.6m wide. Nowhere did the wall survive more than one stone high, so that it is possible that its entire superstructure was built of turf. Inside there were two areas of burning on its peaty floor (contexts 13 and 14), the larger and more deeply burnt (14) towards the east end. There was no clear doorway, but a long slab (1.1m) set low in the outside face on the north side with no matching facing stones on the interior may have been a threshold. No material was found inside this hut. Its deep embedding suggests it is considerably older than the overlying shelter. Immediately east of the circular hut was a second structure (C) which appeared to butt up against it, although there was no absolutely clear stratigraphic connection between the two structures. This structure was represented by alignments of stone blocks laid flat, in places in two courses, to form two adjacent enclosed areas. Only on the east side was the stone alignment more than a single block wide, so that in most areas the blocks formed an interior wall or foundation face only. Hard packed earth outside the stone blocks however suggested that there had probably been an earth and turf superstructure built up around the interior facing blocks. The method of construction, however, was different to that of the oval hut to the north (B) and might suggest that they were not strictly contemporary.

The structure comprised a totally enclosed oval or sub-rectangular space, 2 x 1.2m, at the south end, with a flat slab rather like a threshold forming part of its northern face. The area next to it, across the 'threshold' was U-shaped, 2m x 1.4m, the open end facing north - into the steep slope of Ben Gunnary. It is possible that the builders of this structure utilised the remains of an earlier underlying structure (A) to provide at least some shelter on the north end of the U-shaped space. If they actually rebuilt part of the stone-fronted turf wall it would have increased the area of the northern space to 3.2m x 1.6m. Nowhere inside either space was anything resembling an occupation deposit found, and the floor seemed to be simply the surface of the underlying silty loam (context 11) into which small scraps of burnt material had been trampled. No fire places or areas of burning were found in either space however, and this might suggest that structure C is in fact contemporary with structure B to the north, which had two fire areas. The only finds made in either of the two spaces or rooms of structure C was a small flint flake and two handmade undiagnostic sherds found in the top of the silty loam (context 11). We believe that structures B and C are both later medieval, or very early modern.

Phase 1 (Figs 4.2 and 4.3)
Structure C was built inside the remains of an underlying structure which seems to have been destroyed, probably deliberately robbed, on its western and north-western side during the construction of structure B.

It was a thick-walled oval hut, with external dimensions of 7.5m x 6.75m. Around its south/south-eastern arc, where it was perched on a steep slope, the wall was built entirely of stone to a maximum surviving height on the inside face of almost a metre and up to five courses. This type of construction appears to have continued around the south-west arc too, although here only parts of the foundation course survived.

The east and north-east section of the circuit was built differently, with large stone blocks used to face the wall

inside and out but the core (context 4) constructed of turves. It was still possible to see the outlines of individual turves and they appeared for the most part to be small, mostly between 15cms and 25cms across. The wall averaged 1.3m wide, so that the interior area of the hut measured 5.1 x 4.1m. The door was almost certainly on the east, where there was a gap in the stone facing flanked on the inside by two stone blocks set upright. Between them a flat, slightly worn, slab appeared to be a threshold and there was a similarly worn but larger slab on the outside of the wall. The area between the two slabs was devoid of turf remains and notably worn into a hollow. The door was narrow, no more than 0.5m wide, and could have been easily blocked to keep out the wind.

The interior of the hut was divided into two areas by a roughly laid stone foundation 0.8m wide which ran in an arc from the left of the door towards the rear wall (Fig. 4.2). A turf superstructure could have been erected on this foundation but we observed no signs of one. The foundation followed the line of a low rock face, thus dividing the hut into an upper area immediately inside the door, and a lower or sunken area (about 30cms below the upper level) in the southern end of the hut. Within the sunken area a hearth was found tucked up against the junction of the hut wall and the partition. To the west of the sunken area, and 30cms above its bottom, a rectangular structure, 2.2m x 1m, was set against the inside of the hut wall, marked out by three large blocks set flat and by five blocks set upright at one end. We suggest this may have been a simple box-bed the inside of which would have been filled with heather. Some support for this interpretation is offered by the pollen analysis (see below) of a sample from context 24. The sunken area was filled up to the level of the top of the stones of both the partition and the 'bed' (a total depth of about 45–50cms) with a rich black peaty soil (context 24). There were no visible or clearly defined levels within this fill, but we noted that the pottery and flints found within it tended to occur in horizontal spreads. We interpret the fill and its artifact distribution as probably reflecting intermittent, perhaps seasonal use, over a period of some years. Episodic usage, and possibly periods of abandonment may be suggested by the analysis of a sample of this material (see below).

From this deposit we recovered 34 sherds, mostly of a slightly micaceous fabric with small rounded white grits, fired from buff to grey. One sherd in a dark grey rather laminated fabric had a grass-marked exterior face. In the same level there were also 35 pieces of flint and 2 of chert, of which 18 were small thin flakes. The only other find was a small steatite (?) spindle whorl. We tentatively ascribe this assemblage to the late Norse period on comparison with the much larger assemblage recovered at Cille Pheadair on South Uist, where steatite spindle whorls, grass-marked pottery, and small thin flint flakes from strike-a-lights are more abundant.

When the deposit accumulating in the sunken area had reached the top of the partition stones it began to spread across them towards the door (suggesting that by this time, at least, there was no superstructure on the partition feature). This upper area floor, of soft sandy brown soil (context 22), had been kept clean and clear up to this time, and just two flint flakes were recovered from it. With the partition feature covered, the interior of the hut was re-designed (Fig. 4.3), with a short broad partition built out

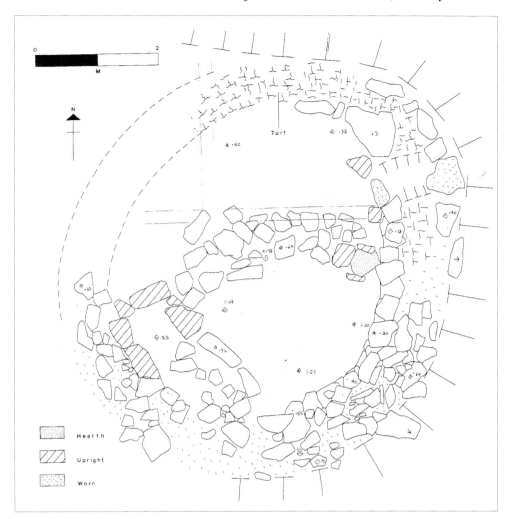

Figure 4.2 The original form of the shieling hut at L15 in phase 1A (Norse?) (spot heights are in cm below datum D)

Figure 4.3 The modified form of shieling hut L15 in phase 1B (Norse?) (spot heights are in cm below datum D)

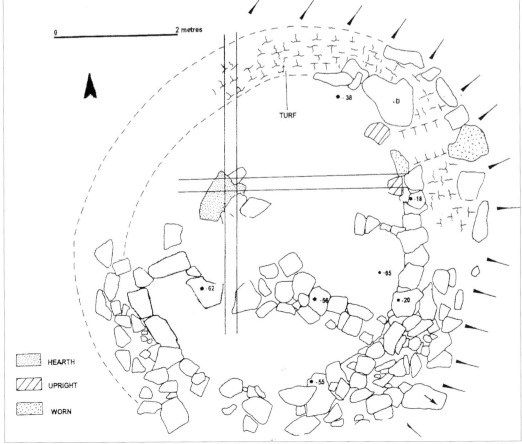

into the room from the south-eastern quarter, and a sub-into the room from the south-eastern quarter and a substantial hearth area (context 16) constructed facing the door but close to the west inner face of the hut. The flat 'bed-box' stones had also disappeared beneath the accumulating deposit, but the upright stones at one end of this feature remained visible and the structure may have been retained in use in some form. This later period of occupation may have been brief, since only 11 sherds of a micacious, hard, thin and somewhat uneven pottery fabric was found in the associated deposit (context 18), along with 3 pieces of flint. The pottery includes the hard uneven 'craggan' ware, similar to that recovered at a shieling in the Borve valley, where rims and decoration on other fabrics are also present, and suggest a medieval date (13th–15th century?) for this material.

The Finds
Pottery
The pottery report for this site will be found, together with that for site B58, at the end of the excavation report on site B58 (below p. 53).

Spindle-whorl (Fig. 4.4)
A discoidal spindle-whorl of steatite (?) was found in context 24. The whorl is 34mm diameter and 12mm thick, with a central perforation 7mm in diameter. It has a well polished surface, with a small chip out of one edge. It is almost identical in every respect to the example found in a tertiary deposit at Alt Chrisal (site T17) in a small rectangular hut.

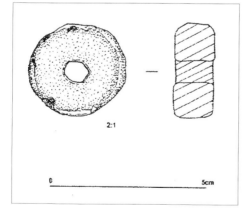

Figure 4.4 A steatite spindle-whorl from L15 phase 1A

2:1

0   5cm

Lithics
by C R Wickham-Jones
The excavations at site L15 produced 43 pieces of flint. The breakdown of the assemblage is given in the table below:

Table 4.1 The lithic assemblage from L15 by context

	Context 11	Context 18	Context 22	Context 24
Chunks		1		19
Debitage Flakes			1	2
Regular Flakes	1	2		15
Core			1	
Re-touched Flakes				1
TOTAL	1	3	2	37

All of the material has resulted from flint working, but the assemblage is of a very different character to those from other of the island sites. In general the pieces are small and irregular, and there is much more evidence for platform knapping than is common elsewhere. The single core (L5) is a small irregular platform core, and nine of the flakes have platform remnants as against only three with signs of bipolar reduction. This is in contrast to most of the other sites in the Barra collection where evidence for bipolar knapping is much stronger. The platforms are generally wide and flat, with slight lips and small bulbs of force. There is little evidence for platform trimming or general core maintenance.

Although there are 18 regular flakes in the assemblage, they are all quite small and generally irregular in shape. In this way they stand out in comparison to the flint flakes from other Hebridean sites. There is only one retouched piece in the assemblage, a fragment from a broken artifact with steep retouch along two sides to form a blunt point (L27). This and several of the other pieces, have steep macroscopic edge damage along one or more sides. This damage is particularly pronounced on L25, an inner flake, but it occurs on both chunks and flakes, apparently indiscriminately. Macroscopic edge damage may result from several different things, including accidental damage, but here it is particularly characteristic of the damage obtained through repeated striking of the flint edge against an iron object for the production of sparks and fire. In light of the apparently more recent date of the site, the excavator suggested that these flints were being used as strike-a-lights, and that would indeed seem to be the case.

Discussion
This assemblage comprises small, irregular pieces, knapped using platform reduction, but with little apparent refinement. The majority of the pieces come from a structure that has been dated on the basis of other artifactual evidence as Norse.

Flint assemblages are not unknown on Norse sites, but there was no great tradition of flint working. In this case the flint is, itself, of interest because, though there are pieces with remnant cortex suggesting the use of pebble flint, most of the pieces are of inner material, and the cortex, where it survives, is minimal. This is unusual for a pebble assemblage and quite distinctive for the Western Isles and one possible explanation could be that the occupants of site L15 were collecting flint artifacts from an earlier site to use as raw material. This might be supported by L27, the tip of a retouched tool which has apparently been re-used as a strike-a-light so that it is damaged all round. There is no clear evidence for two phases of knapping in the assemblage, but this does not always develop.

Existing flint artifacts, and waste, would be a good source of raw material for making strike-a-lights. It could then be knapped down or used as it came, depending on the size of piece available and that desired. The knappers at L15 clearly did some knapping, but they did not apparently have the skill of earlier, west coast knappers. They needed chunky pieces with fairly strong edges, and this is what the bulk of the assemblage comprises, with a few smaller pieces that may represent waste.

There are few flint assemblages associated with sites that post-date the Bronze Age, and those that exist are generally not large. The need for stone tools clearly fell off with refinements in technology and the introduction of new materials. There was, nevertheless, one persistent field in which flint could be of use and that was in the production of sparks for fire. When flint is struck on a cold-iron edge it produces sparks, and at the same time the flint edge is battered in a characteristic way. In order for this to work, a thick flint edge is needed, hence chunky pieces are the best, and that is exactly what is found in the assemblage from L15.

Conclusion

At the time of excavation is it was suggested that the flints might have been strike-a-lights. This would seem the most likely interpretation of the assemblage. The flint may well have come from a pre-existing archaeological site, and some pieces may have been used without modification. Others, however, were crudely flaked – there is some debitage in the assemblage as well as a few small irregular flakes. Certain pieces were then used, and their edges became battered. These pieces are not standardised in form, but they must have served their purpose well enough.

Soil Sample from Context 24
by Charles Frederick

A 200g sample of context 24 (fill of the phase 1 sunken area) was examined in order to determine its composition and how it may have been deposited. Three analyses were undertaken : loss on ignition at 500°C, determination of percentage sand, and sieving of the sand to determine its particle size distribution.

Table 4.2 Analysis of soil sample from context 24. Results at a glance

Loss-on-ignition	18.01
Weight Percent Sand	47.7
Weight Percent Gravel	4.6
Weight Percent Mud	29.69
Moisture Content	35.8%
Dry Munsell Colour	10YR3/2
Moist Munsell Colour	10YR2/1

The organic component

The organic matter within the sample appears to be well-humified, with very few macroscopic plant remains present. The macrobotanical materials that were observed appear to be carbonised. The amount of organic material present was approximated by loss-on-ignition analysis. Two oven-dry splits of the sample were combusted in a muffle furnace at 500°C for 6 hours and the loss-on-ignition was determined gravimetrically. The results of this analysis suggest that the sample contains about 18% organic matter (see Table 4.3).

The mineralic component

In order to estimate the amount of mineralic material present the sample was subjected to a series of procedures that were designed to remove the organic material and then examine the coarse mineral matter. First, a large sample (oven dry mass 112.87g) was digested in 30% hydrogen peroxide to break down organic matter. Next the sand sized component was separated, dried and weighed. This analysis

Table 4.3 Results of loss-on-ignition analysis

Sample number	Oven dry sample mass	Sample mass after ignition at 500° C	Weight loss on ignition	% Loss-on-Ignition	Average Loss-on-Ignition
1	27.29	22.75	4.54	16.64	
2	25.05	20.17	4.88	19.48	
					18.06

indicated that the mineralic sand and gravel comprises about 52% of the sample. This sand was sieved in order to determine the particle size distribution and the results are listed in Table 4.4. The sand present has a mode of 2 phi (0.25mm, medium sand) but it is poorly sorted and not indicative of wind transport. The majority of the coarse fraction appears to be derived from a granite, and is dominated by quartz and feldspar, with lesser amounts of mica and ferruginous material. Some of the larger clasts are clearly granitic rock fragments and exhibit classic granitic textures.

Table 4.4 Results of sieve analysis

Sieve	Weight	% with respect to total sample	% with respect to sand & gravel portion of sample
-1	5.2	4.62	8.81
-0.5	2.66	2.36	4.51
0	3.55	3.16	6.01
0.5	4.24	3.78	7.20
1	7.05	6.27	11.94
1.5	6.97	6.20	11.81
2	7.67	6.82	12.99
2.5	6.49	5.77	10.99
3	6.64	5.90	11.25
3.5	4.55	4.04	7.70
4	4.01	3.56	6.79
Total	59.04	52.48	100.00

Discussion

Overall, if we consider that the sample has 18% organic matter and 52.3% sand and gravel, this implies that the remaining 29.7% must be mud (silt and clay). Therefore this is classified as a peaty loam or peaty sand and most similar to the A horizon of a soil formed from the weathering of a granite bedrock. The colour is typical of such a horizon: the sample has a moist colour of black (10YR2/1) and a dry colour of very dark greyish brown (10YR3/2). The size distribution of the coarse fragments is appropriate for material that has not been subjected to natural transportation. Hence, this deposit is not simply the result of the decomposition of organic matter, but rather is extensively mixed with mineral matter derived from weathered bedrock.

Pollen Sample from Context 24

by Robert Craigie

A sample from context 24 (phase 1, sunken area) was examined to determine the pollen present.

Laboratory procedure

Volumetric samples of $1.0cm^3$ with added Lycopodium clavatum spores (Stockmarr 1971) were treated by standard 10% KOH, 40%HF and acetolysis techniques (Faegri and Iversen 1989). Preparations were mounted in silicone oil of 12500 cSt viscosity. An assessment counting sum of c.250 pollen grains was carried out. Computation achieved with the computer program TILIA (Grimm 1991).

Conclusion

The results of the analysis are shown in Table 4.5:

Table 4.5 Pollen analysis of a sample from context 24

Land pollen types	English Name	%	Absolute numbers (cm^3)
Corylus avelana-type	Hazel + Bog Myrtle	0.4	121
Salix	Willow	0.4	121
Calluna vulgaris	Heather	50.4	14246
Poaceae	Grasses	28.4	8036
Cyperaceae	Sedges	12.1	3409
Solidago virgaurea-type	Daisy family	1.3	365
Lactuceae	Dandelion-like fl.	3.9	1095
Plantago lanceolata	Ribwort plantain	0.4	121
Potemtilla	Cinquefoils	2.2	608
Ranunculus acris-type	Buttercup	0.4	121
Spores			
Selaginella selaginoides	Lesser club-moss	0.9	243
Sphagnum	Sphagnum moss	3.4	974
Pteropsida monolete indt	Ferns	6.5	1826
Damaged land pollen		11.6	3287
Unidentifiable		5.2	1461

The dominant pollen types are Calluna vulgaris 50.4% and Poaceae 28.4%. Calluna is insect pollinated and tends to produce small amounts of pollen, therefore the Colluna found may be consistent with the idea of heather being used for bedding in the shieling hut. The other pollen types are consistent with the local vegetation and probably reflect what was growing outside of the site. The presence of fern spores is interesting as bracken was a prized source of bedding.

Summary: Site Interpretation

An oval shieling hut was constructed on the site, probably in the late Norse period, and occupied sporadically. Its internal features were modified, but occupation continued into the 13th–15th centuries. Subsequently, the remains of the hut were partly robbed, and perhaps partly re-utilised, in the construction of a more complex but less substantial shieling comprising an oval hut with hearths, and a two-chamber oval hut. This structure probably belongs in the late medieval/early modern era. Finally a simple circular shelter was erected on top of the oval hut.

Excavation of VS42 (A boat-shaped setting, South Vatersay

by Patrick Foster

Site VS42 is one of fifteen 'boat-shaped' stone settings located on the low ground west of, and overlooked by, Am Meall at the south-east corner of Vatersay. Stone settings of this type are found on all the islands in the Barra group (though Barra itself has only a single example), and their date and purpose has been discussed in the preceding chapter. It is possible that they do not all belong to the same period and that they did not all serve the same purpose. But the cluster of 15 such settings at the foot of Am Meall does seem likely to represent a coherent group of monuments of similar purpose and date. It was decided to excavate one example in this cluster in the hope that it might throw light on this enigmatic group of monuments. We chose VS42 because it appeared to be related to a relict land boundary. This boundary runs north to south across the low saddle between Am Meall and Ben Cuier, and appears to have been nothing more than a rough alignment of stone blocks and small boulders: it seems to have demarcated a boundary rather than acted as a barrier.

Structure and Stratigraphy

The stone setting was about 7m long and 3m wide, aligned north south, with the pointed 'prow' at the northern end and a broad 'stern' at the southern. The boundary feature runs along the west side of the stone setting. The surrounding land surface slopes down gently to the north and is well drained.

The turf and the richly organic topsoil (context 1), up to 0.15m deep, were removed to reveal the stonework (Fig. 4.5A). It was found that the stones of the boundary rode over the stones of the boat-shaped setting and were associated with an evenly spread brown peaty soil about 0.10m thick (context 2). The stones of the boundary feature were planned and then removed along with context 2. This revealed a faintly layered dark brown organic peat soil (context 3) up 0.23m deep which filled the space between the two sides of the stone setting. When this was removed the stones of the boat-shaped setting were fully revealed down to their bases (Fig. 4.5B), which rested on an apparently undisturbed peaty subsoil (context 4). Excavation did not proceed below this level. Between the stones of the setting, the surface of this underlying soil was more or less level. The central baulk was left in place, unexcavated, and could provide soil samples in future if needed.

No finds of any kind were made during the excavation of contexts 1–3. The natural acidity of the peaty soils would not have allowed the preservation of bone or wood, but

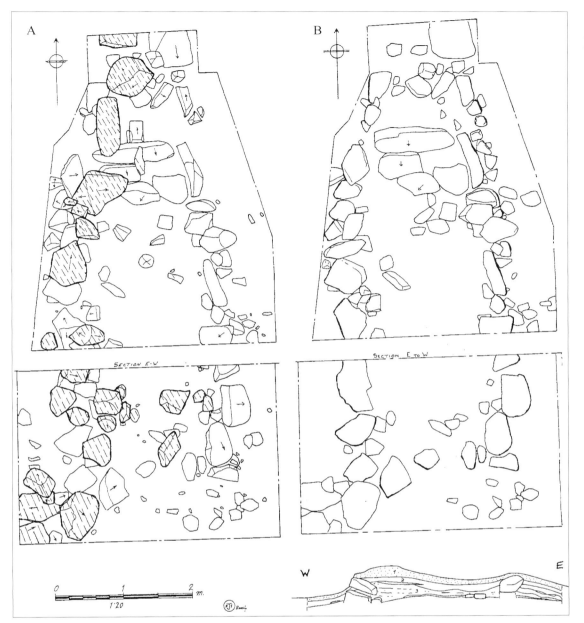

A

B

Figure 4.5 Boat-shaped setting VS42 as revealed by removal of turf and topsoil (A) and after removal of the overlying boundary (B)

SECTION E-W

SECTION E to W

0   1   2 m.

1:20

W   E

there were no traces of artifacts made of clay, stone or metal either. The three slightly different layers of soil appeared to be the result of natural processes of organic decay, downslope movement and a certain amount of wind-blown deposition. None of them suggested a deliberate fill within the confines of the stone setting.

Interpretation

The evidence provided by the excavation of VS42 is entirely of a negative character. This boat-shaped setting was never apparently deliberately filled with earth, turves, or stones. No inorganic materials were deposited within it; due to soil conditions we cannot say whether organic materials were ever placed within it, only that there was no evidence for them.

The stone setting itself has obviously been to some extent disturbed, certainly by the building of a boundary feature over one side of it, which probably involved partly robbing the earlier structure for stone. Nevertheless 'boat-shaped' seems a reasonable description of the stone setting (Fig. 4.6). It very clearly narrows to one end and the large stone block slightly off-centre there may have originally marked

its 'prow'; the other end shows no signs of narrowing and apparently ended in a flat 'stern'.

It would be pointless to repeat the discussion of the purpose of these monuments in the previous chapter, but the salient points about this example may be mentioned.

Figure 4.6 Boat-shaped setting VS42 as excavated

VS42 lies over 100m from the sea and neither its location nor its flat 'floor' would support its identification as a boat noost. There is nothing to suggest it was ever occupied or used for any length of time (its 'floor' for example was not trodden or compacted). Equally, it does not appear to have been deliberately infilled soon after its construction. This leads us to think that its significance may have been more in the act of constructing it than in its 'usage'.

Excavation of site B58 (Shieling structures)

This site was one of four very similar sites in close proximity (sites B56–59), on a flat shelf at 110m OD on the south side of the Borve valley. All four sites were slightly mounded, covered with an enriched turf, and showed traces of embedded stone blocks in roughly circular arrangements of about 3 - 4m diameter. They appeared to be temporary or seasonal huts, and from a rabbit burrow in B58 we recovered a substantial piece of shoulder and rim from a handmade jar. The group were discovered in our first season on Barra in 1988, and B58 was excavated as part of a programme of excavation of different types of seasonal huts or shelters in the Borve valley in 1993. A 4m square area was excavated as four quadrants.

Structure and Stratigraphy

Beneath the turf the dark peaty top soil (context 2) had accumulated over and around some twenty blocks of gneiss, mostly found in a rough arc on the east side of the site. Amongst these stones and in the top soil we recovered 26 sherds of handmade pottery, all but eight from the north east quadrant. At the centre of the area was a hollow or intrusive pit about 20cms deep (context 3), filled with a darker, damper soil.

Below the top soil, a compacted brown soil with very few stones, but with hard blackish patches (context 5) was found over the centre of the area, and beneath some of the gneiss blocks in the north east quadrant (contexts 9 and 10). This deposit was up to 4cms deep, and yielded 24 sherds. Embedded in this deposit and in context 8, a peaty black soil with small red flecks on the west side of the area, were further gneiss blocks. These spread in a reasonably well-defined arc around the eastern quadrants, and were also found in smaller numbers around the western quadrants (Fig. 4.7). Context 8 yielded seven sherds of handmade pottery. South-east of centre was an area about 55 x 30cms with clear signs of burning, the soil coloured orange-red, baked hard and powdery; a stone slab laid on this deposit was in turn covered by a further deposit of powdery orange-

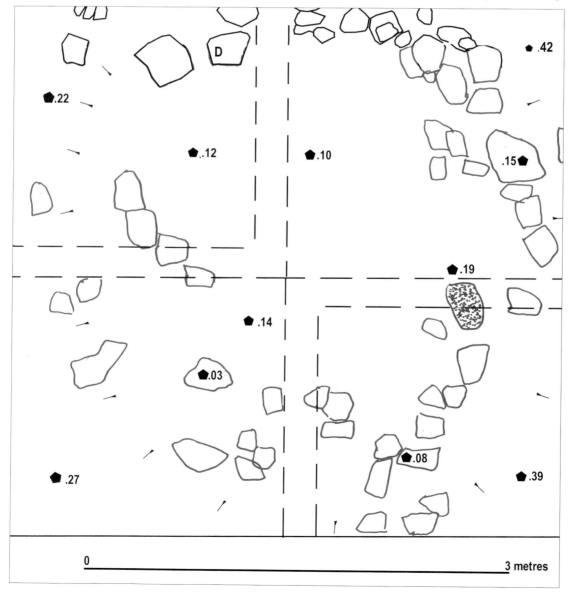

Figure 4.7 The remains of shieling site B58, phase 1 (spot heights are in cm below datum D and north at the top of the page)

red soil. All these deposits sat on a slightly raised, natural hillock.

The Finds

Pottery

by Ewan Campbell

This report includes pottery from sites L15 and B58. This small assemblage is important as it adds to the meagre evidence for medieval/post-medieval pottery in the Hebrides. Although the ceramic tradition in the Western Isles was continuous from the Late Norse period through to the early twentieth century, the typological development is almost unknown, and there are almost no fixed points in the chronology (Young 1966; Lane 1990). Two recent assemblages are known from North Uist, from a post-medieval building at Druim na Dearcraig (Campbell 1997) and from late medieval occupation of the Iron Age site on Eilean Olabhat (Armit *et al* forthcoming). There is also a continuous sequence at the Udal, but only the Late Norse material is published in summary form (Lane 1990; 1983). Otherwise there are a few assemblages in the Inner Hebrides, the best dated of which is from Breachacha Castle, Coll (Turner & Dunbar 1970). Late 'craggan' wares are well-known, but have few dated examples (Cheape 1993).

Most of the material has the usual coarse clamp-fired Hebridean fabric gritted with gneiss fragments, which is found from at least the early first millennium BC through to the early twentieth century, making it difficult to identify particular periods. The best means of distinguishing these wares is by form, decoration and construction technique, but the fragmented nature of the assemblage often makes it difficult to reconstruct forms. The latest wares sometimes have a thinner and harder fabric, perhaps reflecting better kilns, and this seems to be a feature of medieval and later assemblages. The surface of some of these sherds is characteristically uneven, due to thumb smoothing, and is described below as 'craggan type', though as we do not know when it was introduced, this does not necessarily

imply that this fabric is very late. The association with medieval forms in B58 suggests that it could have been introduced at that date. Although most Hebridean pottery is reduced, due to the clamp firing, some of the Barra material is oxidised, perhaps reflecting the influence of imported mass-produced wheel-thrown wares of medieval date. I have noted a similar feature in an unpublished assemblage of hand-made pottery of 12th–13th century date from Lambsdale Leans in Caithness.

Most of the diagnostic sherds from these two sites are from globular jars with upright rims, with decoration on the flat top of the rim (Fig. 4.8). The decoration can be slashes (Nos 3 and 7) or stabbing (No. 8), and two are undecorated (Nos 5 and 9). The rim top decoration, sometimes with a second line at the base of the neck, seems to be characteristic of medieval pottery in the Hebrides. It first appears in 'Late Norse' levels at the Udal (Lane 1983, Fig 20), but the vessel forms here do not have the upright neck which characterises the later medieval material. Recent evidence from the machair excavations in South Uist suggests that the Late Norse pottery of the Udal, especially the flat platters, were still in use as late as the twelfth or thirteenth centuries (Brennand, Parker Pearson & Smith 1998, 36). Very similar forms to the Barra material were present in Phase 4 at Eilean Olabhat, though the vessels there were smaller and in black fabric. I suggest a broad range of thirteenth to sixteenth century for this pottery. A similar form of vessel, but without the stabbed decoration, contained a seventeenth century coin hoard from near Stornaway (Cheape 1993, Fig.8). Related forms, with a different pattern of decoration, are present in the lowest levels at Breachacha Castle which date to the fifteenth / sixteenth century (Turner and Dunbar 1970, Fig. 13, Nos I, 1 and I, 2).

One vessel, the unstratified jar from B58 (No.9) is clearly later than the others, and its form can be paralleled in the 17th/18th century craggan from Breachacha (ibid. Fig. 13, VI, 1). The stabbing decoration on the shoulder is unusual, but a very similar pattern is on an undated example from

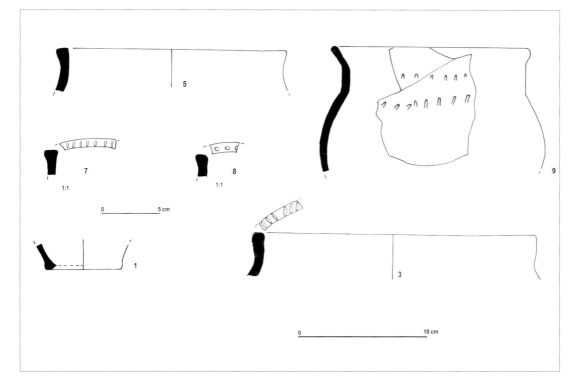

Figure 4.8 Hand-made pottery from sites L15 and B58

Tiree which also has a stabbed rim (Mann 1908, Fig. 2), and scoring on the shoulder is seen on some nineteenth century examples from Lewis (Cheape 1988, Fig. 7). In contrast, another small sherd (No. 4) is in a soft fabric which may be early prehistoric, and would clearly pre-date the rest of the B58 assemblage.

Apart from these examples, there is very little that is diagnostic in either of these assemblages. From site L15, one sherd (No. 2) is a grass-marked base, a technique which is characteristic of Norse period assemblages but not exclusively restricted to that period. Similarly, the small base (No. 1) from L15 is not particularly characteristic of any period, though it is present in Late Norse levels at the Udal (Lane 1983, Fig. 20).

In summary L15 phase I could belong to the Late Norse period, but the one grass-marked sherd cannot be said to be diagnostic. The later phases do not have any diagnostic material. Site B58 Phases I and II seem similar in date, and can be attributed to the late medieval period, with a possible later occupation in the early modern period. It must be emphasised that this is very speculative, especially given the small size of the assemblages, and the fact that residual material is common on all sites.

Catalogue

N.B. Fabrics are only described when they differ from the normal coarse, gneiss-gritted, reduced Hebridean fabric.

The following abbreviations are used throughout: RD: Rim diameter; BD: base diameter; Wt: Weight in grams; sherds illustrated in Fig.4.8 are marked *.

Site L15. Phase 1 (early)
Context 24: 34 sherds, Wt 297g.
1.*   Basal angle of small pedestal-based vessel. BD 6cm.
2.   Flat base sherd, grass-marked exterior.
9 sherds of thick-walled globular vessel; 4 of thin hard fabric.
Site L15. Phase 1 (late)
Context 18: 11 sherds, Wt 43g.
2 craggan type sherds; 2 thin hard fabric.
Site L15. Phase 2
Context 11: 2 sherds, Wt 7g.
Site L15. Phase 3
Contexts 2 and 3: 4 sherds, Wt 15g.
Site B58. Phase 1
Context 5: 18 sherds, Wt 97g.
3.*   Rim of grey jar with upright neck. Rim flat-topped and slightly clubbed, with linear cross-wise slashes. RD 22cm. Context 5, SEQ.
4   Soft grey fabric, linear impressions on interior. May be early prehistoric. Context 5, NEQ.
Context 8: 7 sherds, Wt 29g.
Context 9: 1 sherd, Wt 12g; craggan type.
Context 10: 5 sherds, Wt 57g; all craggan type.
Site B58. Phase 2
Context 2: 24 sherd, Wt 176g.
Context 3: 2 sherds, Wt 10g.
5.*   Rim of jar with upright neck. Rim flat-topped, slight exterior flange, no decoration. Context 2, NEQ.
6.*   Rim of jar with upright neck. Rim flat-topped, no decoration. RD 18cm. Context 2, NEQ.
7.*   Rim of jar with upright neck. Rim flat-topped, expanded, with cross-wise slashes. Fabric oxidised. Context 2, SEQ.

8.*   Rim of jar with upright neck. Rim expanded with circular stab marks. Context 3, NEQ.
Site B58. Unstratified
2 sherds, Wt 71g, recovered from rabbit hole on surface.
9.*   Rim and shoulder of jar with upright neck and slightly everted simple rim. Globular body, with two rows of stab marks, one on neck and one on shoulder. Exterior sooted below the neck. RD 18cm.

Interpretation

A slight natural hillock was utilised in the later medieval period for temporary occupation. The original position and setting of the stone blocks brought to the site cannot be ascertained in detail due to later re-use / modification, but they appear to be distributed in a roughly circular setting about 4m across. In general they form a single line of stone rather than anything resembling a wall foundation. It is unlikely they were ever part of an upstanding stone or stone / turf structure. We think it more likely they are blocks which were simply used to weigh down the edges of a tent-like shelter made of hides or skins.

The hearth feature just off centre was substantial enough, with at least two successive phases of use (separated by a stone slab) to suggest use over a period of time rather than on a single occasion. The natural soil was the only 'floor' surface, but this had been trampled and contained flecks of fire debris. Within the area demarcated by the stone blocks, the limited quantity of pottery was found in all four quadrants, but was notably scarcer in the north west quadrant (10% of the sherds).

A later phase of use appears to be represented by the uppermost stone blocks, which overlie not only the lower stone in some areas, but also the original trampled surface. The upper stones are found mostly in the east and south of the area, and have a more clustered distribution than the linear arrangement of the lower stones. Although clearly disturbed and robbed at some point, they give the impression of having formed part of a simple built feature such as a windbreak. If the pottery distribution represents a focus of activity in this phase, this too suggests a simple structure of limited size in the south and east part of the area, where all but one of the 26 sherds were found. This secondary phase of use appears to belong to the later medieval period too, but how much later than phase 1 is impossible to establish.

The large piece of an early modern jar recovered from a rabbit hole on the surface of the site does not sit easily with the remainder of the pottery from the site. It is possibly to be associated with the robbing of stone from the earlier structures, perhaps during the building of the (pre-19th century?) head-dyke/sheep wall.

In summary, site B58 appears to have been a medieval shieling used sometime between the 13th and 16th centuries AD, with perhaps a change in nature from the site of a seasonal tent emplacement to a windbreak used for even more temporary occupation.

Excavation of site B88 (Shieling mound?)

Site B88 lies about 90m east of site B58, almost at the foot of the steep slope above the plateau on which B58 stands. It is separated from B58 by the head-dyke or sheep wall that runs along the foot of the slope. Although only a little larger in diameter than B58, site B88 is much more upstanding, about 2.5m high. On its summit traces of a stone structure of some sort survive. It was decided to excavate a sample of B88 to see whether it was a multi-period site (as its height might suggest), and whether it was broadly contemporary with B58 and its neighbours.

A trench (A) 4m long x 1.5m was opened running down the north face of the mound (that is facing onto the plateau). The top soil was a fine light brown hill-wash, which overlay a darker brown, slightly clayey soil with charcoal flecks (context 3). This sealed a compacted fine orange-brown soil with very few stones but many charcoal flecks (context 4) from which 11 small, abraded sherds were collected. Embedded in context 4 at the very top (south) of the trench were three slabs of gneiss, set horizontally. A shallow hollow, 2.3m long and 0.6m wide and 25cm deep at its centre, was cut into the surface of context 4 and filled with a rather hard stony soil (context 5). Immediately east of it, and also cut into by it, was a smaller hollow full of soft brown soil with charcoal flecks (context 6). The removal of contexts 5 and 6, followed by that of context 4, revealed a gritty greyish-brown soil (context 7) across the entire area. This in turn overlay natural, an orange-yellow till with many small partly rounded stones.

A second trench (B) was opened along the west edge of the summit of the mound. There were clear traces of rabbit disturbance on the summit, so only a small area 2 x 1m was opened. Beneath top soil a cluster of gneiss blocks was found, penetrated by a rabbit run filled with soft dark brown soil, and set in the compacted orange-brown soil found in trench A (context 4). Two sherds were found in context 4, which sat directly on natural orangey-yellow natural.

The Finds

Pottery

Only 16 sherds were found in the excavation, two of which were from top soil in trench B. None of the sherds came from thick-walled vessels, all were in a coarse gneiss gritted fabric and most were black or dark-brown reduced wares. The sherds from context 4 in trench A were all small and abraded, whereas the two unstratified sherds and the two sherds from context 4 in trench B were larger and less weathered. One small rim fragment from context 4, trench B, with impressions on the top of the rim is comparable to rims from B58 above.

Catalogue

Context 4, Trench A
11 small, heavily abraded sherds all but two in reduced fabric. Wt 15g. No featured sherds.

Context 4, Trench B
Everted rim sherd in oxidised fabric, with finger-nail impressions (?) on top of rim. Wt 15g.
Angled sherd of oxidised fabric, possibly part of a base. Wt 10g.

Context 7, Trench A
Body sherd in reduced fabric. Wt 5g.

Interpretation

The physical appearance of B88 proved to be misleading. It was not a multi-period site but sat on a small but steep-sided natural mound, which one suspects may have resulted from a land slump from the steep slope above at some time in the remote past. On this mound a non-intensive occupation had taken place. The stones edging both the

north and west face of the summit must have been deliberately taken there and used in some sort of temporary structure. It is tempting to think that this was similar to the first phase of site B58 – essentially a ring of stones placed around the periphery of a tent-like structure. Such occupation as there was, was located on the summit of the mound, and displaced material from here (small sherds and fire debris) fell down the slopes of the mound. The pottery fabric is similar to the material from B58, and the rim with impressions on the top finds parallels there. B88 was probably broadly contemporary with site B58 and was one of a group of shieling sites at this location.

Excavation of Site B87 (Shepherd's shelter?)

Site B87 is almost due south of B88, and only some 40m distant, but sits in an elevated position about 35m above B88. In survey it appeared as a collapsed, heavily embedded, roughly square structure attached to the end of a short turf and stone wall which ran across and blocked a steep natural ramp. This ramp ran from the base of the steep slope diagonally across the slope towards the 150m contour. The wall continues the line of a long wall of the same character which runs north–south for over 400m, roughly following the line of the 150m contour. This wall has the appearance of a higher, and more relict, earlier head-dyke in this part of the valley. The structure B87 appeared to be a shelter built against the terminus of this wall. It was decided to excavate the site as an example of the small rectangular built shelter of which other examples exist both in the Borve valley and elsewhere on Barra.

The structure is, surprisingly, built on the down-slope side of the boundary wall, so that it had no existing buttress against slippage (Fig. 4.9). The boundary wall would have offered protection from easterly winds, and the sloping ground would have drained better than the area immediately above the wall, but it was a precarious position in which to build a shelter. This probably explains the relatively thick walls of the shelter. The east wall was the best preserved standing to four stones (one can hardly call them courses) high, and incorporating rough blocks of gneiss between 30 and 60cm in length. This wall was 0.8m wide. The south wall had suffered badly from down-slope

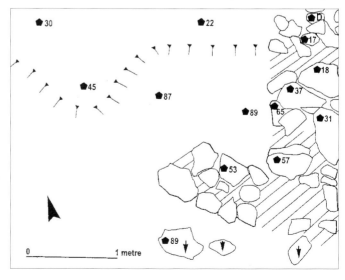

Figure 4.9 Plan of shepherd's shelter B87 (spot heights are in cm below datum D)

slump, and several wall-stones were lying embedded down-slope from the wall. It appeared to be about 70cm wide, but less than a metre's length of it survived. It was probably not much longer, for an expansion of the turf and stone boundary wall projected southwards at the terminus of the boundary, and formed a stunted west 'wall' for the shelter. The area enclosed by the two stone walls and the boundary wall was about 1.8 x 1.2m at its maximum extent. At a depth of 0.9m below the highest stones in the wall, a trampled natural surface was found, flecked with occasional specks of charcoal. This was presumably the 'floor', but there was no trace of a hearth or area of burning in the shelter however. No cultural material of any kind was found in or on this surface, or anywhere in the structure.

The structure is therefore undated, but its heavily-embedded condition and its location on the terminus of the high and apparently early head-dyke suggests that it predates the main head-dyke / sheep wall which runs at the foot of the slope on which this structure is located. Given the nearby location of a much more substantial structure (B60) only 150m away, where there is some evidence for an 18th century date, we tentatively place B87 in the early modern period. It presumably served as a temporary shelter for shepherds in the summer months.

Excavation of site B60 (shepherd's hut/bothey)

Site B60 is located about 180m to the south-west of sites B58 and B88, and as found gave the impression of being a circular hut. It was decided to excavate the site as it appeared to be an example of a small-medium stone hut, clearly more structured than the 'shielings' on the nearby plateau (sites B56–B59) and representative of a number of similar structures elsewhere in the Borve valley. It was also of potential significance because it was built against a relict boundary bank. The dating of such structures is particularly difficult on Barra (for which no pre-1850 maps survive) and the excavation of the hut offered the possibility of securing a *terminus ante quem* for the bank.

The hut sits towards the bottom of a west-facing steep slope, at about 105m OD, in a slight depression which gives it a measure of shelter from north and south winds. It lies about 20m outside the head-dyke/sheep wall. The hut sits against the slight hump of a relict downslope earth bank which runs beneath the head dyke/sheep wall and clearly predates both the hut and the wall. In front of the hut are faint traces of lazy-beds which begin almost outside the hut and again run beneath the head dyke/sheep wall. These lazy-beds swing towards the line of the relict earth bank further downslope but unfortunately both bank and lazy-beds fade out and the relationship between them is therefore uncertain.

The relict earth bank can be traced upslope for a distance of at least 30m, and downslope for rather more, so that it may be considered a boundary bank of some significance. It appears to have been an unfaced bank of mounded earth, perhaps about 1m wide originally. At four points along its line, either side of the hut, there were large stone blocks embedded in the top or on the slope of the bank, and two further large slabs were lying just off the bank upslope. We strongly suspect that the bank was of a type we have noted occasionally elsewhere (Branigan and Foster 2000, 343), characterised by spaced monoliths set in the top of an earth bank. When we excavated the hut, we found amongst the small irregular stones used in its construction three larger

blocks which we believe were removed from the bank against which the hut was built. The hut itself was excavated on a quadrant system. The removal of turf and hillwash (contexts 1 and 2) revealed a stone-built structure, the north side of which was set into the south face of the relict earth bank. We were able to identify three phases of use for the hut.

Phase 3

The final phase of use was a single episode. Sitting on the tumbled remains of the hut wall in the south-west quadrant was a crudely built cist, comprised of five stone blocks set on edge forming three sides of the cist, with the fourth formed by the inside face of the hut wall. The cist measured 1.25 x 0.75m, and had a rather loose fill of blackish-brown soil (context 4) from which we recovered a quantity of well-preserved animal bone. This proved to be the rear quarter of a sheep. The only other find in the cist was a small base sherd from a white china plate of probably later nineteenth / early twentieth century date.

Phase 2 (Fig. 4.10)

The structure into which the cist had been inserted was revealed by the removal of tumbled stone and fine brown, slightly clayey hillwash (context 3). It proved to be D-shaped, about 5.7m square. The curved side of the hut was constructed by cutting into and facing the south side of the relict earth bank with a single line of stone blocks. Presumably the rest of this wall was built in turf, placed on the remains of the old earth bank. The other three walls of the hut were constructed with stone lined inner and outer faces, the space between packed with earth. The east, upslope, wall was the thickest at 1.25m, and its outer face was somewhat irregular, as it was dug into the slope. The downslope west wall was 1m wide, preserved to a height of 0.45m on the outside. On the south side, the wall was only 0.75m wide, and was pierced by a 0.6m doorway, slightly east of centre. The only floor associated with this phase was an old turf surface which had been trampled hard and was mottled brown, black and red in patches (context 5). A small hearth ringed by stones was set in the northeast corner. No artefactual material was found on this surface; the only finds were two small glazed sherds found in the overlying hillwash (context 3), which provide a *terminus ante quem* for this phase.

Phase 1

The turf surface which was utilised as the floor of the phase 2 hut had developed over a fine brown hillwash (context 6) which in turn overlay a slump of clayey orange soil and small stones (context 8). The arc of stones marking the north wall of the phase 2 structure were set on top of this slump material. Beneath the slump was a greyish soil with orange and red flecks (context 9) which appeared to represent an earlier floor level. This could be associated with traces of an earlier, straight wall alignment at the rear (north side) of the hut. Careful examination of the west and south walls also revealed signs of an earlier phase to these walls. The west wall was built more regularly of larger blocks at this lower level, and the south wall had originally been wider, particularly at the doorway, where the wall was over 1m wide. The original structure therefore appeared to be more or less square, rather than D-shaped, and to be somewhat more sturdily built. Two particularly large stone

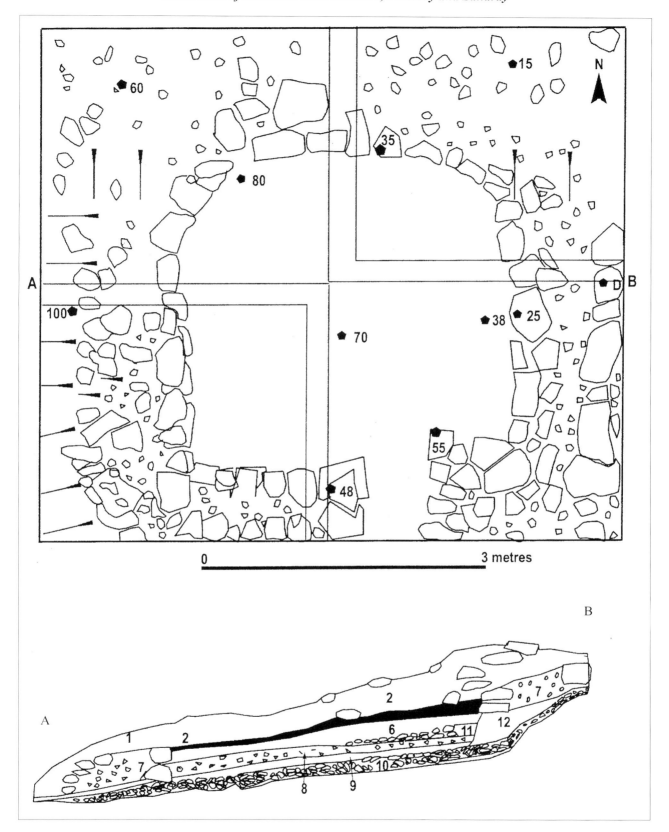

Figure 4.10 Plan and section through site B60, phase 2 (spot heights are in cm below datum D)

blocks were found at the base of the outer face of the east wall, and we suspect these may have been taken from the spaced monoliths that originally sat on top of the boundary bank, against which the hut was built. The only finds were a glazed sherd found in the overlying slump (context 8), which again provides a *terminus ante quem* for this phase, and a handmade sherd found in the hillwash overlying the slump (context 6).

The Finds

Pottery

Only five sherds were found in the entire excavation, but they were well stratified and apart from one clearly residual prehistoric sherd they represented a chronological sequence.

Catalogue
Phase 1
Context 8: 1 sherd, Wt 6g.
Hard fine buff fabric with a good yellow glaze with brown zigzag stripes. Staffordshire 'Tiger' ware. Late 17th-mid 18th-century AD.
Phase 1/2 hiatus
Context 6: 1 sherd, Wt 8g.
Softish coarse buff fabric fired to brownish-red with abundant angular quartz grains; 10mm thick. Prehistoric, and very similar to sherds recovered in the kerbed cairn VS4B (Branigan and Foster 2000, 206) dated by OSL to MBA/LBA.
Phase 2
Context 3: 2 sherds, Wt 8g.
Two sherds apparently from a single vessel. Hard fine white fabric with clear glaze over blue painted trim; rim of a cup or tea bowl. Pearlware. Earlier 19th-century AD.
Phase 3
Context 4: 1 sherd, Wt 7g.
Hard fine white fabric with plain glaze; base fragment of a plate. Late 19th–early 20th-century AD.

Interpretation
The first trace of human occupation on this site is the MBA / LBA sherd found in the slumped/hillwash material sealing phase 1 of the stone hut. No prehistoric sites have been identified on the slopes above the site. The most likely explanation of its appearance is that it was originally incorporated into the earth bank, and had perhaps been dislodged or brought to the surface when the stone blocks were removed from the top of the bank during the construction of the stone hut.

The earth bank with monoliths is the earliest structure on the site. The hut was built over its remains and almost certainly some of the large stones in the hut's walls came from the top of the bank. That is, the bank was apparently relict as a boundary when the hut was built. This provides a likely *terminus ante quem* for the bank of the later 17th century AD. How much earlier it might be is unknown, but similar types of boundary banks have been noted in the vicinity of the broch on Borve headland (sites B5 and B85), of Dun Scurrival (site E15) and of Dun Caolis (site VN 150). These are all, of course, Iron Age sites and it is possible, no more, that the monolith on earth bank boundaries go back to the early first millennium AD.

The hut erected against, and partly over, the edge of the bank is quite a substantial structure, better and more strongly built than the shielings at B58 and B88 (see above), the shieling cabins at T211 (Branigan and Foster 1995, 183) and the shepherd's shelter at B87 (above). In size it provides considerably more space than in shielings T211 and L15 phase 2, about as much as shieling B58, but considerably less than the Norse shieling L15 phase 1. The absence of any adjacent similar structure, the hut's substantial walling, and the absence of any lush grass growth around it, suggest it probably never served as a shieling hut. Equally it seems too small, and probably at too high an elevation, to have been intended as a permanent home of any sort, and the scarcity of occupation debris, and the absence of a hearth or fireplace, or even a substantial and worn floor appear to confirm that view. The purpose for which B60 was built is therefore unclear but we label it a shepherd's hut, suggesting it may have been a hut used

for frequent but short-lived occupation by a lone shepherd, as opposed to the young men and women who took the cattle to the shielings. The single sherd from phase 1 suggests a *terminus post quem* of late 17th–early 18th-century, while the two sherds from phase 2 suggest the modified structure was in use in the early-mid 19th century. In its second phase, when it was rebuilt with less substantial superstructure and with a rounded rear wall it may have been used as shieling hut. A second small insubstantial hut (B61) is located about 100m to the south west, with a characteristic surround of lush grass, and may be a matching structure at this time.

Excavation of Sites K113 and B109 (shelters)
The excavation of these two shelters was undertaken as part of the programme of sampling small field monuments of types usually ignored. As expected they proved to be very simple structures devoid of any material culture.

K113 (NL 660 996) was a western outlier of the thick cluster of shelters mostly of type A found north of Ben Leribreck and east of The Croig. It stood on a low knoll, which was itself only 3m in diameter, surrounded by a water-filled ditch 60cm deep. It is possible that the ditch was deliberately dug, and the soil used to raise the height of the knoll, although that would represent an expenditure of time and effort not normally associated with the construction of a simple shelter. The top of the knoll was encircled by a ring of stone blocks ranging from 20cm to 70cm in size (Fig.4.11). On the north side, facing the rise of the hill behind, the stones formed a single ring, whilst on the south side, facing down-slope towards Nask, the stones were either set two or three across, or were large blocks. K113 was thus something of a hybrid, a cross between shelters of types A and C, with an inside area of 2.1m diameter. It is possible that the stones on the south side could have been built one or two 'courses' higher but any tumble from a low wall would have fallen into the water-filled ditch so this could not be confirmed. The entire area within the stone circuit was deturfed and the soil removed. The thin turf overlay a rooty topsoil which in some areas had accumulated to a depth of 5–7.5cm over some of the stones in the circuit, suggesting perhaps that the structure had gone out of use some time ago. Beneath the topsoil we came immediately onto a sticky black, peaty soil which proved to be undisturbed natural. Whether or not the ditch around the shelter was a natural feature, the construction of the shelter on a steep-sided knoll surrounded by a deep ditch suggests that its purpose was more likely to have been to keep a young animal apart from its mother rather than to provide temporary shelter to a shepherd.

B109 (NF 670 009) was a shelter of type F built against the 'outside' vertical face of a sheep wall running across slope in the upper Borve valley. This was a well-built if simple structure, with walls 0.4 wide with small stone blocks marking both the inner and outer faces, infilled with soil (Fig. 4.11). An entrance 0.4m wide was in the north end wall. The shelter was 2.6 x 1.5m overall, providing an interior space about 1.8 x 1m. On excavation the shelter wall proved to stand just 0.2m high as it survived. The sheep wall, which provided the rear wall of the shelter was more substantial and still stood 0.4m high, but must originally have been higher to be an effective barrier. Beneath the turf there was a shallow topsoil and then a deep brown compacted but not visibly trodden soil which further

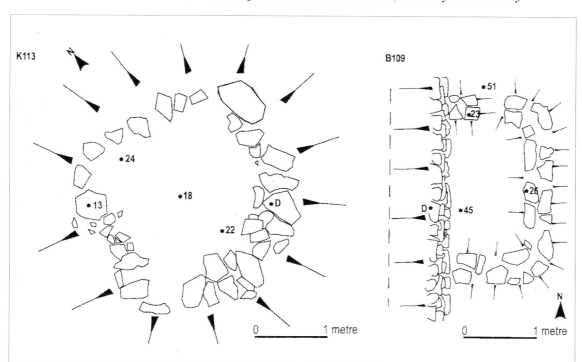

Figure 4.11 Plans of shelters B109 (type F) and K113 (type A) (spot heights are in cm below datum D)

excavation showed to be undisturbed. No cultural material of any sort was found but the shelter was clearly built after the relatively low-lying sheep wall against which it was built. Given that medieval shielings lie outside of this wall (and inside the next sheep wall up the valley) it is possible that this wall is relatively early in the modern sequence.

Excavation of Site E19 (stone building)

by Patrick Foster and Jo Heron

This site was discovered in 1990 during survey of the dune systems between Traigh Mhor and Traigh Eias (Fig. 4.12). A layered palaeosol and cockle shell deposits were noted in the freshly eroded face of a deflating dune at NF6968 0670. Examination of the area immediately to the south revealed the remnants of what appeared to be a substantial stone building, almost completely engulfed by sand. A little further south again a scatter of shells and small sherds denoted the position of a midden deposit (Site 17) in a deflating dune. The decision to excavate was prompted both by the knowledge that somewhere in the dunes here was a lost 'chapel', but also by the active erosion of the old machair surface on which the remains of the building stood. The midden was also sampled. Excavations were supervised by Ms J. Heron, under the direction of Patrick Foster.

The Section

The exposed section was first cut back about 10cm, cleaned and recorded. The layered palaeosol and cockle shell deposits were found to stretch for only about 7.5m along the section, which was approximately the same width as the building appeared to be (Fig. 4.13). The anthropogenic and palaeosol layers (contexts 002 to 008), which were rarely more than 0.20m thick, were covered by up to 0.80m of wind-blown sand (001), especially to the west. The sequence below this blown sand is basically of three deposits. Immediately below the sand was a sandy medium brown soil (002) up to 0.10m thick, which appears to be a post-abandonment palaeosol formed during a long period of sheltered stability within the remains of the building and its

immediate environs. Below this was a dense layer of cockle shells (003) averaging 0.05m in thickness. This seems to have been a compacted floor surface, although shell may also have spilled out of the wall cavities onto this surface in places. Below the shell layer was another, thicker, palaeosol

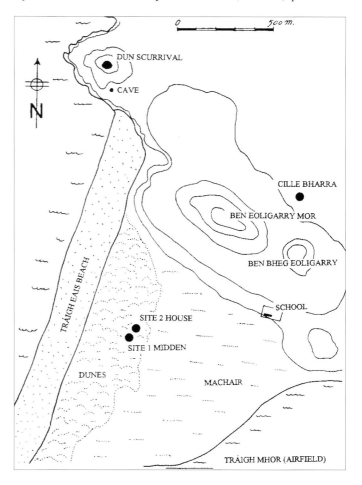

Figure 4.12 Map showing the location of site E19, Eoligarry

59

Figure 4.13 Plan and section of site E19 (spot heights are in cm below datum D)

with upper (004) and lower (005) deposits, divided at the west end by a thin intermittent deposit of shell (006). This palaeosol appeared to be the stabilised machair surface on which the building was erected. A further thin shell deposit (008) at the west end of the section and several centimetres below the lower palaeosol may be a surface scatter of shell midden material of a type commonly and widely found in the dune systems here. An example was excavated in a nearby deflating dune (see below).

Scattered across the section, and almost entirely confined to the upper palaeosol layer (002), are blocks of local stone of various sizes, which may represent the disorganised scatter left after the site had been abandoned and subsequently robbed out. No clearly defined wall stones or settings appeared in the section, but further stones, mostly of modest size, were noted in the deflated dune to the north of the section. A number of rabbit burrows appeared in the section, and the distortion of the various layers in the section may be due to a variety of factors including rabbit disturbance, dune shift and stone robbing.

The Building

To investigate the interior of the building and hopefully define its dimensions a trench 15 x 3m was opened along the axis of the building, its western edge set along the apparent line of the building's west wall. Two further trenches, each 4m long and 1.5 and 1.8m wide respectively were opened at right angles to the main trench, in the centre and towards the south end of the building, to discover its east wall and provide sections across the full width of the building.

It soon became apparent that the isolated pieces of masonry poking through the blown sand were almost all that was left of the original structure of the building (Fig. 4.13). This was not altogether surprising given the size and regularity of the remaining blocks of stone which suggest that this would have been a prime site for stone robbing. Blocks up to 1.2m long, 0.75m wide, and a metre tall were amongst the remaining stones.

The wall blocks were found to rest on the compacted shell layer and where the blocks had been robbed there was no visible trace of their former existence. Fortunately, enough blocks were found *in situ* to establish the interior

width of the building at 5.1m. The east wall, where best preserved towards the south end, was originally a little over a metre wide and at this point formed of two regular blocks placed next to each other. The sole surviving stones of the west wall formed a single alignment, but given the very extensive robbing and the limited area examined, we cannot assume that the west wall was only one stone wide. If the wall was two blocks wide around the whole perimeter then the building's overall width would have been about 7.3m, about the same as the compacted shell deposit on which it stood. Its length is uncertain since the south wall was not found within the excavated area, and the north wall had already been lost in the deflated dune, but it would have been at least 15m overall. By good fortune a doorway was preserved towards the south end of the east wall, framed by large regular blocks (Fig. 4.14). The main stone in the north jamb was 0.7m wide, 0.8m long, and 1.0m tall. The surviving stone on the south side was 0.4m wide, and 0.95m tall; its length is unknown since it was buried in the dune. Three flat slabs set on the shell floor formed a straight alignment across the outer side of the doorway and presumably mark where the door swung shut. Fragments of wooden boards and iron nails in the doorway were probably all that remained of the door itself.

Inside the building, once the overlying sand and the upper palaeosol had been cleared, an occupation level sitting on the compacted shell floor was found, amongst which further small stone blocks from the walls were lying. The occupation debris included sherds of pottery, window and bottle glass, iron nails, a plate from a cast iron stove, and most notably the broken remains of at least four gin traps and a number of copper-sleeved cartridge shells. There were also traces of domestic fires and a deposit of limpet shells. This was the only deposit found on the floor of the building, and below the compacted shell surface there was the earlier palaeosol, overlying natural sand deposits.

Interpretation

The remains at site E19 have several puzzling features. The structure itself was one of the few buildings on Barra built of large regular blocks of masonry. In terms of its construction, it has nothing in common with the island blackhouses and other secular buildings, nor with the

Figure 4.14 The doorway of building E19

church and chapels at Kilbarr, nor with Kisimul Castle and Castle St Clair. Whether the walls were double-faced all round, and how high the walls stood is uncertain, but there is no trace that any mortar was involved in their construction. The building's overall size and proportions are matched by only half a dozen of the nearly 200 blackhouses recorded on the island, and it is larger than St Barr's church at Kilbarr. The floor of the building is more substantial than in any of the seven blackhouses we have examined on Barra, all of which in fact have had nothing but earth floors apart from small selected areas of cobbling. Strangely however, the floor of the Eoligarry building seems to have been laid before the building itself was erected, and its walls stand on the floor! There are no built internal features or structures to suggest that the building had a special agricultural or industrial function. Nowhere close by could we see any trace of a contemporary midden where either household or industrial rubbish was disposed of.

Only the final usage of the building is well-established, both by the finds made on the floor and by oral tradition. The pottery found on the floor is dated to the late 19th / early 20th century. At this time, the Gordon Cathcart estate on Uist and Barra employed rabbit-catchers, and rabbit pelts were sent to the mainland packed in barrels. Local tradition records rabbit catchers resident in Eoligarry, the machair of which was and still is plagued by rabbits. It is said that one of the occupants of this building was an Angus Mackinnon from Uist, who shipped several barrels of rabbit pelts a week. There can be no doubt that at this time, building E19 was occupied by rabbit catchers, who went about their business armed with gin-traps and shot-guns.

But a building of this size and construction can hardly have been built from the first as a rabbit-catcher's hut or bothey. It is likely that building E19 is to be identified with the building shown at this location on the First Edition 6" OS map of Eoligarry, which shares the same orientation and same proportions as E19. There is, however, nothing on the map to indicate the name or nature of this building. The only structure otherwise recorded in the dunes between Traigh Mhor and Traigh Eias is the chapel called 'Kilmoir', referred to by Walter Macfarlane in a description of Barra c.1620 and again by Martin Martin in 1695. Dean Munro does not mention it in his description of Barra in 1549, although he does mention both Cille Bharra itself and Traigh Mhor. It is obviously tempting to identify E19 as this lost chapel, perhaps overwhelmed by the great sand drifts which engulfed this area in the mid-18th century (Walker 1980, 86).

There are, however, good reasons to doubt this identification. The main reason is the size and almost monumental construction of this building, which is bigger than Cille Bharra church and does not really match Macfarlane's description of it as 'ane litle Chappell'. It is also far bigger and more monumentally built than other surviving chapels on Barra and its islands (the north and south chapels at Cille Bharra, the little chapel in the cemetery on Borve headland, and Cille Bhrianain on Vatersay). Furthermore, its orientation north south might be thought to exclude it from consideration as a Christian chapel, and its two opposed doorways (if this *is* the building on the OS map) would also be an unusual feature in churches and chapels in the Western Isles.

The original purpose of building E19 must therefore remain unresolved. The date of its construction is also uncertain,, though we believe it is post-medieval and may have gone out of primary use by the mid-18th century.

The Midden

The midden site was clearly the last remnants of a once extensive midden spread, debris from which disappeared under the flanking dunes. A slightly mounded area about 3m in diameter in the base of the deflated dune had a denser concentration of material and the northern half of this deposit was excavated, to leave an east west section through the deposits. In fact, it rapidly became apparent that even here the midden material was no more than a surface scatter with no depth to it. The shells were almost entirely cockles, and only a dozen small scraps of the gritty red-brown handmade pottery ubiquitous in the Traigh Eias dunes were recovered. To the west of the excavated area, a small flat piece of bronze was picked up from the surface. It was clearly a fragment from a larger item, and was well-preserved with a good patina, polished by wind and sand abrasion. In one surface there were incised lines and small punched dots making up a curvilinear pattern with infilling (Fig. 4.15). Its top and lower edges appear to be possibly original and if so it may have been part of an arc-shaped artefact or flat ring. Both its thickness and its decoration suggest it was a decorative item rather than part of a tool or weapon. We know of no good parallels to this piece; on the basis of the general technique and style we tentatively suggest a middle first millennium AD date.

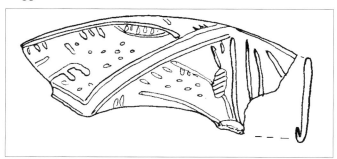

Figure 4.15 A fragmentary decorated bronze artefact from site E17

Excavations at SY13 (a whitehouse at Sheader, Sandray)

by Patrick Foster and Linda Cihakova

The site of Sheader at the north-western corner of Sandray is a complex one, with a long sequence of occupation which has created a miniature 'tell' (Fig. 4.16). The prehistoric occupation of the site was explored by a 'tapestry' excavation of the eroding section facing into Sheader Bay. We reported on this in *From Barra to Berneray* (Branigan and Foster 2000, 278–91). The prehistoric sequence begins with a shell midden C14 dated to the mid-second millennium BC, and is followed by several phases of Iron Age occupation. At the same time as the prehistoric sequence was being examined, a small excavation took place in one of the whitehouses standing on top of the mound which makes up the site.

The standing buildings can be dated precisely because they were built and briefly occupied by some of the

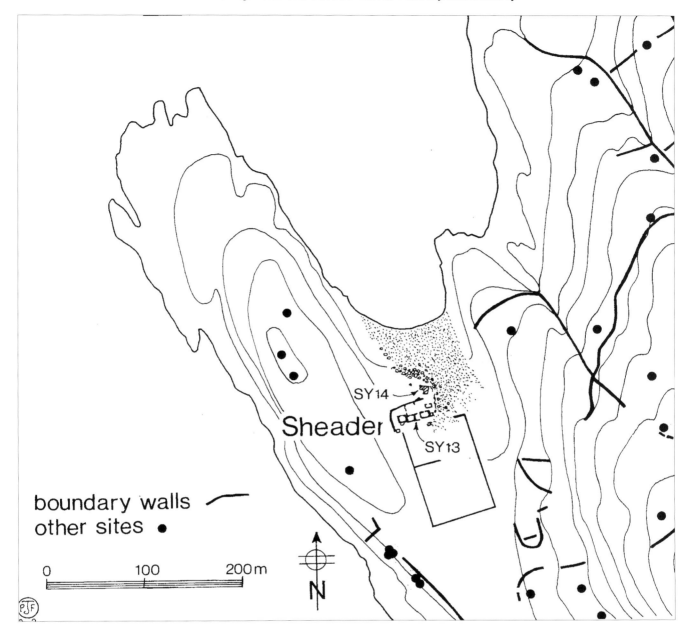

Figure 4.16 A map of Sheader, Sandray

'Vatersay Raiders' from Mingulay, who arrived on Sandray in November 1907 and began to erect houses at Sheader. With the purchase of Vatersay in March 1909, two of the Raiders on Sandray moved to crofts on Vatersay, and two more of the Raiders had returned to Mingulay by April 1910. The last of the Raiders, John Gillies, left Sandray for Vatersay early in 1911.

Our interest in excavating inside one of the Raiders' houses was therefore not to establish its period of use, or to explore the archaeology of the Raiders. We wished to briefly test the deposits beneath the Raiders' houses because it was clear that between the Iron Age settlement and the Raiders' brief occupation, there were other phases of human settlement on the site. These were represented partly by water-worn foundations of rectangular structures on the lower ground to the east of the 'tell', and by other walls and paved ways to the south east and south of the main occupation area. On the 'tell' itself, the Raiders' houses (Fig. 4.17) could be seen to be the last of a sequence of at least four phases of stone-walled structures.

Excavation inside House 4 (Fig. 4.18)

The Raiders' houses were somewhat unusual in that four of the five houses were not freestanding but built up to each other, forming a 'terrace'. All the houses faced north directly onto Sheader bay. We numbered the houses 1–5 from east to west, and decided to sample a small area inside house 4. The turf inside the house was removed across the entire interior to reveal the usual earth 'floor' (context 3) with smears of ash residues in the area immediately in front of the fireplace in the west wall of the house. There were five flat slabs set in the floor in this area providing some paving immediately in front of the fireplace. The rest of the western half of the floor area was devoid of any features, but immediately east of the door an alignment of more stones (context 5) set in the floor surface appeared to be a deliberate feature although their purpose was unclear. They may have simply formed the surfacing of an area which was particularly subject to wear, possibly associated with the structural feature immediately east of them. This was four large stone set in a neat line across the width of the

63

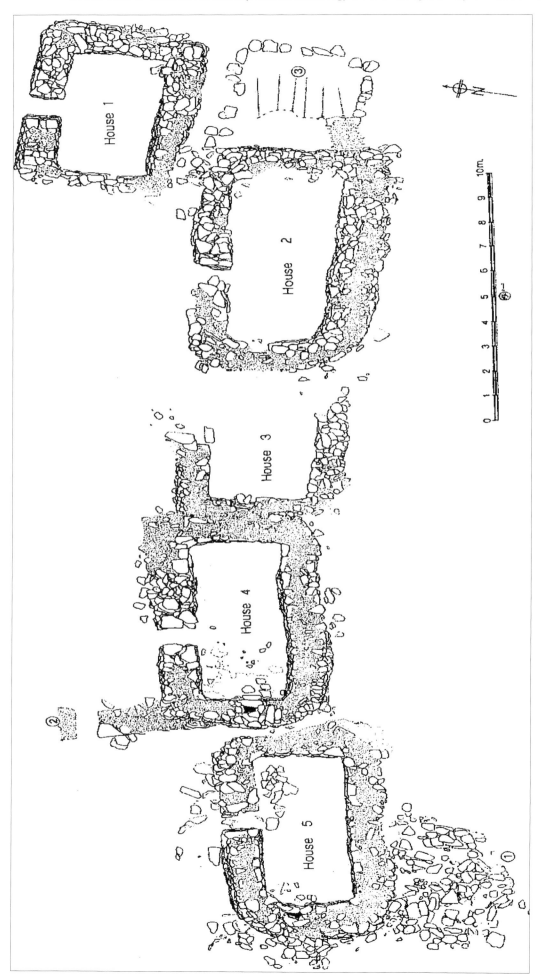

Figure 4.17 Plan of the house built by the 'Vatersay Raiders' at Sheader, Sandray

Figure 4.18 The excavated house (no. 4) at site SY13, Sheader

building (context 6), marking off the eastern third of the house. This is clearly the base of a partition, presumably of wood, and it might be conjectured that its entrance was at its southern end, away from the door of the house, and approached along the stone slabs set in the floor alongside it (context 5). Alternatively these slabs may have been a standing or levelling for a dresser set against the partition wall. This partition base, however, was not constructed by the occupants of the house, but belonged to an earlier structure and was simply re-used. The most northern of the four stones was partly built over by the north wall of the house.

This evidence that the house lay over an earlier structure confirmed indications already visible on the surface outside house 4, where the levelled remains of a wall 1.2m wide ran under the corner of the Raiders' house. A small sondage 2.3 x 2m was opened in the western half of building 4 to examine the deposits immediately below the Raiders' floor. The trampled surface of the floor gave way to a dark brown peaty soil with charcoal flecks (context 7) which surrounded a neatly constructed rectangular hearth (context 8) at the west end of the sondage. This was built of irregular slabs of local stone, which around the perimeter were set on edge. It was 0.7m wide, and at least 1.2m long and was set at an angle to the walls of the Raiders' house, but may have been aligned with the reduced foundations which were seen to run under the wall of House 4. On the other hand it seems unlikely to be associated with the partition base (context 6) being not only on a different

alignment but also set at a somewhat lower level than that feature.

The only direct indicator of a date for this preceding blackhouse occupation is a very worn, almost illegible halfpenny of George III, possibly dated 1776 or 1796, from context 7. No pottery was recovered from context 7. A contemporary of this coin is a halfpenny trade token of Calmac Ryan and Calmac dated 1792, found in our original field survey of the site (Fig. 4.19). The last of the pre-Raiders' occupations on the site of Sheader may have come to an end c.1835, for although nine tenants are recorded on the island in the rental of 1810/11, that of 1836/37 reveals no tenants at all on Sandray, and regular baptisms of

Figure 4.19 A Calmac token of 1792 found at Sheader

children born on the island end in 1835. Thereafter the island, by now designated as grazing for the Vatersay farm, saw occupation by a series of shepherds, but they seem to have lived at Bagh Ban on the opposite, north east corner of the island.

Sheader appears to have a long, if interrupted, sequence of occupations from the Bronze Age through to 1911 and it would undoubtedly repay more extensive excavation. But the site is being continually eroded, not only by direct frontal attack by waves driving down Sheader bay, but also by the scouring effect of waves which break around the 'tell' and erode the sides and even the rear of the site.

5

Balnabodach: the History and Archaeology of a Crofting Township

The township of Balnabodach (Buaile nam bodach) lies immediately south of Loch Obe, a sea-loch, on the east coast of Barra. It was first surveyed by the SEARCH team in May 1992 when the principal monuments noted were the abandoned settlement of blackhouses by the loch side at NGR NF 016 716 and the remains of the old post office just above the causeway at NGR NF 017 712. The group of blackhouses by the loch were of particular interest because there were clearly two successive settlements, separated by the small burn that runs into the loch. This particular location had several advantages that might mean it was a 'preferred site' which could have traces of earlier occupation too. When the SEARCH programme moved on to consider the development of the modern human landscape of Barra in 1995/6, Balnabodach was thus chosen as the location for the excavation of a blackhouse. Subsequently, and with the support of the Balnabodach Preservation Society, it was decided to develop the project further. This would involve not only further excavation at the loch-side settlement but a thorough re-survey of the entire township, the mapping of all traces of agricultural and fishing activity in the township, possible excavations on further sites which might be identified in the new survey, and documentary research including a study of census and parish register data. In 1999 and 2000, two seasons of excavation and survey were undertaken, whilst documentary research was also pursued through the winter. A report was prepared and submitted to Western Isles Council and the Balnabodach Preservation Society in 2001.

The Township
Balnabodach is a township located on the east side of the island of Barra, on the south side of Loch Obe (Fig. 5.1). The line of the modern road neatly divides the township into two contrasting areas. To the south and west of the road are peatlands, whilst to the north and east are the pastures and small areas suitable for cultivation that border the loch.

The peatlands are flat and waterlogged, and have areas of bare rock. The peat-beds here have been exploited extensively by the crofters, an exploitation which has only recently come to an end. Along the southern border of the township are two freshwater lochs, each about 250m long. To the south-west, just beyond the township's boundary is Loch nic Ruiadhe, a somewhat larger loch with a number of small islets, on one of which stand the partially submerged remains of an Iron Age broch. At the south east corner of the township the peatlands extend across the road and slope down to the sea at Bun an t-Sruith. The area is slightly less waterlogged than that to the west, and following clearances on the west coast in the mid-19th century it was occupied by a number of families.

In modern times, occupation has focussed initially close to the lochside and subsequently along the line of the road. The houses alongside the road mostly date from the late-19th century onwards and the earliest of them are whitehouses rather than blackhouses. Between the road and the sea-dyke lies a further small freshwater loch, Loch an Ail, at the bottom of a steep slope. The rest of the land between the road and Loch Obe is gently undulating, with rocky knolls separated by shallow depressions with wet bottoms. On some of the knolls, traces of relict lazy-beds can be seen. A burn runs from a spring to meet the lochside at a small inlet with a shingle shore, and at this point a sea-marsh has formed on which sea-pinks provide a mass of colour at low-tide. To the east of the burn are the reduced and embedded remains of eight blackhouses, whilst to the west are the upstanding walls of six further buildings and an enclosure.

Loch Obe is about 1km long and averages around 250m in width. Although it is a sea-loch, its dramatic and unusual approaches and the freshwater streams which enter it from the south and west, reduce the tidal range, lower salinity, and have created a distinct flora and fauna. The dominant factors in settlement location have probably always been a combination of the well protected access to and from the sea offered by the 400m long sea-dyke (Fig. 5.2), which is rarely more than about 25m wide, and the coincidence of a fresh stream and spring, a relatively sheltered hollow, and a safe mooring for small boats, half way along the south side of the loch.

This location appears to have been a 'preferred' site from early times, but because earlier inhabitants of the area were not constrained by township boundaries, in surveying the township we have included the entire lochside, and we have taken into account sites and monuments discovered just beyond the township boundaries but within the natural catchment of the site.

The History of the Township: 1800–1851
For the 19th century, one might expect that the evidence of archaeology would not simply be supplemented by that of written documents, but would be overwhelmed by them. This is not, in fact, the case anywhere in the Western Isles, but in the case of the Isle of Barra it is particularly untrue. Most of the estate papers of the Macneils have disappeared. Such papers as survive are mostly those concerned with affairs and events in the period c.1822–1840, when the estate was struggling for survival and was eventually sold. Thereafter the estate papers of Gordon of Cluny and Lady Gordon Cathcart include material concerning Barra as a minor element in the records of a much larger estate. Prior to 1820 there are only occasional glimpses of Barra in a wide variety of sources. And by a quirk of fate, the invaluable series of maps of the estates of the Western Isles

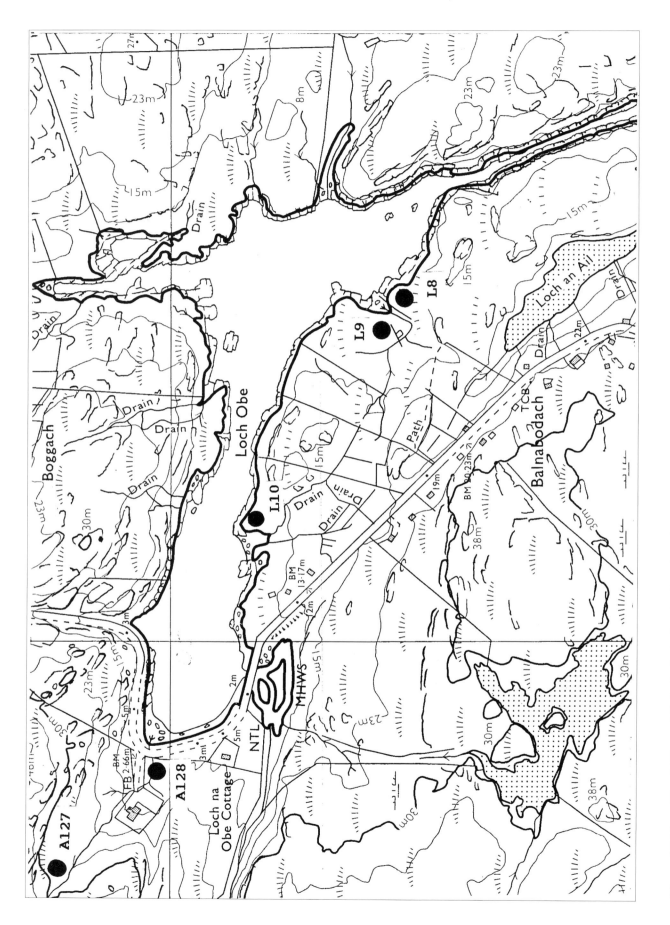

Figure 5.1 Map of Loch Obe and Balnabodach showing location of excavated sites. (Reproduced by kind permission of the Ordnance Survey. Crown Copyright. NC/04/27/869)

Figure 5.2 The 400m long sea-dyke approach to Loch Obe

compiled between 1799 and 1820 are complete, except for the map of Barra, which is lost.

Historical Sources

Given this paucity of documentary evidence for the island before the late 19th century, it is not surprising that a small township like Balnabodach should scarcely appear in the records at all. There are, however, two principal sources which enable us to gain some idea of the size and growth of the settlement in the period c.1800–1850. These are the Barra Parish Register (hereafter BPR), which commences in 1805, and the first census returns, for 1841 and 1851. Even these sources have to be used with care.

We have examined a transcription of the register, and although there are some recognisable and understandable minor errors in the transcription of both personal and place names, there is no reason to think that this transcription is not a reliable and generally accurate copy of the original. The register begins with an entry dated September 23rd 1805 and ends with one on September 11th 1853. There is a complete gap in the records from April 4th 1809 to November 13th 1809, and a much bigger one from August 5th 1810 to September 25th 1812. The first marriage in the register appears only in November 1812. Thereafter marriages are recorded sometimes interspersed amongst births, but sometimes in a separate grouping which covers several years. There are two significant gaps in the record of marriages, however, from November 22nd 1826 to January 17th 1832, and from August 16th 1835 to February 23rd 1840. In the second of these periods, there is in fact

just one marriage recorded (on December 1st 1839), as it happens for an inhabitant of Balnabodach. Deaths are never recorded, **except** between 1815 and 1825, when the average number recorded per year is thirteen. We do not know why the Rev. Angus Macdonald began to record them in 1815, having kept the register without them since 1805, but the decision to exclude them again, may have been taken by his successor, the Rev. Neil Macdonald who replaced him at the end of 1825. Changes in the style, and to some extent the content, of the register seem to be broadly related to changes in the parish priesthood. The register is of course concerned only with Catholics. There were only some 60 Protestants in a population of 2,100 in 1813, but the number had risen to 380 out of 2,400 in 1841, so a small but significant segment of the population are excluded altogether from the register. There is in fact a partial register of Protestants which is notionally for the years 1836–1854. The copy we have seen actually includes information only between 1847 and 1860. Unfortunately the Protestant register usually provides less information per entry than the Catholic one, often omitting the place of residence and never naming sponsors.

Although there was a formal census of the population of Great Britain every ten years from 1801, it was not until 1841 that the census data provided a complete list of the inhabitants of a parish by enumeration district and, crucially, household. The parish of Barra, including of course the islands which surround it and lie to the south, was divided into eight enumeration districts. ED1 includes most of north east Barra - Eoligarry, Vaslain, Fuday and Fuiay, but excludes the Bruernish peninsula. ED1 also includes Balnabodach.

Useful as the census records are, they have to be used with care for several reasons. In the Western Isles we know that people were constantly moving home from one township to another, so that the ten-yearly census may be particularly difficult to use as a source of individual settlement history. It must be remembered that the census represents a snapshot of a particular moment in time - the day on which the individual 'schedules' (forms) were filled in. People temporarily absent were meant to be included but it is thought that many were omitted by choice or by chance. Equally, because the census is a snapshot it reflects the season of the year in which it is taken, in terms both of who is present at the time and the occupation in which they are engaged. Again, the accuracy of the information depended heavily on the honesty and accuracy of the residents who completed the forms. Some might have good reasons for not appearing on a census at all, others might lie or simply be vague about their age. The description of occupation may again reflect not only a seasonal bias but also the whims of the local enumerator. For example on the Tangaval peninsula in the 1851 census no less than 17 women are described as weavers and none as domestic servants; in 1861 there are no weavers but 10 domestic servants. Such a dramatic change almost certainly reflects the way in which the enumerator for that district chose to record the 'occupation' of the women of the households.

Finally it has to be emphasised that census details provide no information on the precise location of a household; it is simply household X in the township of Y. This means there is no way that one can directly correlate a household in the census with the remains of a particular house on the ground. Even with all these caveats however the census records provide very useful snapshots of the changing population of a township, and their occupations, over a period of decades.

In addition to the Balnabodach parish register and the census, there are four other surviving documents that throw some light on the history of Balnabodach. First, we have two surviving rent lists for the estate of Barra, dated to 1810–11 (NAS CS44, Box 446) and 1837 (NAS CS96, 4274), in both of which Balnabodach appears. Second, we have the detailed description of the estate of Barra as prepared for would-be purchasers when the estate was put up for sale in 1837 (NAS CS96, 4275); this too makes reference to Balnabodach. Finally, there is a brief reference to Balnabodach in a letter dated 27/12/1818 from Macneil of Barra to the parish priest, Angus Macdonald (Campbell 1998, 128).

We present the 'raw' data concerning Balnabodach from the BPR (1805–1853) and the Census reports for 1841–1851 in an appendix.

An Outline History of Balnabodach

From these two principal sources, and the others mentioned above, we can outline the development of the township from around 1800 to 1871. In 1810–11 there were just four rent paying tenants in Balnabodach. These were :

Angus Macneil	rent	£5 – 05 - 0
Allan Morison	rent	£5 – 05 - 0
Murdoch Mackinnon	rent	£2 – 12 - 6
Rory Johnston	rent	£2 – 12 - 6

The total rent of the township at £15–15-0 was the lowest of any township on the island but for Skallary (with 3 tenants, and a rental of £13–4-0). We can assume that Mackinnon and Johnston were tenants of only half as much land as Macneil and Morison. We do not know, of course, whether there were already cottars in the township, and if so, how many. On the basis of comparison with the first census data, we might guess that the population in 1810 was around 15–20 persons. Since most Catholic families had several children, the fact that the 13 births between 1814 and 1821 were to 9 different couples, suggests a period of population movement.

What happened to the settlement between then and the 1841 census is unclear but intriguing. The letter from Colonel Macneil to the Rev Macdonald in December 1818 states the intention to rent 'half of Balnabodach on a lease for seven years' to Macdonald's brother. A letter of February 1819 implies the arrangement went ahead (Campbell 1998, 130), so Macdonald may have held half the township until 1825. In a rent list for the island in 1833 (NAS GD244/35, bundle 4), giving rental totals for each township, Balnabodach is conspicuous by its absence. In the BPR, there is a period from October 1825 to December 1834 when no births or marriages were registered in the township. The rental list for 1836–37 shows a total rental value of £25 for Balnabodach, but lists no tenants. Finally, the description of the estate drawn up in 1837 describes Balnabodach as 'a common occupied by the tenants of the said lands of Grean and Cuier'.

Trying to understand what these snippets of information mean in terms of the settlement's history is difficult. By the beginning of 1825, General Macneil's relationship with the

parish priest was rapidly cooling, and it may well be that he decided not to renew Macdonald's brother's lease on half of Balnabodach. The period 1825–1836 coincides with that in which General Macneil was trying to save his estate from bankruptcy. He was trying to lease land on the west side of the island to farmers (Campbell 1998, 143), and we know he planned to move people from the coastal areas in the centre of the island into a new 'fishing village' at Castlebay. One is tempted to speculate that the people of Balnabodach were moved out of the township around 1825 both to make common grazing available to the tenants of Grean and to populate the new fishing village, but we must emphasise that this is speculation. If people were removed from Balnabodach, then to judge from the BPR, at least one family had moved in again by the end of 1834, possibly as cottars or cowherds on land rented by crofters in Grean. Macneil may have encouraged the return of a population to the township, as he needed a large labour force for his chemical works at Northbay, which were just moving into production in 1834/35. However, in the summer of 1836 Macneil was finally declared bankrupt and the estate fell into the hands of Trustees, who ran it until it was eventually purchased in December 1840 by Colonel John Gordon of Cluny.

At the time of the first full census in 1841, the township was populated by 26 persons, living in eight households. Five were crofters, one household were cottars, and there were two lone 'paupers', both very elderly. The biggest family were the Macdugalds, husband and wife, three young children and probably an unmarried (or widowed ?) older sister of the husband. In 1836 the Macdugalds were recorded (in the BPR) as living in Ardveenish, so they were relatively recent arrivals at Balnabodach.

When the potato famine hit Barra in 1846, and continued sporadically for years thereafter, Balnabodach will have been as hard hit as other townships on the island. The island was now in the ownership of Colonel Gordon whose only interest in it was as a source of income. His initial reaction to the disaster was to do nothing, but he was eventually prevailed upon to send some relief. Nevertheless as the famine continued he came to the conclusion that enforced emigration of a significant part of the population on both Barra and his South Uist estate was the only way to be rid of the problem. Forcible emigration began in South Uist and Barra in 1848, and climaxed in 1850 and 1851 on Barra. In 1848 150 people from Barra were sent to Glasgow, in 1850 132 Barra families were removed to the mainland, and in 1851 a further 450 tenants and cottars of Barra are recorded as arriving in Quebec.

Balnabodach was one of many townships marked for clearance. Local oral tradition retains stories of boats arriving in Northbay in 1851 to carry evicted tenants to Lochboisdale where they would board the ship *Admiral*, of people snatched from the fields, of others escaping into the hills, and of families being separated. These accounts, and their veracity, are discussed further in chapter eight.

Tracing the clearances in the documents is much more difficult, because there are no documents which specifically record the events of 1850 and 1851 at Balnabodach. We have to use the clues provided by the census data of 1851 and by the births and marriages recorded in the BPR in the years around 1847–53. The census of 1851 shows an almost total change of population since 1841. Although people were constantly moving around the island, to find that all eight households here in 1841 had moved, and that eleven entirely new families are recorded in 1851, suggests something more than the effects of a normal turnover of population. This view is greatly strengthened by the fact that the township has changed from a settlement with five crofters in 1841, to one with no crofters but four fishers and three boat-builders in 1851. It is surely clinched by the appearance of a 'farmer of 6 acres', an immigrant from the mainland. The census of 1851 surely records an 'improved' township, with the crofting tenants evicted and replaced by a farmer, albeit a small one, and new tenants whose livelihood depends on the sea. There is in fact one surviving family of the pre-clearance (but not the 1841) population. Donald and Christian Macneil were residing in Balnabodach in March 1847 when their daughter Catherine was born, and they appear in the 1851 census. How they came to be spared eviction we do not know.

This eviction however, predates the 1851 Clearance. The census was taken in March, and the eviction notices would have been served at Whitsun. The *Admiral* did not actually take people off until August 11th. The change of population (and occupations!) between 1841 and 1851 must therefore relate to an earlier clearance under Gordon, either in 1848 or 1850. For the most part, the people who left Barra at this time ended up absorbed into the growing industrial centres of the central lowlands.

The population represented in the 1851 census were then cleared and sent on the *Admiral* to Quebec. But as with the previous clearance at Balnabodach, some families seem to have escaped emigration. The families of both Ewan Livingstone and Donald Macneil see further children born at Balnabodach after the 1851 clearance, and both families are resident at Balnabodach in the 1861 census. Between 1851 and 1861 the population doubled to 100, living in 23 households. Fishermen still predominate but some men are described as 'crofter and fisherman', and there are others described as ploughman, labourer, carpenter and grass keeper. Several women are described as domestic servants and one as a dressmaker. There is a clear suggestion here that this burgeoning population relied on providing services as well as farming and fishing. At this point the population stabilises and in 1871 it is recorded as 93 persons in 20 households. Crofters and fishermen are common, but a mason, a gardener and a grocer, and domestic servants and three 'house-keepers', emphasise the continued importance of employment in service.

The Survey Results

A careful survey was made of the surrounds of Loch Obe with a view to recording the location of all archaeological sites and monuments. As expected, the majority of these belong to the last three centuries and are artefacts of the crofting community. We have not individually recorded any buildings which are shown as standing buildings in use or occupation on the Ordnance Survey maps of 1878 and later, with the exception of the settlement west of the burn and the first 'post-office', upslope from the causeway.

The north loch-side of Loch Obe revealed few sites, even of the modern era, whereas south and west of the loch there were several significant sites. All the sites were given catalogue numbers within the sequence established for the whole island, those north of the causeway being given numbers within the A sequence and those south/east of the causeway being given the L prefix. The modern sites recorded are listed below:

A1   (NF 713 019) Two boulder walls built at right angles against a rock cleft to enclose an area 4.3 x 3.3m. Fisherman's store?

A2   (NF 716 022) Turf and stone blackhouse, 8 x 6m, doorway in north west corner.

A3   (NF 716 022) Partly demolished blackhouse, 9 x 6.6m.

A4   (NF 717 019) Two turf and stone walls built out from a low rock face to form a low enclosure 3 x 1.8m. Shepherd's shelter.

A127   (NF 707 022) Two small circular stone structures, 5m apart. A is 2.5m external diam., the wall 0.7m wide, with a door on the east? B is 3m external diam., the wall 0.7m wide, with a door on the south east. Both structures are well embedded. There is a possible third structure south of B. (Excavation, below p. 72–3)

A128   (NF 7080 0201) The disturbed outline of a rectangular structure 11.4 x 5.7m. Almost totally grassed over but some stone blocks visible, especially at the north end. Demolished blackhouse? (Excavation, below p. 73–5)

A129   (NF 7059 0222) Remains of a small structure 2 x 1m, built of stone blocks against a rock face. Shepherd's shelter.

L12   (NF 7105 0182) The remains of a stone-faced building 16.5 x 6.5m long, oriented north east/ south west. There is a door midway along the south east facing wall, and a partition wall creating a small 'rear' room at the north east end of the building. The 1878 OS map records this building as a 'post office'. It was occupied by the Macraes. A measured drawing was made of it.

L10   (NF 7120 0188) A small stone-faced building, 5.6 x 3.95m, close to the lochside with a door in the centre of the north wall. This building is marked as a standing ruin on the 1878 OS map. It was used as an outbuilding, and finally as a chicken shed within living memory. Oral tradition ascribes it to the Johnston's who were one of the four tenants in Balnabodach in 1811 but do not appear in either the BPR or the first census. (Excavation, below p. 75–6)

L9   (NF 7150 0165) A cluster of six houses, four with walls still partly upstanding. The OS map records four of the houses (all without chimneys) as here in 1878, and the remaining two (both with chimneys) appear on the OS map for 1901. The houses are all believed to be post-1850, with the possible exception of houses C and F. House B is that known as the 'plague house' in which two deaths from typhoid are recorded in August 1894. A stone-by-stone drawing of the four wall elevations of this building was made in 1999. The house was abandoned at the time of the tragedy and its windows blocked. We believe the house was built around 1880: it is not on the OS map of 1878, and it is very similar in several respects to a house built 400m to the south, close to the road, by the builders of Northbay school, which opened in 1882. Oral tradition allows us to identify the families occupying all the houses but house F (Excavation, below p. 101–6):

House E	Patrick Macneil	Emigrated to Canada c.1920.
House B	Angus Macdonald	Died 1894. House abandoned.
House A	Michael Mackinnon and Mary Macdonald	Fisherman.
House D	Neil Macneil and Christie Macdonald	
House C	Roderick Boyd	Allegedly a veteran of the Napoleonic wars. The house appears to have been used as a barn associated with a hay-yard in the late 19th century but an earlier domestic occupation is possible.

The midden of this post-1850 settlement is in the salt flat alongside the stream, immediately east of the buildings, and contains much pottery, shoes and other leather items, and some woodwork.

L8　(NF 7154 0163) A cluster of eight blackhouses on the rise east of the stream. None of these survive as standing buildings; all are grassed over foundations. They do not appear on the 1878 OS map. (Excavation, below p. 76–101)

L37　(NF 7152 0095) Grassed over remains of a stone-walled house, 12.2 x 7m, with traces of partition wall towards the east end. The door was probably in the centre of the north wall. A few metres to the east are the traces of a smaller building 4.3 x 3.9m, presumably an outbuilding for the blackhouse.

L38　(NF 7154 0098) Remains of a rectangular structure, 7 x 5.6m, with walls apparently almost entirely of turf. There may have been a door in the west wall. This appears to be similar to a better preserved turf-built house only 150m to the south west, just inside the Rulios township boundary. Oral tradition reports that 'mud-houses' were built here, right down to the shore, by people cleared here from the other side of the island in 1850.

An ancient peat-stack, C14 dated to the Bronze Age, was also recorded at NF 7114 0165 (Branigan et al 2002). In addition to these sites we recorded on the base map all visible traces of crofting activity – lazy-beds, hay-stands, peat cuttings, boat noosts and breakwaters, trackways and water sources. It is notable that whilst there are extensive areas of lazy-bedding around the focus of the 18th–19th century settlement, there are few traces further west and only one certain example on the north shore. The principal peatfields are, of course, above and west of the modern road, although there are smaller areas of relict peat cuttings between the road and the shore and the south-east corner of the township.

Sites which were sampled by excavation, and which are reported on below, include: A127B, A128, L10, L9F, L8A, L8C and L8D.

The Excavations in Balnabodach
Excavation of Site A127B (Round Hut)

This is the easternmost of a pair of small circular structures situated inside a modern sheep fang on a hillside behind the former Northbay schoolhouse, overlooking the west end of Loch Obe. The site is relatively well sheltered from the south, west and north, and is only 30m from a vigorous burn which runs down into the loch. The remains of both structures are heavily embedded. Their location was similar to the pair of huts above the Neolithic occupation site at Alt Chrisal on the south coast of Barra, sites T18 and T19. Excavation of these had shown them to belong to the late Neolithic (Branigan and Foster 1995, 55–60) and it was decided to excavate A127B in the hope that it might throw light on the early history of human settlement around Loch Obe.

A trench 4 x 3m was opened and the turf and top soil removed to reveal the top of the stone wall and an infill of hillwash (context 4) both inside and outside the wall, somewhat compacted by the sheep who occupy the modern fang. At the east (downslope) end of the trench the hillwash was interrupted by an arc of soft blackish silty loam (contexts 5, 6) with some smallish stone blocks embedded within it in a random way. Since this arc followed the line of the circular stone wall it is interpreted as a robber trench from which most of the wall stone had been removed in recent times, presumably in the construction of the fang. Three of the blocks in the inner face of the wall appeared to be in situ, and together with the edge of the robber trench allowed the line of the wall to be ascertained. The structure proved to be circular with an interior diameter of 2m, and a wall about 70cm wide, perhaps a little more on the downslope side (Fig. 5.3). The wall on the north side was revetted against a rock outcrop. Where the robber trench and its fill ended on the south east, there was a gap in the wall stones about 40–50cm wide. This must have been the location of the doorway, since the wall circuit elsewhere was continuous or, in the case of the robbed eastern arc,

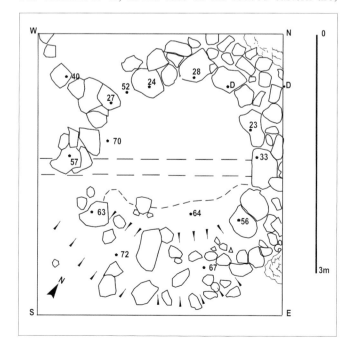

Figure 5.3 Site A127B – a small circular hut. Pictish? (spot heights are in cm below datum D)

any potential exit was blocked by an internal feature described below. There was a further area of robbing on the west side of the hut where a soft blackish fill (context 13) was found behind the wall face, together with some displaced wall stones. Eleven sherds, all but one very small and abraded, were recovered from this fill.

The interior of the hut was filled with a somewhat compacted darkish brown, slightly silty clay loam 3–5cm thick. This overlay a slightly clayey, dark grey soil which formed a reasonably homogenous layer (contexts 8, 10) across the inside of the hut varying from 7–14 cm thick. Seven sherds of pottery were recovered from this material, which we interpret as an occupation deposit. On the east side it abutted an arc of yellowish-brown clayey soil with fibrous material (Context 9). This followed the line of the wall, and was about 30cm wide and 15–20cm deep. It appeared to be the remains of a turf 'bench' placed against the east wall of the hut. The occupation material and 'bench' were found to rest on undisturbed natural.

The pottery
The only artefact material recovered was pottery. Although a total of 18 sherds were collected, all but five were very small (>15mm max. dimension) and abraded. Ten of these abraded fragments came from the 'robber' fill, context 13 and were probably derived from deposits of an unknown nature further upslope. All the pottery is handmade.

1–9 Nine small abraded fragments in a dark grey fabric with a few small angular white inclusions. Three of the pieces are fired to a reddish-brown exterior surface. All the pieces are less than 7mm thick and might come from thin-walled vessels. We believe this fabric to be Iron Age (Branigan and Foster 2000, 334). Context 13.

10 A small abraded sherd in a fine, soft pale grey fabric with no visible inclusions and fired to orange-buff on the exterior; 8mm thick. Context 13.

11 A body sherd 60 x 30mm in a medium hard grey fabric with small white and buff inclusions, and larger brown angular fragments. Fired brownish-orange on the exterior; no decorative features. The most distinctive feature is that it is made of horizontal slabs of clay about 25mm wide, bonded together. This form of construction suggests a Middle Iron Age or Pictish date. Context 13.

12–14 Three small abraded sherds as 1–9 above. Context 8.

15 A sandy orange-brown fabric with many small white, brown and grey rounded inclusions, 11m thick. Five diagonal incisions run across the top half of the sherd. The fabric is closer to Neolithic pottery from Alt Chrisal than it is to Iron Age material, and the decoration with diagonal incisions does not contradict that view. Context 8.

16 A hard dark-grey fabric with few small white inclusions. A simple slightly everted rim with traces of finger-shaping on the outside face. The fabric is more reminiscent of medieval than Iron Age. Context 8.

17–18 Two joining sherds in a hard black fabric with a rather laminated appearance, with mica-like inclusions, fired to brownish-orange on the exterior. The external surface shows traces of 'wiping' but no decoration. Context 8.

This small ceramic assemblage is one of the most difficult to interpret that we have found. Twelve sherds are very small and abraded and are probably residual from earlier occupation nearby. There is some reason for thinking these are Iron Age. One sherd (15) is probably Neolithic and residual, and the small abraded sherd 10 might also be Neolithic. The remaining three pieces – 11, 16, and 17/18 – are all different one from another and variously suggest Iron Age, Pictish or Medieval dates. We believe the absence of any lithic material may be significant, since we have found it on every Neolithic, Bronze Age and Iron Age site we have excavated, including other sites around Loch Obe (see below sites A128, L8A, L8C, L8D and L10). A Pictish or Medieval date is therefore more likely for this site. The technique of sherd 11 favours a Pictish date and the absence of decoration on any of the sherds might lend some support to this view, but this must be regarded as a very tentative dating.

Interpretation
The hut excavated at site A127 is almost certainly too small to have ever been used for permanent or semi-permanent occupation. The absence of any trace of a hearth or burning suggests that any food preparation was done outside. The hut, together with its unexcavated neighbour and a third possible example, was most likely a shieling hut or temporary seasonal hut used by shepherds. The small quantities of artefact material support this view and their variety might suggest sporadic use over a long period of time. The hut is very tentatively dated to the Pictish period, but Neolithic and Iron Age residual material suggests that this may have been a preferred location for shieling-type occupation over many centuries.

Excavation of Site A128 (robbed blackhouse?)
This site lies just to the south of the entrance to Northbay House (formerly Northbay School). Its surface remains showed as a roughly rectangular area outlined by low raised banks with occasional stone blocks showing through the turf. and parchmarks on some parts of the banks. The platform represented by this area fell away steeply to the north and east. The present edge of Loch Obe is 15m from the edge of the platform, and is separated from it by the modern road and its drainage ditch. The east and south sides of the buried structure on the platform had clearly been disturbed, possibly during road building and ditch digging operations, and the banks here were lower and intermittent.

The surface traces suggested a building about 11 x 6m, with walls about 0.8m wide, had stood on the platform. This seemed most likely to be a small blackhouse. No such building, however, is shown on the 1878 OS map , even as a ruin; nor does any building appear in this location on subsequent maps. It appears, therefore, that this building was already demolished and completely embedded by the early- to mid-1870s at the latest. There was therefore the possibility that this was a particularly early blackhouse, the excavation of which might throw light on the early history of both Balnabodach township, and the Barra blackhouse.

A trench 6m x 3m was laid out at the north end of the platform to examine the north end of the structure. It soon became apparent that the structure had been very thoroughly robbed, and only short lengths and fragments of wall survived *in situ* (Fig. 5.4). At only three points, one in

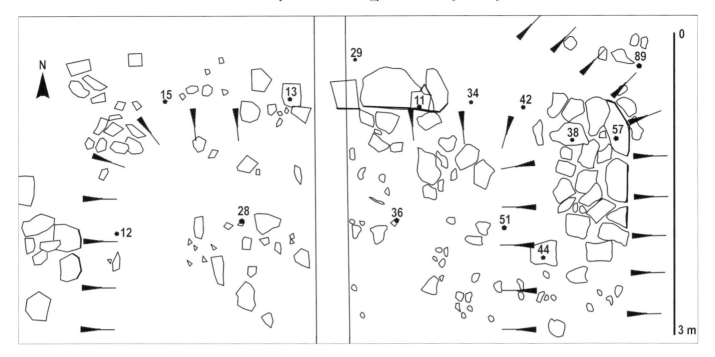

Figure 5.4 Site A128 – the excavated remains of an almost totally destroyed blackhouse (spot heights are in cm below datum D)

the north wall and two in the east wall, did any stones of a second course survive. Most of the facing stones had disappeared, with just two *in situ* in the west wall, six in the north wall, and four or five in the east wall. It was impossible to be certain of the width of the walls, but the east wall appeared to be just over 0.8m wide, and the steep slope on the north means that the north wall can have been no wider. Within the area delineated by the wall remains there was no trace of a floor or floor deposit. The disturbed soils here produced a mixture of flints, a small quantity of 19th century china, five pieces of bottle glass (including one carrying the cast brand name Younger) and a penny of 1916. Such a mixture suggests a complete turning over of the site. However, since the building was apparently demolished and overgrown by the 1870s, the disturbed deposits must have related not to the original robbing of the stone, but to later activity - perhaps associated with road-building, the digging of the drainage ditch, and erection of a fence which ran across the eastern part of the platform.

The Finds
Ceramics
by David Barker
The ceramics from this house are a small mixed group of just 22 19th century sherds. Four whiteware and five grey stoneware preserve jar sherds are of mid- to late-19th century date; one of the former has a moulded body with a hint of under-glaze colour. A single body sherd of refined redware is undiagnostic and may be of either 18th century or 19th century date. Twelve sherds of a pearlware basin or chamber pot have good quality oriental-style blue printed decoration which probably dates to the 1810s or 1820s. There are too few sherds for any firm conclusions, beyond the fact that there seems to be evidence of activity during the second half of the 19th century.

Lithics
by Mark Edmonds
The assemblage from site A128 is very small but shares with the other groups from Balnabodach evidence for bipolar core reduction and for the use of both pebble flint and quartz. Given the small size of the group, there is little basis for inference, particularly in the absence of strongly diagnostic artefacts. However the presence of a spread of primary, secondary and tertiary flakes would seem to indicate the reduction of beach pebbles in the immediate area. Five burnt pieces are also worthy of mention, all of them showing signs of having been worked prior to burning.

Coin
A penny of King George V, minted 1916.

Interpretation
The small quantity of lithic material from the site belongs in the local tradition which extends from the Neolithic into the Early or even Middle Iron Age on Barra. The absence of any coarse handmade pottery, even with such a small lithic assemblage, is unusual on both Neolithic and Iron Age sites on the island (see for example, the small Neolithic and Iron Age deposits under houses L8C and L8A, described below). Enclosure T169 situated right on the edge of the Sound of Vatersay, however, produced a sizeable lithic assemblage with no associated pottery and was carbon-dated to c.800–500 BC (Branigan and Foster 1995, 170-76). An undated enclosure (E11) on the edge of the Sound of Fiaray produced only a handful of lithic material from sampling excavations (Branigan and Foster 2001, 231–3). It is possible that site A128 was another location on the edge of the water where activities involving lithics but no pottery were conducted.

The surviving structural remains appear to belong to a stone-founded building about 11.4 x 5.7m, with walls 0.8–

1m wide. Only the north end of this structure was investigated and it had been almost totally robbed-out and later disturbed by road-building, ditch-digging and fence-building activity so that little more can be said about it. The Ordnance Survey map evidence suggests that it had been robbed and effectively obliterated by the 1870s, but how much earlier it may have been constructed is unknown. The 12 sherds from a single oriental-style bowl/chamber pot could have been from a vessel used in the house but that is not certain.

Although we have assumed that the building was a blackhouse, and it falls well within the normal dimensions of a Barra blackhouse, we should note that its walls at 0.8–1m wide, are somewhat narrow by blackhouse standards, and that the small blocks of stone surviving from the foundation course are unlike the blocks used in most blackhouses. It is of course possible that these blocks were left *in situ* when the building was thoroughly robbed, precisely because they were of small size, and that the missing stones may have been of more massive proportions and therefore worth removing.

Excavation of Site L10 (blackhouse)
by Keith Branigan and Stephen Davis

A small stone-built structure was recorded on this site in the survey of 1992. When the Balnabodach project developed in 1999, the site was revisited and beneath the surrounding ferns we noted the remains of an earth and stone bank, apparently surrounding the building. Although the stone building had clearly been used in relatively recent times (and oral tradition told us it had ended its days as a chicken shed!), we noted that the building appeared on the 1878 O.S. map as an unoccupied ruin. Oral tradition again told us that this was the site of a house owned by a family called Johnston, whilst a rental list for 1811 recorded Rory Johnston as one of four rent payers in Balnabodach at that time. The building was therefore of interest as a relatively early blackhouse with an apparently known occupant, and the bank suggested the possibility of an earlier structure on the site. It was decided to excavate the building and the west half of the embanked area.

The building was first cleared of overlying vegetation and proved to be 5.3 x 3.95m overall, with a door about 0.9m wide in the centre of the north wall, looking out onto the

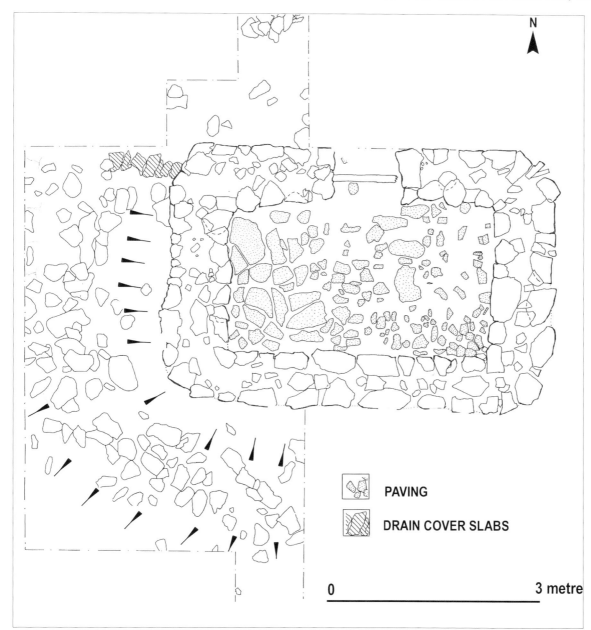

N

PAVING

DRAIN COVER SLABS

0   3 metre

Figure 5.5 Site L10 – a late 19th century outbuilding, apparently constructed on the site of Rory Johnston's blackhouse

loch. With a metre wide wall, the interior measured only 3.3 x 1.95m, which is obviously extremely small for a dwelling house, and is the smallest 'blackhouse' we have encountered anywhere in the islands.

Removing the vegetation and turf, and the peaty subsoil, we found that the interior of the building was differentially paved and cobbled (Fig. 5.5). To the west of the door relatively large blocks and slabs were laid to form a pavement which provided quite a solid 'heavy duty' surface. The central area was more lightly cobbled with smaller stones, less densely set, and these ran from a little inside the doorway to the rear wall, and then in a band about 0.7m wide along the rear wall into the SE corner. The remaining area, east of the door, had only a thin scatter of small lumps of stone, bordered along a line with the edge of the doorway, by four large flat slabs. This differential patterning could be interpreted in different ways, according to whether the building is regarded as a house or some sort of outbuilding.

When we removed the heavy paving west of the door, in the hopes of recovering dating material sealed beneath the blocks, we found that a simple drain, covered with small lumps or slabs of stone, ran from the back wall in a curve towards the north west corner, and then out beneath the wall. It continued for a metre beyond the outside wall of the building, covered by seven further slabs, before giving out into a natural gully leading towards the loch. Five small pieces of white china of later 19th-century date were found beneath the paving, and since there was no trace of an earlier floor it seems likely that they provide a *terminus post quem* for the building's construction.

Excavations outside the house showed that the bank which ran around it had no proper structure. There were some largish blocks of stone mixed with much smaller stones and lumps of rock, and much earth; the stones were not laid in any sense, but were found lying at many different angles. There were patches of burning amongst the debris, and a few small scraps of bottle glass and white china. Beneath the embanked material, and beneath the peaty topsoil and a layer of slightly sandy dark grey subsoil within the embanked area, a dark sticky soil above bedrock contained three small flint flakes but no pottery of any description.

The Finds

Pottery
by David Barker
Five whiteware sherds are undiagnostic but are of mid- to late-19th-century date. One possible cup has a moulded fluted body, while another sherd of indeterminate form has a hint of sponged decoration in purple.

Interpretation
The first usage of the site appears to have been prehistoric, when it may have been used for sporadic, small-scale activities associated with fishing.

The modern building on the site has walls sufficiently sturdy to suggest it was built as a house, but its size is such that it is difficult to believe it could have served such a purpose, even for a single occupant. The drain discovered beneath the paving in the west end of the building also argues that this structure was not a domestic dwelling. Although we have found drains in dwelling houses, they

have always been sited to drain ground water from a high point in the house; in this building there was no inclination of the floor at all – the building is on an entirely level site. We think it likely therefore that the drain was intended to drain urine passed by an animal stalled on the paved area. If so, it would imply that this building was not the 'Johnston house' seen as a ruin on the 1878 OS map but a later building which replaced it near the end of the 19th century, as suggested by the five fragments of china found beneath its floor flags.

Rather, we believe that the rough bank of earth and stone which lies around the surviving building is all that survives of the 'Johnston house'. We interpret this bank of material as the debris left by the demolition and robbing of the ruinous 'Johnston house' to provide the building stone for the new, smaller outbuilding. That is, we believe the bank is essentially the core of the 'Johnston house' wall after most of its stone facing had been removed. If that is correct, then the 'Johnston house' can be identified as a building about 10m x 5m, which falls well within the norms for a Barra blackhouse (Branigan and Merrony 2000, 4–5).

Excavation of Site L8A (blackhouse)

Site L8 has been described in the survey report above and can be seen in Fig. 5.6. The low grass-covered remains of its buildings suggested it was the predecessor of site L9 across the stream. As part of our general study of Barra blackhouses, it was decided to excavate one of the buildings in this group in 1996. House 8A was chosen because it appeared to be the most complex from surface indications. The house stood on a shelf of flat ground, elevated above the other houses in the group. We excavated the whole of the area of the shelf as an open area, and also dug a trench 9m x 1m from the front edge of the shelf, beyond the blackhouse door, downslope towards building 8B.

Architecture (Fig. 5.7)

The structure of the blackhouse revealed at least three main phases of construction, and a late ephemeral structure built into the east end of the abandoned building. All the walls were built in the usual blackhouse method, with an inner and outer stone facing which encased an earth core, but there were notable differences in the width and alignment of various walls, and significant junctions between walls.

The north wall was 1.2m wide where it was well preserved, but its western outer face was badly disturbed. The east wall was notable for its very marked curvature, inside and out, and its width was more irregular, varying from 1.2m to 1.6m. The interior wall dividing the house into two rooms also had a marked curvature inside and out and varied in width from 1.2 to 1.4m. The north end of this wall appeared to be a rather looser build than the rest of it, and we believe it was probably rebuilt during alterations to the house. Several pieces of a leather shoe were found well down in the fill of this (?rebuilt) part of the wall. At the west end of the building, the exterior wall had a well-built curving exterior face, but a straight inside one, so that its width varied from 1.3m at the centre to around 1.1m at either end. The rear wall, as surviving, consisted of two very different parts. The west end, beyond the partition wall, was as broad as any wall in the house, about 1.6m wide. East of the partition wall, the rear wall was very different, barely a metre wide. Its outside face was set back

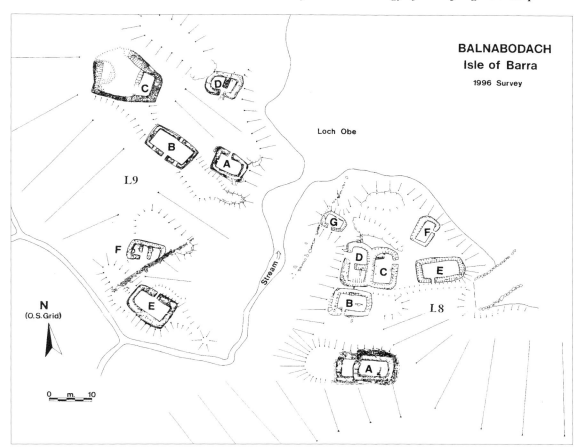

BALNABODACH
Isle of Barra

1996 Survey

Loch Obe

L9

Stream

N
(O.S.Grid)

0   m.   10

Figure 5.6 Plan of the nucleated settlement at Balnabodach, sites L8 (east of stream) and L9 (west of stream)

well inside the line of the outer face of the rear wall west of the partition, but its inside face was set slightly further forward.

Three key wall junctions were well enough preserved to be examined. The junctions of both the east outer wall and the inner partition wall with the narrow section of rear wall

revealed the same story. The narrow section of rear wall simply butted onto the two end walls – in fact, there was in each case a small gap on the inside faces between the south (rear) wall and the walls flanking it. The junction between the west face of the partition wall and the broad section of rear wall was also a butt joint, with the rear wall section

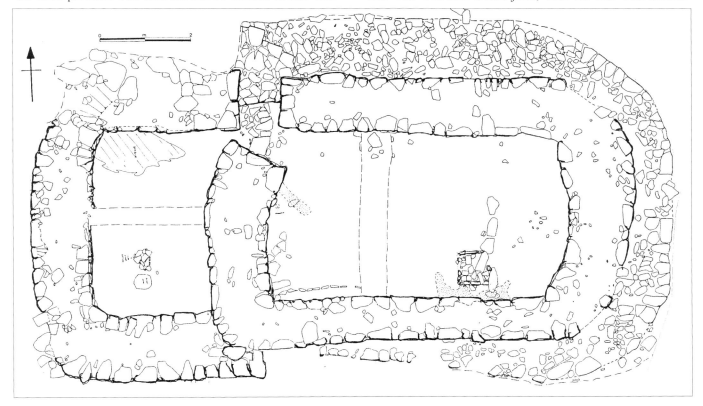

Figure 5.7 Plan of house L8A as revealed by excavation

built up to the curving corner of the partition wall. The significance of these observations, and of the varying nature of the walls, will be discussed in the interpretative section of the report below.

The door to the house was in the north-facing wall, looking out across the houses lower downslope, to Loch Obe. It was 0.9m wide on the outer side and 0.8m on the inside. The rough paving through the doorway was clearly stepped down 2cm about 0.8m in from the front face of the wall, almost certainly to allow the door to close against the ledge thus created, to help keep out winds and draughts. The setting back of the door from the outer face also created a 'porch' 80cm deep to further shelter the doorway. Beyond this 'step', the paving continued, but it ended short of the east side of the doorway. Presumably the door was hung from this side, and swung back to cover this narrow strip alongside the wall.

Immediately inside the door, the end of the partition wall was markedly angled from west to east. This had the effect of allowing enough room for someone entering the house to pass round the open door and into the main room, whilst leaving a very narrow gap for access to the smaller, west room. The open door would also have virtually masked this entrance so that access to the west room could have been relatively private as well as restricted.

Deposits and stratigraphy

When the turf and top soil (contexts 1, 6 and 7) were removed we found, as with other blackhouses, that we had a relatively thin and uniform occupation material resting on the subsoil. This was a sticky black soil (contexts 9 and 12), rarely more than 4cm thick. It was found across the whole area of the east room, across the area immediately inside the door (context 8), and more thinly spread over the west room (context 13), except for the north west corner where an upstanding area of bedrock stood proud of the floor. As noted previously, this occupation material was found to continue beneath the front foundations of the rear (south) wall of the main room (context 10). The occupation soil overlay context 14, a compacted brown soil flecked red, black and orange. It was a thin deposit for the most part, immediately covering bedrock and a few shallow pits in the rock, and was perhaps the original floor surface.

In the main room only two built features or structures were associated with this deposit. The more impressive was an 80cm square hearth (context 11), or fire-stand, built mostly with pieces of yellowish brick and some small slab-like stones. This was very heavily burned, but no significant ash deposit was found on it and it may not have been a hearth as such, so much as a stand for a brazier or fire-box. In the south west corner of the room we found a straight line of small stone slabs, set on edge. There was no trace of any covering slabs, and the feature ended in the corner of the room and was 2m long overall. It was not a drain; and it could never have been wide enough to be the edging for a bed-box. We suggest it is the edging of a dresser stand, which would have been 2m long and 40cm wide. In the smaller, west room, the only built feature was a roughly rectangular area of stone slabs 50 x 30cm, flanked by a heavily burnt area of flooring. Again there was no trace of ashy material at all, and we again envisage a brazier or fire-box with a stand for a kettle or pan alongside.

Only 55 modern sherds were found in the blackhouse occupation deposit, all but two in the larger, east room. Here,

sherds were spread across the floor area, except for the east end of the room, beyond the hearth, from which area no sherds were recovered. There were eight small finds from the occupation material and these are described and discussed below. All of these finds came from the northern half of the main room, three from around the door area, the other five from between the hearth and the wall. The only other finds apart from pottery were two pipe stems and bowls, one from each room, and both immediately adjacent to the hearth/fire-stand.

Alongside the north wall of the house, and apparently continuing beneath it, an irregular depression in the bedrock contained a charcoal-rich, slightly stony dark brown soil (context 15) overlain by context 14. The only finds in context 15 were 100+ handmade sherds and a small flint blade; a few handmade sherds were also found in context 14.

Outside the house, excavation revealed a roughly paved or cobbled surface which ran from the front door along the front wall of the house. The surface was more than a metre wide, and it petered out at the edge of the terrace on which the house stood. At the east end of the building the surfacing narrowed but continued around the end of the house and here had a kerb or built edge of larger blocks. At the rear of the house, the surfacing rapidly narrowed further and petered out. In cleaning this surfacing, we found a bronze thimble which had fallen between two paving stones, just to the east of the door, and a bronze ring in the cobbles on the west side of the door.

West of the house we explored the narrow end of the terrace on which the house stood, with a trench (Z) 9m long and 1m wide, to which a 5 x 2m extension was made at the north west corner. Near the house bedrock was just below the surface, and apart from a few small fragments of glazed pottery there were no finds. At the west end of the trench the soil was deeper, and from it were recovered 22 abraded sherds of handmade pottery, a flint chunk and an end scraper. The extension however found no trace of occupation deposits from which these items might have come.

North of the house, we excavated a 9m x 1m trench (Y) from the edge of the cobbled surface outside the blackhouse door down the slope towards the flatter area on which the remaining blackhouses were built. At the south end of the trench, by the house, we found that there was little soil depth before bedrock was encountered. There was greater depth at the north end, filled with fine hillwash. A scatter of small sherds – from pearl ware, sponge ware, and white ware vessels were found at the top (south) end of the trench but rarely beyond it. They were presumably from floor sweepings thrown out of the front door of the blackhouse. Amongst this material was a single flint flake.

The Finds

Prehistoric pottery
by K Branigan and C Cumberpatch
A total of 263 handmade sherds were found, all but 22 within the confines of the blackhouse, weighing a total of 1,681 grams. The contextual breakdown of this assemblage was as follows (context numbers in brackets):

Topsoil (1)	35 sherds	153 grams
Wall cleaning / tumble (2, 4)	87 sherds	498 grams
Blackhouse occupation soil (12)	4 sherds	50 grams
Blackhouse floor make-up (14)	9 sherds	65 grams
Pre-blackhouse occupation (15)	106 sherds	705 grams
Trench Z (2)	22 sherds	210 grams

The principal fabric was a coarse gritty one containing abundant angular and sub-angular grains of gneiss-derived material, most notably quartz. The size and abundance of inclusions, as well as the hardness of the fabric, varied from sherd to sherd, and sherds came from both oxidised and reduced vessels. Three sherds were of a much finer fabric, with very few, small quartz grits, a smoothed surface and a firm rather than crumbly texture.

There were few decorated sherds in the assemblage. Applied cordons with finger impressions were found on four sherds; two of the cordons were 'wavy'. The largest fragment of a vase, in five joining pieces, had a wavy applied and impressed cordon around the waist, above which were incised angled lines. A further four sherds carried incised decoration in the form of parallel lines, on one of which the vertical parallel lines met an incised cordon filled with short diagonal incisions. Finally, one of the three fine fabric sherds described above had an impressed pattern of at least four chevrons.

Only two rims were found in the assemblage (Fig. 5.8), one slightly everted with a flattened top from a waisted bowl, the other a flat-topped rim from an open bowl with an applied cordon. A single sherd from context 2 appeared to be a fragment from an applied lug, and there were two small sherds from the lower wall/base angle of vessels but too small to be helpful.

The principal part of this assemblage fits well within the Middle Iron Age repertoire of fabrics and decoration in the Outer Hebrides as represented by assemblages from Dun Vulan (Parker Pearson and Sharples 1999), Sollas (Campbell 1991), and Dunan Ruadh, Pabbay (Timby in Branigan and Foster 2000).

The largest profile and decorated piece from an everted rim bowl with an applied and impressed cordon on the waist with linear incised decoration on the shoulder is in a

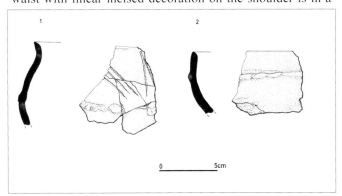

Figure 5.8 Iron Age pottery from beneath house L8A

class of vessels represented at Sollas in periods B1 and B2, (Campbell 1991, ill.17), probably of the first centuries AD.

The three sherds of finer fabric are unlike any Iron Age material we have seen on Barra and were identified at the time of excavation as probably earlier prehistoric. The only decorated sherd of the three has multiple chevrons (at least four). Multiple chevrons are found on Iron Age pottery but usually with only two or three chevrons, and rather irregularly incised. The fine ware sherd from L8A has very evenly impressed lines. Both impressed and incised multiple chevrons,(four to six in number) occur on the Alt Chrisal Neolithic and Beaker pottery, although they are not identical to the L8A sherd. Taking the fabric into account, however, we believe these three sherds are probably of third millennium BC date.

Modern Ceramics
by David Barker
Note: The post-medieval ceramics where discussed in this chapter have been classified by ware type, vessel form and type of decoration, using terminology devised for Staffordshire post-medieval ceramics (Barker et al 2001); this can be broadly applied to most industrially-made refined wares of the late 18th and 19th centuries.

Throughout the post-medieval pottery reports, quantification is based upon a minimum vessel equivalent, which has been determined on the basis of distinctive rims, bases or decoration, or a combination of all three. Each identified vessel has been given an alpha-numeric reference, which is used here in the text. So PLW 1 is pearlware vessel, number 1, and RWE 3 is redware vessel number 3. A separate sequence exists for each house.

House L8A
With 128 sherds, this assemblage is surprisingly small for the largest of the Balnabodach blackhouses, and comprises just 54 vessels, most of which are fragmentary.
Wares
The majority of the vessels (78%) belong to the 'refined' end of the ceramic spectrum. Of these 22% (twelve vessels) are of pearlware and 43% (23 vessels) of whiteware. White salt-glazed stoneware, creamware, soft-paste porcelain, bone china, black basalt, 'Rockingham' ware and yellow ware are each represented by a single vessel.

Only six vessels are coarse earthenware types. Of these, two are probably large storage jars with internal and external black lead glazes; three others are redware dishes, and a further vessel (CEW 3) is of a hard orange-coloured fabric which is identical to BSG 6; its external (?lead) glaze is thin and slightly green in colour; its precise identification is uncertain. There are also six brown salt-glazed stoneware vessels, of which five are probably bottles and one possibly a jug. One of the bottles has a light grey body with dark brown external salt glaze and internal 'Bristol' glaze (BSG 3); the others have bodies varying from orange to brown, with external glazes in shades of brown; one diagnostic sherd has a grey external glaze with light brown speckles on a hard orange-coloured body (BSG 6).
Vessels
Bowls are the dominant form (31%); there are seventeen of these, of which one is pearlware, one yellow ware, and one of English soft-paste porcelain. A sherd of an identical yellow ware bowl was found in House L8D (YWE 1). The remainder are all of whiteware and have sponged (seven),

slip (four), or printed (three) decoration. Two bowl sherds with sponged decoration (WWE 1) have drilled holes from repair.

There is only one definite teapot – of 'Rockingham' ware – but a second cylindrical vessel in black basalt is also likely to be a teapot. There are ten other teaware vessels. Amongst the pearlwares are two teabowls, one cup, and one saucer. The whitewares include two cups and four saucers. Three pearlware body sherds with vertical cable moulding (PLW 12) are of the same type of vessel (or perhaps even of the same vessel) as a base sherd from House L8C (PLW 21) whose form is oval or cylindrical with slightly outward-flaring sides. This may possibly be a teapot.

A creamware dish is probably a baking dish with an everted rim (CWE 1). Three other dishes are of redware, with glazes to the interiors only. Their intended function is quite different to that of the refined wares, and is probably connected with food preparation or dairying activities. Two of these have trailed cream-coloured slip decoration to their interiors, while the other has an internal slip coat (RWE 3). The plates (11%) are all of pearlware. There are five dinner plates (10-inch) of which one is, unusually, undecorated and of the 'bath' edge type; two have blue printed decoration; and two have moulded shell edges coloured blue under the glaze. Another blue-painted shell edge plate, represented by a single rim sherd, is of a smaller size and is perhaps an 8-inch side plate or 'twiffler'.

A single whiteware rim sherd, with pronounced bead moulding to the edge, is of a basin (WWE 20); it has an under-glaze painted band in black in the area of the shoulder. Three further refined earthenware vessels are unidentified. A single white salt-glazed stoneware mug has scratch blue decoration.

There are five brown salt-glazed stoneware bottles and one jug. Stoneware bottles are common finds on all 19th century sites and are frequently likely to have contained beer.

Three black-glazed coarse earthenware vessels are probably jars, of indeterminate function; they would normally be described as storage jars, but in reality they are likely to have been multi-purpose vessels used in a range of food preparation and storage activities.

Decoration

Ninety-three per cent of the refined wares are decorated, with the two most common types of decoration being printed (on 24% of vessels) and sponged (on 29%). Paradoxically, therefore, the most expensive and the least expensive types of decoration occur in similar proportions.

The nine vessels with printed decoration include a teabowl and two saucers, three bowls and two plates. The printed decoration on the pearlwares is all blue, with at least two of the patterns being of oriental type. The printed decoration on the whitewares is also mostly in blue; one probable bowl has a light blue printed pattern which is probably 'Broseley' (WWE 14); another possible bowl has a brown printed landscape-type pattern (WWE 19).

Sponged decoration occurs on one pearlware cup (decoration in green), eight whiteware bowls, two whiteware saucers and on another vessel of indeterminate form. Blue is the most commonly used colour, either as an all-over ground (WWE 4, WWE 5, WWE 7, WWE 23) or as simple cut-sponge designs. Such designs include the stylised flowers of WWE 22 (Fig. 5.9a), which are combined with under-glaze painted bands in blue, the crude overlapping circles of WWE 1, and the irregular ovals-within-ovals pattern of WWE 8, which also has an under-glaze painted band in pink to the rim. WWE 2 has sponged decoration in both blue and green, alongside under-glaze painted bands in pink, while WWE 3 has small sponged stylised flowers in grey / green beneath a single pink under-glaze painted band to the rim. One bowl sherd with sponged decoration in grey (WWE 6) is probably later in date.

The under-glaze painted wares (10%) include one pearlware teabowl, which has a blue oriental landscape pattern (PLW 4); one whiteware saucer with a stylised floral pattern in blue, red and green (WWE 16); and a basin rim with a broad blue / black band just below the rim (WWE 20). The moulded vessel (PLW 12) has under-glaze

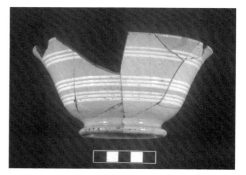

Figure 5.9 Modern ceramics from house L8A

a) sponge-decorated white earthen-ware bowl sherds in blue

b) yellow ware bowl slip-decorated in white and blue

c) miscellaneous wares – soft paste porcelain saucer (left), blue sprigged bone ash china dish (centre), and white salt-glazed stoneware mug with scratch blue decoration (right)

painted decoration comprising a light blue horizontal line, and a sherd of an identical vessel from House L8C has a red band to at least one of the vertical moulded cables. Three pearlware shell edge plates (7%) are coloured blue under-glaze. One other pearlware plate is undecorated; this is unusual in assemblages away from the Western Isles, but several such examples have been noted in early-19th century island blackhouse assemblages.

One bowl rim has over-glaze painted decoration in a distinctive floral and leaf style red, grey / black and green, and also a pink lustre band to the rim. Similarly decorated sherds have been found in Houses L8C (PLW 6) and L8D (PLW 2).

Five (12%) of the bowls have banded or trailed slip decoration, including one of yellow ware (Fig. 5.9b). This latter has three groups of three thin lines of trailed slip with a single broader band of blue slip to the middle of the body. The slip-decorated whiteware sherds are all bowls. One has the suggestion of a wavy trailed pattern in shades of brown applied with a multi-chambered slip bottle (WWE 12), while another (WWE 10) has a band of grey slip with brown and blue speckles, combined with bands of light blue slip.

The soft paste porcelain bowl has under-glaze printed decoration in blue, comprising a floral pattern, while a single bone china dish or plate has blue sprigged decoration ('Chelsea sprig') comprising a flower head and leaves (Fig. 5.9c). A single whiteware cup sherd also has blue-sprigged (?floral) decoration.

A probable teapot in black basalt has engine-turned decoration just below its shoulder, comprising a band of narrow vertical cut ribs.

The decoration of the redware dishes is typical of that found on 19th-century sites in Scotland, the Western Isles and the north-east of England. Two have simple trailed decoration in white coloured slip, while the third has a white slip coat. The white slip has attained a rich cream colour by the addition of a lead glaze.

Dating

At least 30% of the vessels date to before 1830, with pearlwares constituting 23% and dating broadly to c. 1800 - 1830. Diagnostic features of these include blue-printed decoration with the oriental-style subjects suggesting a pre-1820 date. Under-glaze blue painted decoration on a teabowl appears to be of an oriental style building within a landscape, of a type which was widespread between the late-1770s and the 1810s. The moulded shell edges of the pearlware plates appear to be of the more simple scalloped, or slightly scalloped forms which are typical of the period 1810–1840 (Miller and Hunter 1990, 116). A single sherd of a pearlware bowl (PLW 2) has over-glaze painted decoration in the distinctive colours also found in Houses L8C and L8D. These are London shape bowls, a form which was introduced around 1810 or earlier in porcelain but which was adopted by manufacturers of earthenware during the later-1810s.

Only two vessels in the assemblage were definitely produced before 1800 : the scratch blue white salt-glazed

Table 5.1 House L8A ceramics (minimum number of vessels)

	teabowl	cup	saucer	teapot	bowl	jug	dish	mug	basin	plate (dinner)	plate (side)	jar	bottle	unid.	TOTALS
White SGSW															
scratch blue								1							1
Creamware															
undecd.							1								1
Pearlware															
u-gl. printed	1		1							2					4
u-gl. painted	1													1	2
o-gl. painted					1										1
sponged		1													1
shell edge										2	1				3
undecd.										1					1
Whiteware															
u-gl. printed		1			3									1	5
u-gl. painted		1						1							2
sponged		1	2		7									1	11
ind. slip					4										4
blue sprigged		1													1
Rockingham			1												1
Soft paste porcelain															
u-gl. printed					1										1
Bone china															
blue sprigged							1								1
Black basalt				1											1
Yellow ware															
slip-decorated					1										1
Brown SGSW						1							5		6
Coarse redware															
slip-trailed							2								2
slip-coated							1								1
Coarse e' ware												3			3
TOTALS	2	3	5	2	17	1	5	1	1	5	1	3	5	3	54

stoneware mug, most probably dates to the period 1760–1780 and the English soft-paste porcelain bowl dates to c. 1780 (Fig. 5.9c). The engine-turned black basalt vessel was probably produced around 1800, but could be slightly earlier or slightly later. The only creamware sherd from the house is of a baking dish, a form which was common into the 1820s and later; it need not be any earlier than the majority of the assemblage.

However, the majority of the ceramics belong to the period 1830–1850. The whitewares are very much of this period, but are equally difficult to date precisely, having few diagnostic features. The basin rim sherd with pronounced beading and an under-glaze painted band has a close parallel dating to 1835 in a Stoke-on-Trent production group (Burslem Market Place, not published), while the hemispherical bowl forms are more typical of the 1840s and later. These predominantly have sponged decoration which includes simple cut sponge designs, sometimes combined with painted bands, or all-over amorphous patterns in a single colour. During the second half of the 19th century, sponged decoration became more varied with a range of more elaborate cut sponge designs, often using more than one colour. The suggested date of around 1835 for the introduction into Scotland of decoration using cut sponges (Kelly et al 2001, 8) would place the whitewares so-decorated in the later-1830s and 1840s.

The brown salt-glazed stonewares, redwares and coarse earthenwares are impossible to date precisely, and the black glazed coarse earthenwares, at least, could date to either the early- or mid-19th century. The Rockingham wares and yellow wares, however, are standard 19th-century types which become common in domestic archaeological assemblages from the 1830s. The bone china dish or plate has 'Cheslea sprig' decoration in blue, a type which was common from the 1820s into the 20th century and is therefore not closely datable.

The scratch blue mug sherd may indicate earlier activity at Balnabodach, or is possibly from a vessel which remained in use, or which was curated for many years beyond its date of manufacture. While it is difficult to imagine a utilitarian vessel of this kind – albeit decorated – having the status of an heirloom or treasured possession, the same is not true of the soft-paste porcelain bowl which was probably made c. 1780. Although by no means one of the most expensive soft-paste porcelains of its day, there was no such thing as a 'cheap' piece of English porcelain, which retained both its status and its price during the late-18th century. The presence of such an item in a Barra blackhouse is surprising, although it is easy to appreciate that such an expensive item would be treasured and may therefore have been deposited many years after its acquisition.

Only one vessel is definitely later than the middle of the 19th century. This is a bowl with grey sponged decoration (WWE 6) from (002) which probably dates to the mid-1870s or later (Kelly 1996, 20). This sherd was found immediately below the turf and may therefore not relate to the occupation of House L8A.

Discussion

In the interim report it was suggested that this house was built c. 1780, extended c. 1820 (Branigan 2000, 18) and finally abandoned c. 1850. Certainly the bulk of the ceramics date to the period c. 1820–1850, but only two sherds are definitely of 18th-century date. One of these

at least, the relatively expensive soft-paste porcelain bowl, is a strong candidate for curation and does not necessarily point to 18th-century activity at this site. A similar, but less strong, case can be made for the white salt-glazed stoneware mug. On the evidence of these two sherds, however, it is difficult to support the suggestion that the house was built as early as 1780. The ceramic assemblage is a small one upon which to base hypotheses, but the ceramics provide clear evidence for early-19th-century activity and probably occupation evidence, and an early 19th-century date for the house's construction is therefore a strong possibility. It is more difficult to determine whether there was continuity of occupation from this time through to the late 1840s, on account of the paucity of diagnostic material which can be closely dated, but this would seem to be a plausible hypothesis on the basis of the available evidence.

House L8A trenches Z and Y

The ceramics from trenches L8A (Y) and L8A (Z) are probably related to the use of House L8A.

Twenty-eight sherds from L8A (Y) include 1 of prehistoric date. The refined wares are broadly similar in their range and date to the House L8A ceramics. At least 17 vessels are represented, six of which are of pearlware and eleven of whiteware. The pearlwares include three shell edge plates, painted blue; the sherds are a scalloped rim from a 10-inch plate, one from a small, possibly 6-inch plate or 'muffin', also scalloped, while the third is from a large plate or platter whose edge moulding has a hint of the rococo style of the late-18th to early-19th century. One probable bowl has oriental style blue printed decoration, while two others have sponged and painted decoration. One has a sponged ground in blue and yellow, with panel outlined by an under-glaze painted line in brown, within which is a stylised painted pattern in brown, green and orange and below the exterior rim are two painted brown lines; an identically decorated bowl was found in the House L8C assemblage (PLW 19). The second combines under-glaze blue painted lines with a simple blue sponged pattern. A date of c. 1800–1830 seems likely for the pearlwares, with the majority probably dating to the 1820s.

The whitewares are mostly bowls with a mixture of sponged, sponged and painted, and sponged and slip-banded decoration, but there are also at least two blue-printed vessels, one of which is a plate, and one bowl with under-glaze painted decoration in chrome colours. Broadly, the whitewares date to the 1830s–1840s.

Thirty-six sherds from L8A (Z) include 22 of coarse hand-made prehistoric pottery. The 19th century ceramics are of the same date as the House L8A finds, with two pearlware vessels and at least six of whiteware, all decorated. The former are a blue-painted shell edge plate sherd and a bowl with banded slip decoration in blue and black, dating to the 1810s–1820s.

The whitewares include three possible plates, two basins and at least one bowl. Decoration is mostly sponged, but four sherds (at least two vessels) have printed decoration and one vessel has under-glaze painted decoration; none of the sherds are especially diagnostic, but can be broadly dated to the period 1830–1850.

Lithics
by Mark Edmonds

Lithic materials recovered during excavation were identified in several different contexts. Most of these were residual, though a small proportion were recovered from beneath the main blackhouse floor deposit. How far even these were *in situ* remains unclear.

A total of 28 pieces of worked/utilised stone were identified here, the majority (19) taking the form of unmodified flakes. All of these appear to have been created during the working of beach pebbles, and many of the tertiary flakes have the opposed scars or platform crushing commonly associated with bipolar working. Similar characteristics can also be seen on four of the eight cores/core fragments also recovered, from context [002]. Of the remaining cores, two (also from 002] are characterised by two or three removals from split pebbles. The final two core fragments (from 009) are simple platform cores, one of which has been re-used/retouched as an irregular scraper. The majority (12) of the flakes are tertiary, with little or no cortex visible, with four secondary and three primary flakes, one of which is burnt.

Given the small size of the assemblage, there is little that can be said in detail regarding either the character or the chronology of the activities reflected by the stonework. However, given the Iron Age associations for the structure, it is worth noting the relative absence of formally diagnostic tools. This may simply indicate a lack of activities resulting in the deposition of diagnostic material during either the Neolithic or the Bronze Age. Alternatively, it may be that this small assemblage actually reflects the continued use of stone into this later phase. This is by no means certain and little support is offered by the details of context or association. However, it remains a possibility.

Small Finds
by Martin J Dearne

All finds made in the turf level have been excluded from this report, though they are included in the archive. They were all of iron, and to judge from their condition, of relatively recent date. The catalogue is ordered according to material (copper alloy, iron, glass, wood, clay, stone, leather) and the catalogue number and type identification is followed by the context number in brackets. Dimensions are in centimetres, and given with the usual abbreviations (L. = length, W. = width, Di. = diameter, Th. = thickness, Ht. = height; Max. = maximum).

Copper alloy artefacts (Fig. 5.10)

1. ?Token (14). Almost round disc, Di. c. 2.6, Th. 0.2. Corroded, but possible traces of faint incised line across one face.

2. Button (14). Slightly oval button, Di. c. 1.7. Plain face; central cast loop on reverse.

3. ?Stud (3, wall fill). Flat disc, Di. 1.45. Stub of shank.

4. Ring (2). Ring, circular section, Di. 3.4.

5. Hinge plate (9). Rectangular sheet with three circular attachment holes, and two rectangular projections on one long edge, L. 4.4; Max. W. 4.3; Th. 0.06.

6. ?Mitre square (7). L. 3.4; W. 1.9; Th. 0.7. Incomplete wooden strip partly enclosed by copper alloy plates held by small iron rivets, with one concave corner. A third (broken) plate with hidden slanting leading edge is inserted into a slot cut into the thickness of the wood and would have run at right angles to it. There is no sign of any moving mechanism, and the rivets appear to pass

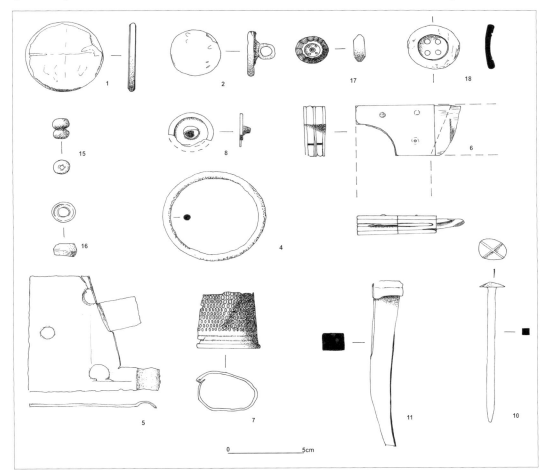

Figure 5.10 Small finds from house L8A

right through the object. It appears to be a fragment of a carpenter's mitre square.

7. Thimble (1). Sheet thimble with basal ridge, and 10 + rings of oval indentations above two bands of fine beading, Ht. 2.1; Di. c. 1.6. Crushed, split and lacking top.

8. Button (2). Button similar to No.2 above, but only stub of loop, Di. 2.1.

9. Sheet frag. (1). Roughly triangular with bottom edge slightly folded; ragged edges, L. 2.8; W. 2.3; Th.0.05.

10. Nail (1). Sub-circular head with ridges, square sectioned shank, L. 5.4.

11. Nail (14). Square head, square sectioned shank, L. 6.3.

Iron artefacts

12. Wedge/chisel (2). Large, circular-section bar, expanding to a broad wedge-shaped end, L. 15; W. 2.5–3.4.

13. Staple (12). Fragment of U-shaped staple with parallel circular- sectioned arms, L. 6.9; Max. W. 4.9.

14. Bar (6). Circular sectioned bar, curving at one end. L. 16.4; Di. 0.6.

Glass artefacts (Fig. 5.10)

15. Bead (4). Opaque pale blue, segmented, with central perforation, L. 0.77; Di. 0.51.

16. Bead (6). Decayed red frit or opaque glass, slightly biconical with large central perforation, L. 0.48; Di. 0.75.

17. Button (14). Translucent cobalt blue, cast button, with four circular holes centrally around ring and dot, Di. 1.04; Th. 0.34. Ridged edge flutes; plain back.

Wooden artefact (Fig.5. 10)

18. Button (8). Circular button with centre of upper face defined by incised ring; four hand-cut holes, Di. 1.67. Polished back.

Clay artefacts

Five fragments from bowls, and three from stems, of clay pipes were found, none with distinctive features or markings.

Stone artefacts

19. Hone (1). Elongated sub-triangular sectioned, tapering whetstone, L. 7.5; W. 2.06. Much abrasion from use; broken at both ends.

20. ? Pestle (2). Elongated oval rounded cobble, L. 9.9; Max. W. 5.4. Polished from use, and with abrasion marks on wider end consistent with use as a pestle or pounder.

21. Rubber (2). Elongated oval gneiss cobble, L. 13; W. 9; Th. 2.8. Rounded on one side, but worn slightly concave on the other with clear abrasion marks.

22. Rubber (2) Half of a circular gneiss cobble, Di. 11; Th. 5.6. Rounded on one side, and worn to concave on other.

23. Net float (9). Oval, rounded lump of pumice with off-centre perforation, and a narrow incised or abraded linear mark at edge, Di. 4.5 - 5.5; Th. 2.6.

Leather artefacts

24. Shoe frags (6). Three non-joining fragments of brittle leather ?sole, secured to a piece of partially overlapping leather by a series of small copper alloy ridge-shanked nails. Largest piece W. 1.4; Th. 0.4.

25. Shoe (16). see report below.

The Shoe
by June Swann
(For specialist terms used here, see Thornton and Swann 1986)

The fragments form part of a youth's shoe of quite thick cattlehide (three pieces form the toe and one side of the upper, the rest missing). The upper is made flesh side out, cut in one piece, seamed centre back with butted seam approximately 8cm high (the top is damaged), stitched at 10 stitches to the inch (shoemakers worked by the inch). The shoe fastened through (probably) 4 pairs of lace holes centre front, the holes distorted, suggesting a leather lace (not found in the excavation). The broken bottom hole may indicate that the lace was knotted at the bottom, and only the single end threaded through the other lace holes, as usual with this style. Toe to throat measures approximately 14cm. The lacing section is 6.5cm long, but one of the two fragments from the toe area appears to have been cut for 3cm, to extend the front opening, presumably for a growing foot. This was a quite common practice found on shoes of most periods, even on good quality work, though footwear, being generally expensive, was usually passed on to other wearers, often lower down the social scale.

Being made flesh out, there is no need for the upper to be lined, though sometimes the bottom edge is reinforced by a thinner, 2cm high side lining. While some fragments have the appearance of side linings, I found no evidence that one was attached. The lack of reinforcement may explain the breaks across the stitch holes in some places, or perhaps the lasting margin was cut too close, as well as long usage.

The throat of the shoe was cut square (the surviving side measures 21mm), as is the toe. The toe upper here measures about 38mm wide, with the sole under it approx. 4cm.

The bottom consisted of an insole (a piece close to the toe survives, together with the matching section of outsole). But this whole area has broken into many pieces, which cannot be reassembled. One piece has the impression of a rectangular oblong, probably the shank piece, which could have been of leather or wood, used to support the waist on a heeled shoe. Thinner fragments may be bottom-filling, inserted between insole and sole. On the sole there are impressions and remains of two rows of hobnails, with others, possibly in rows between, usually restricted to the forepart sole. An unidentified piece of leather with corroded iron in the shape of a small staple may be reinforcement for the waist. Sole length, estimated from the upper pieces: 21.5cm, with width at tread, similarly estimated, 9cm. Because of the fragmentary nature, it is not possible to state whether the shoe was made straight, or shaped left/right, but the latter should be expected.

The heel, 6.2cm from back-front x 7.2cm wide x 18mm high, is of stacked leather of about three lifts, including the top piece, originally with vertical heel breast (the front edge, now damaged with root growth etc, not wedged as drawn in 1996). Like the sole, it has hobnails round the edge, and probably also in the centre. The seat stitches attaching the heel are about $3\frac{1}{2}$ to one inch.

Construction is welted, that is the upper turned in at the sole seam and attached to a welt, with 2–3 pieces of the welt surviving. Stitch-holes indicate it was stitched at 8–10 stitches to the inch to the upper, 3–4 to the inch for the sole, an acceptable average piece of work.

Period and place of manufacture

The style of upper, front lace, with square toe and throat suggested a date of c.1830. The square throat occurs earlier, for instance on a very similar shoe shown on the portrait by Sir John Watson Gordon (in the Scottish National Portrait Gallery) of John Taylor, Captain of the Hon. Company of Edinburgh Golfers. Dated c.1825, it is 4–5 hole front lace, with the earlier blunt toe, but a very shiny black leather; though the Barra shoe would have been polished, a high gloss is unlikely on flesh-out leather. Also a quite wide toe is seen in Sir William Allen's oil, *The Ettrick Shepherd's House Heating*, c.1823/5 (SNPG). The square toe, seen occasionally in the 1820s, becomes general wear in 1830.

The 3-hole front lace shoe was very common through the 1820s–30s, with 4-holes not unusual. It was particularly popular for boys, and only slightly less so for men, competing in their case with the more expensive knee boots for general wear. One somewhat unusual feature is the one piece upper with no side seams. This was normal on children's shoes, but less common on adult men's, partly because it fits less accurately. Two similar boys' shoes can be seen in Baynes and Baynes (1979, 35). But this pattern is used for a 15" shoe for a 'giant' in Taunton Museum, worn c.1828 (died 1829), as well as for the sword dancers' shoes of the Perth Glovers Incorporation of c.1820. I would also not expect quite such heavy hobnailing on this style, though that could have been added after manufacture, during repair work, or even when new, as extra protection for demanding wear.

Although I have quoted some Scottish references as more appropriate, there is nothing regional about either the style or workmanship. The latter looks a reasonable average, if a little skimpy at the sole seam. But the general appearance is of smart but sturdy wear, with no elaboration to make it more expensive. I see no reason why it cannot have been made by a shoemaker on Barra, but it could equally well be from a thrifty shoemaker elsewhere in Britain.

The place of concealment

Concealment of shoes in walls is not uncommon. Research has shown (Swann 1996) showed that 'walls' are the third most common place of concealment, at 18.8%, the chimney being the most common at 26.2%, with between-floors at 22.86%,and the roof yielding one less example than walls. However, both between-floors and 'walls' are misleading : shoes may be concealed under a floor or above a ceiling, strictly two hiding places, though often difficult to specify when rubble falls. Similarly, wall find spots may be close to a chimney, door or window, all areas popularly chosen, though usually unknown to the individual finder.

Position within the wall could be determined by the history of alterations: an extension, rebuilding of damage, insertion of floor, door or window, and so on. For most concealments are made at the time of alterations, and it is rare that the date of the shoe relates to the date of the original building. It is likely that this shoe was concealed on Barra when the original outer wall became an internal partition when the house was extended sometime between 1820 and 1840. Most of the shoes found, like this one, are singles, and all but twenty of the 1,600 or so concealments recorded are of old, worn-out shoes, similar to this shoe from Balnabodach. Although the date of making is likely to be c.1830 or a year or two later, it is difficult to estimate how long it was worn, because of the fragmentary state of the sole and almost half the upper being missing. But even given the conditions on Barra, I think it unlikely to have been discarded until towards the end of the 1830s.

Very rarely I have been able to record that the occupier of the house was asked to supply an old shoe, but there is more evidence for concealments being made secretly without the knowledge of the occupier, and thus supplied by the workman or builder. Unless there is other evidence with the shoe it is impossible to decide. Nor are the reasons for concealment known with any certainty. Some appear to be merely an affirmation of the owner's existence; others are frequently said to be for good luck. But protection from evil is a much stronger motive, and disturbing the spirit of the house a good reason to make a token sacrifice.

Interpretation

The site occupied by blackhouse L8A appears to have been previously utilised in the Middle Iron Age. The quantity of sherds, and the stratified location of almost half the assemblage beneath the blackhouse floor in an undisturbed deposit, suggest some sort of occupation on this platform. The recovery of about 80 sherds from the wall fill and tumble suggests that deposits in the centre of the area occupied by the blackhouse were dug out to provide material for the core of the blackhouse wall. No structural remains associated with the Iron Age deposit survived however.

Other material found in the blackhouse excavation which might have originally been associated with this Iron Age occupation include the two gneiss rubbers (SFs 21–22) and the pestle (SF 20), which were all found in the wall fill. The pumice net float (SF 23) might also be suspected of prehistoric origin, as pumice was collected and used at Iron Age Dun Vulan and Sollas.

Much thought was given to the interpretation of the structural evidence for the blackhouse and the recognition of a three-phase history for the building as it survives seemed inescapable (Fig. 5.11). The narrow section of rear wall must be a complete rebuild, slotted between the existing partition wall and the east exterior wall, on new foundations. This was confirmed during excavation of the floor deposit, which continued under the front of the rear wall whilst butting against the bottom of the east and partition walls; a sherd was recovered from under the wall which joined others found in the floor deposit of the main room. Equally, the broad western section of the rear wall, and presumably the west wall of the building too therefore, must be an addition to an existing building, since it is butted to the south west corner of the partition wall. We suggest that the lines of its inner and outer face represent the lines of the original rear wall which the narrow foundation replaced.

This series of deductions leads to an architectural history for house L8A which begins with a small, rounded-end blackhouse about 9.5 x 6.6m. There is no trace of a blocked doorway for this house. The door could have been in the south wall – and consequently all trace of it obliterated in the total rebuild of that wall; this is possible but unlikely. The slope behind the house would have offered some protection from the elements, but where blackhouses are built on slopes, they almost always look seawards or across a valley rather than into the hill slope. The only alternative is that a door existed in the eastern section of the front wall but that no trace of it remains – presumably due to a rebuild of this wall too, possibly when the house was altered in

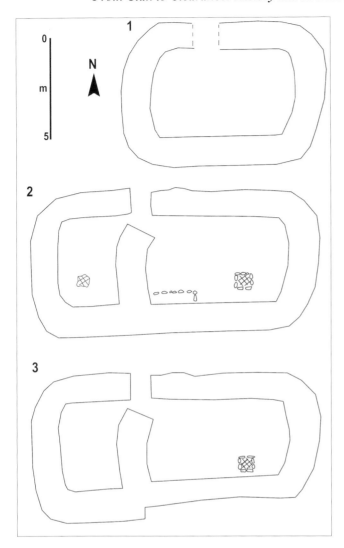

Figure 5.11 The constructional sequence of house L8A

phase 2. We know that blackhouse walls were frequently rebuilt, though it was usually the end wall that received this treatment.

The house was extended by building an extra room onto the west end of the existing house. The extended rear wall was butted on to the south west corner of the original blackhouse, but the building of the new front wall and the modification of the former west wall of the house to form an internal partition was more complex. As noted above, it seems likely that the old front wall of the house was rebuilt at this time, obliterating the original doorway. The door to the house was now situated at the point of the internal partition. The doorway into the additional room was exceptionally narrow, only a little over 20cm wide at the wall base, though it would have probably widened higher up. This very narrow doorway, the presence of a fire-stand in the middle of the new room, and the absence of a drain, all argue against interpreting the room as a byre. Furthermore there is both archaeological and documentary evidence (Branigan and Merrony 2000) that most Barra blackhouses housed only humans. We suggest the room was added for human use.

A final, major structural phase in the building's history was the rebuilding of the rear (south) wall. As rebuilt this was the narrowest wall in the entire structure, and it was butt-jointed to the original end walls of the building. There

is no indication what might have required this renovation work. The fact that the floor deposit in the main room was both overlain by the new wall and butted up against it clearly implies, however, that the rebuild was done whilst the building was in occupation rather than following a period of abandonment.

A final phase of use is represented by the line of stone blocks set up towards the east end of the main room, enclosing an area about 2.3 x 1.3m. The blocks are set on a thin soil overlying the occupation deposit and the hearth, but they could have been erected not long after the abandonment of the building. They are a feature found in many abandoned blackhouses and probably represent the use of the abandoned houses as lambing pens.

Putting a date to the main phases of use of the building is not easy, despite the presence of the remains of over 50 ceramic vessels. The continuous build-up of occupation deposit, the problem of estimating how long vessels were in use before they were broken, and the overall short period of occupation, all make the interpretation of the pottery evidence in terms of chronology very difficult. Only two sherds definitely pre-date 1800 in manufacture; another 34 *could* have been made before 1820, but only six of them need have been. On the other hand about 25% of the assemblage was manufactured before 1830 (and the 'floor sweepings' in trench 8Y included 28% pre-1830). If one takes the median dates of production and plots them on a histogram, then the first significant period represented is after 1815, with low quantities in the 1830s and then an increase in 1840 leading to a peak in 1845. Only one sherd later than 1850 has been identified, and that in the topsoil; significantly there is not a single sherd of ironstone ware from the house, supporting the abrupt story told by the histogram. We therefore argue with some confidence that the house was abandoned c.1850. Its foundation date is less certain but appears to be around 1820.

Dating the two phases within these brackets from the pottery evidence is even more difficult, but there are two possible pointers. The rebuild of the wall that became the partition between the main room and the extension incorporated a substantial part of a shoe which was probably made c.1830. The shoe was incomplete and presumably redundant when it was deposited, and the specialist report says it is 'unlikely to have been discarded until towards the end of the 1830s', so that phase 2 is unlikely to be earlier than c.1837–40. The rebuilt section of the rear (south) wall was constructed over the existing occupation material, and from this deposit *beneath* the rebuild was recovered a substantial sherd of the yellow ware bowl (YWE 1), other pieces of which were in the occupation deposit in the main room (context 9). This bowl is dateable only as 'mid-19th century' but is almost certainly post 1830, and probably 1840 or later. This is a likely *terminus post quem* for phase 3.

How does this tentative dating sequence compare with the documentary evidence for the settlement in the period from 1810 to 1851? If the first, simple house was built around 1815–20 it may have been abandoned c.1825/26 if, as we suggested above, the population was removed by Macneil at that time. Re-occupation in the later 1830s, as suggested by the ceramic material and shoe, would be in line with the growth of the settlement as indicated by the 1841 census. Abrupt abandonment in c.1850 is supported by the oral tradition and can be plausibly related to Gordon of Cluny's clearance of Balnabodach and other Barra townships in 1850/51. But there is the possibility that the building was re-occupied very soon after 1851 and the rebuilding of the entire south wall could be associated with such a re-occupation. The absence of any pottery clearly later than c.1850 however suggests that any re-occupation was short-lived.

We might offer one further speculative thought. House L8A is the largest of the blackhouses in the group at site L8, and has a room added, apparently for human occupation, sometime probably in the later 1830s. Of the eight households recorded at Balnabodach in the 1841 census, two might be considered as likely occupants of house 8A. Hector Macdugald, his wife, and three children also accommodated his older sister, Flory, for whom the additional room might have been provided. An alternative might be John Macmillan, who in addition to his wife and two children, housed a 90-year old 'pauper' Kirsty Shaw. If the shoe found in the wall build came from a youth living in the settlement in the later 1830s, the only candidates (from the 1841 census) would be either Angus Macmillan or Silas Macneil, both aged 20 in 1841.

Discussion of furnishings, diet, and standard of living as represented by artifact material, will be pursued after the description of the excavations of houses 8C, 8D, and 9F.

Excavation of Blackhouses L8C and L8D

by Keith Branigan and Colin Merrony

The excavation of these two houses is described in a single section of this report, because the houses were built back-to-back as a single unit, and in addition a pre-blackhouse occupation of the site extended beneath both buildings. These two houses were selected for excavation because they represented a different type of complexity to that of L8A. Whereas L8A appeared (and proved) to have a complex history in itself, L8C and L8D were physically related to one another and both the chronological and functional relationship between them might prove interesting. At the same time, in themselves they appeared to be simple one-phase structures that would provide a contrast to the complex sequence of L8A. House L8D was the first excavated, in 1999, and House L8C was excavated the following year. Both houses were excavated under the direction of Colin Merrony.

Architecture of House L8D (Fig. 5.12)

This house was set with its long axis more or less north south, with a door in its western wall facing onto the stream and mud-flat. Externally it was 10.5m long, and taking its rear, party-wall with House 8C, as a full wall it was 7.3m wide. The walls survived to a maximum height of 0.95m, and were of usual blackhouse construction, faced with unworked stones inside and out and with an earth core. Sections taken through the wall fill showed that the core was almost entirely of soil, with very few stones and no traces of turf. The walls were 1.4–1.5m wide, except for the rear, party-wall, which was 1.7m. A single door was placed towards the north end of the west wall, and was 0.8m wide at the point where the door was apparently set. This was marked by a slight offset on the north face of the entrance and two flat slabs on the floor against which the door had probably closed. North of the door, the west wall broadened as it approached the doorway, to provide a little extra protection from the wind.

The interior of the house was 8m x 4m. but an internal partition wall, visible before excavation, divided the interior into two rooms. This wall was 1.2m wide, of similar construction to the exterior walls, and apparently butt-jointed to the rear (east) wall. A metre wide doorway gave access to the inner, southern room, but there was nothing to demonstrate that a door had ever been mounted here. The southern room measured 4 x 2.8m, and the northern was almost 4m square. When turf was removed and the tumble cleaned, a second less substantial partition wall was found in the southern room, dividing it into two cells. The wall was only 0.5–0.6m wide and 1.7m long, butted against the main partition wall. A metre-wide gap gave access to the inner, east, cell which was just 1.5m wide, and 2.8m long. The outer, west, cell was 2.2m wide and 2.8m long.

Since one of the reasons for excavating houses 8C and 8D was to explore their relationship, the party wall between the two houses was explored at the time of the excavation of house L8D. Two 1m square soundings were taken into the fill of the wall (context 20), one at the southern junction of the two houses and the second just south of the main partition wall.

These revealed no earlier, buried, facing stones belonging to an original outer face of either house, and there was no obvious structural evidence from within the wall that one house preceded the other. However, the fill of the wall produced a large quantity of mid-19th century pottery (as well as some prehistoric material), and this, together with the different stratigraphy and quantities of material from the two houses, suggests that they were not both built and occupied at a single point in time. This is discussed further below.

Deposits and Stratigraphy in House L8D

The turf and underlying topsoil (contexts 003–008) was stripped off the interior of the house, revealing only a small quantity of tumbled stone, mostly in the southern room. Beneath 5cm of topsoil, a thin medium-brown soil with small stones (up to 3–4cm lth/diam.) was found across the interior of the building (contexts 041, 047, 052, 053 and 062). This in turn sat on similar material that was much more compacted and appeared to represent the original floor of the house. In the northern room there were odd patches of stones set in this surface, most notably just inside the door where they were presumably intended to prevent either wear or a muddy patch developing. Against the main partition wall there was a roughly circular pit, about 0.8m wide at the top and 18cm deep, filled with a clayey soil burnt to orange and brown. It appeared to be a hearth or fire-pit, which pre-dated the main partition wall, which ran over one end of the pit. It appeared to be contemporary with the original floor material, which did not cover it.

In the southern room, there were sufficient stones embedded in the floor of the eastern cell to suggest that this was a deliberate if partial surfacing of the floor. The western cell had only a few patches of stone, except alongside the small partition wall where four substantial slabs and a dozen smaller pieces of stone 'paved' a 0.5m wide strip across the room. When the surfacing (context 046) in the east cell was removed, a pale-brown slightly stony soil was found to overlie bedrock and infill some small hollows within it. In the fill of one of these hollows

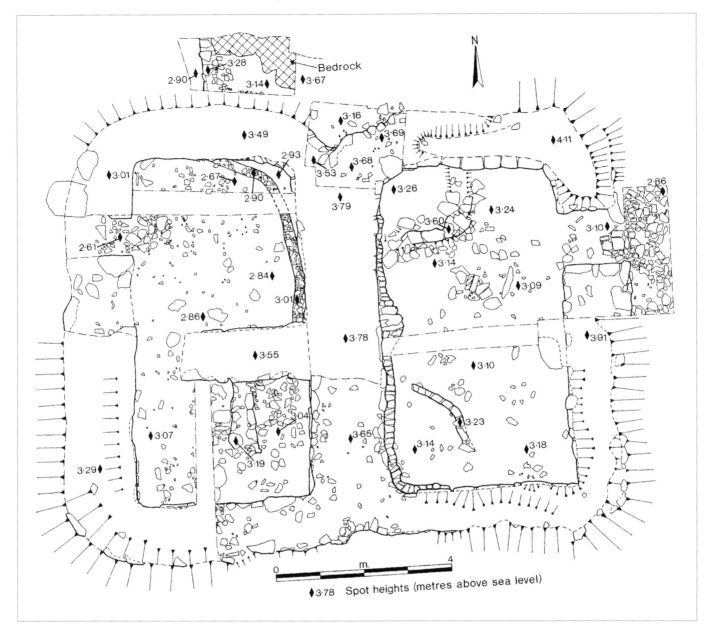

Figure 5.12 Plan of houses L8C (right) and L8D (left) as revealed by excavation

(context 066) a large sherd of a painted pearl-ware bowl was found (Fig. 5.15d). This soil appears to be the subsoil which was trampled into a floor surface elsewhere in the building, and the small partition wall was built over it.

When the floor material was removed from the rest of the building, it was found to lie on bedrock. Cut into the bedrock, and visible in the floor surface, was a linear feature. This was a narrow gully, from 15–25cm wide and 7–10cm deep, which ran in a curving line from the rear (east) wall until it disappeared under the north wall. It was filled with small rocks, amongst which were found two flint flakes, and a short piece of an iron nail was found embedded into the top of the gully. It ran up to, and appeared to run under, the main partition wall.

The interpretation of the structures and deposits will be discussed alongside that of house L8C, as will the pottery and lithics from this house.

Architecture of House L8C (Fig.5.12)

House L8C was built back-to-back with house L8D and obviously shared its north south axis. Its single doorway was near the north end of the east wall, and faced eastwards towards the entrance to Loch Obe. Overall it was 10m long and 7.4m wide, taking its rear party-wall as a full wall. The walls were generally well preserved on the inside faces, but less well on the outside. They stood to a maximum preserved height of 1.1m and were of the usual stone-face and earth-core (context 009) construction. The front (east) wall was notably wider at 1.2m than the end walls (north and south) which were 1m wide. The east wall broadened as it approached the doorway to reach a maximum width of 1.5m, creating the deep-set entrance noticed on many blackhouses. Outside the 1.2m wide doorway there was a rough paving or surfacing of stones (context 057), the most regular area of paving being immediately in front of the door. Part of an iron hinge apparently from the door was found in the paving stones by the foot of the wall. A single room 7.5 x 4.2m occupied the whole of the interior of the house with no trace of any partition of any kind, except for a boulder built structure in the north west corner which was obviously a late feature.

Deposits and Stratigraphy in House L8C

When the turf and top soil were stripped off, the structure in the north west corner could be seen to form a small 'pen' 2m x 1.6m, constructed by arranging large blocks of stone around the inside corner of the house. The bottom of these stone blocks was surrounded by the bottom of the top soil and the scatter of stone blocks and stone lumps from the house wall, and it appeared that this structure had been inserted into the house not long after it was abandoned.

Below top soil was a compacted dark-brown sandy-silt, averaging 5–6cm thick, and with a scatter of small- to medium-sized angular stone lumps. This ran across the entire interior and into the doorway (contexts 032, 033, 035 and 038). This contained a considerable quantity of pottery and appears to have been the uppermost deposit associated with the occupation of the house. As this level was removed it merged into a dark reddish-brown sandy-silt, with small angular lumps of stone, and patches of red and black charred areas (contexts 037, 039, 040 and 043). This lower occupation deposit produced considerably less pottery than the upper deposit.

Three clear features were associated with it. The most prominent was a shallow gully running alongside the foot of the west wall, covered with blocks and small slabs of stone, and clearly forming a drain. It ran the length of the house, following the wall around the south west corner and then turned and ran under the south wall itself, to give out into the deep gully between House L8C and House L8B. The second feature was a curving arc of small stone blocks set into context 039 'enclosing' an area in the south west corner of the house. This was a single line of small blocks, which could never have been built up into a significant structure, and yet there can be no doubt that they were a deliberate arrangement. They presumably represent some notional partitioning of space in this corner - perhaps as sleeping area ? - but there was nothing in the nature or wear of the deposit here to suggest that anything substantial had stood on the 'enclosed' area.

The third feature set in 039 was an oblong area 66 x 44cm, in the south east corner of the house, which was burnt dark red, quite hard, with many small pieces of charcoal embedded in it (context 41). On excavation it proved to be only 4cm deep. There were no deposits of ash around it, and it seems most likely to have been an area where a fire-basket or brazier had been stood.

In the northern half of the house, this occupation deposit (context 037) was mostly thin, sitting immediately on bedrock, whereas as in the southern half it was deeper, up to 10cm. Here it merged into a further deposit of occupation material, dark-brown rather sticky, flecked with red and black (context 48). In the surface of context 048 were six very clear areas of burning (contexts 050–054, and 056). Each of these was sectioned and excavated. Contexts 050 and 051 were very shallow, really little more than irregular burn marks on the deposit beneath. The other four areas were larger and deeper:

052   50 x 40cm, 25cm deep; set against a block of stone, and with two burnt stones collapsed into its lower levels.

053   37 x 34cm, 6.5cm deep; small pieces of burnt stone and three bright red lenses in the fill.

054   90cm long, 40–21cm wide; 8.5cm deep; yellowy clayey material.

056   39cm diam.; 5cm deep; yellowy clayey material.

All these features appeared to be truncated. Context 048 produced further sherds of 19th-century pottery, but also sherds of handmade prehistoric pottery, and two handmade sherds were found in the fill of context 054. Context 048 sat on a thin undisturbed natural soil and bedrock.

Outside the house, on the east, we excavated a 2m square to see if the pre-house deposits continued eastwards, but although handmade sherds were found there, there was no significant deposit below top soil before bedrock was reached.

The Finds

Apart from pottery and lithics, only two small finds were made in House 8D and none in 8C. From 8D were recovered a short length of clay pipe stem, and a small spherical blue glass bead 6mm in diameter.

Handmade pottery
by Keith Branigan

Excavations in houses L8C and L8D yielded 93 handmade sherds of pottery, of which 90 are identified as Neolithic and three as medieval/early modern. Nine fabrics are represented in this sample, of which Fabrics 1–7 are Neolithic and 8–9 are medieval/early modern.

Fabric 1:   dark buff-brown sandy fabric, with small white and buff rounded inclusions, surface smoothed. Fired hard-medium. Mostly 10–15mm thick, no decorated sherds. Simple, upright or slightly flaring rims from bowls.

Fabric 2:   similar to 1, but more small inclusions and some larger, angular white inclusions. No surface treatment, fired medium-soft. Mostly 10–15mm thick. No decorated or rim sherds. Large vessels.

Fabric 3:   grey-brown fabric with large white angular inclusions, no surface treatment. Fired medium-hard to pale brown. Mostly 10mm+ thick. No decorated or rim sherds. Large vessels.

Fabric 4:   grey-black fabric with many small white, pinkish-brown inclusions and a few larger angular white or buff. Smoothed micaceous surface, fired medium-hard to a grey surface. 5–10mm thick. Occasional incised lines, no rims. Bowls ?

Fabric 5:   black to brown fabric with small rounded white inclusions. Surface self-slipped and low burnish, fired medium-hard. Mostly 3–7mm thick. Incised linear decoration. Carinated bowls.

Fabric 6:   buff-brown fabric with a few rounded pink-brown inclusions. Smoothed surface, fired medium. 8mm thick, incised linear decoration. Open bowl?

Fabric 7:   dark brown very sandy fabric with many small rounded white and grey inclusions, and larger angular white ones. Slipped and burnished dark brown/black surface, fired soft-medium. 10–22mm thick. No decorated sherds, horizontal lug. Thick storage bowls or jars?

Fabric 8:   dark grey fabric with many small white and grey inclusions. No surface treatment, fired hard. 4–5mm thick. No decoration; everted sharp-edged rim.

Fabric 9:   dark grey sandy fabric with a few large angular white/grey inclusions. Smoothed surface, fired to hard brick-red. 8–10mm thick. No decoration or rims.

Of the Neolithic sherds, 16 (wt 251gms) were recovered in house L8D and 74 (wt 850gms) from L8C. Only three prehistoric sherds came from the earth fill of the walls; 35 came from the pre-blackhouse levels (066 in 8D and 048 in 8C) and 2 from the fill of the fire-pit 054. The rest came from the blackhouse occupation deposits, presumably resulting from the disturbance and churning of the original prehistoric deposits when they were levelled for the blackhouse floor.

It is estimated that the sherds represent a minimum of 23 vessels, broken down by fabric as follows

Fabric 1:   5 vessels (bowl?)
Fabric 2:   2 vessels (large jars?)
Fabric 3:   1 vessel (large jar?)
Fabric 4:   4 vessels (bowls ?)
Fabric 5:   7 vessels (bowls)
Fabric 6:   3 vessels (bowls)
Fabric 7:   1 vessel (large jar?)

The fabrics are very similar to those found, in much larger quantities, at Alt Chrisal (Gibson, in Branigan and Foster 1995, 100–115), and the few decorated sherds and rims can be paralleled in the Alt Chrisal assemblage, as indicated in the following list of illustrated sherds (Fig. 5.13). All sherds except H come from house 8C.

A	Fabric 1	open bowl	Gibson 6, 33, 109, etc	context 037
B	Fabric 1	open bowl	Gibson 37, 62	context 032
C	Fabric 1	deep bowl?	Gibson 1, 21, 29, etc	context 037
D	Fabric 6	open bowl	Gibson 110, 111, 117 etc	context 037
E	Fabric 4	open bowl?	Gibson 88 - 92, etc	context 048
F	Fabric 4	open bowl	Gibson 71, 116	context 009
G	Fabric 5	carinated bowl	Gibson 70, 77, 89 etc	context 048
H	Fabric 5	open bowl with lug	Gibson 90	context 8D, 064

These fabrics and forms were dated at Alt Chrisal by C14 to c.5,200 BP, and Gibson quotes other comparable Hebridean assemblages with broadly similar dates. Unlike Alt Chrisal, however, the Balnabodach site has no Beaker material and to judge from the limited quantity of pottery and lithics, and small area of occupation, was a relatively short-lived settlement.

The three sherds ascribed to the medieval/early modern era are in very different fabrics, and the everted jar rim is similar though not identical to sherds from the medieval shieling site of B58.

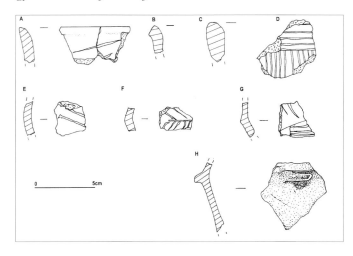

Figure 5.13 Neolithic pottery from beneath houses L8C and L8D

Modern Pottery from House L8C
by David Barker

With 520 sherds and 129 vessels, this is the largest of the Balnabodach groups, but coming from the smallest, and structurally least complicated of the houses. House L8C is unusual, however, for being part of a semi-detached pair with the slightly larger House L8D. The relationship of the two is clearly of interest. Unlike its neighbour, the wall fills of House L8C produced few ceramic sherds, which amounted to just three sherds of a single redware dish (RWE 2), sherds of which are almost certainly present in a range of occupation and other contexts. Like its neighbour, however, the ceramics are fairly consistent across the areas of the site and across the contexts. The lower (037 and 039) occupation deposits, contain exactly the same range of pearlwares, whitewares, Rockingham wares, coarse earthenwares and redwares as those contexts above and below. The ceramics from the lowest of the occupation contexts (043 and 048), sitting directly upon Neolithic contexts, have little to distinguish them from the remainder of the site assemblage. A small number of sherds (32 or 6%) of the assemblage are from outside the house. These represent nine vessels, seven of whiteware, and one each of pearlware and Rockingham ware. A relationship to the house is indicated by a cross-join of one whiteware sherd with another from one of the occupation deposits (038).

Wares

There are just two creamware vessels in this group (1.6% of the assemblage). The majority of the ceramics are of pearlware (22 vessels or 17%) and whiteware (62 vessels or 48%). There are very few vessels in Rockingham ware (three or 2.3%), bone china (two), blackware and drab coloured earthenware (one each).

Brown salt-glazed stonewares are represented by seven vessels (5.4%) and there are three vessels (2.3%) of grey 'Bristol' glazed stoneware. Nine coarse earthenware vessels constitute 7% of the assemblage, the highest proportion in any of the house assemblages, but not significantly so, while six redwares constitute 4.7% of the vessels.

Vessels

There are two teapots – one in Rockingham ware (RCK 1), and one in a refined blackware (BWE 1). A pearlware base sherd from an oval or round vessel (PLW 21) may possibly be from another teapot. It has vertical cable moulding to the exterior, and the body is slightly flaring. Three body sherds of this type are present in the L8A group (PLW 12); they may belong to the same vessel as the L8C sherd.

Other tewares include two teabowls and three saucers in pearlware, and five cups and ten saucers in whiteware; there is a further cup in drab ware and one teabowl and one saucer in bone china. All the teaware forms together make up 21% of the assemblage.

Twenty-eight bowls constitute 22% of the vessels of the assemblage. The majority (sixteen) are in whiteware, eight are in pearlware, and there is a probable Rockingham example. Three redware bowls, of uncertain function, are also present.

More numerous than the bowls in this group are plates (Fig. 5.14a), which number 33 (26%). Six of these are of printed, over-glaze painted and shell edged pearlware; one of the latter is a smaller side plate or 'twiffler'. The remainder are in whiteware with a mixture of printed (including 'Willow' pattern), sponged, shell edge and undecorated vessels. Two of the whiteware plates have moulded edges; one has a small floral pattern with a beaded edge (WWE 33); the other has an overall flower-head pattern typically found on moulded so-called 'children's' plates with printed and painted decoration (WWE 32).

Mugs are not common finds at Balnabodach, but three – all in whiteware – are present here. They are decorated with under-glaze painting, sponging and slip banding. There are two basins in whiteware, one with printed decoration. Another small basin or, more probably, a dish (WWE 43) has a light moulded shell-type rim pattern identical in form to one found in the L8D group (WWE 17). A further probable dish has blue printed decoration.

Three of the group's four jugs are in pearlware. One has under-glaze painted decoration, a second has slip decoration, and the third is decorated with turned bands to its body. The whiteware jug (WWE 49) has a moulded body and printed floral decoration in purple.

Bottles are all in stoneware, seven in brown salt-glazed stoneware and one in a grey 'Bristol'-glazed stoneware. Two grey stoneware jars may be preserve jars. Coarse earthenware forms also include jars, probably storage jars (seven in number), and two dishes. There are also two dishes in redware as well as three bowls, a jar and two unidentified forms.

Decoration
Eighty-three per cent of the refined wares are decorated. Printed decoration occurs on 30 vessels (29% of the refined wares), with blue being the most common colour (Fig. 5.14b). Printed patterns are also found in purple, lilac, mulberry, and grey. Eight whiteware plates are decorated with 'Willow' pattern in blue; there are also two possible examples of 'Two Temples' or 'Broseley' (in light blue), and two of 'sea leaf' (in grey on a bowl and a saucer). Other patterns are predominantly floral designs (PLW 1, WWE 16, WWE 49), but there is at least one European-type landscape (WWE 2) and a bowl with the pattern 'Exhibition' (WWE 71).

Under-glaze painted decoration is present on 17% of the refined wares in both blue (PLW 11, PLW 12) and polychrome (Fig. 5.14c). One pearlware bowl is decorated with the earlier muted earth colours (PLW 9), but there are several vessels with painted decoration in the bright chrome

colours of the late-1820s onwards in both pearlware (PLW 10, PLW 13) and whiteware (WWE 36, WWE 37).

There are just two slip-decorated vessels (2% of the refined wares) – a pearlware jug with light blue and fawn-coloured wormed or cable decoration, on a pea green ground (Fig. 5.14d), with additional olive green banding (PLW 3), and a mug or bowl with blue banded decoration or a blue slip coat (WWE 25).

Sponged decoration is present on 22% of the refined wares of both pearlware and whiteware (Figs 5.14e and 5.14f). Simple cut sponge designs of diamonds, stars, leaves, overlapping circles or ovals, and scroll motifs are well-represented in blue, red and purple (e.g. PLW 2, WWE 8); on several vessels the use of blue cut sponge designs is combined with blue painted bands (e.g. WWE 17 – 20), or with thin light blue washes which form a ground for the sponged pattern (e.g. WWE 6, WWE 22). All-over amorphous sponged grounds are also used (WWE 1). Eight of the 22 sponge-decorated vessels are bowls.

The diagnostic olive green, red and grey over-glaze painted decoration noted above in the House L8A group, and also present in that from House L8D, occurs on a pearlware bowl (PLW 6) which, on the evidence of bowl PLW 2 from L8D, is likely to be of London shape (Fig. 5.14g); the same decoration occurs on a smaller pearlware bowl or cup (PLW 7), and a pearlware dinner plate (PLW 5). Other over-glaze decorated vessels are a pearlware teabowl, painted in pink (PLW 20), and a whiteware saucer, painted in green and pink / red, possibly lustre (WWE 51).

Dating
The only 18th century sherd in the group is an over-glaze painted creamware (CWE 1); this dates to c. 1765–75, and is considerably earlier than the majority of the material. The other creamware vessel is probably of 19th century date. The pearlwares date to the period c. 1810 to 1830, with the likelihood of the majority of the vessels belonging to the decade 1820 to 1830. The presence of a London shape bowl (PLW 6) supports this and the mixture of shell edge plate types includes regularly scalloped edges and plates with little or no scalloping; the move away from scalloped edges was under way by 1840. Some of the moulded edges are reminiscent of the new moulded varieties (with embossed grass, leaf fronds, etc.) introduced in the 1820s, which aimed to revive interest in a type whose popularity was waning; this variant type was produced into the early 1840s (Miller and Hunter 1990, 116).

Nineteen per cent of the ceramics are likely to pre-date 1830, but the predominance of whitewares (47%) suggests significant activity at House L8C after 1830. Many of these are difficult to date precisely, but the large number of sponge-decorated wares suggests a date of manufacture closer to, or in the 1840s. It has been suggested that the technique of decoration using cut sponges was invented in Scotland around 1835 (Kelly et al 2001, 8), while its introduction into the Staffordshire potteries has been suggested in the late 1840s (Miller 1991, 6). It is clear, however, that sponged decoration was in use before this date in Staffordshire, albeit less commonly and with a more restricted range of decorative motifs. It is probably safe to suggest that sponge decoration using cut sponges became widespread during the 1840s.

The whitewares with under-glaze painted decoration are also consistent with a post 1830 date. These use the brighter, chrome colours which first appear during the late1820s and thereafter become the norm into the 20th century.

Figure 5.14 Modern ceramics from house L8C

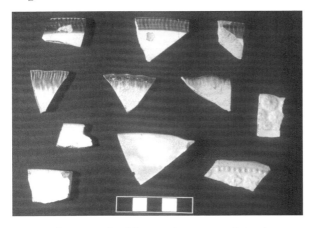

a) pearlware and white earthenware plate rims

b) printed white earthenwares, with 'Exhibition' pattern top right

c) under-glaze painted wares

d) pearlware jug sherd with banded slip decoration in green and brown and worming in blue and cream

e) above, white earthenware bowl sherds with under-glaze painted and sponged decoration in blue

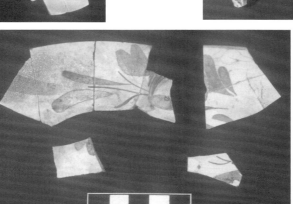

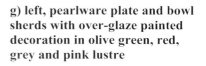

f) above, sponge-decorated white earthenware plate sherds in blue

g) left, pearlware plate and bowl sherds with over-glaze painted decoration in olive green, red, grey and pink lustre

Table 5.2 House L8C: ceramics by context

Turf and Topsoil	No. of sherds
001	107
002	24
003	1
004	44
Occupation	**No. of sherds**
032	67
033	6
035	22
038	55
040	1
057	15
Lower Occupation	**No. of sherds**
037	1
039	49
Top of Neolithic Occupation	No. of sherds
043	1
048	7
Wall Fill	**No. of sherds**
007	3
008	3
Outside House	**No. of sherds**
058	32
Other	**No. of sherds**
025	7
026	29
028	3
030	36
031	2
060	1
Unstrat	4
Total	520

Amongst the printed wares are prints in colours other than blue, including lilac, mulberry and grey. These coloured prints were introduced in the late 1820s (Shaw 1829, 234). The House L8C printed sherds are not diagnostic but are likely to date to the 1840s. It is a blue-printed sherd, however, which provides the one definite date. This is a bowl rim with part of a pattern referred to as 'Exhibition' (WWE 71) (I am grateful to Henry Kelly for this identification) which was made by Robert Cochran & Co. of the Verreville Pottery, Glasgow, as well as by J. & M P Bell of the Glasgow Pottery and other Staffordshire potteries, such as that of Thomas Godwin (Coysh and Henrywood 1982, 132). Depicting the Great Exhibition Pavilion, it would seem that this piece must date to 1851 or later. However, at least one exterior view of the Crystal Palace was registered for use as a printed pattern on pottery – by Crosse and Blackwell – in October 1850 after Paxton's

design for the Pavilion had been accepted (Mortimer 2003, 83). It is just possible, therefore, that this bowl was acquired and discarded by the occupants of House L8C prior to Cluny's clearance of 1851, but a date for its discard shortly after this event seems more likely. The sherd was found in (057) on the cobbles immediately outside the blackhouse door.

As mentioned above, Rockingham wares, yellow wares and brown salt-glaze stonewares are difficult to date precisely, but the three 'Bristol-glazed' grey stoneware vessels must post-date 1831, when this felspathic glaze type was first introduced (Green 1999, 159). It is more likely that they post-date 1835 when the Bristol glaze became more widely used (*ibid.*). The blackware vessel (BWE 2) is possibly of the second half of the 19th century, but it is difficult to be certain.

The coarse earthenwares and redwares are difficult to date precisely; the former changed little stylistically over time, and the vessels here could belong to the earlier-19th century or later. Certainly similar wares have been found in small quantities in pre-Clearance contexts (i.e. pre-1827) at Airigh Mhuillin in South Uist, and similarities in the fabrics of some of the South Uist vessels and some of those from Balnabodach (especially L8A CEW 1, L8C CEW 5, and others from L8D) suggest that they might be from the same manufacturing source. The diagnostic features of these are pronounced throwing rings to the exteriors of large jars, with fabrics which are of red-purple and cream-coloured clays laminated together.

In view of the homogeneity of the ceramics across the site and its identifiable phases of occupation, it is reasonable to suggest a comparatively late construction date, possibly in the mid-to late-1830s. The ceramics seem not to indicate a long period of occupation, and there is little to suggest significant activity here beyond the early 1830s.

House L8D

At 8.2 x 4m. internally, L8D is only slightly larger than its semi-detached neighbour House L8C, but secondary internal dividing walls make it a more complex structure with internal spaces being clearly defined and separated from each other. The excavation of the house produced 230 sherds or 74 vessels, making this the second largest of the pre-1850 excavated groups. However, 49 of the sherds came from the wall fill of the house, with 32 being from the party wall with L8C (contexts 020A and 020B) and the remainder being from the other fill contexts 020 (15 sherds) and 021 (two sherds). These represent twenty vessels, which would therefore make the number of vessels recovered from the occupation contexts of the house smaller even than that from L8A, where none of the vessels were from the wall fills.

Wares

Three creamware vessels account for just 4% of the group; seventeen pearlwares constitute 23%; while the dominant type is whiteware, with 33 vessels or 45% of the group. Other refined wares include two blackware vessels (3%), two of Rockingham ware (3%), one of yellow ware, one of bone china and a single oriental porcelain vessel.

There are also six brown salt-glazed stoneware vessels (8%) and one of grey stoneware. The coarsewares include two (3%) of redware and four (5%) of coarse earthenware.

Vessels

There are three teapots, one in blackware and two in Rockingham ware. There appear to be no cups in the group, but there are three pearlware teabowls, as well as two saucers in pearlware, five in whiteware and another in bone china.

Bowls are the dominant form, with eighteen examples accounting for 24% of the vessels; these are all decorated. The eleven whiteware bowls are of hemispherical form, but a large over-glaze painted pearlware bowl (PLW 2), and a smaller pearlware bowl with slip decoration (PLW 4) are of London shape. The slip-decorated yellow ware bowl is very similar to the bowl YWE 1 from the L8A group, and may even be from the same vessel.

Next in proportion are plates, with ten dinner plates and one side plate, together forming 15% of the vessels. There is also a single platter in whiteware. One whiteware plate sherd has an impressed maker's mark 'SCOTT', beneath an asterisk, on its underside.

Jugs are better represented than in the other pre-1850 groups from Balnabodach. There is one in whiteware, one in blackware, two in brown salt-glazed stoneware and a single coarse earthenware example. There is one basin in whiteware (WWE 5) which has pronounced bead moulding of the same type as WWE 20 in the L8A group. There is a single whiteware mug and what appears to be a porringer, with a rounded body, narrower neck and flaring rim, an unusual form in whiteware. The moulded form of the porcelain vessel is uncertain, but may be a plant pot or similar.

Repairs are evident to two vessels – a pearlware saucer with over-glaze painted pink lustre-decoration (PLW 8) and a whiteware bowl with sponged and painted decoration (WWE 2).

Decoration

Fourteen vessels (23% of the refined wares) have printed decoration, blue being the most common colour. Printed patterns are also found in brown and purple. 'Willow' pattern is not obviously present, but two saucers are decorated with 'Two Temples' or 'Broseley' in light blue, and there are two examples of 'sea leaf' in blue. Other patterns include floral designs (PLW 9) and an oriental-type landscape (PLW 16). A single jug in refined blackware has over-glaze printed decoration in ochre, with additional painted decoration (BWE 1).

Sponged decoration occurs on eleven vessels (18% of the refined wares), all whiteware, in a wide range of types in blue, brown, lilac and red. There are perhaps three examples of neat, cut sponge designs, but the majority are cruder. Overlapping ovals or rough concentric circles, amongst others, are combined with under-glaze blue painted bands (Fig. 5. 15a). A saucer has brown sponged inverted 'V' pattern to its rim and a simple floral motif to its interior centre. One sherd has an amorphous yellow all-over sponged ground. Six of the sponge-decorated vessels are bowls.

Slip decoration is present on six bowls (10%), three of pearlware, two of whiteware and one of yellow ware. The most diagnostic of these is a London shape bowl which is decorated with two wavy bands of trailed slips in four colours (brown, light brown, dark brown and blue), separated by a single band of trailed blue slip (PLW 4); the slips have been applied from a four-chambered slip bottle (Fig. 5.15b).

Under-glaze painted decoration is present in a range of colours. A pearlware teabowl is decorated with a floral pattern in earth colours (PLW 10), and a pearlware handle

Table 5.3 House L8D: ceramics by context

Turf and Topsoil	No. of sherds
003	13
004	7
006	25
007	1
008	18
Occupation	**No. of sherds**
046	18
047	3
050	2
053	24
062	48
Pre-building	No. of sherds
066	21
Wall Fill	**No. of sherds**
20	15
20A	24
20B	8
21	2
Other	**No. of sherds**
52	1
Total	230

sherd has a brown design running down its length; a pearlware bowl has a blue-painted landscape pattern, probably in oriental-style (PLW 16). The later chrome colours (Fig. 5.15c) are present on at least three whiteware bowls (WWE 4, WWE 15, WWE 19). A single shell edge pearlware plate rim has under-glaze blue painted decoration.

One London shape pearlware bowl (PLW 2) has the distinctive over-glaze painted decoration in olive green, red and grey, noted above in Houses L8A and L8C (Fig. 5.15d). A pearlware saucer also has over-glaze decoration which may be of a different type (PLW 12).

One bone china saucer (BCH 1) has over-glaze painted decoration in red and green, comprising floral sprigs.

Dating

There are no vessels of 18th century date in this group, although 27% of the ceramics are likely to pre-date 1830. These are three creamware vessels and the pearlwares, the majority of which probably date to the 1810–1830 period. A single shell edge plate in pearlware has the scalloped edge which can be dated to c. 1810–1840 (Miller and Hunter 1990, 116). As noted above, the London shape does not appear in earthenware until the later 1810s, and is more likely to suggest a date in the 1820s or later. In this group there are at least two London shape bowls in pearlware (PLW 2 and PLW 4) which are broadly contemporary, as well as other later examples in whiteware. PLW 4 has slip-trailed decoration applied using a four-chambered slip bottle, the patent for which was taken out in 1811 (Carpentier and Rickard 2001, 126). The over-glaze painted pearlware bowl (PLW 2) is particularly important;

Figure 5.15 Modern ceramics from house L8D

a) white earthenwares with under-glaze painted and sponged decoration in blue

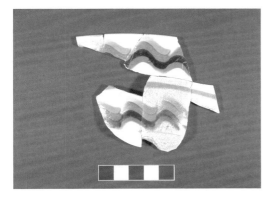

b) pearlware bowl with trailed slip decoration in three shades of brown and blue

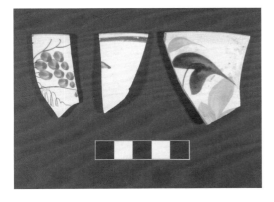

c) white earthenwares with under-glaze pointed decoration in olive, green, red and grey

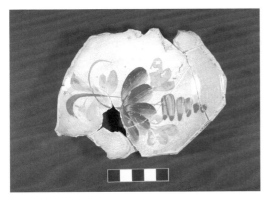

d) pearlware bowl base with over-glaze painted decoration

however, as its stratigraphic position beneath the blackhouse floor suggests strongly that it was deposited prior to the floor's construction and, consequently, before the construction of the house. If this was the case, then a construction date of c. 1830 would be possible for House L8D.

The predominance of whitewares suggests that the main period of activity at House L8D was after c. 1830. The decoration of the whitewares is entirely consistent with a date in the 1830s and 1840s. This includes under-glaze painted decoration using the bright chrome colours which were being used from the late 1820s, and printed decoration in colours other than blue, such as brown and purple, which, again, were much used after the late 1820s. At least one vessel (from 062) having the more simple, cruder, printed decoration – in brown – which was a feature of lower quality printed wares from the 1840s onwards. The most common type of decoration on the whitewares is sponged in a style which is still fairly simple, even when used in conjunction with under-glaze blue painted decoration. Although difficult to date precisely, these are consistent with a date in the later 1830s or 1840s. This dating of the whitewares is supported by the find of a whiteware plate base with an impressed maker's mark, 'SCOTT'. Godden (1991, 587) dates the use of this at the Southwick Pottery, Sunderland, to 1838–1854.

Rockingham and yellow wares are not easy to date precisely, but again are typically becoming more common finds on domestic sites throughout mainland Britain from the 1830s. There are several sherds of at least one vessel – a large storage jar – of black glazed coarse earthenware of the type discussed above; these have pronounced external throwing rings and the laminated red-purple and cream fabric. This, and at least three other coarse earthenwares, as well as the redware vessels, could date to the early- or mid-19th century.

At least one of the two vessels of blackware, or jet ware to use the contemporary term, is later in date. Black glazed wares are difficult to date precisely and teapots and jugs were important products at many of the smaller factories during the second half of the 19th century, if not earlier. The term jet ware, however, seems to be first used during the late 1870s when the wares described form a distinctive group of good quality wares, frequently with over-glaze printed or over-glaze painted decoration, or a combination of the two. They are rarely marked with a maker's mark, but the occasional use of design registration numbers or the 'ENGLAND' mark (post-1881) puts them firmly in the period 1880 or slightly earlier to 1900 or later. The single printed jug sherd (BWE 1) here is certainly of this period. A grey stoneware cylindrical jar with a Bristol glaze may possibly be a preserve jar, in which case it is likely to date to the later-19th century.

Houses L8C and L8D: Discussion
These two assemblages have a similarly varied range of wares to that from House L8A, but their relationship to each other is evident. Despite some differences in the size of the two groups, their composition is broadly comparable with most of the ware types represented in similar proportions. This is not entirely true for the printed whitewares of the 1830–1850 period, however, of which there are 26 vessels (20%) in House L8C, in contrast to just nine vessels (12%) in the House L8D group. Further difference can be seen in the presence amongst the House

Table 5.4 House L8C ceramics (minimum number of vessels)

	teabowl	cup	saucer	tea-pot	bowl	jug	mug	dish	basin	plate (dinner)	plate (side)	jar	bottle	unid.	TOTALS
Creamware															
o-gl. painted														1	1
undecd.														1	1
Pearlware															
u-gl. printed			1		1					2					4
u-gl. painted	1		1		4	1								1	8
o-gl. painted	1				2					1					3
sponged			1		1										2
ind. slip						1									1
shell edge										2	1				3
turned						1									1
Whiteware															
u-gl. printed		1	6		3	1		1		4			2		18
u-gl. printed - willow										7	1				8
u-gl. painted		2			5		1		1						9
o-gl. painted		1													1
sponged		4	3		7		1			5					20
ind. slip							1								1
shell edge										4					4
moulded decn.								1		2					3
undecd.			1						1	4					6
Drab ware		1													1
Blackware															
undecd.			1												1
Rockingham			1		1							1			3
Bone china															
undecd.	1		1												2
Brown SGSW													7		7
Grey St' ware												2	1		3
Coarse redware					1								1		2
slip-trailed					1			2							3
slip-coated					1							1		1	3
Coarse e' ware								2				7			9
TOTALS	3	6	16	2	28	4	3	6	2	31	2	11	8	7	129

L8C printed wares of plates with the 'Willow' pattern, a design which is not present in either the L8D or the L8A groups. Unfortunately the significance of this is not clear and may simply relate to the much higher proportion of plates in the L8C group, which is 26% in contrast to 10% in House L8D. Overall, though, the similarities between the two groups and the dates assigned to the ceramics suggest that the two houses were occupied at the same time, and probably abandoned together. A single sherd of a later 19th century date from House L8D need not contradict this suggestion.

The precise date of their construction, however, must remain a matter of conjecture as the ceramic evidence does not significantly add to the available historical evidence. Wall fill, occupation and pre-occupation contexts all contain a similar broad range of ceramics with no clear compositional or chronological difference between them; creamwares, pearlwares and other pre-1830 ceramics are present in similar proportions across the site; this is also true of the whitewares and other post-1830 wares which are found in the same contexts as earlier material.

Twenty one sherds were found in a context (066) which is thought to pre-date the construction of House L8D, as this is sealed beneath what was the blackhouse floor. Amongst these is the large painted bowl base PLW 2 which dates to the 1820s, probable further sherds of which were also found in the occupation deposit context (062) and in the fill of the wall between the two houses (020A). On the strength of this one piece and other undiagnostic pearlwares from (066) a possible construction date of c. 1830 or later is suggested for House L8D, but the picture is complicated by the presence in the same context of whiteware sherds which include one of a hollow ware of indeterminate form which is decorated with the printed 'sea leaf' pattern in blue, which is generally thought to date to the late 1840s and later.

On the evidence of the ceramics, it seems likely that the two adjoining blackhouses were probably not built until some time in the 1830s, and that they were occupied until no later than the early 1850s.

Lithics

by Mark Edmonds

As with L8A, the lithics associated with structures L8C and L8D were for the most part recovered as residual material. Given that these two structures were so closely related, it is reasonable to combine the description and discussion of the worked stone in one section.

Table 5.5 House L8D ceramics (minimum number of vessels)

	teabowl	saucer	tea-pot	bowl	porrin-ger	mug	jug	dish	basin	plate (dinner)	plate (side)	platter	pre-serve jar	jar	bottle	unid.	TOTALS
Creamware																	
ind. slip				1													1
undecd.										1	1						2
Pearlware																	
u-gl. printed	2	1														1	4
u-gl. painted	1			1												2	4
o-gl. painted		1		1			1		1								4
ind. slip				3													3
shell edge										1							1
undecd.													1				1
Whiteware																	
u-gl. printed		4								4						1	9
u-gl. painted		1		3												1	6
sponged		1		6	1	1				2							11
ind. slip				2													2
moulded decn.								1	1								2
undecd.										1		1	1				3
Blackware																	
o-gl. printed							1										1
undecd.		1														1	2
Rockingham		2															2
Porcelain																	
u-gl. painted																1	1
Bone china																	
o-gl. painted		1															1
Yellow ware																	
ind. slip				1													1
Brown SGSW							2								4		6
Grey St' ware													1				1
Coarse red-ware																	
slip-decorated								1									1
slip-coated								1									1
Coarse e' ware							1							3			4
TOTALS	3	9	3	18	1	1	5	4	2	9	1	1	3	3	4	7	74

Once again, the assemblage is dominated by flakes, which account for 98 out of a total of 162 pieces. The remainder includes three blades, 22 cores/core fragments and some 15 retouched pieces. Here too there is consistent evidence for the working of beach pebbles, resulting in the creation of both regular flakes and more irregular chips, chunks and spalls. All stages in a generalised reduction sequence are represented, and many flakes bear attributes consistent with bipolar working. Not surprisingly, this is a pattern repeated with the cores and core fragments, where split pebbles and pieces with extensive scars from bipolar working are common. That said, platform cores are also present in several contexts, though in smaller numbers, reflecting the use of several different reduction strategies in the immediate area. While three blades were identified, the lack of any comparable working on the cores suggests that these were either fortuitous removals, or no more than a minor component of the reduction strategies pursued.

A total of 17 pieces of burnt flint were also recorded. All showed signs of having been worked prior to exposure to heat and with the exception of one burnt bipolar core, all took the form of secondary and tertiary flakes.

Retouched forms show a measure of variety in character. Simple points and scrapers are the most common, made for the most part on secondary and tertiary flakes and present in a number of different contexts. These are all diminutive in size, rarely exceeding 15–20mm in their maximum dimensions, the one exception being a more extensively retouched point or fabricator from L8C [032] which is 25mm in length. The scrapers are for the most part circular or sub-circular in plan, and broadly similar to those found in many Neolithic and Bronze Age contexts in the Western Isles. One exception to this is a well defined endscraper on a primary beach pebble flake from L8C [037]. Beyond these, there are two retouched forms worthy of note. These include a 'part-made' barbed and tanged arrowhead from L8C [033] and another barbed but tangless form recovered from L8D [004]. In the latter case, the concave curve between the two barbs is very pronounced, and matches a small number of similar projectile points found in Scotland (Green, 1980).

While beach pebble flint dominates the assemblage, there is evidence for the use of other raw materials. The most common of these is quartz, which is represented by crude flakes and simple 'cores' – pieces from which removals have been struck, albeit unsystematically. Difficulty in identifying any formal attributes on this material, beyond the fact that they have been worked, most likely stems from

Figure 5.16 Lithic artefacts from beneath houses L8C and L8D (scale in cms)

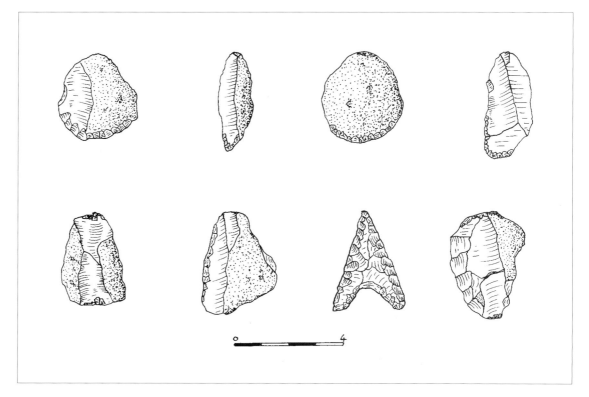

the poor quality of the quartz itself. As it is very difficult to recognise worked quartz, particularly when it is of poor quality, it is likely that at least some material has 'slipped through the net'. Beyond quartz, two secondary flakes are sufficiently coarse grained and of a mottled grey colour to warrant identification as chert, and there is one small scarred chunk which is most likely bloodstone. Coarse stone tools are represented by a heavily worn square sectioned whetstone and two worn rubbers, all of a fine grained sandstone.

Discussion of the Lithics from A128, L8A and L8C and L8D

The lithic assemblages recovered from excavations on four sites at Balnabodach comprise a total of 221 pieces of worked stone. Though a few were associated with contemporary features, the majority were recovered as residual elements during the digging of much later, historic, structures.

Table 5.6: Basic composition of assemblages by type

FORM	L8A	L8C	L8D	A128	TOTAL
Pebbles	1	5	3	1	10
Cores	8	17	5	7	37
Flakes	19	67	31	20	137
Blades	-	2	1	-	3
Chunks	-	14	2	1	17
Re-touched	-	11	4	2	17
TOTAL	28	116	46	31	221

Even when combined, the assemblages described above are limited in size and this places considerable constraints upon interpretation, a problem exacerbated by the lack of much in the way of secure contexts and associations. That said, it is worth noting that the range of materials and forms present across the structures (particularly in the case of L8C/D) are consistent with the sorts of patterns of stone-working and use seen on many Neolithic and Bronze Age sites in the Western Isles (e.g. Wickham-Jones 1995).

In raw material terms, the vast majority of the artefacts recovered are made of flint from local beach pebble sources. Core fragments, chunks and primary and secondary flakes all retain areas of the original cortex, which shows the heavy abrasion and smooth curved surfaces characteristic of these sources. Complete and near complete pebbles indicate that whilst larger pieces were certainly favoured, even pebbles as small as 20mm across were consistently worked. The size ranges of flakes, chunks and retouched pieces is entirely consistent with these patterns of selection. With one exception, other utilised raw materials are also likely to be local. The most common of these is quartz, which could also be won as pebbles from the beach or through the more direct exploitation of *in situ* veins.

The bulk of working appears to have been directed towards the splitting and bipolar working of beach pebbles, from which useable flakes could be struck. Where possible or appropriate, split pebbles were sometimes worked down

Table 5.9: Raw material composition of assemblages

Material	Number of Pieces
Beach Pebble Flint	173
Flint (uncertain source)	3
Quartz	38
Chert	2
Bloodstone	1
Coarse stone	4
TOTAL	221

Table 5.7: Density of worked stone by context

L8A Context	Number of Pieces	L8C Context	Number of Pieces	L8D Context	Number of Pieces	A128 Context	Number of Pieces
002	26	001	12	004	1	002	13
004	1	004	3	006	5	003	16
009	2	009	2	008	1		
		015	2	020	4		
		018	5	021	1		
		025	11	041	1		
		026	2	046	2		
		030	1	053	1		
		032	9	062	21		
		033	3	065	3		
		037	9	066	3		
		038	2				
		039	2				
		040	2				
		043	2				
		048	33				
		057	3				
		058	5				
		059	1				

Table 5.8: Composition of assemblages

Type	L8A	L8C	L8D	A128
Pebbles	1	5	3	1
Platform cores	4	3	-	-
Bipolar cores	4	10	4	4
Irregular / amorphous cores (inc. quartz)	-	4	1	3
Blades	-	2	1	-
(primary)	-	-	-	-
(secondary)	-	2	-	-
(tertiary)	-	-	1	-
Flakes	19	67	31	20
(primary)	3	10	3	7
(secondary)	4	24	12	3
(tertiary)	12	33	16	10
Chunks	-	14	2	1
(primary)	-	2	-	-
(secondary)	-	6	1	1
(tertiary)	-	6	1	-
Endscrapers	-	1	-	-
Side scrapers	-	1	-	1
Circular / sub-circular scrapers	-	3	2	1
Awls / points	-	3	1	-
Fabricator	-	1	-	-
Barbed and tanged points	-	1	-	-
Barbed points	-	-	1	-
Unifacial retouched flakes	-	1	-	-
Bifacial retouched flakes	-	-	-	-

from simple and largely unprepared platforms, an even more 'ad hoc' approach being taken to the working of lumpsof quartz of varied quality. Though a small number of blades have been identified, there is little else to suggest that this more controlled form of reduction was a consistent concern. All areas contain evidence for both manufacturing and use, though the small size of some of the assemblages means that this impression may not be altogether reliable.

Interpretation

The most surprising feature of houses L8C and L8D is that they appear to sit squarely on top of a prehistoric occupation site, as did house L8A (Middle Iron Age) and the blackhouse we excavated at Alt Chrisal (T26: Neolithic). As discussed above, the prehistoric pottery from L8C and 8D is of Neolithic date. The Neolithic occupation is limited, on present evidence to the area beneath these two houses and is focussed in fact in house L8C. Most of the sherds came from this area, and the only features and significant deposits of Neolithic date are found within L8C. No structural remains were noted, but four contemporary features survived. One, 052, appears to have been a fire-pit with a considerable amount of fire debris within it, whilst 053 may also have been a hearth or fireplace. The remaining two features were somewhat different being of yellow clayey material but without any traces of variegated burning. They have clearly been levelled during the construction and occupation of the blackhouse and we have only the bases of them. The size and shape of 054, however, suggests something more than a simple hearth and it is possible we have the base of a clay oven or something similar.

These various features and the depth of the Neolithic deposit in the south half of house 8C suggest that a roofed structure stood in this area. There are no features which appear to be truncated post holes, so we must assume that such a building was constructed of stone or turf, or quite possibly a combination of the two. The fall-off in material in house 8D and also the absence of any occupation deposit in the sounding made east of house 8C, suggests that no more than a single modest building stood on this part of the site at Balnabodach. It is of course possible there were other Neolithic buildings elsewhere on the site, although excavations in house L8A and house L9F revealed no Neolithic deposits, and just three sherds from the site of L8A.

The structural sequence in the two blackhouses is relatively simple and easy to establish. That one house was added onto the rear of the other seems clear for several reasons. Firstly the north and south walls of the two houses do not form a continuous straight alignment as might be expected if they were built as a single structure, but betray the remains of the original rounded corners at the ends of the party wall. Secondly the quantity of contemporary pottery found in the fill of the party wall suggests the prior existence of a good occupation deposit, presumably associated with a building, on this site before one or the other of the houses was erected. Thirdly, the thickness and richness of the occupation deposit in L8C and the sparseness of it in L8D suggests that L8C had a somewhat longer occupation than its neighbour. We believe that 8D was the secondary building, with the outside face of the rear (west) wall of L8C demolished, rebuilt further west and the core of the enlarged party wall filled with soil

scooped both from the area to be occupied by house 8D and perhaps by re-levelling the floor in 8C.

In house 8C the only recognisable internal features are the 'fire-stand', which in the absence of any other hearth must have been the focus of the house, and the curious arc of small stone blocks / slabs set in the floor in the south west corner. As we remarked above, we can only assume this demarcated an area for some purpose. The drain which runs along the rear wall, turns and then exits through the south wall must be a secondary feature associated with the construction of house 8D. It is of course matched by a similar, if differently constructed feature, in house 8D. It is unusual to get drains which run along the side of a room rather than across it, but its explanation here is obvious. With the building of house 8D on the back of 8C, they would now have shared what was, in effect, a valley gutter between their two roofs. That is the rain would have run straight down into the party wall, percolated down through the wall and then out into the rooms on either side. The drains were built to carry this water away and prevent the floors inside becoming wet and muddy.

House 8D was first constructed as a one-roomed building with a central hearth. There were no underlying occupation deposits here, although both Neolithic and modern pottery was found in pockets in the bedrock beneath the floor of the blackhouse. There was equally little occupation deposit built up on the earth floor of the house, and none of the usual flecks of charcoal and fire debris in the material. It appears that domestic occupation of house 8D may have been short-lived, which might explain the relative dearth of pottery from its occupation debris.

A partition wall was inserted and ran across part of the hearth, presumably indicating the hearth was no longer in use. The southern of the two rooms created was at some point sub-divided, and the smaller eastern cell was given a roughly cobbled floor. It may be therefore that building 8D was converted to farming use, with a stall at one end and a storage shed/barn at the other, although we should note no drain was inserted in the floor of the stall.

The dating of buildings L8C and L8D is difficult, despite the considerable quantity of modern pottery recovered. The pottery is mostly dateable to the period c.1830–1850, and it is likely the main history of the two buildings can be fitted into this short time frame. The clearest evidence we have is for the date of the construction of building 8D. From beneath its floor came a large piece of an attractive painted bowl manufactured c.1820–30. A rim sherd of the same vessel was found in the fill of the party wall with house 8C. This seems to confirm that in the building of a new, widened, wall soil was scraped up from the area west of 8C to provide material for the core of the wall. There were many more sherds from this same wall fill (context 020–21) and they form an interesting group. The eight latest are dated c.1840–50, and they must imply that the party wall, and house 8D, was constructed some years after 1840. But the earlier sherds in the wall fill include four made c.1800–1820, eight manufactured c.1800–1830, two made c.1810– 1830, and four dated c.1820–30. If we are right in believing that in order to obtain enough material to fill the core of the new party wall soil was levelled off from the occupation material in house 8C, this earlier material seems most likely to have come from there. The construction date of house 8C however must still be relatively late, because the fill of its east wall yielded two sherds from vessels manufactured c.1830–50.

It seems we must try to relate this archaeological evidence to the documentary evidence for the site's history. If house 8C is not built until some years after 1830, then it seems most likely it was built during the re-occupation of Balnabodach c.1837 and was one of the eight households in the township in 1841. House 8D was added after 1840, and after a very short-lived occupation was modified for farm use. This may have been following evictions in 1848, or the bigger removals of 1850. Both 8C and 8D were, we believe, abandoned when Balnabodach was subjected to the final clearance by Gordon in 1851. There is nothing in their occupation deposits which documents usage after that date. But we know that some families were not removed, and continued to live in the township, and further that by 1861 the townships population had grown to twice the size it was before the 1851 clearance. The abandoned houses could have been re-used for a short time, and indeed in 8C we believe that the lambing pen was inserted not long after the building had been abandoned as a home. But the post-1850 sherds (and there are only a handful) come from topsoil

deposits and there is nothing to indicate any significant re-occupation or re-use of these two houses.

Excavation of Site L9F (blackhouse)
by Keith Branigan and Colin Merrony

Site L9 has been described in the survey report above. The houses here are all still partly standing structures and clearly postdate the houses across the stream at site L8. It was decided that one of the houses on site L9 should be excavated to try and establish its foundation date and subsequent history, which could in turn be linked to the abandonment of the buildings east of the stream. House F was chosen because it was clearly a multi-period structure, but showed no trace of a built fireplace and chimney and might therefore be one of the earlier buildings on site L9.

Architecture (Fig. 5.17)
House L9F proved on excavation to have originally been 8.7m x 6.3m overall, with a door in the centre of its southern wall. Its rear wall was 1.3m wide, its front wall 1.1m wide, and the its east and west walls only 0.9m wide. The rear wall, built against a rock outcrop stood to a height

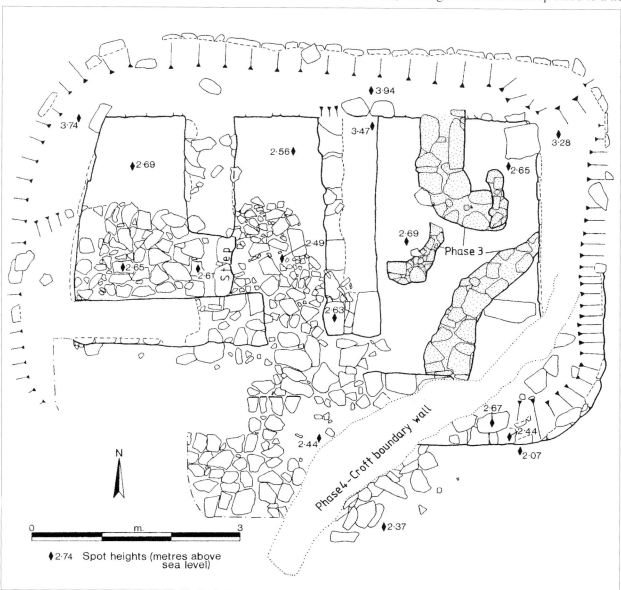

Figure 5.17 Plan of house L9F in its final form

about 1.3m, and other walls were less well preserved the further south they went. The interior of the house measured 6.7m x 4m. The door was probably widened in its later history, but may have been about 0.8m wide originally. The western half of the front (south) wall was subsequently reduced to its footings and a new wall erected to replace it, set back about 1.4m north of its original line. This wall was only 0.7m wide, the same as two internal partition walls which divided the interior of the building into an eastern room (4m x 2.4m) and a western room with two 'cells' (each 2.8m long and 1.4m–1.3m wide). The eastern room had two or three small, rather irregular, walls built into its corners. Outside the doorway of the building was a wide and substantial area of paving. A stone boundary wall was eventually built across the east wall and south east corner of the building.

Deposits and Stratigraphy

Beneath turf and topsoil the eastern room and the central cell had a dark brown silty loam (contexts 09, 048 and 014) in which were embedded some stone blocks tumbled from the wall faces. In the western cell, topsoil was found to immediately overlie the stone slabs and blocks with which the southern half of the room was paved (context 043). When the dark loam in the central cell was removed, the southern half of this cell was also found to have a stone surfacing though many of the stones were notably smaller than in the end cell. In the eastern room, the removal of the dark loam revealed three rather flimsy, narrow walls one in an arc around the south east corner, one enclosing the north east corner, and a short length of wall which enclosed a narrow strip alongside the partition wall. The dark loam continued in the spaces between these walls and merged into an underlying dark grey silty loam with small- to medium-sized angular lumps of stone (context 069), which was apparently contemporary with the walls. In the limited area for excavation between the flimsy walls, context 069 was found to overlie a 2cm thick deposit of yellowish-white sand. Whether this deposit predated the main partition wall is uncertain, but it appeared to run below the flimsy wall structures in the room. Throughout the house, the lowest deposit was a medium-brown slightly clayey soil somewhat hard and lying on bedrock. This appears to be the original floor of the building.

The Finds

Although there was a quantity of glass and corroded iron pieces lying in the vegetation in the ruins of the building, below turf the only finds made were sherds of modern pottery, but for a single piece of tobacco pipe stem.

Modern Pottery

by David Barker

With 628 sherds or 118 vessels, the House L9F assemblage is large. House L9F is a complex structure which has been substantially modified at least twice during its life. Three phases of use have been identified, during which time the building may have served first as a blackhouse, then a store or workshop, and finally as stalls for animals (Branigan 2000, 17). A date contemporary with the other excavated houses has been suggested for its initial construction (*ibid.*), but the ceramic evidence casts doubt upon this hypothesis and suggests a much later period of occupation.

Wares

Eighty (68%) of the ceramic vessels are of whiteware, with ten bone china vessels (9%) forming the next largest group of refined wares; the others include two porcelain vessels

(2%), and A single vessel each of parian ware and blackware or jet ware, and four Rockingham vessels (3%). The remainder of the wares belong to the coarseware end of the ceramic spectrum and include six vessels of brown stoneware (5%), of which five are salt-glazed; two each of coarse earthenware and redware; and ten of grey stoneware (9%).

Vessels

Teawares are well-represented in this group, with two definite teapots, fifteen cups and 26 saucers. By contrast, there are 20 bowls and 19 plates, one of which is a side plate. Vessels which are present in modest numbers include jugs (four), dishes (four), and bottles (six), the latter being in brown stoneware, but a significant new form not seen in any quantity in the other houses is the grey, 'Bristol' glazed stoneware preserve jar, of which there are at least nine. In addition, there is one basin in whiteware, an egg cup in bone china and an unidentified vessel in parian ware. Two storage jars in coarse earthenware, and a further jar in grey stoneware complete the catalogue of vessels.

Decoration

Seventy per cent of the refined wares are decorated, a figure which rises to 78% if moulded wares and vessels with coloured glazes are included. Twenty-six per cent of the refined wares have printed decoration which is mostly in blue, but other colours such as red, pink, grey and brown are also present. Identifiable named patterns include 'sea leaf' and 'Broseley'. Twenty-four per cent of the refined wares have sponged decoration in a range of colours – blue, red, green, and grey – many used with under-glaze painted bands or lines. Plates (four), saucers (six) and bowls (thirteen) and a single cup are the vessels so-decorated (Figs 5.18a–5.18e).

Under-glaze painted decoration, without accompanying sponged patterns, is also common, occurring on 14% of the refined earthenwares, or on 15% of the refined wares including a further porcelain vessel. While there are some examples of the floral patterns in bright chrome colours, which were still very popular at the end of the 19th century, the majority of the under-glaze painted decoration is confined to bands or lines, in pairs or threes, applied to the rims of plates, saucers and bowls.

Other forms of decoration are poorly represented. There are just two vessels with over-glaze painted decoration, a whiteware bowl and a porcelain vessel of indeterminate form, and just two (2%) whiteware bowls with slip decoration. A single moulded jug has red majolica glaze, and a further six whiteware vessels have moulded decoration.

Dating

The character of this group is somewhat different to that of the other Balnabodach assemblages, the result of its later date. There is ample evidence here to date the ceramics to the late 19th century, with the possibility that deposition did not occur until early in the 20th century.

Perhaps the clearest dating evidence are two vessels with the printed maker's mark 'J. & M. P. Bell & Co. L^D.', a mark which was not used by the Bell factory until after (Kelly 1999, 109), while other printed saucers which do not obviously relate to the maker's marks are stylistically of a similar, or slightly later date. One (WWE 11) has an art nouveau style design which is unlikely to date to before c. 1885, and is more likely to be of the 1890s, while another

Figure 5.18 Modern ceramics from house L9F

a) white earthenware bowl rims with under-glaze painted and sponged decoration. Note drilled hole from repair in top centre

b) white earthernware bowls with under-glaze painted and sponged decoration in green, blue and red

c) sponge-decorated white earthenware plate sherds

d) white earthenware saucer sherds with under-glaze painted and sponged decoration

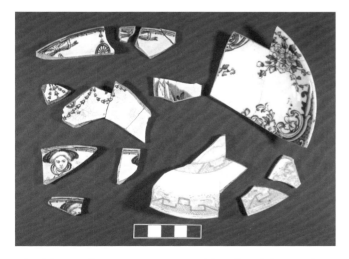

e) white earthernware saucers with printed decoration in blue and light blue

f) underside of grey stoneware preserve jar with impressed eagle mark of Eagle Pottery, Bridgetown, Glasgow

Table 5.10 House L9F ceramics (minimum number of vessels)

	cup	saucer	teapot	bowl	jug	dish	basin	plate (dinner)	plate (side)	egg cup	pre-serve jar	jar	bottle	unid.	TOTALS
Whiteware															
u-gl. printed	6	8		1	1		1	7							24
u-gl. painted	2	7		3				2							14
o-gl. painted				1											1
gilding		1													1
sponged	1	6		13				4							24
ind. slip				2											2
col. glaze					1										1
moulded decn.	1				1			4							6
undecd.		2				1		1	1		2				7
Blackware															
o-gl. printed				1											1
Rockingham			2										2		4
Porcelain															
u-gl. painted														1	1
o-gl. painted														1	1
Bone china	5	2				1				1				1	10
Parian														1	1
Brown SGSW													5		5
Brown St' ware													1		1
Grey St' ware											9	1			10
Coarse redware						2									2
Coarse e' ware												2			2
TOTALS	15	26	2	20	4	4	1	18	1	1	11	3	6	6	118

has a bold floral and scroll design which is rather rococo in style in the darker blue which was increasingly in use during the 1890s (Fig. 5.18e). Other printed wares can be dated to the 1880s–1890s, including a pink-printed saucer with an aesthetic style pattern, and a blue-printed cup (WWE 80) which features a Japanese figure within an otherwise indeterminate pattern; neither are likely to be any earlier than the mid-1880s.

A similar date is suggested by an impressed mark of an eagle on the underside of a grey stoneware jar. This is the mark of Frederick Grosvenor's Eagle Pottery in Bridgeton, Glasgow, which changed its name from the Bridgeton Pottery in 1882 and continued in production until 1923 (Fig. 5.18f). A Rockingham ware base sherd has a mark moulded in relief which is almost certainly also from the Eagle Pottery; a more complete example of this was found on the island of Pabbay.

The sponged wares have little to distinguish them apart from a brighter range of colours than found in the other Balnabodach assemblages. There are, however, sherds of two plates with the grey sponged Grecian pattern, which was one of the most common sponged patterns used; it dates to after 1875 (H. Kelly, pers. comm.).

Discussion
The ceramics point to the main period of use of House L9F being the late 19th century. Indeed the finds suggest that this may have been the only period of use, despite the complex structural evidence, for there are no ceramics of an earlier date to suggest that the house was constructed in the mid-19th century.

Interpretation
Building L9F appears to have begun life as a simple blackhouse, 8.6m x 5.7m externally (Fig. 5.19). It is in most respects a 'typical' Barra blackhouse in terms of size, floor space, and a single central doorway. Its walls are perhaps a little narrower than most Barra blackhouses we have examined, but another of the houses excavated in the Balnabodach project (A128) also has walls only 0.8–0.9m wide. If the building's interpretation as a blackhouse is correct, then the absence of a built fireplace and chimney in an end wall suggests the building was probably built before c.1870–1880, when they were becoming commonplace. The so-called 'plague house' in the settlement (house L9B) had a large fireplace and chimney at each end, as did a further similar house 400m to the south east. Both of these houses are known to have been erected c.1880. We believe this house was built in the mid-19th century, but there was no occupation deposit on its original floor and only three sherds from the house are firmly dated to that period.

It is possible that the building had a central partition from the first, but on balance we believe not. The fact that the partition is butt-jointed to the rear wall and built on the same deposit as made up the original floor surface of the building are by no means unequivocal indicators

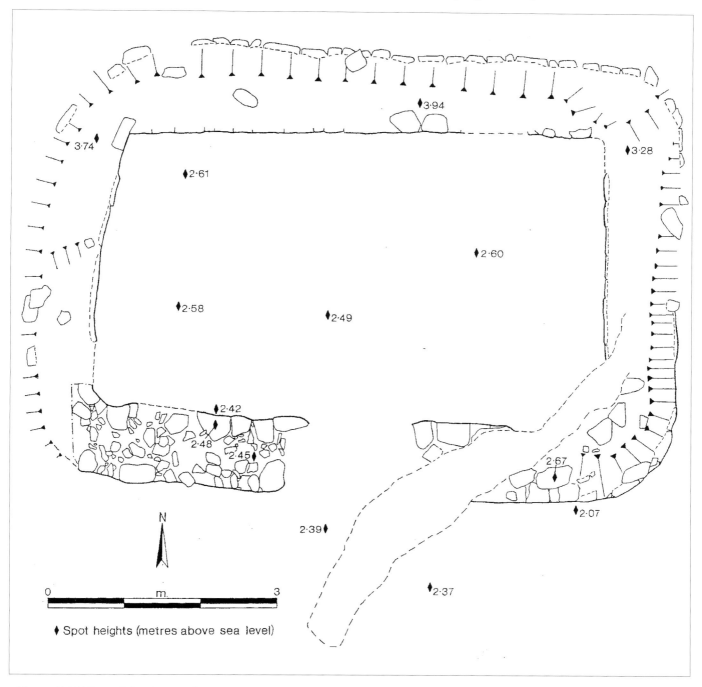

Figure 5.19 The original plan of building L9F

that the partition was a later addition. But the construction and size of the wall are similar to the clearly later rebuild of the west end of the front (south) wall and we think it likely that the central partition wall is part of the considerable modification of building L9F. There is clearly a complete change of use of the building at this time, and it is possible that the original house had been abandoned for a time before modification took place. The levelling of the west end of the south wall is somewhat puzzling and might be explained if it had collapsed or been partly robbed during a period of abandonment. Its replacement by a slightly narrower wall, set back 1.4m is also difficult to explain. This did, however, have the effect of providing a completely separate entrance to each of the two rooms now created, though why that should have been thought desirable is unclear.

The scattered 'paving' outside the old front door was now expanded and made a good deal more solid, so that it was almost like a small paved roadway leading into the building. One would be tempted to think that perhaps wheeled carts were to be brought to the building, but the immediate topography makes that impossible. The other obvious reason for laying down a substantial surfacing is that animals were to be brought to the building. There are no drains, however, to suggest its use as a byre, and the 'cells' in the western room were too small for the overwintering of cows.

The paving inside the building is also curious. It extends from the old front wall and doorway, through the new door and then across the southern half of each cell. The northern half of each cell is still a bare earth floor. It is possible

105

that some sort of timber partition was set across each cell at the point where the paving ended but if so there was no surviving trace of them. Our tentative interpretation of these cells is that they might have been used either for lambing or as milking pens.

As to the east room, that appears to have been initially left undivided, with a narrower door (only 0.5m wide) than that to the west room. The only clue to this room's use is that the bulk of the pottery (78%) found within the building (excluding material in topsoil) was found in this room. In general terms we suggest that the east room of the modified building was used for human activities, as opposed to the use of the west room and its two cells for animals. Whether it was ever used as living space, even by a single individual, is open to doubt but it is possible. Certainly the pottery found in this room is a 'domestic' assemblage, dominated by cups, saucers, bowls and plates. Subsequently, the room had three small 'bins' built into it partitioned off with flimsy walls. Their purpose is unknown.

The modification of building L9F seems to have taken place c.1880/1890, and its last use as an outbuilding almost certainly extended into the 20th century. Its ruins were finally used as a dumping ground.

Balnabodach – An Overview

The focus of early settlement around Loch Obe seems to have been at the site occupied in the 19th century by two successive clusters of blackhouses (sites L8 and L9). A Neolithic settlement was established east of the stream. It was relatively short-lived and small to judge from the depth and extent of the Neolithic deposits. The absence of any Beaker pottery suggests it was abandoned before the mid-3rd millennium BC. Further prehistoric activity in the area is indicated however by the cut peat stack dated to the mid-second millennium BC (Branigan et al 2002), and perhaps by the lithic scatters without associated pottery at sites A128 and L10. Site L8 was re-occupied in the Middle Iron Age, again perhaps by a single family in a house beneath blackhouse L8A and again for a relatively short period. This occupation might overlap with the broch built on an island in Loch nic Ruaidhe, now almost entirely submerged. Activity around Loch Obe in the mid-first millennium AD may be marked by the two (possibly three ?) small shieling huts at site A127. At present there is no evidence from Balnabodach for Norse settlement, which is surprising given the excellent harbourage offered by Loch Obe; the nearest known Norse site is the shieling at site L15 about 1.5kms to the south. The only traces of any activity in the medieval and early modern era are a few sherds of pottery found in excavations on site L8.

The history of the nineteenth century settlement has been discussed in some detail above, based on documentary sources. The excavations and field survey perhaps allow for some further interpretation of the evidence. Since there were four tenants at Balnabodach in 1810, but little evidence of occupation much earlier, the township crofts were probably created by Roderick the Gentle shortly before or after 1800. It is likely that houses A128 and L10 were houses on two of the original crofts, and it is possible that house L8A (in its first form) was occupied by 1810. The township's growth was apparently stunted by its renting out as pasture to tenants in Grean c.1825–1835, and the removal of its population elsewhere. The restoration of

tenants to Balnabodach was probably undertaken by the Trustees of the estate c.1836–37 at which point the settlement by the stream expanded, with new houses (L8C and L8D) joining a re-occupied house L8A. Under Gordon the tenants at some point lost their crofts and some were probably removed. House L8D may have been abandoned as a home at this time and adapted for farm use. By the census of 1851 the tenants were fishermen and boat-builders rather than crofters, with a solitary immigrant 'farmer' of 6 acres. Soon after this the township was cleared, and the excavated houses at site L8 were abandoned at this time.

The excavations of blackhouses L8A, L8C, and L8D have provided some insights into the material culture of the people living at Balnabodach at this time, though not as many as one might have hoped. Their homes were well adapted to the local environment in terms of both building materials and the protection they provided from the elements. Their single deep-set doors and small windows beneath the eaves excluded draughts (and daylight) from the interior. The floors were of trampled earth, sometimes spread with a little sand; we found no evidence for floor coverings of any kind. The hearth was surprisingly small in L8A, and so was the fire-pit in L8D. There was also very little trace of ash deposits around the hearths, and it may be that fires were contained within a brazier or fire-box. Contemporary visitors to Barra noted how sparsely furnished the blackhouses were (above, p. 22), and this is the impression gained from the excavated houses at Balnabodach. Buchanan and Nicholson both mentioned the rarity of beds, for example, and none of the excavated houses revealed evidence of a bed-box, or a setting for one. In only two houses (T26 and L8A) was there any evidence for built furnishings of any kind – in each case probably a standing for a dresser facing the doorway.

The dresser and its contents may have been the one item of 'display' in the house, though David Barker rightly expresses doubts about the availability of even simple dressers in the earlier 19th century Western Isles. The pottery which seems to have been favoured by the people of Balnabodach (and elsewhere) was mostly bright and cheerful, if at the cheap end of the range. A few more expensive items, like the soft-paste porcelain bowl from house L8A, appear to have been treasured as they are mostly decades older than the bulk of the pottery. Of pottery vessels in the Balnabodach blackhouses whose shape could be identified the most common were bowls followed by plates. Teacups, tea-bowls, and saucers were sufficiently common at Balnabodach to confirm a taste for tea, but there were remarkably few fragments of tobacco pipes, given the alleged partiality of the Barramen for tobacco. One of General Macneil's complaints against his tenants was that the fishermen bartered their catch for 'inferior and dear tobacco', and the Rev. Nicholson commented how 'extremely addicted' the Barramen were to smoking tobacco. But apart from a single piece in house 8D only house 8A yielded pipe fragments; this may be coincidence but this, the largest house in the cluster, was the only house to produce even a handful of other personal belongings.

The assemblage of personal items from house 8A was hardly impressive, however, amounting to four buttons, two beads and a thimble. The hinge plate and bronze ring (and possibly the bronze stud) may have come from a small box or casket. Otherwise the only items found were simple tools – stone hones and rubbers, a pestle and an iron wedge or chisel. Only the fragment of a mitre square suggests perhaps both the need and the resources to acquire something just a little out of the ordinary. There can be little doubt that in material terms, the people of Balnabodach led an impoverished existence, and even that was taken from them in the traumatic events of 1848–1851.

APPENDIX

A list of births and marriages recorded at Balnabodach in the Barra Parish Register between 1805 and 1853, and census returns for 1841 and 1851.

The first surviving volume of the parish register begins with an entry dated September 23rd 1805 and ends with one on September 11th 1853. There is a gap in the records from April 4th 1809 to November 13th 1809, and a much bigger one from August 5th 1810 to September 25th 1812.

The first marriage in the register appears only in November 1812, but subsequently they appear regularly. Deaths on the other hand are never recorded, except between 1815 and 1825, when the average number in the parish per year is thirteen. We do not know why the Rev. Angus Macdonald began to record them in 1815, having kept the register without them since 1805, but the decision to exclude them again, may have been taken by his successor, the Rev. Neil Macdonald who replaced him at the end of 1825.

The Register is of course concerned only with Catholics. There were only some 60 Protestants in a population of 2,100 in 1813, but the number had risen to 380 out of 2,400 in 1841, so a small but significant segment of the population are excluded altogether from the register. There is in fact a partial register of Protestants which is notionally for the years 1836 - 1854. The copy we have seen actually includes information only between 1847 and 1860. Unfortunately the Protestant register usually provides less information per entry than the Catholic one, often omitting the place of residence and never naming sponsors.

From these two sources we have listed all the recorded births, and marriages which are of people living in Balnabodach at the time of the event. Only one death was *recorded* in Balnabodach in the entire period. In the list of births, we give entries under the date of registration first, followed by the date of birth where it is given. We then give the christian name of the child, followed by the father's christian name and then the father's surname. This is followed by the christian name and surname of the mother. The register almost always follows this with the names of the sponsors, and sometimes with their place of residence, but we do not include this information here.

We have worked from a transcription of the original register in which there are some obvious minor errors which occurred either in transcription or in typing. There are also the usual range of variations of spelling names (e.g. Marion and Marian). We have adopted a single spelling for each name here, and similarly have followed the convention that surnames beginning with 'Mac' have a capital only for the first letter of the name (e.g. Macneil). The difficulties of using the census data are discussed above (p. 69–70).

BIRTHS REGISTERED AT BALNABODACH

CATHOLIC

Registered	Birth Date	Name	Father	Surname	Mother	Surname
18/1/14	3/1/14	James	John	Macneil	Marion	Gillis
2/6/15		Cathrine	John	Macneil	Marion	Gillis
22/7/16		Beag	Allan	Macarthur	Catherine	Macdonald
16/11/16		Donald	John	Macneil	Marion	Gillis
16/11/16		Margaret	John	Macneil	Marion	Gillis
5/5/18		Catherine	Donald	Macdonald	Ann	Macneil
21/10/18		Effie	Donald	Macneil	Marion	Maclean
17/6/19		Mary	John	Macneil	Catherine	Maclean
23/11/19		Donald	Roderick	Macneil	Mary	Macmillan
23/8/20		Christian	Neil	Macneil	Ann	Mackinnon
16/4/21		Mary	John	Macneil	Marion	Mackinnon
24/4/21		Christian	Donald	Macneil	Ann	Maclean
19/10/21		Donald	John	Macneil	Catherine	Maclean
27/10/25		Donald	John	Macdougal	Ann	Macdonald
26/12/34		Michael	Eoin	Mackinnon	Mary	Macleod
19/2/35		Finlay	Duncan	Macphee	Christian	Macphee
27/8/37	26/8/37	Murdoch	Donald	Macneil	Mary	Macmillan
20/6/40	7/6/40	Ranald	Hector	Macdougal	Ann	Macdonald
23/7/40	19/7/40	Murdoch	Donald	Macneil	Mary	Macmillan
13/10/42	13/10/42	Alexander	Donald	Maclean	Catherine	Macneil
28/12/42	27/12/42	Neil	Hector	Macdougal	Ann	Macdonald
5/4/43	4/4/43	Ann	Donald	Macneil	Catherine	Macneil
30/3/47	28/3/47	Catherine	Donald	Macneil	Christian	Macneil
9/4/40	1/4/50	Christian	Michael	Macdonald	Mary	Macleod
9/5/50	7/5/50	Rachel	Donald	Macneil	Christy	Macneil
9/6/50	8/6/50	Mary	Roderick	Macdonald	Christian	Macneil
18/11/50	17/11/50	Mary	Neil	MacNeil	Margaret	Macdonald
26/4/51	26/4/51	Ann	Angus	Macdonald	Catherine	Mackinnon
19/5/51	12/5/51	Marion	Donald	Macneil	Mary	Macneil
29/8/51	28//8/51	John	Ewen	Livingstone	Mary	Macneil
16/2/53	15/2/53	Catherine	Donald	Macneil	Mary	Macneil
3/5/53	29/4/53	Donald	Farquhar	Macneil	Flora	Macleod
20/5/53	18/5/53	Donald	Angus	Macdonald	Catherine	Mackinnon

PROTESTANT
None registered

MARRIAGES OF RESIDENTS OF BALNABODACH

CATHOLIC

Date	Groom	residence	Bride	residence
26/9/15	John Morrison	Balnabodach	Jane Campbell	Rulios
20/10/18	Roderick Macneil	Balnabodach	Mary Macmillan	Bruernish
30/1/23	Rory Macneil	Balnabodach	Ann Macneil	Mingulay
1/12/39	Roderick Macmillan	Balnabodach	Isabella Macinnes	Rulios
16/2/41	Donald Macneil	Balnabodach	Flora Macneil	Balnabodach
16/1/42	Donald Maclean	Craigston	Catherine Macneil	Balnabodach
16/1/42	Neil Macneil	Balnabodach	Peggy Macdonald	Hellisay
22/8/43	Roderick Macneil	Balnabodach	Christian Macinnes	Rulios
18/1/46	Donald Macneil	Bruernish	Mary Macneil	Balnabodach
17/2/46	Donald Macneil	Balnabodach	Chirsty Macneil	Borve
14/9/47	Neil Mackinnon	Earsary	Chirsty Macneil	Balnabodach
17/4/49	Farquhar Macneil	Balnabodach	Flora Macleod	Bruernish

PROTESTANT

12/4/54	Hugh Macleod	Balnabodach	Catherine Macneil	Bruernish

CENSUS OF BALNABODACH: 1841

Sched.	Indiv.	Name	Age	Sex	Occupation	Birthplace
24	117	John Macmillan	65	M	Crofter	Scotland
24	118	Mearon Macmillan	55	F -		Scotland
24	119	Angus Macmillan	20	M -		Scotland
25	120	Hector Macdugald	30	M	Crofter	Scotland
25	121	Anne Macdugald	30	F -		Scotland
25	122	Peggy Macdugald	3	F -		Scotland
25	123	Michael Macdugald	5	M -		Scotland
25	124	Ranald Macdugald	1	M -		Scotland
25	125	Flory Macdugald	35	F -		Scotland
26	126	Niel Macdugald	80	M	Pauper	Scotland
27	127	Effy Macneil	55	F	Crofter	Scotland
27	128	Elisa Macneil	25	F -		Scotland
27	129	Mary Macneil	23	F -		Scotland
27	130	Silas Macneil	20	M -		Scotland
27	131	Andrew Buchanan	5	M -		Scotland
27	132	John Macdonald	3	M -		Scotland
28	133	Donald Macneil	30	M	Cottar	Scotland
29	134	Flora Macneil	25	F -		Scotland
30	135	Donald Macneil	30	M	Crofter	Scotland
30	136	Mary Macneil	30	F -		Scotland
30	137	Murdo Macneil	10m	M -		Scotland
31	138	John Macmillan	43	M	Crofter	Scotland
31	139	Eliza Macmillan	40	F -		Scotland
31	140	Marion Macmillan	35	F -		Scotland
31	141	Flory Macneil	6	F -		Scotland
31	142	Chirsty Shaw	90	F	Pauper	Scotland

CENSUS OF BALNABODACH: 1851

Sched.	Indiv.	Name	Age	Sex	Occupation	Birthplace
1	1	Jonathan Macneil	62	M	Boat builder	Barra
1	2	Catherine Macneil	67	F	Wife	Barra
1	3	Michale Maclean	16	M	Nephew/Apprentice	Barra
2	4	Donald Macneil	36	M	Boat builder	Barra
2	5	Christina Macneil	32	F	Wife	Barra
2	6	Cathrine Macneil	4	F	Daughter	Barra
2	7	Jane Campbell	10	F	Niece	Barra
3	8	Cathrine Macdonald	28	F	Cottars wife	Barra
3	9	John Macdonald	4	M	Son	Barra
4	10	Rodrick Macdonald	50	M	Fisherman	Barra
4	11	Elizabeth Macdonald	27	F	Wife	Barra
4	12	Marion Macdonald	19	F	Daughter	Barra
4	13	Cathrine Macdonald	17	F	Daughter	Barra
4	14	William Macdonald	13	M	Son	Barra
4	15	Michale Macdonald	11	M	Son	Barra
4	16	Mary Macdonald	2m	F	Daughter	Barra
5	17	Ewen Livingstone	38	M	Fisherman	Barra
5	18	Cathrine Livingstone	36	F	Wife	Barra
5	19	John Livingstone	10	M	Scholar	Barra
5	20	Cathrine Livingstone	11	F	Daughter	Barra
5	21	Ewen Livingstone	2	M	Son	Barra
6	22	Neil Macneil	35	M	Fisherman	Barra
6	23	Margaret Macneil	35	F	Wife	Barra
6	24	John Macneil	6	M	Son	Barra
6	25	Donald Macneil	4	M	Son	Barra
6	26	Michael Macneil	2	M	Son	Barra
6	27	Mary Macneil	6m	F	Daughter	Barra
6	28	Ann Macdonald	12	F	Niece	Barra
7	29	Cathrine Maclean	30	F	Outdoor labourer	Barra
8	30	Angus Macneil	82	M	Pauper	Barra
8	31	Marion Macneil	24	F	Daughter	Barra
8	32	Alexander Macneil	2	M	Grandson	Barra
9	33	Duncan Macrae	61	M	Farmer, 6 acres	Kintail
9	34	Margaret Macrae	25	F	Daughter	Kintail
9	35	Mary Macrae	22	F	Daughter	Kintail
9	36	Ann Macrae	18	F	Daughter	Kintail
10	37	Farquhar Macneil	30	M	Boat builder	Barra
10	38	Flora Macneil	28	F	Wife	Barra
11	39	Donald Macneil	36	M	Fisherman	Barra
11	40	Mary Macneil	41	F	Wife	Barra
11	41	John Macneil	4	M	Son	Barra
11	42	Jonathan Macneil	3	M	Son	Barra
11	43	Michael Macneil	2	M	Son	Barra

6

Pottery Usage in a Crofting Community: an Overview

David Barker

Introduction

The excavated assemblages from the Balnabodach blackhouses (Fig. 6.1) are important. The paucity of blackhouse excavations in the Western Isles – only 14 are known by the writer to have produced significant groups of material culture – means that there that there is still little reliable archaeological evidence for their origins, structural development and variations between islands, and the role of material culture and the manner of its use is still poorly understood and cannot easily be reconciled with contemporary documentary evidence. Only one other Barrra blackhouse has been excavated, that at Alt Chrisal from which were recovered ceramics dating to between the late-18th century and the 1820s (Foster 1995). The Alt Chrisal ceramics are contemporary with a small proportion of the finds from three of the Balnabodach houses (L8A, L8C and L8D), but offer no evidence for occupation beyond 1830. Consequently the finds are not contemporary with the main period of activity at Balnabodach and the small size of the group leaves some doubt as to the completeness of the assemblage.

The study of the ceramics from the Balnabodach blackhouses contributes to the third of the archaeology project's objectives, namely 'to gain a greater insight into the life of the people of Balnabodach during the eighteenth and nineteenth centuries' (Branigan 2000, 2). By their relevance to perhaps the most important of domestic activities – eating, drinking and food preparation – the ceramics introduce us to the very heart of the household and provide direct contact with their users. The ceramics can reasonably be expected to shed light upon the foodways of the people of Balnabodach, but they may also provide evidence for a wider range of domestic activities.

Ceramics are used by archaeologists as indicators of 'status', however this may be defined. By the 19th century, however, they provide real evidence for the economic means of a household, or at least the ability of its members to spend on ceramics. Differences in the composition of the ceramic assemblages of the four excavated Balnabodach houses may be significant, perhaps reflecting their occupants' position within the community, their economic means, the size and composition of households, the uses to which houses were put and, of course, any change over time. The impact of the Clearance of populations in the Western Isles was such that significant differences may well be evident in pre- and post-Clearance assemblages, although the situation at Balnabodach is not so clear cut. The need for close dating of the ceramics is therefore self evident, and while ceramics present problems in this respect, at Balnabodach they are the best material evidence available. Their role in establishing the contemporaneity of houses, in dating the length of their occupation, and in helping to understand structural changes is crucial.

Finally, it is all too easy to focus upon the site under discussion while ignoring its place in a wider regional, national or global context. The island of Barra is

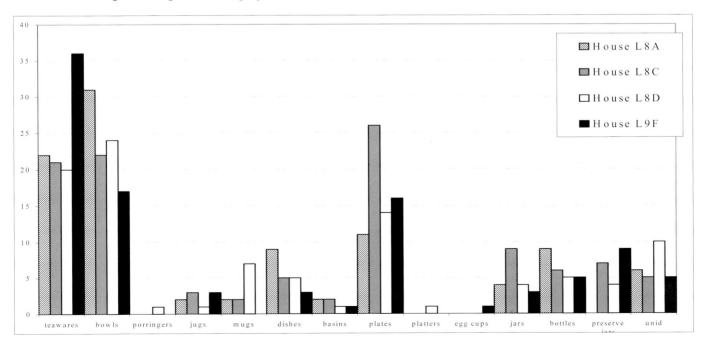

Figure 6.1 Ceramic forms at Balnabodach by percentage

geographically remote, but the ceramics are an important reminder that neither it nor its neighbouring islands were completely isolated during the post-medieval period. The ceramics were not made locally, but were brought to the island in a variety of ways, providing evidence for communication with mainland Britain and for trade, whether *ad hoc* or organised. The potential to identify the sources of manufacture for some of the ceramics extends the picture beyond the activities of middlemen and places Barra and its neighbours in the wider context of an industrial Britain which was changing patterns of ceramic consumption during the later-18th and 19th centuries. Something of this wider context is illustrated by a number of casual ceramic finds made on the neighbouring islands of Pabbay, Sandray, Mingulay and Fuiay which are referred to here in the discussion (Fig 6.2).

Context

While it is important to understand the social and economic context in which industrially-made ceramics from mainland Britain first came to be used, the evidence is scant. Only in the late-18th century do the Western Isles emerge from historical obscurity as travellers began to visit the islands and to record their observations. These include the Reverend John Walker in the 1760s (McKay 1980), the Reverend John Lane Buchanan in the 1780s (Buchanan 1793) and, of course, Dr Samuel Johnson and James Boswell whose travels among the islands of the Inner Hebrides in 1773 are well known (McGowan 1996). All of these made important records of a people who were, in effect, still part of a feudal society. More detailed, and more thorough accounts of the economy and way of life in the islands were compiled for the *Statistical Accounts of Scotland* of 1791–1799, which are now a valuable source of evidence.

From an archaeological perspective, it is evident that there are too few excavated sites of post-medieval date, and from too narrow a geographical area, to inspire confidence that interpretations of structures and assemblages of material culture will withstand serious scrutiny. On the sites excavated, the absence of significant quantities of industrially made ceramics dating to before 1800 might suggest that it was not until the early years of the 19th century that this material became widely available to the mass of the population, in which case its appearance coincides with a period of relative prosperity for the islands. This was the heyday of kelp production, the islands' own industrial revolution, but one which appears to have benefited the local population little. On the contrary, the higher wages paid to the workers labouring seasonally in kelp production were largely swallowed up by increased rents, while the landlords' need for a guaranteed workforce led them to reduce the size of their tenants' cultivation plots to a point where self-sufficiency was impossible and work in kelp burning became a necessity (Gray 1957, 131–134).

The lack of 18th century ceramics might also be due to the fact that sites of this date have not been identified and targeted by excavation. The earlier ceramics from Balnabodach are too few in number to be other than ambiguous, whereas a slightly more substantial group of 18th century sherds excavated in one of the Airigh Mhuillin (South Uist) blackhouses has been interpreted as belonging to occupation of the house by a tacksman (J Symonds, pers. comm.). Whatever the precise context for the use of these

wares in South Uist, it is evident that small quantities of ceramics were reaching the Western Isles before the last quarter of the 18th century. It is easy to imagine the landowners and, to an extent, the middle classes (the tacksmen), with both a position and a distance from sub-tenants to maintain, embracing the material culture of mainland Britain as it became available, and adopting elements of a more mainstream British lifestyle. Visiting the islands of Skye, Raasay, Coll, Staffa and Mull in 1773, Dr. Samuel Johnson and James Boswell enjoyed a good standard of hospitality – from the landowners and well-to-do - and found a lifestyle and domestic comforts which were entirely familiar to them (McGowan 1996). When the population at large accepted industrially made mainland ceramics, and precisely why are questions which cannot yet be answered. The way in which new ceramic items were used is also problematic, and there is no documentary evidence to suggest whether these new wares accompanied, or brought about significant changes in food preparation, drinking and dining practices. Did they replace, or supplement, locally-made ceramic vessels or else a body of utensils of other materials?

For the 19th century, there is a significantly larger body of evidence, both archaeological and historical. The detailed contemporary accounts of the Western Isles, their economy and their people, contained in the *New Statistical Account* provide limited, but nonetheless valuable evidence for the blackhouses and the condition of their occupants, but significantly at a time after the collapse of the kelp industry. Typically the contributors to the *Account*, who were the local clergymen, are dismissive of a lifestyle which they did not properly understand, and make no attempt to hide their disgust at conditions within the houses which they considered to be 'sordid' or 'indescribably filthy' (Cameron 1833, 128). Although these writers were not concerned to describe the material culture of the blackhouse *per se*, some useful information may be gained. For example, on Barra, 'The common buildings of the peasantry are of a most miserable description…The natives have little or no idea of cleanliness or comfort. They seldom have much furniture to boast of; sometimes not a chair to sit upon, a bed to sleep on, or bed clothes to cover them from the severity of the night air…'(Nicolson 1840, 212).

Islands Foodways

A brief reference of 1840 shows that the diet of the people of Barra was closely comparable with that in the other islands: 'Food is barley-meal, potatoes and milk and at times fish. The fishermen export catches of cod and ling to Glasgow and other markets, reserving such fish as is not fit for market for their own families. In very scarce years, e.g. 1836 and 1837, they subsist upon cockles and other shell fish, with very little bread and milk' (Nicolson 1840, 209). All such contemporary descriptions make no mention of meat or else emphasise its absence in the daily diet of the islanders. On Harris, 'Their food principally consists of potatoes, fish and meal. They seldom can indulge themselves in the luxury of either beef or mutton' (Macivor 1841, 156–157), while the South Uist diet was described as 'barley-bread, potatoes, milk, oat-gruel (brochan), and occasionally fish, and shell fish in summer. In good seasons they have abundance of bread and potatoes' (Maclean 1837, 189). Cockles were also part of the diet in Barra where, 'Sometimes they eat them when boiled, out of the shell, at other times, such as have milk, boil it and the cockles together, making them into a soup, which they consider a very nutritious diet' (Nicholson 1840, 203).

The limited diet, the absence of furniture and domestic comforts in general, combined with the repeated references to the islanders' poor circumstances, do not provide a convincing context for the widespread use of a range of industrially made ceramics from mainland Britain. Indeed, the predominance of bowls in ceramic assemblages from the Scottish Highlands and Islands has been noted (Kelly 1996, 68; Symonds 2000, 207), and suggests that a more limited range of vessel forms was required by the inhabitants of these more remote communities. This view is reinforced by G W Brownlow's painting, *The Humble Meal*, which shows a mother in a poorly furnished (? Highland) cottage dispensing a meal from a single iron pot standing over an open peat fire to expectant children, each of whom holds a single bowl. The bowl is the ideal vessel from which to eat meals prepared in a single pot, and a spoon would seem to be the appropriate utensil for such food. The bowl might also have had a significant role in view of the importance of milk in the island diet.

The association of bowls with poverty is often made. In the context of 19th century plantation sites in the southern states of the USA, excavations have shown that bowls typically form a significantly higher proportion of the ceramic vessels recovered in the cabins of the plantation's slaves than in the houses of either the overseer or the plantation owner (Otto 1977). The slaves, and to an extent the overseers, he suggests, were mostly eating slow-simmer foods cooked in a single pot and served in bowls, while the plantation owners were eating roasts, vegetables and soups presented at the dining table on platters and in tureens, and eaten from a wider variety of contemporary table wares (Otto 1984, 167). A similar picture emerges from a study of lower-class free Afro-American sites in New England suggesting that single-pot cooking was more widely practised than simply amongst the slaves of the southern states. Otto recognises the need for a wider comparative study to determine whether this manner of cooking and the resulting preponderance of bowls were the result of class or race (*ibid.*, 175), and the relevance of the situation in the Western Isles is clear.

Island Ceramics

While it does not necessarily follow that form dictates function, the number of bowls in the Balnabodach assemblages, and in the other excavated groups from the Western Isles, is striking and accords well with preconceptions about ceramic use within the island blackhouses. Bowls are the dominant vessel form in two of the three pre-1850 assemblages from Balnabodach. In House L8A, 31% of the ceramics are bowls, while in House L8D bowls make up 24% of the vessels; in House L8C they are second in proportion (21%) to plates. Even in the late-19th century group from House L9F bowls are somewhat less numerous, but still constitute 17% of the vessels present.

The presence of a significant number of plates in all of these groups is somewhat surprising, however, given a diet that is supposedly based upon stews, broths and oatmeal porridge, and may suggest that our preconceptions of foodways in the Western Isles may not be entirely well founded. The 33 plates out of an assemblage of 129 vessels from House L8C is a considerable proportion (26%), while in House L8A plates make up 11% of the group, and in L8D plates and a platter make up 15% of the vessels. In the later assemblage from House L9F 16% of the ceramics are plates. The Balnabodach assemblages are not unusual in this respect, and the picture presented here is broadly in keeping with other blackhouse assemblages excavated on South Uist and on the Shiant Islands; in all of these plates were considerably more numerous than might have been expected and were a significant proportion of vessels.

It seems that the date of an assemblage has little bearing upon the presence or otherwise of plates, and the idea that plates may have appeared at a later date to supplement a limited range of ceramics already in use can be discounted. True, 36% of the vessels identified in the small pre-1830 group from Alt Chrisal on Barra were bowls, in contrast to plates which formed just 8%, but no other assemblages support this interpretation. In the Balnabodach House L8A group, all five of the plates are in pearlware, whereas fourteen of the seventeen bowls are in whiteware, which could be interpreted as suggesting that bowls were the later form. Of course this is not the case, and the size of a group will inevitably determine its worth as a representative sample of wares. In the Balnabodach L8C group, there are six plates in pearlware, but there are also 27 in whiteware, and in the L8D group there are two in creamware, two in pearlware and seven (and one platter) in whiteware. It seems, therefore, that in all of the Barra blackhouse assemblages, except that from Alt Chrisal, plates constituted a significant proportion, if not the greatest proportion, of the vessels in use from the first appearance of industrially made ceramics there. Indeed, the proportions of plates in all of the blackhouse assemblages from South Uist and the Shiant Islands, all of which are largely pre-1830 in date, confirm this. Plates are not under-represented in the late-19th century Balnabodach L9F group; in this the number of bowls (20) only just exceeds the number of plates (19).

Our preconceptions about the domestic habits and material culture of the Western Isles are also challenged by material evidence which points to tea-drinking on Barra during the first half of the 19th century, even though it is stated to have been largely unknown at this time. On their travels in 1773, Johnson and Boswell, 'found tea here [Cissipol, Col], as in every other place, but our spoons were of horn' (McGowan 1996, 107), but it should be remembered that their hosts were men of some means. Sixty years later, Reverend William Macrae wrote of the people of Barvas on Lewis, 'Their domestic economy is frugal and modest beyond conception. The produce of a foreign soil, as tea, coffee, and sugar, and the common conveniences of art, as knives, forks, &c. are to them alien' (Macrae 1836, 147), while in 1840 the Reverend John Mackinnon complained of the recent introduction into Skye of tea drinking, 'formerly unknown to the lower orders', as 'gipsies, rag-men, vendors of crockery, tinsmiths, egg-dealers, and old-clothes-men' pored into the island as a result of improvements in communication between the island and Glasgow (Mackinnon 1840, 313). Skye was clearly better placed than the Western Isles to benefit from such improvements, and it might be expected that the arrival of tea in any quantity here occurred at a somewhat later date. As late as 1863 Isabella Bird, visiting a house on Berneray, commented that, 'Its inmates seemed entirely dependent on their own resources; tobacco and tea, and the last used not as a beverage, but as a luxury, appeared the only exotic articles' (Mair 1978, 143). In 1888, however, Mrs. Murray, remarked upon the presence in a house on Mingulay of a 'three-legged pot, and kettle, not to omit the never-failing friend of every old wife in the kingdom, the brown teapot standing by the fire' (Mair 1978, 87).

The fact that teawares (15 cups, 26 saucers and 2 teapots) constitute 36% of the vessels in the Balnabodach House L9F group is no cause for surprise, given its late-19th century date, since by this time tea was probably in widespread use as Isabella Bird indicates. It is probably significant, however, that teawares are well represented in the other, earlier Balnabodach assemblages. In House L8A they account for 22% of the vessels; in the House L8C group they are 21%; and in the L8D group they form 20% of the vessels. In House L8A there are two teabowls, three cups, five saucers and one teapot; in L8C, three teabowls, six cups, 15 saucers and two teapots; and in L8D, three teabowls, nine saucers and three teapots. The evidence seems clear; even if one were to attempt to explain away teabowls, cups and saucers as forms which might be put to other uses, the presence of teapots in all of the earlier groups suggests that tea was, at the very least, a luxury which was enjoyed to a certain extent in Barra before 1850. Moreover, there is no convincing evidence that tea drinking belonged to the main period of activity at Balnabodach, that is during the 1830s and 1840s, for tea wares are present in all of the House groups in the appropriate proportions of early (i.e. pre-1830) to later (i.e. 1830s–1840s) ware types.

Another feature shared by Balnabodach, South Uist and Shiants blackhouse assemblages is the paucity of coarse earthenware vessels, particularly those which were likely to have been used for storage. Most British post-medieval sites produce large quantities of coarse lead-glazed earthenware cylindrical, or near-cylindrical jars, which were probably multi-purpose storage vessels, as well as deep flaring pancheons, jugs, and pans or milk pans. There are three coarse earthenware jar forms from each of Balnabodach Houses L8A and L8D, seven from House L8C, and just two from House L9F. These present a consistent proportion of between 4% and 6% of the vessels in the earlier houses, while in the later House L9F group coarse earthenware jars account for just under 2% of the ceramic vessels.

Such a low proportion of these vessels on a 19th century British site is striking, but these items would have been both heavy and difficult to transport; given their low value a significant trade in these would probably not have been economical. However, it is equally possible that there was no great need for ceramic storage vessels, as vessels in other materials, such as baskets, would probably have been used for storing the bulk of domestic foodstuffs and other commodities, while potatoes would have been stored in the ground. Smaller-scale storage, especially of liquids, is possibly indicated by jars and bottles of brown salt-glazed stoneware which are present in all of the Balnabodach houses, although equally they may have been used to transports such commodities as beer and whisky.

Dishes which may have been used as milk pans are found in all of the Balnabodach houses in redware with or without some form of slip decoration, which is either a trailed cream-coloured slip, or a slip coat in the same colour. There are two such dishes in each of the Balnabodach houses, except L8A in which there are three, while there are also two dishes in a lead-glazed coarse earthenware in the House L8C assemblage which may also have been used as milk pans. Given the importance of milk to the diet of the islanders, the small number of possible dairying vessels is striking, but again vessels in other materials may well have answered the need here.

The ceramic assemblage from House L9F is somewhat different from those of the other Balnabodach houses. This is to a great extent due to its later date; ceramics became more widely available as industrial manufacture expanded in mainland Britain, not least in Scotland, and as improvements to the transport infrastructure facilitated the movement of manufactured goods throughout the whole of Britain. The later date of the House L9F assemblage accounts for the greater quantity of teawares amongst the ceramics, as more people in the islands had access to tea in the second half of the 19th century; the number of vessels of bone china reflects the increased occurrence throughout the country of this fine translucent ware in domestic ceramic assemblages at the lower end of the socio-economic scale in this period; and the large number of grey stoneware preserve jars illustrates the extent to which these were being produced by a number of industrial ceramic factories in Scotland and England during the final quarter of the 1880s.

If the types of vessel present in excavated assemblages can shed some light upon foodways and the manner in which food was consumed, the types of decoration on ceramics have the potential to provide evidence for the economic means of their users. George Miller has shown how the price of ceramics is directly related to the type of decoration used (Miller 1980; Miller 1991), and any form of decoration will have raised the price of wares to some extent.

In all of the Balnabodach house assemblages the majority of the refined wares are decorated in some fashion. While this may indicate a real preference for decorated wares, it is also reasonable to look for a connection between the composition of assemblages and the ability or willingness of the consumer to acquire decorated in preference to undecorated wares.

In the House L8A group 93% of the refined wares vessels (73% of the sherds) are decorated; in the House L8C and L8D groups the figure is 84% and 80% of the vessels respectively; and in the later House L9F group 70% of the vessels are decorated, a lower figure which is largely due to the late-19th century preference for undecorated bone china vessels, ten of which are present here. This is a consistently high proportion across all the houses, and one which compares well with the other excavated blackhouse assemblages; decorated ceramics seem to have been acquired for preference in the Western Isles, a situation which is broadly true of 19th century sites in Britain as a whole. So we must consider the types of decoration represented in these blackhouse assemblages.

The preponderance in the Western Isles of ceramics with sponged decoration has been commented upon (Webster 1999, 60–61, 68; Kelly 1996, 68), but there are important factors at work here other than a suggested overwhelming preference for the products of Scottish factories (Webster 1999, 67–68). In fact, the majority of these sponge-decorated wares are very difficult to attribute to a manufacturing centre (see below), although their earlier introduction by Scottish factories has been claimed (Kelly *et al* 2001, 8). On the other hand, it is clear that from the time of their manufacture on a large scale, perhaps during the 1830s, they became widely used on sites in the Western Isles. There is little price information available for sponge-decorated wares, but where this does exist it shows that for their period they were usually the cheapest decorated type of pottery available (Miller 1991, 6). It would appear that during the 1830s and 1840s sponge-decorated wares to a great extent replaced slip-decorated wares at the bottom end of the price range. These 'dipped' wares (the contemporary term) were themselves the cheapest decorated hollow wares available until the widespread manufacture and use of sponge-decorated wares (Miller 1991, 6).

At Balnabodach, more than a third of the refined wares from House L8A are of the cheapest decorated types of their day; slip-decorated wares account for 10% of the refined wares, while sponge-decorated wares constitute 29%. In House L8C, 2% of the refined wares are slip-decorated, while 22% are sponge-decorated, and in House L8D these figures are 11% slip-decorated, compared to 18% sponge-decorated. In these earlier assemblages, it is the whitewares which are most likely to have sponged decoration, which is consistent with its growing popularity from the 1830s onwards. In the later L9F group, just 2% of the refined wares are slip-decorated, while 24% are sponge-decorated. This figure effectively illustrates the decline in popularity of slip-decorated wares in the later-19th century. The high proportion of the cheapest decorated wares goes some way towards reinforcing the notion of a population with limited resources to spend on ceramics, but the picture is not so clear.

Most of the houses also have a significant proportion of wares with printed decoration. In House L8A 12% of the refined wares are printed, while in House L8C this figure is 29% and in House L8D it is 21% or 23%, depending upon whether an over-glaze printed blackware vessel is included. In the later House L9F group, the percentage of printed wares is exactly the same (26%) as that of the two cheaper types of decoration combined. During the 19th century, wares with printed decoration were generally the most expensive type on the Staffordshire potters' price fixing lists (Miller *et al* 1994, 234), and their presence in quantity in these houses indicates that the people of Balnabodach were not merely acquiring the cheapest wares. Whatever the motivation, and whatever the limitations on choice which resulted from difficulties in supply, deliberate choices were being made to purchase more expensive ceramic items in preference to cheaper items of the same form.

Miller has demonstrated how the differential in price between decorated and undecorated ceramics narrowed as the 19th century progressed (Miller 1991; Miller 1994). In 1814, for example, printed ten-inch plates were 3.33 times more expensive than undecorated equivalents (Miller 1991, 14). However, as competition increased within the ceramics industry, and as it continued to produce more than the market could consume, prices fell; by 1854 printed plates were only 1.86 times more expensive than undecorated ones (*ibid.*), and consequently decoration – even printed decoration – came within reach of a larger sector of the pottery buying public. This is true of all forms of

decoration. The result was that printed wares are now a significant feature of all excavated assemblages dating to the middle of the 19th century and later, and thereafter undecorated wares are a rarity in these groups.

While printed decoration in early 19th century assemblages is worthy of note on account of its higher price, the same is also true of over-glaze painted decoration, which was more expensive on account of the additional firing – or firings – required to harden on the decoration. A number of vessels so decorated are amongst the earlier ceramics from Balnabodach Houses L8A, L8C and L8D and, while perhaps not the most attractive items to the modern eye, these bowls and a plate were not cheap items. In the 1820s and 1830s the price of bowls with over-glaze painted decoration was broadly comparable to that of printed wares (*ibid.*, 22).

Ceramics for Display?

The high proportion of decorated ceramics in assemblages from the Western Isles requires some consideration of their display potential. Dressers were an important item of furniture in Highland houses and their role in the display of ceramics is well known (Grant 1961, 173), although the date by which they come to be widely used seems open to further enquiry. The presence of dressers in the Western Isles is also reasonably well documented during the second half of the 19th century and is typified by the well stocked example in the blackhouse No. 42 at Arnol in Lewis. However, the Arnol blackhouse was not constructed until c. 1875 (Fenton 1995, 25) and it would be a mistake to conclude that, simply because dressers were an important feature of later 19th century houses, they were commonly used for the displaying ceramics in the early 1800s (Webster 1999, 57). On the contrary, the documentary evidence for the use of dressers, and therefore for the display of ceramics, within the blackhouses of the Western Isles is lacking before the middle of the 19th century. References to a general absence of *any* significant items of furniture and of other material possessions are numerous and this situation would seem to preclude a need for, and the use of dressers at this time.

In 1828, for example, in a house on Berneray David Stevenson, 'found several women and a number of children all squatting on the ground round a fire of peats on the floor and without any chimney, and except for a few cooking materials we saw no other articles of furniture whatever. In the other apartment was a large box-bed and a rude weaving loom. There 4 or 5 children of the family made their bed of straw on the floor, with only a single plaid to cover them'(Mair 1978, 143).

The situation of Skye may have been different in the earlier 19th century, being closer to, and more easily accessible from the mainland, although descriptions of blackhouses made in 1840 suggest a similarly poor level of furnishing. Houses at Kilmuir comprised three rooms, 'The middle apartment is the one principally occupied by the family, who have the fire in the centre of the floor, over which the crook is suspended from the rafters above. On one side of the fire, a wooden bench or rude sofa is placed, of sufficient size to contain five or six people, while on the other side is found the good-wife's 'sunnag' or rustic arm chair, of plaited straw, near which are the cradle, spinning wheel, 'amraidh' or cupboard, a large covered pot containing the kelt for family dress, undergoing the slow process of indigo dye, and the other paraphernalia which are indispensable for immediate family use. The inmost apartment serves the purpose of barn or bedroom, sometimes both, while that next the door is occupied by the cattle' (MacGregor 1840, 268). The same basic layout is followed at Snizort with one room given over to animals; 'Of the other two apartments, one is the sittingroom of the family, and the other both bedroom and barn; but some have a separate place for thrashing their corn. The fire is placed in the middle of the floor, and the smoke finds its way through a hole in the roof, or by the door. The leading articles of furniture, which is of the humblest description, consist of a table of very rough workmanship, a few stools, two or three chairs, and an easy chair called a *sunnag*, made of straw, and the sole property of the good wife. In the more respectable houses, there is along the wall a bench made in the form of a sofa, on which half a dozen people can sit. In the want of this convenience, there is a row of stones covered with turf' (MacLeod 1840, 292). At Duirinish, 'Houses are wretchedly filthy…The furniture is very scanty and rude. A couple of bedsteads, filled with straw or heather or ferns, a few chairs, and a table, generally complete the list. Such of the family as cannot find room in the beds sleep on the floor, and a stone is always a good substitute for a chair. Indeed, there are some houses where no chair is used, stones, pieces of dried turf, and one or two small stools or settles constituting the only seats.' (Clerk1840, 345–346).

In describing the blackhouses of western Lewis in 1866, Captain Thomas writes, 'in the middle of the floor; on the right is a bench of wood, stone or turfs, on which the men sit; on the opposite side the women perform their domestic duties. Tables and chairs are almost unknown, but the evident modern luxury of bedsteads and a dresser are quite usual. I am not sure of the date of their introduction; but they cannot have been long in use, from the former scarcity of wood, at least planks' (Thomas 1866, 155–156). His plans of Lewis blackhouses, when they show the position occupied by the dresser, invariably show them at right angles to the far wall of the house (i.e. that without the doorway) along the line dividing the human and animal halves of the house; this is not the case at Arnol. Visiting a house on Berneray in 1863, Isabella Bird comments that it was, 'finished with tables, benches, boxes, beds and stools of driftwood', but makes no mention of a dresser (Mair 1978, 143). Even in the 1880s, dressers were by no means ubiquitous, as Mrs Murray remarked on the absence of one in a Mingulay house, 'A little table but no dresser; one small chair, one three-legged pot, and kettle…' and 'Three stout kists, the property of the girls of the family who had just returned from fishing at Peterhead. This is about all' (Mair 1978, 87).

The date of the first use of dressers in the Western Isles must, therefore remain a matter of conjecture, but their early use cannot be supported by the available evidence. Nevertheless, at the Alt Chrisal blackhouse on Barra, a rectangular cobbled area of 3.3 x 1.4m. was marked out by a stone kerb. Its position directly opposite the house's main entrance - the position occupied by the dresser at the Arnol blackhouse - has led to its interpretation as a stand for a dresser (Branigan and Merrony 2000, 11–12). This cannot be substantiated.

Repaired Ceramics

The high incidence of ceramic vessels which have been repaired has already been noted in the excavated assemblages from blackhouses at Airigh Mhuillin on South Uist (Symonds 2000, 207) and House Island, one of the Shiants. The ceramics from Balnabodach also include sherds which have been drilled as part of the repair process, with sherds being joined using what were, in effect, metal staples. There are two sherds from House L8A, four from House L8C, two from House L8C, and one from House L9F.

The practice was commonplace well into the 20th century, until the introduction of epoxy adhesives and evidence can be seen in many modern collections where it tends to be porcelains or good quality earthenwares and stonewares which have been repaired in this way. Archaeologically the practice is well-known on ceramic vessels from the Roman period onwards, and by the early post-medieval period glass vessels were also being repaired in this way (Willmott 2001). Archaeological finds of 19th century ceramics with evidence for repair are rare on sites in mainland Britain, but are more commonplace in remote situations such as the Western Isles. In North America, a high incidence of repaired ceramics has been noted in the 19th century seasonal shore based fishing station on Saddle Island in Red Bay, Labrador (Burke 2000).

Given the more frequent occurrence of repaired ceramics in remote locations, it is possible that difficulties of supply might have necessitated the repair of broken items, as replacements may have been some time in arriving, especially when adverse seasonal weather conditions might make contact with the outside world dangerous or even impossible. This is not a factor which is relevant to Willmott's consideration of repairs to 22 17th century glass vessels from London, Surrey and Oxford (Willmott 2001, 102–103). He discounts their repair for functional purposes, and offers three possible explanations : repair for display, for the retention of the 'antique' and for purely personal reasons, or the 'heirloom factor'.

These explanations might be relevant to any group of material culture so treated, but the quantity of repaired vessels from blackhouse sites in the Western Isles suggests that they cannot all have had value as heirlooms, and indeed many of them had no great age to them at the probable time of their discard; they are unlikely, therefore, to have been regarded as antiques. The possible role of industrially made wares as items for display in the 19th century, defining and strengthening a cultural identity in the Western Isles, has been discussed in the context of the dresser (Webster 1999), and this hypothesis may withstand scrutiny for the later 19th century when dressers were more a feature of houses. For the first half of the 19th century, however, the evidence does not appear to support display as a primary reason for repair, although a large repaired pearlware bowl from Pabbay has good quality over-glaze painted decoration (Fig. 6.2a) and was almost certainly an expensive piece with display potential. Typically, though, repaired vessels are just as likely to be undecorated as they are decorated, and they are mostly standard domestic wares. At Balnabodach, the repaired vessels from House L8A are both sponge-decorated bowls in whiteware (one being WWE 1); in the House L8C group there are two undecorated whiteware sherds, possibly of bowls, and two whiteware plates, one undecorated (WWE 27) and one with

Figure 6.2 Modern ceramics from Pabbay, Fuiay and Sandray

a) pearlware bowl from Pabbay with over-glaze painted decoration in red, blue green, purple and black, with drilled hole from repair c 1820

b) pearlware sherds from a blackhouse on Fuiay: note bowl sherds (centre) with trailed slip decoraction applied from a four-chambered slip bottle

c) white earthenwares from a blackhouse on Fuiay, with sponged and painted decoration in blue, 1840s

d) white earthenware bowl with sponged decoration in grey from Sandray, late 19th century

e) white earthenware sherds with sponged decoration from Pabbay late 19th century

printed 'Willow' pattern decoration (WWE 12); the House L8D group has a pearlware saucer with over-glaze painted decoration (PLW 8) and a whiteware sponged and painted bowl (WWE 2). There is a single sponged and painted bowl in the L9F group (Fig. 5.18a). A further undecorated body sherd of pearlware was amongst the material recovered from a blackhouse on Fuiay. Chronology has no obvious bearing upon the incidence of repair, especially in view of the level of repair seen at Airigh Mhuillin where the majority of the finds date to the 1810s and 1820s.

A further factor which may influence a decision about whether or not to repair a piece, and one which is difficult to substantiate with the sort of evidence available, is poverty and the inability of island populations to afford replacements on a regular basis. Making do in this way, would be consistent with a lack of ready money, and tenants had difficulty in acquiring capital as a result of high rents and the fragility of the local economy which could vary dramatically from year to year (Gray 1957, 53). At best, however, we can get but a general view of the changing economic fortunes of the islands during the first half of the 19th century. Hardship there certainly was, with shortages and famines, the intermittent failure of inshore fishing, and the decline and eventual collapse of the kelp industry after the Napoleonic wars did nothing to help matters (Macinnes 1988, 86). Contemporary commentators, however, often wrote less of the poverty of the islanders than of their happy state: 'Though the people, in general, have not the many comforts which others in the south enjoy, they have fewer wants and are easily satisfied' (Cameron 1833, 130), and 'Their simple cottages are abodes of happiness and contentment' (Macrae 1836, 147).

Sources of the Ceramics

It can be very difficult to determine the sources of 18th and 19th century refined wares, unless they are marked, although decoration – particularly printed decoration – may be helpful in this regard. The problem is simply that by the early 19th century Staffordshire industrially made earthenwares, stonewares and bone chinas were effectively the industry standard (Barker 2001, 78). Identical wares were made by manufacturers throughout Britain, using identical processes and raw materials, moulds, copper plates, tools and equipment purchased from suppliers in Stoke-on-Trent, and often using Staffordshire workmen. This was not copying, *per se*; rather manufacturers simply produced in the style of their day the wares that would sell and, consequently, the wares of the majority of factories were to a great extent interchangeable.

The development of transport routes within Britain during the later 18th and 19th centuries, in particular improved river navigation, the turnpiking of roads, and the construction of canal and railway networks, greatly facilitated the movement of goods and increased access to items from a wide range of sources. These improvements facilitated the distribution of Staffordshire wares throughout Britain, and encouraged the export of ever greater quantities from the ports of Liverpool and Hull. There is evidence, however, that Staffordshire ceramics were also shipped out through the ports of Glasgow (Greenock) and Leith (Quail 1983–4, 44). Other manufacturing centres may also have done the same, using Glasgow and other Scottish ports as the point of shipment

to Europe, the Caribbean, North America, and perhaps also for the coasting trade. Further research is needed in this area.

In assessing the likely source of industrial wares excavated within and outside Britain, the balance of probability will generally favour a north Staffordshire origin, where there was by far the largest concentration of manufacturers, unless there are local reasons which dictate that the situation should be otherwise. However, such vague assumptions are not helpful in considering the sources of ceramics found in the Western Isles. Many of the Balnabodach pearlwares would not be out of place in north Staffordshire production groups, but other sources cannot be ruled out. Given the rise of pottery production in Scotland, and in Glasgow in particular, during the first half of the 19th century, it would be surprising if Scottish products were not well-represented in Hebridean ceramic assemblages of this date, and as the majority of the contact between the Western Isles and mainland Scotland seems to have been through Greenock and Glasgow, the products of Glasgow potteries should be better represented than those of the Forth potteries.

Despite the difficulty of identifying the products of individual factories and manufacturing centres during the first half of the 19th century – a situation exacerbated by the paucity of good excavated production groups of this date outside north Staffordshire – there is evidence of probable Glasgow-made ceramics amongst the three early Balnabodach house groups. For example, one vessel from House L8C with the blue-printed pattern 'Exhibition' (Fig. 5.14b) was probably made in Glasgow by J Cochran & Co. of the Verreville Pottery (H Kelly, pers. comm.), although a version of this design was also made by Glasgow potters J & M P Bell & Co. and by the Caledonian Pottery, also in Glasgow (Kelly 1999, 58), while in Stoke-on-Trent it was used by Thomas Godwin of Burslem, (Coysh and Henrywood 1982, 98). Surprisingly, none of the other printed wares can be positively assigned to a specific manufacturing centre, a sad indictment of the current state of research into the ceramics of this period.

However, there is also evidence that some of the slip-decorated wares are Scottish in origin. It has been suggested that trailed slip decoration in four colours, applied with a four-chambered slip bottle, is a distinctive Scottish practice (J Rickard, pers. comm.), and finds from Scottish production sites would seen to support this. The use of a four-chambered slip bottle to decorate near identical London shape bowls in pearlware can be seen in the House L8D assemblage from Balnabodach (Fig. 5.15b) and amongst the surface collection sherds from a blackhouse site on Fuiay (Fig. 6.2b); slip-decorated sherds recovered from production waste at the Verreville factory site provide exact parallels for these (H Kelly, pers. comm.).

There are other close similarities with sherds found on the Verreville site, the most striking of which are with the pearlwares with over-glaze painted decoration in a dull olive green, red and black, such as PLW 2, from House L8A, PLW 5, 6 and 7 from House L8C and the London shape bowls PLW 2 and PLW 11 from House L8D (H. Kelly, pers. comm.). No comparable pieces have been found in Stoke-on-Trent and a Scottish origin therefore seems probable for these distinctive vessels.

Figure 6.3 Modern ceramics from Pabbay, Mingulay and Sandray

a) white earthenware base sherds with printed marks of J and M P Bell & Co Ltd in blue (from Balnabodach house L9F)

b) base sherd of Rockingham ware vessel from Pabbay with maker's mark moulded in relief; Eagle Pottery Bridgeton, Glasgow. Late 19th-early 20th-century

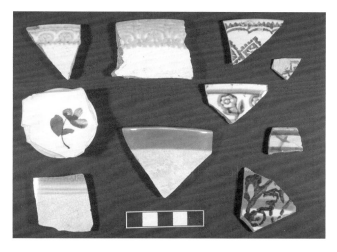

c) sponged and painted white earthenwares, Mingulay, late 19th-century. Top left: two plate rims with 'Grecian' pattern

d) white earthenware bowl from Sandray with sponged decoration in red; possibly made at the Clyde Pottery, Greenock, late 19th-century

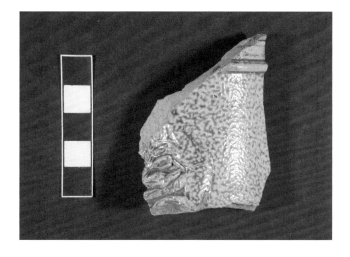

e) Rhenish stoneware bottle with applied bartmann-type face mask, from Sandray, late 17th-early 18th-century

The vast majority of all sponged wares are unmarked and are consequently difficult to assign to a manufacturing centre. However, given the probable widespread manufacture of sponged wares in Scotland from at least the 1830s (Kelly et al 2001, 8), it can be assumed with some confidence that a significant proportion of the sponged wares from Balnabodach are Scottish in origin, but proof will not be forthcoming until identical decorated wares are found on production sites or else with maker's marks. The Balnabodach sponged wares, such as the blue sponged bowl WWE 22 from House L8A, are of types not yet found in significant quantities in north Staffordshire before 1850, but there are close similarities amongst the material found on the Verreville factory site (H Kelly, pers. comm.).

The Scottish pottery industry expanded tremendously from the middle of the 19th century, and given the scale of production at some of the very large factories such as Bell's Glasgow Pottery and Cochran's Verreville and Britannia Potteries also in Glasgow, it would be surprising if later ceramic groups from the islands did not contain a significant proportion of Scottish-made ceramics.

Indeed it seems likely that the majority of the ceramics from the later House L9F at Balnabodach are Scottish. Amongst these are certainties such as the printed vessels with marks of J & M P Bell of Glasgow (Fig. 6.3a), and a Rockingham vessel with a possible moulded eagle mark such as that used by the Eagle Pottery in Bridgeton, Glasgow (Kelly 1999, 89). Another Rockingham vessel from Pabbay is definitely from this factory, as it bears, in relief, a partial moulded mark incorporating the text 'GROSVENOR / FIREPROOF / ...', with an eagle facing right between the two lines of the inscription (Fig. 6.3b). The Eagle Pottery was founded as the Bridgeton Pottery by Frederick Grosvenor in 1869 (Kelly 1999, 89). The factory changed its name to the Eagle Pottery in 1882 and thereafter sometimes used an eagle as a trade mark. The firm became Grosvenor & Son in 1889 upon Frederick's son Donald becoming a partner. The factory closed in 1923. Rockingham ware was produced at many Scottish potteries during the 19th century, but such clear indications of origin are rare. An impressed eagle mark on the underside of a grey stoneware preserve jar from Balnabodach House L9F (Fig. 5.18f) is also from the Eagle pottery and of the same late-19th to early-20thcentury date (H. Kelly, pers. comm.).

The House L9F sponged wares are quite unlike documented Staffordshire sponged wares of the same date, although the body of evidence to support this assertion is not great. A Scottish origin for the majority of these seems likely, especially for the sherds of the grey sponged 'Grecian' pattern (Fig. 5.18c) which was made at a number of Scottish factories, including Bell's Glasgow Pottery (Kelly 1999, 12), Cochran's Britannia Pottery, Glasgow, (*ibid.*, 36, 41), the Bo'ness Pottery (*ibid.*, 25), and the Bridgeness Pottery, also in Bo'ness (*ibid.*, 30). 'Grecian' pattern sponged sherds have also been found amongst the material recovered from the area of the village on the island of Mingulay (Fig. 6.3c). Another Glasgow factory may be the source of a whiteware bowl with sponged decoration in red

comprising four-petalled flowers with fringes found in the north dunes of Sandray (Fig. 6.3d); Kelly et al (2001, 236) illustrate an unmarked bowl with an identical sponged design, but state that vessels with this motif have been attributed to the Clyde Pottery of Greenock.

Many of the ceramics from Balnabodach and the nearby island groups cannot be sourced with any confidence. If the refined wares are difficult to place, the unrefined vessels are the more so. The majority of the 19th century redwares, coarse earthenwares, yellow ware, brown salt-glazed stonewares and other stonewares are likely to be Scottish-made, and indeed are common finds in the Western Isles, but without exact parallels it is difficult to be certain.

Some of the ceramics from Balnabodach and the nearby islands, however, are clearly not Scottish products. One sherd, at least, originates from the north-east of England. This is the whiteware plate from House L8D at Balnabodach which has an impressed maker's mark 'SCOTT', indicating manufacture at Anthony Scott & Co.'s Southwick Pottery at Sunderland, during the period 1838–1854 (Godden 1991, 587).

The white salt-glazed stoneware mug from House L8A (Fig. 5.9c) is a type which was made in north Staffordshire until the end of the 18th century, although numerous other centres, including Prestonpans (Kemp, 1981; Quail 1986) and Liverpool, were also making white salt-glazed stonewares at the same time. A Liverpool source is almost certain for the soft-paste porcelain bowl from House L8A (Fig. 5.9c) which was probably made at Seth Pennington's factory (M. Hillis, pers. comm.). Amongst the earlier wares from the nearby island sites, there are from Sandray trailed and combed slipwares of Staffordshire or Bristol type, although a provenance in other English manufacturing centres is a remote possibility, and a brown salt-glazed stoneware bottle from the Rhineland from Sheader on Sandray (Fig. 6.3e).

Vessels of Chinese porcelain, present in some quantity at Airigh Mhuillin on South Uist, are barely represented at all at Balnabodach. Where they do occur, such as PLN 1 from Balnabodach House L8D, they are not teawares, as was consistently the case in the earlier South Uist blackhouses. This is simply a matter of chronology. The formal importation of Chinese porcelains by the East India Company ceased in 1791 (Godden 1988, 21–25, 29), and while individual ships' masters were able to continue importation on a small scale, by the end of the 18th century British pottery factories came to satisfy the demand for decorated teawares, especially with their pearlwares.

Ceramic assemblages excavated on Hebridean sites are characterised by a fairly uniform range of wares. While this may be an indication of a strong local preference for certain vessel forms or types of decoration (Webster 1999, 63–69), it is more probably a reflection of the methods of acquisition and their limitations. These are islands without shops and with few settlements of any size, and the potential for exercising consumer choice within a recognisable market seems remote. Supply on a small scale would have had the effect of restricting choice, while creating the semblance of a strong cultural preference, which may be misleading when archaeological assemblages are interpreted. Ceramics acquired at the factory gate, for example, might well have included a number of identical pieces which could, through the agency of travelling peddlers carrying only small quantities of wares, reach their final destination as an intact parcel of goods. In this way, a single factory's wares, or the wares of one manufacturing centre, could easily dominate assemblages of excavated ceramics in remote settlements supplied predominantly in this way.

It is difficult to find documentary evidence that relates directly to the trade in ceramics to the islands, but there is evidence to indicate that packmen or travelling peddlers were important to the local economy, selling small quantities of a range of goods, which almost certainly included pottery. In Skye, 'vagrants, such as gipsies, rag-men, vendors of crockery, tinsmiths, egg-dealers, and old-clothes-men' were said to be responsible for introducing tea drinking, tobacco chewing and smoking – which were previously unknown – amongst the lower orders of society, following improvements in communications with the mainland and, particularly, with Glasgow (Mackinnon 1840, 313). In South Uist, egg dealers took their goods to Glasgow and Greenock in small boats, returning home with, amongst other things, tobacco and crockery (Maclean 1837, 193).

The idea that the Western Isles were isolated from the mainland and from mainland culture does not withstand scrutiny. Besides the movements of peddlers and small dealers in various commodities, there were important regular contacts in many areas of business which were essential to the survival of the islands' economies. The people of Barra, for example, were well known as fishermen (Nicolson 1840, 209) and maintained close contact with the mainland as the market in which they sold their fish. From the late-18th century the sea around Barra supported 20 or 30 fishing boats (MacQueen, E. 1794, 335), and fish and oil were sent to Glasgow (*ibid.*, 149). Forty years later there were a similar number of boats taking ling and cod to Glasgow and Greenock : 'country boats ply at all seasons of the year to Glasgow with fish and other such articles as the country produces' (Nicolson 1840, 214).

Of equal importance to the economy of the Western Isles was the trade in cattle. Since the 17th century, the cattle had been the islands' main export and it was from their sale that much of the islanders' income was generated (Shaw 1980, 195). The cattle trade was conducted at fairs or markets which were held on the islands at least annually, if not more often. These were attended by cattle dealers who shipped the cattle purchased across to Skye (for example, MacQueen, A. 1794, 306; Maclean 1837, 194). On Barra, 'The only markets are in the summer and autumn for disposing of surplus cows and horses to dealers from the mainland, who carry them to the southern markets' (Nicolson 1840, 216), while in the late-18th century at these fairs between 200 and 500 cattle were sold to drovers and 100 hides of beef were sent to Glasgow (MacQueen, E. 1794, 341). No trade is one-way; it is inconceivable that cattle dealers would have visited the islands with empty vessels, but precisely what their cargoes might have been can only be guessed at.

The kelp trade, too, brought the islands into close and regular contact with vessels from a number of mainland ports, and in particular Glasgow. In the heyday of kelp production there would have been a significant coming and going of vessels; in 1799, for example, it is recorded that 200 tons of kelp were sent annually from Barra to Liverpool and Leith (MacQueen, E.1794, 341), while in 1840, long after the collapse of the kelp trade, four vessels were engaged in taking kelp out of Barra (Nicolson 1840, 213–214).

Further contact with the outside world – mainland Britain and beyond – would have occurred as a result of the extensive fishing of the waters by outside fishing fleets. The fisheries also provided employment opportunities for both men as crews and women as fishwives and resulted in both spending protracted periods away from home (Gray 1957, 53; Clerk 1841, 347).

Many other opportunities existed for islanders to gain experience of the wider world. Seasonal employment as agricultural labourers on the farms of Lowland Scotland was available to many and the employment of islanders is well-documented (for example, Mackinnon 1840, 308; Gray 1957, 53). There was also military service, which attracted many thousands of Highlanders during the 18th and 19th centuries.

Conclusion

In broad terms, the Balnabodach ceramic assemblages are similar to those from excavated blackhouses on other islands of the Outer Hebrides, and are a fair representation of what was available in the market at the time. A high proportion of the less expensive wares is evident in all cases, but there is no shortage of more expensive ceramics with printed or over-glaze painted decoration, raising questions about the economic means of the islanders and the motives behind consumer choice. A limited, but consistent range of wares is present in all cases; bowls are common, suggesting a diet based upon stews or gruels, but so too are plates in a range of sizes, with connotations of a more English style of dining involving tables and chairs; teawares are also found at all of the sites, although in differing proportions, despite evidence to suggest that tea was not widely available before the middle of the 19th century. All of the assemblages contain ceramics from a variety of sources, although the growing importance of the trade in Scottish-made ceramics is evident by the mid-19th century, if not earlier; by the late-19th century it appears that the ceramics used in the Western Isles were almost entirely from Scottish factories. All sites exhibit a limited range of decorative patterns which may be consistent with a restricted supply on a limited scale, and the frequent occurrence of repaired vessels would also seem to suggest that there may frequently have been difficulties in acquiring new supplies of goods from the mainland.

What we see at Balnabodach are ceramics which would not be out of place in households on mainland Britain, albeit with a distinctive character in the composition of the assemblages. An embracing of at least the trappings of a mainland Anglo-Scottish way of life seems to have been complete early in the 19th century, but the precise way in which mainland British material culture was employed within the blackhouse is still uncertain. Here was a domestic environment which had no obvious history of consumerism, and in which people would have had only a limited awareness of the culture which they were buying into with these industrially made goods. The available evidence suggests that this is not the obvious environment in which factory made ceramics would readily find a place, and yet here they are in quantities, and in a variety of styles and forms, which necessitates further investigation.

Acknowledgements
I should like to thank Henry Kelly, Jonathan Rickard, Maurice Hillis and Don Carpentier for helpful comments on the ceramics; James Symonds and Keith Branigan for encouragement and an abundance of practical support; and Miranda Goodby for her patience during the writing of this piece. Some of the background research on these and other related assemblages was undertaken with an AHRB Research Exchange Grant. Without this award, this work would have been the poorer and Chapter 6 could not have been written.

7

The Rise and Fall of the Kelping Industry in the Western Isles

J M Bumsted

The kelping industry, which flourished in the western Highlands and Islands of Scotland between 1770 and the 1830s, has always had a rather negative reputation, chiefly because in the wake of its demise some of the nastiest clearances of the region were conducted. The industry clearly encouraged an overpopulation of the lands adjacent to the shores where the kelping was conducted, and when it could no longer support that population, it was replaced by other improvement strategies, nearly all of which included large-scale evictions of people. Most of those evicted ended up emigrating to Canada. Whether the industry deserves all the opprobrium which has been heaped upon it is another matter, however. It is certainly true that kelp provided a handful of Highland landlords with a handsome income for many years. It is equally true that the changing state of the kelping industry led to one of the great reversals of landlord policy in Highland history, from a fierce hostility to loss of population through emigration before 1815 to an equally fierce determination to depopulate through emigration, especially after 1830. But kelping was in the ascendancy for over half a century, from 1770 to about 1825, and thus could hardly be described as an ephemeral business.

With hindsight we can see that, as Eric Richards (1982, 133) has put it, the kelp industry 'possessed no long-term foundation'. The income from it was 'squandered', and the human society it created may have become far too dependent on its continuation. On the other hand, if neither landlords nor people planned for kelp's decline, this failure was no different for kelping than for most other extractive industries based on natural resources, which could either run out of raw material or find demand for them disappear. (1) If kelping encouraged exploitation of workers and excessive profit-taking among owners, it was merely evoking typical and familiar patterns among both groups. Moreover, the kelp industry was a perfect example of an industry which was entirely dependent upon government trade policy. It was destroyed not by its own internal logic or by inefficiency – indeed, it became increasingly efficient in response to competition – but by a public decision not to protect it from that competition.

Kelp and Kelp Making

The manufacture of kelp extracted from the seaweed an alkaline ash which was used in various industries. 'Kelp' was at the time and since used interchangeably to describe both the seaweed and the calcined ashes of the seaweed.(2) The ashes contained lower grade vegetable alkali, useful in the manufacture of soap, alum, glass, and in bleaching and calico-printing. But kelp contained other valuable salts and ingredients. The soap-makers got from it a salt called 'muriate of potash', which they sold to the alum-makers, and other simple processes would later distil iodine, once its medical importance was understood in the later 19th

century (Anderson 1831)(3) The making of kelp started around 1735 on North Uist, having been imported from Ireland, and after 1750 was in operation on several places. The raw material was a variety of seaweeds – tangle or red ware, prickly tang, black tang, bell-wrack – which grew on the rocks between low and high water marks. Different weeds produced better kelp for some purposes than for others, and much depended on what the ultimate usage would be. As we shall see, that usage changed over time. What did not change is that kelp-making was a classic 'cottage industry', for it could be conducted on a part-time basis from the home of the producer.

Kelp was manufactured on many shores in the British Isles, but principally on the Isle of Aran, in the Shetland Islands, on the Isle of Orkney, and in the western Highlands and Islands, particularly the Hebrides (Jameson 1798; Thompson 1983; Waddell et al 1994). It was seemingly an ideal Hebridean enterprise, since the raw material was one of the few natural resources readily available on the islands. Most of the kelp made in the Golden Age of the kelp industry, from 1770 to 1830, came from the Outer Hebrides. The process of manufacture was labour intensive, requiring neither great skill nor capital investment in physical plant, and the ultimate product was sufficiently concentrated as to be relatively easily stored without spoiling until transported out of the region by water. The weed was cut from around rocks with hooks and sickles by workers standing in ice-cold water, often up to their waists, or working from boats. Or it was gathered as 'drift' on the beaches; before 1840 harvested kelp was regarded as of superior quality to drift and gathering each type was often the right of a different class of residents. In the early period, the weed on the sheltered or eastern side of the islands was held to be far superior to that on the western side, although the eastern side was often much more difficult of access overland than the west. The weed was carried to the beach in creels or barrows, and it was then spread out to be dried by the sun and wind on shore.

The harvesting was not easy work. One contemporary wrote, 'If one figures to himself a man, and one or more of his children, engaging from morning to night in cutting, drying, and otherwise preparing the seaweeds, at a distance of many miles from his home, or in a remote island; often for hours together wet to his knees and elbows; living upon oatmeal and water with occasionally fish, limpets and crabs; sleeping on the damp floor of a wretched hut; and with no other fuel than twigs or heath; he will perceive that this manufacture is none of the most agreeable' (MacGillivray 1831, 301). Several generations earlier, the missionary John Lane Buchanan had observed 'the meagre looks and feeble bodies of the belaboured creatures, without the necessary hours of sleep, and all over in dirty ragged clothes, would melt any but a tyrant into compassion, yet if any quantity of their set complement of kelp remained unfinished, the deficiency must be accumulated to their former debts to make up the pretended loss to the cruel men' (Buchanan 1793, 198).

The dried weed was then hauled by Highland ponies (which grazed all year round upon the machair) to a primitive kiln. The traditional process of manufacture was described by one observer in the *Old Statistical Account*:

> The kilns that are made use of for this purpose, are either erected with stones in the sand, or dug in the beach, of a circular form, and about twelve inches deep, and about four feet broad. In these [the kelpers] make holes for the free circulation of air. [when] they imagine they have about one third of a tun of kelp, they begin to stir it strongly, or to rake it with a clumsy instrument of iron formed for the purpose. Much of the excellence of the kelp depends on the perfection of this operation. Great care must be taken to keep it free of sand, of stones, and every sort of extraneous liquid. The contents of the kiln must be made perfectly liquid, and somewhat resembling the metal in a furnace; and in this state it is sometimes very difficult to preserve it of the requisite purity. The liquid requires to be left in the pit to cool, which it generally does in about two days, when it congeals and hardens into a solid ponderous mass, which is broken and piled up on the shore, till an occasion occurs to ship it for the market

(Shapinsay, Orkney in *The Statistical Account of Scotland* (Sinclair 1791–7), 14, 233–4; for excavation plans of kilns on Barra, Branigan and Foster 1995, 94ff).

The gradual burning was done on peat fires and stirred with long iron tools known as clatts until it turned into what another observer called a 'hot pasty mess'. As John Lane Buchanan described the procedure, 'After one floor full is burnt of the kelp, or ware, two men work the red hot liquid with irons made for the purpose, until it becomes hard; and then they burn another stratum above, and the same operation is gone through, until that also is hardened into a solid body, and so on from one stratum to another' (Buchanan 1793, 80). In the period before 1840, each individual harvester or family of harvesters burnt their own kelp. Tending peat fires for long hours was very hard on the eyes.

When completely cooked and cooled, the result was a brittle many-coloured substance less than one-twentieth the weight of the original weed. Since the kelp was desirable because of its alkaline content, its quality depended upon the alkaline percentage in the cooked product. This percentage in turn depended on the amount of alkali in the raw material, which varied from shore to shore, and on the care taken in reduction, which varied from harvester to harvester. Kelp was a more heterogeneous compound than its foreign competitors, such as barilla, and the quantity of free alkali ranged from 2 to 16 percent, mostly on the low end of the range (Anderson 1831, 21). The majority of kelp came from and was prepared on the Long Island, stretching from Lewis through Harris to the Uists to Barra, although some kelp was made on the mainland, in the Shetlands, in the Orkneys, and on the west coast of Ireland. In general, the alkali content improved the further north the kelp was harvested and made. The 'burnt' kelp was then hauled to a wharf – usually belonging to the landlord – or collected by boats on the beaches, whence it was shipped south to Hull, Leith, Liverpool, or other destinations in England and Lowland Scotland. The season for kelping was summer – June, July, and August, when the water was warm enough to wade in and the weather sufficiently dry for the manufacturing process.(for general background on kelping, Gray 1951; 1957; Hunter 1976, passim; Youngson 1973, especially 134–40) According to John McCulloch, 'the differences in the declivity of the shores, and the greater or less rise of the tides, together with more or less shelter from the prevalent surge, constitute the chief bases of the variations in a kelp estate' (MacCulloch 1824, I, 122).

The Origins and Early Development of Kelping

A combination of circumstances produced an increasingly great demand for burnt or made kelp after 1750. Industrial need for alkalines increased in the second half of the eighteenth century, and there was legislative protection against foreign substitutes such as potash and salt. Moreover, the constant warfare of the period often interrupted supplies of alkalines from overseas, especially barilla from Spain, previously the principal source for the British market. As a result, kelp prices edged inexorably upward, from £2 per tun in 1750 to £8 during the American war to £10 in 1800 and a high of £20 in 1810 (Youngson 1973, 135f; for a yearly run of prices 1768–1797, Cregean 1964, 188). The demand for kelp was greatly increased after 1808, and prices were at their highest from that year until the end of the Napoleonic Wars. Within this broad upward trend, prices were variable, depending on the quality of the kelp produced and the business acumen of those dealing with the southern markets. The Duke of Argyll frequently complained that his kelp was selling at far lower prices than other large landlords were receiving, and the best prices were probably consistently received by Clanranald and Lord Macdonald. But in general, the high prices encouraged an increasing emphasis on kelp-making until the market collapsed fairly abruptly in the 1820s.

There are a number of series of kelp prices in the archives and the secondary literature. One early series is from the Island of Mull (Cregeen 1964, 188):

1770–79	£4. 3
1780–89	£5
1790	£5. 15
1791	£4. 15
1792	£3. 15
1793	£3. 10
1794	£4. 10
1795	£6. 6
1796	£8. 4
1797	£8. 8

Another set from one Highland estate covers the later period (Youngson 1973, 138):

1815	£10. 10
1816	£9
1819	£10. 10
1820	£9. 15
1821	£8. 15
1822	£6. 15
1823	£7. 10
1824	£7
1825	£7
1826	£6
1827	£5. 10
1828	£4. 15
1829	£4. 17
1830–36	£4

Figures from the Clanranald papers (NAS GD 201/5/1232/2; NAS GD 201/5/1232/1) demonstrate that not all estates were receiving exactly the same average price at the same time:

Clanranald average prices	Lewis sales in Liverpool	
1811	£7. 25	
1812	£6. 11	
1816	£7	
1817	£8	
1818	£11. 2	£8. 16. 4
1819	£8. 10	£10. 12. 2
1820	£7. 15	£10. 12. 10
1821	£6. 7	
1824	£5. 8. 9	L£. 4
1825	£4. 12	£8. 33
1826		£6. 4. 9
1827		£5. 15. 9
1832	£4. 8	

What all evidence of kelp prices does suggest is that overall prices constantly increased until reaching an extreme (and untypical) high of £20 per tun around 1810, and then levelled off at a lower figure – somewhere around £10 per tun -- until 1820. The prices were lower during the decade of the 1820s, and began reaching the bottom in the early 1830s.

The Duke of Argyll's early experience with kelp was not untypical of that of the larger Highland lairds. As late as 1770, kelp made little contribution to the Duke's income; Tiree's rental of £852 was paid largely out of sales of whisky and barley. By 1806, however, Tiree's rental was £2,606 and the island's kelp sales worth £2,613. In 1799 the Duke advised his baillie on Tiree, 'As you inform me that small tenants can afford to pay more rent for farms on Tiry [sic] than gentlemen-farmers, owing to the manufacture of kelp, this determines me to let the farms to small tenants which have been and are at present possessed by tacksmen who reside upon farms in Mull' (Cregeen 1964, 48). Other lairds on the western coasts had similar experiences and similar reactions, especially with regard to the elimination of farming tacksmen and the emphasis upon small holders. As early as 1775, Colin Macneil of Boisdale admitted that kelp 'is our chief dependence here' (NAS GD201/5/1232/1). Tacksmen acting as kelping agents or ground officers remained on some estates, however. By 1800, five thousand tuns of kelp were being produced annually in the north-west, mainly on the estates of Macdonald of Clanranald, Lord Macdonald, the Earl of Seaforth, and the Duke of Argyll on Lewis, Harris, the Uists and Benbecula, the Outer Hebrides, Skye, Mull, and Tiree. At the high point of kelping around 1810, Clanranald was selling 1,000 tuns per year, Lord Macdonald 1,200, Seaforth 900, and the Duke of Argyll 400 (Gray 1951, 205). Between 1807 and 1809, Clanranald made an average profit of £9,454 per year from kelp, while his rentals brought in only £5297 (NAS GD 201/5/1332/7a). As prices gradually fell after 1810, the great kelping lairds pushed to increase the production of their estates, and Clanranald's rose to a high of £497 tuns in 1820 (NAS GD 201/6/2).

Whether prices were rapidly rising or merely substantial, they led to three developments in the kelping regions : landlords attempted increasingly to gain complete control of the industry; they encouraged subdivision to smallholders; and they encouraged or at least permitted the residence of people – pendiclers, cottars, and scallags – with whom they had no formal land relationships, but who provided labour to help manufacture the kelp (for overviews of life in these regions, Symonds 1999, 101–22; 2000, 197–210). Let us look at each of these developments in turn.

As the laird began to recognize the value of kelping, he sought to control it in his land dealings. The larger tacksmen had often been among the first to recognize the value of kelp. By 1776, Seaforth tacks on Lewis were specifying that the tacksman was not 'to cut any seaware fit for making kelp' (Grey 1951, 129ff). While the great kelping proprietors moved to control the manufacture and marketing of the kelp for themselves, other lairds with smaller amounts treated it as a resource to be let out to the highest bidder. According to one account from the western Highlands in the *Old Statistical Account of Scotland*, 'upon the shore of the glebe, which extends about ¾ of a mile, grows a profusion of sea-weed, of the sort fittest for kelp: to this the present incumbent thought he had a right; and that he might convert this seaweed to his own benefit, as a small addition to his small stipend; but in this he unexpectedly found himself opposed by the family of Reay, who thought fit to dispose of this very sea-weed, as well as the rest on their estate, by lease to a Peterhead Company'. He was forced to defend himself in court of session against a suit for damages, and lost the case, thus not only depriving him of kelping income but of the seaweed which was used to manure his land and pasture his cattle (the parish minister at Eddrachillis, in *The New Statistical Account of Scotland*, 6, 281).

Most of the great kelping lairds reorganized their estates in the last quarter of the eighteenth century to emphasize the manufacture of kelp. As early as 1763, Sir James Macdonald recognized that on his North Uist estate, kelping had 'enabled many people to keep families independent of lands'. Unlike his successors, he worried about 'a redundance of people who had multiplied to a greater degree than the profit of the community will support' (quoted in Richards 1982, I, 130). Despite Macdonald's concerns, leases and agreements increasingly dealt with the minutia of kelping. In 1798, the Clanranald factor recommended the rental of the farm of Miltun on South Uist to a tacksman for £200 sterling, allowing him the making of the kelp on the western shore. Factor Robert Brown explained his recommendation at enormous length, solely in terms of the kelping.(4) The Clanranald kelp contract in 1802, for example, bound the tenants leasing a farm 'to manufacture the kelp under such regulations as might be agreed on for the melioration of the kelp and good government of the Estate'. The tenants were to manufacture the kelp 'in a proper season' and 'in a good and sufficient & honest manner and well burnt and wrought without adulteration by allowing it to be mixed with stone gravel or clay sand or mud and shall be carefully preserved from damp or wet by the respective makers until the same is taken off their hands in the usual manner'. The penalty for neglect of appropriate manufacture was the market price of the kelp not made, with bad kelp to be destroyed (NAS GD 201/5/1232/1) Similar stipulations were written into Seaforth leases on Lewis (Macdonald 1978, 91). An ultimate sanction was removal from the estate in the next sett of the lands.

Kelping was generally recognized to be injurious to agriculture, partly because it produced smallholdings inadequate for livestock and extensive cultivation, but also because it kept the people fully engaged throughout the period they should have been tending their crops. James Macdonald noted in his book on Hebridean agriculture in 1811 that 'on kelp estates the land is almost entirely sacrificed to that manufacture and is at best, with regard to its agriculture, in a stationary condition....In this state of agriculture the land is considered as of no further value than merely to accommodate the kelp manufacturers with some milk, a few carcases of lean sheep, horses, or cattle, and a wretched crop of barley, black oats, and potatoes. Turnips and all other green crops demanding attention in summer, are (excepting potatoes) quite out of the question' (Macdonald 1811, 119f). Clanranald's trustees argued in 1815 that 'it is impossible that the tenants can give that attention to the production of the land which to secure a decent return is indispensably necessary' when tenants 'were almost uniformly called off, and that in the best weather, too,' to make kelp (NAS GD 201/5/1233/6130).

The Organisation of Kelping

The local organization of the early kelpmaking industry varied from estate to estate. There were several possible arrangements. One was for the tenants to have a share in the shore of their farms and to work their own shores for the kelp, thus, as the Chamberlain for Mull and Morvern explained, having 'employment to them at their doors during a time of the year at which the other labour of their farms does not require so much of their attention' (quoted

in MacArthur 1990, 30). A consequence of this arrangement was that the manufacturers were at the mercy of the market for the price they received for their kelp. This arrangement was most common on estates where the amounts manufactured were relatively small and it was not worth the proprietor's effort to take a more active part. Another arrangement was for the proprietor to control the kelp rights on the shores, but to allow (or even require) the tenants to make kelp on them. This more often happened on estates where kelpmaking was a major industry and especially in districts where extensive subdivision of lands had occurred based on the importance of kelping. In the second case, the kelpmakers controlled their own production and sold the finished product ('made kelp') to the proprietor, usually at a price fixed in the leases. Many estates had mixtures of the two systems. On the Clanranald estate of South Uist, for example, the tacksmen were allowed to control kelp manufacture on the less important western shore of the island.(NAS GD 201/5/1232/9) On few estates in the period 1770-1830 did the proprietor merely hire the residents on wages to manufacture kelp. The lairds typically dealt with the kelpmakers as independent small producers. This was an important matter of status among a proud people.

There were also a variety of different arrangements in existence for the kelp payment. On the Clanranald estate, the 'lands were let to the tenantry with a view to the rents being paid in a great measure by kelp manufacture' (quoted in Gray 1951, 131). Kelping contracts were made with the tenants as part of their leases. The Clanranald factor theoretically paid the kelpmakers in cash, deducting arrearages and other charges (such as for imported meal). On Tiree, the factor simply balanced the return due for kelp against the amount due in rent, and sent any surplus to the kelpmakers. On many estates, as in Clanranald's, much of the kelp earnings were taken back in the book-keeping for arrears for supplied meal or other advances.(ibid) In Lewis, 'Tacksmen, Tenants and Subtenants bind themselves … to cut and burn and sufficiently manufacture and put on Ship Board the whole Kelp growing on the Shores of the lands occupied by them respectively, for which they shall receive the rate of wages usually paid therefore on the tracts of their respective farms'(ibid). Whether this meant that the Lewis kelping was totally on an employer - employee basis is not clear. Whatever the arrangement, the factor for North Uist and Harris observed in 1841 in the report on emigration the main point that the tenants 'certainly made a great deal of money by manufacturing kelp; they paid their rents entirely by it'.

Not all the kelpworkers were tenants. The 'landless' class seldom appears in the formal records of any estate, because its members did not formally have any relationship with the laird or even with the major tacksmen, but at best some understanding with the possessors of small farms. These people usually cultivated **some** land, but did not have the right or the facilities to raise livestock. Crofters, the most established of the subtenants, might have had some rights to summer grazing, but without an outfield they could hardly winter stock. The crofter category is a particularly difficult one, its origins and development shrouded in uncertainty. In the rationalisation and subdivision of estates, individuals might become tenants of the laird without proper grazing land – this frequently happened in newly-created coastal villages and helps explain why people were not drawn to them – and thus become crofters. Crofters would become the typical small possessors in the Highlands only in the 19th century, and not before (Hunter 1885). The numbers of the technically landless only increased on the kelping estates throughout the kelping period. On Skye in 1837 there were 1,300 families paying no rent, most of them relatives of the tenants, 'sometimes two or three of them are on the lot'. On another Skye estate, it was calculated there were two cottar families for every tenant one. On Harris, there were about as many cottars as tenants. On Barra, less than half of those who held a bit of land were officially registered in the rental book (Devine 1988, 8). On one unnamed estate, claimed a witness to the emigration enquiry of 1841, each small croft was inhabited by an average of two families of five persons each (Select Committee 1841, 9).

Most of the subtenant class were in effect landless labourers, whose bit of arable land helped support them but who had little opportunity to accumulate wealth in the form of livestock. There was a whole hierarchy of such people, ranging from cottars at the top to a numerous bottom. In the Hebrides this bottom layer of society was usually called scallags, individuals who had a hut, worked five days for a master and on the sixth cultivated a bit of ground. The casual traveller who knew no Gaelic seldom understood about such people, and often assumed that **they** were the tenantry. One witness to the 1841 emigration enquiry explained the process of subdivision in the following terms : '… If an honest Highlander…happened to have a son, he did not object to his son marrying and settling in life early, and giving him a part of his holding, where young Donald settled with his wife, and soon had a family; and if he, the original crofter, had a daughter, she married, and there was a further partition of the original croft; and this practice was continued till most of the crofts, originally intended for one family, had on them two or three, and sometimes four families. The proprietors…did not put a stop to this practice; they found they had full employment for all who settled on their estates, in consequence of the kelp trade and herring fishery' (ibid, 4). (5)

Missionary minister John Lane Buchanan insisted in his *Travels in the Western Hebrides*, published in 1793, that what he called the scallag – whose labour was essential to the kelp industry – was far worse off than the Negro slave, for neither the laird nor his employer had any obligation to him whatsoever.(Buchanan 1793, especially 195ff; also Gailey 1961, 57–76) According to the *Gentleman's Magazine,* which reviewed Buchanan's book, the author had written to the Duke of Clarence and William Wilberforce, begging them to 'take up the cause of the oppressed Hebrideans' (Gentlemen's Magazine 1793, 927–30). Unfortunately, exploitation in distant colonies was always easier to oppose than suffering at home. Moreover, Buchanan did not make sufficiently clear in his book that the scallags were not always directly oppressed by what contemporaries normally regarded as the landlord class – the lairds and tacksmen – but were often exploited by the possessor or tenant class by whom they were usually employed, especially in kelping. Instead, his thesis was that most exploitation was by the tacksmen.

On the other hand, Clanranald agreements with tenants by 1802 reserved to the laird 'the liberty to employ at the manufacturing of Kelp from cast ware or black ware on the sand shores all such persons who may not hold lands on the said farm or pendicles' (NAS GD 201/5/1232/1). More than one external observer instinctively compared the kelping labourer with the blacks, usually to the latter's advantage. (e.g. Hall 1807, II, 548, where the author writes that in comparison with the kelpers, 'the state of our Negroes is paradise'). In any event, the subtenant class constituted some unknown portion of the population of the Hebrides, although it is impossible to be precise about their numbers because no contemporary population data can be broken down by classes and estate records usually do not list them. These subtenants were a marginal population, theoretically easily drawn to emigration to America. In fact, they were in most cases far too poor to be able to pay the cost of passage and often far too oppressed to have much ambition or desire for change. Eventually they would in many cases have to be assisted (or driven) to depart the islands.

This growth in the subtenant class was obviously closely related to one of the outstanding features of Hebridean development in the kelping period, the constant increase in population. While an increase occurred in all major Highland counties, the areas of greatest growth were the western islands and coastal mainland of Sutherland, Ross-shire, Inverness-shire, and Argyll. Here the total percentage increase 1755–1800 was 44.4 percent, with an average annual growth rate of 0.8 percent (Flinn 1973, 47–64). As Table 7.1 illustrates, the islands experienced a much greater growth than the mainland. Nevertheless, some islands grew even more rapidly in population than these figures suggest; Tiree, for example, more than doubled its population between 1750 and 1808 (Cregeen 1964, xxviii-xxix).

Table 7.1 Population increases in the Western Islands and adjacent mainland, 1755–1801 (adapted from Flinn (1973, 48))

	% increases in intercensal periods	Annual % compounded rate
Islands		
Outer Hebrides	59.9	1.02
Skye	40.3	0.74
Mull	61.5	1.04
Others	84.0	1.33
TOTAL	**56.2**	**0.97**
Mainland		
Sutherland	11.9	0.24
Ross	48.3	0.85
Inverness	49.8	0.88
Argyll	11.1	0.23
TOTAL	**29.3**	**0.56**

This considerable increase in population occurred despite emigration (and most Highland emigrants 1775–1815 came from this region) and with no obvious changes in technology. It appears to have been the product of a combination of subtle factors, of which the most important were the widespread use of smallpox inoculation and vaccination, the introduction of the potato, and perhaps most significant of all, a generally improved standard of living based upon new sources of income for the inhabitants, including kelping.

Inoculation with harmless cowpox had become fairly general practice in the Highlands by the 1790s (Smout 1969, 253f). The potato was introduced into Uist in 1743. It was commonly grown in Skye and throughout the Hebrides by 1770, and had spread all through the Highlands by the 1780s. The tuber was exceptionally easy to cultivate, even by kelp manufacturers who spent most of the summer in kelp production. Once planted in the late spring, it required no care until harvest in the autumn. It helped prevent scurvy, and usually survived bad weather (Salaman 1949, 344–85; Flinn 1973). One knowledgeable observer in 1811 insisted that potatoes provided eighty percent of the nourishment of the residents of the Hebrides (Macdonald 1978, 232).

The introduction of new wealth came in various forms, the result of the integration of the Highlands into the larger Scottish and British economies. New wealth did not necessarily mean prosperity in the modern sense, for Highlanders responded to it by expanding family size and distributing the new income among members of the extended family, enabling more people to live at a subsistence level. Apart from kelping, the new sources of money came from the sale of black cattle in the British market, and cash remittances from those who had left the region to find employment, either in Lowland cities, in military service, or in colonial services such as the East India Company or the Hudson's Bay Company. Military service not only represented a cash infusion for the region, but also in turn increased the subdivision of holdings among several kelping proprietors who allocated land in return for enlistment. Lord Macdonald, the Earl of Seaforth, and the Duke of Argyll all raised regiments before 1815, the abortive Canadian regiment had recruited in the Hebrides, and Argyll had actually created four fencible regiments during the Napoleonic wars. Many of Argyll's returned veterans were allotted land on Tiree.

To what extent did these new factors simply encourage population growth, and to what extent were they also a response to it ? Only the introduction of inoculation was obviously independent of the population curve. The market for black cattle in the south also had no transparent connection with the trends of Highland population. However, the other factors – the potato and the new employment opportunities – existed in a constantly reciprocal relationship with population growth. Kelping, particularly, developed as much because there was an excess population as it helped to create one. In short, it was really quite impossible to separate cause from effect as far as kelping and population growth was concerned. What is clear is that the major factor limiting population growth, of course, was emigration.

Kelping and Emigration: the Early Period

Although emigration to North America had been occurring from the Western Highlands and Islands from 1770, it was not until an armistice was finally and unexpectedly negotiated with the French in 1801 that the great landlords attempted to do more about the exodus than merely protest it. This cessation of hostilities came at a particularly crucial point in the shifting economic system in the region. Improvement was in high gear. Estates were being carefully surveyed to increase landlord income. In the Hebrides, those surveys and subsequent setts of the estates were generally designed to maximize the manufacturing of kelp.

Conditions in the kelping regions, where much of the talk of emigration was centred, were particularly tense. A series of bad harvests had occurred, prices for meal were up, rents were increasing, and several of the principal properties were being administered for one reason or another by trustees to the south and stewards or factors on the spot (prices: Flinn 1977, 497; rents: Grant 1979; for a provocative argument on the importance of bad harvests to emigration Dixon 1978, 753). The outside administrators tended to work with the mentality of accountants rather than the paternalism of ancient clan chieftains, and they listened with care to the opinions of the local factors, whose interest was always with 'the estate' rather than either its laird or its inhabitants. The lands they supervised – particularly those on the outer Hebrides estates of the Earl of Seaforth, Lord Macdonald, and Clanranald – were the most vulnerable to the winds of disenchantment blowing through the western Highlands with the sudden arrival of peace. The mix of conditions was highly volatile, as contemporaries fully recognized. Although everywhere leases were expiring and new setts of estates – where all farms were up for bidding before reletting – were prevalent throughout the western Highlands in 1801, the situation was most serious on Skye, the outer Hebrides (especially the Long Island), Arisaig, and Moidart. Here most of the lands were controlled by Lord Macdonald (who held half of Skye and all of North Uist), Clanranald (who at one time held South Uist, Benbecula, and much of Arisaig and Moidart), and the Earl of Seaforth (who owned Lewis). In all three cases estates in financial trouble were being managed by trustees or commissioners. The Clanranald heir was a minor at Eton, Lord Macdonald was off serving with his Regiment of the Isles, and Seaforth was governing an island in the West Indies. While a laird in control of his own affairs might well accept a deficit balance sheet as an unavoidable part of his life, the lawyers and merchants who were trustees were far less likely to tolerate red ink, which implied a failure of their administration. They were thus extremely responsive to proposals from the local factors for increasing income, whatever the local implications.

In Lord Macdonald's case, a favourable net balance in 1797 and 1798 had alarmingly turned to substantial losses in 1799 and 1800. These deficits were occurring despite a great increase in kelping proceeds, which had grown from £3,935 in 1797 to £6,304 in 1800, and were caused by new expenses, particularly for construction, a regiment, and farm improvement (NAS GD 221/40). Since Lord Macdonald's two principal sources of income were from rents and kelping, his administrators were quite open to any suggestions for an increase, and had even employed special surveyors in 1799 to investigate the possibilities. In his report of May in that year, John Blackadder carefully distinguished between Skye and North Uist, although on both islands he advised caution. On Skye he recommended 'new and better customs and methods of management' to increase rental, although he had been quite struck by the conservatism of the population there and the need to move slowly, 'for no man gives up readily what he has without a substitute equal or better'. He noted the tenantry's 'adherence to inveterate opinions and old uncorrected customs', which operated 'powerfully against improvements or even alterations'. Blackadder recognized that any sudden changes would dispossess large numbers of people who might well turn to emigration unless 'all reasonable allowances' were made. For North Uist, where kelp-making was the major objective of the landlord, he emphasized the need for continued subdivision. But, he insisted, the Uist people also had 'a spirit for rejecting new Modes of Improvement, and an independent cast of mind which will not be bound down (as the Farmers in other Countries generally are) by Covenants in leases to do what other people think right for them to do, if they do not think the thing proposed right themselves' (NAS RH 2/8/24; the trustees also employed Robert Reid, a Perthshire land surveyor : Moisley 1961, 89-92). Despite Blackadder's cautions, the very fact of his presence started rumours of major changes among Lord Macdonald's tenantry. There was particular concern about what would happen on Skye in the next major sett of the estate in 1801, when indeed 267 tenants on 56 farms were dispossessed (NAS GD 221/51).

As with Lord Macdonald, Clanranald held both kelping and agricultural land. The heir's Edinburgh tutors found 1800 a particularly difficult year, for one of their principal kelp merchants had gone bankrupt while owing over £2,300 to the estate, and there were additional heavy outlays for the purchase of the Island of Muck, as well as a slight depression in kelp prices (NAS GD 202/5/1233/35). (6) As a result, the tutors were much concerned to increase the quantity and quality of kelp while reducing the cost of manufacture. After consultation with local factor Robert Brown, a number of related actions were undertaken in 1800 and 1801 to achieve these goals. The annual meeting of the tutors in March 1799 had discussed Brown's recommendations for improving kelp manufacture. These included earlier sowing of crops and an enforced end to agriculture when the kelping season began, divisions of the shore to the tenants most successful at making kelp, and the removal from the estate of any manufacturing a low quality product. Some of these points made their way into the new leases. The meeting also agreed to augment the rates paid to the kelpers 'a little', especially for those 'most deserving'. Tacksmen outside the Clanranald kelping arrangement were to be requested to join in some 'measure for equalizing their prices and of giving similar prices to that paid by Clanranald', and some tacksmen were to be eliminated entirely (NAS GD 201/5/1233/31). A year later, the tutors agreed to prosecute anyone carrying off seaweed for manure, and removed the tenants of two large farms who were not producing sufficient kelp. More significantly, they agreed to fix the price paid to workers for manufactured kelp, with a substantial fine for anyone paying more (NAS GD 202/5/1233/35). The emphasis of the tutors was clearly upon the kelping income, and they agreed with factor Brown in 1801 that Moidart and Arisaig were overcrowded and 'would be the better' if an exodus occurred. But any emigration from Uist 'would injure the interest of the Landlords', for 'the manufacturing of the kelp depends entirely on the number of the people' (NAS GD 201/51). As a result, at least on the Long Island, subdivision was entrenched.

The laird of Lewis – the Earl of Seaforth – was another major kelping proprietor in the Hebrides in financial difficulty. According to his Edinburgh 'man of business', Seaforth's estate deficit in 1800 alone was over £1,000, and

Colin McKenzie applauded the Earl's colonial appointment as one which would in a few years enable him 'to pay off all your debt & preserve your noble Estate in your Family' (NAS GD 46/17/14)(7) The appointment was a better solution than the earlier suggestion by one John Mackenzie to sell off part of the Lewis property.(58) It is not clear what had caused Seaforth's 'pecuniary distress', although the cost of his 78th Regiment probably played a large role. But whatever the problem, it was certainly not Lewis, which had been returning a kelping profit of never less than £1,104 and as much as £2,452 between 1794 and 1799; together with rents in 1800 it showed a net credit balance of £3,833 (NAS GD 46/13/126; and NAS GD 46/1/326).

Smaller lairds had difficulties as well. Part of the problem for Murdoch Maclean of Lochbuy on Mull was that his estate was not well situated for kelping. Despite his successful efforts to recover the shore rights from tenants, Lochbuy was informed that just over thirty tuns of kelp was the maximum the shore could yield (NAS GD 174/1012/1). Rumours that Maclean was trying to sell were common among his tenants after 1799, and the people attempted – without success – to secure their positions through longer leases (NAS GD 174/964).

Throughout the Outer Hebrides, kelping was clearly the principal reality both for lairds and their tenants. The proprietors wanted as high a production as they could get at the lowest possible cost to themselves. The tenants obviously would not view the situation in the same light. A revealing glimpse of the typical small tenant's financial situation in the Outer Hebrides – a five to twenty mile wide ridge of land and rock running 180 miles in length off the western coast of Scotland, comprising Lewis, Harris, both Uists, Benbecula, Barra, and innumerable small islands – was provided by the minister of North Uist in the *Old Statistical Account* for 1794. This smallholder, wrote Reverend Allan MacQueen, could with the assistance of his family earn about L6 annually from kelping (this was the remuneration for about 3 tuns of made kelp, about average for the Clanranald estate). He owned the equivalent of six grown cows, and could sell one annually for £2. 8. 0. This total of £8. 8. 0 was his basic income, out of which he paid £5. 4. 0 rent, maintained six horses for drawing kelping carts and other jobs at £1. 5. 5 per year, and usually found himself buying outside meal (one boll costing an average of seventeen shillings). After paying his expenses, he was left with twelve shillings, not much of a margin and hardly sufficient to think seriously about emigration (MacQueen 1794, 310–319).

Clear limitations existed on the extent to which any small tenant family could increase the quantity of kelp they manufactured. Most contemporaries put the maximum per family at four tuns (a tun was usually calculated at 120 pounds to the hundredweight and twenty-one hundred weight to the tun, or 2,520 pounds), although one South Uist crofter told the Napier Commission he had once made five tuns. A fully-loaded horse and cart could carry perhaps 1,000 pounds of wet weed, which when reduced would produce little more than fifty pounds of manufactured kelp. Fifty cartloads were thus required to produce a single tun of finished kelp, and to cut sufficient weed with small sickles in knee-high or even waist-high water to fill a cart was no easy task, particularly given the shortness of the season. Small wonder that the kelpers often took as much beached weed as possible, although it was generally regarded as of inferior quality and often 'belonged' to somebody else. Small wonder they often mixed the burning kelp with sand and rock, which of course reduced the alkaline content of the finished product and thus its value. Even smaller wonder that tenants were not happy with the concerted efforts of the great lairds to keep prices paid for kelp down while increasing rentals. But tenants had few weapons at their disposal. If they protested they were simply dispossessed at the expiration of their leases, and often before.(8) As we have seen, the lairds increasingly wrote the price to be paid for the kelp into their agreements, and even provided penalties for unsatisfactory manufacture.

About the only alternative for the discontented small tenant at the turn of the century was to sell his livestock and meagre possessions, which would in the years 1801–3 just about bring him sufficient money to pay for his family's passage to British America aboard one of the emigrant vessels recruiting in the western Highlands. Reverend MacQueen's small tenant would receive less than fifteen pounds for his cattle, and perhaps another five for his horses. If the tenant's family consisted of himself, a wife, and two or three children, the revenue received from the liquidation of the family's property would not leave much over after the purchase of passage at £3 to £4 per adult. Crofters and cottars, of course, did not have even this option, for they seldom owned much beyond the wooden beams they employed to raise their huts, and could only aspire to taking over a holding from a tenant either emigrating or dispossessed. In both the islands and the non-kelping districts of Skye and the mainland, the pressure of population was so great that new tenants could easily be found to replace any departing, although the kelping lairds preferred as much labour force as possible for the short season of manufacture.

The kelping lairds (or rather, their administrators) employed a number of strategies for preventing emigration departures from their estates. One was through harassment, legal and otherwise, against those who were itinerating the region recruiting emigrants. A judicial investigation in October of 1802 on Benbecula, for example, determined that agents Archibald Maclean and Roderick Mclellan had led tenants to sign agreements to convey them to America in ignorance of the precise contents, which were written in an English the signatories did not understand (Bumsted 1982, 114–39). When kelping agreements were written in English that was apparently another matter. Another possible strategy was to offer better terms to tenants. Clanranald's factor, Robert Brown, suggested in 1802 'the propriety of having a new sett of the lands…occupied by small tenants to obtain for such of the farms as can afford it a small augmentation and to allow the farms already highly rented to remain at the present rent to take none but good tenants – to give a lease during Clanranald's minority to the Tenants of each farm – these leases to specify the regulations of the farm particularly with regard to the manufacturing of the kelp as to which the Tenant should be carefully taken bound to manufacture it during his lease' (NAS GD 201/5/1233/37). (9)

As well as the local carrot and stick, the kelping lairds succeeded in rousing the Highland Society of Edinburgh to action. The society advocated both a Highland improvement programme to provide for employment at home for potential emigrants, and a legislative regulation of the transatlantic passage of those departing, on the grounds that they were being treated inhumanely on many of the vessels carrying them. The resultant legislation, hastily passed without debate by Parliament in May 1803, was received quite paradoxically in Scotland. While the Highland lairds applauded the Passenger Vessel Act – as it was often called – for its humane concern about the health and well-being of the victimized Highlanders, the objects of the altruism bitterly condemned the legislation as an ill-disguised effort to halt their departure for North America by greatly increasing the cost of passage (Bumsted 1978a, 171–88). As Lord Selkirk pointed out in 1805, the weekly food minimums required by the Act – particularly for meat – bore no relationship to the standard diet of oatmeal and water which never bothered the humanitarians when consumed on their own estates. The net effect of the legislation was not only to require better conditions of treatment for Highlanders at sea than they had ever enjoyed on land, but to enforce standards far superior to those the government provided for Highlanders when it transported them as soldiers (Selkirk 1805; reprinted in Bumsted 1984, 148–156). The Act, whatever the pious pronouncements of public rhetoric, was privately acknowledged by the ruling classes of Scotland as an attempt to halt emigration until the effects of the Highland improvement programme of 1803 could be felt (Bumsted 1978a, 171–88). Probably none of the defensive strategies was as successful in staunching the flow of emigration from the Highlands as the resumption of warfare against the French in 1803. A trickle of departures continued throughout the wartime period, but for the duration of the hostilities, the kelping estates were relatively safe from depopulation.

After 1815

By the final conclusion of peace after the Battle of Waterloo, however, the situation in the kelping districts was beginning to catch up with the rest of the Western Highlands. Several years of bad harvests, particularly that of 1811, had demonstrated how tenuous was the kelpmakers' ability to avoid starvation, given the continual subdivision of the estates. Moreover, new British trade policies demonstrated how equally tenuous was the continuation of the kelping proprietor's high profits during the years of war. Kelp was economic to make only so long as the alternatives were denied entry to Britain or exposed to high duties. When the Newcastle glass manufacturers asked for a reduction of import duties on Norwegian kelp in 1813, the proprietors met in Edinburgh and had managed to persuade the government not to act (NAS GD 221/33 and NAS GD 221/33). But it became increasingly clear that the various duties which made kelp competitive were likely to end. As they had in 1802, the proprietors turned to the Highland Society of Scotland, which appointed a committee to investigate the future of the industry. The committee reported early in 1815 that more information on kelp and its manufacture was needed, and recommended experimentation with burning techniques, including proper kilns, and with cutting kelp at various stages of growth. It offered a premium of fifty guineas for the best essay on the management of kilns, and another prize for the best essay on the comparative value of kelp and barilla (NAS GD 201/6/3). Premiums were later offered by the Society for making quality kelp in the Hebrides (NAS GD RH4/00188). Nevertheless, as late as 1816, Clanranald's managers hesitated to further subdivide on South Uist because of fears of 'stirring up a spirit of emigration' by attempting 'to introduce too generally a change to which the inhabitants, from attachment to old habits are very averse' (NAS GD 201/5/1233/64-73).

A printed 'Memorial of Proprietors of Kelp-Shores… assembled at Edinburgh, 13th day of February 1818' against a reduction of the salt duties insisted that kelpmaking employed the poor, prevented emigration, bred seamen, and brought money into circulation. The proprietors described the total manufacture of kelp at between fifteen and twenty thousand tuns, employing 10,000 families and from 150 to 200 vessels of 60 to 100 tuns burden transporting kelp to London, Liverpool, Bristol, Hull and Newcastle. In some places, the kelp money bought imported grain because of bad harvests and a drop in the price of black cattle (NAS GD 237/12/4). A crisis over the reduction of Spanish barilla duties in 1818 led proprietors to panic. They told the government, 'Many persons have purchased their estates relying on the permanency of kelp, and others have lent money on the security of the annual returns from it (NAS GD 201/6/4). True as this statement might have been, it was not a totally compelling reason for changing a government policy. A succession of governments paid considerably less attention to the kelping interests after 1815 than they had in 1802–3. As Mr. McLeod of Harris wrote to the Secretary of State in 1829, after referring to the competition to Scottish kelp from barilla and various ashes, 'Up to the year 1822 considerable duties were leviable on all the commodities just enumerated; but in that year the duty on salt was lowered from 15s to 2s a bushel. Shortly afterwards the impost on barilla was considerably reduced. This measure was quickly followed by a repeal of the remainder of the salt duties and of the duty on alkali made from salt. Close upon this followed a considerable reduction in the duty on pot and pearl ash and an entire removal of that on ashes from Canada, and this last step was accompanied by a diminution of the duty on foreign sulphur from 15s to 10s a tun' (Select Committee 1841, 2). Part of the reason for the change of policy was the perception that the lairds had reaped excessive windfall profits during the war. But more significantly, Scotland no longer enjoyed the political clout in Westminster that it had while managed by Henry Dundas earlier in the century. In the long run the danger was not from Spanish barilla but from 'British barilla', manufactured by refining salt mined at home (Anderson 1831). This manufacture was based upon the 'Leblanc process', discovered in France in 1791, for converting common salt into alkali. It was first used in Liverpool by James Muspratt (1795–1886) in 1823 and in Glasgow by Josias Gamble (1776–1846) in 1825 (Ihde 1964, 446f). (10) After 1815, probably in response to the publication of the report of the Highland Society, the kelping lairds and their administrators became far more conscious of the need to understand the workings of their industry. Clanranald's people produced increasingly sophisticated data on kelping, obviously designed at least partially for policy purposes. From this material it is possible to gain some notion of what a complex business kelp had become. In 1816, for example, Clanranald's kelp crop was shipped on 24 vessels, with 6 sailing to Liverpool, 2 to Queensferry, 5 to Hull, 9 to Greenock, and 2 to Leith. The total shipped was 1,321 tuns, and 1,134 tuns were delivered, suggesting some unexplained losses in shipping The shipping costs included insurance charges of £101. 17, agents' commissions of £199. 5. 4, interest of £60. 17. 6, stamp and postal charges of £31. 13. 3, and the remainder in freight charges (NAS GD 201/6/4). The average price per tun was £6. 8, although there were considerable variations in price depending on the port involved and the time of shipping. Liverpool, where the customers were local soap-boilers, consistently offered the best prices, and the Scottish ports the worst. Cargoes shipped early in the season obtained better prices than those shipped later, partly because there was some competition for the first shipments, partly because the later ones were for inferior kelp made mainly from driftware. Between 1816 and 1820, the Clanranald estates had increased kelping production from 1,134 tuns sold to 1,496 tuns sold, with the production of 1820 representing an all-time high (NAS GD 201/6/2).

Although annual average prices for kelp varied, the prices held up fairly well until the mid-1820s, when they began a sharp decline that persisted until the mid-1830s, when they seemed to bottom out. The less expensive alternatives included Spanish barilla, British barilla, and various ashes. At the high end of the market, the Crown glass manufacturers preferred very prime Irish kelp or kelp from the Orkneys (NAS GD 201/5/1232/3/31). Kelp had value to glass manufacturers apart from its alkaline content, but Hebridean kelp was disliked by Crown glass makers because it was held to contain residue that coloured the glass. Most of the costs to the proprietor were relatively fixed. The cost of manufacture was set in the rental agreements, and there were few ways to cut the costs of shipping. Clanranald's bean-counters understandably were most concerned with the bottom line, the 'Nett Produce' to the estate of the annual crop. When that figure began shrinking, from an average of £4,589. 10. 11 in the years 1816–1820 to £2,263. 18 in 1833, the question of 'net proceeds per tun' became increasingly critical, as the managers and the factors began wondering whether some other utilization of the lands of the estate might be more profitable. An unsigned note on kelp markets in the Clanranald Papers for 1827 noted that kelp was now only barely defraying its cost of manufacture and shipping charges. The lowest price for manufacturing was £2. 12. 6 per tun, and the price of shipping added nearly another L per tun, making the total cost of production £3. 16. At a sale price of £3. 10 per tun, Clanranald was losing 6d per tun (NAS GD 201/1232/1/15).

After 1815 as well, the local managers of the kelping lairds had come to begin to appreciate the doubled-edged nature of the socio-economic structure they had created in the kelping districts. In 1818, Clanranald factor Duncan Shaw testified before Major James Macdonald, JP, that the estate he supervised was divided into very small portions, more than the land could support even in ordinary seasons. Many of the more than 4,000 people on the estate paid no rent and consumed the provisions of tenants; their poverty put emigration beyond reach. The parish of South Uist furnished more men to the militia and reserve than any other in Inverness County. Shortfalls of food because of crop failure from 1812 to 1817 had forced Clanranald to import food, both at his own expense and from the government. The price of black cattle was low, and cattle and horses were lost through the crop failures of 1812, 1816, and 1817 (NAS GD 201/6/5). In 1823, Seaforth wrote to a correspondent that given the decline in kelp prices, the lairds would eventually have to do something 'for their wretched tenantry either by giving them the means of other employment or of emigrating ere it is too late. And convinced I am that before five years have expired, this they will be driven to under increased difficulties, and then without even the semblance of benevolent and human feeling towards the starving mass of whom in the interval they will make use, so their applications will lose power and sordid motives will be too justly laid to their charge (NAS GD 46/17/44). By 1827, Duncan Shaw had come to recognize the need for a revenue apart from kelp, chiefly from sheep farming. He saw the handwriting on the wall for the kelping industry, and argued, 'if the kelp is given up the small tenants cannot continue to pay the present rents, because the work they got enabled them to pay for portions of ground so small that they could pay nothing from the produce (NAS GD 201/4/97). He wanted to ship out 3,000 people to North America. The trustees agreed (NAS GD 201/5/1217/46; NAS GD 201/4/97). Government assistance was sought, but the authorities were not keen to help (Select Committee 1826–7, 500-8). So Shaw decided to begin in the middle of South Uist. He added acreage to the farm of Miltun, where the tenant had recently taken possession and offered a substantial rent, planning to use the land for sheep. Sheep, wrote Shaw, would give Clanranald 'a well paid money rent and a certain income independent of kelp (NAS GD 201/1/338).

Improving the Kelp

Those effectually running the great kelping estates, who continued for the most part to be Edinburgh managers rather than the kelping proprietors themselves, had become quite sensitive to the economics and technology of their industry. 'Chemistry is the true enemy of kelp and we can only last as long as its advance to perfection is going on', wrote Lord Seaforth to his Liverpool kelp agent in 1827 (NAS GD 46/176/41). Thus the proprietors and their agents were quite responsive to a 'Proposal for Improving the Manufacturing of Kelp in the Highlands of Scotland', sent them in October of 1829 by Dr. John W. Anderson and Mr. D. Mccrummen (NAS GD 201/5/1232/5). Anderson was a professional chemist, and he concentrated on the question of the alkaline strength of the kelp. Best-made Highland kelp averaged a 6percent alkaline content, he argued, and could not compete with either Tenerife barilla or 'British barilla (salt ash made cheaply with salt mined at home), both of which were now being supplied to the soap trade. In terms of its alkaline strength, Anderson maintained, kelp was overpriced in 1829 at £5 per tun; it should really have been selling for £2. 14. At such a low price, the kelping lairds would abandon the industry and expose their people to destitution. However, in response to the Highland Society's premium offer, Mr. Mccrummen of Leith had experimented on an improved process for making kelp, and had demonstrated that the alkaline content could be raised to at least 13 percent. Anderson further asserted that the soap makers liked foreign barilla and salt ash because of its consistent alkaline content. The present manufacture of kelp by 'ignorant and careless' workmen produced a product of mixed and uncertain character. Chemical principles must be applied, wrote Anderson. Kelpmaking must follow standards carefully, must use improved kilns,

and must apply the proper amount of heat in order to get the highest alkaline content.

While Anderson's proposal sounded promising, not everyone was totally convinced. Although Anderson wrote about 13 percent content, by his own admission Mccrummen's 1822 experiments had only raised the percentage to 8.25 percent. Although it was understandable that Anderson was not very specific about his techniques, he was quite clear that he wanted a percentage of one-sixth of any improvements. Clanranald factor Duncan Shaw was sceptical. He suspected any improved process would be very expensive, and he doubted that Anderson and Mccrummen could much improve on present quality (NAS GD 201/5/1232/5). Shaw was reluctantly prepared to support a trial, based upon comparisons of the results Anderson and Mccrummen could obtain with the results of normal estate practice (NAS GD 201/5/1232/5). Clanranald's kelp merchants at Liverpool were equally dubious, arguing that improving the alkaline content of kelp would be difficult and adding that Liverpool ash costing £7. 10 per tun and containing 20 to 25 percent alkali was delivered daily to the soap makers (NAS GD 201/5/1232/5). Nevertheless, the principal kelping lairds and their agents could not resist the possibility of an improved alkali content. At a meeting in Edinburgh on 8 May, Clanranald and Lord Macdonald agreed to hire Anderson and Mccrummen to supervise kelp manufacture on the Long Island for the ensuing season, at a rate of 2 guineas per day during the period from June to August (NAS GD 201/5/232/5).

The resultant experiment was a fiasco. According to Mr. Mccrummen, the new procedures and kilns required a consolidation of the kelp of various producers, but the people were hostile (understandably) to combining their small lots of weed, so that it was hard to get enough kelp together. Most of the makers were unwilling to try new kilns, and the factors set up their own kilns in competition against his efforts to raise heat and regulate it better. Mccrummen had harsh words for the existing procedures and insisted that most of the local population – factors and makers – were more concerned to defend their existing methods than to try new ones (NAS GD 201/5/1232/6). Factor Duncan Shaw of Benbecula told quite a different story. He agreed that Mccrummen thought that the Islanders 'are much wedded to old customs, and consequently averse to improvements and innovations'. But he insisted that the tenants on North and South Uist had not only been told of the new procedures in April, but advised that on those improvements their future livelihood would depend. The protests of the makers were usually against their weed being 'so ill burnt as not to be workable', because of the application of too much heat. Shaw insisted he had to pay off some kelpers right on the spot because their weed had been ruined. Moreover, in any direct comparisons with the work of the outsiders, argued Shaw, the locals were able to produce kelp of a higher alkaline content. To some extent, of course, this was a classic demonstration effect (NAS GD 201/5/1232/9).

More to the point was Shaw's insistence that the estate had greatly improved production techniques in recent years, introducing cast iron bottoms for kilns, premiums for best manufacture, the eviction of any sloppy makers, and the appointment of kelping officers to supervise the work. The officers were all Protestants from Skye and North Uist, and no South Uist Catholics were included. Shaw believed that 'wilful adulteration of kelp is now unknown on the Long Island' (NAS GD 201/5/1232/6). The behaviour of Dr Anderson seemed to substantiate Shaw's case. Even Mccrummen admitted that Anderson had returned to Edinburgh in mid-summer, saying that after personal experience he did not think that the value of the improvement was worth the difficulties. According to factor Shaw, Anderson had admitted that he had been deceived about the state of kelp manufacture on the Long Island, believing it much more primitive than it was. Anderson continued to work for the proprietors for several years (NAS GD 201/5/1232/9). As for Mccrummen, who spent a full 88 days in the field at 2 guineas per day plus expenses, he had considerable trouble collecting his money. Dr. Anderson travelled to the kelp buyers in England to discover how they employed kelp, and reported to the proprietors in 1830 (NAS GD 201/5/1232/5). He also published at his own expense the pamphlet *The Barilla Question Discussed* in 1831. The pamphlet was not a best-seller, and he attempted in 1835 to sell the remainders to the kelping proprietors to recover his costs (NAS GD 201/5/1232/9). In the pamphlet, Anderson insisted that government policy towards *Spanish* barilla was essentially irrelevant to the kelp industry, since the real enemy was 'British barilla', black ash made from local salt from which the duties had been removed. Anderson insisted that the use of Hebridean kelp depended largely on the price of the various alkalis relative to their alkaline content. He offered an illustrative table:

	Alkali percent	Price
Foreign barilla	25	£17
Ditto	20	£15
Crystals of soda	21.6	£15–16
Salts of soda	44	£22
British barilla	22	£8
Best kelp	10	£5
Average kelp	7	£4 to £4 .4
Inferior kelp	3	£2–3

So long as the relationship between alkaline content and price was in kelp's favour, it would continue to sell. But Anderson maintained that proposed reductions in the salt duties would make 'British barilla' the alkali of preference over the next few years. He had visited the kelping islands, wrote Anderson, and was satisfied that the proprietors could hope for no chemical discovery that would add to the value of their material. The material had been improved as much as it could be. The islands of South Uist and Benbecula contained 8,000 people dependent on kelp manufacturing who would be put out of work and would have to be removed from their lands. Kelp was the only exportable produce of the islands, and the lots were barely adequate in good seasons to supply the tenants' own wants. 'We recollect the tumult and insurrection, occasioned by the attempted forcible removal of about seventy families, in the comparatively accessible counties of Ross and Sutherland [the evictions associated with Patrick Sellar]; and what must be the consequence of a similar attempt, to remove so many from their native islands, to go they know

not whither. The means of emigration they do not possess; nor have they any inducement to come to the Low Country to compete with the shirtless and shoeless myriads from Ireland'. Force would be required to transport the former kelpmakers, wrote Anderson, and 'it is, unquestionably, the duty of society, in a case of this kind, to interpose, in some way or other, to prevent what may *even* be a general blessing from becoming a particular curse' (Anderson 1831, 10–20). Despite these warnings, the government persisted in lowering the salt duties.

The 1830 Long Island experiment was only one of several new efforts to improve kelp production. Another was begun by Colonel Macneil of Barra in 1830. Macneil was apparently introduced to the scheme in a visit to Glasgow or Liverpool. It involved a chemical reprocessing of kelp into muriate of potash and carbonate of soda, and could be profitable only if attempted on a very large scale, since the margins were very small. In order to find the money to buy large quantities of outside kelp, Macneil reputedly cut every property on his island in half without reducing the rent (but see below p. 143). Many of the tenants decided to emigrate. Duncan Shaw wrote that it was difficult to learn much about 'Barra's Discovery', although he had been told that it took four tuns of made kelp to create a tun of ash, which was then sold at £10 per tun. As Shaw noted, 'even if three Tuns of Barra kelp are required for the quantity of Ashe the profit is very questionable' (NAS GD 201/5/1232/7)(11) Clanranald and Lord Macdonald held out against selling Macneil any of their kelp until 1834, and then only provided kelp of less desirable quality that could not find a market elsewhere. But they did sell on credit. Macneil became one of the major customers for made kelp, and by 1834 probably reprocessed more kelp on Barra than was sold to the south. The word was that the process was very successful, but the Macneil had been deeply in debt for a generation. Since the Barra proprietor had been teetering on the verge of bankruptcy for years, it is impossible to know whether the failure of his kelp scheme drove him over the edge in 1837. The same sort of processing plant was subsequently set up on South Uist, but on a smaller scale (Select Committee 1841, 81).

The failure of the Macneil's Barra scheme was really one of the last gasps of a declining industry, although some would hold out longer before reaching the inevitable conclusions. In 1839, Lord Macdonald's North Uist factor wrote: 'Kelp is not now a productive manufacture. The population on the Estate is greater than the Land, kelp being abandoned, can maintain. Tenants are so small that they cannot maintain their Families and pay the Proprietor the rent which the Lands are worth if let in larger Tenements. It becomes necessary therefore that a number of the small tenants be removed; that that part of the Estate calculated for grazings be let as grazings; and that the allotments, on that part better calculated for small tenants, be so enlarged as to enable the Tenants to raise a surplus of produce for the payment of the rents. In this way the yearly rent of the Estate will not be materially, if at all, diminished' (NAS GD 221/38103). The 1841 emigration enquiry heard that some proprietors continued the manufacture of kelp, although the returns to the estate were negative, in order to provide income for the inhabitants. But within a few years of 1836, all the kelping lairds were gone, most of those on the Long Island replaced by a rich Aberdonian named John Gordon of Cluny, reputed to be the 'richest commoner in Scotland'.

Cluny was the son of an Aberdeen improver and land speculator whose father had been long known for his ability to squeeze a penny (Bulloch 1911). The younger Gordon initially entered the Islands picture early in 1836, when he was wooed by Clanranald's trustees as a potential purchaser of the estate. The administrators hoped to sell for between £110,000 and £120,000 before the kelp market collapsed completely, although Alexander Hunter admitted that it would take £30,000 in improvements to double the rental (NAS GD 201/5/1223). The administrators refused an offer of £100,000, although Robert Brown subsequently maintained that there was no point in haggling over price while the income of the estate fell short of expenditures by £500 per year, as it had done for the past six years (letter from Robert Brown to Messrs Hunter &c., 10 Feb. 1838, in private collection). Cluny did not counteroffer, but instead years later opened direct negotiations with Clanranald himself, who had declared that he personally did not want to sell, but his administrators, who had the final say in the matter, did. Clanranald insisted that the debt on the estate of £45,000 had been caused by bad management and neglect, thus suggesting that if the laird were an active one, the situation would improve. Clanranald made what was in effect the counteroffer, proposing to borrow the amount of the debt from Cluny on the security of the estate and declaring touchingly that he wanted to spend the remainder of his life 'among the affectionately disposed tenantry' of the Long Island (NAS GD 201/5/1223).

In the east of Scotland, Gordon was regarded as a tough but fair landlord. Why he moved west is not clear, but he purchased in the space of three years Benbecula, South Uist and Barra. Gordon ultimately spent £163,799 in acquiring property in the Western Isles which yielded £8,223 rent per annum. In the early years Gordon was said to be interested in maintaining the present population, but even if this were true he soon was converted by the crisis of the mid-1840s to clearance and subsidised emigration. Gordon apparently had bought his island estates in the understanding that they had been mismanaged and undercapitalised, and could be easily turned around with proper care and administration. Such a belief was certainly encouraged by a report on Benbecula and South Uist prepared for Colonel Gordon in 1839 by outside surveyor John Fleming. (12) This report offers an alternative explanation for Gordon's reluctance to clear his estate immediately upon taking possession. It recommended the continuation of kelp manufacture on these islands as the best way to provide employment for much of the population, insisting, 'If the kelp is not continued to be manufactured, or extensive improvements carried out to give work to the small tenants it will be vain to expect them to pay the rents they promise in the meantime'. In the short run, argued Fleming, the extensive population could be employed in making the improvements, especially the construction of roads. After the 'necessary improvements are completed', the excess population – especially the sub-tenants that paid no rent – could be forced to emigrate.

The First Decline of the Kelping Industry and its Implications

Although all the secondary literature on kelping, emigration, and clearance notes in passing the government

reductions in the salt and barilla duties, it is not typically emphasized that the decline of the kelp industry was a direct product of deliberate government trade policy after 1820. The problem was not so much reduced barilla duties as reduced salt duties. While it would be unfair to blame the problems associated with the end of kelpmaking solely on a liberal government committed to freer trade, it was nevertheless true that the government could have maintained high Hebridean kelp sales (and helped support the 10,000 kelpmakers) at any time through simple trade policy, and equally true that the government was warned of the disastrous effects on the Highlands of an open competition in alkaline substances. Had the culprit been Spanish barilla, the government might have been more sympathetic to the kelping industry. But the enemy was salt – a commodity used by most of the population – and the government was willing to sacrifice a few thousand Highlanders for the greater good of the greater number. According to one expert, Cheshire salt mines and the shipping industry were among the chief beneficiaries of the removal of the salt duties, although the agricultural interests had supported the removal and all consumers had benefited, not least from the lowered cost of soap (Select Committee 1841, 169). According to another witness, the whole of the British alkalis that eliminated kelp were manufactured with sulphuric acid containing substantial quantities of arsenic, which in turn contaminated the final products (ibid, 76). Not surprisingly, the emigration committee of 1841 did not wish to touch this issue with a ten-foot pole. Nevertheless, a recurrent subtext to the main theme of the need for emigration in the testimony before the committee on emigration was the insistence of many of those associated with the kelp business that since the government was responsible for the plight of the former kelp manufacturers, it had some duty to relieve their misery. Contemporaries understood full well that deliberate government policy had been the culprit. The Reverend Donald Campbell wrote of the kelp manufacture in the Parish of Kilfinichen and Kilviceun (the Ross of Mull and Iona) in the *New Statistical Account* : 'In previous years this manufacture employed and gave bread to many thousands in the Highlands and Islands, and the price it drew brought money to the country…which now goes to enrich the foreigner at the poor Highlander's expense; a measure of policy which cannot be too strongly condemned' *(New Statistical Account of Scotland*, 7 (1845)).

We must not be led by the excessive profits made by the kelping lairds in the halcyon days of the industry into thinking that the lairds or their managers continued to insist on such levels of return. The economic calculation was whether lands excessively divided to support a large population manufacturing kelp could be made more profitable by being consolidated and used for something else, such as sheep farming. When the 'nett return' on kelp completely disappeared, obviously almost any other policy would pay better. The lairds had cashed in on excess profits for many years, but all they or their managers wanted after 1830 was the prospect of a reasonable net return for the future, and such a return would have had a substantial socio-economic effect in the kelping regions. For better or worse, the Hebridean kelp industry is a perfect example of an industry in a region with few alternatives destroyed by free trade policies which exposed it to the unregulated market. This point was emphasized by the *Inverness*

Courier in 1850 when it editorialised, 'the kelp trade, which promoted a large population, was destroyed by legislative enactment' (*Inverness Courier*, 19 December 1850). For the British government in the late 1840s to tell proprietors like Colonel John Gordon that the starving tenants were solely their responsibility, was hardly playing fair.

The decline or loss of kelping income did not drive the kelping lairds into receivership. Many years of living beyond their means, the cost of heritable indebtedness, and expensive litigations over inheritances were responsible for much of the financial state of the proprietors.(13) Almost all of the major kelping estates were in the hands of outside administrators long before 1830. These administrations were all judicial ones authorized by a court, in which the administrators felt greatly constrained about what they could do; one man of business testified before the 1841 emigration enquiry that trustees doubted they had competency to assist tenants and others through emigration or to provide outdoor relief out of the funds of the estate (Select Committee 1841, 14). Heritable debt was allowed to grow, so long as no creditor demanded his money. The convention had grown up that such a debt was really like invested capital, safe so long as the estate continued to bring in money and pay the interest on the debt. The decline of kelping income to some extent did threaten the security of the debt, of course.

In any event, the great kelping lairds themselves were not responsible for the major clearances or exodus of people from the Hebrides after 1815, and were not even directly responsible for the sale of their estates to those, like John Gordon of Cluny or James Matheson or Sir John Campbell Orde, who ultimately did most of the clearing. Those sales had been decided upon and executed by an interlocking directorate of Edinburgh 'men of business' and lawyers, the same men who had been administering the estates for years. As the *Scotsman* observed in 1849, 'When the lands are heavily mortgaged, the obvious, though harsh resource, is dispossessing the small tenants, to make room for a better class able to pay rent, and this task generally devolves on south country managers or trustees, who look only to money returns, and cannot sympathise with the peculiar situations and feelings of the Highland population' (*The Scotsman*, 25 August 1849). At least one laird, Clanranald, did not want to sell and found his estate sold despite his protests (NAS GD 201/5/612/1). The result was that most of the Hebrides had by 1851 passed into the hands of outside 'capitalists' (the term is that used by *The Inverness Courier*, 19 December 1850). Whether the kelping lairds – given their record of reckless expenditure – would have managed the emergency conditions of the 1840s any better than their successors is a purely hypothetical question.

Finally, the loss of kelping income was only one of a number of major economic setbacks for people in the Hebrides attempting to survive on inadequate landholdings. The decline in the market for black cattle, a period of relative peace which cut down on military remittances, and especially the failure of the potato crops in the 1840s, all combined with the decline of kelping to produce the major exodus of population from the islands. Had nothing else gone wrong, however, the region might well have adjusted to the loss of the kelping income, which it must be noted did not entirely disappear as a cash crop (Gray 1957, 156–8). On the other hand, had the government supported its

Hebridean kelping industry with appropriate trade policies, the region would have been in a much better position to withstand the famine years. Certainly before the famine struck full strength, an experienced investor like John Gordon of Cluny thought that good management could turn the Long Island around, and perhaps it could have done so, had not the series of disasters come together within a very short time.

The Resurgance(s) of the Kelp Industry
Most writing on the Highlands and Islands suggests that the kelp industry came to an abrupt end sometime between the 1820s and the 1840s. To some extent the terminal date depends on the estate involved. A few sources have allowed that a small amount of kelping was carried on after 1840, but the brief resurgence in the Hebrides of kelping in the later 1860s and early 1870s has gone virtually unchronicled (e.g. Devine 1988; Richards 1982; the later kelping is mentioned briefly in MacArthur 1990, 132). One of the major reasons for this neglect is because the Napier Commission, receiving testimony within a half dozen years of great kelping activity, especially on South Uist and Benbecula, heard very little about this recent kelping from its witnesses (Napier 1884, xxxii–xxxvi). The careful reader of the testimony would discover that kelping on the Gordon Cathcart estate had terminated only a few years earlier, but little said by the witnesses suggested the volume of the manufactory. Only a handful of witnesses even hinted at a large industry. Angus Macdonald of Griminish insisted that the suffering of the past few years had been caused by the want of kelpmaking. 'I may say kelp was the sole support of the people here; and although they had not a good deal of wages for doing it, still the whole were turned out doing it, and there were stores of meal in the country, and no destitution while the kelp was going on. They would get plenty of meal when they were at the kelp' (ibid question 11975). In answer to a question from one of the commissioners, he insisted that cessation of kelpmaking was more injurious to the people than the removal of hill pasture complained of by most South Uist witnesses before the Royal Commission (ibid question 11976). The Cluny chief factor, Ranald Macdonald, admitted that he bore the responsibility for the policy of the reclamation of waste lands that were another chief item of complaint, justifying it on the grounds that because of the failure of the kelp industry, it was necessary in the early 1880s to find alternate employment for the population (ibid question 12052).

The reason for the renewed interest in kelp had nothing to do with its alkali content, but because it was also the raw ingredient of iodine. Iodine had been discovered by Bernard Cortois (1777–1838) in 1813, but only became commercially important in the 1860s (Partingtun 1964, IV, 86–90). The factor's letter-books for the Hebridean estate of the Gordons of Cluny provide a window into this later kelping world.(14) In mid 1872, the Gordons hired a new factor for the Hebrides. James Drever was a native of the Orkneys, and was a highly experienced kelp manager. For the next four years, Drever would build on the work of his predecessor and make kelp manufacture the central feature of his management. While the letter-books do not contain many of the detailed accounting records for the estate, they do emphasize the importance of kelp. According to Drever, the Cluny estate in the Hebrides, which consisted of South

Uist, Benbecula, and Barra, was still capable of the manufacture of between 800 and 1,600 tuns of kelp annually. In 1874 – the best year under Drever's management – it actually shipped over 1,300 tuns of kelp to Glasgow, a figure which compares most favourably with Clanranald figures in the Golden Age of kelping. Shipments were sent, as had traditionally been the case, on small vessels carrying cargoes of less than 60 tuns each. The purchasers organized most of the shipping. Between 1871 and 1876, kelpmaking returned a substantial annual profit to the estate.

By the 1860s, when kelp had become again commercially valuable mainly for its iodine content, the nature of kelping was substantially altered, for the red weed cast on shore as drift had a higher iodine content than the cut-weed. Good drift-weed kelp yielded ten to fifteen pounds of iodine per tun, while cut-weed kelp yielded only three or four pounds per tun (Newton 1931, ix). While the different eventual use of the kelp explains the preference for drift-weed over cut-weed, it does not explain the changes in the organization of the industry on the Cluny estate. In the earlier period, as Alexander Macneil of Smerclett had emphasized to the Napier Commission, 'we did not cut the weed for the proprietor; we ourselves manufactured the kelp' (Napier 1884, questions 11709–11716). Macneil was 80 years old in 1883 and therefore familiar with the industry at its height. He added that 'We never sold a pound of it but to the proprietor', and were paid by the weight. In the 1870s, however, the kelpmaking was subdivided into different tasks (collecting and drying tangle, drying drift-weed, burning drift-weed) and the crofters and cottars were paid separately and appropriately for each task, although burning remained the responsibility of individual manufacturers. Angus Macdonald spoke about 'wages', not 'payments (ibid question 11975). In some ways the difference seems inconsequential. In either case, the bulk of the money came back to the laird as rent or was applied to arrears. But in the earlier industry the kelpmaker could see himself as an independent producer, while in the later arrangement he was little more than a wage labourer. The reluctance of the crofters on South Uist in the 1870s to turn from their agricultural activities to kelpmaking was probably at least in part a result of the more industrial organization of the industry.

The market for South Uist kelp in the 1870s was an extremely limited one. Only Messrs Montgomery Paterson, Chemists, of Glasgow, and the British Seaweed Company, also of Glasgow, actually purchased kelp in this period. The latter preferred to deal directly with the kelpmakers whenever possible. The BSC went temporarily bankrupt in 1877, the year in which iodine from South America totally undercut the British kelpmakers and once again destroyed the industry. Given the limited numbers of purchasers, it was not surprising that the kelp producers were at their mercy, both in terms of price and in terms of the conditions of sale.

In the years immediately before 1877, kelpmaking served two purposes for the Gordon estate. In the first place, it provided welcome additional revenue for the estate, for it was still the case that kelping required little capital investment. Any revenue beyond the payment to the kelpmakers and the costs of shipping was pure profit. In the second place, it provided income for crofters, and hence indirectly enhanced the rentals of the estate. Successful

kelpmaking greatly improved rental collections, as Drever well recognized. Given these considerations, Drever's instincts were to make as much kelp as possible throughout the year regardless of its quality, arguing that if kelp were to be manufactured at all, the people needed to be provided with meal and employed regularly.

The chemists in Glasgow, on the other hand, wanted only the highest quality kelp, which from their standpoint meant drift-weed kelp made before August of each year. Messrs Montgomery Paterson were not much interested in cut-weed kelp made later in the season. Annual bargaining between the estate and the purchasers got more and more protracted and complicated each year. The estate in 1875 successfully resisted a suggestion that the purchasers not be bound to take delivery if the price of iodine fell below the contracted price of the kelp. Drever also opposed payment according to the quality of each parcel, on the grounds that the making of kelp was so dependent on weather and raw materials that quality control was almost impossible. He insisted that, although South Uist kelp did not contain as high a proportion of the valuable 'insoluble matter' as that manufactured in the Orkneys or in Ireland, this was more than compensated for by its lower price. In 1873, Orkney kelp delivered in Glasgow sold at £7 per tun, and South Uist kelp at £4. 14 per tun similarly delivered.(15) By 1876, however, the purchasers managed to introduce a differential price structure, with drift-weed manufactured before 1 August and that manufactured afterward purchased at a different rate; there was also a much lower price for cut-weed. Drever was nonetheless prepared to make cut-weed at a loss in order to keep his operation intact, and would have continued to do so had the bottom not fallen completely out of the market after 1876.

Most of the kelp manufactured on the Cluny estate came from South Uist and Benbecula. The people on Barra had shifted into the east coast fishery and were, for the most part, no longer available for kelpmaking. The Barra kelpmaking concession was let to an Irishman who produced only about 30 tuns a year. The North Uist estate of Lord Macdonald was involved in kelping, although its shores had been let to the British Seaweed Company, which dealt directly with the kelpmakers itself. Only on South Uist and Benbecula was kelpmaking still directly controlled by the landlord. Drever emphasized the need to collect seaweed blown on the beach, especially tangle, throughout the year. The tangle was to be piled up and cross-stacked, so that the wind could blow through it and help dry it before it was burnt in the spring. The crofters were reluctant to take time from their agricultural pursuits to deal with the tangle, however, and Drever often threatened to evict those who refused to become involved. He provided meal to kelpmakers as an incentive. Later in the year, drift-weed was collected, transported in hand barrows, and spread by men, women, and children on large drying grounds scattered throughout the estate, where it was subsequently burned.(16) At the end of the season, weed was cut and then burned., but the cut-weed was not of much value.

The bulk of the payments to the kelpmakers were applied to their rentals and meal accounts, although Drever recognized the need for incentives. He fought for a higher payment for the workers, insisting that if something were left over to the workers after their annual accounts were cleared, they would be more willing to participate in the kelpmaking. Subsequently, in 1874, Drever succeeded in persuading the laird to reintroduce a prize system for kelpmaking. Both quantity made and quality were rewarded. The estate was broken down into four districts, and the individuals in each district who delivered the largest quantity of the best drift-weed kelp won prizes of £5 each, a substantial bonus for the time. The overall winner had 'delivered the largest quantity of the best quality of drift-weed kelp all over the estate' (James Drever to John Gordon, 14 January 1875, South Uist Estate Papers). The total was over twelve tuns, which suggests the extent to which the organization of manufacturing had been altered. Four prizes of decreasing value were awarded in each district. Drever expected the prizes not only to motivate the individual kelpmakers, but to stir up a spirit of competition among the districts. As he wrote to one of his ground officers in 1875, 'although you carried off the prize last year you had better be up and doing lest the 'Men of the North' who are on the alert snatch it from you this season' (ibid Drever to Donald McInnes, 21 January, 1875). This strategy was soon ended, however, by the total collapse of the market. After 1877 kelpmaking was virtually unmentioned in the letters of the factor.

The Final Demise

After 1877, the Gordon estates of the Hebrides no longer emphasized kelp manufacture. New administrators were brought in who concentrated on agricultural improvement, especially land reclamation and game management. As the testimony before the Napier Commission had shown, these new policies were among the greatest grievances of the people of South Uist and Benbecula. By the early 1880s, the major products of the estate were potatoes and carrots. The new managers were prepared to consider a reintroduction of kelping, and occasionally discussed it, for it still promised to provide additional income for the crofters. But beyond leasing the shores of the estate to a Glasgow firm in the early 1880s – which was supposed to pay crofters for tangle at the rate of 4d per yard, the yard to be 3 feet long each way and 2 feet deep – little was ever done about kelping by the laird. Kelp was subsequently made in the traditional way, however, although the amounts shipped by the leaseholder were much smaller than had earlier been produced by the estate. The schoolmaster F G Rea, who came to South Uist in 1889, recorded in his autobiography :

> the long line of the western shore was spaced out with columns of smoke rising high into the clear air. When I made inquiries I heard that these were the fires of the kelp burners. During the gales of the winter much seaweed from the Atlantic is thrown up on the western shores, and among it the long thick 'tangle' or roots as thick as, or thicker than, a man's wrist. The men hasten to the shore with long forks and drag this wrack from the waves high up on to the shore out of the reach of the sea; here it is piled up and left in heaps until spring. As soon as dry weather comes it is burnt in a kiln or kind of pit, the resultant ash being left to cool and solidify. This is the kelp from which iodine, soda and otherproducts are obtained at the chemical works in Glasgow (Rea 1997, 77). (17)

The Great War brought a renewed demand for iodine, and as late as the early 1920s, the British Chemical Company was still taking between 50 and 100 tuns of kelp out of South Uist annually, making small payments directly to individual producers. By this point technology had changed, and the burnt kelp was exported as ash in bags rather than in the earlier blocks. Relations between the British Chemical Company and the kelpmakers were not good, with the Company convinced that insufficient care was being taken to produce a good product and the kelpmakers convinced that the Company was exploiting them.(18) A subsequent employment of kelp as a source of alginates rejuvenated the industry after World War II, and the last kelp manufacturer did not finally disappear from the Hebrides until the late 1990s. The possible value of kelp to the food industry has kept the possibility of a return to kelp manufacture alive into the 21st century, but by this point, not many people were holding their breaths. As one observer on South Uist put it, 'the people had been disappointed too often by the kelp'.

Notes

1 As in recent years has been the case with the cod fishing industry of Newfoundland, or the coal-mining industry almost everywhere in the world.
2 It might be better to distinguish kelp, the raw seaweed, from the kelp burnt by the harvesters, which could be called 'made kelp'. A third distinction could also be added of reprocessed 'made kelp', which could perhaps be called manufactured kelp.
3 Anderson was a manufacturing chemist who ran an alkali manufacturing plant (using salt as its raw material) in Leith. Although this pamphlet was probably financed by the great kelp proprietors and its policy analysis must be understood in this light, Anderson had nonetheless studied kelp and alkalines with more care than anyone else in Britain at the time; see Dr J W Anderson to John Bowie, 9th February 1835 (NAS GD 201/5/1232/9).
4 The principal argument was that the kelp on the western shore was far inferior to that on the eastern.
5 John Bowie had been employed by Lord Macdonald as factor for many years.
6 At the time of the institution of the trusteeship, Clanranald's debts were in excess of £70,000. See SCA, Oban Letters, Box 16.
7 Colin Mackenzie to Earl of Seaforth, 21 June 1800. A similar comment was made by his attorney to the wife of Seaforth's successor in 1835: 'I do most sincerely hope some good Colonial Appointment may be offered to Seaforth, for I see no other way for his & our extrication'. William McKenzie to Mrs McKenzie, 1 June 1835 (NAS GD 46/1/204).
8 See, for example, the marginal notation on Crofters of Salem to Murdoch Maclaine, 27 April 1799 (NAS GD 174/964), that protestors were let 'at their liberty 2 May 1799'.
9 Minutes of Sederunt of Clanranald's Tutors, 1 July 1801. This would not only placate the tenants, but, argued a later sederunt, would tie down them down so they 'could not possibly leave their farm without the consent of the Proprietor'.
10 Leblanc's process involved adding limestone (calcium carbonate) to the heating of common salt with sulphuric acid. He made nothing from the development of the process because the French government forced him to disclose his secrets and then published them. He committed suicide in 1806.

12 'A Report to Colonel John Gordon of Cluny, 1839, by John Fleming, concerning the present state of the Estates of Benbecula and South Uist and proposed alterations and improvements', typescript (from a lost original) in South Uist Historical Museum.

13 It is not possible to calculate the costs of litigation over the inheritance of estates to the proprietors of the Hebrides, but given the amount of documentation on litigation in their surviving papers, it must have been considerable.

14 These letter-books survive in the estate office in South Uist at Askernish. The first volume begins on 5th July 1872.

15 The 'tun' involved in these shipments was 2,250 pounds.

16 One of these drying grounds survives and has been studied by the Sheffield archaeological team.

17 Another contemporary account, probably from the late 19th century, is recorded by Lawson (1991, II, 13–14).

18 James S Paul (of the British Chemical Company) to Mr Mcdonald (factor of the estate), 18th October 1921, in loose papers relating to the kelp industry held in the estate office, South Uist.

8

General Macneil and Colonel Gordon: Collapse and Clearance (Barra from 1822 to 1851)

The 41st and last ancestral chieftain of the Clan Macneil succeeded to the title when his father died in Toxteth, Liverpool, on April 24th 1822. General Roderick Macneil (or as he then was, Lieutenant Colonel Macneil) was born in 1790, the eldest son of Roderick the Gentle (Fig. 8.1). He was brought up in Liverpool and on Barra, where his father had built the Adams-style mansion at Eoligarry. In March 1808 he joined the 52nd Regiment of Foot as Ensign, explaining to his maternal grandfather that 'an intelligent and skilful officer in the army is as respectable a character as any' (NAS GD/1/736/88-90). His father met his expenses and paid off debts of £500 when he joined the army. In July his regiment embarked for Spain, and in January 1809 he fought under Sir John Moore at Corunna, where he was wounded. After convalescence he rejoined

Figure 8.1 General Roderick Macneil of Barra c. 1860 (from a portrait by an unknown artist: photographic copy in the Regimental Museum of the Queen's Highlanders

his regiment and fought through the rest of the Napoleonic campaigns, being raised to Lieutenant in the 91st Regiment, and then Captain in the 60th, before transferring to the 23rd Light Dragoons early in 1815. With the Dragoons he fought at Quatre Bras and at Waterloo. Paradoxically, the fall of Napoleon, in which Roderick Macneil played his part, led in turn to the fall in the demand for, and the price of, kelp and therefore hastened, perhaps even instigated, the collapse of his own estate!

By 1818 Roderick, like so many officers, was on half-pay, but in that year he made an advantageous marriage with Isabella, daughter of Lieut. Colonel Charles Brownlow of Lurgan, Armagh. Brownlow was a wealthy man with an annual income of £15,000 a year, and he settled a dowry of £6,000 on Macneil. The following year Roderick the Gentle purchased a new commission, as Major in the 1st Life Guards, for his son and continued to meet at least some of his son's accumulating debts. Between 1813 and 1819, the chief claims to have spent £10,685 on purchasing promotions and paying off the personal debts of his heir (who we hereafter refer to as General Macneil).

The Estate in 1822

Roderick the Gentle was, however, running up debts of his own and when he died in 1822 he owed in excess of £30,000. These included not only the usual debts of a gentleman, but some significant heritable bonds. Furthermore his will required his son to pay annuities to each of his unmarried sisters of £450. Yet, in 1820 he had registered a disposition 'in favour of Sir Ewan Cameron of Fassifearn [his father-in-law] and others disposing to them the Estate of Barra in Trust' (NAS TD85/63/A8), so that the new chieftain had no control of the estate from which he was expected to find the means to meet these obligations. It is hardly surprising that in his first (surviving) letter to the parish priest, General Macneil should rail against the 'ruinous nature of the Deeds executed by my late father'. He continued 'I was literally tied to the stake, having no alternative but to reduce them or consign myself and my family to penury' (Campbell 1998, 135). These debts, obligations, and restrictions, however, were only one of four mounting problems which faced the new chief.

The decline in the demand for Hebridean kelp which was mentioned in the previous chapter gathered speed from 1822, when the duty on salt was cut from 15/- to just 2/- a bushel. In quick succession there followed a reduction in the duty on barilla, repeal of all duties on salt, a reduction in the duty on pot and pearl ash, the removal of duty on ashes from Canada, and a reduction in the duty on foreign sulphur (Select Committee 1841, question 10). At the same time in 1823 the 'Leblanc process' for converting salt into alkali was introduced in Liverpool, one of the principal markets for Hebridean kelp (see above p.131). Thereafter the price of kelp fell rapidly.

This was a double-edged sword, for as we noted earlier, tenants throughout the highlands and islands had seen rents raised on the back of the surge in kelping between 1790 and 1815, so that as prices for kelp fell and the landlords paid less for its harvesting and processing, so tenants fell increasingly into rent arrears. The fall in rent income was exacerbated by a continuing loss of rent-paying tenants to emigration. There was a steady flow of emigrants, as demonstrated in the following chapter, punctuated by episodes of large-scale migration. After the loss of about 300 people in 1817, a further 350 left on the *Harmony* in 1821, and another shipload was to leave in 1826. These emigrants represented a loss to the landlord of both rents and kelping activity.

Paradoxically, the fourth problem which faced the new chief was Barra's overpopulation. We noted in a previous chapter that between 1755 and 1821 Barra's population doubled, despite considerable emigrations. At 2,300, the population was well in excess of what the islands could really support by farming and fishing alone. Maculloch in 1816 noted that 'everything arable ...is already in a state of cultivation. Indeed in any other circumstances, the cultivation of Barra would be judged excessive and injudicious' (in Campbell 1998, 101). In other words Barra had no further arable which it could exploit if the population rose further, and it was very vulnerable to any shortfall in food supplies caused by bad weather. In fact, Barra (and the rest of the Hebrides) suffered a series of 'bad years' – 1795/6, 1806/7, 1816/17 were particularly bad. More were to come – in 1826/27 and 1836/7. Just how marginal was the subsistence base on Barra is emphasised in a letter from Neil Macdonald, parish priest, to his predecessor (Angus Macdonald) in October 1827: 'people were actually starving, fainting away in different parts of the island. Had it not been for the cockles of Traigh Mhor there would have been hundreds dead this day in Barra' (SCR B12/128). A similar scene was played out in 1836/7 according to the Statistical Account for 1840. The constant but unpredictable threat of having starving tenants and cottars on his estate must have added to Macneil's concerns.

General Macneil's Strategy

In such circumstances what was the General to do? He seems to have initially set about the task of improving his and the estate's financial circumstances with some zeal. By November 1822 he had issued a summons of reduction against the estate's Trustees (and every relative he could think off - the summons lists 34 individuals). Although the process was slow, and fought hard by those named in the summons, the estate was finally removed from the Trustees and placed in the General's hands in February 1826 (NAS TD 85/63/A8). Furthermore in February 1828 he bought back the superiority of Barra from the Macdonalds, in whose hands it had rested since 1695, under the burden of £999 (*ibid*). Given his circumstances, this was the action of a proud man!

At the same time as he took legal action to secure control of the estate, he was wise enough to court the support of the parish priest, Angus Macdonald. He clearly understood just how important the support of the priest would be in securing the acquiescence, or better, the willing participation of his overwhelmingly Catholic tenantry in his plans for the estate. Indeed in March 1824 he plainly said as much to Macdonald, 'possessing as you do unbounded influence over your flock, I look to you for the most cordial cooperation' (Campbell 1988, 137). He promised to look after the priest's interests, adding conspiratorially 'what I shall do for you is quite between ourselves'. Over the next three years he grew increasingly disillusioned about Macdonald's role in events on Barra, but when Macdonald was (remarkably) translated from parish priest to Rector of the prestigious Scots College in Rome in 1825, he sought the support of the new priest with a mixture of stick and carrot (SCR B12/127, 128, 132).

Meanwhile, the General was developing a strategy, or at least a programme of action, to put the estate on a sounder footing. There were four principal strands to this programme. One was to clear small tenants from the better arable and low pasture on the machair and adjacent lands on the west coast, and to turn these over to farmers. The second, which was to some extent dependent on the first, was to create additional crofts on the relatively sparsely occupied east side of the island.

These would provide both an additional source of rent income, and a home for the displaced tenants from the west coast. The third strand in the General's strategy was to develop the potential of the fishing industry. This was to be achieved by ensuring that more of the population were engaged in fishing, that deep-sea fishing and exploitation of the further banks was developed, by creating a 'fishing village' in Castlebay, and by taking central control of the sale of the catch. Fourthly, Macneil decided there was still potential in the kelp market, and decided to invest in the building of a 'soda factory' which would re-process made kelp to produce 'soda ashes' with a much higher market value.

How and when this programme came to be formulated is not entirely clear, but as we shall see it may have owed something to advice from elsewhere. Macneil's interest in realising the potential of the fishing around Barra emerges in several of his letters to Angus Macdonald in 1824 and 1825. Though he mentions kelping twice in letters of this period, the first mention of the plan to build a factory is in a letter to Angus Macdonald from the new parish priest in July 1828 (SCR B12/132). As for removals from the west coast, although he threatens removals in letters in 1824 and 1825, these are general threats against those who do not pay their rents or do his bidding. The first intimations of possible clearances on the west side of the island are in an enigmatic reference to Craigston township in a letter of February 1825. It was around this time that crofter Roderick Macneil later claimed (in 1871) that he was evicted from Grean and his house burned. According to him 'all the lands of the townland were given to the lowland farmer beside us' (CG III, 111). Further, in October 1827, Neil Macdonald writes to his predecessor in Rome saying that 'McStuart is no longer here...he left after unroofing all the houses in Borve, Tangasdale and Allasdale' (SCR B12/128).

The 'McStuart' mentioned is in all probability the same man as the Stewart who is described as 'my factor' in Macneil's last two letters to Angus Macdonald, written in July and October 1825. There is reason to think that this man is Alexander Stewart of Scowrie, for in a letter of January 1840 Stewart of Scowrie writes '**My plan to**

Colonel Macneil [our emphasis] was to remove the hordes of small tenantry from the west to the east side so as to get at the most valuable of the pasture for stock and to put down fishing settlements on the south and east for the purpose of putting employment in fishing ling and cod within reach of the greater part of the population. He admitted my plan to be a good one, and commenced, but unfortunately he had neither capital nor perseverance to go on with it'. Stewart adds that Macneil 'subsequently got hold of a Welsh chemist who commenced manufacturing soda and neglected the natural productive quality of the island for sheep and black cattle' (NAS D593K, 1/3/28 Jan). Stewart of Scowrie was writing to none other than the notorious Patrick Sellar, who had been brought to trial (but acquitted) in 1816 for nothing less than the culpable homicide of evicted tenants in Strathnaver. As factor of Scowrie in 1840 Stewart had become a confidant of Sellar and seems to have shared some of Sellar's views on how to deal with unprofitable estates!

West Coast Clearances?

The confirmation that Macneil did indeed at least begin to pursue his or Stewart's strategy is partly documentary and partly archaeological. The clearance of some of the west side townships had certainly taken place by the time of the 1841 census but when, and therefore under whose direction, is not easily pinpointed. The 1841 census reveals that Craigston, Alasdale, Grean and Cleat townships had all become farms, mostly populated by people described in the census as agricultural labourers. A fourth west coast township, Cuier, was the glebe of the Protestant minister. The only document that throws any light on when this action had taken place is a rental list for the year 1836 - 1837 (NAS CS96/4274), which should have been agreed whilst Macneil was still, just, in charge of his estate. The rental does not describe the status of its rent-payers, it simply lists their names. Throughout the island, not surprisingly, one can match most of the tenants on the 1836–37 rental with households living in the same townships in 1841. In the case of the west coast townships just named, at least 75% of the tenants listed on the 1836–7 rental can be found still in residence in the 1841 census. These rent payers in 1836/7 were presumably paying rents for their crofts, and in fact there are almost the same number of rent payers in each of these townships as there were in the 1811 rental (NAS CS44/446). It appears that the number of crofting tenancies in these townships remained more or less unchanged between 1811 and 1836/37. But if farms were created from townships, and their populations became agricultural labourers, then the crofts must have disappeared **after** Whitsun 1837 – in the time of either the trustees administration of the estate or at the beginning of Colonel Gordon's ownership. This would square with the testimony given many years later at the Napier Commission, that the only clearances undertaken by the Macneils were of the townships of Rolls and Kilbar, probably cleared by Roderick the Gentle in creating his Eoligarry home farm (Napier 1884, 633, question 10320). Taking into account the evidence of Roderick Macneil of Grian, Neil Macdonald's letter of October 1827, Stewart's letter to Sellar, the 1836/7 rental list, and the 1841 census, it appears that under Stewart's influence the General planned and began a clearance of west coast townships in 1825–27. He then had second thoughts, possibly under the threat of a

second mass emigration to follow that of 1826 (John Chisholm to Angus Macdonald: SCR B12/127). At this point Stewart left Barra (SCR B12/128), and Macneil turned his energies to implementing the remaining elements of his grand strategy.

Fishing and Fishermen

His determination to increase the income derived from fishing was already apparent in May 1824 when he told Angus Macdonald that those tenants who chose to market their catch themselves in Glasgow, or barter it with passing merchants, would be 'turned off my lands'. A year later he gave the fishermen of Barra just 48 hours in which to 'bend their energies to the daily prosecution of their calling as fishermen' (Campbell 1998, 138, 145). He bought new tackle, and by 1825 had begun to build his new fishing village (*ibid*, 142, 147). At the same time he explored the possibility of bringing in fishermen from elsewhere, partly out of exasperation with his own men, but also to utilise experience of deep-sea and further bank fishing. He told Macdonald he would bring in Irish fishermen (ibid, 144), though there is little evidence for any of them in either the Parish register or the 1841 census. But in November 1826 he also sent a factor to Mackenzie of Seaforth 'to learn if any of your tenants can be induced to establish themselves in my fishing village' (NAS GD 46/17/Vol.70). According to the Select Committee on Emigration in 1841, he also 'brought fishermen from Peterhead to teach the people the art of deep-sea fishing (Select Committee 1841, question 2720). Having waved the stick before his native fishermen in 1825, he then apparently resorted to the carrot in 1827, making them 'very fair offers about their fishing, which they accepted' (Chisholm to Macdonald SCR B12/127). Chisholm wryly observed 'I doubt much they will be inclined to implement their part of the bargain', and sure enough in 1828 Neil Macdonald recorded that the fisherman and Macneil were 'at variance for their having given a part of their fish away to procure provisions'. By 1830, it seems the General had finally decided that the lack of cooperation from his fishermen together with the removal of the fishing bounty meant that fishing could no longer contribute significantly to solving his problems : '(Macneil) will have no more to do with the fish' Neil Macdonald wrote to his predecessor in January of that year (SCR B12/136).

Macneil's Chemical Factory

By now, the General was investing all his energies, hopes, and not inconsiderable amounts of capital in his soda works at Northbay. Stewart clearly stated that the decision to re-process made kelp was made after the reversal of the decision to clear some of the west coast townships, and there is no mention of the factory in any source earlier than July 1828. At this time, the decision to build the factory had been made, the bricks to build its chimneys were already stacked at Northbay, but the work had not yet begun (SCR B12/132). In January 1830 Neil Macdonald reported that 'the great work at Bahierva is a building and will, in course of the spring, if well, be fit for work', and in March pronounced the work finished (SCR B12/136; 138). But the slow process of building, seems to have been followed by an equally slow process of putting the works into production. A memorandum prepared for Colonel John Gordon in 1835 claims that work actually only began in the factory 'within these few past months' and that they are 'now for the first time in full operation' (NAS GD 244/35/4). But production must have commenced earlier for Macneil was buying made kelp for the factory from the Clan Ranald estate in 1833. In 1834 he imported 387 tons of kelp from Clan Ranald, and in 1835 537 tons (NAS GD201/Pt 5/1232/8-9). Nevertheless, production only began eleven years after the General succeeded his father, and a full five years after he invested considerable capital in materials and labour to build the works.

The physical remains of the works have been described in an earlier chapter. They were clearly on a very considerable and ambitious scale (Fig. 8.2) and apart from producing a return on re-processed kelp would also provide work for a large number of the islanders. One report suggested as many as 500 were employed in the 'manufacture of alkali' (IC 19/12/1850, 4), but such a number is only feasible if it includes those crofters, cottars and others who cut kelp on Barra, as well as those employed in the factory. There is also a report that the people were removed from Berneray and probably from Mingulay to work in the chemical factory (Stevenson 1838) and the designation of one of the buildings at Northbay as a 'barracks' might possibly refer to accommodation provided on site for workers who did not live locally.

The large scale of the venture was probably determined by the small profit margins involved; if Macneil was to revive his fortunes he needed to re-process a lot of kelp. The results of a contemporary and similar venture on the Clan Ranald estate on South Uist, undertaken on a trial basis in 1830, did not bode well for Macneil (see above p. 132). The process used in Macneil's factory seems to have differed from that tried by Anderson and Mccrummen on South Uist, although at the time it was a source of speculation and somewhat shrouded in mystery. Anderson and Mccrummen tried to produce what may be described as enhanced kelp (with an improved alkali content of somewhere around 10%, and a selling price of perhaps £5 or £6 per ton) by the use of improved kelp furnaces and closer control of the process. Macneil's factory on the other hand was thought to use a chemical process to 'manufacture soda ashes from kelp'. The economics of the venture can be broadly identified. Macneil was buying-in made kelp from Clan Ranald at a price of around £2-10-0 to £2-15-0 a ton, though he presumably was also using Barra kelp which cost him much less. No one knew for certain how much made-kelp was needed to produce a ton of the soda ashes, though 'some say as high as four tons'. This enhanced kelp was sold at a price 'varying from £10 to £18 a ton', the entire production being sold in Liverpool and Manchester (NAS GD 244/35). Given the costs of manufacturing, and the shipping charges to the Mersey, the product could only make a substantial profit when it was selling at somewhere in the top end of its price range. Whether the 'chemical factory' ever made an operating profit we do not know, although it should be noted that for three years (1833–35) Macneil purchased large quantities of made-kelp from Clan Ranald, and that right up to the time he was declared bankrupt in 1836, he was still negotiating to buy as much as a further 500–600 tons. This

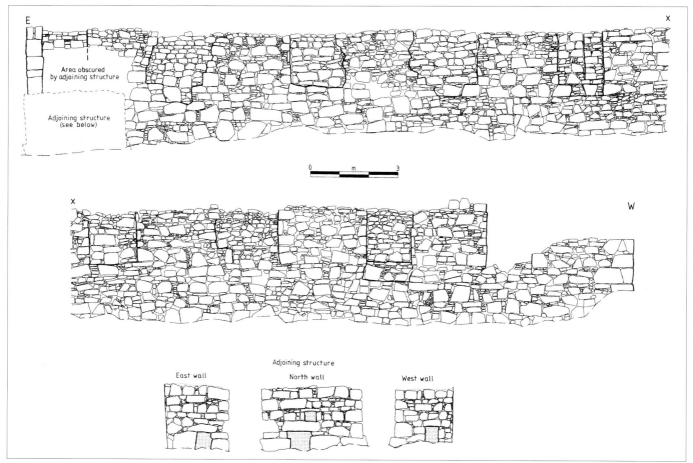

Figure 8.2 Measured elevation of the external wall of Macneil's 'chemical' factory at Northbay showing the portals through which kelp was offloaded into the factory

might suggest that the works were indeed beginning to turn over a profit, though the fact that Macneil was failing to pay the bills for the Clan Ranald kelp has also to be taken into account! Overall, however, the 'chemical factory' must have been yet a further drain on Macneil's resources, given the capital needed to build it. A considerable part of this, somewhere around £40,000, had been raised in a heritable bond and a loan secured on the factory from two manufacturers or merchants in Liverpool and Manchester (NAS GD 244/35).

Rent Increases

It is also claimed that to finance his factory Macneil 'divided every croft in Barra in two, charged the same rent for a half croft as had formerly been paid for a whole croft, and thus doubled the apparent value of the property' (Hunter 1976, 35-6). It is not clear what the evidence for this assertion is, although the agent sent by the Trustees to Barra in 1836 reported that 'it is understood that Macneil raised the rents because he gave the tenants work at the Soda Works and thus, in a manner, had their labour for nothing' (NAS CS96/4274, p25). We can get some general impression of the rise in rents and rent payers between 1811 and 1836 by comparing the rental lists for those two years (table 8.1).

From this table it is clear that between 1811 and 1836 rents in many townships doubled, and in a few they trebled. But in most townships the number of tenants barely changed at all. Increased numbers are to be found in the east coast townships (Fig. 8.3), where overall the number increased from 39 to 67, with big increases in Bruernish and Brevig. The other significant increase is with the creation of Glen township with 25 tenants. We do not know when the rent increases were made; over a twenty-five year period it is likely that they were raised several times rather than just once. Nevertheless there can be little doubt that at least some of the increase, and probably the greater part of it, came during the General's stewardship of the estate. On the other hand it is clear that we certainly cannot substantiate the claim that the General divided all his crofts in two and collected twice as many rents. Even in Bruernish, Earsary and Brevig, where the number of tenants doubled between 1811 and 1836 we cannot be sure that the General was solely responsible for the increase. Equally we do not know if the increased number of tenancies represents new areas of land not previously rented, rather than the subdivision of existing crofts.

New Tenants

Nevertheless it is equally clear that by 1836 there were a significant number of new tenancies on Barra, mostly down

Table 8.1: Tenants and rents for Barra townships in 1811 and 1836 (sources: NAS CS44/B446; CS46/4274)

Township	1811 Tenants	1811 Rents	1836 Tenants	1836 Rents
Northend/Eoligarry	52	£225 – 05 - 0	-	(home farm)
Hellisay	5	£75 – 10 - 0	8	£56 – 14 - 0
Northbay	1	£24 – 00 - 0	1	£24 – 00 - 0
Bruernish	9	£58 – 10 - 0	17	£117 – 12 - 0
Balnabodach	4	£15 – 15 - 0	1?	£25 – 00 - 0
Rulios	4	£19 – 16 - 0	6	£37 – 07 - 0
Earsary	3	£24 – 00 - 0	8	£55 – 00 - 0
Skallary	3	£13 – 04 - 0	4	£41 – 00 - 0
Brevig	10	£49 – 04 - 0	23	£145 – 05 - 0
Glen	-	-	25	£169 – 15 - 0
Kentangaval	14	£58 – 10 - 0	11	£85 – 10 - 0
Nask	3	£20 – 16 - 0	-	-
Tangasdale	16	£55 – 02 - 6	14	£100 – 00 - 0
Borve	27	£160 – 16 - 0	31	£222 – 00 - 0
Craigston	13	£48 – 00 - 0	15	£112 – 11 - 7
Allasdale	18	£96 – 00 - 0	18	£140 – 09 - 0
Grean	26	£123 – 04 - 0	27	£165 – 07 - 0
Cleat	10	£57 – 10 - 0	12	£107 – 07 - 0
Cuier	1	£34 – 00 - 0	-	-

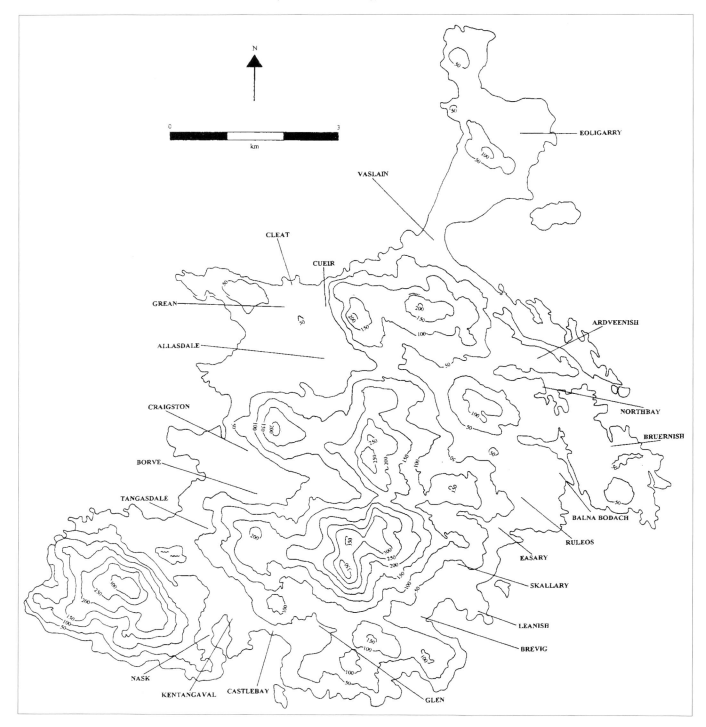

Figure 8.3 The location of the townships of Barra listed in the 1851 and 1861 census records

the east coast and at the south east corner in Glen. This might support the view that the General pressed ahead with putting tenants on the previously sparsely occupied east coast, even if he did not remove them there from the west coast townships. If so, where did these new tenants come from? The answer is found in several sources.

In his letters to parish priest Angus Macdonald, the General raised the spectre of bringing in tenants from elsewhere on several occasions, though interestingly the first reference to this possibility clearly lays the blame for initiating this policy elsewhere. '*Others* again, to my knowledge, encouraged Mr Mcniven with the view of introducing Protestants into the shoes of the deluded

Roman Catholics'. Mcniven was an emigration agent, and those who encouraged him to recruit Catholics for emigration might have included either the Protestant minister or the 'Robertson' referred to a little earlier in the same letter (Campbell 1998, 141). At this time (February 1825) the General says that he would 'much prefer rowing in the same boat with the natives of the soil', but he was soon to revise this view. In July of the same year he wrote to Macdonald 'if one set of servants (tenants at will, are nothing else) won't do, the master must try others'. By August the threat was quite explicit: 'if I don't on my arrival find them heart and hand engaged in fishing, *I pledge you my honour* they shall tramp, and the Land shall be this ensuing spring occupied by *strangers.*' *(ibid* 144, 147). Macneil clearly followed up the threat with action, for Angus Macdonald's successor, Neil Macdonald, reported to him in October 1827 'North Uist and Tiree people are daily flocking in' (SCR B12/128). In fact Macneil's hand may have been forced since in 1826 there was a group emigration from Barra (of which more in the following chapter), organised by Mcniven and Colonel Fraser, another well-known emigration agent. Nevertheless, the General soon grew disillusioned with at least some of his new tenants, and by January 1830 he had ordered a list of North Uist men to be made with a view to removing them. A year later some at least were still on Barra, for Neil Macdonald reported again 'they are to be sent off' (SCR B12/136, 138).

Some impression of both the scale of immigration to Barra under Macneil, and the directions in which he cast his net for new tenants, can be gained by careful use of the 1841 and even the 1851 census data. Colonel Gordon, in seeking to justify his large-scale clearance of the island in 1850 went so far as to claim that 'the majority of the present inhabitants of Barra were not originally natives of Barra but brought there by the late proprietor from neighbouring islands'. The 1851 census therefore, which took place after the 1850 clearance, but before further removals in 1851, might be expected to reflect this mass immigration, and the 1841 census should certainly reveal immigrant families. The 1841 census, however, records the place of birth of individuals only by county so that any immigrants from the Outer Hebrides, and the whole swathe of mainland Inverness, would not be distinguished from natives of Barra. Nevertheless, analysis of the 1841 and 1851 census records, noting particularly the date and place of birth of children, allows us to identify a notable number of immigrant families. In 1841, 146 individuals (in a population of 2,363), including 30 heads of families, are recorded as having been born outside Inverness. Of the 30 heads of families, 18 can be identified as having arrived in Barra during General Macneil's stewardship, and 3 in that of the Trustees. In the 1851 census there are 119 individuals (including 27 heads of family) born outside Inverness. Taking into account families already recorded in the 1841 census, the two census records together allow us to identify 22 heads of non-Inverness families who established themselves in Barra during the General's time. Because the 1851 census identifies people's place of birth to a specific location, we can also identify now people who came to Barra from other parts of Inverness. They number 144 individuals, including 25 heads of family. Eleven of the latter certainly arrived during the General's time and 4 after 1840. Altogether then, we can identify at least 33 immigrant families under General Macneil; there are a further 12 who probably arrived before 1836. Given that Macneil may have removed some of the immigrant North Uist families around 1830, the evidence does suggest a serious attempt by the General to bring in families from elsewhere, many of whom were non-Catholic.

As to where he sought his recruits, the principal points of origin for immigrant individuals in the 1851 census were : South Uist 55, Tiree 54, North Uist 46, Skye 16, Lowlands 16, and Argyll 13, although not all of these necessarily arrived in Barra under the General. Despite these numbers, however, there is certainly no evidence to support Gordon's claim that the majority of inhabitants in 1850 were

immigrant to the island. Nor is it likely that the General's new tenants were ever sufficient in numbers to replace the groups who left in 1821 and 1826, and the individual families who emigrated in the years between 1822 and 1836. Certainly the 1831 census shows that between 1821 and 1831 Barra suffered a net loss of over two hundred inhabitants. By 1841 there had been a net gain of about sixty, but some of these were immigrant families brought in by the trustees of the estate after 1836.

Other Measures

In addition to the principal measures described above, by which the General attempted to turn around the fortunes of his estate, there were other steps he took for the same purpose. Some were trifling. Early in his ownership he tried to increase the amount of work he got from his tenants by forcing the priest to reduce the number of holidays (Campbell 1998, 138)! Other measures were more significant. Chief amongst these was probably an aggressive policy towards collecting rents. Allowing rent arrears to accumulate had become commonplace in many highland estates in the period after 1815 (Devine 1988, 25). The General complained in May 1824 'that little or no rent has been paid' (Campbell 1998, 138). By 1827, with Stewart apparently in charge, it was 'determined that every penny of rent would be paid at the term'. Those who could not or would not pay in 1827 had their cattle seized, and this practice continued for in 1830 Neil Macdonald reported that the land officers 'are continually collecting the tenantry's cattle' (SCR B12/136). It was during this period that John Macpherson recalled seeing his mother's sheep seized and sent to Vatersay (Napier 1884, question 10578). Things appear to have come to a head in 1831, when the General himself led his ground officers to seize cattle and horses and eventually even calves, all of which were sent to the home farm at Eoligarry. At the same time, he ordered 'every sheep in Barra should be killed', and Neil Macdonald says this was done but for a few which some of the North Uist tenants refused to yield up (SCR B12/138). It should be noted however that the Trustees of the estate in November 1836 recorded over 2,000 sheep amongst Macneil's own stock (NAS CS96/4274), whilst evidence was given to the Napier Commission that in 1838 there were 7,600 sheep on Barra, including 4,000 on the home farm (Napier 1884, question 10945).

In addition to trying to enforce the payment of rents, Macneil seems to have attempted to raise quick cash by considering the sale or rental of his own home farm, and its stock, in 1825 (Campbell 1998, 140, 143). He also took back the farm of Vatersay, which had been in the hands of Macneil tacksmen since at least the 17th century. In 1827 Hugh, the eldest son of the incumbent tacksman Donald, wrote from Liverpool to Angus Macdonald in Rome to say that 'our family has left their native home being forced from the place by that monster of ingratitude the Colonel' (SCR B12/129). Hugh and the other children had all left the Hebrides, but he makes no mention of his father or mother. It may be that Macneil had forewarned the family that on the death of Donald the farm would be taken back by the General. Donald did not die until 1830, and his wife was allowed to stay 'in possession of the house, garden and park, with grass of 8 cows, 2 horses and a few sheep, rent free' (NAS CS96/4274, p27). Perhaps the General had a conscience after all. Furthermore, by 1831

Hugh Macneil had returned to Barra and put up a shop in Castlebay; in addition he had taken the tenancies of the public houses on the island. He could only have done this of course with the General's permission. The General in return received a handsome rent of £200 a year for these properties (SCR B12/138); hard cash could melt even the General's heart!

In summary, the General inherited the estate with considerable heritable bonds attached, no direct control of its affairs, an impoverished and growing population, at a time when the opportunities for tenants and landlords alike to earn an income were in sharp decline. With a mixture of commonsense, bravado, cunning, and a times malevolence, he set about restoring his fortunes through a planned programme of 'improvements' and an *ad hoc* set of other practices. He grew increasingly frustrated with his tenants, perhaps with some justification at times, and by 1830 was becoming desperate.

His energies and capital were poured into the great white hope of his chemical works. It might just possibly have paid off in time, but in October 1836 time ran out.

Sequestration and the Trustees

General Macneil's debts, both heritable bonds and personal debts, had been steadily accumulating. Creditors had been exerting pressure and threatening action for several years. One of them, Colonel John Gordon of Cluny, had looked into Macneil's affairs in 1835 and concluded 'on the best information that he can obtain' that Macneil 'if not hard pressed by creditors will in a short time succeed in relieving himself from his difficulties' (NAS GD 244/35). By mid 1836 Gordon had changed his mind and pursued a debt of £3,500, resulting in Macneil being commanded in July of that year to pay this sum plus the interest accruing. A final command was issued on September 16th, and when Macneil failed to pay up, he was 'horned and poind'. This was not as physically painful as it sounds, but was socially and financially ruinous. The Messenger at Arms went to the Market Cross in Edinburgh and there publicly proclaimed Lieutenant Colonel Roderick Macneil 'his Majesty's rebel' and 'put him to the horn by three blasts thereof' (horning). At the same time the law officers were empowered to seize his moveable possessions (poinding). On September 28th a warrant was issued for Macneil's arrest and imprisonment, but when the Messenger at Arms eventually tracked Macneil down to his Edinburgh address (apparently in lodgings) he was found to have absconded!

Serious as this process was, at this time only his 'moveables' were in danger of seizure. But with Macneil's agreement, his wine merchant (to whom he owed nearly £400) petitioned on October 7th for his estate to be sequestrated. Macneil had finally given up his attempt to rescue his estate and was now intent on avoiding imprisonment, total disgrace and dismissal from his one remaining source of both social standing and income, the army. The petition by Messrs Bell Rennie of Leith opened up the whole pandora's box of Macneil's debts.

A meeting of creditors was held in Edinburgh on October 19th, and it emerged that the General's total debts, at that time, were thought to be £115,395-17s-4d! Of these, heritable bonds secured on the estate came (with interest) to £66,395; the rest were personal debts (NAS CS 96/4274). Of the dozen heritable bonds, eight seem to have originated in Roderick the Gentle's time, and these accounted for half

of the debts found on heritable bonds. On the other hand, the personal debts (amounting to nearly £50,000) were all down to the General, and included the sort of debts that any self-respecting gentleman might be expected to carry – to his tailor, boot maker, and wine-merchant, among others. But this huge burden of personal debt was not entirely due to a lavish lifestyle, for no less than £30,000 was owed to Harold Littledale of Liverpool, and this loan had been used to finance the soda works. This money was secured specifically on the soda factory itself, and was loaned on the understanding that Macneil would regularly send an unspecified quantity of soda ashes to Littledale (NAS GD 244/35).

At the meeting of creditors an accountant, Charles Murray Barstow, was elected as interim factor of the estate, and he subsequently became chairman of the small group of trustees appointed to oversee the estate's sequestration, the recovery of assets, and the sale of the estate. Three volumes of Sederunt Books record the activities of the Trustees between October 1836 and August 1839 (NAS CS 46/4274; 4275; 4276) and the following account is based on these records.

Their first priority was to seize all of Macneil's assets that they could lay hands on. By October 28th, a very detailed list of the contents of Eoligarry House had been received by the Trustees, right down to items like Mrs Macneil's tumbler, cup and jug. Reading through the list one is struck by the poverty of a highland chieftain's home, and so were the Trustees! They immediately demanded that Macneil meet with them in Edinburgh for an 'examination' (i.e. interrogation) on December 8th, but when they convened there was a letter from Macneil's solicitor explaining that 'stress of weather' prevented the General from attending; he asked for an adjournment. Meanwhile they learned (somehow) that the General had sent a large number of wooden crates to the mainland. On the 16th December 1836 John Campbell of the Sheriff's Office at Fort William searched the property of Michael Mceachen a cattle dealer at Arisaig, the house of Elizabeth Fraser, Innkeeper in Arisaig, and the sloop *Adelaide*. He found 71 assorted crates, boxes and packages, apparently belonging to the General, along with carpets, and various items of furniture including a pianoforte. Campbell does not list (and perhaps at this time had not examined) the contents of most of the crates and packages, which were simply seized and taken as they were. One exceptionally large barrel was opened however, and found to contain about sixty items of crockery, but nothing of notable value. These items were all subsequently sold at a public auction.

But Macneil had shipped more than furniture and crockery off the island. When the Trustees' agent, Charles Shaw, went to Barra to make an inventory of the estate, the home farm and the soda factory, he discovered just how devious the General could be. He was received at Eoligarry House by Macneil, who harangued him for coming too soon, said he was not prepared, and told him to come back in eight or ten days time. There was a lengthy conversation, at the end of which it was agreed that Shaw could begin work the next day. But as he was leaving Eoligarry House he was informed (presumably by a disaffected servant) that at that very moment Mceachen was taking on board between 50 and 60 stots. Shaw challenged Macneil to stop the shipping, but the General said he had sold the animals to Mceachen some time ago and simply allowed them to graze at Eoligarry till Mceachen could take them to the mainland. While they argued the boat sailed. (The animals were later seized in Arisaig and sold on behalf of the creditors). Next day Shaw set out for Vatersay to make an inventory of the sheep, but on his way to Castlebay he was informed that the previous day nearly 200 head of cattle had been taken off Vatersay and were now dispersed in the hills on Barra. They were eventually tracked down, with Macneil claiming that they too had been sold to Mceachen and suggesting that perhaps Shaw could take 50 or 60 of the cattle if the rest could be allowed to go quietly. Shaw declined the offer, and seized all the animals. When Shaw decided to visit the soda factory, Macneil had four crates of furniture removed from the works and hidden in a blackhouse nearby – but again Shaw's secret informant gave Macneil away. Eventually, everything that Shaw had diligently inventoried and seized was sold by auction, at Eoligarry House on May 23rd 1837.

By this time after much procrastination the General had finally submitted to an 'examination' by the trustees in March 1837. The verbatim accounts of this examination, and of another conducted in November of the same year, reveal a lot of verbal sword-play, with the Trustees thrusting and Macneil parrying. They demanded an explanation of why the furniture had been shipped to Arisaig. Why, to protect **all** his creditors said Macneil; he had heard that the Glasgow creditors were planning to seize it for themselves. But why, asked the Trustees, did he not inform either Shaw or the Trustees? Because the shipping had taken place before the General heard of their appointment, he replied. The Trustees were very suspicious that the inventory of Eoligarry House included no silver plate (or indeed much else of value). Macneil, perhaps choosing his words carefully, said that at the time of sequestration he did not possess any silver plate. He admitted the sale of 'stots' to Mceachen, and of a bull to Macneil of Canna, but said these had all been in June or July (before sequestration); he had sold no animals to anyone after August 1836. In July 1837 the Trustees were still concerned about that silver plate, and wrote to Macneil demanding an explanation of its disappearance. He replied (from Dublin) that he had never owned much plate. When Macneil appeared in person for another examination they pressed him yet again on his missing silver, but he was adamant 'he neither bought, sold or possessed plate since he left London'. It seems they were still chasing the elusive silver in May 1838, when Colonel Gordon very sensibly told the Trustees that the value of any plate was too small to bother with. As far as we can see, the Trustees never did lay hands on Macneil of Barra's silverware!

They tried one last rather spiteful trick, perhaps in exasperation. They wrote to the War Office and asked them to appropriate some of Macneil's pay. He was an unattached colonel at this time and on half pay in any case, so it was hardly worth the effort. But it was a mean thing to do to the man who had fought through the Napoleonic wars; or perhaps it was what one might expect of the bean-counters who were in charge of the sequestered estate. In any event, to their credit, the War Office would have none of it.

While this endless wrangling was going on over relatively trifling amounts of property and money, the Trustees were also grappling with the management of the estate. The Sederunt Books, being concerned essentially with the sequestration of the estate and recovery of assets, only occasionally throw any light on this management activity. Such action as was taken seems to have been mostly initiated by Charles Shaw. He suggested that kelp manufacture be continued, at 250 tons a year, and that if they could, they should rent out the soda factory. Apart from raising cash, he stressed that both measures would provide employment for the crofters. Similarly, he urged the Trustees to supply people with fishing materials, and to recover the costs from selling the catch; after deduction of the expenses and rents, the surplus should be passed to the crofters. In 1837 he persuaded the Trustees not to collect rents from the 'small tenants', though in the spring of the following year the trustees decided to recover not just rents but arrears by deducting it from the crofters income from kelp production. The New Statistical Account of 1840 confirms that crofters at this time were still bound by their rental agreements to cut kelp in the summer months. One other decision made by the Trustees is recorded not in the Sederunt Books but in the *Reports on Northern Lighthouses* (NLS Acc. 10706/93) for 1837. This was that tenants removed from Berneray and Mingulay should return to these islands and take up tenancies again.

On the broader strategy of managing the estate, the Trustees decided as early as January 1837 to try to lease out the home farm of Eoligarry, initially for one year. They may also have been responsible for establishing the 'few farms...now let to graziers, who seldom crop much of their ground' referred to in the Statistical Account, which also reports that the only new sheep stock introduced to the island arrived 'last year', i.e. in 1838 (the report was written, as opposed to published, in 1839). The main issue, however, was of course the sale of the entire estate, and Shaw had written to the Trustees in November 1836 urging them to sell it as soon as possible, and warning them they could expect a low price.

The Sale of the Estate of Macneil of Barra

The General, in the statement of his affairs that he prepared for the Trustees when the estate was sequestered, put its value at £85,000, and claimed that he had been offered £75,000 plus payment of annuities amounting to £1,400 p.a. in August 1836. In the light of subsequent events, the valuation seems highly optimistic, and the alleged offer highly suspect.

The Trustees took the decision to sell the estate at their meeting on January 6th 1837, and set an auction date of April 19th. Adverts were placed on the front page of the *North British Advertiser* on February 18th, and on two subsequent occasions. The upset price was £65,000, suggesting that the Trustees had little regard for Macneil's valuation. Nor, apparently, did the speculators and entrepreneurs; no bids were received at the upset price and the sale was adjourned. The Trustees did however manage to sell a portion of Macneil's most remote island property, Berneray, to the Commissioners for Northern Lights for £491-8-0.

The estate was advertised for a second time, in the *Edinburgh Advertiser* of April 28th, to be sold at public auction on May 24th, with a reduced upset of £60,000. But at a meeting of the Trustees on April 27th, a fly had appeared in the ointment! It was discovered that Mr J Fraser held some of the old titles, and attempts to get them back had met with no response. By the time the Trustees met again on May 11th they had before them a copy of the *Edinburgh Advertiser* for May 5th containing notice of a public auction for the estate of Barra to be held in September. Whilst the wording of the advert was taken almost verbatim from their own advert a week earlier, it concluded 'title deeds may be seen in the hands of J. J. Fraser'. Also on the table at the meeting was a letter from Mr Law acting on behalf of Mr Fraser, claiming that the Trustees had no right to be in possession of the titles to the Estate of Barra, that they should be returned at once, and that their forthcoming sale was illegal!

One can imagine the concern, even consternation, of the Trustees at this news. But Colonel John Gordon was able to set their minds at rest. His representative, Mr Hunter, produced a conveyance showing that Fraser's heritable bond was now legally held by Gordon. The Trustees, no doubt in righteous indignation, decided at once to take Fraser to court! They also went ahead with arrangements for the May auction, placing further adverts in the *North British Advertiser* on May 13th and 20th. Again, however, there were no bidders and the sale of the estate had once again to be adjourned.

The estate was offered for the third time on October 18th 1837. The upset price was £59,800, with the superiority offered separately (once the estate was sold) for £200,because it had a separate burden of debt of £999 on it. Yet again there were no takers, and a week later the Trustees decided to reduce the upset to £55,000. There appears to have been no further attempt to sell the estate by public auction, before the Trustees decided in March 1838 to further reduce the upset to a mere £45,000. At meetings in July and August 1838, there was much debate about the upset to be asked for the next sale, scheduled for October 10th. This sale appears never to have taken place, and at further Trustees meetings on October 20th and 27th it was decided to sell the estate 'next day' at £47,000 by 'private bargain' and if not sold by December 19th to offer it at £45,000. Still there were no buyers and when the Trustees met with the Commissioners on January 17th 1839 it was agreed they would put the estate up for sale with an upset now reduced to £36,000, under burden of the £900 annuities for the Misses Macneil.

On March 6th, in the coffee house of the Royal Exchange, Edinburgh, the estate of Barra was up for public auction for the fourth time with an upset of £36,000. The bidding was opened by Captain Duguid (for Colonel Gordon) with an offer of £36,000. Two other buyers then entered the fray, Mr Warrington of Godstone (Surrey) and Mr Menzies ('Writer in Edinburgh'). The bidding gathered pace, and Duguid offered £40,200, topped by Warrington with £42,000, and this by Menzies with £42,050. At this point the half-hour sand-glass ran out, and Mr Menzies was declared the purchaser of the estate of Barra.

Menzies paid his £100 deposit, but then failed to find any acceptable 'cautioner' as security for this bid, within the required 30 days. Barstow therefore quite rightly offered the estate to the next highest bidder, Mr Warrington. Warrington accepted and said he had no need of a 'cautioner' – he would pay the price. A Metropolitan Bank cheque for £10,000 duly arrived, but the trustees were suspicious. Enquiries showed he was not the intimate acquaintance, as he claimed, of various 'people in high life'. The Metropolitan Bank were surprised to learn that Warrington had established a credit of £10,000 with them,

said they had not a sixpence belonging to Warrington, and refused to honour the cheque. And so the estate was offered to Colonel Gordon at £40,200.

But Gordon immediately claimed that since both Menzies and Warrington had submitted fraudulent bids, he should pay no more than his opening bid of £36,000. Barstow sought Counsel in what threatened to become a legal nightmare. Counsel advised that since Menzies' bid appeared to have been genuine and based on expectation of support from his 'cautioner' (Mr Fraser Graham of Morphie), Gordon did not have a strong case.

Gordon then wrote to say he would not pay £40,200, but would not oppose a new auction of the estate. Barstow's response was to serve a 'protest' on Gordon and Duguid for them to provide security in the sum of £40,200 within fourteen days. On June 24th, 1839, Gordon was informed that his bid had failed, and the estate would be offered again. Barstow further wanted to seek damages of £8,040 from Gordon for failure to secure his bid, but Counsel sensibly told him he had no chance of success.

Indeed, by this time a good case had emerged that Gordon should be offered the estate at his opening bid of £36,000, for Menzies bid had been exposed as anything but genuine. Mr Menzies was found to be 'merely a clerk of a Writer to the Signet in Edinburgh'. It subsequently emerged that Mr Menzies' employer was none other than J J Fraser, the unhappy former holder of one of Macneil's heritable bonds. Menzies had clearly been acting on behalf of Fraser probably to cause disruption rather than as a genuine bidder. That did not prevent Menzies raising a summons of damages against the Trustees in July 1839 whereupon he was offered the estate again at £42,050 and given fourteen days to pay. The offer was not taken up, and in August Barstow turned yet again for advice from Counsel. That advice was clear – not to continue with the sale at that time because of the unsettled claims.

And so the sale of the estate dragged on, although there appear to be no further Trustees' minutes after August 1839. But a discharge and assignation of December 1840 records that the estate of Barra 'having been exposed to public roup ...upon the sixteenth day of December 1840 was purchased by Lieutenant Colonel John Gordon of Cluny at the price of £38,050 (NAS GD 244/35). The legal niceties were not finally completed until a disposition in favour of Gordon was signed on May 14, and the instrument of sasine was produced on September 21st, 1841.

Gordon of Cluny takes Charge

John Gordon of Cluny was born c.1774, the son of Charles Gordon, in turn the heir of John Gordon of Cluny who founded the dynasty. All three were noted for their obsessive penny-pinching, it being said of Charles that towards the end of his life he even refused to get out of bed on the grounds that he couldn't afford it (*The Times* 23/7/1858)! Their careful management of their money, together with an eye for a bargain and a passion for acquiring property nevertheless allowed them to build a large family fortune, so that Colonel Gordon was said to be the richest commoner in Scotland, and possibly in the whole of the United Kingdom. The estates which his father and grandfather acquired were all in eastern Scotland, and Colonel Gordon continued to accumulate property there. But in the mid 1830s he turned his attention to the Hebrides where Clanranald was in dire financial straits and the estate in the hands of trustees. Gordon made his opening moves for South Uist and Benbecula early in 1836 (NAS GD 201/5/1223), but only eventually acquired them in October 1838 at the upset price of £96,000. The disposition of the estate was finally signed in May 1839 (NAS GD 201/5/612/1). By this time Gordon had made his bid for Barra at the March auction. He had not previously shown any public interest in acquiring Barra, so it might be thought that his bid in March 1839 was initiated by the purchase of Uist.

There is, however, the possibility that Gordon had kept his eye on Barra some years in advance of its purchase. He had acquired a financial interest as early as 1832, having in April of that year bought-out part of Macneil's debt, in a heritable bond, to J J Fraser (NAS GD 244/35/B4). As we have seen above, that deal was to be of importance in dismissing Fraser's claim to the titles of Barra in 1839. As one of Macneil's creditors, albeit a relatively minor one, Gordon now began to take an interest in the Barra estate. In 1835 he prepared his memorandum on the estate (NAS GD244/35/B4), urging creditors not to press Macneil too hard since it might prevent the soda factory becoming a profitable concern, and the creditors getting their money. Nevertheless it was he who initiated proceedings against Macneil in 1836, although significantly he did not seek sequestration of the estate but the seizing of moveables to pay off the debt against the heritable bond. When Macneil's wine merchant petitioned for the sequestration of the estate on October 7th 1836, Gordon's agent, John Hunter, wrote to him the next day saying that to ensure Gordon got his money, the estate would need to sell for about £53,000 (NAS GD 244/34/B1). This suggests that at this point Gordon was interested only in recovering the loan and interest. At the meeting of Trustees on April 3rd 1837, Gordon was represented for the first time (by Hunter). Amongst the items discussed was a summons of 'ranking and sale' issued by Miss Clarke, a creditor of £1,000, a loan which was the first heritable debt on the estate. (It had been made in 1815 to Roderick the Gentle by Archibald Macneil and others, and purchased by Miss Clarke in 1825). At the meeting of the Trustees on July 26th, Hunter announced that to resolve the problem posed by Miss Clarke's petition, Colonel Gordon had purchased the debt from Miss Clarke. He then proposed that the estate be offered at the upset of £55,000. When the auction took place, in October 1837, there were no bidders as we have seen. This was the third attempt to sell the island, and Gordon had made no bid or shown any interest in purchasing the estate. Neither did he make any move to acquire the estate during the next eighteen months, before he bought Uist and Benbecula.

So was his only interest up until 1839 in recovering his loans? It would appear so, except for three letters written in 1837. The first, from a Mr Macmillan at Castlebay, Barra, was written on August 14th to Colonel Gordon at Cluny Castle, and begins : 'in consequence of being informed that you propose being the purchaser of the estate of the island of Barra' (NAS TD 85/63/A8). It mentions that Gordon himself has visited the island, and then goes on to the discuss the real value of the island, expresses the view that it would be best to ship most of the crofters off to America, and concludes by asking Gordon not to mention his name! The second letter does not apparently survive, but it was an important one for it was from Gordon himself, was written

within a few days of receiving Macmillans' letter, and clearly asked for more detailed information, particularly about sheep grazing. In other words Gordon was expressing an immediate interest in the island and its potential for 'improvement'. Macmillan replied to it, this time from Skye, and described the pastures at some length, said his father estimated that the estate could maintain sixteen thousand sheep (twice the number on it at the time), and that 'if well managed there would be no sheep in the islands that would compete with them'. These letters must raise the possibility that by mid 1837 Gordon was positively interested in acquiring Barra and that he was simply waiting in the hope of acquiring the estate at the lowest price possible. If that was indeed his aspiration, he seems to have succeeded.

By the time he acquired Barra, Gordon already had at hand various assessments as to the potential and problems of the estate, apart from those of Macmillan. Charles Shaw had reported to the Trustees that little profit could be expected from crofters rents and had firmly stated in 1836 that 'the only mode of putting matters upon a proper footing would be to send two-thirds of the population to America' (NAS CS/96/4274, 25). Similar views were expressed in evidence given to the Select Committee on Emigration, whose report was published in 1841. Gordon was recommended to assist his people to emigrate, and a specific target of a thousand emigrants was proposed (Select Committee 1841, questions 184, 258). It is possible that Gordon was tempted. At this time over half the households on Barra were not even in the rent book (Select Committee 1841, 95), so there was certainly a 'surplus' population who would not be contributing to Gordon's profits.

But there were no discernible evictions or removals of tenants in the early 1840s and the claim made by William Yorstoun in 1842 that Gordon 'wishes to keep them all' may have been true. Yorstoun reported that Gordon intended to move the 'redundant population of the coast' and re-settle them in the interior (*J. Agriculture* 1842, 541). It has been said that 'Gordon's first years as owner of Barra are notable for their apathy', and that initially at least he had no strategy for exploiting his new estate (Newby 2000, 139). Certainly there is no hard evidence for extensive changes in either the pattern of tenancies or the general management of the estate between 1840 and 1846. But when it came to making a profit, Gordon had never previously been apathetic, and there are perhaps some indications that important initiatives were taken. A description of Barra in 1845 said that 'hundreds of acres of drift land and sandy plains have, of late, been reclaimed and converted into arable fields', and it specifically refers to drift land on the west coast (*Inverness Courier* 3/12/1845). It may be that, in the west coast townships of Craigston, Allasdale, Grean and Cleat, the conversion of crofts into fa*l*rms with large numbers of agricultural labourers, noted above in the 1841 census data, points to the beginning of this activity. If so, Gordon was quick off the mark, but as we have seen he had been seeking and taking advice on Barra since 1837 and he may have known exactly what he intended to do with the island when he acquired it. It was generally acknowledged that Gordon invested in improving the estates he acquired (Richards 1982, 405), and there is some evidence that he followed this path on Barra. Gordon himself claimed that between 1839 and 1846 he spent almost £27,000 on his new estates in the Hebrides, making a meagre profit of just £10,000 over the ten year period (*Witness*, 22/11/1848).

In some respects, however, he followed the practices of both General Macneil and the Trustees. Like the General before him, he was keen to collect his rents, and willing to have his ground officers seize tardy tenants' livestock (Napier 1884, question10185 ; Campbell 1988, 199). He was also happy to find new tenants from outside Barra. The 1851 census reveals at least 16 families, and possibly another half dozen, that were brought into Barra from the Uists and Tiree between 1841 and 1851. Equally he was not unwilling to remove tenants from one part of the island and move them to another, and in 1846–7 he set about creating new farms, turning the people 'off their small holdings and locating them on the sea coast, where they received coarse land which would grow potatoes and nothing else' (CRD 1847, 294–300). In Allasdale a North Uist man, Archibald Macdonald, who had migrated to Barra during the days of the Trustees, took the lease on a farm of 30 acres (Napier 1884, 1883, question 10253). Grean and Cleat were taken by Dr Macgillivray, the tenant of the home farm at Eoligarry. It was later recorded that the township of Borve alone took in 19 people from the clearance of Grean, Cleat, Allasdale and Craigston (Napier 1884, question 10250). Neighbouring Tangasdale seems to have absorbed some of the removed families too, its population jumping from 60 to 137 between 1841 and 1851. Another township which almost certainly took in many people removed from the west coast was Ruleos, the population of which rose from 46 to 124 in the same period. The last traces of the 'turf houses' (blackhouses with walls entirely of turf) which these people built were discovered here by us in 1998 (Branigan and Foster 2000, 19, L34). Around the coastline of the Bruernish peninsula we also found the remains of blackhouses (Figs 8.4 and 8.5) in locations which exactly mirrored those described in the 1847 report (e.g. ibid, 12, A6-A10). By some of these houses one could still see the remains of pathetic cultivation patches where the thin soil had been lazy-bedded for potatoes.

Famine and Clearance

But by 1846 the potato blight had hit the Western Isles, and the precarious subsistence base of the island populations was shattered. People all over Barra were faced with severe shortages and hunger, none more than those on the west coast. Once again the cockle beds on Traigh Mhor were all that stood between hundreds of inhabitants and starvation. Reports of the dire situation in Barra appeared in the *Scotsman* in October 1846, and in December the same paper reported two deaths from starvation on the island.

By now an alarmed government had established a team under Sir Edward Pine Coffin to oversee the provision of relief from bases at Portree and Tobermory. In a letter he received from the Assistant Secretary to the Treasury, Sir Charles Trevelyan, on December 28th 1846, it was noted that though relief of famine had been satisfactorily arranged in many parts of the highlands and islands that was not so in 'Colonel Gordon's portion of the Long Island'. Coffin was instructed to write to Gordon. Further, said Trevelyan, 'it appears to be desirable that no time should be lost in inspecting Colonel Gordon's estate' (NAS AD/58/81). Coffin sent Gordon a strongly-worded letter in which he warned the Colonel that if necessary he would take the relief measures necessary and leave it to parliament to decide 'whether or not you should be legally as well as morally responsible' (CRD, 294-300). Gordon replied with a mixture of anger, irritation, and protestations of innocence, but crucially an acknowledgment that he accepted responsibility for feeding his tenants in time of crisis. By June 1847 Coffin was able to report that Gordon had spent significant sums of money, had remitted large arrears of rent, and sent considerable quantities of food (NAS HD6/2). Nevertheless, when the Reverend Norman MacLeod visited in August that year he described how 'on the beach the whole population of the country seemed to be met, gathering the precious cockles...starvation on many faces.' (MacLeod in Campbell 1998, 221). Worse, the blight persisted in the Western Isles and there was a general failure of the potato crop again in 1848 and 1849. Devine

Figure 8.4 A blackhouse on the edge of the sea on the Bruernish peninsula (site L7)

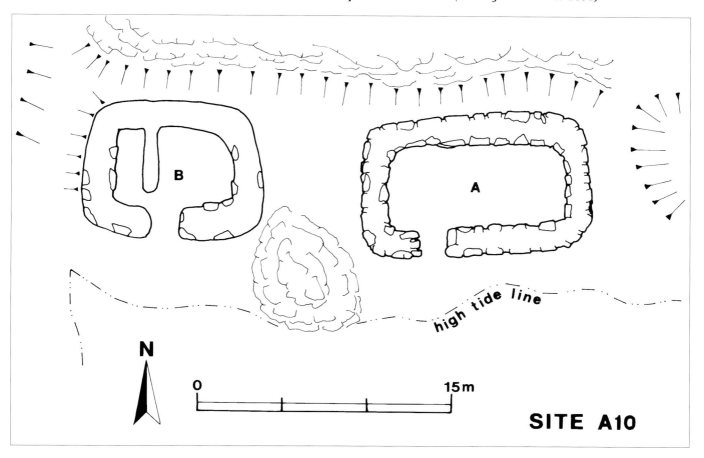

Figure 8.5 A blackhouse and another building (possibly a second blackhouse) at site A10 on the coast of Bruernish

(1988, 45) has abstracted the figures for the numbers of people receiving relief in these years. On South Uist it was 62% and 67% respectively; on Barra it was a staggering 89% and 85%!

Gordon's response to the on-going crisis, and demands on his pocket in 1848, was to ship 270 tenants, mainly from South Uist, to Canada. But 150 from Barra were sent to Glasgow, where Gordon's agent eventually offered them temporary accommodation and a passage to Canada (Richards, 2000, 214; *Scotsman* 5/8/1848). Gordon no doubt did his sums, and taking his plans for the future 'improvement' of the islands into account must have concluded that assisted emigration was the best course of action to follow in future. In 1849 he sent off about 900 of his tenants, though there is no evidence these included any from Barra (Devine 1988, 326). In 1850 the potato crop failed completely in Barra and the Uists, and Gordon removed 132 families from their crofts in Barra and initially shipped them to Tobermory. (The figure of 660 individuals in this party is clearly an estimate based on an assumed five persons per family). From there they dispersed – 37 families were recorded arriving in Glasgow, others in Edinburgh, and 65 individuals eventually turned up in Inverness. Many of the families who went to Glasgow and Edinburgh seem to have disappeared into the industrial centres of the lowlands. Those in Inverness were eventually (in 1853!) offered a free passage to Australia but only two families took up the offer (*Scotsman* 18/12/1850; 5/2/1851; *Inverness Courier*, 6/1/1853).

Any goodwill that Gordon's relief activities in 1847 had generated amongst the ranks of the press, the government

or the opinion-formers in Glasgow and Edinburgh was dissipated by the removals of 1849–1850 and the way they were conducted. Reports appeared in the press describing how the Barra people were removed from their houses in May, the houses then being destroyed. When they erected tents of blankets, or slept in their boats, they were warned to move on, their tents were demolished and their boats broken up. Their condition by the time they arrived in Glasgow and Edinburgh was pitiful, and there for all to see, for they were destitute on the streets. A deputation of 'gentlemen' held an urgent meeting with the City Council in Glasgow in mid-December to urge the provision of relief for the people from Barra. One of the deputation, a Mr Ross, had written to Colonel Gordon to ask him what he proposed to do about his starving tenants, and with admirable promptitude Gordon had replied on December 14th. But by accident, or perhaps design, his Scrooge-like reply was not published by the *Scotsman* until Christmas Day: 'In answer to your enquiry 'what do I propose doing with them – I say – nothing'. He explained that over the past three years he had suffered a net loss of almost £2,000 on the estate of Barra, that he had recently sent his tenants a cargo of Indian corn, but that he would do no more.

The more significant part of Gordon's letter, however, is where he denied any knowledge of, or part in, their removal from Barra. 'They must have left Barra of their own free will' he asserted and railed against 'the false assumption that the Barra people now in Glasgow were needlessly turned out of their dwellings by me or by my orders' (*Scotsman* 25/12/1750). His denials gained a certain degree of support in ensuing months. An investigation ordered by Sir John Macneil concluded that many Barra people had been led to 'misrepresent their circumstances'. Even the censorious correspondent of the *Banffshire Journal* conceded that 'it may be true that neither Colonel Gordon, nor any of his underlings ever actually took them by the shoulders and drove them out of his dominions' (quoted in the *Scotsman* 5/2/1851). But on this occasion there is little reason to believe Gordon, for it is in this letter than he goes on to claim 'the majority of the present inhabitants of Barra were not originally natives of Barra but brought there by the late proprietor'. We have already seen earlier (above p. 145) that whilst Macneil certainly brought in tenants from elsewhere they numbered at most a few hundred, and we have seen above that Gordon himself certainly took in new tenants from North and South Uist and Tiree. Gordon reveals himself in this letter as quite willing to distort the truth.

Undaunted by the criticisms levelled at him in 1850, in 1851 he arranged a clearance and emigration on an unprecedented scale, sending 1,700 tenants from South Uist and Barra to Quebec. According to a statement issued by 70 of the Barra emigrants when they arrived in Quebec, Colonel Gordon had not only offered to defray the cost of the passage, but had promised that on arrival in Quebec they would be transported free to Upper Canada and there given both work and land (Mackenzie 1883, 258). These of course were promises which would cost Gordon nothing, and which he could not possibly ensure were implemented by the Canadian authorities. Nevertheless, on the basis of these promises, some Barra tenants and cottars had 'signed' for the passage. Gordon's factor on South Uist, John Fleming, told the emigration office in Quebec that the people had heard such good accounts of Canada from those who had emigrated two years previously that they too were keen to emigrate (CPRIC 1854, 81). So it was, presumably, that Gordon's largest tenant on Barra, Dr Macgillivray, was able to put a further gloss on this and tell the Napier Commission in 1883 that 'the people of South Uist and Barra had petitioned in a body to be helped away and Colonel Gordon helped them'. The assistance included not only the provision of a passage but 'clothing for scores of them' (Napier 1884, question 10797). This too was a specific claim made at the time by John Fleming, who told emigration officer A. C. Buchanan in Quebec, that Gordon had provided both clothes and shoes for the emigrants. This was confirmed by the captain of one of the ships chartered by Gordon, but he also said that when Gordon's agent inspected the passengers before the ship sailed, he decided they were clothed well enough, and ordered the clothes to be taken off again (Report by G. Douglas in CPRIC 1854, 17).

Gordon chartered five ships to undertake this clearance and emigration. As far as we can tell, the *Brooksby, Montezuma, Perthshire* and *Liskeard* were primarily hired to carry about 1,300 people from South Uist. The remaining ship, the *Admiral*, seems to have been intended purely for a group of about 450 people from Barra. Although Macgillivray says that Gordon sent a ship to Barra, the *Admiral* appears to have anchored at Lochboisdale on South Uist. According to Fleming, who supervised the boarding of the ships, the *Brooksby* and the *Montezuma* sailed in late July, followed by the *Perthshire*. The Chief Emigration Officer in Quebec recorded the arrival of the *Brooksby* on August 28th (with 285 passengers) and the

Montezuma on the 30th (with 442 passengers). The *Perthshire* arrived on September 10th (with 437 passengers). *The Admiral* eventually boarded passengers on August 11th, almost certainly a few days later than intended. The delay was caused by the problems which Gordon's officers and the constables had in persuading many of the intending emigrants to board ship, and the time that had to be spent in rounding up those who had changed their minds – or simply replacing them with any other tenants they could lay hands on.

Some of the evidence for what occurred at this time was oral tradition first written down between thirty and more than a hundred years after the event. These memories are recorded in the Napier Commission (1883), Mackenzie (1883), Macpherson (1992), and Craig (1990). The Barra people were required to take themselves to Lochboisdale and were threatened with a £2 fine if they failed to appear. Some of those who arrived in Lochboisdale decided, on the spot, not to embark. At this point they were seized and bound and carried on board. A good many others simply stayed at home on Barra, so Gordon's men came to find them. Boats put into Northbay and stood off Balnabodach while the officers and constables went about their work. Oral tradition says that a young man living with his grandparents at Balnabodach, Michael Maclean, escaped by hiding on a ledge on a cliff, but that Jonathan Maclean was overpowered on the shore of Ardveenish. A young woman milking a cow at Balnabodach was seized and carried off with only the clothes she was wearing. A widow living at Vaslain was cleared as she was cooking potatoes over her fire, and John (Iain Muillier) Macdougall, an old man, was taken for emigration but his sisters escaped into Ben Cliad overlooking Vaslain and Traigh Eias.

In so far as we can check these oral traditions against documentary sources they seem reliable. Michael Maclean, for example, appears in the 1851 census for Balnabodach (taken only a few months before the clearance) and is a 16 year old apprentice, living not with his grandfather but his uncle. Jonathan Maclean too is in the census, a 38 year-old cottar, living in Bruernish, just south of Ardveenish. The 1851 census return shows only two families living at Vaslain, but one of them is a 40-year old widow, Margaret Macnash. The splitting of families by the enforced emigration of some members and successful flight of others is specifically mentioned in the passengers' statement given in Quebec, as is the hunting of people by officers and constables. As for the seizure of people with no possessions but what they were wearing, that is confirmed by reports from Canada: 'they were in rags' (*Dundas Warder* 2/10/1851), and 'destitute of clothing' (medical superintendent Quebec, Richards 2000, 222). George Douglas (quoted by Richards *ibid*) describes how the wife of the *Admiral's* master spent the voyage making makeshift clothing for the emigrants.

In the end Gordon's men managed to ship out 413 people on the *Admiral*, which left Lochboisdale on August 11th. On arrival in Quebec they were hungry and penniless, and the local authorities had to provide food and shelter for them. Anyone suspected of being infected with typhus or cholera was put into quarantine on Grosse Ile in the St Lawrence river, with the risk they would be permanently separated from their family. The rest were given passage on river steamers to carry them upriver into Ontario. Some of Gordon's tenants from Barra and Uist went to London,

Ontario or Williams and Stephens townships, others to Toronto and Hamilton, where they were expected to take work on the railway. Some sought and obtained grants of land locally, but it is has always been thought likely that some Barra people eventually drifted eastwards seeking a place to settle in Cape Breton where so many Barra people had settled before them. In fact, Buchanan specifically noted in his report for 1853 that many highlanders who had lived in Cape Breton for years had moved west into Ontario in 1852 (CPRIC 1854, 25). Buchanan tried to recover part of the costs of transporting his former tenants from Quebec to Ontario from Colonel Gordon. Gordon, of course, refused to pay.

We have identified six of the families (numbering about 40 individuals) sent to Canada on the *Admiral*, out of the 413 on board. These include the leader of the passengers who signed the statement at Quebec, Hector Lamont. He and his family can be found in the 1851 census, taken shortly before the clearance, a crofter in Brevig. Neither he nor his wife were natives of Barra. They had come from Tiree with three daughters and a son in 1837–38. Further sons had been born on Barra in 1839 and 1843, and a fourth daughter Jessie had been born late in 1850. Other families on the *Admiral* include those of Jonathan Maclean of Bruernish, Donald Johnston of Northbay, Farquhar Johnston and John Macneil of Glen, and John Macneil of Tangasdale. These families reveal clearances in at least five townships, and by careful use of the census data from the 1841, 1851 and 1861 census records we can get some idea of which townships saw extensive clearance (Fig. 8.6). We

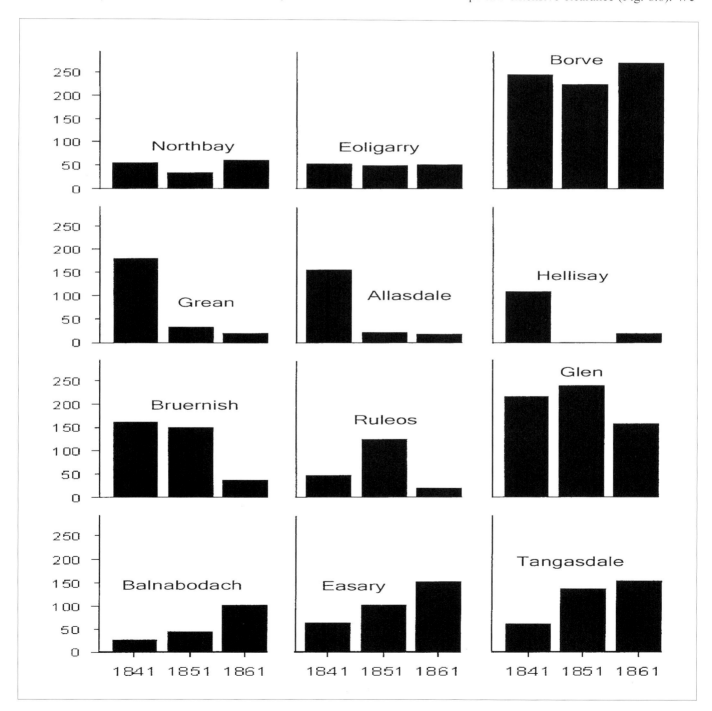

Figure 8.6 The populations of 12 townships on Barra as recorded in the census data for 1841, 1851 and 1861

must bear in mind that the total number of about 1,200 people cleared from Barra includes 150 in 1848, c. 660 in 1850, and 413 in 1851.

Places apparently cleared in 1848 or 1850 include the west coast townships of Allasdale, Grean and Cleat, which were reduced from 70 families and 436 individuals (almost all agricultural labourers on new farms) to just 10 families and 54 individuals. The island of Hellisay (and its neighbouring smaller islands) lost its entire population (109 people in 15 households) before the 1851 census too. There may been some clearance too in Northbay, Brevig and Kentangaval. But as Devine has warned us, we have to be aware that people are moved around within a parish as well as forced abroad. The census data from the small township of Balnabodach, together with the use of the parish register, reveals that although the population of Balnabodach was bigger in 1851 than it was in 1841, only one of the 1841 families was still there. Furthermore five crofting families and a cottar had been replaced by three boat-builders, four fishermen, and a farmer from Kintail. Apparently the 1841 crofting families of Balnabodach had been cleared and replaced by a farmer, and fishing and boat-building families. But at least two of these new families had themselves been already removed from Hellisay, emphasising that clearances can be more complex than we might assume.

As for the clearances of 1851, we can see significant reductions in population as represented by the 1851 and 1861 figures, even allowing for population renewal in the decade after 1851. This time the west coast has the biggest changes, with Bruernish and Ruleos having just 56 people and 12 families in 1861 compared to 274 and 54 respectively in 1851, just before the arrival of the *Admiral*. There were probably further clearances too in Glen and Brevig, and at the Napier Commission Farquhar Macneil recalled the emigration from Brevig c.1851 (Napier 1884, questions 10932-4). Beyond these townships where population figures, even ten years later, were so depressed at to suggest substantial clearance in 1851, we must assume that cottars and small tenants, particularly those with rent arrears, throughout the island were prime targets for Gordon's officers in 1850 and 1851. Gordon's net swept widely and cruelly and there can scarcely have been a family on Barra that was not affected by it.

9

Emigration from Barra to British North America: 1770–1850

Horrendous as it was, the enforced emigration of 400 Barra people to Canada in 1851 was just one in a long series of large-scale emigrations from the island to British North America (hereafter, for convenience, Canada). This final chapter of our book examines the evidence for earlier emigrations and has three objectives. The first is to identify the various agencies which stimulated and encouraged emigration, and the way the differing roles of each changed through time. The second is to try and establish some idea of just how many emigrants to Canada Barra provided between 1770 and 1850. The third objective is to gain an understanding of what transformations emigration brought for the emigrants and their families.

The sources of evidence on which we have to rely are a very mixed bunch. Government records such as customs reports, accounts, and correspondence to and from the Colonial Office and Treasury, are generally reliable but are so voluminous that it is a long and difficult to track down those relevant to emigration from Barra. Census data is more easily available but much more difficult to use. Obituaries and cemetery records occasionally provide valuable evidence but the former can be the proverbial needle in a haystack, and the latter are not always easily available. The records of the Catholic church, mostly correspondence to bishops and priests, are rather patchy. Passenger lists for ships are relatively scarce, considering how many ship crossed the Atlantic in this period. Records of land petitions and grants are better preserved in some cases, but the information they provide varies widely. Finally there are personal records ranging from rare but invaluable contemporary letters, receipts etc, to family histories, and oral traditions. Many of these have been collected and brought together in various locally-focussed parish or township histories in Canada, such as Archibald Mackenzie's (1984) *History of Christmas Island Parish*. Valuable as they are, family histories and oral traditions inevitably accumulate some uncorroborated additions and factual errors through time.

We have attempted to utilise all of these resources, and some of the problems encountered in using them are briefly discussed in the introduction to Appendix 2. Some immigrants undoubtedly made their way to Canada either as lone individuals, or as part of a 'small-group' emigration, ranging from four or five siblings or a single nuclear family to groups of three or four families. However, most information inevitably concerns large-scale or group emigrations, and it is likely that many individual emigrants for whom we have little information beyond their name originally emigrated as part of a group. In the discussion which follows, therefore, we inevitably focus mainly on group emigration.

Emigration in the Eighteenth Century

The earliest Barra men to see America were almost certainly soldiers, and the earliest of all may have been a 'soldier' in Bonnie Prince Charlie's army at Culloden. Roger Macneil of Vatersay was one of only two Barra men known to have fought at Culloden, and he was seized and transported from Tilbury to the American colonies in 1747 (Seton and Arnot 1929; Livingston 1984). When the French war began in Canada however three highland regiments were recruited and sent to support the attack on the fortress of Louisbourg, on the tip of Cape Breton, which commanded the entrance to the Gulf of St. Lawrence. After its capture in 1758, the same highland regiments proceeded down the St. Lawrence to Quebec where they spearheaded the British attack on the Heights of Abraham. It was here that General Macneil's grandfather was killed. According to Walker (1980, 86), who visited Barra in 1764, 31 Barra men fought with the highland regiments in the French war in Canada, six of whom had returned to Barra by the time of Walker's visit, the rest having died during the war. It is possible that some of the 25 who didn't return in fact survived the war and took up land grants when the regiments were disbanded in 1763. Many soldiers followed this course of action, and when the American War of Independence broke out in 1776 a new Royal Highland Emigrant Regiment was raised, to be recruited initially amongst former soldiers of the highland regiments who had taken land in Canada (Stanley 1976). One of the two battalions was raised in Nova Scotia, and after demobilisation in 1783 many of the soldiers took up new land grants in Nova Scotia. Between 1785 and 1790 at least 15 Barra men who had served in the recent war took up grants on the north coast of Nova Scotia between Malignant Cove and Cape George. Most were Macneils but there were two Camerons, a Campbell and a Mackinnon. The amount of land granted to each depended on his rank. Matthew Macneil, a private, got 100 acres; John Macneil, a sergeant, got 300 acres.

How significant a contribution military service made to early emigration from Barra to Canada is debateable. The people of Barra were mostly impoverished and they could not undertake self-funded emigration for much of the eighteenth century. The opportunities provided by military service both to earn money and to acquire a grant of land were perhaps one of the few channels for emigration open to them. Given the small number of Barra men apparently recruited to the highland regiments serving in America (if Walker's figure of 31 is broadly accurate for the period of the French war) the number who took up land grants is relatively high. Further, although the 31 soldiers mentioned by Walker is a small number, it probably represents about 10% of all men of serviceable age on Barra c.1760. In addition, according to both Walker and Mackenzie, some

Barra soldiers returned home, and they were able to give the islanders first-hand accounts of the colonies. In particular, Mackenzie claimed that three soldiers who had taken part in the capture of Louisbourg had visited the Bras D'Or and when they returned to Barra they had extolled its virtues (Mackenzie 1984, 167). On the other hand it is very unlikely that any of the veterans who had taken up land grants on Cape George were able to write letters to inform relatives back home about their new farms and how successful, or otherwise, they were. Further, Devine (1994, 179) has pointed out that whilst wars may have increased opportunities for military service, they also created a dramatic reduction in civilian emigration. With two wars affecting transatlantic shipping between 1755 and 1780, and with the Napoleonic wars beginning in 1793, it may be that the negative affects of war on emigration outweighed the positive ones in this period.

Civilian emigration from Barra had certainly commenced in the 'window of opportunity' between the capture of Quebec and the American War of Independence, although for the Barra families involved it was a particularly opportunistic episode. The settlement of Scottish Catholics organised by John Macdonald of Glenaladale has been extensively researched by Bumsted (1979) and Lawson (1991) and need not be examined in depth here, except perhaps for the part played by the Barra people. The motivation for this group emigration was provided by the attempts in 1769 of Colin Macdonald of Boisdale to force his Catholic tenants on South Uist to abandon their religion or face removal. The Catholic church were extremely concerned by this development, which rapidly began to spawn imitators on Inner Hebridean islands. Two bishops proposed that the Church should sponsor an emigration of Catholics from South Uist with the intention not simply of placing them beyond repression, but also quite explicitly to frighten off Boisdale and other Protestant lairds from further persecutions. John Macdonald of Glenaladale, a Catholic tacksman of Clanranald, agreed to organise and lead the emigrant group. Through the good offices of Bishop Macdonald he managed to purchase the 20,000 acres of Lot 36, on the Island of St John (hereafter referred to as PEI, Prince Edward Island) from James Montgomery, Lord Advocate of Scotland. He paid £600 for the Lot, with repayment terms which were generous. The charter of the ship *Alexander* cost a further £600 and the total cost of the whole venture has been calculated by Bumsted to have amounted to over £2,000. The Church provided half of the costs of transportation and provisions, and the remainder came from the emigrants themselves.

To make the venture worthwhile and the new settlement viable, Glenaladale needed about 200 emigrants. Initially of course these were to be mainly from South Uist, where more than thirty families were thought likely to be involved, together with some families from the mainland. The latter were important since they, unlike the South Uist people, could probably afford to pay for their passage and supplies. But Boisdale, initially with black propaganda and subsequently by a more lenient attitude, undermined the apparently already shaky determination of the Uist families. In the end only eleven families from South Uist embarked on the *Alexander*, the rest came from the mainland, a small group from Eigg, and eight men (probably with their families) from Barra. The Barra emigrants, like those from Eigg, have been considered as late stop-gap additions to the

group when recruitment on South Uist fell well short of the mark (Lawson 1991, 35-6), but two letters in the Scottish Catholic Archives might suggest otherwise. On September 14th 1770, writing to Bishop Hey about acquiring land on PEI, John Macdonald says that he has had a letter from 'Mr Alexander' on Barra. This may be Alexander Macdonald, the parish priest at this time. Glenaladale is pressing Alexander to visit him, but Alexander does not want to undertake the journey. In November a further letter from Macdonald says that 'Barra is as much exposed to danger as Uist' and that Mr Alexander is well-connected and well-equipped to do any business with Mr Geddes, with whom Glenaladale and Hey negotiated much of the arrangements for the emigration. It looks as if recruitment of Barra people may have been intended from the start of the venture.

The Barra contingent is known from two documents which survive not in the Scottish Catholic Archives but in the Public Archives of PEI. The first is the original agreement between Glenaladale and the Barra emigrants, signed on their arrival in PEI on June 24th 1772 (Fig. 9.1). Being unable to write, the Barra men put their mark or cross by their names, led by Allan Mackinnon who is described as a carpenter. This remarkable document provides each of the emigrants with a plot of 150 acres, on a lease which would run from Whitsunday 1772 for 'three thousand full and complete years'! To men who were used to renting three or four acres, a year at a time, with eviction at the whim of the laird always hanging over them, this must been a lease beyond their wildest dreams. The rent too was a revelation – a penny per acre per year for the first three years, rising to three-pence an acre thereafter for seven years. Further stipulated rises meant that after 27 years, the rental per acre would reach 1/6d – but that it would stay at that level for the remaining 2973 years of the lease! These generous terms, together with provisions and equipment given to the assisted emigrants, and the recruitment of a priest to accompany the group and minister to them in their new home, demonstrate Glenaladale's understanding of the principal concerns of the emigrants - namely long-term security and freedom of religion.

But there was one further concern which Glenaladale failed to recognise. As we saw in chapter 2, following the '45 there was a rapid acceleration of the collapse of the old clan system and its loyalties. The clan chieftains were brought, by a mixture of coercion and enticement, to become gentlemen. They became increasingly distanced from their clansmen. But if, as is often claimed, the clansmen were bewildered by the changing relationship between them and their laird, some at least may soon have overcome it. There is no evidence that as early as 1770, the young Roderick the Gentle was persecuting his Catholic tenants. Those families who emigrated on the *Alexander* may have been encouraged by the parish priest, but their reasons for going may have been as much about personal and economic freedom as religion. The reason for thinking so is that, despite the remarkably generous terms of their leases from Glenaladale, within three months they had paid a penalty and left their lands on Lot 36. The second document in the PEI archives (PAPEI 2664/156) is the one they signed to free them from their leases, and allow them to seek a future where they were nobody's tenant.

The situation which had arisen in 1770 on South Uist was to a lesser extent repeated on Barra in 1790. According to Burke (1881) Roderick the Gentle became 'arbitrary and

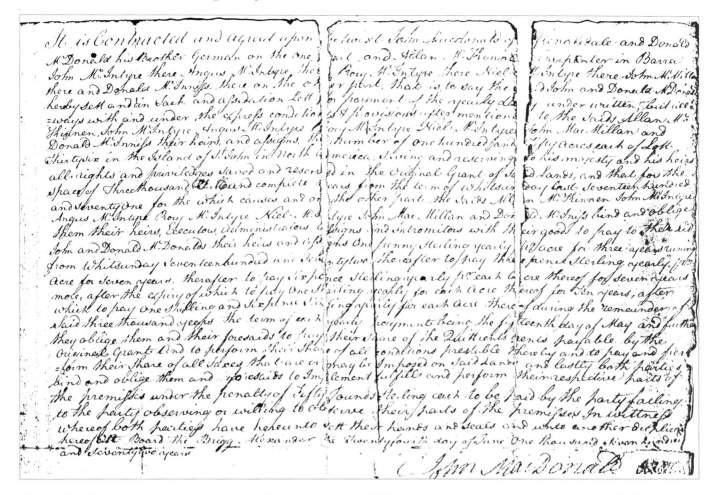

Figure 9.1 The agreement signed between John Macdonald of Glenaladale and eight Barra men on June 24th 1772 leasing them each 150 acres of land for 3,000 years! (PAPEI 2664/148. Reproduced by permission of the Public Archives and Records Office of Prince Edward Island)

despotic' in his attitude to his Catholic tenants and refused them permission to build a new church. Things came to a head on March 9th 1790, when Macneil had a furious argument with four Catholics who were looking at a possible site for their new church. As a result, if we are to believe Burke, 'all Macneil's Catholic tenants gave him notice that they had decided to give up their holdings and leave the country'. This must surely be an exaggeration, since in 1794 (even after two successive emigrations) Barra had almost 1,600 Catholics. Nevertheless a significant number certainly chose to leave the island. In referring to this episode, MacQueen in the Statistical Account of 1794, mentions that the emigrants were tempted by 'promises of the undisturbed profession of their religion'. Furthermore we may recall too that by the end of the decade Macneil was again at loggerheads with the priest (above p.15), so there is some evidence to support the outlines of Burke's account. Indeed there is even a specific echo of the 1772 emigration since it was Bishop Macdonald who put the would-be emigrants of 1790 in touch with an emigration agent. This was Simon Fraser, who seems to have been active in selling passages to Scottish emigrants between 1790 and 1830 (assuming it is one and the same man throughout).

According to Burke he required 350 passengers, but it is unlikely that he found that many, even by extending his net to the Uists as Burke claims. But Burke is quite explicit in saying that 28 Barra families were involved, which might mean somewhere between 100 and 150 persons. We know the names of 22 individuals, and the 'leader' of the group, as in 1772, was a Mackinnon. The ship on which the emigrants sailed was the *The Queen (of Greenock)*, a 200 ton brig of good repute (Dobson 2002, 138). According to Burke *The Queen* sailed from Tobermory early in July, with the intention of setting its passengers down in Louisbourg, Cape Breton. This is not implausible, since the latest first-hand accounts of Canada to have arrived in Barra would have come from the mouths of the returning soldiers who had fought at Louisbourg and seen the Bras D'Or lake for themselves. However, severe storms drove the ship off course, and eventually it anchored in Charlottetown PEI on September 20th. Initially they settled at Princetown, but in 1792 they moved to Grand River.

It appears that they were followed, in 1792, by a second group. The accounts of this emigration are rather vague, but they do appear to be a quite separate group from the first. Fraser was again involved, and on this occasion seems to have either bungled the operation or wilfully absconded. MacQueen in the 1794 Statistical Account reported that 'within the last two years upwards of 200 left the island, some to PEI and Nova Scotia'. But others, presumably when their passage did not materialise, went to Glasgow to work in the cotton mills, and some then returned home. This story is confirmed by a report in a PEI newspaper *The Examiner* (9/8/1882), that says that about two years after the 1790 emigration from Barra 'another band came out, making their homes in Lot 18 and Indian River'.

Taken together, these emigrants of 1790 and 1792 along with a small number of individual families who appear to have been on the ships arriving from Tobermory and the Western Isles in PEI in 1791, Barra may have sent about 300 of its people to Canada in this three-year flurry of activity. But according to MacQueen, by 1794 'the spirit for emigration is happily and totally suppressed', and this accords with the evidence in our database of emigrants.

The *Dove*, the *Sarah* and the *Hector*: 1801–1802

With the opening of the 19th century, however, Barra once more became a rich breeding ground for emigrants. It may indeed have been the relative prosperity of the crofting families at this time which stoked the fires of both discontent and ambition. With the Napoleonic Wars waging, and no end to them in sight, the price of kelp was rising steeply and offering the crofters new ways of paying their rent and even accumulating a surplus. There were too the renewed opportunities for military service and the monetary rewards that went with it. At the same time the cost of a transatlantic passage was low, and the volume of half-empty ships travelling westwards to bring back full loads of much-needed timber was high. For those with the ambition to emigrate it was a time of perhaps unparalleled opportunity. At the same time, we may recall Macneil had been in dispute with the parish priest, had sub-divided some crofts, was keen to undertake 'improvements', and had raised rents (above p. 15–16). His tenants may have become restless.

In 1801 we confront a mysterious episode in the history of emigration from Barra. This is the voyage of the *Sarah* and the *Dove* from Fort William to Pictou. In essence, the mystery is this : we have complete passenger lists for these two vessels, including the place of origin of each and every one of the 569 passengers; not one of them comes from Barra. Yet there is a persistent tradition that a large number of Barra people (possibly as many as 500) were taken on board (probably after the ships left Fort William). To attempt to find the truth about this episode we have to investigate the way in which the emigration was organised, the principal persons involved, and the evidence of the emigrants themselves.

The initiative seems to have begun in Nova Scotia, and to have been the brainchild of Hugh Denoon. Denoon was a Scotsman by birth but he had emigrated to Nova Scotia in his late teens and by 1784 at the age of 22 had already obtained land at Pictou. He continued to acquire land including plots from former veterans around Merigomish, built a mill, and became Collector of Impost and Excise in Pictou. He appears to have been a man of ambition and ability, and something of an entrepreneur. But he was not, before or after 1801, an emigration agent. Exactly why he chose in that year to return to Scotland and organise a mass emigration is unknown. It may be that he intended to establish himself as an agent but that the difficulties that he experienced in 1801 decided him against repeating the experience.

In any event, he arrived in western Scotland early in 1801 and applied himself with vigour to the task of recruiting emigrants. He initially chartered two ships, the *Sarah* of Liverpool and the *Dove* of Aberdeen. By late April it was reported he had already engaged '300 persons

and their families' to take passage at Fort William in May or June (NAS CE 62/2/7/142). There now began a frantic attempt by those who opposed emigration by the small tenantry to make life difficult for Denoon and, at best, to prevent his ships from sailing. These machinations have been well-documented and described by Bumsted (1982, 88–93). Amongst the measures they attempted to impose was an inspection of the ships to make sure they were not overcrowded (NAS GD 248/3416/3) and a requirement that a full passenger list for each ship be provided three weeks prior to sailing. Denoon in prolonged and skilful argument with the Customs finally persuaded them that it was unfair to count children as full passengers because they needed less space and less provisions than adults. Whilst not an unreasonable claim in itself, the final method they used to calculate the number of 'full passengers' was a triumph for Denoon. The ages of all passengers under the age of 16 were added together and divided by 16, this number then being added to the number of adult passengers. As a result the *Dove* which had 219 people on board was recorded as carrying 176 passengers, and the larger *Sarah* carried 350 souls, recorded as only 250 passengers. In this way, Denoon managed to persuade the authorities that the ships were not overcrowded.

As we noted above, however, the passenger lists submitted to the Customs officers in Fort William reveal not a single person from the island of Barra (or indeed anywhere in the Western Isles) on board either ship. But the story persists that after the ships left Fort William they took on a large number of Barra emigrants, and the present writer has himself mentioned this in print (Branigan and Foster 2002, 143). The account appears to have been first put on paper by R L Macneil of Barra in 1923 (Macneil 1985, 134–5) who probably took some of his information from Patterson's *History of the County of Pictou* since they both mistakenly refer to the second ship as the *Pigeon*, and both say that the *Sarah* sailed with 700 souls rather than the 350 on the passenger list. Patterson, however, did not claim that the additional passengers came from Barra. Is there any truth in this undocumented assertion?

The evidence is, frankly, confusing. In the first place, the ships were already fully loaded when they left Fort William. If the *Sarah* had taken on another 350 passengers, she would have been carrying two passengers per ton, about twice the usual complement, even before the Passenger Act of 1803 reduced the number. It was calculated at the time that the two ships together, if employed in the slave trade, would have been restricted to a total of 489 passengers against the 569 souls they actually carried (*Highland Society Sederunt Books*, III, 483-99). In other words, they were packed in like sardines! The idea that they could have taken on almost as many again is simply unrealistic.

But the Highland Society (who were opposed to emigration and successfully pressing the case for the new Passenger Act) and Hugh Denoon did agree on one point. They both said that in 1801 two of Denoon's ships took 700 emigrants to Pictou. Denoon made this admission in a petition for land in 1810, actually using it as part of his case to acquire 500 acres in Sydney County (Fig. 9.2). He says that in 1801 he took 'about seven hundred emigrants in two ships to this country and through that emigration a number followed that year and the two following seasons'. Both the Highland Society and Denoon, for quite different reasons, were keen to quote the highest possible number of

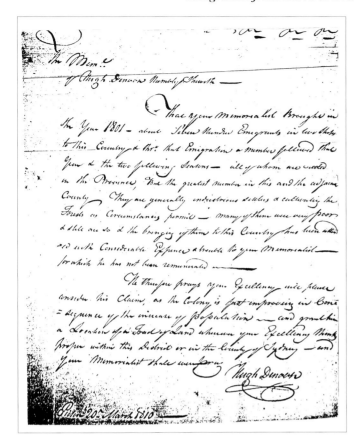

Figure 9.2 Hugh Denoon's petition of 1810 referring to his emigrant ships of 1801 (Reproduced by permission of the Public Archives of Nova Scotia)

emigrants on the ships, so it is likely that 'about 700' is if anything a rounded-up figure. Nevertheless, it suggests that there were perhaps a hundred or so emigrants who did not appear on the passenger lists. One possible explanation of the discrepancy is that Denoon's brother George had a third smaller vessel, the *Hope of Lossie,* carry 100 'full passengers' (the actual number of souls was in excess of 122) to Pictou later in 1801 (Fraser 1802, 19). These passengers would take the total of emigrants the Denoons took to Pictou in 1801 up to around 700. But the contemporary account of this vessel says that the passengers included 122 from an estate in Strathglass alone, so it is unlikely that there could have been more than a handful of Barra people amongst the notional 100 'full passengers'. But this may be the vessel he had in mind when he says that 'a number followed that year' (i.e. additional to the original 700) and there is no reason why he should have said two vessels if three were involved.

The possibility that perhaps around 100 Barra emigrants were picked up after the ships left Fort William might also be suggested by the claim made by the Highland Society that a third tier of bunks had been inserted into the *Sarah,* hidden behind a partition, to house passengers boarded after the ship had cleared customs. Barra oral tradition, as recounted by Neil Macphee of Vatersay to A A MacGregor (nd., 188–93), might also support a limited number of Barra emigrants on the ships. Macphee's account alleged that when Barra men enquired at Greenock about a passage there were not enough places left to meet the demand so that some were disappointed. But some allegedly sailed on

the ships, including Roderick Og Macneil of Brevig and James Macneil of Earsary, of whom more later. So it is tempting to think that there was a group emigration from Barra on Denoon's two ships in 1801, although it was much smaller than Macneil, relying on Patterson, suggested. A final word of support for a number of Barra emigrants in 1801 comes from the Rev. D. Rankin of Iona, Cape Breton, who told J L Campbell that 'in 1801 several people from Barra came to what is now Iona' (Campbell 1998, 129). It may be that these people were aboard two unnamed ships that Fraser (1802, 33) records arriving at Pictou from 'northern Scotland' in 1801, calling to collect a cargo of timber but bringing with them 400 more emigrants.

There is a caveat to enter however. Emigrant families have a propensity to claim a place amongst the first 'pioneers' and to therefore allow as early a date as possible for their own migration. Yet strangely, apart from Roderick and James Macneil, there is not a single Barra migrant who later claimed, or is known, to have emigrated in 1801, whereas there are dozens who are believed or known to have emigrated in 1802.

The emigration of 1802, to which so many Barra families laid claim, is in its way just as mysterious as that of 1801. Indeed, it is a mirror image of it in the sense that on this occasion we have documented emigrants, but the ship itself does not appear in the records. The principal source for the story behind the emigration is Neil Macphee. According to the oral tradition recounted by Macphee, one of the two cousins who sailed on Denoon's ships in 1801, James Macneil, returned to Barra at the beginning of 1802 to organise a second and more substantial emigration. These were, presumably, the families who had intended to sail in 1801 but for whom a passage on Denoon's ships could not be found. James, however, drowned in The Minches and it was left to his brother Hector Ban Macneil to organise the emigrant party. According to Macneil (1985, 135) Hector Ban actually owned a ship in which he embarked 370 Barra people in 1802 and took them to Pictou. This ship is believed to have been the *Hector,* a name recorded by Mackenzie (1984, 155) in 1926.

Although the details of this story have no documentary evidence to support them, its general outlines do seem to be confirmed by several strands of evidence. Fraser's manuscript, written at the close of that year, reports emigrants from several estates including Barra (Fraser 1802, 21), and later elaborates claiming at one point (p.23) that 600 people left Barra in 1802, and at another that the number was 1,000 (p.32). Though these numbers seem high at a time when the population just before the 1801 emigration was recorded as 1,925 people, they clearly imply a significant migration. The role of Roderick Og Macneil and James Macneil also seems plausible. They were the sons of the tacksmen of Brevig and Earsary respectively, and tacksmen at this time were certainly restive and others elsewhere were actively involved in promoting emigration. Significantly, two tacksmen of Clanranald, Archibald Maclean and Roderick Maclellan were recruiting emigrants for Hugh Denoon in 1801. They may have been involved therefore in the passages secured by Roderick and James, and perhaps some other Barra people, in the *Sarah* and the *Dove* or the two timber ships. In 1802 they were again very active in promoting emigration from the Western Isles, so much so that prompted by the Lord Advocate, the sheriff of

Invernesshire arrested them and hauled them off to Inverness gaol for questioning (Bumsted 1982, 117). Although they were later released, it is possible that due to their incarceration, and his brother's death, Hector Ban Macneil had to step in and take over more of the organisation of the emigration than he had anticipated. Whether he had a ship of his own, capable of taking nearly 400 passengers across the Atlantic is unknown but highly unlikely. Tacksmen were moderately affluent, but tacksmen of a small township on a small estate like Barra were unlikely to have had the means (or the inclination) to acquire a ship of this size.

There is certainly no recorded ship called the *Hector* taking emigrants to Nova Scotia around 1800, although Lloyds List records ten ships of this name afloat in 1802. But in 1802 there are several other ships known to have carried families from the Western Isles to Pictou and Sydney. The *Tweed* and the *Aurora* carrying respectively 70 and 128 passengers to Pictou, seem too small for the Barra emigration, but the *Northern Friends*, a ship of 245 tons carrying 340 passengers to Sydney is a contender. Fraser, who in preparing his 1802 manuscript obtained information from the Revenue Collectors about departing ships and their passengers noted that no lists were kept at Greenock in 1801/2 and that as a result 'not all ships from the west coast and isles were known' (Fraser 1902, 25). It is believed the Barra people landed at Pictou (Patterson 1877), but Kennedy believes they put in at Sydney (Kennedy 1995, 248). Other ships are known to have called first at Sydney and then at Pictou, so the two accounts are not incompatible. In addition, there are two further ships of unknown name recorded as carrying 900 emigrants from Uist and Barra to Pictou in 1802 (Brown 1806, appendix). The ship on which the Macneils of Brevig and Earsary sailed could be one of these, and it could have been called the *Hector*.

Patterson records that when the Barramen arrived in Nova Scotia they were provided with some assistance by Governor Wentworth, and by other Barra emigrants who had arrived a decade earlier, before a small group of them moved eastwards to Antigonish and into Cape Breton the following spring. The Cape Breton land petitions for 1803 include those from at least seven Barra families (Fig. 9.3). There are further petitions from natives of Barra over the next several years, up to as late as 1809, in which the petitioners say they arrived in Cape Breton in 1804. This accords with Patterson's account, in which he says that about twenty families followed the original group from Pictou to the Bras D'Or in 1804. Altogether, we have identified over fifty Barra families who claim to have emigrated in 1802. It is interesting to note that whereas the group migrations in 1772 and 1790 had been lead by Mackinnons and had few Macneils amongst them, forty of the fifty-three families who claim to have emigrated on the *Hector* in 1802 are Macneils. This provides a measure of support for Macphee's account, that the emigration of 1802 was organised by Macneil tacksmen. Their support for the emigration may have been crucial, but we should not ignore the important role of the emigration agents - Denoon, Maclean and Maclellan - in stimulating the emigration fever which seems to have gripped the Western Isles at the beginning of the century. There is also the possibility that the parish priest encouraged, and even accompanied, the emigration of 1802 (Fraser 1802, 32, 121).

The passing of the Passenger Act in May 1803 lowered emigration fever considerably, raising the price of a transatlantic passage from around £3 to £10 a head. Furthermore war had again broken out with France, with all the threat to British ships that that implied. The records show that ships continued to sail from Scotland to Canada in 1803, but the pace was falling off and to some extent there must have been a change in the type of families that were emigrating. The crofter with two or three acres, few personal possessions and a large family – in fact the typical Barra tenant at this time – could not afford the new fares. Equally, the difficulty of obtaining freehold land grants in Cape Breton at this time (Hornsby 1992, 23, 48) may have deterred would be emigrants who above all, were anxious to free themselves from the obligations and uncertainties of being tenants. Nevertheless, there is evidence in land petitions and family records that there was a continuing drain of individual migrations from Barra through the rest of the decade.

The *William Tell* and the *Hope*: 1817

With the end of the Napoleonic war, the emigration fever again seized Barra, and this time it is documented in shipping records, in land petitions, in official correspondence and in the letters of Macneil of Barra to the parish priest Angus Macdonald. The bare facts about this group emigration are reasonably clear. Two ships, the *William Tell* (256 tons) and the *Hope* (a brig of 190 tons) sailed from Greenock, early in May 1817, for Sydney and then onward to Pictou. The *Hope* arrived in Sydney on July 23rd, with 161 passengers, and the *William Tell* arrived two

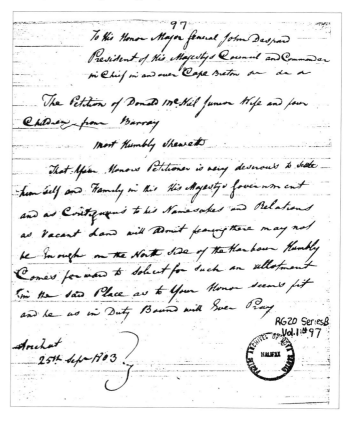

Figure 9.3 A petition for land on behalf of Donald Macneil Jnr, wife and four children, dated September 25th 1803 (Reproduced by permission of the Public Archives of Nova Scotia)

days later with 221 passengers (PANS RG.1/Vol.239/Doc.109). Lieutenant Governor Ainslie reported their arrival to Lord Bathurst at the Colonial Office (PRO CO 217/135) and sent him also a statement drawn up by one of the passengers which along with other information reports that 'the greater part of the passengers lived at Barra'. Many of the passengers seem to have disembarked at Sydney, but a petition signed at Pictou on 31/7/1817 reveals that 92 passengers on one of the ships sailed on to Pictou (PANS RG5,GP.Vol7, 7; Punch 1985). Sixty-three of these petitioners have surnames which were unknown on Barra in the first half of the nineteenth century, and they appear to be that part of the emigration group which did not originate from Barra. The remaining 29 passengers on the petition could have come from Barra to judge by their surnames, and eight of them certainly did. These are Roderick Gillies, his wife and six children, who emigrated from Borve and were granted land at Antigonish in 1818 (BPR; NSLP 1818). It seems clear that the majority of Barra emigrants disembarked at Sydney and then made their way to the Bras D'Or. This is confirmed by further official records as we shall see below. In contrast the bulk of the non-Barra migrants continued to Pictou and presumably settled along the Gulf Shore of Nova Scotia.

It seems likely that there were about 300 Barra emigrants in all on the two ships. From land petitions in Cape Breton and Nova Scotia, together with the petition for relief referred to above, and a couple of surviving personal documents, we can identify 200 individual emigrants who arrived in Cape Breton in 1817 and who were almost certainly passengers on the *William Tell* or the *Hope*. Ten of the Cape Breton land petitioners specifically mention that they arrived on the *William Tell*, and three individuals are named on a bill of passage for the *Hope* (Fig. 9.4). Most petitions simply gave 'Scotland' as the place of origin but some were more specific and gave Barra. Other Barra petitioners give away their origins by the names they give for their new plots of land – Kilbar and Borve for example.

The real interest of the 1817 emigration, however, is not its size but rather the evidence that it provides for the complex interplay of various agencies in reviving the 'spirit of emigration' in that year. The first intimations of an impending emigration come a full year earlier in a letter from Macneil of Barra to his parish priest, Angus Macdonald. In June 1816 he wrote 'reports have come to me of a spirit of emigration from your parish; but having no hint from you on the subject I paid them little attention.... A considerable number have signed with a Mr Fraser' (Campbell 1998, 122). So emigration agent Fraser was already actively recruiting passengers, and Macneil perhaps hints that he suspects the priest was deliberately keeping him in the dark. Two further letters follow in quick succession, and in all three letters Macneil insists he is anxious to help those of his tenants who wish to emigrate, and that he is concerned that they are being over-charged and given false promises by Fraser. In the third of these letters however, written on August 8th 1816, he also expresses his irritation at his tenants lack of confidence in him, and even their suspicions of him, and mentions unspecified threats which they have apparently made. It may be that his tenants views and actions were made known to him by Macdonald in the two letters he mentions he has received from the priest. Macneil would certainly have been expecting the priest to have put his offers of assistance to emigrate to his flock, and indeed to have had a significant influence on their behaviour. We have to suspect that Macdonald may not have been open with, or helpful to, Macneil in his involvement in the emigration issue. As we shall see (below p. 164), a decade later he is certainly involved in encouraging and actively assisting a large number of tenants to emigrate.

As for emigration agent Fraser, Macneil plainly believes that he has overcharged his passengers and has made them spurious promises. Further, he has apparently threatened them with having to pay an unlawful penalty if, having signed, they withdraw (Macneil in a letter of 25/6/1816; Campbell 1998, 124). Macneil's concerns are in fact born out by both Governor Ainslie's letter to the Colonial Office, and the statement made by the passengers of the ships. Ainslie writes 'I possess no means to afford them the supplies of provisions with which Mr Fraser deceived them

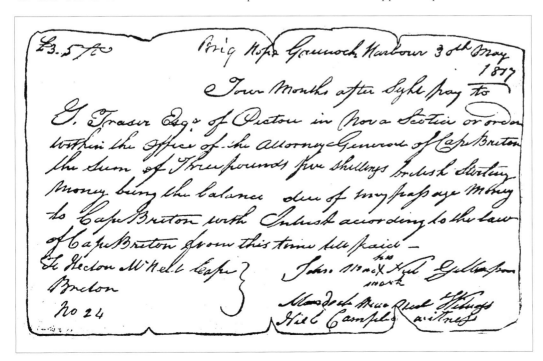

Figure 9.4 A promissory note for £3-5-0 signed by John Macneil, this being the balance of his fare for passage on the Hope from Greenock to Cape Breton in 1817 (Copy made in 1923 of an original then in the possession of Rev J Macneil of Cape Breton)

with hope of, and for giving them the implements of agriculture they expect. They have been much deceived'. The passengers' statement gives more details about Fraser's promises, and also the fares he charged. 'He [Fraser] informed them that Colonial Governments had the authority to give them on arrival three years' provisions , what land they wanted, farming and agricultural implements'. Fraser offered a fare of 8 guineas per person, and 6 guineas for children under 7 years of age, with the passengers to be picked up at Barra itself. In the event, however, when the time came, they were told to make their way to Tobermory, and on arrival there were directed to make their way on to Greenock. Small boats were provided by Fraser to take them to Tobermory and Greenock, but he charged them an additional 4/- per adult, and 2/- per child. Whilst the fares were not excessive, given that the Passenger Act was still in force, Fraser certainly appears to have promised a package of benefits that he could not deliver. But in the light of Government support for emigration to Canada only the year before, such promises may have looked entirely reasonable. In 1815, following the attempted American invasion of 1812, the British government had sponsored an emigration programme to encourage settlers in Upper Canada (*Caledonian Mercury* 25/2/1815). It is surprising, nevertheless, that Earl Bathurst and his colleagues in the Colonial Office also appear to have been very actively involved in assisting the emigration from Barra to Cape Breton in 1817. Cape Breton and Nova Scotia were already well populated and well defended both by land and sea-based forces and reasonably well populated, albeit mostly by leaseholders and, effectively, squatters. Bathurst himself was far from convinced of the wisdom of large-scale emigration, and at this time the government were forcing the Colonial Office to drastically reduce its expenditure (Thompson 1999, 110, 187). But Ainslie's report to Lord Bathurst of the arrival of the *William Tell* and the *Hope* is in itself unusual; the Lieutenant Governor did not report the arrival of every immigrant ship in this way. More significant, however, is Ainslie's assurance at the beginning of the letter that 'your Lordship's recommendation received, no effort shall be wanting on my part to afford them my protection and support' (PRO CO 217/135). Clearly, prior to the ships' arrival, Ainslie had received a request from the highest levels of the Colonial Office to provide assistance.

The involvement of the Colonial Office is confirmed by minutes tucked away in the Treasury Notebooks detailing correspondence from the Colonial Office. A record of April 25th 1817 records that Bathurst had requested that 'facility may be afforded for the embarkation of a considerable number of persons who wish to proceed as settlers from the Isle of Barra to Cape Breton, and of the provisions necessary for their subsistence and... my Lords desire that every possible facility may be afforded to them to take with them any provisions and articles of husbandry or furniture which they may have provided free of any duties to which they may legally be liable' (PRO T11/58). The Treasury replied on April 30th, and informed Bathurst that they had asked the Scottish customs officers to afford these privileges to the Barra people (PRO CO/384/2).

But why had Bathurst sanctioned this special treatment for the emigrants from Barra ? The letter to the Treasury on April 25th explains the action by referring to 'the particular circumstances in which the individuals about to proceed

from Barra are placed'. But we have no records of poor crop yields and famine in 1816–1817, nor of any persecution of Macneil's Catholic tenants. There is nothing in the Macneil letters to Angus Macdonald to point in this direction. The explanation may perhaps be found in a further entry in the Treasury Notebooks (PRO T29/148/ entry 8015). This refers to a letter from Henry Goulburn, Bathurst's Under Secretary for the Colonies, dated April 18th, which apparently enclosed one from the emigration agent Mr Fraser! Here too there is a reference to the circumstances in which the Barra people find themselves. Since there is no further explanation it seems probable that those circumstances were explained in Fraser's letter. If so, one can only imagine that Mr Fraser had spun a tale to get such support for his emigrants.

It is possible, but unlikely, that the Colonial Office went even further to help the Barra emigrants in 1817. Their records contain two lists of agricultural implements, one dated March 27th 1817, and the other July 2nd (PRO CO/3842). They are headed 'Order for the use of settlers in Canada'. The lists are impressive in both the range and quantity of materials to be provided, and the quantities were increased between March and July. By July, for example, there were to be 3,000 each of felling axes, scythes and sickles. Tempting as it is to link these with the correspondence about the Barra emigrants it seems unlikely there is any connection. The first list was compiled a month before the first reference to Barra, the second is compiled almost two months after they had sailed. Furthermore they are said to be for 'Canada', a term which the Colonial Office would certainly not be expected to use for Cape Breton, and of course the quantities are far in excess of what 400 emigrants (perhaps 80 families) would need! They are perhaps late assistance for the people sent out under the government sponsored scheme of 1815.

The extent to which Ainslie complied with Bathurst's request to afford assistance to the emigrants on the *William Tell* and *Hope* is indicated by a series of warrants from Ainslie in August 1817 to pay various local boat owners for taking Scottish emigrants from Sydney to the Bras D'Or (PANS RG/11/1, 178-9). The extant warrants record payments of between £5 and £10 per trip (presumably varying according to the size of the boat and the number of families carried). A £5 passage took 4 families, so the total bill of £31 may refer to transport for about two dozen families. A copy of a letter to Bathurst on October 1st 1817 records a payment of £44 – 71 for conveying highland emigrants to the Bras D'Or together with a large quantity of fishing nets, implements and spinning wheels – presumably the sort of items they had been allowed to bring duty free from Barra! A further warrant from Ainslie records payments to local merchants for the supply of provisions (pork, mutton, and flour) for the emigrants. A note at the bottom of the warrant says that these charges are to be met from His Majesties Gypsum Fund.

From these various records we can see the part played by a variety of agencies in the emigration of 1817. Support was offered by the Colonial Office in London, and significant assistance was given by the governor of Cape Breton in response to instructions from London. But these were not the prime movers. That role appears to have fallen to Fraser, who was actively signing up Barramen already in 1816. The passengers' statement says explicitly, referring to Fraser's promises, that 'such inducements encouraged many to sell their little property and emigrate'. There has to be a suspicion that the priest, Angus Macdonald, at the very least did not discourage them. It is possible he went further. In 1818 he wrote to Macneil apparently promoting the activities of a William Macmillan, who seems to have been planning a further group emigration. In his reply (which is what survives) Macneil scorns Macmillan's ability to organise such a venture but concludes 'however as you seem to take an interest in this man, if he makes an offer on proper terms by your interference I will return you an answer' (Campbell 1998, 128–9). Macdonald is here plainly involved in negotiations about an emigration, a year after the *William Tell* and the *Hope*. As for the laird, Macneil initially seems to have been in the dark about the plans for an emigration, but then to have offered the would-be emigrants - perhaps through the offices of Angus Macdonald - whatever assistance he could to find a cheaper passage. When his help was rejected he was somewhat aggrieved, but was still able to tell Macdonald in a letter of May 28th 1817 'the loss of so very many decent people is to be regretted' (Campbell 1998, 126). These 300 people were of course at the very centre of the events of 1816 and 1817, yet they are often disregarded when the dynamics of the emigration are considered. It is well to remember that for all the promises of Fraser, the encouragement of the priest, the support of the Colonial Office and the assistance of Governor Ainslie, neither persons nor circumstances forced these people to sign up for emigration in 1816–17. It was not a time of starvation, there were no clearances. The Napoleonic Wars had come to an end but the price of kelp was at this point still high, and money saved by returning soldiers was perhaps still unspent. In fact, it may have been a time of opportunity - the coincidence of relatively well-off tenants, a persuasive emigration agent with an attractive package, a well-disposed Colonial Office and a new opportunity to acquire freehold land in Cape Breton. The decision to emigrate in 1817 should perhaps be seen as a positive choice made by people with an ambition to better themselves, rather than as a desperate attempt by an oppressed and manipulated people to free themselves from bondage.

Group emigrations 1820–1845

We have already noted above that in 1818 there appear to have been further plans for an organised emigration from Barra in which a William Macmillan was involved. Governor Ainslie's report to Earl Bathurst in 1817 mentioned that Fraser too had 'announced another ship load or two next year' and said that he would warn Fraser not to deceive his would-be clients. However, although we have records of individual emigrants from Barra in 1818 there is no evidence of a group migration. In fact even where we can identify migration groups over the next twenty-five years the evidence is often thin.

This applies particularly to the emigration of 1821. The ship *Harmony* is recorded as having sailed from Barra to Sydney in 1821 with 350 passengers (Dobson 1998, 55; CNSHS 23.45). This one ship accounts for the all the Scots emigrants recorded by the Customs at Sydney in 1821 (Martell 1942). We know little else about this emigration, except that in our database we have about 150 Barra people who are known, or who claimed, to have settled in Cape Breton in 1821. There is thus little reason to doubt that this group emigration took place, but we have no evidence,

direct or otherwise, as to what stimulated it. It was, however, a bleak end to the chieftainship of Roderick the Gentle, in whose time the *Alexander*, the *Queen*, the *Sarah* and the *Dove*, the *Hector*, the *William Tell* and the *Hope*, and finally the *Harmony*, had carried off large numbers of his clansmen and tenants.

With the succession of the General to the chieftainship, the context in which emigration took place changed. Roderick the Gentle had generally treated his tenants well, and had offered to assist those who wished to emigrate, whilst regretting their going. In contrast Roderick the General expected his tenants simply to obey his orders in the same way that his troops did, and was determined to prevent them emigrating. In February 1825 he wrote to Angus Macdonald : 'I have little fear of emigration. I shall certainly in all the various ways in my power (and they are not a few) oppose it'. It appears that those who were opposed to his plans for the estate had used the threat of emigration in an attempt to deter him (Campbell 1998, 141). Five months later it seems that an emigration was imminent. He wrote to Macdonald (30/7/1825) and asked him to read aloud a proclamation at the next Sunday service. He had a message for emigrants : 'say to those who are about to emigrate that I sincerely wish them well ... and assure those who have signed and repented that their repentance comes too late - So help me God they shall go'. The General was resigned to the inevitable.

In fact there is no evidence of a group emigration in 1825; it follows in 1826, but it may be that an agent was signing up passengers a full year in advance. That agent was probably the self-same Simon Fraser who had followed this procedure in 1816 for the emigration of 1817, although his name does not appear in the records concerning **this** emigration until February 1827. But parliamentary papers report that in April of 1826 1,600 potential emigrants from various parts of the highlands and islands, including Barra, were enquiring if they would receive assistance to emigrate to British North America that summer.

By June 400–500 people from Uist and Barra had applied for the means to join their friends 'who had emigrated in 1817'. The *William Tell* and the *Hope* were clearly still fresh in the memory. One ship arrived in early September with 400 emigrants from the Hebrides, and at that time two further vessels with about the same number of people were imminently expected (PANS Vol.335, Doc 64). One of the two latter vessels may have been the *Northumberland* which actually sailed into St Andrews, New Brunswick with Hebridean emigrants in 1826 (MacDonald 1936, 45). These are unlikely to be the Barra people, although many of the *Northumberland*'s passengers are said to have moved to Inverness Co. in Cape Breton, so the possibility should not be discounted. But the Barra people probably sought a passage direct to Cape Breton, and Governor Sir James Kempt reported to Wilmot Horton at the Colonial Office on September 14th that nearly 500 Scots had arrived in Cape Breton, landing at Sydney and other unspecified places (PANS CO 217/146). Bishop Angus Maceachern of PEI confirmed the arrival of the Barramen in Cape Breton in December 1826 when he wrote to Angus Macdonald, by now somewhat mysteriously translated to the Rectorship of the Scots College in Rome: 'many of your flock from Barra came to Cape Breton this last season' (SCR Box 12/109). Our database includes about 50 individuals who are known, or claimed, to have arrived in Cape Breton in 1826 but we have no clear indication from the brief mentions in the Canadian sources as to how many emigrants from Barra arrived in total.

The most interesting aspect of this emigration is the role that Angus Macdonald may have played in it. By August 1825 the General had firmly come to the conclusion that his father had only vaguely grasped – that he simply couldn't trust the priest. On the 8th of August he wrote to Macdonald with a mixture of anguish and anger: '[I] endeavoured to avail myself of the good offices of the Pastor with his flock....he proffered me his cordial cooperation....I saw that you possessed influence almost unbounded over your flock...what then am I to think when I find the fishermen slothful...the kelpers also are in a state of disgraceful insubordination. What then, I repeat, am I to think? ...either you are not free from prejudice yourself or your feelings lead you to encourage it in others'. In fact, it appears that Macdonald may have been encouraging not simply resistance to Macneil's plans, but the spirit of emigration.

The clues to this activity come both in letters from Macdonald himself, and in letters to him, sent by John Chisholm, priest on South Uist, and by Neil Macdonald, the new priest on Barra. In a letter to the Rev. Andrew Scott at the Catholic Chapel in Glasgow, Angus Macdonald appears to implicate himself in emigration affairs as early as March 1825 (SCA BL5/170). He says he has passed on 'papers belonging to emigrants of the famous Robertson', some of whom are in Cape Breton and others in Barra. This may be James Robertson of PEI, who had previously been involved in organising some controversial emigrant ships around 1810 (Bumsted 1978, 201–1; Campey 2001, 52–4). Macdonald goes on to say 'powers of attorney were sent me from Cape Breton, other powers to the same effect drawn in this country were lodged with me'. He appears to have been attempting to recover lost monies for would-be emigrants whose passage had not materialised: 'the poor people at home constantly make enquiry about their money and I am at a loss what to tell them'. In March 1826 he informed Bishop Patterson that his parishioners were so enraged by Macneil's tyrannical behaviour that they had 'come to a determination of rescuing themselves from such intolerable measures'. Emigration agents had appeared and 'more than one half of the whole population of the island' has subscribed for Cape Breton (SCA BL5/192). After Macdonald had been transferred to the Scots College in Rome, John Chisholm in August 1826 wrote to him: 'I look upon all of them as on the wing to emigrate if they possibly can. The ferment you left, and perhaps fermented among them, has not as I find in the least subsided'. He also refers to 'our emigration agents' who again 'promise largely to the people' (SCR Box 12/127). Neil Macdonald in 1827 reports to Macdonald 'I had in my possession that of your money, a little more than £13, all recovered from the emigrants of last year' (SCR Box 12/128). None of this is explicit, but it suggests that Macdonald had been actively stoking the fires of emigration fever, had acted on behalf of emigrants, had perhaps been making small loans to would-be emigrants, and had even been in some way involved with emigration agents. In this connection, we can recall his involvement with William Macmillan in 1818, and Colonel Macneil's disquiet that Macdonald had said nothing to him of Mr Fraser's recruiting activities in 1816. It may be coincidence, but it was none other than Fraser who was the agent involved in the 1826 saga.

Fraser had a bad track record as far as emigrations from Barra goes, ranging over a period of about 40 years, from 1790 to 1828. Whilst the 1790 emigration seems to have been relatively trouble-free, that of 1792 saw many would-be emigrants left without the passage they had paid for. In 1817 Fraser had failed to meet his promises to pick up the passengers from Barra, and had made promises which were not his to make and he was unable to keep. So too, in 1826 things went wrong. Government assistance seems not to have materialised for Governor Kempt reported that the 500 emigrants to Cape Breton that year had travelled at their own expense. Neil Macdonald in 1827 reported to Angus Macdonald that only half of those who had enlisted were able to go 'either for means of sufficient money on their part or want of fidelity of the agents' (SCR Box 12/128). The story was confirmed by Hugh Macneil of Vatersay who laid the blame at Fraser's door: 'those emigrants that engaged with Col Fraser have been sadly disappointed as he was unable to send them off to America, and I am told the poor wretches are going about from place to place looking for some place to rest themselves' (SCR Box 12/129).

Fraser must by now have been an elderly man, but he continued to seek recruits for passage to Canada by now working in tandem with an emigration agent from Skye, Archibald Mcniven. John Chisholm told Macdonald that in 1827 Colonel Fraser and another agent called Mcniven had recruited four families from South Uist (SCR Box 12/131). Emigrants from South Uist and Barra were allegedly among the 193 passengers of the *George Stephens* from Tobermory to Sydney in 1827. Neil Macdonald reported in July 1828 that just two Barra families had emigrated that year (SCR Box 12/132). The disappointments of 1826 had clearly suppressed the enthusiasm for emigration and in 1830 Neil Macdonald was able to write 'there is no incitement for emigration here just now'. He puts this down to two developments - bad news from America and the ruination of the agents. In the same letter he reports both that 'very bad accounts have been of late received from America' and that 'Macniven the flying d...l will become this year a complete bankrupt. Poor unfortunate Fraser is long ago knocked up. He is either still in prison or in the begging way' (SCR Box 12/136). On what charges 'poor unfortunate Fraser' had been incarcerated we do not know, but he seems at the end of his long career as an emigration agent to have acquired the status of a loveable rogue.

From 1830 until Gordon's clearances there is little hard evidence for group emigrations, but there are indications that significant numbers of Barramen were still leaving the island. Poor weather and low crop yields in 1836–37 seem to have stimulated a new outflow of tenants from the Western Isles in 1837 when six ships sailed from Stornoway, Tobermory and Greenock with a total of 600 emigrants. There were almost certainly Barramen amongst them, for in the *Second Statistical Account*, Nicholson reported that 'emigration to Cape Breton and Nova Scotia carried off the island a great many almost every year. In some years several hundreds leave it for those places'. The Select Committee on Emigration (Select Committee 1841, question 1012) also heard that 'emigration has taken place lately, both in Barra and South Uist...but the scale was not sufficiently extensive, as the births are generally much greater than the deaths'. Nicholson said the reason for the fall-off in emigration was that due to the fall in kelp prices most tenants were 'unable to betake themselves to any other country by emigration'. Shortly after, in 1843, there appears to have been the first and only genuinely voluntary group emigration under Colonel Gordon's ownership of Barra. A group of 70 Barra people are reported as emigrating, without assistance, to Canada (Leavit and Smout 1979, 48). Further group emigration from Barra under Colonel Gordon's supervision, would be 'assisted' in more ways than one as we saw at the end of the previous chapter!

What emerges from a survey of group emigration from Barra between 1770 and 1851 is that it involved a multiplicity of agencies whose attitudes and roles changed though time. It was not a story only about lairds and clansmen, though they certainly held centre stage. The Macneils were happy to see their clansmen recruited into the army for North America, but between 1780 and 1830 loath to see whole families emigrating, denying them rents and crofting income. Their tenants' enthusiasm ebbed and flowed, dependent on the changing currents of relative affluence and poverty, of religious persecution (real or imagined), of the availability or denial of government assistance, and of the lairds' good will or contempt. The Catholic church at times played on the tenants' fears to pressure lairds and government to adopt more tolerant policies to the church, whilst the parish priests sought to use emigration to protect their flock not only from religious intolerance but economic exploitation. Whilst tacksmen did not play a large part in the life of Barra by the late 18th century, their traditional loyalty to their chief was tested by their growing disillusionment, loss of prestige, and perhaps loss of income. On Barra this may have led them into taking on a major role in the emigrations of 1801–3. The emigration agents were perhaps the only individuals involved who were unequivocal about their role. They were businessmen who made a living from emigration. Finally there was the Government, both in London and in Canada. Its impact on emigration is difficult to overestimate. Through its growing imperial ambitions it provided Barramen with opportunities both to earn money and to see North America for themselves. Its struggles with Revolutionary France and Napoleon created conditions for an economic boom in the Western Isles, but its enactment of the Passenger Act imposed a major restriction on emigration. Its reduction of taxes on a whole series of products in the 1820s led to the collapse of the kelp industry and a growing destitution in the islands which both promoted a spirit of emigration and denied tenants the means to follow it. At the same time it repealed the Passenger Act making transatlantic passages cheaper. From the end of the Napoleonic Wars onwards it also became directly involved in emigration as it offered assistance to various emigration schemes, including specific involvement in the emigrations from Barra in 1817. Its successive Commissions investigating the problems and opportunities presented by emigration led to further schemes of assistance, and also meant that when famine hit the Western Isles in the late 1840s it already had a great deal of information about prospects for emigrants at its fingertips. Although the Colonial Office in London may have had little or no direct involvement in Gordon's deportation of hundreds of Barramen in 1850/51, the Government officials in Canada certainly played a crucial role in assisting these people to begin a new life in North America.

The Pattern and Scale of Emigration from 1770 to 1851

In discussing the changing patterns of emigration and the number of people involved, we need to bear in mind the problems which beset compiling a database of emigrants. These are discussed at some length in the introduction to the database itself. One factor which is perhaps worth mentioning specifically here is the probable under-representation of those emigrants who quickly moved into urban settlements, particularly those with an industrial base (such as Sydney, Cape Breton). Our database includes no more than one or two such individuals, yet there must have been others, even if most emigrants became farmers or fishermen.

Two aspects of the pattern of emigration from Barra to British North America stand out clearly from even a cursory glance at the evidence. These are the changing destinations of the emigrants and the episodic nature of the emigrations (Fig. 9.5). We know of two, probably three, group migrations between 1770 and 1800, and our database contains details of about 60 individual emigrants who were involved in one or the other of these. Both of the documented group migrations, and the third less certain example of 1792, took people to Prince Edward Island. These ships may have taken about 350 Barramen there in total, and it seems to have been quite clearly the preferred destination in this period, although the preference may have been that of the emigration organisers rather than the emigrants (as the 1772 emigration in the *Alexander* certainly was). We should recall, however, that in 1790 the *Queen* was allegedly intended to put into Louisbourg and only went to PEI as a result of being driven off course. If that is true, it suggests an early interest in Cape Breton as a destination. Three individuals who emigrated in 1790 / 91, and were therefore probably on the *Queen*, ended up in Nova Scotia and others amongst the hundred or so untraced passengers may have joined them. Otherwise, the only Barramen known to have taken up land in Nova Scotia in the 18th century were the veterans who settled at Malignant Cove and Cape George, north of Antigonish in the 1780s. In their case their location was determined by the Colonial Government. The first recorded Barra emigrants into Cape Breton landed in Pictou in 1799 and made their way to the Bras D'Or in 1800.

The new century opened a new chapter in Barra emigration. Whereas somewhere between 80–90% of the pre-1800 emigrants had gone to PEI and the rest to Nova Scotia, between 1800 and 1840, about 97% went to Cape Breton! This figure is based on the c.900 individuals in the database who emigrated between 1800 and 1840 for whom a destination is known. All of the known group emigrations in this period sailed into either Sydney (CB) or Pictou (NS), but the vast majority of their passengers ended up in Cape Breton. A few stayed in Nova Scotia, around Antigonish or Pictou, and a handful sailed across to PEI, but otherwise Cape Breton absorbed them all.

This dramatic change of direction cannot be explained in terms of current government policy at the time, particularly as the government was restricting the acquisition of freehold land grants in Cape Breton at the time. It may owe much to the initial large-scale emigration of 1802, and the steady trickle which followed it to the Bras D'Or, and this emigration may of course have been inspired, and at least partly organised, by

Figure 9.5 Map of Cape Breton, Nova Scotia and Prince Edward Island showing main ports of landing for immigrants and some principal places of settlement

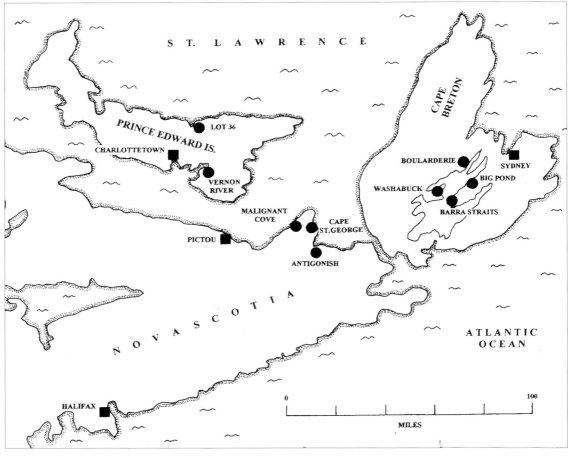

Barramen themselves. Thereafter, both the strength of the Barra tradition in the area, and perhaps the attractions of a landscape which was in some respects more similar to their homeland than was PEI, continued to pull Barra emigrants to Cape Breton and the Bras D'Or in particular (Fig. 9.6).When this pattern changed again, in the 1840s, it was due largely to government policy both in London and Canada. Although some claimed that Cape Breton could still absorb more settlers (RCPC, 148), between 1815 and 1838 its population had swollen from 6,000 to 38,000 (MacLean 1976, 115). Upper and Lower Canada on the other hand were still relatively empty (particularly the former) and government was willing to provide support and encouragement to would-be emigrants. The people cleared by Gordon had no choice as to where they made their landfall and initially, at least, few options as to where they first settled. They were given passage from Quebec up the St Lawrence and into Ontario. There they could find temporary work as servants and labourers if they could not yet acquire land. Some made their way east again to seek out relatives or friends in Cape Breton; the Johnstons settled in Red Islands for example. But most of the families on the *Admiral* appear to have remained in Upper Canada.

Changes in the chronological pattern of emigration may at first appear to have been just as abrupt as those in spatial patterning. Emigrations from Barra to British North America seem to be essentially episodic. There are a series of well spaced major emigrations – 1772, 1790/92, 1802, 1817, 1821, 1826, perhaps 1843, and of course 1848/51. As we have discussed above, these can be related to a variety of factors - religious, military, economic, and social – the value or force of each of which changed through time. But we should not assume that in between each of these group

emigrations the flow of emigrants dried up. From 1800 onwards, there is a steady leakage of emigrants from the reservoir in Barra, punctuated by times when the dam burst. This is hinted at in a number of contemporary sources some of which have been mentioned earlier (e.g. *Second Statistical Account* and Select Committee 1841), and it is confirmed by the evidence of our database. In the 38 years between 1801 and 1837 we have emigrants from Barra recorded in all but five years, from amongst the c. 660 Barramen for whom we have a date of emigration. There are 300 further emigrants for whom we do not have an emigration date, amongst whom of course there may be a few who would fill one or more of those five empty years. Emigration was clearly continuous, though seasonal, and between the peak years, even on our very incomplete database, one can see smaller surges (e.g. 1813, 1822, 1828, and 1836) in the general swell.

It is the small-scale on-going emigrations which make it difficult to estimate just how many people emigrated from Barra to British North America between 1770 and 1851. Even though we have been unable to trace many of the people involved in the group emigrations, we often have a reasonably accurate total figure from contemporary official sources. But emigrations by individuals or single families normally went unrecorded except in family histories, and as a result many of these emigrants remain unrecognised. If we consider only the known group emigrations we can arrive at a minimum figure. We tabulate these below (table 9.1); note that we round up or down to the nearest ten in all cases. We must also note that we have no identified individuals from the emigrations of 1792, 1843, and 1848, but we believe they took place. Finally we also note that some figures are estimated from a known number of

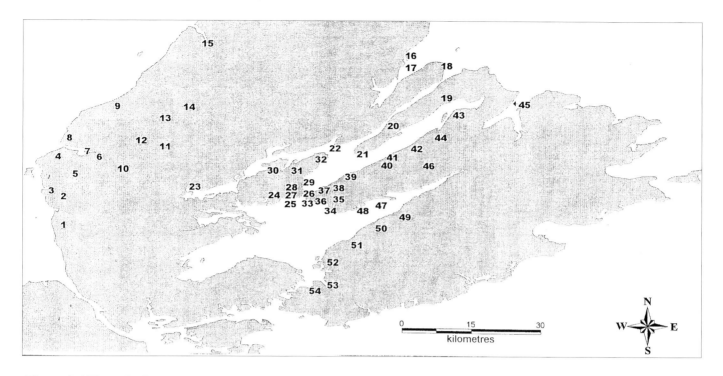

Figure 9.6 Places in Cape Breton settled by emigrants from Barra

Key: 1. Judique 2. Little Judique 3. Port Hood 4. Little Mabou 5. South West Mabou 6. Mabou 7. Mabou Harbour 8. MacKinnon's Brook 9. Broad Cove 10. Miramichi 11. West Lake Ainslie 12. Mount Young 13. North Ainslie 14. Upper Margaree 15. East Margaree 16. Indian Brook 17. Red Island 18. Cape Dauphin 19. Goose Cove 20. Boularderie 21. Point Clear 22. Baddeck 23. Whycocomagh 24. MacKinnon's Harbour 25. Jamesville 26. Iona 27. Barra Glen 28. St Columba 29. Gillis Point 30. South Cove 31. Upper Washabuck 32. Lower Washabuck 33. Grand Narrows 34. Piper Cove 35. Benacadie 36. Coopers Pond 37. Christmas Island 38. Goose Pond 39. Big Beech 40. Shenacadie 41. Beaver Cove 42. Boisdale 43. Macneil's Beach 44. Barrachois 45. Sydney Mines 46 Rear Boisdale 47. Eskasoni 48. Castle Bay 49. Big Pond 50. Middle Cape 51. Irish Cove 52. Red Islands 53. Soldiers Cove 54. Barra Head

'families' (assuming an average of 5 per family), and the figure for the 1801 *Sarah/Dove* is based on the discussion above (p. 158–9).

The figures for 'identified' individuals in these group emigrations include those who are recorded as arriving in the year of that particular emigration but are not specifically recorded as being on the ship in question. We think the total figure for these group emigrations is reasonably accurate.

Trying to translate the number of identified individuals who were not **apparently** part of a group emigration, into an estimated total number of non-group emigrants over the period is obviously difficult but we believe that some attempt should be made. We have to recognise first that some of the emigrants for whom no date of emigration is known were, nevertheless, almost certainly involved in a group emigration. We also have to recognise that some of the apparently independent emigrants may also have arrived in a group. The most remarkable example to illustrate this point is John Gillis who petitioned for land in 1835, and in the absence of other information might be assumed to be a recent arrival. But in his petition he mentions that he arrived on the *William Tell* in 1817, when he was just four years old! To balance these individuals, we have to bear in mind that it is more difficult to trace emigrants who really do travel on their own or with just their immediate family. In that sense, the number of non-group emigrants is probably under-represented compared to those who came in a group emigration.

For our purposes we are assuming that the pros and cons of these factors cancel each other out. To estimate the total of individual non-group emigrants that the 300 individuals in our database represent, we suggest multiplying them by a factor derived from our identified group emigrants. This factor we might call our Percentage Identification Rate

Table 9.1 Estimated number of Barra emigrants in group emigrations 1772–1851

Year	Ship	Passengers	Identified
1772	*Alexander*	40	10
1790	*Queen*	140	22
1792	-	200	0
1801	*Sarah/Dove*	80	2
1802	*Hector*	370	99
1817	*William Tell/ Hope*	300	137
1821	*Harmony*	350	141
1826	-	200	26
1843	-	70	0
1848	-	150	0
1851	*Admiral*	410	43
Total		**2,310**	**480**

(PIR) – that is, the % of the total of group-emigrants (calculated at about 2,300) that we have traced and include in our data-base. A crude PIR figure would be 21%, but we think that would be misleading. The identification rate for emigrants going to Upper and Lower Canada and to PEI is much lower than that for those going to Nova Scotia and Cape Breton. For the first two areas it is around 7–8%, whilst for Nova Scotia/Cape Breton it is 30%. In the case of PEI the identification rate is low partly because the emigrations are too early to allow us to identify all or most of the individuals in a family, so we have only a head of household identified. The figure is also depressed for PEI because of the different land-tenure system there which did not create the same petition and land-grant records that we have for Nova Scotia and Cape Breton. The figure for Ontario is depressed for different reasons. The number of Barramen who emigrated to Ontario between 1840 and 1851 was a tiny fraction of the total number of emigrants flooding into the area, and the area itself of course was huge. Furthermore the emigrants of this period were more likely to move on or disappear into the emerging towns, and thus be difficult to trace. We have barely skimmed a small selection of land grant and census records for a handful of townships. For these reasons, we think it best to exclude the early PEI and late Ontario group emigrations when calculating our PIR, and to use the Nova Scotia / Cape Breton figure of 30% for our purposes.

Applying this to the 300 non-group emigrants in our database, we estimate that this may represent an original total of about 1,000 individuals who emigrated singly or in small family groups between 1800 and 1840. There were probably small numbers before 1800 and others between 1840 and 1850 but very few. We estimate therefore that the total number of Barra emigrants to British North America between 1770 and 1851 was perhaps c.3,500 men, women and children.

Three of the group emigrations coincide more or less with census years. These allow us to grasp something of the impact that emigration may have had on Barra. In 1801/2 the island lost about 24% of its population to Canada, in 1821 it lost 15%, and in 1851 it lost 22%. But we must remember that 1821 had been preceded by the emigration of 1817, which had removed 13% of the people, and that 1851 had been preceded not only by an emigration in 1848, but also by the removal to the Scottish mainland of 600 people in 1850. In four years 1848–1851, Barra lost half its population. Small wonder the episode left such deep and bitter memories, as well as the abandoned blackhouses and outbuildings, shielings and enclosures whose ruins still inhabit the landscape.

Transformations and Traditions

Until the clearances of 1848–51 most emigrants from the isle of Barra had moved from one island on the eastern margin of the Atlantic to another island on the western side of the same ocean. But in many respects Cape Breton and Barra could not be more different. Barra is a small island of less than 25 square miles, whereas Cape Breton covers 4,000 square miles. The central core of Barra is made up of bleak high hills rising to 200–400m, whereas the centre of Cape Breton is occupied by the huge Bras D'Or lake. By the 19th century (and indeed long before) Barra was treeless, and much of it covered with blanket peat or rough pasture, whilst Cape Breton was still thickly forested but

possessed good deep soils. The forests were populated by moose, deer, caribou, bear, and smaller mammals, none of which were to be found on Barra. Only in the fishing were there similarities, and even here Cape Breton's rivers and lakes provided large quantities of freshwater fish not found in Barra. Samuel Holland, who surveyed Cape Breton between 1765 and 1767 for the British government, following its cession to Britain in 1763, recommended it for settlement: 'The soil is in general good, nay in some places luxuriantly so; the woods afford a great quantity of excellent timber; the many rivers, rivulets, creeks, lakes, coasts etc abound with fish; the game that resorts here at different seasons through the year is innumerable' (Harvey 1935, 85). Holland had little to say about the climate, apart from commenting that most of Cape Breton did not suffer the summer fogs and excessively cold winters that beset Louisbourg. But this was relative. Cape Breton has far colder winters, with deep snows, iced-over lakes and harbours, and low temperatures that Barra, warmed by the Gulf Stream, avoids.

One way in which the Barramen coped with this alien landscape was to familiarise it, and even appropriate it, with their own place-names. Around the Bras D'Or we find Barra Straits and Barra Head, Barra Glenn and Castlebay. Individual plots were given names like Sandray, Kilbar, Borve and Craigston. Other natural features were named after early pioneer families - MacKinnon's Harbour and Mackinnon's Point, Gillis Point and Gillis Lake, MacDougall's Point, and Roderick Head, and of course Macneil's Beach and Macneil's Vale.

If the physical geography of Cape Breton presented emigrants from Barra with a genuinely 'new world', so did the human geography. The population of Barra was an overwhelmingly Gaelic-speaking, Catholic society drawn largely from its own islands but with some families whose origins lay elsewhere in the Highlands and Islands. It was in many ways a very close society, not only because of the many family relationships but also because a relatively large population occupied a small part of a very small island. Notionally, population density in 1800 was about 80 persons to the square mile, but because most of the island was uninhabited, the actual density was much greater than this. In contrast, Cape Breton in 1784 had a population of about 1,250 people, with a density of about 0.3 per square mile (PANS Vol.44, 48). This small population was also a very diverse one, made up, in descending numerical order, of French, Irish, immigrant American, native American, and English peoples. In 1766, there were just 6 Scots in the whole of Cape Breton!

It is hard to imagine the psychological impact of the new physical and human environment in which the first Barra settlers around the Bras D'Or found themselves. They had come from an open landscape in which everything in sight – even the most distant peaks on Skye – was known and familiar, to an enclosed landscape where the claustrophobic forest blanketed everything as far as the eye could see. From a society where mutual support and family relationships were always close at hand, they had removed to one where apart perhaps from a handful of friends and relatives, other human beings were few and far between, and spoke a different language and possessed an alien culture. Some sense of the feelings of sadness and cultural dislocation experienced by the emigrants is captured in the Gaelic songs and poems which some of them composed.

None perhaps conveyed it better than Bard Maclean:

'a hidden grief has overfilled me since I've been doomed to stagnate here for the rest of my life with little amusement in this gnarled forest and without anyone to ask me if I'll sing a song. That was not my custom in early days; then I used to be frolicking at every table, happy and contented among cultured companions, passing our time without any care' (Dunn 1953, 59)

And Maclean and other migrant poets were less sanguine than Samuel Holland about 'the surly winter' with its 'bitter and biting winds' and 'deep snow in every valley', and much less enthusiastic about the 'tyrannous forest'.

The forests of course did not simply surround the plots of land which the emigrants were granted - they covered them. And these plots were not the two or three acres they had rented from Macneil, they were rarely less than 100 and for a family were normally at least 200 acres in extent. In every respect these plots represented both an opportunity and a challenge. At least in the early days of the colonisation of Cape Breton, emigrants seem to have been able to settle on a plot of land before actually petitioning for the grant of it. John Macneil of Little Judique for example submitting his petition in 1803 for the right and title to the land, said that he had settled the land three years previously, and since then had improved the land and built a house and outbuildings (CBLP 100). Submitting a petition for a grant of land immediately involved the emigrants in expense, since they were not capable of producing a written document in English, let alone one couched in the appropriate 'legalese'. They also needed to employ a surveyor to mark out the boundaries of the plot they were given, as described in the Land Grant document. Surviving receipts issued to Hugh Gillis of Judique (Fig. 9.7) reveal a payment of £5 to one Hugh Maceachen for submitting his petition to the governor at Sydney, and another payment of £2 - 6 - 0 to W. Proctor for a survey (PANS MG/12).

The conditions under which the grants were made came to be both stringent and specific. A typical Crown Grant document of the 1820s first described the location and the boundaries of the plot in some detail, usually accompanied by a sketch map. It then set out what the grantee was entitled to from the plot – timber, fishing, water, hunting etc – and what the Crown reserved for itself – coals, gold, silver and other minerals. The document then assigns the plot to the grantees and their heirs 'for ever, in free', subject to an annual payment of two shillings per acre. Recognising the financial constraints of newly arrived settlers, however, this payment was not to commence for two years from the time of the grant. At the same time the grantee was required, within three years of the grant, to put three cattle on every fifty acres of 'barren' land, and within five years of the grant, to cultivate at least three out of every fifty acres of land considered cultivable, or to drain three acres of marsh land. If the land was particularly difficult to work, the grantee was required to employ 'an able hand' for three years to cut wood and clear the land. Failure to meet these requirements, or of course to pay the annual fee, would see the land revert to the Crown. A final requirement stated that should any of the land prove suitable for cultivating hemp or flax, then the grantees were bound and obliged to plant a 'proportionable part of

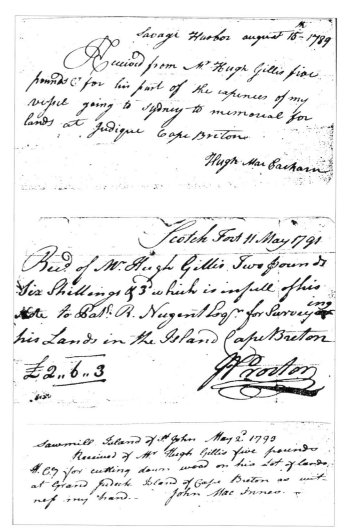

Figure 9.7 Receipts given to Hugh Gillis for payments for services in claiming and clearing his grant of land in Cape Breton (Reproduced by permission of the Public Archives of Nova Scotia)

the lands' with those crops. One can only imagine that this was to help meet the needs of His Majesty's Royal Navy.

Clearing the land, primarily of trees but also in some areas of stone, was a major task for the new settlers. The list of agricultural and other implements sent by the Colonial Office for the emigrants of 1817 (PRO CO384/2) is dominated by items such as felling axes, various saws, and pick axes, and spades. Bard Maclean put into verse what many a Barraman must have felt as he laboured to clear his newly acquired land:

'Before I make a clearing and raise crops and tear the tyrannous forest up from its roots by the strength of my arms, I'll be worn out' 'Piling tree-trunks on top of each other in bonfires has strained every muscle in my back' (Dunn 1953, 28–9)

Robert MacDougall in *The Emigrants Guide to North America* published in 1841, devotes a whole chapter to offering advice on how to clear the virgin forest. Although he points out that an experienced logger could fell trees twice as fast as a newly arrived emigrant, he does not recommend hiring a hand to help with clearing the forest. This was certainly a common practice in the mid 19th century in Upper Canada (Duncan 1976, 69–70), and although we might suppose it was beyond the means of the early emigrants to Cape Breton, some at least adopted this course of action. Hugh Gillis of Grand Judique Island, for example, paid John Macinnes £5 (Fig. 9.7) for clearing wood from his 'lot' in 1795 (PANS MG/12). If Macinnes was paid at the going rate for labourers of 2/6d a day, then the sum represented about 40 days work, which on MacDougall's estimates would mean Macinnes cleared between three and four acres of land, assuming he was a skilled logger. After the trees were felled there was still hard work to be done, trimming and burning the branches and leaves, and arranging for the logs either to be taken to a mill for sawing into useful lengths and planks for building, or to be dragged into piles to be burnt. In either case a team of four men and a yoke of oxen were required. MacDougall claimed that such a team could clear an acre of fallen logs in a day, so the plot cleared by Macinnes might have needed another 16 man-days of work to actually clear the ground of fallen trees.

When the ground was cleared, even with stumps and roots still in place, it was sowed with oats, barley and potatoes. Wherever there was pasture cattle and sometimes sheep and horses were raised. Census returns for early settlers reveal their gradually accumulating agricultural prosperity. In the 1811 Census for Cape Breton Hector Macneil has 20 cattle and 10 sheep, Donald Macdonald 45 cattle, 30 sheep, and 3 horses, and Malcolm Macdonald 8 cattle, 12 sheep and a horse. There is no information given about crop yields. Forty years of hard work on the 100 acres acquired by Roderick Macneil at Vernon River PEI in 1802 brought more significant rewards. The PEI census of 1841 revealed that the farm, now in the hands of his son, supported 14 cattle, 12 sheep, 10 pigs, and 2 horses, and yielded 14 bushels of wheat, 4 of barley, 325 of oats, and 450 of potatoes.

The produce of these farms brought financial rewards when it was sold to local merchants and businesses. A batch of receipts issued by William Campbell, Superintendent of Mines, and John Leaver JP, merchant, in 1807 and 1812 respectively (PANS RG 11/2), reveal a thriving market for the settlers' oats, potatoes and dairy products. For example:

From Neil Macneil (Dec.8th, 1807)

12.5 bushels of oats @ 2/ 6d	£1 – 11 - 6
10 bushels of potatoes @ 2/ -	£1 – 00 - 0
43lb of butter @ 1/ -	£2 – 03 - 0
Total	**£4 – 14 - 6**

From James Macneil & others (Oct. 31st, 1812)

57 bushels of potatoes @ 2/ 6d	£8 – 02 - 6
23.5 bushels of oats @ 4/ -	£4 – 14 - 0
Total	**£12 – 16 - 6**

Whereas back in Barra almost every penny that was earned by kelping and raising one or two cattle was spent in paying the rent, in Nova Scotia, PEI and Cape Breton there was sufficient income to allow the purchase of luxuries on a scale unknown in Barra. The fortuitous survival of a PEI merchant's ledger (Morris 1991) provides glimpses of the sort of things that Scottish emigrants were buying with the proceeds of their labours. Duncan Gillis purchased powder and shot, crockery, silk, muslin and cotton materials, and considerable quantities of rum, which were paid for by a mixture of cash, hay and oats. Roderick Macdonald bought tea, sugar, crockery, knives and forks, buttons and threads, handkerchiefs, muslin, tobacco and large quantities of rum. Whilst the menfolk indulged their traditional taste for tobacco and strong liquor, the women were able to acquire new and better materials, and household items normally beyond their reach.

It was in housing, however, that material transformations were most apparent. Earlier in this volume we have described the blackhouses from which Barra families emigrated to Canada. They were thick-walled structures of earth and stone, with little natural lighting, a bare earth floor and a fireplace in the middle of the floor. All activities took place in a single room. Emigrant families found themselves building timber or log cabins with a fireplace and chimney in one end wall, two or three windows, and timber flooring (Fig. 9.8). The expectation that they would

Figure 9.8 A replica of an immigrant log cabin (The Highland Village, Iona, Cape Breton

learn carpentry skills to build and furnish their homes presumably underlay the Government provision not only of tree-felling tools for emigrants but also hammers, adzes, chisels, augurs, and huge quantities of nails (PRO CO384/2). In one respect, however, the early timber cabins may have sustained the social behaviour of the blackhouse, being mostly one-roomed buildings.

As families cleared more land, raised more cattle or grew more crops, however, they were able to accumulate sufficient resources to build or buy houses of a very different sort. They were built not of logs but of boards and planks, with three rooms downstairs, a large attic capable of subdivision, and decent windows allowing in plenty of daylight. The main downstairs rooms each had a fireplace with a shared central chimney. The Macdonald house, built in 1829 and preserved in the Highland Village at Iona (CB), is a good example of the type (Fig. 9.9). How much it cost to erect in 1829 is not known, but similar houses were being offered to new emigrants in Manitoba in the 1880s for about £65 (NAS AF51/30). Homes of this sort must, it seems, have encouraged new patterns of domestic social behaviour with separate rooms for eating, sleeping, cooking and working. They threatened to undermine the very basis of the island family more effectively than any of the luxuries purchased from the merchants' stores.

Yet their influence was countered by the fierce loyalty of the emigrant islanders to their religion, their language and their Gaelic culture. In PEI, where there were many Irish as well as Scottish settlers, by 1803 there were reported to be several Catholic chapels (Walsh 1984, 13), and Burke describes the building of a timber church by the Barra settlers at Grand River West in 1810 (Burke 1881). In Cape Breton, the first church on the Bras D'Or was probably that at Christmas Island, built of logs and completed and in use by 1815 (MacKenzie 1984, 6); by 1825 Cape Breton boasted eight Catholic chapels (Johnston 1960, II, f p. 374). The influx of Barramen in the group emigrations of 1817 and 1821, as well as other Catholic settlers, made heavy demands on Father Angus Maceachern, whose enormous parish included not only much of Cape Breton but PEI and eastern Nova Scotia. In 1824 he wrote to the Rector of the

Scots College in Rome, Paul Macpherson, that Cape Breton had so many Catholics that it needed four priests to look after their spiritual needs (SCR Box 12/106). There was at least one volunteer to serve them – Angus Macdonald of Barra! In March 1826 he wrote to Bishop Patterson, reporting the forthcoming emigration of that summer, and claiming that so many were going that 'I shall next year be without a congregation'. Furthermore 'not only the present emigrants but those that went before them cry for my going along with them'. After all 'if I should go to Cape Breton I should only be serving the very congregation I had before' (SCA BL5/192). Within weeks, Macdonald had been transferred from his priesthood on Barra (which had lasted 21 years) and had been posted abroad. But not to Cape Breton – rather to Rome where he replaced Macpherson as Rector of the prestigious Scots College. By a strange twist of fate, Macdonald did indeed now take on some responsibility for his former flock who had fled to Cape Breton, for the official representative of the Canadian bishops to the Vatican was, *ex officio*, the Rector of the Scots College. Thus, Bishop Maceachern of PEI, as he now was, wrote to Macdonald in December 1826 reporting the arrival of the new Barra emigrants, who were 'thickly settled on the Bras D'Or and I may say all over Cape Breton' (SCR Box 12/109). By 1828 William Fraser of Antigonish reported to Macdonald that there were 15,000 Catholics in Cape Breton alone ,almost half its total population (SCR Box 12/112). The presence of so many Catholics, served by Gaelic-speaking priests, ensured that Gaelic not merely survived but thrived amongst the emigrant communities. In turn the survival of both the Gaelic language and the oral tradition which it communicated strengthened the faith and the resolve of the exiles.

The Gaelic tradition in Canada has been explored by Dunn (1953) and Emmerson (1976), and in different ways more recently by Bitterman and Kennedy (1999) among others. Alongside its role as the language of their faith, Gaelic was used by the emigrants to preserve their tales of the homeland but also to express their emotions and record their experiences of the New World. Many Gaelic poets

Figure 9.9 An Emigrant's house of 1830 – the Macdonald House (Highland Village, Iona, Cape Breton

emigrated to Canada, and others were raised there, and their poems reveal not only the continued vibrancy of the language, but the maintenance of Gaelic values and Gaelic traditions. Bard Maclean, who had become reconciled to the pleasures of his new homeland, spoke with joy of the news 'that has awakened my mind to verse to be invited to go to a gathering of the Gaels at the beginning of Spring' (Kennedy 199, 282). When Bard Maclean died in 1848 an elegy recalled:

> 'you were a generous dispenser when your guests were seated around, and the loveliest songs would flow smooth from your lips; you were renowned as a poet'

When a friend and neighbour left Pipers Glen, Angus Macfarlane recalled the times 'when friends would gather in your room ... there would be merriment a-plenty and music and Gaelic songs' (Dunn 1953, 131). The strength of the Gaelic song tradition in Cape Breton was captured by John Lorne Campbell in his *Songs Remembered in Exile*, where he gathered together 60 songs from the Gaelic singers of Cape Breton and Antigonish in the years either side of the Second World War. These were ballads, mostly in the Barra tradition, which for the most part were originally composed in, and were about, the Western Isles. The singing of the ballads down the decades not only sustained the Gaelic tradition in music and poetry, but also of course maintained and created the memory of the homeland.

Alongside these traditional ballads were others composed in Cape Breton and Nova Scotia which, as we have seen, celebrated the survival of the Gaelic tradition in Canada. And to these were added other ballads which spoke of the trials and tribulations, the pleasures and benefits, of the new life. The maintenance of the Gaelic tradition did much to enable the Barra and other Highland emigrants to cope with the otherwise overwhelming transformations which their removal to Canada involved. One contemporary observer in 1832 wrote:

> 'wherever the Highlanders form distinct settlements, their habits, their system of husbandry, disregard for comfort in their houses, their ancient hospitable customs, and their language, undergo no sensible change. They frequently pass their winter evenings reciting traditional poems in Gaelic, which have been transmitted to them by their forefathers ... At their weddings, and often at their dances ...the piper is considered indispensable' (M'Gregor 1832, 184–6)

Kennedy has rightly emphasised the importance of the group or community migration, and what he calls 'chain migration' – the successive waves of emigrants who were encouraged to follow and join with the pioneer groups. This ensured that there was 'a remarkably complete transfer of old communities and old cultural forms to Prince Edward Island and Nova Scotia' (Kennedy 2003, 40). As we have seen earlier in this chapter, group emigration was certainly a major feature of the migrations from Barra. Equally, from government and private correspondence, land petitions, and township and family histories, it is abundantly clear that 'chain migration' played an important part both in stimulating emigration from Barra and in determining the destination of the migrating groups and individuals. The great majority of Barra emigrants between 1800 and 1840 went to Cape Breton, and a majority of those settled around the Bras D'Or. There they created a new life which in many physical and material respects was very different from that they had left behind. But it was embedded in social values, cultural traditions, and a sense of identity which were rooted in a small island three thousand miles away.

10

Epilogue

In numerical terms, emigration reached a peak on Barra in the years 1848–1851 when about 550 islanders were packed off to Canada, and another 600 went to the mainland. It is a tragic irony that whereas the Barra families who had been loath to board the *Admiral* and sail to Quebec in 1851, arrived safely (if destitute) and eventually established themselves and prospered in Canada, a shipload of willing English and Irish emigrants, paying their own passage to Quebec, were ship-wrecked on the rocks of Bagh Siar, Vatersay, just two years later (Charnley 1992). The *Annie Jane*, a brand new ship making its return journey to Quebec from Liverpool, with 434 souls on board was driven onto the rocks at midnight September 24th, 1853. There were just 101 survivors; the dead were buried in pits in the dunes which fringe the beautiful west beach of Vatersay, and remain there to this day beneath a stone cross erected in their memory (Fig. 10.1).

Figure 10.1 The memorial to the emigrants on board the Annie Jane, who died when it was wrecked on Vatersay in 1853

Whilst the tragedy of the *Annie Jane* provided a chilling reminder of the dangers of the Atlantic crossing, it failed to deter Barramen from continuing to emigrate to Canada, albeit in smaller numbers than earlier in the 19th century. Encouragement from both government and estate owners continued sporadically through the later 19th century, and there was a steady but unspectacular trickle of emigrants from Barra during this period. But just as earlier emigrations had failed to stem the growth of population on the island, so did this continuing haemorrhage. Before Gordon's clearances the population of Barra stood at 1,977 (1841 census); in 1861, despite having lost over 1,100 people by clearance, it stood at 1,569. By 1881 it had recovered to 1,854, and by the beginning of the new century it had accelerated to reach a new peak of 2,417 people.

With the estate, first under Colonel Gordon, then under his son, and finally under Lady Gordon Cathcart, favouring the creation of larger farms, the land pressure on the small tenants grew ever more oppressive. There was growing and widespread discontent throughout the highlands and islands, culminating in riots in Skye in 1883, and the government established the Napier Commission to investigate the conditions of the crofters and cottars. It visited Barra on May 26th 1883 and met in the schoolhouse in Castlebay (Fig. 10.2) where it took evidence from six witnesses selected by the townships, as well as from Dr Macgillivray (the unpopular tenant of the Eoligarry farm) and from the (equally unpopular) factor. The outcome of the Commission's work was the passing of the Crofters' Holding Act in 1886, which provided security of tenure, compensation for tenant's improvements, and fair rents. When the Crofters' Commissioners, who were responsible for fixing fair rents, visited Barra in 1890 and 1891, virtually every crofter in the island applied for a review of their rent. The rent burden was reduced from £814 to £532, the average rent falling from around £3 to rather less than £2.

Nevertheless the Act of 1886 did not of itself relieve the pressure on the land and further Government action was needed to resolve the problem. After cottars had invaded and squatted on the farms of Northbay and Eoligarry in 1900, 3,000 acres of the Eoligarry farm was purchased in 1901 and divided into 58 new holdings. This still left dozens of cottars without land, and in 1903 sixty acres on Vatersay were acquired and divided into potato plots for cottars from Castlebay and Glen. Having gained a foothold on the island, the cottars began to build houses in 1906 and took cattle over to graze on the excellent pastures of the island. Families from Mingulay joined them, and some built new homes on the adjacent island of Sandray. They were all, of course, acting illegally, and Lady Gordon Cathcart did not hesitate to press charges against the Vatersay

Figure 10.2 Castlebay School, where the Crofting Commission met in 1883

Raiders. In June 1908 ten of them were sentenced to prison for two months. A wave of sympathy and support for the Raiders swept the country, and within a month the Congested Districts Board and Lady Gordon Cathcart had come to terms. By the end of the year 37 families had moved to Vatersay and 5 to Sandray. Vatersay was formally purchased in March 1909 and 58 new crofts established.

The rest of the Barra estate remained in Lady Gordon Cathcart's hands until she died in 1932. After long and protracted negotiations, it was purchased in 1937 by Robert Lister Macneil, who had matriculated Arms and Supporters as Chief of the Clan Macneil in 1915. He spent much of his life, and most of his modest fortune, restoring Kisimul Castle. In 2004, his son and successor, Ian Roderick Macneil, gave the crofting estate to the Scottish nation.

Bibliography

MANUSCRIPTS AND WORKS CITED IN
    ABBREVIATION
(PP = Parliamentary Papers)

BPR :   Barra Parish Register.
CBLP :   Cape Breton Land Petitions.
CG :   Carmina Gadelica
CNSHS :   Collections of the Nova Scotia
                 Historical Society
CPRIC :   Correspondence and Papers Relating
                 to Immigration in Canada (PP, 1854)
CRD :   Correspondence Relating to the
                 Measures Adopted for the Relief of
                 Distress in Ireland and Scotland (PP
                 LIII, 1847)
ENAC :   Correspondence Relative to
                 Emigration to the North American
                 Colonies (PP XXXIII,1852)
IC :   *Inverness Courier.*
NAS :   National Archives of Scotland,
                 Edinburgh (for which details where
                 not included in footnotes in chapter 4
                 as follows)
GD 46   (Seaforth Papers)
NAS GD 46/1/326 'Copy State of Rental Public Burdens
                 1800 Island of Lewis'.
NAS GD 46/13/126 'State of the Lewis Kelp 1794 to
                 1799'.
NAS GD 46/17/14 John Mackenzie to Earl of Seaforth,
                 24 April 1799
NAS GD 46/17/44 Seaforth to J. Gladstone, 11 June
                 1823.
NAS GD 46/176/41 Seaforth to A. Mossman, 2 October
                 1827.
GD 174
NAS GD 174/964   Crofters of Salem to Murdoch
                 Maclaine, 27 April 1799.
NAS GD 174/1012/1 'State of the kelp, Lochbuy, 4 July
                 1801'.
GD 201   (Clanranald Papers)
NAS GD 201/1/251/9(27) 'Report as to sundry matters
                 South Uist, 28 September 1798'
NAS GD 201/4/97 D. Shaw to A. Hunter, 25 Feb. 1827.
NAS GD 201/1/338 Factor's report, 19 Nov. 1827.
NAS GD201/5/1232/1 Colin McNeill to William
                 MacDonald, Nuntown, 19 January
                 1775.
NAS GD 201/5/1332/7a Abstract of Clanranald's Kelp, n.d.
NAS GD 201/5/1232/1 Kelp contract, Ardivecher, 1802,
                 Clanranald Papers.
NAS GD 201/5/1232/9 Duncan Shaw to Messrs Hunter et
                 al., 18 Nov. 1836.
NAS GD 201/5/1232/1 Kelp Contract, Ardivecher, 1802.

NAS GD 201/5/1233/31.'Minutes of Sederunt of the Tutors
                 of Ranald George Macdonald Esqr. of
                 Clanranald,' 17 March 1799.
NAS GD 201/5/1233/64-73 Minutes of Clanranald Trustees.
NAS GD 201/5/1232/3/31 John MacLellan Greenock to
                 Messrs Hunter &c., 22 July 1825.
NAS GD 201/5/1232/5 D. Shaw to Messrs Hunter &c, 11
                 November 1829.
NAS GD 201/5/1232/5 D. Shaw to Messrs Hunter &c., 28
                 June 1830, 12 May 1830.
NAS GD 201/5/1232/5 Macdonald and Ravenscroft to
                 Duncan Shaw, 3 April 1830.
NAS GD 201/5/232/5 Minutes of Meeting at Edinburgh
                 McKay's Hotel 8 May 1830.
NAS GD 201/5/1232/6 Journal by D. McCrummen on
                 Long Island; Report of D
                 McCrummen.
NAS GD 201/5/1232/9 'List of those who receive annuities
                 from Mr. Shaw for inspecting Kelp
                 shores and weighing Kelp &c,' n. d.
NAS GD 201/5/1232/6 D. Shaw to John Bowie, 2 October
                 1730.
NAS GD 201/5/1232/9 J. W. Anderson to John Bowie, 9
                 Feb. 1835.
NAS GD 201/5/1232/5 Dr Anderson kelp report, 1830.
NAS GD 201/5/1232/7 D. Shaw to Messrs Hunter, 25 May
                 1832.
NAS GD 201/5/1223 Alexander Hunter to D. Shaw, 24
                 May 1836.
NAS GD 201/5/1223 R. G. Macdonald of Clanranald to
                 John Gordon, 2 May 1839.
NAS GD 201/5/612/1 Memorial & Queries for Robert
                 Brown, Esq., 1 May 1839.
NAS GD 201/6/4   'Account Sales of Kelp Crop 1816
                 from the Estates of Clanranald'.
NAS GD 201/6/2   'Abstract Shewing the Produce of
                 Clanranald's Kelp 1816-1820'.
NAS GD 201/6/5   Testimony of Duncan Shaw, 2
                 December 1818.
NAS GD 201/6/4   'Account Sales of Kelp Crop 1816
                 from the Estates of Clanranald'.
NAS GD 201/6/2   'Abstract Shewing the Produce of
                 Clanranald's Kelp 1816-1820'.
NAS GD 201/6/5   Testimony of Duncan Shaw, 2
                 December 1818.
NAS GD 201/51   'Minutes of Sederunt of Clanranald's
                 Tutors,' 1 July 1801.
NAS GD 221/38   Report of North Uist factor, 14 Dec.
                 1839, Lord Macdonald Papers.
GD 202
NAS GD 202/5/1233/35 Minutes of Sederunt of
                 Clanranald's Tutors,' 14 March 1800.
GD 221   (Lord Macdonald Papers)

NAS GD 221/33   'Memorial of the Kelp Proprietors, 1813'.

NAS GD 221/40   'Abstract or View of Lord Macdonald's Income & Expenditure, 1795-1800'.

NAS GD 221/51   'List of Tenants Warned by the Chamberlain 1801'.

GD 237

NAS GD 237/12/4   Memorial of the kelp proprietors, Feb. 1818.

GD RH4   (Highland Society minute books)

NAS GD RH4/00188   Minutes of Meeting, 1 April 1813, Highland Society Sederunt Book, 1815-21.

NLS :   National Library of Scotland.

NSLP :   Nova Scotia Land Petitions.

PANS :   Public Archives of Nova Scotia, Halifax.

PAPEI :   Public Archives of Prince Edward Island.

PRO :   Public Record Office (now The National Archives), London

RCPC :   Reports, Correspondence and Papers Relating to Canada, 1825–32 (PP, 1832)

SCA :   Scottish Catholic Archives.

SCR :   Scots College in Rome.

MANUSCRIPTS CITED IN FULL IN TEXT AND FOOTNOTES

South Uist Historical Museum (A Report to Colonel John Gordon of Cluny, 1839 (typescript)).

South Uist Estate Office, Askernish (Factor's Letter-books, 1872 ff).

PUBLISHED WORKS, THESES AND REPEATEDLY CITED UNPUBLISHED SOURCES

Anderson, A. 1922 *Early Sources of Scottish History* Edinburgh, Oliver and Boyd.

Anderson, J W. 1831 *The Barilla Question Discussed, in a letter to the Right Honourable Lord Althorpe, Chancellor of the Exchquer, Shewing the Effect of the Late Order in Council, Reducing the Duty on Foreign Barilla on the Manufacture of Kelp and Oother British Akalies, with Observations Relative to the Manufacture of Soap and Window Glass* Edinburgh, Self Published.

Armit, I. (ed.) 1990 *Beyond the Brochs: Changing Perspectives on the Later Iron Age in Atlantic Scotland*, Edinburgh, Edinburgh University Press.

Armit, I. 1996 *The Archaeology of the Western Isles and Skye* Edinburgh, Edinburgh University Press.

Barker, D. and Dawson, D. 1989 *A Comparison Between Staffordshire and Bristol Yellow* Unpublished research notes.

Barker, D. 2001 ''The usual classes of useful articles': Staffordshire ceramics reconsidered' *Ceramics in America* 1, 72-93.

Barker, D. (*et al*) 2001 *Staffordshire Post-Medieval Ceramics* Unpublished notes for English Heritage training course.

Baynes, K. and Baynes, K. 1979 *The Shoe Show*, London, Crafts Council Cassin-Scott.

Bitterman, R. 1999 'On remembering and forgetting : memories within the maritime diaspora' in M. Harper and M. Vance *Myth, Migration and the Making of Memory*, Halifax and Edinburgh, Fernwood and John Donald, 253–66.

Borgstrom, C. 'The Norse place-names of Barra' in Campbell, J. L. 1998, 226–232.

Branigan, K. 1995 'The archaeological survey of the Tangaval peninsula' in Branigan and Foster 1995, 31–48.

Branigan, K. 1995a 'Sampling excavations on the Tangaval peninsula' in Branigan and Foster 1995, 161–86.

Branigan, K. 1995b 'Human settlement on the Tangaval peninsula' in Branigan and Foster 1995, 199–207.

Branigan, K. 2000 *The Buaile-nam-Bodach Project*, Unpublished report for the Buaile-nam-Bodach Preservation Soc.

Branigan, K. and Foster, P. 1995 *Barra : Archaeology on Ben Tangaval*, Sheffield, Sheffield Academic Press.

Branigan, K. and Foster, P. 2000 *From Barra to Berneray*, Sheffield, Sheffield Academic Press.

Branigan, K. and Foster, P. 2002 *Barra and the Bishop's Isles*, Stroud, Tempus.

Branigan, K. and Merrony, C. 2000 'The Hebridean blackhouse on the isle of Barra' *Scottish Archaeol. J.* 22:1, 1–16.

Brown, R. 1806 *Strictures and Remarks on the Earl of Selkirk's Observations on the Present State of the Highlands*, Edinburgh, Self Published.

Buchanan, J. L. 1793 *Travels in the Western Hebrides : From 1782 to 1790*, London, C. & J. Robinson.

Bulloch, J. M. 1911 *The Gordons of Cluny*, Buckie, Privately Printed.

Bumsted, J. M. 1978 'Highland emigration to the island of St. John and the Scottish Catholic church 1769–1774' *Dalhousie Review* 58, 511–27.

Bumsted, J. M. 1978a 'Settlement by chance : Lord Selkirk and Prince Edward Island', *Canadian Historical Review* 59, 171–188.

Bumsted, J. M. 1982 *The People's Clearance : Highland Emigration to British North America 17701–815*, Winnipeg, University of Manitoba Press; Edinburgh, Edinburgh University Press.

Bumsted, J. M. (ed.) 1984 *The Collected Writings of Lord Selkirk, I*, Winnipeg, Manitoba Record Society.

Burke, C. A. 2000 *Nineteenth Century Ceramics from a Seasonally Occupied Fishing Station on the Labrador Coast*, unpublished paper presented at the Council for Northeast Historical Archaeology, Halifax, Nova Scotia.

Burke, E. 1880 'The mission of St. Patrick, Grand River West' *Public Archives of Prince Edward Island* 2353: 245.

Buxton, C. B. 1995 *Mingulay : An Island and its People* Edinburgh, Birlinn.

Cameron, Rev. J. 1833, 'The parish of Stornoway', *The New Statistical Account of Scotland* 14 (1845), 115–140.

Campbell, E. 1997 'Pottery' in I. Armit 'Excavation of a post-medieval settlement at Druim na Dearcag, and related sites around Loch Olabhat' *Proc. Soc. Antiq. Scot.* 127, 909-13.

Campbell, J. L. 1998 *The Book of Barra*, Stornoway, Acair (first published 1936).

Campbell, J. L. 1999 *Songs Remembered in Exile*, Edinburgh, Birlinn (Revised Ed.).

Campbell, J. L. 2000 *A Very Civil People*, Edinburgh, Birlinn.

Campey, L. 2001 *'A Very Fine Class of Immigrants'. Prince Edward Island's Scottish Pioneers 1770–1850*, Toronto, Natural Heritage Books.

Charnley, B. 1992 *Shipwrecked on Vatersay* Portree, Maclean Press.

Cheape, H. 1988 'Food and liquid containers in the Hebrides : a window on the Iron Age' in A. Fenton and J. Myrdal (eds) *Food and Drink and Travelling Accessories. Essays in Honour of Gosta Berg* Edinburgh, John Donald, National Museums of Scotland, Skansen and Nordiska Museet, 6–27

Cheape, H. 1993 'Crogans and Barvas ware: handmade pottery in the Hebrides' *Scottish Studies* 31 (1992–3), 109–27.

Bibliography

Clerk, Rev. A. 1841 ' The parish of Duirinish', *The New Statistical Account of Scotland* 14 (1845), 322–360.

Coysh, A. W. and Henrywood, R. H. 1982 *The Dictionary of Blue and White Printed Pottery 1780–1880*, Woodbridge, Antique Collectors' Club.

Crawford, B. 1987 *Scandinavian Scotland* Leicester, Leicester University Press.

Cregeen, E. (ed.) 1964 *Argyll Estate Instructions 17711–805*, Edinburgh, Scottish History Society.

Cruden, S. 1960 *The Scottish Castle* Edinburgh, Birlinn.

'Dalraid' [Lord Colin Campbell] 1885 *The Crofter in History*, Edinburgh, William Brown.

Devine, T. M. 1988 *The Great Highland Famine : Hunger, Emigration and the Scottish Highlands in the Nineteenth Century*, Edinburgh, John Donald.

Devine, T. 1994 *Clanship to Crofters War* Manchester, Manchester University Press.

Dixon, G. A. 1977 'Letter to the editor', *New Scientist*, 77, 753 (16 March 1978).

Dobson, D. 1998 *Ships from Scotland to America 1628-1828 Vol. 1*, Baltimore, Genealogical Publishing Co.

Dobson, D. 2002 *Ships from Scotland to America 1628-1828 Vol. 2*, Baltimore, Genealogical Publishing Co.

Dodgshon, R. A. 1998 *From Chiefs to Landlords*, Edinburgh, Edinburgh University Press.

Donaldson, G. 1978 *Scotland : James V–VII*, Edinburgh, Mercat (first published 1965).

Dunbar, J. 1978 'Kisimul Castle, Isle of Barra', *Glasgow Archaeol J.* 5, 25–43.

Duncan, A. 1975 *Scotland : The Making of the Kingdom*, Edinburgh, Oliver and Boyd.

Duncan, K. 1976 'Patterns of settlement in the east' in W. Stanford Reid (ed.) *The Scottish Tradition in Canada*, Toronto, McClelland and Stewart, 49–75.

Dunn, C. 1953 *Highland Settler : A Portrait of the Scottish Gael in Nova Scotia*, Toronto, Toronto University Press.

Emerson, G. 1976 'The Gaelic tradition in Canadian culture' in W. Stanford Reid (ed.) *The Scottish Tradition in Canada*, Toronto, McClelland and Stewart, 232–47.

Faegri, K. and Iversen, J. 1989 *Textbook of Pollen Analysis*, Chichester, John Wiley & Son.

Fenton, A. 1995, *The Island Blackhouse*, Edinburgh, Historic Scotland.

Fisher, I. 2001 *Early Medieval Sculptures in the West Highlands and Islands*, Edinburgh, Royal Commission on the Ancient and Historical Monuments of Scotland.

Flinn, M. W. 1973 'Malthus, emigration and potatoes in the north west, 1770–1870', in L. M. Cullen and T. C. Smout (eds) *Comparative Aspects of Scottish and Irish Economic and Social History 1600–1900*, Edinburgh, J. Donald , 47–65.

Flinn, M. W. (ed) 1977 *Scottish Population History from the 17th Century to the 1930s,* Cambridge, Cambridge University Press.

Foster, P. J. 1995 'Excavations at Alt Chrisal 1989–94' in Branigan and Foster 1995, 49–160.

Foster, P. J. 1995 'The early modern pottery' in Branigan and Foster 1995, 117–18.

Foster, S. and Smout, T. (eds) *The History of Soils and Field Systems*, Aberdeen, Scottish Cultural Press, 66–74.

Fraser, E. 1802 *On Emigration from the Scottish Highlands and Islands*, Unpublished Mss, National Library of Scotland 9646.

Gailey, R. A. 1961 'The role of subletting in the crofting community', *Scottish Studies* 5, 57–76.

Gentleman's Magazine 1793, LXIII, part 2, 927-930.

Gilbertson, D. Kent, M. and Grattan, J. (eds) 1996 *The Outer Hebrides. The Last 14, 000 Years,* Sheffield, Sheffield Academic Press.

Godden, G. A. 1988 *Mason's China and Ironstone Wares*, Woodbridge, Antique Collectors' Club.

Godden, G. A. 1991 *Encyclopaedia of British Pottery and Porcelain Marks*, London, Barrie & Jenkins (Revised Ed.).

Graham-Campbell, J. and Batey, C. 1998 *Vikings in Scotland : An Archaeological Survey* Edinburgh, Edinburgh University Press.

Grant, I. F. 1961 *Highland Folk Ways*, London, Routledge & Kegan Paul.

Grant, I. 1979 *Landlords and Land Management in North-Eastern Scotland, 1750-1850*, unpublished Ph.D. thesis, University of Edinburgh.

Gray, M. 1951 'The kelp industry in the highlands and islands', *Economic History Review*, 2nd s., 4, 197–209.

Gray, M. 1957, The *Highland Economy, 1750–1850*, Edinburgh, Edinburgh University Press.

Green, C. 1999 *Fulham Pottery Excavations, 1971–1979*, London, HMSO.

Green, H. S. 1980 *The Flint Arrowheads of the British Isles*, Oxford, British Archaeological Reports British Series 75.

Grimm, E. 1991 *TILIA and TILIAGRAPH*, Springfield, Illinois State Museum.

Haggerty, G. 1996 'Newbigging pottery, Musselburgh, East Lothian', *Scottish Pottery Hist. Rev.* 18, 15–38.

Hall, J. 1807 *Travels in Scotland by an Unusual Route*, London, J. Johnson.

Harvey, D. 1935 *Holland's Description of Cape Breton Island* Halifax, Public Archives of Nova Scotia.

Hunter, J. 1976 *The Making of the Crofting Community*, Edinburgh, John Donald.

Ihde, A. J. 1964 *The Development of Modern Chemistry*, New York, Harper and Row.

Jameson, R. 1798 *An Outline of the Mineralogy of the Shetland Islands and Island of Aran with Appendix on Peat, Kelp, Coal*, Edinburgh, W. Creech.

Johnson, S. 1775 *A Journey to the Western Isles of Scotland* London, T. Cadell (reprinted).

Kelly, H. E. 1996 'Crockery: red and white earthenware', in N. Emery, *Excavations on Hirta*, Edinburgh, HMSO, 19–20, 68–70, 120–123, 153–154.

Kelly, H. E. 1999, *Scottish Ceramics*, Atglen, Schiffer.

Kelly, H., Kowalsky, A., and Kowalsky, D. 2001 *Spongewear 1835–1935: Makers Marks and Patterns*, Atglen, Schiffer.

Kemp, R. 1981, 'Are Prestonpans stilts unique?', *Scottish Pottery Hist. Rev.* 6, 4–6.

Kennedy, M. 1999 'Lochaber no more: a critical examination of highland emigration mythology' in M. Harer and M. Vance (eds.) *Myth, Migration and the Making of Memory*, Halifax and Edinburgh, Fernwood and John Donald, 267–97.

Kennedy, M. 2003 'The people are leaving : highland emigration to Prince Edward Island', *The Island Magazine* 53, 31–41.

Lane, A. 1983 *Dark-Age and Viking-Age Pottery in the Hebrides with Special Reference to the Udal, North Uist*, Unpublished PhD thesis, University College London.

Lane, A. 1990 'Hebridean pottery : problems of definition, chronology, presence and absence' in Armit 1990, 108–30.

Lawson, B. 1991 *Croft History Isle of South Uist, Volume 2*, Northtun, Harris.

Lawson, J. 1991 'Passengers on the Alexander' *The Island Magazine*, 29, 34–39.

Livingston, A. 1984 *Muster Roll of Prince Charles Edward Stuart's Army 1745–46*, Aberdeen.

M'Gregor, J. 1832 *British America*, Edinburgh, Blackwood.

MacArthur, E. M. 1990 *Iona : the Living Memory of a Crofting Community 1750–1914*, Edinburgh, Edinburgh University Press.

MacCulloch, J. 1824 *The Highlands and Western Isles of Scotland*, London, Longmans.

MacDonald, C. 1936 'Early highland emigration to Nova Scotia and PEI from 1770–1853', *CNSHS* 23, 41–48.

Macdonald, D. L. 1978 *Lewis, A History of the Island*, Edinburgh, G. Wright.

MacDougall, R. (ed. E. Thompson) 1998 *The Emigrant's Guide to North America*, Toronto, Natural Heritage (first published 1841).

MacGillivray, W. 1831 'Report on the Hebrides', *Transactions of the Highland Society*, n. s., 2.

MacGregor, Rev. R. 1840, 'The parish of Kilmuir', *The New Statistical Account of Scotland* 14 (1845), 237–287.

Macinnes, A. J. 1988, 'Scottish Gaeldom : the first phase of clearance', in T. M. Devine and R. Mitchison (eds), *People and Society in Scotland Vol. 1, 17601–830*, Edinburgh, John Donald.

Macivor, Rev. J. 1841 'The parish of Harris', *The New Statistical Account of Scotland* 14 (1845), 155-159.

MacKenzie, A. 1883 *History of the Highland Clearances*, Inverness, A. & W. MacKenzie.

Mackenzie, C. 1998 'Catholic Barra' in Campbell J. L. 1998, 1–25.

Mackinnon, Rev. J. 1840, 'The parish of Strath', *The New Statistical Account of Scotland* 14 (1845), 300–317.

Maclean, Rev. R. 1837 'The parish of South Uist', *The New Statistical Account of Scotland* 14 (1845), 182–97.

MacLean, R. 1976 'The highland Catholic tradition in Canada' in W. Stanford Reid (ed.) *The Scottish Tradition in Canada*, Toronto, University of Toronto Press, 93–117.

Maclean Sinclair, A. 1907 'The Macneils of Barra', *Celtic Review* 3.

Macleod, M. 2003 Review of Branigan and Foster 2002, *Y. A. T.* 2002, 344–6.

MacLeod, Rev. R. 1840 'The parish of Snizort', *The New Statistical Account of Scotland* 14 (1845), 287–295.

Macneil, R. L. 1964 *The Castle in the Sea*, London and Glasgow, Collins.

Macneil, R. L. 1985 *The Clan Macneil*, West Virginia, Scotpress (first published 1923).

MacPherson, J. (ed. J. L. Campbell) 1992 *Tales from Barra* Edinburgh, Birlinn.

MacQuarrie, A. 1992 *Cille Bharra*, Worcester, Grant Books.

MacQueen, Rev. A. 1794 'The parish of North Uist', *The Statistical Account of Scotland* 13, 300–325.

MacQueen, Rev. E. 1794 'The parish of Barray', *The Statistical Account of Scotland* 13, 326–342.

Macrae, Rev. W. 1836 'The parish of Barvas', *The New Statistical Account of Scotland* 14 (1845), 141–150.

McDonald, R. A. 1997 *The Kingdom of the Isles*, Edinburgh, Tuckwell Press (Scottish Hist. Rev. Monograph No. 4).

McGowan, I. (ed.) 1996, *Journey to the Hebrides*, Edinburgh, Canongate Classics.

McGregor, A. not dated *Summer Days Among the Western Isles*, Edinburgh, Nelson.

McKay, M. 1980 (ed.) *The Reverend John Walker's Report on the Hebrides of 1764 and 1771*, Edinburgh, John Donald.

Mair, C. 1978, *A Star for Seamen: the Stevenson Family of Engineers*, London, J. Murray.

Mann, L. 1908 'Report on a pottery churn from the island of Coll, and remarks on Hebridean pottery', *Proc. Soc. Antiq. Scot.* 44, 326–8.

Martell, J. 1942 *Immigration to and Emigration from Nova Scotia 1815–38*, Halifax, Public Archives of Nova Scotia Publication 6.

Martin, M. 1994 *A Description of the Western Isles of Scotland*, Edinburgh, Birlinn (first published in London 1703).

Miller, G. L. 1980 'Classification and economic scaling of 19th century ceramics' *Historical Archaeology* 14, 1–40.

Miller, G. L. 1991 'A revised set of cc index values and economic scaling of English ceramics from 1787 to 1880' *Historical Archaeology* 25:1, 1–25.

Miller, G. L. 1993 'Thoughts towards a user's guide to ceramic assemblages: pt 4 some thoughts on classification of white earthen-wares' *Council N. E. Hist. Archaeol. Newsletter* 26, 4–7.

Miller, G. L. 1994 *Demand Entropy as a Byproduct of Price Competition: a Case Study from Staffordshire*, unpublished paper presented at the School of American Research seminar, The Historical Archaeology of Capitalism.

Miller, G. L. and Hunter, R. R. Jr. 1990 'English shell edged earthenware: alias Leeds ware, alias feather edge', *Proceedings of the 35th Wedgwood International Seminar*, 107–136.

Miller, G. L., Smart Martin, A. and Dickinson, N. S. 1994 'Changing consumption patterns. English ceramics and the American market 1770 to 1840' in C. E. Hutchins (ed.), *Everyday Life in the Early .Republic*, Winterthur, Henry Francis du Pont Winterthur Museum, 219–48.

Moisley, H. A. 1961 'North Uist in 1799', *Scottish Geographical Magazine* 77, 89–92.

Morris, D. 1991 'Tales from a ledger', *The Island Magazine* 30, 30–36.

Mortimer, K. V. 2003 *Pot-Lids and other Colour-Printed Staffordshire Wares*, Woodbridge, Antique Collectors' Club.

Muir, T 1885 *Ecclesiological Notes on Some of the Islands of Scotland*, Edinburgh, Douglas.

Munro, D 1994 *A Description of the Western Isles of Scotland Called The Hybrides. An Account of 1549*, Edinburgh, Birlinn (first published 1774).

Munro, R. W. 1979 *Scottish Lighthouses*, Stornoway, Thule.

Napier 1884 *Report and Evidence of the Commissioners of Inquiry into the Conditions of the Crofters and Cottars in the Highlands and Islands of Scotland 1884* ('The Napier Report') London.

New Statistical Account of Scotland 1845, Edinburgh, W. Blackwood & Sons.

Newby, A. 2000 'Emigration and clearance from the Island of Barra', *Trans. Gaelic Soc. Inverness* 61, 116–48.

Newton, L. 1931 *A Handbook of the British Seaweeds*, London, Natural History Museum.

Nicolson, Rev. A. 1840 'The parish of Barray', *The New Statistical Account of Scotland* 14 (1845), 198–217.

Otto, J. S. 1977 'Artifacts and status differences – a comparison of ceramics from planter, overseer, and slave sites on an antebellum plantation' in S. South (ed.) *Research Strategies in Historical Archaeology*, New York, Academic Press, 91–118.

Otto, J. S 1984, *Cannon's Point Plantation, 1794–1860 : Living Conditions and Status Patterns in the Old South*, New York, Academic Press.

Owen, O and Dalland, M. 2000 *Scar : A Viking Boat Burial at Sanday, Orkney*, East Linton, Tuckwell Press.

Partington, J. E. 1964 *A History of Chemistry*, London, St. Martin's Press.

Pringle, D. (ed.) 1994 *The Ancient Monuments of the Western Isles*, Edinburgh, Historic Scotland.

Punch, T. 1985 'Scots to Nova Scotia in 1817', *Nova Scotia Genealogist* 3:2, 91–2.

Quail, G. 1983-4, 'The Verreville pottery', *Scottish Pottery Hist. Rev.* 8, 44-62.

Quail, G. 1986 'The Old Kirk pottery of Prestonpans', *Scottish Pottery Hist. Rev.* 10, 58–72.

RCAHMS 1928 *The Outer Hebrides, Skye and the Small Isles*, Edinburgh, HMSO.

Rea, G. F. 1997 *A School in South Uist : Reminiscences of a Hebridean Schoolmaster, 18901–913*, Edinburgh, Birlinn.

Richards, E. 1982 *A History of the Highland Clearances : Agrarian Transformation and the Evictions 1746–1886*, London, Croom Helm.

Salaman, R. N. 1949 *The History and Influence of the Potato*, Cambridge, Cambridge University Press.

Select Committee 1826–7 *Third Report from the Select Committee on Emigration*, London.

Select Committee 1841 *First Report from the Select Committee on Emigration, Scotland*, London.

Selkirk, Earl of 1805 *Observations on the Present State of the Highlands of Scotland* (reprinted in Bumsted 1984, 101–241).

Seton, B. G. and Arnot, J. G. (eds) 1929 *Prisoners of the '45*, Edinburgh, Scottish History Society 3rd s. 13–15.

Sharples, N and Parker Pearson, M. 1999 'Norse settlement in the Outer Hebrides', *Norwegian Archaeol. Rev.* 31:1, 41–62.

Shaw, F. J. 1980, *The Northern and Western Islands of Scotland – Their Economy and Society in the Seventeenth Century*, Edinburgh, Donald.

Sinclair, Sir J. 1791–7, *The Statistical Account of Scotland*, Edinburgh, (16 volumes).

Smout, T. C. 1969 *A History of the Scottish People 1560–1830*, London, Collins.

Stevenson, R. 1838 *Report on Northern Lighthouses to the Commissioners of Northern Lights*, unpublished report, National Library of Scotland Acc. 10706/94.

Stockmarr, J. 1971 'Tablets with spores used in absolute pollen analysis' *Pollen et Spores* 13, 615–21.

Swann, J. 1996 'Shoes concealed in buildings', *Costume* 30, 56–69.

Symonds, J. 1999 'Toiling in the vale of tears : everyday life and resistance in South Uist, Outer Hebrides, 1760–1860', *International Journal of Historical Archaeology* III:2, 101–122.

Symonds, J. 2000 'The dark island revisited : an approach to the historical archaeology of Milton, South Uist' in J. A. Atkinson, I. Banks and G. MacGregor (eds) *Townships to Farmsteads. Rural Settlement Studies in Scotland, England and Wales*, Oxford, British Archaeological Reports British Series 293, 197–210.

Symonds, J. 2001 'South Uist : an island story', *Current Archaeol.* 175, 276–280.

Thomas, F. W. L. 1866 'On the primitive dwellings and hypogea of the Outer Hebrides', *Proc. Soc. Antiq. Scot.* 7 (1866–1868), 153–95.

Thompson, F. 1974 *The Uists and Barra*, Exeter, David & Charles.

Thompson, N. 1999 *Earl Bathurst and the British Empire*, Barnsley, Cooper.

Thomson, W. 1983 *Kelpmaking on Orkney*, Stromness.

Thornton, J. and Swann, J. 1986 *A Glossary of Shoe Terms*, Northampton, Northampton Shoe Museum.

Turner, D. and Dunbar, J. 1970 'Breachacha Castle, Coll: excavation and field survey 1975–71' *Proc. Soc. Antiq. Scot.* 102, 155–87.

Vance, M. 1992 'The politics of emigration: Scotland and assisted emigration to Upper Canada, 1815–26' in T. Devine (ed.) *Scottish Emigration and Scottish Society*, Edinburgh, John Donald, 37–60.

Waddell, J., O'Connell, J. W. and Korff, A. (eds) 1994 *The Book of Aran*, Newtownlynch, Irish books and Media.

Walker 1980: see McKay 1980.

Webster, J. 1999 'Resisting traditions : ceramics, identity, and consumer choice in the Outer Hebrides from 1800 to the present', *International Journal of Historical Archaeology* 3:1, 53–73.

Welsh, E. (ed. Holman, H.) 1984 'An account of Prince Edward Island in 1803' *The Island Magazine* 15, 9–13.

Wickham-Jones, C. 1995 'Flaked stone tools' in Branigan and Foster 1995, 120–37.

Willmott, H. 2001 'A group of 17th century glass goblets with restored stems : considering the archaeology of repair', *Post-Medieval Archaeology* 35, 96–105.

Young, A. 1956 'Excavations at Dun Cuier, Isle of Barra, Outer Hebrides' *Proc. Soc. Antiq. Scot.* 89, 290–328.

Young, A. 1966 'The sequence of Hebridean pottery' in A. L. F. Rivet (ed.) *The Iron Age in Northern Britain*, Edinburgh, Edinburgh University Press, 45–58.

Youngson, A. J. 1973 *After the Forty-Five : The Economic Impact on the Scottish Highlands*, Edinburgh.

Appendix 1

A list of MacNeils petitioning for land in Cape Bretton 1807–1826 not *known* to be from Barra

Although the following petitioners gave no information concerning their origin, the majority of them were probably from Barra. The discussion in chapter 9 and the data in Appendix 1 demonstrate the overwhelming preference of Barra emigrants (50% of them, Macneils) for Cape Breton in the years from 1800 to 1840. They are listed here in the hope and expectation that further genealogical research might identify their origins.

Petition	Year	First Name	W/F/M	Children	Other information
325	1807	Neil 'Ban'	-	-	@ Coopers Pond
423	1808	Donald	-	-	@ E Bay Grand Lake
424	1808	Norman	-	-	-
425	1808	Hugh	-	-	@ Little Judique
426	1808	John Jnr	-	-	@ Little Judique
428	1808	Neil	-	-	-
515	1809	Donald Snr	-	-	On PEI since 1806
515	1809	Donald Jnr	-	-	Ditto
515	1809	Roderick	-	-	Ditto
515	1809	James	-	-	Ditto
515	1809	Neil	-	-	Ditto
515	1809	Donald	-	-	Ditto
515	1809	John	-	-	Ditto
516	1809	John	M	-	Age 21
742	1811	Hugh	F	-	@ Judique since 1795
743	1811	William	-	-	In PEI 1810; age 55
856	1812	Mary	-	7	@ River Bay
858	1812	Neil	W	1	@ Low Point; age 25
859	1812	Roderick	W	1	Age 23
947	1813	John	-	-	@ Red Island; emig.1808
948	1813	Neil	W	2	Emig.1811
1057	1814	Donald	W	1	@ Narrows; emig.1805
1057	1814	Donald Snr	-	-	Ditto
1236	1815	Alexander	-	-	@ Red Island; emig. 1809; age 25
1237	1815	Alexander	-	-	@ Bras D'Or; emig.1805
1238	1815	Alexander	-	-	@ Red Island; emig.1810; age 22
1239	1815	Donald	-	-	@ Benacadie
1240	1815	Donald	-	-	@ Mabou; emig. 1803
1241	1815	Hugh	-	-	Emig. 1811
1242	1815	John	-	-	@ Red Islands; emig. 1812

Cont'd

1419	1816	John	-	-	@ Narrows; age 60.
1420	1816	Alexander	-	-	@ Bras D'Or; emig.1809
1421	1816	Alexander	-	-	@ Broad Cove
1422	1816	Hugh	W / F	-	Emig. 1810
1423	1816	Mary	-	-	@ Benaccadie since 1806; age 70
1424	1816	Roderick	W / F	2	Emig. 1806; age 27
2011	1818	James	-	-	Emig. 1805; age 22
2012	1818	John	-	-	@ Red Island; age 29
2230	1819	Alexander	-	-	@ Broad Cove
2234	1819	John	W	4	@ Red Islands; age 29
2235	1819	John	-	-	@ Benaccadie;emig. 1817; age 26
2236	1819	John	W	-	Emig. 1817; age 31
2237	1819	John	W	4	Emig. 1812; age 34
2239	1819	Neil	W	5	Emig. 1816?; age 36
2493	1820	James	-	-	@ Mabou; emig.1812; age 29
2495	1820	Lachlan	-	6	Emig. 1811; age 70
2748	1821	Ann	-	5	@ Red Islands; age 50
2749	1821	Hector	-	-	@ Goose Pond; age 25
2750	1821	John	W	12	@ Benaccadie; emig. 1813; age 60
2752	1821	John	M	3S	@ Shenaccadie; emig.1818
2753	1821	Lachlan	-	6	Emig. 1812; age 60
2869	1822	Alexander	W	1	@ Mabou; age 25
2870	1822	John	W	6	Emig. >1814; age 35
2871	1822	John	-	-	Age 24
2952	1823	John	-	-	Emig. 1823; age 29
2952	1823	Donald	W	4	Emig. 1823; age 31
2953	1823	Kate	-	8	Emig. 1822; H died on voyage
3071	1825	Angus	-	-	Age 26; @ head of River Denys
3072	1825	Neil	W	7	Lived 8 years @ Mabou; age 42
3073	1825	Neil	W	5	@ Shenaccadie; age 38
3143	1826	Alexander	W	4	@ River Denys basin; age 35
3144	1826	Alexander	W?	3	@ Little Baddeck Bay; age 29

(Note : 2752 John Macneil was accompanied by 3 siblings – a brother and two sisters)

Appendix 2

A catalogue of named emigrants from the Isle of Barra to British North America: 1772–1851

INTRODUCTION

It is important to read this introduction before using the database presented in the catalogue.

The purpose of compiling and presenting this database of emigrants is two-fold. It has provided information about the numbers, origins, destinations and emigration dates for about 1050 individuals, which has allowed us to study the changing patterns of emigration over the period 1772–1851. Its publication provides both a database for further research, and a useful source and point of entry for those who wish to trace a Barra emigrant ancestry.

The database has been compiled from a variety of sources of varying accuracy, reliability, and detail. These include: Land and General Petitions, Land Grants, census records, cemetery records, shipping lists, township and family histories, the Barra parish register and personal communications.

ERRORS

The process has been complicated, difficult and certainly open to error. **It is important to remember when using the database that it will certainly contain errors, and equally that it is not of course 'complete'.** We have, perhaps, the names of about one in four of the total emigrant population in the period in question. Unfortunately, we do not know where the errors are, but we can identify the likely sources of error and it is well to comment briefly on these at this point.

LAND PETITIONS: Land petitions may give the place of origin, date of emigration, even the name of the ship, and the number of dependents. But the date of the petition is often some years after the date of emigration, which means that the number of dependents may include some children born in BNA rather than Barra.

CENSUS RECORDS: These always have to be used with care, but especially so when only heads of family are named, because as a glance at the database will demonstrate, there may be many John or Roderick Macneils, who may have emigrated to the same part of e.g. the Bras D'Or, even in the same year. In the case of the British census records certainly, the handwritten enumerator's books may contain errors resulting from the enumerator misunderstanding the Gaelic names he was given.

CEMETERY RECORDS: Many cemeteries have not yet been recorded and published, so the evidence is patchy. Dates of birth are not always accurate, and women are usually recorded by their married name, whereas they may be known in the parish records by their maiden name.

LAND GRANTS AND GENERAL PETITIONS: These do not usually provide much useful information on their own; they may provide confirmation and further details for individuals who can be recognised in land petitions or other sources.

TOWNSHIP AND FAMILY HISTORIES: These are very patchy in quality, and in particular the sources of information used are rarely recorded, and therefore are difficult to assess. They often rely heavily on oral tradition, and to some extent on family bibles and other family records. In general, where we have been able to check the oral/family traditions against other sources we have found them generally accurate. There are, inevitably, however, some errors or confusions that have crept in over the years. We can identify some of these errors, but must assume there are others that elude us at present. One problem with many family histories is that the children of an emigrant couple are listed, but it is not known or stated where these children were born. Where we can cross-check against a petition, we may be able to say that e.g. three out of nine children were born post-emigration, but we may not be able to say which three. We also have to bear in mind the natural tendency of emigrant families to place their ancestors among the 'pioneers', and to recall earlier dates for their emigration than was actually the case.

BARRA PARISH REGISTER: This is an immensely useful document for tracing births and marriages, but it has some significant limitations. The surviving register only keeps records of births from September 1805, and it has a gap (for unknown reasons) from August 5th 1810 to September 25th 1812. This is an important gap, because the big group emigrations of 1817, 1821, and 1826 must have included children born in these years. In some other years there appear to be markedly low numbers of births, and several consecutive months with none recorded, which suggest there may be other 'gaps' and other unrecorded births. For many years, the actual date of birth was not recorded, but rather the date of baptism - this could be the same day, or weeks, or in some cases months, later (for further details see below in the description of the database headings).

As for marriages, the first records do not begin until November 1812, and are then somewhat patchy. Deaths are rarely recorded, and only it appears between January 1st 1815 and December 31st 1825. There are also occasional transcription errors in the copy of the Register available.

CHILDREN: One problem arising from using the BPR is that we can often trace the children of an emigrant couple, even if there is no record of their offspring emigrating in the documentation. Where we have children under sixteen years of age at the time of their parents emigration we have assumed that they emigrated with their parents, even though we may have no direct evidence of this. Almost certainly there will have been a few children that didn't take passage with their parents, but of course identifying them would be a difficult and very time-consuming task. Given that the vast majority of children (from those families where we have records) seem to emigrate with their parents, we think the assumption is justified.

DUPLICATION: Given the large number of people with the same name, emigrating over a relatively short period of time, it is possible that some individuals in the database are duplicated. The risk of duplication is obviously greatest where we have the least information about individuals. We have cross-checked as thoroughly as we can, and believe that there are few possible duplicates left in the database.

THE HEADINGS IN THE CATALOGUE

The database has been designed to provide as much information as possible within the very real limits of the space available. **We must again emphasise that it is important to read the following explanations of the column headings before using the database.**

SURNAME: The database is ordered alphabetically by surname. Surnames have been standardised where there are slightly variant forms (e.g. Gillies and Gillis appear as Gillis). Women are given their maiden surname (which helps in tracing their parents and siblings), though they are of course cross-referenced to their husbands so that their married surname can be easily found. Women for whom only their married surname is known (mostly from cemetery records) have an asterisk after their christian name.

CHRISTIAN NAME: Christian names are given **as recorded** in the primary source. This is done in the hope that it **may** help in the difficult problem of separating out people with the same christian and surname, if the form in which the name is recorded is that by which they were known within the family. Thus, for example, we record Ians and Johns, Rodericks and Rorys, Christys, Chirstys, and Christinas. We also record any known nick-names for the same reason.

DoB = BIRTH/BAPTISM: Where possible we have given a precise date of birth or baptism, usually taken from the Barra Parish Register. The dates provided there are for date of baptism between 23/9/1805 and 28/5/1826. From 30/5/1826 to 1/8/1835 a date is given with no description as to its significance (i.e. it says neither baptised nor born, but we must assume it refers to baptism - the point at which a record is made). From 12/8/1835 the register gives both the date of birth and the date of baptism. Where dates before 1805 are given they are derived either from family or cemetery records (in either of which cases they may be specific), or from land petitions, where the age at the time of petitioning is often given (providing dates to within a year). In general therefore, a precise date between 23/9/1805 and 1/8/1835 will indicate the date of baptism not birth; all other dates will be to date of birth.

ORIGIN: Under this heading we try to give a precise place of origin within the parish of Barra. This is often a township on the island of Barra itself, or it is one of the smaller islands. Because people often moved from one township or island to another several times in a lifetime we have sometimes had to choose between several possible 'origins'. In general for children we have put their place of birth, for adults the place where they are recorded as living as near the time of emigration as records allow. Where we have no specific place of origin known, we have inserted Barra, to distinguish them from a small number of emigrants who were born elsewhere (e.g. Tiree) but who had moved to Barra and emigrated from there.

PORT OF ARRIVAL: This is the port into which the ship on which an emigrant sailed first put in, where the ship is known, or the port of arrival as recorded in family history.

FATHER'S NAME: We include this information partly because it was of course of particular significance in the Gaelic oral tradition, and partly because it will help to distinguish between people with the same christian and surname.

DATE OF EMIGRATION: Where a specific year is provided by a source it is given. In others cases a *terminus ante quem* may be provided by, for example, a land petition (i.e. if someone submits a land petition in Cape Breton in 1822 they had obviously emigrated by 1822). These dates are indicated thus : >1822. Equally we can sometimes get a *terminus post quem* from, for example, birth records in the BPR (i.e. if a family are known to have emigrated, then the last recorded birth in that family in Barra will provide a date after which they emigrated). These dates are indicated thus : <1822.

SHIP: It is a sobering and surprising fact that only ONE of the c. 1050 people on our database are named in an original 'passenger list' (as opposed to a 'reconstituted' one, put together from non-shipping sources). We identify the ship on which an emigrant sailed from a combination of land petitions and grants which, occasionally, name the ship, from various other official documents, and from family and township histories. In certain years when there was a group emigration in a known ship, we give the name of that ship alongside emigrants for that year, since it is highly likely that this was the ship they sailed on. But we precede the name with a question mark, thus: ?*William Tell*.

DESTINATION: In this entry we supply the name of one location where the emigrant settled. Depending on the information available it may be the place where they stayed for a few years immediately after arrival, it may be (most commonly) where they took land and settled permanently, or it may be the place where they died. It is intended primarily as a starting point for those trying to trace ancestors.

All places referred to are in Cape Breton unless followed by: NS = Nova Scotia; PEI = Prince Edward Island; ONT = Ontario.

REFERENCES: We provide as full a list of references which relate to an individual as possible. The list of abbreviations used follows below.

NOTE:

Any entry preceded by a question mark implies that there is a degree of uncertainty over the information provided.

We will be pleased to provide any further information that we hold on individuals in the database (e.g. dates of marriages, acreage of land-holdings, information about the township of origin on Barra) to those requesting it by post from:

Prof. K. Branigan, Dept of Archaeology, University of Sheffield, Northgate House, West Street, Sheffield, S1 4ET, England. **Note: we are unable to deal with enquiries sent by e-mail.**

ABBREVIATIONS USED FOR REFERENCING

ACIH   *All Call Iona Home* S. R. MacNeil, Antigonish, 1979.

AHM   Antigonish Heritage Museum files.

AN   *Antiquaries Notes - Historical, Genealogical, and Social* C. F. MacKintosh (1865) 2nd Edition Inverness, 1913.

AR   *Abegweit Review.*

BCB   *Barra to Cape Breton* Melissa MacNeil, (thesis), Beaton Institute, UCB, Sydney.

BPR   Barra Parish Register.

BSGN   *Barra Settlement in Grand Narrows 1804-1904* M. Rothe, (thesis), Beaton Institute, UCB, Sydney.

Casket   *The Casket.*

CBLP   Cape Breton Land Petitions (PANS).

CCB   Census of Cape Breton (in *Holland's Description of Cape Breton Island and Other Documents* ed D. Harvey, Halifax, 1935).

CM   Calum MacNeil, Barra, pers. comm.

CMC   *Clan MacNeil in Canada Newsletter.*

CMH   Colleen MacNeil, Hawaii, pers. comm.

CNS   Census of Nova Scotia.

DW   *A Dictionary of Scottish Emigrants to Canada Before Confederation* Vol.1 D. Whyte, Toronto, 1986.

DW2   Ditto Vol.2 Toronto, 1995.

DW3   Ditto Vol.3 Toronto, 2002.

EHE   *Early Highland Emigration* C. S. MacDonald, Halifax, 1936.

Galley   *The Galley* (Clan Macneil Association of America).

HB   *To the Hill of Boisdale* A. J. Macmillan, Sydney, 1986.

HCA   *History of the County of Antigonish* D. J. Rankin, Georgeville, 1929.

HCP   *History of the County of Pictou* G. Patterson, Montreal, 1877.

HIC   *History of Inverness County* J. L. MacDougall, Nova Scotia, 1923.

HMER   *History of Merigomish* L. Maudsley & K. MacIntosh, Antigonish, 1972.

HMHC   *History of Casumpec* J. Hudson & G. Muggison, 1979.

ICR   Iona Cemetery Records, Highland Village, Iona.

INVJ   *Inverness Journal.*

ISLAND   *The Island Magazine.*

JGA   Jocelyn Gillis, Antigonish, pers. comm.

KM   Karen MacNeil, Indiana, pers. comm.

LLSNS   *Loyalists and Land Settlers in Nova Scotia* PANS, Halifax, 1980.

MCI   *MacKenzie's History of Christmas Island Parish* A. MacKenzie, Sudbury, Ontario, 1984 (Rev. Ed).

MG   Mary Gumlak, Massachusetts, pers. comm.

MHA   *History of Antigonish* R. MacLean, Antigonish, 1976.

MHHC   *History of the Highland Clearances* A. MacKenzie, Edinburgh 1991 (Rev. Ed).

MNB   *The Clan MacNeil* R. L. MacNeil, New York, 1923.

MP   *Mabou Pioneers* A. MacDonald, Halifax NS, 1998 (Rep. Ed.).

NCTC   *Na Caimbeulaich The Campbells* M. E. Macneill 1970.

NMD   Letters of Father Neil MacDonald to Angus MacDonald (Archives of the Scots College in Rome).

NMP   Niall MacPherson, pers. comm.

NSG   *Nova Scotia Genealogist* (1983-).

NSGP   Nova Scotia General Petitions (PANS).

NSLP   Nova Scotia Land Petitions (PANS).

OC   Census of Ontario (Ontario Provincial Archives, Toronto).

PAPEI   Public Archives of Prince Edward Island.

PEIC   Prince Edward Island Cemetery Index (PAPEI).

QT   *Quebec Times*

RANS   *Reports and Articles on Nova Scotia 1931-33* D. Harvey (PANS).

REF   *A Register of Emigrant Families from the Western Isles of Scotland to Ontario, Canada Pt.1* B. Lawson.

RG   *Royal Gazette.*

RM   Raymond MacNeil, Pennsylvania, pers. comm.

SC   Census of Scotland (NAS).

SCP   *The Story of St.Columba Parish, Iona* R. MacNeil *et al*, Iona, 1994.

SGSH   *The Scottish Gaelic Settlement History of PEI* M. Kennedy (PhD thesis) Edinburgh University, 1995.

SICB   *Scottish Imigration to Cape Breton 1758-1838* B. Kincaid (MA thesis) Dalhousie University, Halifax, 1964.

SMC   St Mary's Roman Catholic Cemetery (Master Index, PAPEI).

SPE   *Scottish Immigration to PEI from the Death Notices and Obituary Notices* PEI Geneol.Soc., Charlottetown, 1990.

SRE   *Songs Remembered in Exile* J. Campbell, Stornoway, 1998.

TPC   Terence Punch, Halifax NS, pers. comm.

VCDR   *Victoria County Death Records 1867-1870* Archives of the Highland Village, Iona.

VM   Vincent Macneil, Bedford NS, pers. comm.

WMGN   William McGurk MacNeil, Vernon River PEI, pers. comm.

Note: the following abbreviations are used to denote relationships between individuals in the catalogue.

B	brother of	H	husband of
D	daughter of	M	mother of
F	father of	S	son of
		W	wife of
		Z	sister of

BROWN

ID	Name	Father	D.o.B / D.o.E	Origin / Ship	Port of Arrival / Destination	Relations	References
1	Alexander		/ 1790	Barra / Queen	Charlottetown / PEI, Grand River W		PAPEI, 2353, 24, 25

CAMERON

ID	Name	Father	D.o.B / D.o.E	Origin / Ship	Port of Arrival / Destination	Relations	References
2	Alexander		1772	Barra	PEI, Grand River		HMHC, 288
3	Archibald		c1785	Barra	Antigonish, NS		HIC, 410
4	Archibald		/ 1790	Barra / Queen	PEI, Grand River W		PAPEI, 2353, 24, 25
5	Flora		c1817-19	Cliad	S Boularderie	W: 234; M: 229, 237	HB, 230-313

CAMPBELL

ID	Name	Father	D.o.B / D.o.E	Origin / Ship	Port of Arrival / Destination	Relations	References
6	Ann(ie)	John	c1791 / >1830	Barra	MacNeil's Vale	W: 636	ACIH, 155; BSGN; VM
7	Donald	Ian 'Jnr'	1791	Barra / ?Dunkeld	Pictou / Antigonish, NS		HB, 59
8	Donald		>1819	Barra	Little Bras d'Or		SICB, 137
9	Donald		c1766 / >1826	Barra	NE Scotch Narrows		CBLP, 3095
10	Donald		<1830	Barra	Scotch Narrows		DW2, 1139; SICB, 137
11	George	Hugh	31/8/1820 / 1820-21	Kyles	Boisdale	S: 13, 1005	ACIH, 289; BPR; VCDR; VM
12	Hector		c1801 / >1826	Barra	NE Scotch Narrows		CBLP, 3095
13	Hugh		c1793 / 1820-21	Kentangaval	Boisdale	H: 1005; F: 11	ACIH, 289; BPR; VCDR; VM
14	Ian 'Jnr'	Ian 'Jnr'	1791	Barra	Pictou / Morristown, NS	H: 551	HB, 58-59
15	Jane		1822	Mingulay	?Sydney / Boisdale	W: 959; M: 500	HB, 481; BPR
16	John		?1785	Barra	Cape George, NS		MHA, 123

CAMPBELL

ID	Name	Father	D.o.B D.o.E	Origin Ship	Port of Arrival Destination	Relations	References
17	John	?Peter	<1821	Barra		H: 593	BRP; VM; NAS, CS44, Bx 446
18	Malcolm	John		?Brevig	Cape Breton	H: 662	VM, 25/04/03
19	Margaret		1799	Barra	Iona	W: 684; M: 715	ACIH, Intro
20	Mary	John	c1792 ?1821	Brevig	Iona	M: 533, 678, 697	VM,

GALBRAITH

ID	Name	Father	D.o.B D.o.E	Origin Ship	Port of Arrival Destination	Relations	References
21	Catherine		c1817	Barra	Castle Bay	W: 223; M: 212, 221, 225, 228	MCI, 57; BPR; SRE, 83
22	Mary		c1822	Cliad	Boisdale	W: 1042; M: 1028, 1030, 1031, 1034, 1037, 1038, 1040	HB, 577; BPR

GILLIS

ID	Name	Father	D.o.B D.o.E	Origin Ship	Port of Arrival Destination	Relations	References
23	Alexander		1823 c1830	Barra	Soldiers Cove		CASKET, 27/7/1899, 5
24	Angus	Donald	1786 1790	Barra Queen	Charlottetown PEI, Grand River W, Lot 14	S: 39, 322; B: 51, 61	WMGN
25	Angus	Donald	c1770 1790	Barra Queen	Charlottetown PEI, Mills Point, Lot 18		WMGN
26	Angus	Roderick	3/10/1816 1817	Borve William Tell	Sydney Antigonish, NS	S: 73, 232; B: 28, 32, 41, 70	NSG, iii, 2, 91; BPR; NSLP, 1818; NSGP, 7, 7
27	Angus	Hugh	1821	Barra Harmony	Sydney Christmas Island	S: 45, 833; B: 34, 47, 63, 64, 68, 75	MCI, 31
28	Ann	Roderick	13/12/1814 1817	Borve William Tell	Sydney Antigonish, NS	D: 73, 232; Z: 26, 32, 41, 70	NSG, iii, 2, 91; BPR; NSLP, 1818; NSGP, 7, 7
29	Ann	Archibald	14/3/1815 c1832	Cliad	Barrachois Pond	D: 30, 179; Z: 37, 38, 46, 56, 58, 69	HB, 87; BPR
30	Archibald		c1832	Cliad	Barrachois Pond	H: 179; F: 29, 37, 38, 46, 56, 58, 69	HB, 87; BPR
31	Catherine	Hugh	c1816-17	Kilbar	Shenacadie	D: 231; Z: 43, 48, 52, 59, 74	ACIH, 325-6; JGA
32	Catherine	Roderick	19/12/1809 1817	Borve William Tell	Sydney Antigonish, NS	D: 73, 232; Z: 26, 28, 41, 70	NSG, iii, 2, 91; BPR; NSLP, 1818; NSGP, 7, 7

GILLIS

ID	Name	Father	D.o.B D.o.E	Origin Ship	Port of Arrival Destination	Relations	References
33	Catherine		?1817	Kilbar	Mabou	W: 120; M: 140, 143, 145, 153, 154	MP, 419; BPR; CM
34	Catherine	Hugh	1821	Barra Harmony	Sydney Red Island	D: 45, 833; Z: 27, 47, 63, 64, 68, 75	MCI, 31
35	Catherine		c1784 1824	Greian	Cape Breton	M: 537, 632, 789, 840, 933	CBLP, 1824; BPR
36	Catherine	Ewan	1/4/1807 1851	Kilbar Admiral	Quebec Red Islands	W: 86; M: 78, 82, 92, 93	VM, 25/4/03; BPR
37	Chirsty	Archibald	?1811-12 c1832	?Cliad	Barrachois Pond	D: 30, 179; Z: 29, 38, 46, 56, 58, 69	HB, 87; BPR
38	Christian	Archibald	13/7/1819 c1832	Cliad	Barrachois Pond	D: 30, 179; Z: 29, 37, 46, 56, 58, 69	HB, 87; BPR
39	Donald		1748 1790	Barra Queen	Charlottetown PEI, Grand River W, Lot 14	H: 322; F: 24, 51, 61	PAPEI, 2353, 24, 25; DW3, 571; WMGN;
40	Donald		1802	?Hector	?Pictou Antigonish, NS		NSLP, 1818
41	Donald	Roderick	8/10/1807 1817	Borve William Tell	Sydney Antigonish, NS	S: 73, 232; B: 26, 28, 32, 70	NSG, iii, 2, 91; BPR; NSLP, 1818; NSGP, 7, 7
42	Duncan		1766 1817	Barra ?William Tell	Sydney Near Red Islands		CBLP, 1914
43	Flora	Hugh	c1816-17	Kilbar	MacKinnon's Harbour	D: 231; Z: 31, 48, 52, 59, 74	ACIH, 325-6; JGA
44	Hugh	John	1797 1821	Kilbar Harmony	Sydney Shenacadie	H: 480	HB, 86; CBLP, 1822; BPR
45	Hugh		1821	Caolis Harmony	Sydney Christmas Island	H: 833; F: 27, 34, 47, 63, 64, 68, 75	MCI, 31
46	Ian	Archibald	1804 c1832	Cliad	Barrachois Pond	S: 30, 179; B: 29, 37, 38, 56, 58, 69	HB, 87; BPR
47	James	Hugh	19/10/1806 1821	Kyles Harmony	Sydney Christmas Island	S: 45, 833; B: 27, 34, 63, 64, 68, 75	MCI, 31
48	Jane	Hugh	c1816-17	Kilbar	Shenacadie	D: 231; Z: 31, 43, 52, 59, 74	ACIH, 325-6; JGA
49	Janet	Murdoch	21/2/1821 1821	Caolis ?Harmony	?Sydney S Boularderie	D: 67, 127	HB, 82
50	John	Donald	c1755 1790	Barra Queen	Charlottetown PEI, Grand River W	H: 522; F: 76	PAPEI, 2353, 24-25; DW3, 574; WMGN

GILLIS

ID	Name	Father	D.o.B / D.o.E	Origin / Ship	Port of Arrival / Destination	Relations	References
51	John	Donald	1780 / 1790	Barra / Queen	Charlottetown / PEI, Grand River W, Lot 14	S: 39, 322; B: 24, 61	WMGN
52	John 'Ban'	Hugh	26/11/1806 / c1816-17	Kilbar	Jamesville	S: 231; B: 31, 43, 48, 59, 74	ACIH, 325-6; JGA
53	John		1797 / 1817	Barra / William Tell	Sydney / S Boularderie	B: 72	CBLP, 1920; CBB, 1818
54	John		1813 / 1817	Barra / William Tell	Sydney / Straits of Barra		NSLP, 1835
55	John		1826	Vaslain	Nova Scotia		NMD, 4/3/31
56	John	Archibald	17/12/1808 / c1832	Cliad	Barrachois Pond	S: 30, 179; B: 29, 37, 38, 46, 58, 69	HB, 87; BPR
57	John		1793	Barra	PEI, Indian River	H: 805	PEIC, LOT18, CEM, I, 288
58	Lawrence	Archibald	18/8/1823 / c1832	Cliad	Barrachois Pond	S: 30, 179; B: 29, 37, 38, 46, 56, 69	HB, 87; BPR
59	Margaret	Hugh	c1809 / c1816-17	?Kilbar	Jamesville	D: 231; Z: 31, 43, 48, 52, 74	ACIH, 325-6; JGA
60	Marion		?1851	Barra / ?Admiral	?Quebec	W: 183; M: 195	NMP
61	Mary	Donald	1778 / 1790	Barra / Queen	Charlottetown / PEI, Grand River W, Lot 14	S: 39, 322; B: 24, 51	WMGN
62	Mary		1808	Kilbar	Mabou	W: 496; M: 586, 648, 703, 765, 808, 971	MP, 767; CBC, 1818; HIC, 557; BPR
63	Mary	Hugh	1821	Barra / Harmony	Sydney / Christmas Island	D: 45, 833; Z: 27, 34, 47, 64, 68, 75	MCI, 31
64	Mary	Hugh	1821	Barra / Harmony	Sydney / Red Island	D: 45, 833; Z: 27, 34, 47, 63, 68, 75	MCI, 31
65	Mary	Hugh	1821	Caolis / Harmony	Sydney / Washabuck	W: 261	MCI, 64-65; BPR
66	Murdoch		1817	Barra / ?William Tell	Sydney / Antigonish, NS		NSLP, 1818; NSGP, 7,7
67	Murdoch		1821	Caolis / ?Harmony	?Sydney / S Boularderie	H: 127; F: 49	HB, 82
68	Peggie	Hugh	1821	Barra / Harmony	Sydney / Christmas Island	D: 45, 833; Z: 27, 34, 47, 63, 64, 75	MCI, 31

GILLIS

ID	Name	Father	D.o.B D.o.E	Origin Ship	Port of Arrival Destination	Relations	References
69	Peter	Archibald	10/12/1806 c1832	Cliad	 Barrachois Pond	S: 30, 179; B: 29, 37, 38, 46, 56, 58	HB, 87; BPR
70	Rachel	Roderick	13/12/1805 1817	Borve William Tell	Sydney Antigonish, NS	D: 73, 232; Z: 26, 28, 32, 41	NSG, iii, 2, 91; BPR; NSLP, 1818; NSGP, 7, 7
71	Roderick	Donald	1752 1790	Barra Queen	Charlottetown PEI, Grand River, Lot 13		PAPEI, 2353, 24-25; DW3, 581; WMGN
72	Roderick		1795 1817	Barra William Tell	Sydney S Boularderie	B: 53	CBLP, 1922;
73	Roderick		 1817	Borve William Tell	Sydney Antigonish, NS	H: 232; F: 26, 28, 32, 41, 70	NSG, iii, 2, 91; BPR; NSLP, 1818; NSGP, 7, 7
74	Rory	Hugh	c1816-17	Kilbar	Jamesville	H: 354; S: 231; B: 31, 43, 48, 52, 59	ACIH, 325-6; JGA
75	Sarah	Hugh	1821	Barra Harmony	Sydney Christmas Island	D: 45, 833; Z: 27, 34, 47, 63, 64, 68	MCI, 31
76	William	John	c1786 1790	Barra Queen	Charlottetown PEI, Grand River W	S: 50, 522	PAPEI, 2353, 24-25; DW3, 1202; WMGN

JOHNSTON

ID	Name	Father	D.o.B D.o.E	Origin Ship	Port of Arrival Destination	Relations	References
77	Alexander	Farquhar	1778 c1807	Barra	 Red Islands	B: 79, 83, 94	CBLP, 854; CCB, 1818; VM, 25/4/03
78	Alexander	Farquhar	1848 1851	Glen Admiral	Quebec Red Islands	S: 36, 86; B: 82, 92, 93	VM, 25/4/03; BPR
79	Angus	Farquhar	1770 c1807	Barra	 Butt Harbour	B: 77, 83, 94	CBLP, 854; CCB, 1818; VM, 25/4/03
80	Angus	Donald	3/12/1828 ?1850-51	North Bay ?Admiral	Quebec Red Islands	S: 84, 581; B: 81, 85, 89, 91, 97	VM, 25/4/03; BPR
81	Catherine	Donald	24/2/1819 ?1850-51	Kilbar ?Admiral	Quebec Red Islands	D: 84, 581; Z: 80, 85, 89, 91, 97	VM, 25/4/03; BPR
82	Catherine	Farquhar	1841 1851	Glen Admiral	Quebec Red Islands	D: 36, 86; Z: 78, 92, 93	VM, 25/4/03; BPR
83	Donald	Farquhar	1768 c1807	Barra	 Red Islands	B: 77, 79, 94	CBLP, 854; CCB, 1818; VM, 25/4/03
84	Donald	John	c1795 ?1850-51	Kilbar ?Admiral	?Quebec Red Islands	H: 581; F: 80, 81, 85, 89, 91, 97	VM, 25/4/03; BPR
85	Donald	Donald	8/12/1825 ?1850-51	Ardveenish ?Admiral	?Quebec Red Islands	S: 84, 581; B: 80, 81, 89, 91, 97	VM, 25/4/03; BPR

JOHNSTON

ID	Name	Father	D.o.B D.o.E	Origin Ship	Port of Arrival Destination	Relations	References
86	Farquhar	?John	c1806 1851	Glen Admiral	Quebec Red Islands	H: 36; F: 78, 82, 92, 93	VM, 25/4/03; BPR
87	Flora	Roderick	c1805 1817	S Uist ?William Tell	?Sydney Red Islands	D: 94, 1045; Z: 88, 90, 95	CBLP, 1650; VM, 25/4/03; 1/5/03
88	John 'Red'	Roderick	c1803 1817	Barra ?William Tell	?Sydney Red Islands	S: 94, 1045; B: 87, 90, 95	CBLP, 1650; VM, 25/4/03; 1/5/03
89	Lauchlin	Donald	17/10/1830 ?1850-51	North Bay ?Admiral	?Quebec Red Islands	S: 84, 581; B: 80, 81, 85, 91, 97	VM, 25/4/03; BPR
90	Margaret	Roderick	c1811 1817	Barra ?William Tell	?Sydney Red Islands	D: 94, 1045; Z: 87, 88, 95	CBLP, 1650; VM, 25/4/03; 1/5/03
91	Mary	Donald	7/5/1821 ?1850-51	Kilbar ?Admiral	?Quebec Red Islands	D: 84, 581; Z: 80, 81, 85, 89, 97	VM, 25/4/03; BPR
92	Mary	Farquhar	1836 1851	Glen Admiral	Quebec Red Islands	D: 36, 86; Z: 78, 82, 93	VM, 25/4/03; BPR
93	Neil	Farquhar	1845 1851	Glen Admiral	Quebec Red Islands	S: 36, 86; B: 78, 82, 92	VM, 25/4/03; BPR
94	Roderick	Farquhar	c1776 1817	Barra ?William Tell	?Sydney Red Islands	H: 1045; F: 87, 88, 90, 95; B: 77, 79, 83	CBLP, 1650; VM, 25/4/03; 1/5/03
95	Roderick 'Red'	Roderick	c1813 1817	Barra ?William Tell	?Sydney Red Islands	S: 94, 1045; B: 87, 88, 90	CBLP, 1650; VM, 25/4/03; 1/5/03
96	Roderick		c1835	Barra	Cape Breton		SRE, 69
97	Roderick	Donald	19/9/1823 ?1850-51	Kilbar ?Admiral	?Quebec Red Islands	S: 84, 581; B: 80, 81, 85, 89, 91	VM, 25/4/03; BPR

LAMONT

ID	Name	Father	D.o.B D.o.E	Origin Ship	Port of Arrival Destination	Relations	References
98	Alexander	Hector	c1837 1851	Tiree Admiral	Quebec Ontario	S: 100, 105; B: 99, 101, 102, 103, 104, 106	QT 9/1851; 1851 CENSUS
99	Allan	Hector	c1843 1851	Tiree Admiral	Quebec Ontario	S: 100, 105; B: 98, 101, 102, 103, 104, 106	QT 9/1851; 1851 CENSUS
100	Hector	Hector	c1803 1851	Tiree Admiral	Quebec Ontario	H: 105; F: 98, 99, 101, 102, 103, 104, 106	QT 9/1851; 1851 CENSUS
101	Jessie	Hector	1850 1851	Tiree Admiral	Quebec Ontario	D: 100, 105; Z: 98, 99, 102, 103, 104, 106	QT 9/1851; 1851 CENSUS
102	John	Hector	c1839 1851	Tiree Admiral	Quebec Ontario	S: 100, 105; B: 98, 99, 101, 103, 104, 106	QT 9/1851; 1851 CENSUS

LAMONT

ID	Name	Father	D.o.B / D.o.E	Origin / Ship	Port of Arrival / Destination	Relations	References
103	Margaret	Hector	c1831 / 1851	Tiree / Admiral	Quebec / Ontario	D: 100, 105; Z: 98, 99, 101, 102, 104, 106	QT 9/1851; 1851 CENSUS
104	Mary	Hector	c1835 / 1851	Tiree / Admiral	Quebec / Ontario	D: 100, 105; Z: 98, 99, 101, 102, 103, 106	QT 9/1851; 1851 CENSUS
105	Mary*		c1807 / 1851	Barra / Admiral	Quebec / Ontario	W: 100; M: 98, 99, 101, 102, 103, 104, 106	QT 9/1851; 1851 CENSUS
106	Nancy	Hector	c1833 / 1851	Tiree / Admiral	Quebec / Ontario	D: 100, 105; Z: 98, 99, 101, 102, 103, 104	QT 9/1851; 1851 CENSUS

MACARTHUR

ID	Name	Father	D.o.B / D.o.E	Origin / Ship	Port of Arrival / Destination	Relations	References
107	Allan		/ 1828	Nask		H: 406; F: 108, 109, 110, 111, 112, 113	NMD 13/7/28; BPR
108	Archibald	Allan	16/12/1824 / 1828	North Bay		S: 107; B: 109, 110, 111, 112, 113	NMD 13/7/28; BPR
109	Beag	Allan	22/7/1816 / 1828	Balnabodach		S: 107; B: 108, 110, 111, 112, 113	NMD 13/7/28; BPR
110	Jane	Allan	27/2/1807 / 1828	Earsary		D: 107, 406; Z: 108, 109, 111, 112, 113	NMD 13/7/28; BPR
111	Janet	Allan	11/7/1814 / 1828	Nask		D: 107; Z: 108, 109, 110, 112, 113	NMD 13/7/28; BPR
112	Margaret	Allan	14/12/1818 / 1828	Torrun		D: 107; Z: 108, 109, 110, 111, 113	NMD 13/7/28; BPR
113	Mariana	Allan	9/4/1821 / 1828	Torrun		D: 107; Z: 108, 109, 110, 111, 112	NMD 13/7/28; BPR

MACDONALD

ID	Name	Father	D.o.B / D.o.E	Origin / Ship	Port of Arrival / Destination	Relations	References
114	Alasdair		c1802	Barra		B: 133, 146, 175	HB, 217
115	Alex	John	9/8/1823 / 1826	Berneray	Mount Young	S: 156, 579; B: 135, 173	HB, 230; CBLP, 3123
116	Alexander	Michael	1817	Kilbar / William Tell	Sydney / Mabou	S: 169, 233; B: 125	ACIH, 356; BPR; HIC, 613
117	Alexander		c1794 / 1822	?Rulios	S Boularderie	H: 330	HB, 230; CBLP, 3123; SICB, 149; BPR
118	Alexander		c1805 / 1826	Barra	S Boularderie		HB, 230; CBLP, 3123; SICB, 149

MACDONALD

ID	Name	Father	D.o.B / D.o.E	Origin / Ship	Port of Arrival / Destination	Relations	References
119	Alexander	John	?1788	Barra	Washabuck		VCDR, 1868
120	Allan	Iain 'Og'	?1817	Kilbar	Mabou	H: 33; F: 140, 143, 145, 153, 154; B: 124, 136, 139, 141, 141	MP, 419; BPR; CM
121	Angus		1776 / >1826	Tangusdale	S Boularderie	H: 437; F: 130, 137, 155, 168, 170, 172	HB, 230; CBLP, 3132; DW2, 4777; SICB, app 150
122	Ann	Donald	1802	Barra / ?Hector	?Pictou / Grand Narrows	W: 614	MCI, 157; DW2, 7498
123	Ann	Neil		Kilbar	Mabou	D: 481; Z: 126, 129, 150, 151, 157, 161, 167, 174	MP, 414; BPR
124	Archibald	Iain 'Og'	20/12/1806 / ?1817	Barra	Pictou / Mabou	B: 120, 136, 139, 141	MP, 414, 420; BPR
125	Archibald	Michael	1817	Kilbar / William Tell	Sydney / Mabou	S: 169, 233; B: 116	ACIH, 356; BPR; HIC, 613
126	Archibald	Neil		Kilbar	Mabou	S: 481; B: 123, 129, 150, 151, 157, 161, 167, 174	MP, 414, 417
127	Catherine	John	1821	Tangusdale / ?Harmony	S Boularderie	W: 67; M: 49	HB, 82
128	Catherine	John	<1830	Craigston	Victoria Co.	W: 383; M: 289, 297, 331, 333, 366, 377	VCDR, 23/4/68; BPR
129	Catherine	Neil		Kilbar	Bras d'Or	D: 481; Z: 123, 126, 150, 151, 157, 161, 167, 174	MP, 414, 418
130	Christian	Angus	12/8/1818 / >1826	Langinish	Boularderie	D: 121, 437; Z: 137, 155, 168, 170, 172	HB, 230; CBLP, 3132; DW2, 4777; SICB, app 150
131	Christina	John	c1808	Barra	Boularderie		VCDR, 1868
132	Donald		1790	Barra / Queen	PEI, Grand River W, Lot 14		PAPEI, 2353, 24, 25
133	Donald		1786 / c1802	Barra	Mount Young	B: 114, 146, 175	HB, 217
134	Donald	Alistair	?1811	Barra	St Columba	B: 144, 147, 169, 177	ACIH, 356, 367; HIC, 613
135	Donald	John	6/4/1825 / 1826	Sandray	S Boularderie	S: 156, 579; B: 115, 173	HB, 230; CBLP, 3123

MACDONALD

ID	Name	Father	D.o.B / D.o.E	Origin / Ship	Port of Arrival / Destination	Relations	References
136	Donald	Iain 'Og'		Barra	Mabou Harbour	B: 120, 124, 139, 141	MP, 422
137	Elizabeth	Angus	17/9/1823 / >1826	Brevig	Boularderie	D: 121, 437; Z: 130, 155, 168, 170, 172	HB, 230; CBLP, 3132; DW2, 4777; SICB, app 150
138	Elizabeth	John	18/6/1808	Barra	Baddeck		VCDR, 1869
139	Eoin	Iain 'Og'		Barra	Mabou / S Mabou Harbour	B: 120, 124, 136, 141	MP, 414, 422
140	Finlay	Allan	18/10/1807 / ?1817	Eoligary	Mabou	S: 33, 120; B: 143, 145, 153, 154	MP, 419; BPR; CM
141	Finlay	Iain 'Og'		Barra	Mabou	B: 120, 124, 136, 139	MP, 426
142	Flora		>1816	Vaslain	Near Red Islands	W: 866; M: 735, 857, 919	CBLP, 2238; BPR
143	Flora	Allan	4/7/1813 / ?1817	Kilbar	Mabou	D: 33, 120; Z: 140, 145, 153, 154	MP, 419; BPR; CM
144	Flora	Alistair	>1817	Barra	Washabuck	Z: 134, 147, 169, 177	ACIH, 356
145	Flory	Allan	1/10/1806 / ?1817	Kial	Mabou	D: 33, 120; Z: 140, 143, 153, 154	MP, 419; BPR; CM
146	Hector		1802 / c1802	Barra	Mount Young	B: 114, 133, 175	HB, 217
147	James	Alistair	c1803 / ?1811	Barra	St Columba	H: 560; B: 134, 144, 169, 177	ACIH, 356, 365; HIC, 613
148	Jane	Alistair	?1817-19	Barra	Boisdale		HB, 230-313
149	Janet	John	1817	Tangusdale / ?William Tell	?Sydney / Benacadie	W: 339; M: 340	MCI, 94; BPR
150	Janet	Neil	29/10/1815 / ?c1830	Kilbar	Mabou	D: 481; Z: 123, 126, 129, 151, 157, 161, 167, 174	MP, 414; BPR; CM
151	Jessie	Neil		Kilbar	MacKinnon's Brook	D: 481; Z: 123, 126, 129, 150, 157, 161, 167, 174	MP, 414, 418
152	John		1790	Barra / Queen	Charlottetown / PEI, Grand River W, Lot 14		PAPEI, 2353, 24, 25
153	John	Allan	7/12/1808 / ?1817	Cliad	Mabou	S: 33, 120; B: 140, 143, 145, 154	MP, 419; BPR; CM

MACDONALD

ID	Name	Father	D.o.B / D.o.E	Origin / Ship	Port of Arrival / Destination	Relations	References
154	John	Allan	26/10/1816 / ?1817	Kilbar	Mabou	S: 33, 120; B: 140, 143, 145, 153	MP, 419; BPR; CM
155	John	Angus	8/11/1815 / >1826	Tangusdale	Boularderie	S: 121, 437; B: 130, 137, 168, 170, 172	HB, 230; CBLP, 3132; DW2, 4777; SICB, app 150
156	John		1790 / 1826	Vatersay	S Boularderie	H: 579; F: 115, 135, 173	HB, 230; CBLP, 3123
157	John	Neil		Kilbar	Mabou	S: 481; B: 123, 126, 129, 150, 151, 161, 167, 174	MP, 415
158	John 'Mor'			Barra	W Mabou		HIC, 284
159	Jonathan		1802	Barra	Pictou	B: 162, 171	MCI, 38
160	Louisa			?Hector	Grand Narrows	W: 206; M: 207, 214, 226	HIC, 531; BPR
161	Lucy	Neil	1831	Kilbar	W Lake, Ainslie	D: 481; Z: 123, 126, 129, 150, 151, 157, 167, 174	MP, 414, 418
162	Malcolm		c1775 / ?1802	Barra	W Lake, Ainslie	B: 159, 171	CBLP, 499; SICB, 156; MCI, 38
163	Marion	John	?1826	Tangusdale	S Grand Narrows / Point Clear, Boularderie	W: 301; M: 290, 296, 327, 365	HB, 335; BPR
164	Mary		1802	Barra / Hector	Pictou / Red Islands	W: 668; M: 669	CBLP, 946; CCB, 167; CMC, 29,4,6-11
165	Mary		c1780 / <1806	Barra	PEI		DW3, 914; NPEIGS, 19/4, 12
166	Mary		c1784 / ?1817-19	Barra	Boisdale		HB, 230-313
167	Mary	Neil	c1804 / ?1825-26	Vaslain	Mabou	W: 1027; D: 481; Z: 123, 126, 129, 150, 151, 157, 161, 174	MP, 418, 804; HIC, 614; BPR; CM
168	Mary	Angus	21/6/1810 / >1826	Tangusdale	Boularderie	D: 121, 437; Z: 130, 137, 155, 170, 172	HB, 230; CBLP, 3132; DW2, 4777; SICB, app 150
169	Michael 'Mor'	Alistair	1817	Kilbar / William Tell	Sydney / Mabou Mines	H: 233; F: 116, 125; B: 134, 144, 147, 177	ACIH, 356; BPR; HIC, 613
170	Murdoch	Angus	16/6/1814 / >1826	Tangusdale	Boularderie	S: 121, 437; B: 130, 137, 155, 168, 172	HB, 230; CBLP, 3132; DW2, 4777; SICB, app 150

MACDONALD

ID	Name	Father	D.o.B	D.o.E	Origin	Ship	Port of Arrival	Destination	Relations	References
171	Neil			1821	Barra	Harmony	Sydney	Grand Narrows	B: 159, 162	MCI, 38
172	Ranald	Angus	10/5/1821	>1826	Langinish			Boularderie	S: 121, 437; B: 130, 137, 155, 168, 170	HB, 230; CBLP, 3132; DW2, 4777; SICB, app 150
173	Roderick	John	16/9/1821	1826	Vatersay			S Boularderie	S: 156, 579; B: 115, 135	HB, 230; CBLP, 3123
174	Roderick	Neil	26/12/1818		Kilbar			Mabou	S: 481; B: 123, 126, 129, 150, 151, 157, 161, 167	MP, 414; BPR
175	Ronald		c1802		Barra			Mount Young	B: 114, 133, 146	HB, 217
176	Rory		c1806		Barra			Cape Breton		SRE, 64
177	Rory	Alistair	?1811		Barra			Upper Washabuck	B: 134, 144, 147, 169	ACIH, 356, 371; HIC, 613

MACDOUGALD

ID	Name	Father	D.o.B	D.o.E	Origin	Ship	Port of Arrival	Destination	Relations	References
178	Ann	Neil		>1826	Glen			Rear Goose Pond	W: 635; M: 519, 751, 813	CBLP, 3145; BPR
179	Anne		c1832		Cliad			Barrachois Pond	W: 30; M: 29, 37, 38, 46, 56, 58, 69	HB, 87; BPR

MACDOUGALL

ID	Name	Father	D.o.B	D.o.E	Origin	Ship	Port of Arrival	Destination	Relations	References
180	Adam	Malcolm	<1802		Barra			Cape North	B: 182, 186, 187, 197, 203	MCI, 44
181	Alexander	John	1802		Barra	?Hector	?Pictou	Christmas Island	S: 190; B: 191, 201, 202	MCI, 44
182	Archibald	Malcolm	1779		Barra			Grand Narrows	H: 589; B: 180, 186, 187, 197, 203	MCI, 44; MG, 3/3/03
183	Barr		c1790	?1851	Barra	?Admiral	?Quebec		H: 60; F: 195	NMP; MHHC, 256
184	Catherine	Donald	c1801		Barra			Rear Big Pond	W: 968; M: 649, 687, 766, 850; D: 186, 351; Z: 188, 189, 194, 198, 199, 200	BPR; CNS, 1871; VM, 30/4/2004
185	Christy			>1826	Barra			New Campbelltown	W: 750	RM, 28/6/1998

MACDOUGALL

ID	Name	Father	D.o.B D.o.E	Origin Ship	Port of Arrival Destination	Relations	References
186	Donald 'Miller'	Malcolm		Barra	Rear Big Pond	H: 351; F: 184, 188, 189, 194, 198, 199, 200; B: 180, 182, 187, 197, 203	BPR; CNS, 1871; VM, 30/4/2004
187	Hector 'Red'	Malcolm	1802	Barra ?Hector	?Pictou Christmas Island	B: 180, 182, 186, 197, 203	MCI, 44
188	Hector	Donald	24/11/1807	Allasdale	Rear Big Pond	S: 186, 351; B: 184, 189, 194, 198, 199, 200	BPR; CNS, 1871; VM, 30/4/2004
189	James	Donald	29/1/1818	Allasdale	Rear Big Pond	S: 186, 351; B: 184, 188, 194, 198, 199, 200	BPR; CNS, 1871; VM, 30/4/2004
190	John	John 1802		Barra ?Hector	?Pictou Big Beach	F: 181, 191, 201, 202	MCI, 44
191	John 'Ban'	John 1802		Barra ?Hector	?Pictou Christmas Island	S: 190; B: 181, 201, 202	MCI, 44
192	John		1784 1827	Barra	Nova Scotia		NSLP, 1833
193	John	Barr	c1818 1851	Barra Admiral	Quebec		NMP
194	John	Donald	15/9/1815	Allasdale	Rear Big Pond	S: 186, 351; B: 184, 188, 189, 198, 199, 200	BPR; CNS, 1871; VM, 30/4/2004
195	Jonathan	Barr	1818 ?1851	Barra ?Admiral	?Quebec	S: 60, 183	NMP; MHHC, 256
196	Malcolm		1823	Barra Emp. Alexander	Sydney Cape Breton		INVJ, 30/1/1824
197	Margaret	Malcolm	1760's ?1802	Barra ?Hector	?Pictou Grand Narrows	W: 671; M: 558, 657, 691; Z: 180, 182, 186, 187, 203	MCI, 44, 145
198	Margaret	Donald	12/8/1820	Allasdale	Rear Big Pond	D: 186, 351; Z: 184, 188, 189, 194, 199, 200	BPR; CNS, 1871; VM, 30/4/2004
199	Marion	Donald	10/1/1810	Allasdale	Rear Big Pond	D: 186, 351; Z: 184, 188, 189, 194, 198, 200	BPR; CNS, 1871; VM, 30/4/2004
200	Michael	Donald	15/9/1815	Allasdale	Rear Big Pond	S: 186, 351; B: 184, 188, 189, 194, 198, 199	BPR; CNS, 1871; VM, 30/4/2004
201	Neil	John 1802		Barra ?Hector	?Pictou Christmas Island	S: 190; B: 181, 191, 202	MCI, 44
202	Rory	John 1802		Barra ?Hector	?Pictou Christmas Island	S: 190; B: 181, 191, 201	MCI, 44

MACDOUGALL

ID	Name	Father	D.o.B / D.o.E	Origin / Ship	Port of Arrival / Destination	Relations	References
203	Sarah	Malcolm	<1802	Barra	Christmas Island	Z: 180, 182, 186, 187, 197	MCI, 44
204	Sarah	Malcolm	<1816	Vaslain	PEI	W: 334; M: 293, 335, 355, 356	MCI, 100; BPR

MACINNIS

ID	Name	Father	D.o.B / D.o.E	Origin / Ship	Port of Arrival / Destination	Relations	References
205	Alex	Roderick	12/8/1813 c1817	Kial	Iona	S: 227, 530; B: 209, 211, 217, 222	MCI, 57; VM, 7/4/2003; BPR
206	Angus 'Og'	Angus	1831	Rulios	W Lake, Ainslie	H: 160; F: 207, 214, 226	MP, 660; HIC, 531; BPR
207	Angus	Angus	1829 1831	Rulios	W Lake, Ainslie	S: 160, 206; B: 214, 226	MP, 660; HIC, 531; BPR
208	Ann		1802	Barra ?Hector	?Pictou Coopers Pond	W: 313; M: 287, 292, 311, 323, 353, 371, 384	MCI, 98; SRE, 83; ACIH, 465
209	Ann	Roderick	4/12/1814 c1817	Kilbar	Iona	D: 227, 530; Z: 205, 211, 217, 222	MCI, 57; VM, 7/4/2003; BPR
210	Ann	Neil	23/3/1817 c1817	Sandray	Castle Bay	D: 224, 592; Z: 213	MCI, 57; BPR
211	Catherine	Roderick	31/3/1808 c1817	Hellisay	Iona	D: 227, 530; Z: 205, 209, 217, 222	MCI, 57; VM, 7/4/2003; BPR
212	Catherine	Michael	23/3/1817 c1817	Sandray	Castle Bay	D: 21, 223; Z: 221, 225, 228	MCI, 59; BPR; SRE, 83
213	Charles	Neil	13/1/1815 c1817	Sandray	Castle Bay	S: 224, 592; B: 210	MCI, 57; BPR
214	Charles	Angus	13/4/1826 1831	Rulios	W Lake, Ainslie	S: 160, 206; B: 207, 226	MP, 660; HIC, 531; BPR
215	Donald		1772	?Barra Alexander	PEI, Lot 36		PAPEI, 2664, 148, 156; ISLAND, 29, 34-9
216	Donald	Rory	c1817	Barra	Benacadie	B: 223, 224, 227	MCI, 57
217	Donald	Roderick	29/1/1810 c1817	Hellisay	Iona	S: 227, 530; B: 205, 209, 211, 222	MCI, 57; VM, 7/4/2003; BPR; VCDR, 1868
218	Donald		1826	Vaslain			NMD, 4/3/31
219	Flory	Angus	c1799 <1827	Bruernish	Big Pond	W: 936; M: 580, 660, 802, 814, 842, 886	ACIH, 115; BPR; CNS, 1871; VM, 29/4/2004

MACINNIS

ID	Name	Father	D.o.B / D.o.E	Origin / Ship	Port of Arrival / Destination	Relations	References
220	John		c1768 / 1780	Barra	PEI		EXAMINER, 11/1/1858
221	John	Michael	11/10/1807 / c1817	Sandray	Castle Bay	S: 21, 223; B: 212, 225, 228	MCI, 59; BPR; SRE, 83
222	Michael	Roderick	30/9/1806 / c1817	Hellisay	Iona	S: 227, 530; B: 205, 209, 211, 217	MCI, 57; VM, 7/4/2003; BPR
223	Michael	Rory	c1817	Sandray	Castle Bay	H: 21; F: 212, 221, 225, 228; B: 216, 224, 227	MCI, 59; BPR; SRE, 83
224	Neil	Rory	c1817	Sandray	Castle Bay	H: 592; F: 210, 213; B: 216, 223, 227	MCI, 57; BPR
225	Neil	Michael	c1812 / c1817	?Sandray	Castle Bay	S: 21, 223; B: 212, 221, 228	MCI, 59; BPR; SRE, 83
226	Neil	Angus	11/12/1823 / 1831	Kilbar	W Lake, Ainslie	S: 160, 206; B: 207, 214	MP, 660; HIC, 531; BPR
227	Roderick	Rory	c1817	Hellisay	Iona	H: 530; F: 205, 209, 211, 217, 222; B: 216, 223, 224	MCI, 57; VM, 7/4/2003; BPR
228	Stephen	Michael	18/10/1813 / c1817	Sandray	Shenacadie	S: 21, 223; B: 212, 221, 225	MCI, 59; BPR; SRE, 83

MACINTYRE

ID	Name	Father	D.o.B / D.o.E	Origin / Ship	Port of Arrival / Destination	Relations	References
229	Allan	Donald	19/11/1814 / c1817-19	Cliad	S Boularderie	S: 5, 234; B: 237	HB, 230-313; BPR
230	Angus		1772	Barra / Alexander	Charlottetown PEI, Lot 36		PAPEI, 2664, 148, 156; ISLAND, 29, 34-9
231	Ann		c1816-17	Kilbar	Jamesville	M: 31, 43, 48, 52, 59, 74	ACIH, 325-6; JGA
232	Ann		1817	Borve / William Tell	Sydney Antigonish, NS	W: 73; M: 26, 28, 32, 41, 70	NSG, iii, 2, 91; BPR; NSLP, 1818; NSGP, 7, 7;
233	Catherine	Allan	1817	Cliad / William Tell	Sydney Washabuck	W: 169; M: 116, 125	ACIH, 356; BPR; HIC, 613
234	Donald	Ian Rory	c1817-19	Cliad	S Boularderie	H: 5; F: 229, 237	HB, 230-313; BPR
235	James		1802	Barra / ?Hector	?Pictou Troy	H: 972	CMC, 29,4,6-11
236	John		1772	Barra / Alexander	Charlottetown PEI, Lot 36		PAPEI, 2664, 148; ISLAND, 29, 34-9

MACINTYRE

ID	Name	Father	D.o.B D.o.E	Origin Ship	Port of Arrival Destination	Relations	References
237	John	Donald	9/5/1817 c1817-19	Cliad	S Boularderie	S: 5, 234; B: 229	HB, 230-313; BPR
238	Lachlan		1790	Barra Queen	Charlottetown PEI, Grand River W, Lot 14		PAPEI, 2353, 24, 25; DW3, 1029
239	Neil		1772	Barra Alexander	Charlottetown PEI, Lot 36		PAPEI, 2664, 148, 156; ISLAND, 29, 34-9
240	Roderick	Allan		Cliad	St Columba		ACIH, 416
241	Rory		1772	Barra Alexander	Charlottetown PEI, Lot 36		PAPEI, 2664, 148, 156; ISLAND, 29, 34-9

MACKEEGAN

ID	Name	Father	D.o.B D.o.E	Origin Ship	Port of Arrival Destination	Relations	References
242	Ms ?		1821	Barra Harmony	Sydney Christmas Island		MCI, 64

MACKENZIE

ID	Name	Father	D.o.B D.o.E	Origin Ship	Port of Arrival Destination	Relations	References
243	Alexander	Donald		Barra	Christmas Island	S: 251, 600; B: 252, 254, 256, 258, 265, 269, 272, 278	MCI, 75; BPR
244	Angus	Alexander	1826	Vatersay	Red Island	H: 1014; F: 245, 253, 264, 280; B: 262, 276	MCI, 84
245	Ann	Angus	13/11/1809 1826	Vatersay	Red Island	D: 244, 1014; Z: 253, 264, 280	MCI, 84
246	Archibald	Hector	c1776 1821	Kentangaval ?Harmony	Washabuck	H: 306; F: 247, 249, 250, 259, 260, 266, 268, 274, 277, 279; S: 255; B: 251, 261, 263, 267, 271	MCI, 64; CBLP, 2856; ACIH, 425; BPR
247	Catherine	Archibald	1821	Barra ?Harmony	Washabuck	D: 246, 306; Z: 249, 250, 259, 260, 266, 268, 274, 277, 279	MCI, 64; CBLP, 2856; ACIH, 425; BPR
248	Catherine	Jonathan	19/9/1814 1821	Glen Harmony	?Sydney Sydney Mines	W: 392; D: 263, 439; Z: 270, 273, 275	MCI, 64; BPR
249	Christie	Archibald	17/4/1820 1821	Glen ?Harmony	Sydney Mines	D: 246, 306; Z: 247, 250, 259, 260, 266, 268, 274, 277, 279	MCI, 64; CBLP, 2856; ACIH, 425; BPR

MACKENZIE

ID	Name	Father	D.o.B / D.o.E	Origin / Ship	Port of Arrival / Destination	Relations	References
250	Donald	Archibald	1821	Barra / ?Harmony		S: 246, 306; B: 247, 249, 259, 260, 266, 268, 274, 277, 279	MCI, 64; CBLP, 2856; ACIH, 425; BPR
251	Donald	Hector	c1774 / ?1821	Glen	Christmas Island	H: 600; F: 243, 252, 254, 256, 258, 265, 269, 272, 278; S: 255; B: 246, 261, 263, 267, 271	MCI, 75; BPR; NSLP, Bk U, 83
252	Donald	Donald	4/2/1807 / ?1821	Glen	Christmas Island	S: 251, 600; B: 243, 254, 256, 258, 265, 269, 272, 278	MCI, 75; BPR
253	Donald	Angus	25/1/1806 / 1826	Vatersay	Red Island	S: 244, 1014; B: 245, 264, 280	MCI, 84; IONA CEMTY, 1886
254	Finlay	Donald	c1805 / ?1821	Barra	Christmas Island	S: 251, 600; B: 243, 252, 256, 258, 265, 269, 272, 278	MCI, 75; BPR
255	Hector	Archibald	c1821	Kentangaval	Christmas Island	F: 246, 251, 261, 263, 267, 271	MCI, 63
256	Hector	Donald	2/4/1820 / ?1821	Glen	Christmas Island	S: 251, 600; B: 243, 252, 254, 258, 265, 269, 272, 278	MCI, 75; BPR
257	James	Donald	1809 / 1821	Barra / Harmony	Sydney / Christmas Island		MCI, 236
258	James	Donald	1812 / ?1821	Barra	Christmas Island	S: 251, 600; B: 243, 252, 254, 256, 265, 269, 272, 278	MCI, 75; BPR
259	John	Archibald	9/2/1809 / 1821	Kentangaval / ?Harmony	Washabuck	S: 246, 306; B: 247, 249, 250, 260, 266, 268, 274, 277, 279	MCI, 64; CBLP, 2856; ACIH, 425; BPR
260	John	Archibald	12/6/1816 / 1821	Glen / ?Harmony	Washabuck	S: 246, 306; B: 247, 249, 250, 259, 266, 268, 274, 277, 279	MCI, 64; CBLP, 2856; ACIH, 425; BPR
261	John	Hector	1821	Glen / Harmony	Sydney / Washabuck	H: 65; S: 255; B: 246, 251, 263, 267, 271	MCI, 64-65; BPR
262	John	Alexander	1826	Barra	Christmas Island	B: 244, 276	MCI, 84
263	Jonathan	Hector	c1787 / 1821	Glen / Harmony	?Sydney / Washabuck	H: 439; F: 248, 270, 273, 275; S: 255; B: 246, 251, 261, 267, 271	MCI, 64; BPR
264	Margaret	Angus	28/11/1807 / 1826	Vatersay	Red Island	D: 244, 1014; Z: 245, 253, 280	MCI, 84

MACKENZIE

ID	Name	Father	D.o.B / D.o.E	Origin / Ship	Port of Arrival / Destination	Relations	References
265	Marian (Sarah)	Donald	27/4/1821 ?1821	Glen	Christmas Island	D: 251, 600; Z: 243, 252, 254, 256, 258, 269, 272, 278	MCI, 75; BPR
266	Marion	Archibald	3/12/1813 1821	Glen ?Harmony	Washabuck	D: 246, 306; Z: 247, 249, 250, 259, 260, 268, 274, 277, 279	MCI, 64; CBLP, 2856; ACIH, 425; BPR
267	Mary	Hector	1817	Glen ?William Tell	?Sydney Big Beach	W: 736; M: 881; D: 255; Z: 246, 251, 261, 263, 271	MCI, 64, 140; BPR
268	Mary	Archibald	18/10/1817 1821	Glen ?Harmony	Upper Washabuck	D: 246, 306; Z: 247, 249, 250, 259, 260, 266, 274, 277, 279	MCI, 64; CBLP, 2856; ACIH, 425; BPR
269	Mary	Donald	27/11/1815 ?1821	Lower Glen	Christmas Island	D: 251, 600; Z: 243, 252, 254, 256, 258, 265, 272, 278	MCI, 75; BPR
270	Mary	Jonathan	18/8/1818 1821	Glen Harmony	?Sydney Washabuck	D: 263, 439; Z: 248, 273, 275	MCI, 64; BPR
271	Murdoch	Hector	1817	Glen ?William Tell	?Sydney Washabuck	H: 782; S: 255; B: 246, 251, 261, 263, 267	MCI, 63-64, 86; ACIH, 437
272	Murdoch	Donald	24/3/1818 ?1821	Glen	Christmas Island	S: 251, 600; B: 243, 252, 254, 256, 258, 265, 269, 278	MCI, 75; BPR
273	Murdoch	Jonathan	12/9/1816 1821	Glen Harmony	?Sydney Washabuck	S: 263, 439; B: 248, 270, 275	MCI, 64; BPR
274	Neil	Archibald	1821	Barra ?Harmony	Washabuck	S: 246, 306; B: 247, 249, 250, 259, 260, 266, 268, 277, 279	MCI, 64; CBLP, 2856; ACIH, 425; BPR
275	Neil	Jonathan	11/7/1820 1821	Glen Harmony	?Sydney Washabuck	S: 263, 439; B: 248, 270, 273	MCI, 64; BPR
276	Neil	Alexander	1822	Vatersay	Christmas Island	B: 244, 262	MCI, 84
277	Rory	Archibald	2/6/1806 1821	Kentangaval ?Harmony	Washabuck	S: 246, 306; B: 247, 249, 250, 259, 260, 266, 268, 274, 279	MCI, 64; CBLP, 2856; ACIH, 425; BPR
278	Rory	Donald	c1800 ?1821	Barra	Christmas Island	S: 251, 600; B: 243, 252, 254, 256, 258, 265, 269, 272	MCI, 75; BPR
279	Sarah	Archibald	1821	Barra ?Harmony	Washabuck	D: 246, 306; Z: 247, 249, 250, 259, 260, 266, 268, 274, 277	MCI, 64; CBLP, 2856; ACIH, 425; BPR

MACKENZIE

ID	Name	Father	D.o.B	D.o.E	Origin	Ship	Port of Arrival	Destination	Relations	References
280	Stephen	Angus	16/9/1813	1826	Vatersay			Red Island	S: 244, 1014; B: 245, 253, 264	MCI, 84

MACKILLOP

ID	Name	Father	D.o.B	D.o.E	Origin	Ship	Port of Arrival	Destination	Relations	References
281	Ann			1817	Barra	?William Tell	?Sydney	Red Island	W: 867; M: 565, 688	CBLP, 1754; BPR

MACKINNON

ID	Name	Father	D.o.B	D.o.E	Origin	Ship	Port of Arrival	Destination	Relations	References
282	Alex		c1755	1790	Barra	Queen	Charlottetown	PEI, Grand River, Lot 14		PAPEI, 2353, 24, 25; SPE, 31; DW3, 1091
283	Alex			1802	Barra	Hector	?Pictou	PEI, Indian River, Lot 18		DW2, 6486; SPE, 2; SMC, 1, 256
284	Alex	Neil	10/6/1817	1821	Fuiay	Harmony	Sydney	Christmas Island	S: 376, 1008; B: 309, 321, 380	MCI, 64; BPR; HB, 335, 351
285	Alexander			1802	Barra	?Hector	?Pictou	PEI, New Annan, Lot 19		WMGN
286	Allan			1772	Barra	Alexander	Charlottetown	PEI, Lot 36		PAPEI, 2664, 148; ISLAND, 29, 34-9
287	Allan	Donald		1802	Barra	?Hector	?Pictou	MacKinnon's Harbour	S: 208, 313; B: 292, 311, 323, 353, 371, 384	MCI, 98; SRE, 83; ACIH, 465
288	Allan	John	c1796	1817	Barra	?William Tell	?Sydney	W Bolactrie	S: 336	DW2, 6489; CBLP, 2214; SICB, 171
289	Allan	Roderick	<1830		Fuiay		Victoria Co.		S: 128, 383; B: 297, 331, 333, 366, 377	VCDR, 23/4/68; BPR
290	Angus	Archibald	22/3/1820	?1826	Gortien		Boularderie		S: 163, 301; B: 296, 327, 365	HB, 335; BPR
291	Angus			1827	Barra		Woodbine			CASKET, 01/1907
292	Ann	Donald		1802	Barra	?Hector	?Pictou	Piper's Cove	D: 208, 313; Z: 287, 311, 323, 353, 371, 384	MCI, 98; SRE, 83; ACIH, 465
293	Ann	John	27/11/1806	<1816	Vaslain		PEI		D: 204, 334; Z: 335, 355, 356	MCI, 100; BPR
294	Ann	Hector	c1811	?1821	Barra		Christmas Island		D: 992; Z: 307, 320, 358, 374	VM 24/4/2003, 1/5/2003; BPR
295	Ann	Murdoch	18/6/1820	c1821	Kentangaval	?Harmony	?Sydney	Big Pond	D: 370, 836; Z: 317, 326, 361	EBPR; VM

MACKINNON

ID	Name	Father	D.o.B / D.o.E	Origin / Ship	Port of Arrival / Destination	Relations	References
296	Ann	Archibald	30/3/1822 / ?1826	Gortien	Boularderie	D: 163, 301; Z: 290, 327, 365	HB, 335; BPR
297	Ann	Roderick	<1830	Fuiay	Victoria Co.	D: 128, 383; Z: 289, 331, 333, 366, 377	VCDR, 23/4/68; BPR
298	Ann		c1807 / c1837	Brevig	Eskasoni	W: 318; M: 367, 369	BR, 2/2004; BPR
299	Anne		1817	Gortien / William Tell	Sydney / Boularderie Island	W: 1021; M: 1019	CBLP, 1766; HB, 541; CM
300	Archibald	Archibald			Sydney / Shenacadie		MCI, 99
301	Archibald	Neil	1821	Barra / Harmony	Point Clear, Boularderie	H: 163; F: 290, 296, 327, 365	HB, 335; BPR
302	Catherine	Philip	1817	Barra / ?William Tell	?Sydney / Gillis Point	W: 626	ACIH, 95
303	Catherine	John	3/3/1817	Vatersay	Rear MacKinnon's Harbour	D: 342, 401; Z: 315, 324, 373, 379, 385	MCI, 96; BPR
304	Catherine	John	<1817	Borve / ?William Tell	?Sydney / Bras d'Or	W: 627; M: 567, 661, 676, 882	CBLP, 2008; BPR
305	Catherine	John	<1821	Barra	Benacadie Glen	W: 653; M: 800, 810, 834	MCI, 157
306	Catherine		1821	Kentangaval / ?Harmony	Washabuck	W: 246; M: 247, 249, 250, 259, 260, 266, 268, 274, 277, 279	MCI, 64; CBLP, 2856; ACIH, 425; BPR
307	Catherine	Hector	20/12/1809 / ?1821	Nask	Christmas Island	D: 992; Z: 294, 320, 358, 374	VM 24/4/2003, 1/5/2003; BPR
308	Catherine	Donald	16/11/1819 / ?1821	Earsary	Washabuck	D: 316, 835; Z: 375	VCDR, 1868; BPR
309	Catherine	Neil	2/4/1809 / ?1821	Allasdale / Harmony	Sydney / Christmas Island	D: 376, 1008; Z: 284, 321, 380	MCI, 64; BPR; HB, 335, 351
310	Catherine	Archibald	c1825	Borve	Scotch Hill		HIC, 375; BPR
311	Charles	Donald	1802	Barra / ?Hector	?Pictou / MacKinnon's Harbour	S: 208, 313; B: 287, 292, 323, 353, 371, 384	MCI, 98; SRE, 83; ACIH, 465
312	Charles			Barra	Merigomish, NS		HMER, 15

MACKINNON

ID	Name	Father	D.o.B	D.o.E	Origin	Ship	Port of Arrival	Destination	Relations	References
313	Donald 'Ban'			1802	Barra		?Pictou	Coopers Pond	H: 208; F: 287, 292, 311, 323, 353, 371, 384	MCI, 98; SRE, 83; ACIH, 465
314	Donald		1796	1817	Barra	?Hector	Sydney	Point Clear, Boularderie	S: 337	HB, 335; CBLP, 1729
315	Donald	John		<1817	Barra	William Tell		Rear MacKinnon's Harbour	S: 342, 401; B: 303, 324, 373, 379, 385	MCI, 96; BPR
316	Donald	Finlay	1786	?1821	Borve			Washabuck	H: 835; F: 308, 375	VCDR, 1868; BPR
317	Donald	Murdoch	6/12/1814	c1821	Kentangaval	?Harmony	?Sydney	Big Pond	S: 370, 836; B: 295, 326, 361	EBPR; VM
318	Donald	Roderick	12/12/1807	c1837	Hellisay			Eskasoni	H: 298; F: 367, 369; B: 347	BR, 2/2004; BPR
319	Donald 'Mor'	Donald			Barra			MacKinnon's Harbour		ACIH, 486
320	Elizabeth	Hector	10/8/1813	?1821	Kentangaval			Christmas Island	D: 992; Z: 294, 307, 358, 374	VM 24/4/2003, 1/5/2003; BPR
321	Elizabeth	Neil	19/10/1820	1821	Fuiay	Harmony	Sydney	Christmas Island	D: 376, 1008; Z: 284, 309, 380	MCI, 64; BPR; HB, 335, 351
322	Flora		1790		Barra	Queen	Charlottetown	PEI, Grand River W, Lot 14	W: 39; M: 24, 51, 61	PAPEI, 2353, 24, 25; DW3, 1094; WMGN;
323	Flora	Donald	1802		Barra	?Hector	?Pictou	Coopers Pond	D: 208, 313; Z: 287, 292, 311, 353, 371, 384	MCI, 98; SRE, 83; ACIH, 465
324	Hector	John	31/7/1814	<1817	Vatersay			Highland Hill	S: 342, 401; B: 303, 315, 373, 379, 385	MCI, 96; BPR
325	Hector	John	5/3/1813	1821	Nask	?Harmony	?Sydney	Beaver Cove	S: 343, 801; B: 329, 344, 345, 359, 378, 382	MCI, 90; DW2, 6542; BPR
326	Hector	Murdoch	22/10/1816	c1821	Kentangaval	?Harmony	?Sydney	Big Pond	H: 816; S: 370, 836; B: 295, 317, 361	EBPR; VM
327	Hector	Archibald	18/4/1818	?1826	Gortien			Boularderie	S: 163, 301; B: 290, 296, 365	HB, 335; BPR
328	Ian 'Mhor'			?1821	Alt Easdal	?Harmony	?Sydney	Cape Breton		VM, 24/4/2003, 1/5/2003; BPR
329	James	John	27/4/1817	1821	Gortien	?Harmony	?Sydney	Beaver Cove	S: 343, 801; B: 325, 344, 345, 359, 378, 382	MCI, 90; DW2, 6542; BPR
330	Janet	John		>1826	Greian			S Boularderie	W: 117	HB, 230; CBLP, 3123; SICB, 149; BPR

MACKINNON

ID	Name	Father	D.o.B / D.o.E	Origin / Ship	Port of Arrival / Destination	Relations	References
331	Janet	Roderick	<1830	Tordu	Victoria Co.	D: 128, 383; Z: 289, 297, 333, 366, 377	VCDR, 23/4/68; BPR
332	Janet		c1836	Craigston	Rear Beaver Cove	W: 484; M: 476, 479, 482, 485, 486, 488, 489, 490	MCI, 111
333	Jean	Roderick	<1830	Fuiay	Victoria Co.	D: 128, 383; Z: 289, 297, 331, 366, 377	VCDR, 23/4/68; BPR
334	John		<1816	Vaslain	PEI	H: 204; F: 293, 335, 355, 356	MCI, 100; BPR
335	John	John	21/11/1816 <1816	Vaslain	PEI	S: 204, 334; B: 293, 355, 356	MCI, 100; BPR
336	John		c1764 1817	Barra ?William Tell	?Sydney Boularderie	F: 288	HB, 362; CBLP, 2216
337	John		c1767 1817	Barra William Tell	Sydney Point Clear, Boularderie	F: 314	HB, 335; CBLP, 1729
338	John		>1817	Barra	Straits of Barra		SICB, app 172
339	John	Neil	1817	Barra	Benacadie	H: 149; F: 340; B: 372	MCI, 94; BPR
340	John	John	13/1/1816 1817	Tangusdale ?William Tell	?Sydney Christmas Island	S: 149, 339	MCI, 94; BPR
341	John		?1817	Barra	Big Pond	H: 828	VM, 7/4/2003
342	John 'Og'		<1817	Vatersay	Rear MacKinnon's Harbour	H: 401; F: 303, 315, 324, 373, 379, 385	MCI, 96; BPR
343	John	John	1821	Gortien ?Harmony	?Sydney Beaver Cove	H: 801; F: 325, 329, 344, 345, 359, 378, 382; S: 346	MCI, 90; DW2, 6542; BPR
344	John	John	8/10/1808 1821	Nask ?Harmony	?Sydney Beaver Cove	S: 343, 801; B: 325, 329, 345, 359, 378, 382	MCI, 90; DW2, 6542; BPR
345	John	John	23/5/1815 1821	Gortien ?Harmony	?Sydney Beaver Cove	S: 343, 801; B: 325, 329, 344, 359, 378, 382	MCI, 90; DW2, 6542; BPR
346	John 'Iain Og'		<1821	Barra	Cross Point	F: 343	HB, 318
347	John	Roderick	8/6/1810 c1837	Hellisay	Eskasoni	B: 318	BR, 2/2004; BPR
348	Laughlin		1790	Barra Queen	Charlottetown PEI, Grand River W, Lot 14		PAPEI, 2353, 24, 25

MACKINNON

ID	Name	Father	D.o.B D.o.E	Origin Ship	Port of Arrival Destination	Relations	References
349	Margaret		1813	Barra	Barra Falls	W: 954; M: 547, 561, 622, 686, 733, 787, 823, 955, 973, 978	ACIH, 1
350	Marian		1828	Fuday	Irish Cove	W: 752; M: 665, 843, 907	CASKET, 29/8/1901,5
351	Marion		c1802	Barra ?Hector	?Pictou Rear Big Pond	W: 186; M: 184, 188, 189, 194, 198, 199, 200	BPR; CNS, 1871; VM, 30/4/2004
352	Marion		c1797	Gortien	Cape North	W: 767; M: 666, 768, 913	BPR; CNS, 1871; VM, 30/4/2004
353	Mary	Donald	1802	Barra ?Hector	?Pictou Iona Rear	D: 208, 313; Z: 287, 292, 311, 323, 371, 384	MCI, 98; SRE, 83; ACIH, 465
354	Mary	Donald	1816-17	Kentangaval	Jamesville	W: 74	ACIH, 326; BPR
355	Mary	John	21/10/1805 <1816	Vaslain	PEI	D: 204, 334; Z: 293, 335, 356	MCI, 100; BPR
356	Mary	John	28/2/1814 <1816	Vaslain	PEI	D: 204, 334; Z: 293, 335, 355	MCI, 100; BPR
357	Mary		1818	Barra Dunlop	Pictou Inverness Co.	W: 389; M: 423	HIC, 462; DW2, 6680;
358	Mary	Hector	7/5/1806 ?1821	Nask	Christmas Island	D: 992; Z: 294, 307, 320, 374	VM 24/4/2003, 1/5/2003; BPR
359	Mary	John	14/4/1819 1821	Gortien ?Harmony	?Sydney Beaver Cove	D: 343, 801; Z: 325, 329, 344, 345, 378, 382	MCI, 90; DW2, 6542; BPR
360	Mary		c1821	Gortien	Boisdale	W: 393; M: 404, 415, 417, 418, 424, 442	HB, 379-80; BPR
361	Mary	Murdoch	14/4/1813 c1821	Kentangaval ?Harmony	?Sydney Big Pond	D: 370, 836; Z: 295, 317, 326	EBPR; VM
362	Mary		>1822	Vatersay	Iona	W: 960; M: 501, 536, 576, 630, 747, 788, 839, 885, 906, 974	ACIH, 194-216; BPR
363	Mary	John	>1822	Vaslain	Red Islands	W: 390; M: 395, 410, 425, 428, 435, 445, 456	MCI, 101; BPR
364	Mary	John	>1826	Glen	NW Scotch Narrows	W: 634	SICB, app 182; CBLP, 3149
365	Mary	Archibald	12/7/1816 ?1826	Gortien	Boularderie	D: 163, 301; Z: 290, 296, 327	HB, 335; BPR

MACKINNON

ID	Name	Father	D.o.B / D.o.E	Origin / Ship	Port of Arrival / Destination	Relations	References
366	Mary	Roderick	<1830	North Bay	Victoria Co.	D: 128, 383; Z: 289, 297, 331, 333, 377	VCDR, 23/4/68; BPR
367	Mary	Donald	29/1/1833 / c1837	Brevig	Eskasoni	D: 298, 318; Z: 369	BR, 2/2004; BPR
368	Michael		<1836	Barra	Cape Breton		HNS, iii, 194
369	Michael	Donald	27/7/1834 / c1837	Fuiay	Eskasoni	S: 298, 318; B: 367	BR, 2/2004; BPR
370	Murdoch		c1791 / c1821	Kentangaval / ?Harmony	?Sydney / Big Pond	H: 836; F: 295, 317, 326, 361	EBPR; VM
371	Neil	Donald	1802	Barra / ?Hector	?Pictou / Coopers Pond	S: 208, 313; B: 287, 292, 311, 323, 353, 384	MCI, 98; SRE, 83; ACIH, 465
372	Neil 'Ur'	Neil	?1817	Crubisdale	Barra Glen	B: 339	MCI, 95
373	Neil	John	<1817	Barra	Highland Hill	S: 342, 401; B: 303, 315, 324, 379, 385	MCI, 96; BPR
374	Neil	Hector	28/1/1808 / ?1821	Nask	Christmas Island	S: 992; B: 294, 307, 320, 358	VM 24/4/2003, 1/5/2003; BPR
375	Neil	Donald	19/8/1817 / ?1821	Earsary	Washabuck	S: 316, 835; B: 308	VCDR, 1868; BPR
376	Neil		1821	Allasdale / Harmony	Sydney / Christmas Island	H: 1008; F: 284, 309, 321, 380	MCI, 64; BPR; HB, 335, 351
377	Niel	Roderick	<1830	Fuiay	Victoria Co.	S: 128, 383; B: 289, 297, 331, 333, 366	VCDR, 23/4/68; BPR
378	Peter	John	2/6/1821 / 1821	Alt Easdal / ?Harmony	?Sydney / Beaver Cove	S: 343, 801; B: 325, 329, 344, 345, 359, 382	MCI, 90; DW2, 6542; BPR
379	Rachel	John	<1817	Barra	Rear MacKinnon's Harbour	D: 342, 401; Z: 303, 315, 324, 373, 385	MCI, 96; BPR
380	Rachel	Neil	3/3/1814 / 1821	Allasdale / Harmony	Sydney / Christmas Island	D: 376, 1008; Z: 284, 309, 321	MCI, 64; BPR; HB, 335, 351
381	Roderick		1773 / 1790	Barra / Queen	Charlottetown / PEI, Grand River W, Lot 14		SPE, 33; DW2, 6577; RG 20/2/1849
382	Roderick	John	22/11/1806 / 1821	Nask / ?Harmony	?Sydney / Beaver Cove	S: 343, 801; B: 325, 329, 344, 345, 359, 378	MCI, 90; DW2, 6542; BPR
383	Roderick	Donald	<1830	Allasdale	Victoria Co.	H: 128; F: 289, 297, 331, 333, 366, 377	VCDR, 23/4/68; BPR

MACKINNON

ID	Name	Father	D.o.B	D.o.E	Origin / Ship	Port of Arrival / Destination	Relations	References
384	Rory	Donald	1802		Barra / ?Hector	?Pictou / MacKinnon's Harbour	S: 208, 313; B: 287, 292, 311, 323, 353, 371	MCI, 98; SRE, 83; ACIH, 465
385	Rory	John		<1817	Barra	Highland Hill	S: 342, 401; B: 303, 315, 324, 373, 379	MCI, 96; BPR

MACLEAN

ID	Name	Father	D.o.B	D.o.E	Origin / Ship	Port of Arrival / Destination	Relations	References
386	Alex	Malcolm		<1816	Caolis	Middle Cape	B: 394, 397, 400, 412, 421, 440, 452, 464	MCI, 103; CM
387	Alex	Roderick	1817		Barra / ?William Tell	?Sydney	S: 460, 1007; B: 402, 422, 433, 441	HB, 375; CBLP, 2219; SICB, 175; BPR
388	Alex	Hector	?1818		Borve	Little Mabou	H: 830; B: 409, 431, 434	MP, 727; HIC, 276
389	Alexander		1768	1818	Barra / Dunlop	Pictou / S Wycoccough	H: 357; F: 423	HIC, 462; DW2, 6680; TPC, 10/2/1992
390	Alexander			>1822	Vaslain	Red Islands	H: 363; F: 395, 410, 425, 428, 435, 445, 456	MCI, 101; BPR
391	Alexander	Lachlan			Barra	Washabuck	S: 432, 990; B: 419, 436, 447, 448, 453, 458, 461	SCP, 15; ACIH, 487-8
392	Allan	Donald	12/3/1816		Glen	Washabuck	H: 248; B: 443, 455	BPR; MCI, 64; CCB, 1871
393	Angus	Ian	c1821		Barra	Boisdale	H: 360; F: 404, 415, 417, 418, 424, 442	HB, 379-80; BPR
394	Ann	Malcolm	19/3/1809	<1816	Caolis	Middle Cape	Z: 386, 397, 400, 412, 421, 440, 452, 464	MCI, 103; CM
395	Ann	Alexander	9/1/1814	>1822	Vaslain	Red Islands	D: 363, 390; Z: 410, 425, 428, 435, 445, 456	MCI, 101; BPR
396	Anna	Angus	?1821		?Glen	Beaver Cove	Z: 399, 444	HB, 313
397	Archibald	Malcolm		<1816	Caolis	Benacadie Glen	B: 386, 394, 400, 412, 421, 440, 452, 464	MCI, 103
398	Archibald				Barra	Iona	F: 413, 429, 450, 457, 459, 462	ACIH, 526
399	Catherine	Angus		<1807	Eriskay	Washabuck	W: 877; M: 730; Z: 396, 444	MCI, 135; BPR
400	Catherine	Malcolm	31/5/1816	<1816	Caolis	Middle Cape	Z: 386, 394, 397, 412, 421, 440, 452, 464	MCI, 103; CM

MACLEAN

ID	Name	Father	D.o.B D.o.E	Origin Ship	Port of Arrival Destination	Relations	References
401	Catherine		<1817	Vatersay	Rear MacKinnon's Harbour	W: 342; M: 303, 315, 324, 373, 379, 385	MCI, 96; BPR
402	Catherine	Roderick	15/5/1807 1817	Kilbar ?William Tell	?Sydney Barrachois	D: 460, 1007; Z: 387, 422, 433, 441	HB, 375; CBLP, 2219; SICB, 175; BPR
403	Catherine	Neil	29/5/1816 1819	Earsary	Washabuck	D: 453, 532; Z: 449	ACIH, 487-8; BPR
404	Catherine	Angus	15/3/1810 c1821	Kyles	Boisdale	D: 360, 393; Z: 415, 417, 418, 424, 442	HB, 379-80; BPR
405	Catherine	Neil	3/11/1819 1821	Craigston Harmony	Sydney Shenacadie	D: 454, 987	MCI, 64, 105; BPR
406	Catherine		1828	Earsary		W: 107; M: 110	NMD 13/7/28; BPR
407	Catherine	Jonathan	c1846 1851	?Bruernish Admiral	Quebec Ontario	D: 430, 804; Z: 416, 426	BUCHANAN, 1942, 36-7; BPR
408	Catherine	Donald	1786	Earsary	Baddeck	M: 420	VCDR, 1869; BPR
409	Charles 'Gobha'	Hector	?1817-18	Barra	Washabuck Bridge	B: 388, 431, 434	MP, 727; CBLP, 2768
410	Christie	Alexander	>1822	Barra	Red Islands	D: 363, 390; Z: 395, 425, 428, 435, 445, 456	MCI, 101; BPR
411	Christina		<1811	Hellisay	Christmas Island	W: 785; M: 559, 878	MCI, 141; BPR; MG, 3/3/2003
412	Christy	Malcolm	<1816	Caolis	Middle Cape	Z: 386, 394, 397, 400, 421, 440, 452, 464	MCI, 103; CM
413	Dan	Archibald		Barra	MacKinnon's Harbour	S: 398; B: 429, 450, 457, 459, 462	ACIH, 526
414	Donald	Hugh	c1790	Barra	Cape George, NS		HCA, 312; MHA, 121; NSLP, 1809
415	Donald	Angus	17/2/1815 c1821	Gortien	Boisdale	S: 360, 393; B: 404, 417, 418, 424, 442	HB, 379-80; BPR
416	Donald	Jonathan	13/1/1849 1851	Bruernish Admiral	Quebec Ontario	S: 430, 804; B: 407, 426	BUCHANAN, 1942, 36-7; BPR
417	Hector	Angus	15/12/1813 c1821	Kyles	Boisdale	S: 360, 393; B: 404, 415, 418, 424, 442	HB, 379-80; BPR
418	Hector	Angus	20/1/1818 c1821	Gortien	Boisdale	S: 360, 393; B: 404, 415, 417, 424, 442	HB, 379-80; BPR

MACLEAN

ID	Name	Father	D.o.B / D.o.E	Origin / Ship	Port of Arrival / Destination	Relations	References
419	Jan	Lachlan		Barra	George River	D: 432, 990, Z: 391, 436, 447, 448, 453, 458, 461	SCP, 15; ACIH, 487-8
420	Jane		27/2/1827	Earsary	Baddeck	D: 408	VCDR, 1869; BPR
421	John	Malcolm	<1816	Caolis	Middle Cape	B: 386, 394, 397, 400, 412, 440, 452, 464	MCI, 103; CM
422	John	Roderick	2/7/1813	Kilbar ?William Tell	?Sydney Barrachois	S: 460, 1007; B: 387, 402, 433, 441	HB, 375; CBLP, 2219; SICB, 175; BPR
423	John	Alexander	1818	Barra Dunlop	Pictou Inverness Co.	S: 357, 389	HIC, 462; DW2, 6680; TPC, 10/2/1992
424	John	Angus	c1821	Gortien	Boisdale	S: 360, 393; B: 404, 415, 417, 418, 442	HB, 379-80; BPR
425	John	Alexander	>1822	Barra	Red Islands	S: 363, 390; B: 395, 410, 428, 435, 445, 456	MCI, 101; BPR
426	John	Jonathan	24/9/1836 1851	Bruernish Admiral	Quebec Ontario	S: 430, 804; B: 407, 416	BUCHANAN, 1942, 36-7; BPR
427	John		1794	Barra	Iona		IONA CEM, 1880
428	Johnnathan	Alexander	>1822	Barra	Red Islands	S: 363, 390; B: 395, 410, 425, 435, 445, 456	MCI, 101; BPR
429	Johnnathan	Archibald		Barra	Iona	S: 398; B: 413, 450, 457, 459, 462	ACIH, 526
430	Jonathan	Roderick	2/7/1813 1851	Kilbar Admiral	Quebec Ontario	H: 804; F: 407, 416, 426	BUCHANAN, 1942, 36-7; BPR
431	Kate	Hector	?1817-18	Barra	Washabuck	Z: 388, 409, 434	ACIH, 525
432	Lachlan		1728	Barra	Washabuck	H: 990; F: 391, 419, 436, 447, 448, 453, 458, 461	SCP, 15; ACIH, 487-8
433	Lucy	Roderick	1817	Barra ?William Tell	?Sydney	D: 460, 1007; Z: 387, 402, 422, 441	HB, 375; CBLP, 2219; SICB, 175; BPR
434	Malcolm	Hector	?1779 c1818	?Borve	Mabou Harbour	B: 388, 409, 431	MP, 727; VCDR, 1866
435	Malcolm	Alexander	>1822	Barra	Christmas Island	S: 363, 390; B: 395, 410, 425, 428, 445, 456	MCI, 101; BPR
436	Malcolm	Lachlan		Barra	Washabuck	S: 432, 990; B: 391, 419, 447, 448, 453, 458, 461	SCP, 15; ACIH, 487-8

MACLEAN

ID	Name	Father	D.o.B D.o.E	Origin Ship	Port of Arrival Destination	Relations	References
437	Margaret		>1826	Tangusdale	S Boularderie	W: 121; M: 130, 137, 155, 168, 170, 172	HB, 230; CBLP, 3132; DW2, 4777
438	Margaret		1826	Brevig	S Shore, Boularderie		HB, 230; CBLP, 3123; SICB, 50
439	Marion (Sarah)	Hector	c1790-95	Borve Harmony	?Sydney Washabuck	W: 263; M: 248, 270, 273, 275	MCI, 64; BPR
440	Mary	Malcolm	<1816	Caolis	Middle Cape	Z: 386, 394, 397, 400, 412, 421, 452, 464	MCI, 103; CM
441	Mary	Roderick	12/4/1815 1817	Kilbar ?William Tell	?Sydney Barrachois	D: 460, 1007; Z: 387, 402, 422, 433	HB, 375; CBLP, 2219; SICB, 175; BPR
442	Mary	Angus	28/11/1807 c1821	Kyles	Boisdale	D: 360, 393; Z: 404, 415, 417, 418, 424	HB, 379-80; BPR
443	Mary	Donald	c1804 ?1821	?Kentangaval	Grand Narrows	Z: 392, 455	CCB, BC pers comm
444	Mary	Angus	1821	Earsary Harmony	?Sydney	W: 1000; M: 984, 989, 991, 998, 999, 1009; Z: 396, 399	BPR; MCI, 197
445	Mary	Alexander	>1822	Barra	Red Islands	D: 363, 390; Z: 395, 410, 425, 428, 435, 456	MCI, 101; BPR
446	Mary		<1830	Barra	Washabuck	W: 890	ACIH, 115
447	Mary 'Mhor'	Lachlan		Barra	Washabuck	D: 432, 990; Z: 391, 419, 436, 448, 453, 458, 461	SCP, 15; ACIH, 487-8
448	Mary 'Og'	Lachlan		Barra	Margaree	D: 432, 990; Z: 391, 419, 436, 447, 453, 458, 461	SCP, 15; ACIH, 487-8
449	Michael	Neil	2/1/1814 1819	Nask	Washabuck	S: 453, 532; B: 403	ACIH, 487-8; BPR
450	Michael	Archibald		Barra	Iona	S: 398; B: 413, 429, 457, 459, 462	ACIH, 526
451	Mildred		1813	Barra	Lower Washabuck		IONA CEM, 1889
452	Neil	Malcolm	<1816	Caolis	Middle Cape	B: 386, 394, 397, 400, 412, 421, 440, 464	MCI, 103; CM
453	Neil	Lachlan	1819	Barra	Washabuck	H: 532; F: 403, 449; S: 432, 990; B: 391, 419, 436, 447, 448, 458, 461	ACIH, 487-8; BPR

MACLEAN

ID	Name	Father	D.o.B / D.o.E	Origin / Ship	Port of Arrival / Destination	Relations	References
454	Neil	Rory	1821	Craigston / Harmony	Sydney / Shenacadie	H: 987; F: 405	MCI, 64, 105; BPR
455	Neil	Donald	c1809 ?1821	?Kentangaval	Baddeck	B: 392, 443	CBCD; BC pers comm
456	Neil	Alexander	>1822	Barra	Red Islands	S: 363, 390; B: 395, 410, 425, 428, 435, 445	MCI, 101; BPR
457	Neil	Archibald		Barra	Iona	S: 398; B: 413, 429, 450, 459, 462	ACIH, 526
458	Peter	Lachlan		Barra	Washabuck	S: 432, 990; B: 391, 419, 436, 447, 448, 453, 461	SCP, 15; ACIH, 487-8
459	Peter	Archibald		Barra	Iona	S: 398; B: 413, 429, 450, 457, 462	ACIH, 526
460	Roderick		c1779 1817	Kilbar / ?William Tell	?Sydney / Barrachois	H: 1007; F: 387, 402, 422, 433, 441	HB, 375; CBLP, 2219; SICB, 175; BPR
461	Roderick	Lachlan		Barra	Washabuck	S: 432, 990; B: 391, 419, 436, 447, 448, 453, 458	SCP, 15; ACIH, 487-8
462	Rory	Archibald	17/8/1790	Barra	Rear Ottawa Brook	S: 398; B: 413, 429, 450, 457, 459	ACIH, 526
463	Rory			Barra	MacKinnon's Harbour		VCDR, 1869
464	Sarah	Malcolm	<1816	Caolis	Middle Cape	Z: 386, 394, 397, 400, 412, 421, 440, 452	MCI, 103; CM
465	Sarah	Donald	<1824	Berneray	Rear Christmas Island	W: 1004; M: 995, 997, 1001, 1002, 1010	MCI, 196; BPR

MACLELLAN

ID	Name	Father	D.o.B / D.o.E	Origin / Ship	Port of Arrival / Destination	Relations	References
466	Donald		1790	Barra / Queen	Charlottetown / PEI, Grand River W, Lot 14		PAPEI, 2353, 24-5
467	John		1790	Barra / Queen	Charlottetown / PEI, Grand River W, Lot 14		PAPEI, 2353, 24-5

MACLEOD

ID	Name	Father	D.o.B / D.o.E	Origin / Ship	Port of Arrival / Destination	Relations	References
468	Ann					W: 645	ACIH, 164
469	Donald	Roderick		Barra	Iona	S: 473, 474; B: 470, 471	MCI, 109

MACLEOD

ID	Name	Father	D.o.B D.o.E	Origin Ship	Port of Arrival Destination	Relations	References
470	John	Roderick		Barra		S: 473, 474; B: 469, 471	MCI, 109
471	Malcolm	Roderick		Barra		S: 473, 474; B: 469, 470	MCI, 109
472	Ms ?	John	c1807	Barra	Georgeville, NS		AHM, D003.015
473	Roderick			Barra	Grand Narrows	H: 474; F: 469, 470, 471	MCI, 109

MACLEOD*

ID	Name	Father	D.o.B D.o.E	Origin Ship	Port of Arrival Destination	Relations	References
474	Sarah			Barra	Grand Narrows	W: 473; M: 469, 470, 471	MCI, 109

MACMILLAN

ID	Name	Father	D.o.B D.o.E	Origin Ship	Port of Arrival Destination	Relations	References
475	Ann		1817	Craigston ?William Tell	?Sydney Mabou	W: 737; M: 825	MNB, 206; SICB, 183; CCB, 152; DW, 7522; BPR
476	Ann	John	2/2/1819 c1836	Craigston	Rear Beaver Cove	D: 332, 484; Z: 479, 482, 485, 486, 488, 489, 490	MCI, 111; BPR
477	Anne		?1818	Kilbar	SE Mabou	W: 677; M: 545, 569, 682, 742, 829, 970, 982	DW, 8887; MP, 770; HIC, 557
478	Catherine		1835	Bruernish	Rear Beaver Cove	W: 1026; M: 1039	HB, 571; SRE, 69; BPR; CM
479	Catherine	John	1/12/1812 c1836	Bruernish	Rear Beaver Cove	D: 332, 484; Z: 476, 482, 485, 486, 488, 489, 490	MCI, 111; BPR
480	Christian	Hugh	1821	Bruernish Harmony	Sydney Shenacadie	W: 44	HB, 86; CBLP, 1822; CM; BPR
481	Emily		1821	Kilbar	Mabou	M: 123, 126, 129, 150, 151, 157, 161, 167, 174	MP, 414
482	Ewan	John	15/2/1815 c1836	Craigston	Rear Beaver Cove	S: 332, 484; B: 476, 479, 485, 486, 488, 489, 490	MCI, 111; BPR
483	John		1772	Barra Alexander	Charlottetown PEI, Indian River		PAPEI, 2664, 148, 156; ISLAND, 29, 34-9
484	John		c1836	Craigston	Rear Beaver Cove	H: 332; F: 476, 479, 482, 485, 486, 488, 489, 490	MCI, 111; BPR
485	John	John	12/6/1822 c1836	Craigston	Rear Beaver Cove	S: 332, 484; B: 476, 479, 482, 486, 488, 489, 490	MCI, 111; BPR

MACMILLAN

ID	Name	Father	D.o.B / D.o.E	Origin / Ship	Port of Arrival / Destination	Relations	References
486	Malcolm	John	28/5/1820 / c1836	Craigston /	/ Rear Beaver Cove	S: 332, 484; B: 476, 479, 482, 485, 488, 489, 490	MCI, 111; BPR
487	Mary		1851 /	Glen / Admiral	Quebec / Stephen, Ontario	W: 758; M: 582, 658, 759, 815, 911, 939	SC, 1851; OC, 1861e, 71; BPR
488	Roderick	John	16/2/1825 / c1836	Craigston /	/ Rear Beaver Cove	S: 332, 484; B: 476, 479, 482, 485, 486, 489, 490	MCI, 111; BPR
489	William	John	30/8/1817 / c1836	Craigston /	/ Rear Beaver Cove	S: 332, 484; B: 476, 479, 482, 485, 486, 488, 490	MCI, 111; BPR
490	William	John	28/2/1828 / c1836	Flodday /	/ Rear Beaver Cove	S: 332, 484; B: 476, 479, 482, 485, 486, 488, 489	MCI, 111; BPR

MACNEIL

ID	Name	Father	D.o.B / D.o.E	Origin / Ship	Port of Arrival / Destination	Relations	References
491	Alasdair 'Mor'		1821 /	Barra / Harmony	Sydney / Gillis Point	H: 571; F: 510, 512, 654, 763, 807, 862, 898, 918, 975	ACIH, 129
492	Alasdair		c1821 /	Barra / ?Harmony	?Sydney / Boisdale		HB, 486
493	Alex	Donald	1802 /	Barra / ?Hector	?Pictou / Shenacadie	S: 610, 820; B: 515, 597, 720, 772, 819, 909, 952	MCI, 192
494	Alex		1802 /	Barra / ?Hector	Pictou / Mabou	H: 976; F: 495, 544, 546, 644, 777, 780, 849, 864, 900, 942	DW, 8852; MP, 766
495	Alex	Alex	1802 /	Barra / ?Hector	Pictou / Mabou	S: 494; B: 544, 546, 644, 777, 780, 849, 864, 900, 942	DW, 8852; MP, 766
496	Alex 'Sergeant'		c1778 / 1808	Kilbar /	/ Mabou	H: 62; F: 586, 648, 703, 765, 808, 971	DW, 8855; MP, 767; HIC, 557; CBC, 1818; BPR
497	Alex		>1811 /	Barra /	/ Mabou		HIC, 610
498	Alex		1787 / 1817	Brevig / ?William Tell	?Sydney / Goose Pond	H: 564; F: 893, 917	DW2, 7486; MNB, 206; SICB, 182; CBLP, 1817,1752
499	Alex 'K'		c1820 /	Barra /	/ PEI		AR, 8, ii, 45
500	Alex	Rory	5/8/1821 / 1822	Mingulay /	?Sydney / Boisdale	S: 15, 959	HB, 481; BPR
501	Alex	Rory	20/12/1809 / >1822	Vatersay /	/ Rear Iona	S: 362, 960; B: 536, 576, 630, 747, 788, 839, 885, 906, 974	ACIH, 194-216; BPR

MACNEIL

ID	Name	Father	D.o.B / D.o.E	Origin / Ship	Port of Arrival / Destination	Relations	References
502	Alex	Angus	24/10/1819 / >1824	Vaslain	S Little Bras d'Or	S: 517, 595	DW2, 7489; SICB, 182; BPR
503	Alexander	John B	c1791 / 1794-1801	Barra	Red Islands	S: 590, 771; B: 714	VM
504	Alexander	Rory	c1794 / >1801	Barra	Big Pond	S: 947, B: 523, 601, 607, 719, 836, 948	BPR; EBPR; VM
505	Alexander	Barra	1813	Barra	Christmas Island	S: 549, 969; B: 562, 623, 693, 734, 853, 854, 879, 910	ACIH, 29
506	Alexander	Malcolm	c1790 / ?1817	Hellisay	S Little Bras d'Or		VM 24/4/2003; ?CBLP, 2219
507	Alexander	Neil	c1787 / 1817	Brevig	?Sydney / Barra Straits	H: 568; F: 883, 915	BPR; CBLP, 2229
508	Alexander	Rory	19/6/1815 / 1821-22	Kentangaval / ?William Tell	Shenacadie	S: 957, 1015; B: 628, 629, 832, 869, 958	MCI, 178; BSGN; BPR
509	Alexander	Charles	c1797 / 1821	Borve		S: 837; B: 535, 572, 573, 594, 698, 745	BPR; CNS, 1871; CBCD; NAS, CS44, Bx446; VM
510	Alexander 'Jnr'	Alasdair		Barra	Gillis Point	S: 491, 571; B: 512, 654, 763, 807, 862, 898, 918, 975	ACIH, 129
511	Allan 'Og'		?1821-22	Cueir / ?Harmony	?Sydney / Boisdale	H: 916; F: 574, 920, 959	HB, 481; BPR
512	Allan	Alasdair		Barra	Gillis Point	S: 491, 571; B: 510, 654, 763, 807, 862, 898, 918, 975	ACIH, 129
513	Angus		1772	Barra / Alexander	Charlottetown / PEI, Indian River		PAPEI, 2664, 156; ISLAND, 29, 34-9
514	Angus		1802	Hector	Pictou / Christmas Island		MCI, 155
515	Angus	Donald	1802	Barra / ?Hector	?Pictou	S: 610, 820; B: 493, 597, 720, 772, 819, 909, 952	MCI, 192
516	Angus	Malcolm	c1786 / ?1817	Hellisay	Benacadie E / Benacadie	H: 1024; F: 812, 826; B: 566, 696, 903	VM 4/4/2003; BPR; CBLP, 1753
517	Angus		<1824	Vaslain	S Little Bras d'Or	H: 595; F: 502	DW2, 7489; SICB, 182; BPR
518	Angus	Roderick	1797-98 / 1824	Barra	Little Bras d'Or	S: 932	SICB; CBLP, 3258
519	Angus	Donald	23/4/1821 / >1826	Vaslain	Rear Goose Pond	S: 178, 635; B: 751, 813	CBLP, 3145; BPR

MACNEIL

ID	Name	Father	D.o.B D.o.E	Origin Ship	Port of Arrival Destination	Relations	References
520	Angus	Peter	2/4/1826 >1830	Pabbay	Rear Big Beach	S: 578, 912; B: 699, 891	MCI, 171; BPR
521	Angus	Donald		Barra	Cape George, NS	S: 642; B: 541, 585, 643, 680, 764, 863, 899	DW 8866; HCA, 333
522	Ann		1790	Barra Queen	Charlottetown PEI, Grand River W	W: 50; M: 76	PAPEI, 2353, 24-25; DW3, 574; WMGN
523	Ann	Rory	>1801	?Barra		D: 947; Z: 504, 601, 607, 719, 836, 948	BPR; EBPR; VM
524	Ann		1802	Barra ?Hector	?Pictou Coopers Pond	W: 874	MCI, 161
525	Ann		1802	Barra ?Hector	Pictou Christmas Island	W: 950	MCI, 163-4
526	Ann	James	1802	Barra ?Hector	?Pictou Big Beach	D: 555, 690; Z: 616, 721, 822, 904	MCI, 173
527	Ann	Hector	1802	Barra Hector	Pictou Piper's Cove	D: 670; Z: 557, 617, 722, 784, 796, 953	HB, 474; MCI, 114; BCB
528	Ann		?1817-21	Brevig	Rear Boisdale	W: 779; M: 570, 744, 776, 859	HB, 501; BPR
529	Ann	James	18/12/1815 1817	Borve William Tell	Pictou Nova Scotia	D: 695, 1016	NSGP, 7,7; BPR; DW, 7514
530	Ann	Malcolm	c1788 c1817	Hellisay		W: 227; M: 205, 209, 211, 217, 222	MCI, 57; VM, 7/4/2003; BPR
531	Ann	Neil	1819	Earsary Ann	Sydney Washabuck		ACIH, 487, 488; BPR
532	Ann	Neil	1819	Earsary Ann	Sydney Washabuck	W: 453; M: 403, 449	ACIH, 487-8; BPR
533	Ann		8/11/1820 ?1821	Brevig	Iona	D: 20; Z: 678, 697	VM,
534	Ann		c1821-22	Cliad	Boisdale	W: 1035; M: 1029, 1032, 1033, 1036, 1041, 1043, 1044	HB, 574; BPR
535	Ann	Charles	13/3/1807 1821	Borve		D: 837; Z: 509, 572, 573, 594, 698, 745	BPR; CNS, 1871; CBCD; NAS, CS44, Bx446; VM
536	Ann	Rory	25/1/1806 >1822	Vatersay	Rear Iona	D: 362, 960; Z: 501, 576, 630, 747, 788, 839, 885, 906, 974	ACIH, 194-216; BPR

MACNEIL

ID	Name	Father	D.o.B D.o.E	Origin Ship	Port of Arrival Destination	Relations	References
537	Ann	Neil	c1784 1824	Greian	Cape Breton	D: 35; Z: 632, 789, 840, 933	CBLP, 1824; BPR
538	Ann		6/9/1815 >1824	Greian	Shenacadie	D: 577; Z: 633, 790, 841, 934	CBLP, 3073; BPR
539	Ann		1787-88	Barra	Georgeville, NS		AHM, D001.45
540	Ann	Roderick		Berneray	Benacadie	W: 966	MCI, 179; BPR
541	Ann	Donald		Barra	Cape George, NS	D: 642; Z: 521, 585, 643, 680, 764, 863, 899	DW 8866; HCA,333
542	Ann	James	10/2/1818	Mingulay	Big Pond	D: 705, 809; Z: 588, 651, 707, 770, 901, 943	ACIH, 115; BPR; CNS, 1871; VM, 29/4/2004
543	Ann*		<1827	Barra	Red Islands	W: 887; M: 888	CNS, 1871; RCM; RCML; VM
544	Anne	Alex 1802		Barra	Pictou Mabou	D: 494; Z: 495, 546, 644, 777, 780, 849, 864, 900, 942	DW, 8852; MP, 766
545	Anne	Hector ?1818		?Hector ?Barra	Mabou	D: 477, 677; Z: 569, 682, 742, 829, 970, 982	DW, 8887; MP, 770; HIC, 557
546	Anne	Alex		Barra	Mabou	D: 494, 976; Z: 495, 544, 644, 777, 780, 849, 864, 900, 942	DW, 8852; MP, 766
547	Annie	Rory 1813		Barra	Barra Glen	D: 349, 954; Z: 561, 622, 686, 733, 787, 823, 955, 973, 978	ACIH, 1
548	Anthony	Roderick		Kilbar	Boisdale	B: 641, 967, 980	HB, 515
549	Barra	Donald 'Og'	>1759 1813	Barra	Rear Big Beach	H: 969; F: 505, 562, 623, 693, 734, 853, 854, 879, 910	ACIH, 29
550	Barra		c1776 1816-26	Sandray	Little Bras d'Or	H: 811; F: 563, 624, 694	CBLP, 3185; BPR
551	Catherine		1791	Barra	Pictou Morristown, NS	W: 14	HB, 58-59
552	Catherine		?1802	Barra Hector	Big Beach	D: 817; Z: 608, 656, 689, 818	MCI, 164
553	Catherine	Roderick 1802	1780's	Brevig Hector	Pictou PEI, Vernon River	D: 923; Z: 667, 778, 795, 922	AR, 9, i, 1-20

MACNEIL

ID	Name	Father	D.o.B / D.o.E	Origin / Ship	Port of Arrival / Destination	Relations	References
554	Catherine		1802	?Brevig / ?Hector	?Pictou / PEI		WMGN
555	Catherine	Philip	1802	Barra / ?Hector	?Pictou / Big Beach	W: 690; M: 526, 616, 721, 822, 904	MCI, 173
556	Catherine		1802	Barra / ?Hector	?Pictou	W: 667	AR, 9
557	Catherine	Hector	1802	Barra / Hector	Pictou / Piper's Cove	D: 670; Z: 527, 617, 722, 784, 796, 953	HB, 474; MCI, 114; BCB
558	Catherine	Hector	c1796 / ?1802	Barra / ?Hector	?Pictou / Grand Narrows	D: 197, 671; Z: 657, 691	MCI, 44; VM 12/10/2004
559	Catherine	Malcolm	24/12/1807 / <1811	Hellisay	Christmas Island	D: 411, 785; Z: 878	MCI, 141; MG, 3/3/2003; BPR
560	Catherine		?1811	Barra	St Columba	W: 147	ACIH, 356, 365; HIC, 613
561	Catherine	Rory	1813	Barra	Barra Glen	D: 349, 954; Z: 547, 622, 686, 733, 787, 823, 955, 973, 978	ACIH, 1
562	Catherine	Barra	1813	Barra	Big Beach	D: 549, 969; Z: 505, 623, 693, 734, 853, 854, 879, 910	ACIH, 29
563	Catherine	Barra	5/2/1816 / 1816-26	Sandray	Goose Island	D: 550, 811; Z: 624, 694	CBLP, 3145; BPR
564	Catherine		1817	Brevig / ?William Tell	?Sydney / Goose Pond	W: 498; M: 893, 917	DW2, 7486; SICB, 182; CBLP, 1752; BPR
565	Catherine	Murdoch	24/2/1817 / 1817	Rulios / ?William Tell	?Sydney / Red Island	D: 281, 867; Z: 688	CBLP, 1754; BPR
566	Catherine	Malcolm	24/12/1807 / ?1817	Hellisay	Cape Breton	Z: 516, 696, 903	VM 7/4/2003
567	Catherine	Donald	5/5/1813 / 1817	?Borve / ?William Tell	?Sydney / Bras d'Or	D: 304, 627; Z: 661, 676, 882	CBLP, 2008; BPR
568	Catherine	Allan	1817	Cueir / ?William Tell	?Sydney / Barra Straits	W: 507; M: 883, 915	BPR; CBLP, 2229
569	Catherine	Hector	?1818	?Barra	Mabou	D: 477, 677; Z: 545, 682, 742, 829, 970, 982	DW, 8887; MP, 770; HIC, 557
570	Catherine	Lachlan	4/6/1817 / ?1821	Brevig	Rear Boisdale	D: 528, 779; Z: 744, 776, 859	HB, 501; BPR

MACNEIL

ID	Name	Father	D.o.B D.o.E	Origin Ship	Port of Arrival Destination	Relations	References
571	Catherine			Barra	Sydney Gillis Point	W: 491; M: 510, 512, 654, 763, 807, 862, 898, 918, 975	ACIH, 129
572	Catherine	Charles	c1801 1821	Harmony		D: 837; Z: 509, 535, 573, 594, 698, 745	BPR; CNS, 1871; CBCD; NAS, CS44, Bx446; VM
573	Catherine	Charles	c1809 1821	Borve		D: 837; Z: 509, 535, 572, 594, 698, 745	BPR; CNS, 1871; CBCD; NAS, CS44, Bx446; VM
574	Catherine	Allan	1822	Barra	Boisdale	D: 511, 916; Z: 920, 959	HB, 481; BPR
575	Catherine	Jonathan	17/8/1818 1822	Pabbay	Piper's Cove	D: 773, 994; Z: 746, 838	MCI, 162; BPR
576	Catherine	Rory	>1822	Barra	Beaver Cove	D: 362, 960; Z: 501, 536, 630, 747, 788, 839, 885, 906, 974	ACIH, 194-216; BPR
577	Catherine	?Gillis	c1784 >1824	Greian	Shenacadie	M: 538, 633, 790, 841, 934	CBLP, 3073; BPR
578	Catherine	Michael	c1826-30	Sandray	Rear Big Beach	W: 912; M: 520, 699, 891	MCI, 171; BPR
579	Catherine		1826	Berneray	Boularderie	W: 156; M: 115, 135, 173	HB, 230; CBLP, 3123; SICB, 153
580	Catherine	Roderick	24/7/1818 <1827	Bruernish	Big Pond	D: 219, 936; Z: 660, 802, 814, 842, 886	ACIH, 115; BPR; CNS, 1871; VM, 29/4/2004
581	Catherine		?1850-51	Allasdale ?Admiral	?Quebec Red Islands	W: 84; M: 80, 81, 85, 89, 91, 97	VM, 25/4/03; BPR
582	Catherine	John	22/8/1844 1851	Glen Admiral	Quebec Stephen, Ontario	D: 487, 758; Z: 658, 759, 815, 911, 939	SC, 1851; OC, 1861e, 71; BPR
583	Catherine			Barra	Christmas Island	Z: 640, 663, 762	ACIH, 164
584	Catherine	James	c1845	Barra	Boularderie		DW3, 1204
585	Catherine	Donald		Barra	Cape George, NS	D: 642; Z: 521, 541, 643, 680, 764, 863, 899	DW 8866; HCA, 333
586	Catherine	Alex		Barra	Mabou	D: 62, 496; Z: 648, 703, 765, 808, 971	DW, 8855; MP, 767; HIC, 557; CBC, 1818; BPR
587	Catherine	Rory 'Red'		Sandray	Boisdale	W: 1011; M: 985, 988	VM, 1/5/2003; BPR

MACNEIL

ID	Name	Father	D.o.B / D.o.E	Origin / Ship	Port of Arrival / Destination	Relations	References
588	Catherine	James	29/7/1814	Mingulay	Big Pond	D: 705, 809; Z: 542, 651, 707, 770, 901, 943	ACIH, 115; BPR; CNS, 1871; VM, 29/4/2004
589	Catherine	John 'Dubh'	c1793	Barra	Grand Narrows	W: 182	CBCD, 1873; MCI, 44
590	Catherine*		1794–1801	Barra	Red Islands	W: 771; M: 503, 714	VM
591	Charles	Donald	1817	Barra / ?William Tell	?Sydney / Mabou	S: 625; B: 673, 741, 868, 914, 956	MCI, 137; ACIH, 286
592	Christian		c1817	Glen	Castle Bay	W: 224; M: 210, 213	MCI, 57; BPR
593	Christian	Roderick, Jnr	<1821	Berneray	Cape Breton	W: 17	BPR; VM
594	Christian	Charles	1821	Borve		D: 837; Z: 509, 535, 572, 573, 698, 745	BPR; CNS, 1871; CBCD; NAS, CS44, Bx446; VM
595	Christian		>1824	Vaslain	S Little Bras d'Or	W: 517; M: 502	DW2, 7489; SICB, 182; BPR
596	Christian	John	28/10/1820	Mingulay	Irish Cove	D: 769, 993; Z: 650, 659, 774, 851, 908, 979	BPR; NCTC; VM, 29/4/2004
597	Christie	Donald	1802	Barra / ?Hector	?Pictou / Christmas Island	D: 610, 820; Z: 493, 515, 720, 772, 819, 909, 952	MCI, 192
598	Christie		?1766 / >1809	Sandray	Benacadie Pond	M: 620	CBLP, 2491
599	Christie	Murdoch	1821	Barra / Harmony	Sydney / Gillis Point		ACIM, 24
600	Christie	Rory	c1773 / ?1821	Barra	Christmas Island	W: 251; M: 243, 252, 254, 256, 258, 265, 269, 272, 278	MCI, 75; BPR; FHL, 1278878, pg 36, 205
601	Christina	Rory	>1801	?Barra		D: 947; Z: 504, 523, 607, 719, 836, 948	BPR; EBPR; VM
602	Christina	Neil	1802	Barra / Hector	Pictou / Mabou		DW, 8864; MP, 704, 754
603	Donald 'Black'		>1785	Barra	Malignant Cove, NS		MHA, 122
604	Donald		>1785	Barra	Cape George, NS		MHA, 122
605	Donald		>1785	Barra	Malignant Cove, NS		MHA, 122; LLSNS

MACNEIL

ID	Name	Father	D.o.B D.o.E	Origin Ship	Port of Arrival Destination	Relations	References
606	Donald	Rory	1799	Barra	Pictou / Iona	H: 794; F: 946	GALLEY, VI, 25, 15; SCP, 5-6
607	Donald 'Breac'	Rory	>1801	Barra	/ Big Pond	H: 977; S: 947; B: 504, 523, 601, 719, 836, 948	BPR; EBPR; VM
608	Donald		?1802	Barra / Hector	/ Big Beach	S: 817; B: 552, 656, 689, 818	MCI, 164
609	Donald	Rory	?1802	Fuday	/ Beaver Cove	S: 951; B: 685	CM, 2001
610	Donald 'Og'	Rory	1802	Barra / ?Hector	?Pictou / Christmas Island	H: 820; F: 493, 515, 597, 720, 772, 819, 909, 952	MCI, 192
611	Donald		1802	Barra / ?Hector	Pictou / Christmas Island	H: 710	MCI, 165
612	Donald 'Red'		1802	Barra / ?Hector	?Pictou / Grand Narrows		MCI, 150
613	Donald	Donald	?1802	Barra / ?Hector	?Pictou / Christmas Island	H: 821	MCI, 156
614	Donald	Ian	1802	Barra / ?Hector	?Pictou / Grand Narrows	H: 122	MCI, 157; DW2, 7498
615	Donald	Rory	1802	Barra / ?Hector	?Pictou / Jamesville		MCI, 147
616	Donald	James	1802	Barra / ?Hector	?Pictou / Big Beach	S: 555, 690; B: 526, 721, 822, 904	MCI, 173
617	Donald	Hector	1802	Barra / Hector	Pictou / Piper's Cove	S: 670; B: 527, 557, 722, 784, 796, 953	HB, 474; MCI, 114; BCB
618	Donald		>1803	Barra	/ Mabou		SICB, app 182; CBLP, 98
619	Donald 'Jnr'		>1803	Barra	/ N Mabou		SICB, app 182; CBLP, 97
620	Donald		>1809	Barra	/ Benacadie Pond	S: 598	CBLP, 2491
621	Donald	Rory	>?1812	Barra	/ Big Beach		MCI, 172; ?CBGP, 854
622	Donald	Rory	1813	Barra	/ Barra Falls	S: 349, 954; B: 547, 561, 686, 733, 787, 823, 955, 973, 978	ACIH, 1

MACNEIL

ID	Name	Father	D.o.B / D.o.E	Origin / Ship	Port of Arrival / Destination	Relations	References
623	Donald	Barra	1813	Barra	Big Beach	S: 549, 969; B: 505, 562, 693, 734, 853, 854, 879, 910	ACIH, 29
624	Donald	Barra	1816-26	Rulios	Goose Island	S: 550, 811; B: 563, 694	CBLP, 3145; BPR
625	Donald	John 'Piper'	1817	Barra / ?William Tell	?Sydney / Christmas Island	F: 591, 673, 741, 868, 914, 956; B: 670, 877, 949	MCI, 137; ACIH, 286; ?CBLP, 2009
626	Donald	Neil	1817	Barra / ?William Tell	?Sydney / Gillis Point	H: 302	ACIH, 95
627	Donald		1817	?Borve / ?William Tell	?Sydney / Bras d'Or	H: 304; F: 567, 661, 676, 882	CBLP, 2008; BPR
628	Donald	Rory	5/11/1812 / 1821-22	Berneray	Shenacadie	S: 957, 1015; B: 508, 629, 832, 869, 958	MCI, 178; BSGN; BPR
629	Donald	Rory	6/7/1813 / 1821-22	Kentangaval	Shenacadie	S: 957, 1015; B: 508, 628, 832, 869, 958	MCI, 178; BSGN; BPR
630	Donald	Rory	>1822	Barra	Rear Christmas Island	S: 362, 960; B: 501, 536, 576, 747, 788, 839, 885, 906, 974	ACIH, 194-216; BPR
631	Donald 'Farmer'	Rory	1822	Barra	Barra Glen		MCI, 172
632	Donald	Neil	c1784 / 1824	Greian	Cape Breton	S: 35; B: 537, 789, 840, 933	CBLP, 1824; BPR
633	Donald		20/7/1807 / >1824	Greian	Shenacadie	S: 577; B: 538, 790, 841, 934	CBLP, 3073; BPR
634	Donald		c1800 / >1826	Glen	NW Scotch Narrows	H: 364	SICB, app 182; CBLP, 3149
635	Donald	Roderick	>1826	Berneray	Rear Goose Island	H: 178; F: 519, 751, 813	CBLP, 3145; BPR
636	Donald	Ian	>1830	Barra	MacNeil's Vale	H: 6; B: 704, 871, 890, 962	ACIH, 155; BSGN; VM
637	Donald		<1830	Barra	Doctors Brook, NS		DW, 8872; HCA, 327
638	Donald	John	28/3/1842 / 1850-51	Tangusdale / Lord Nelson	Quebec / Brantford, Ontario	S: 756; B: 701, 757, 803, 846, 938	KM, 9/2/2000; BPR
639	Donald	Rory		Barra	Cape Breton	S: 965; B: 702, 761, 848, 897	MCI, 180

MACNEIL

ID	Name	Father	D.o.B D.o.E	Origin Ship	Port of Arrival Destination	Relations	References
640	Donald 'Ban'			Barra	Iona	B: 583, 663, 762	ACIH, 164
641	Donald	Roderick		Kilbar	Boisdale	B: 548, 967, 980	HB, 515
642	Donald 'Og'			?Barra	Cape George, NS	F: 521, 541, 585, 643, 680, 764, 863, 899	DW 8866; HCA,333
643	Donald	Donald		Barra	Cape George, NS	S: 642; B: 521, 541, 585, 680, 764, 863, 899	DW 8866; HCA,333
644	Donald	Alex		Barra	Mabou	S: 494; B: 495, 544, 546, 777, 780, 849, 864, 900, 942	DW, 8552; MP, 766
645	Donald			Barra	Iona	H: 468	ACIH, 164
646	Donald	Hector		Barra	PEI, Cape Traverse		SGSH, 251
647	Donald		c1800	Barra	PEI, Brae, Lot 9		SPEI, Lot 9, Cem 2, Stone 82
648	Donald	Alex		Barra	Mabou	S: 62, 496; B: 586, 703, 765, 808, 971	DW, 8855; MP, 767; HIC, 557; CBC, 1818; BPR
649	Donald	Rory	17/6/1826	Allasdale	Rear Big Pond	S: 184, 968; B: 687, 766, 850	NCTC; BPR; VM, 29/4/2004
650	Donald	John	18/5/1807	Mingulay	Irish Cove	S: 769, 993; B: 596, 659, 774, 851, 908, 979	BPR; NCTC; VM, 29/4/2004
651	Donald	James	31/10/1819	Mingulay	Big Pond	S: 705, 809; B: 542, 588, 707, 770, 901, 943	ACIH, 115; BPR; CNS, 1871; VM, 29/4/2004
652	Duncan		>1826	?Barra	New Campbelltown		RM, 28/6/98
653	Edward		<1821	Sandray	Benacadie Glen	H: 305; F: 800, 810, 834	MCI, 157; BPR
654	Elisabeth	Alasdair		Barra	Gillis Point	D: 491, 571; Z: 510, 512, 763, 807, 862, 898, 918, 975	ACIH, 129
655	Eliza	Malcolm	23/8/1821 1828	Sandray	?Cape Breton	D: 792, 844; Z: 683, 889	NMD, 13/7/1828; BPR
656	Elizabeth		?1802	Barra Hector	Big Beach	D: 817; Z: 552, 608, 689, 818	MCI, 164
657	Elizabeth	Hector	c1800 ?1802	Barra ?Hector	?Pictou Grand Narrows	D: 197, 671; Z: 558, 691	MCI, 44; VM 12/10/2004

MACNEIL

ID	Name	Father	D.o.B D.o.E	Origin Ship	Port of Arrival Destination	Relations	References
658	Elizabeth	John	19/4/1837 1851	Glen Admiral	Quebec Stephen, Ontario	D: 487, 758; Z: 582, 759, 815, 911, 939	SC, 1851; OC, 1861e, 71; BPR
659	Elizabeth	John	16/5/1818	Mingulay	Irish Cove	D: 769, 993; Z: 596, 650, 774, 851, 908, 979	BPR; NCTC; VM, 29/4/2004
660	Ewan	Roderick	3/12/1816 <1827	Bruernish	Big Pond	S: 219, 936; B: 580, 802, 814, 842, 886	ACIH, 115; BPR; CNS, 1871; VM, 29/4/2004
661	Finla	Donald	9/5/1806 1817	?Borve ?William Tell	?Sydney Bras d'Or	S: 304, 627; B: 567, 676, 882	CBLP, 2008; BPR
662	Flora			Barra	Iona	W: 18	ACIH, 164
663	Flora			Barra	Iona	Z: 583, 640, 762	ACIH, 164
664	Frederick		1772	Barra ?Alexander	?Charlottetown PEI, Malpeque		CMH 10/2000
665	George	John	20/1/1819 1828	Hellisay	Irish Cove	S: 350, 752; B: 843, 907	BPR
666	George	John	20/1/1819	Hellisay	Cape North	S: 352, 767; B: 768, 913	BPR; CNS, 1871; VM, 30/4/2004
667	Gilleonan	Roderick	>1780 1802	Brevig ?Hector	?Pictou	H: 556; S: 923; B: 553, 778, 795, 922	AR, 9
668	Hector 'Ban'	Hector 'Og'	c1770 1802	Earsary Hector	Pictou Red Islands	H: 164; F: 669	?CBLP, 946; CCB, 167; CMC, 29, 4, 6-11
669	Hector	Hector	15/9/1795 1802	Earsary Hector	Pictou Red Islands	S: 164, 668	CCB, 167; CMC, 29, 4, 6-11
670	Hector	John 'Piper'	c1763 1802	Barra Hector	Pictou Piper's Cove	F: 527, 557, 617, 722, 784, 796, 953; B: 625, 877, 949	HB, 474; MCI, 114; BCB
671	Hector	James	c1764 ?1802	?Craigston ?Hector	?Pictou Grand Narrows	H: 197; F: 558, 657, 691	MCI, 145; ACIH, 256; CBLP, 518 & 2010; DW3, 120(
672	Hector	Neil	1813	Barra	Gillis Point	H: 797; F: 880	ACIH, 86
673	Hector	Donald	1817	Barra ?William Tell	?Sydney Castle Bay	S: 625; B: 591, 741, 868, 914, 956	MCI, 137; ACIH, 286
674	Hector 'Mhor'		c1781 1817	Kilbar ?William Tell	?Sydney SE Mabou	H: 986; F: 708, 929, 981	CBLP, 2232; CM; BPR
675	Hector	Malcolm	?1817	Hellisay ?William Tell	?Sydney Bras d'Or		VM, 7/4/2003

MACNEIL

ID	Name	Father	D.o.B D.o.E	Origin Ship	Port of Arrival Destination	Relations	References
676	Hector		24/7/1815 1817	?Borve ?William Tell	?Sydney Bras d'Or	S: 304, 627; B: 567, 661, 882	CBLP, 2008; BPR
677	Hector		?1818	Barra	SE Mabou	H: 477; F: 545, 569, 682, 742, 829, 970, 982	DW, 8887; MP, 770; HIC, 557
678	Hector		5/5/1817 ?1821	Brevig	Iona	S: 20; B: 533, 697	VM,
679	Hector		c1787 >1826	?Barra	Cape Dauphin		RM, 28/6/98
680	Hector	Donald		Barra	Cape George, NS	S: 642; B: 521, 541, 585, 643, 764, 863, 899	DW 8866; HCA,333
681	Hector		c1815	Barra	Cape Breton		VM, 1/5/2003
682	Hugh	Hector	?1818	?Barra	Mabou	S: 477, 677; B: 545, 569, 742, 829, 970, 982	DW, 8887; MP, 770; HIC, 557
683	Hugh	Malcolm	23/7/1823 1828	Sandray	?Cape Breton	S: 792, 844; B: 655, 889	NMD, 13/7/1828; BPR
684	Ian		1799	Barra	Pictou Iona	H: 19; F: 715	ACIH, Intro
685	Ian	Rory	?1802	Fuday	Cape Breton	S: 951; B: 609	CM, 2001
686	Ian	Rory	1813	Barra	Barra Glen	S: 349, 954; B: 547, 561, 622, 733, 787, 823, 955, 973, 978	ACIH, 1
687	Isabel	Rory	3/2/1835	Allasdale	Rear Big Pond	D: 184, 968; Z: 649, 766, 850	NCTC; BPR; VM, 29/4/2004
688	Isabella	Murdoch	26/2/1815 1817	Rulios ?William Tell	?Sydney Red Island	D: 281, 867; Z: 565	CBLP, 1754; BPR
689	James		?1802	Barra Hector	Big Beach	S: 817; B: 552, 608, 656, 818	MCI, 164
690	James		1802	Barra ?Hector	?Pictou Big Beach	H: 555; F: 526, 616, 721, 822, 904	MCI, 173
691	James	Hector	c1798 ?1802	Barra ?Hector	?Pictou Grand Narrows	S: 197, 671; B: 558, 657	MCI, 44; VM 12/10/2004
692	James		>1803	Barra	N Mabou Harbour		CBLP, 99; SICB, 183

MACNEIL

ID	Name	Father	D.o.B	D.o.E	Origin	Ship	Port of Arrival	Destination	Relations	References
693	James		1813		Barra			Big Beach	S: 549, 969; B: 505, 562, 623, 734, 853, 854, 879, 910	ACIH, 29
694	James		21/9/1807	1816-26	Barra	Sandray		Goose Island	S: 550, 811; B: 563, 624	CBLP, 3145; BPR
695	James	Neil	1817		Borve		Pictou	Nova Scotia	H: 1016; F: 529	NSGP, 7,7; BPR
696	James	Malcolm	15/5/1806	?1817	?Hellisay	William Tell		Castle Bay	B: 516, 566, 903	CMC, 29,4,6-11
697	James		19/10/1819	?1821	Brevig			Iona	S: 20; B: 533, 678	VM,
698	James	Charles	c1801	1821	Borve				S: 837; B: 509, 535, 572, 573, 594, 745	BPR; CNS, 1871; CBCD; NAS, CS44, Bx446; VM
699	James	Peter	15/4/1824	>1830	Pabbay			Rear Big Beach	S: 578, 912; B: 520, 891	MCI, 171; BPR
700	James			>1838	Barra			Benacadie		NSLP, 1838
701	James	John	5/6/1844	1850-51	Tangusdale	Lord Nelson	Quebec	Brantford, Ontario	S: 756; B: 638, 757, 803, 846, 938	KM, 9/2/2000; BPR
702	James	Rory			Barra			Cape Breton	S: 965; B: 639, 761, 848, 897	MCI, 180
703	James	Alex			Barra			Mabou	S: 62, 496; B: 586, 648, 765, 808, 971	DW, 8855; MP, 767; HIC, 557; CBC, 1818; BPR
704	James	Ian			Barra			Big Pond	B: 636, 871, 890, 962	ACIH, 155; BSGN; VM
705	James	Jonathon	c1782		Barra			Big Pond	H: 809; F: 542, 588, 651, 707, 770, 901, 943; B: 936	ACIH, 115; BPR; CNS, 1871; VM, 29/4/2004
706	Jane		1790		Barra	Queen		PEI, Grand River W		PAPEI, 2353, 24-25
707	Jane	James	6/6/1822			Glen		Big Pond	D: 705, 809; Z: 542, 588, 651, 770, 901, 943	ACIH, 115; BPR; CNS, 1871; VM, 29/4/2004
708	Jean	Hector	1/6/1808	1817	Kilbar	?William Tell	?Sydney	Mabou	D: 674, 986; Z: 929, 981	CBLP, 2232; CM; BPR
709	Jennie/Jane	John	c1830	>1848	Barra			Margaree	Z: 937	KMH, 25/7/2003
710	Jessie		1802		Barra	?Hector	Pictou	Christmas Island	W: 611	MCI, 165

MACNEIL

ID	Name	Father	D.o.B D.o.E	Origin Ship	Port of Arrival Destination	Relations	References
711	John		>1785	Barra			MHA, 1,122
712	John 'Brown'		>1785	Barra	Cape George, NS		HCP, app. D; MHA, 62
713	John 'Breac'		>1789	Barra	Malignant Cove, NS		MHA, 62; AHM, MF44/54/720
714	John	John B	c1794 1794-1801	Barra	Malignant Cove, NS Red Islands	S: 590, 771; B: 503	VM
715	John	Ian	1799	Barra	Pictou Iona	S: 19, 684	ACIH, Intro
716	John		1799	Barra	N Side, Narrows	F: 717	GALLEY, VI,25,13-14
717	John	John	1799	Barra	N Side, Narrows	S: 716	GALLEY, VI,25,13-14
718	John		1800	Barra	Little Judique		CBLP, 100
719	John 'Mor'	Rory	>1801	Barra		S: 947; B: 504, 523, 601, 607, 836, 948	BPR; EBPR; VM
720	John	Donald	1802	Barra ?Hector	?Pictou Christmas Island	S: 610, 820; B: 493, 515, 597, 772, 819, 909, 952	MCI, 192
721	John	James	1802	Barra ?Hector	?Pictou Big Beach	S: 555, 690; B: 526, 616, 822, 904	MCI, 173
722	John	Hector	1802	Barra Hector	Pictou Piper's Cove	S: 670; B: 527, 557, 617, 784, 796, 953	HB, 474; MCI, 114; BCB
723	John	Hector	1802	Barra Hector	Pictou Grand Narrows		MCI, 147
724	John 'Black'		>1803	Barra	N Mabou Harbour		CBLP, 101; SICB, 183
725	John 'Brown'		>1803	Barra	N Mabou Harbour		CBLP, 101A; SICB, 183
726	John 'Jnr'		1780-81 >1804	Barra	NE Narrows		CBLP, 517; SICB, 183; DW3, 1208
727	John		>1804	Barra	?Pictou Grand Narrows		DW, 7520; MNB, 95; SICB, 183
728	John		c1785 1805	Barra	Bras d'Or		CBLP, 512

MACNEIL

ID	Name	Father	D.o.B D.o.E	Origin Ship	Port of Arrival Destination	Relations	References
729	John		c1765 c1807	Barra	Benacadie Pond		CBLP, 857; SICB, 181; DW, 7521
730	John	Neil	13/10/1807 <1807	Eriskay	Washabuck	S: 399, 877	MCI, 135; BPR
731	John 'Snr'		1755 >1808	?Barra	Little Judique		CBLP, 427; SICB, 183; CCB, 152
732	John 'Snr'		1809	Barra	Judique River		CBLP, 1060
733	John	Rory	1813	Barra	Barra Glen	S: 349, 954; B: 547, 561, 622, 686, 787, 823, 955, 973, 978	ACIH, 1
734	John	Barra	1813	Barra	Big Beach	S: 549, 969; B: 505, 562, 623, 693, 853, 854, 879, 910	ACIH, 29
735	John	Murdoch	2/1/1810 >1816	Vaslain	Near Red Islands	S: 142, 866; B: 857, 919	CBLP, 2238; BPR
736	John 'Red'	Donald	1817	Rulios ?William Tell	?Sydney Big Beach	H: 267; F: 881	MCI, 64, 140; BPR
737	John		1817	Craigston ?William Tell	?Sydney Mabou	H: 475; F: 825	MNB, 206; SICB, 183; CCB, 152; DW, 7522; BPR
738	John		1788 1817	?Borve ?William Tell	?Sydney S Little Mabou Harbour		CBLP, 2236
739	John		1793 1817	?Glen ?William Tell	?Sydney Little Mabou Harbour		CBLP, 2235
740	John	Michael	17/1/1807 1817	Sandray ?William Tell	?Sydney N Mabou Harbour	S: 858, 1023; B: 798	CBLP, 2189; BPR
741	John	Donald	1817	Barra ?William Tell	?Sydney Christmas Island	S: 625, B: 591, 673, 868, 914, 956	MCI, 137; ACIH, 286
742	John	Hector	?1818	?Barra	Mabou	S: 477, 677; B: 545, 569, 682, 829, 970, 982	DW, 8887; MP, 770; HIC, 557
743	John	Murdoch	1821	Barra Harmony	Sydney Gillis Point		ACIH, Intro
744	John	Lachlan	28/7/1815 ?1821	Brevig	Rear Boisdale	S: 528, 779; B: 570, 776, 859	HB, 501; BPR
745	John	Charles	c1799 1821	Borve	Shenacadie	S: 837; B: 509, 535, 572, 573, 594, 698	BPR; CNS, 1871; CBCD; NAS, CS44, Bx446; VM

MACNEIL

ID	Name	Father	D.o.B / D.o.E	Origin / Ship	Port of Arrival / Destination	Relations	References
746	John	Jonathan	27/5/1817 / 1822	/ Pabbay	Piper's Cove	S: 773, 994; B: 575, 838	MCI, 162; BPR
747	John	Rory	>1822	/ Barra	Rear Iona	S: 362, 960; B: 501, 536, 576, 630, 788, 839, 885, 906, 974	ACIH, 194-216; BPR
748	John	James	19/11/1817 / 1823	Tangusdale	Gillis Point		BPR; Iona Cemetery
749	John 'Capt'		c1797 / 1825	/ Barra	Cape Mabou		CASKET, 23/2/1899, 8
750	John		1797 / >1826	/ Barra	New Campbelltown	H: 185	RM, 28/6/1998
751	John	Donald	30/6/1825 / >1826	/ Glen	Rear Goose Pond	S: 178, 635; B: 519, 813	CBLP, 3145; BPR
752	John	Rory	1828	/ Fuday	Irish Cove	H: 350; F: 665, 843, 907	CASKET, 29/8/1901; BPR
753	John	Rory	1/8/1825 / 1832-33	/ Kyles	Christmas Island	S: 964; B: 781	MCI, 179; BPR
754	John		1804 / >1838	/ Barra	Alexander Pond, NS		NSLP, 1838
755	John		>1838	/ Barra	Benacadie		NSLP, 1838
756	John	Angus	18/7/1810 / 1850-51	Allasdale / Lord Nelson	Quebec / Brantford, Ontario	F: 638, 701, 757, 803, 846, 938	KM, 9/2/2000; BPR
757	John	John	16/12/1835 / 1850-51	Tangusdale / Lord Nelson	Quebec / Brantford, Ontario	S: 756; B: 638, 701, 803, 846, 938	KM, 9/2/2000; BPR
758	John		1801 / 1851	Glen / Admiral	Quebec / Stephen, Ontario	H: 487; F: 582, 658, 759, 815, 911, 939	SC, 1851; OC, 1861e, 71; BPR
759	John	John	20/7/1846 / 1851	Glen / Admiral	Quebec / Stephen, Ontario	S: 487, 758; B: 582, 658, 815, 911, 939	SC, 1851; OC, 1861e, 71; BPR
760	John			/ Barra	Iona		ACIH, 164
761	John	Rory		/ Barra	Cape Breton	S: 965; B: 639, 702, 848, 897	MCI, 180
762	John			/ Barra	Pictou	B: 583, 640, 663	ACIH, 164

MACNEIL

ID	Name	Father	D.o.B / D.o.E	Origin / Ship	Port of Arrival / Destination	Relations	References
763	John	Alasdair		Barra		S: 491, 571; B: 510, 512, 654, 807, 862, 898, 918, 975	ACIH, 129
764	John	Donald		Barra	Washabuck	S: 642; B: 521, 541, 585, 643, 680, 863, 899	DW 8866; HCA, 333
765	John	Alex		Barra	Cape George, NS	S: 62, 496; B: 586, 648, 703, 808, 971	DW, 8855; MP, 767; HIC, 557; CBC, 1818; BPR
766	John	Rory	4/9/1828	Allasdale	Mabou	S: 184, 968; B: 649, 687, 850	NCTC; BPR; VM, 29/4/2004
767	John 'Ban'	Rory	c1798	Barra	Rear Big Pond	H: 352; F: 666, 768, 913	BPR; CNS, 1871; VM, 30/4/2004
768	John	John	16/4/1812	Balnabodach	Cape North	S: 352, 767; B: 666, 913	BPR; CNS, 1871; VM, 30/4/2004
769	John			Mingulay	Cape North	H: 993; F: 596, 650, 659, 774, 851, 908, 979	BPR; NCTC; VM, 29/4/2004
770	John	James	23/5/1816	Mingulay	Irish Cove	S: 705, 809; B: 542, 588, 651, 707, 901, 943	ACIH, 115; BPR; CNS, 1871; VM, 29/4/2004
771	John B		c1760 / 1794-1801	Barra	Big Pond	H: 590; F: 503, 714	VM
772	Johnathan	Donald	1802	Barra / ?Hector	Red Islands	S: 610, 820; B: 493, 515, 597, 720, 819, 909, 952	MCI, 192
773	Jonathan	John	1822	Pabbay	?Pictou	H: 994; F: 575, 746, 838	MCI, 162; BPR
774	Jonathan	John		?Mingulay	Benacadie W	S: 769, 993; B: 596, 650, 659, 851, 908, 979	BPR; NCTC; VM, 29/4/2004
775	Jonathan	James	c1822	Barra	Piper's Cove		VM; RCM; RCML
776	Julian	Lachlan	27/8/1806 / ?1821	Brevig	Irish Cove	S: 528, 779; B: 570, 744, 859	HB, 501; BPR
777	Katie	Alex		Barra	Red Islands	D: 494, 976; Z: 495, 544, 546, 644, 780, 849, 864, 900, 942	DW, 8852; MP, 766
778	Lachlan	Roderick	1802	Brevig / Hector	Rear Boisdale	S: 923; B: 553, 667, 795, 922	AR, 9, i, 1-20; DW, 7524; MNB, 206
779	Lachlan		?1821	Brevig	Pictou / PEI, Vernon River	H: 528; F: 570, 744, 776, 859	HB, 501; BPR

MACNEIL

ID	Name	Father	D.o.B D.o.E	Origin Ship	Port of Arrival Destination	Relations	References
780	Lauchlin	Alex		Barra	Mabou	S: 494, 976; B: 495, 544, 546, 644, 777, 849, 864, 900, 942	DW, 8852; MP, 766
781	Laughlin	Rory	7/11/1831 1832-33	Greian	Christmas Island	S: 964; B: 753	MCI, 179; BPR
782	Louisa	Donald	1817	Rulios ?William Tell	?Sydney Washabuck	W: 271	MCI, 63-64, 86; ACIH, 437
783	Malcolm 'Black'		>1785	Barra	Malignant Cove, NS		MHA, 61-2
784	Malcolm	Hector	1802	Barra Hector	Pictou Piper's Cove	S: 670; B: 527, 557, 617, 722, 796, 953	HB, 474; MCI, 114; BCB
785	Malcolm	?Malcolm	<1811	Hellisay	Christmas Island	H: 411; F: 559, 852, 878, 977	MCI, 141; MG, 3/3/2003; BPR
786	Malcolm	Ian 'Ban'	1813	Barra	Barra Glen	H: 823	ACIH, 235
787	Malcolm	Rory	1813	Barra	Barra Glen	S: 349, 954; B: 547, 561, 622, 686, 733, 823, 955, 973, 978	ACIH, 1
788	Malcolm	Rory	>1822	Barra	Rear Iona	S: 362, 960; B: 501, 536, 576, 630, 747, 839, 885, 906, 974	ACIH, 194-216; BPR
789	Malcolm	Neil	c1784 1824	Greian	Cape Breton	S: 35; B: 537, 632, 840, 933	CBLP, 1824; BPR
790	Malcolm		2/2/1810 >1824	Greian	Shenacadie	S: 577; B: 538, 633, 841, 934	CBLP, 3073; BPR
791	Malcolm		c1803 1826	Barra	NW Scotch Narrows		CBLP, 3149
792	Malcolm		1828	Mingulay	?Cape Breton	H: 844; F: 655, 683, 889	NMD, 13/7/1828; BPR
793	Malcolm	Ian	<1830	Barra	MacNeil's Vale		ACIH, 115; BSGN
794	Margaret		1799	Barra	Pictou Iona	W: 606; M: 946	ACIH, Intro
795	Margaret	Roderick	1802	Brevig Hector	Pictou PEI, Vernon River	D: 923; Z: 553, 667, 778, 922	AR, a, I, 1-20

MACNEIL

ID	Name	Father	D.o.B D.o.E	Origin Ship	Port of Arrival Destination	Relations	References
796	Margaret	Hector	1802	Barra Hector	Pictou Piper's Cove	D: 670; Z: 527, 557, 617, 722, 784, 953	HB, 474; MCI, 114; BCB
797	Margaret		1813	Barra	Gillis Point	W: 672; M: 880	ACIH, 86
798	Margaret	Michael	12/3/1809 1817	Sandray ?William Tell	?Sydney N Mabou Harbour	D: 858, 1023; Z: 740	CBLP, 2189; BPR
799	Margaret	Murdoch	1821	Barra Harmony	Sydney Gillis Point		ACIH, 24
800	Margaret	Edward	23/7/1815 <1821	Gortien	Benacadie Glen	D: 305, 653; Z: 810, 834	MCI, 157; BPR
801	Margaret		1821	Gortien ?Harmony	?Sydney Beaver Cove	W: 343; M: 325, 329, 344, 345, 359, 378, 382	MCI, 90; DW2, 6542; BPR
802	Margaret	Roderick	18/12/1824 <1827	Bruernish	Big Pond	D: 219, 936; Z: 580, 660, 814, 842, 886	ACIH, 115; BPR; CNS, 1871; VM, 29/4/2004
803	Margaret	John	12/12/1839 1850-51	Tangusdale Lord Nelson	Quebec Brantford, Ontario	D: 756; Z: 638, 701, 757, 846, 938	KM, 9/2/2000; BPR
804	Margaret	John	24/6/1813 1851	Kentangaval Admiral	Quebec Ontario	W: 430; M: 407, 416, 426	BUCHANAN, 1942, 36-7; BPR; 1851 CENSUS
805	Margaret		1792	Barra	Charlottetown PEI, Indian River, Lot 18	W: 57	DW2, 7550; SPE, 12; PEIC, LOT18, CEM, I, 288
806	Margaret		c1816	Barra	Christmas Island		CASKET 24/10/1901, 5
807	Margaret	Alasdair		Barra	Gillis Point	D: 491, 571; Z: 510, 512, 654, 763, 862, 898, 918, 975	ACIH, 129
808	Margaret	Alex		Barra	Mabou	D: 62, 496; Z: 586, 648, 703, 765, 971	DW, 8855; MP, 767; HIC, 557; CBC, 1818; BPR
809	Margaret		c1786	Barra	Big Pond	W: 705; M: 542, 588, 651, 707, 770, 901, 943	ACIH, 115; BPR; CNS, 1871; VM, 29/4/2004
810	Marian	Edward	9/10/1821 <1821	Nask	Benacadie Glen	D: 305, 653; Z: 800, 834	MCI, 157; BPR
811	Marion	Donald	1816-26	Sandray	Little Bras d'Or	W: 550; M: 563, 624, 694	CBLP, 3145; BPR
812	Marion	Angus	2/6/1816 ?1817	Hellisay	Benacadie	D: 516, 1024; Z: 826	VM 4/4/2003; BPR; CBLP, 1753
813	Marion	Donald	20/6/1823 >1826	Glen	Rear Goose Pond	D: 178, 635; Z: 519, 751	CBLP, 3145; BPR

MACNEIL

ID	Name	Father	D.o.B / D.o.E	Origin / Ship	Port of Arrival / Destination	Relations	References
814	Marion	Roderick	29/3/1820 / <1827	Bruernish	Big Pond	D: 219, 936; Z: 580, 660, 802, 842, 886	ACIH, 115; BPR; CNS, 1871; VM, 29/4/2004
815	Marion	John	13/3/1835 / 1851	Glen / Admiral	Quebec, Stephen, Ontario	D: 487, 758; Z: 582, 658, 759, 911, 939	SC, 1851; OC, 1861e, 71; BPR
816	Marion	Roderick	29/3/1820	Bruernish	Glengarry	W: 326	BPR; VM
817	Mary			Barra		M: 552, 608, 656, 689, 818	MCI, 164
818	Mary		?1802	Barra / Hector	Big Beach	D: 817; Z: 552, 608, 656, 689	MCI, 164
819	Mary	Donald	1802	Barra / ?Hector	?Pictou / Christmas Island	D: 610, 820; Z: 493, 515, 597, 720, 772, 909, 952	MCI, 192
820	Mary		1802	Barra / ?Hector	?Pictou / Christmas Island	W: 610; M: 493, 515, 597, 720, 772, 819, 909, 952	MCI, 192
821	Mary	John	?1802	Barra / ?Hector	?Pictou / Christmas Island	W: 613	MCI, 156
822	Mary	James	1802	Barra / ?Hector	?Pictou / Big Beach	D: 555, 690; Z: 526, 616, 721, 904	MCI, 173
823	Mary	Rory	1813	Barra	Barra Glen	W: 786; D: 349, 954; Z: 547, 561, 622, 686, 733, 787, 955, 973, 978	ACIH, 1, 235
824	Mary	John	c1796 / c1815-20	Barra	Malignant Cove, NS		AHM, D002.219
825	Mary	John	16/12/1816	Craigston / ?William Tell	?Sydney / Mabou	D: 475, 737	MNB, 206; SICB, 183; CCB, 152; DW, 7522; BPR
826	Mary	Angus	7/5/1813	Hellisay	Benacadie	D: 516, 1024; Z: 812	VM 4/4/2003; BPR; CBLP, 1753
827	Mary		?1817	Barra / ?William Tell	?Sydney / Bras d'Or		VM, 7/4/2003
828	Mary	Malcolm	c1792 / ?1817	?Hellisay / ?William Tell	?Sydney / Big Pond	W: 341; M: 930	VM, 7/4/2003; BPR
829	Mary	Hector	?1818	?Barra	Mabou	D: 477, 677; Z: 545, 569, 682, 742, 970, 982	DW, 8887; MP, 770; HIC, 557
830	Mary		?1818	Borve	Little Mabou	W: 388	MP, 727; HIC, 276

MACNEIL

ID	Name	Father	D.o.B / D.o.E	Origin / Ship	Port of Arrival / Destination	Relations	References
831	Mary		1819	Barra	PEI, Prince Co.		DW, 7529; SPE, 39; ISLANDER 3/5/1845
832	Mary	Rory	29/8/1817 / 1821-22	Kentangaval	Shenacadie	D: 957, 1015; Z: 508, 628, 629, 869, 958	MCI, 178; BSGN; BPR
833	Mary		1821	Caolis / Harmony	Sydney / Christmas Island	W: 45; M: 27, 34, 47, 63, 64, 68, 75	MCI, 31
834	Mary	Edward	31/8/1817 / <1821	Kyles	Benacadie Glen	D: 305, 653; Z: 800, 810	MCI, 157; BPR
835	Mary	Neil	?1821	Earsary	Washabuck	W: 316; M: 308, 375	VCDR, 1868; BPR
836	Mary	Rory	c1791 / c1821	Barra	Big Pond	W: 370; M: 295, 317, 326, 361; D: 947; Z: 504, 523, 601, 607, 719, 948	BPR; EBPR; VM
837	Mary		1821	Borve	Sydney / Shenacadie	M: 509, 535, 572, 573, 594, 698, 745	BPR; CNS, 1871; CBCD; NAS, CS44, Bx446; VM
838	Mary	Jonathan	15/12/1819 / 1822	Pabbay	Piper's Cove	D: 773, 994; Z: 575, 746	MCI, 162; BPR
839	Mary	Rory	15/2/1808 / >1822	Vatersay	Rear Iona	D: 362, 960; Z: 501, 536, 576, 630, 747, 788, 885, 906, 974	ACIH, 194-216; BPR
840	Mary	Neil	c1784 / 1824	Greian	Cape Breton	D: 35; Z: 537, 632, 789, 933	CBLP, 1824; BPR
841	Mary		3/10/1812 / >1824	Greian	Shenacadie	D: 577; Z: 538, 633, 790, 934	CBLP, 3073; BPR
842	Mary	Roderick	23/8/1816 / <1827	Bruernish	Big Pond	D: 219, 936; Z: 580, 660, 802, 814, 886	ACIH, 115; BPR; CNS, 1871; VM, 29/4/2004
843	Mary	John	16/4/1821 / 1828	Balnabodach	Irish Cove	D: 350, 752; Z: 665, 907	CASKET, 29/8/1901; BPR
844	Mary	Rory 'Snr'	1828	Sandray	?Cape Breton	W: 792; M: 655, 683, 889	NMD, 13/7/1828; BPR
845	Mary	John	15/12/1819 / 1828	Pabbay	Irish Cove		CASKET, 29/8/1901, p5; BPR
846	Mary	John	11/9/1846 / 1850-51	Tangusdale / Lord Nelson	Quebec / Brantford, Ontario	D: 756; Z: 638, 701, 757, 803, 938	KM, 9/2/2000; BPR
847	Mary	Ben		Barra	Rear Big Beach	W: 894	MCI, 171

MACNEIL

ID	Name	Father	D.o.B D.o.E	Origin Ship	Port of Arrival Destination	Relations	References
848	Mary	Rory		Barra	Cape Breton	D: 965; Z: 639, 702, 761, 897	MCI, 180
849	Mary	Alex		Barra	Mabou	D: 494; Z: 495, 544, 546, 644, 777, 780, 864, 900, 942	DW, 8852; MP, 766
850	Mary	Rory	16/1/1831	Allasdale	Rear Big Pond	D: 184, 968; Z: 649, 687, 766	NCTC; BPR; VM, 29/4/2004
851	Mary	John	1/11/1815	Mingulay	Irish Cove	D: 769, 993; Z: 596, 650, 659, 774, 908, 979	BPR; NCTC; VM, 29/4/2004
852	Mary	Malcolm	c1788	Hellisay	Big Pond	D: 785	VM; CASKET 14/7/1891
853	Mary (I)	Barra	1813	Barra	Big Beach	D: 549, 969; Z: 505, 562, 623, 693, 734, 854, 879, 910	ACIH, 29
854	Mary (II)	Barra	1813	Barra	Big Beach	D: 549, 969; Z: 505, 562, 623, 693, 734, 853, 879, 910	ACIH, 29
855	Mary*		c1791	Barra	Georgeville, NS		AHM, D001.77
856	Matthew		>1785	Barra	Malignant Cove, NS		LLSNS; HCP, app D
857	Michael	Murdoch	6/6/1815 >1816	Vaslain	Near Red Islands	S: 142, 866; B: 735, 919	CBLP, 2238; BPR
858	Michael		1787 1817	Sandray ?William Tell	?Sydney N Mabou Harbour	H: 1023; F: 740, 798	CBLP, 2189; BPR
859	Michael	Lachlan	13/8/1808 ?1821	Brevig	Rear Boisdale	S: 528, 779; B: 570, 744, 776	HB, 501; BPR
860	Michael	Murdoch	1821	Barra Harmony	Gillis Point		ACIH, 24
861	Michael	John 'Ban'		Barra	Grand Narrows		CNS, 1871; MCI, 151
862	Michael	Alasdair		Barra	Gillis Point	S: 491, 571; B: 510, 512, 654, 763, 807, 898, 918, 975	ACIH, 129
863	Michael	Donald		Barra	Cape George, NS	S: 642; B: 521, 541, 585, 643, 680, 764, 899	DW 8866; HCA,333
864	Michael	Alex		Barra	Mabou	S: 494; B: 495, 544, 546, 644, 777, 780, 849, 900, 942	DW, 8852; MP, 766

MACNEIL

ID	Name	Father	D.o.B / D.o.E	Origin / Ship	Port of Arrival / Destination	Relations	References
865	Murdoch		>1785	Barra	Malignant Cove, NS		LLSNS; HCP, app D
866	Murdoch		>1816	Vaslain	Near Red Islands	H: 142; F: 735, 857, 919	CBLP, 2238; BPR
867	Murdoch		1817	Rulios	?Sydney / Red Island	H: 281; F: 565, 688	CBLP, 1754; BPR
868	Murdoch	Donald	1810-11 / 1817	Barra / ?William Tell	?Sydney / Washabuck	S: 625, B: 591, 673, 741, 914, 956	MCI, 137; ACIH, 286
869	Murdoch	Rory	1821-22	?Berneray	Shenacadie	S: 957, 1015; B: 508, 628, 629, 832, 958	MCI, 178; BSGN; BPR
870	Murdoch	Neil	c1825	Borve	Scotch Hill		HIC, 375; BPR
871	Murdoch	Ian	<1830	Barra	PEI	B: 636, 704, 890, 962	ACIH, 115; BSGN
872	Murdoch		1834/1835	?Tangusdale	Iona		ICR 10/10/1909; BPR
873	Neil	?Donald	>1785	Barra	Cape George, NS		MHA, 122
874	Neil 'Ban'		1802	Barra / ?Hector	?Pictou / Coopers Pond	H: 524	MCI, 161; ?CBLP, 325
875	Neil		c1770 / 1802	Barra / ?Hector	?Pictou / PEI, Lot 19		WMGN, 5/2003
876	Neil		1793 / 1802	Barra / ?Hector	?Pictou / Mabou		DW 8924; MP, 754; HIC, 601
877	Neil	John 'Piper'	<1807	Barra	Washabuck	H: 399; F: 730; B: 625, 670, 949	MCI, 135; BPR
878	Neil	Malcolm	6/8/1806 / <1811	Hellisay	Christmas Island	S: 411, 785; B: 559	MCI, 141; MG, 3/3/2003; BPR
879	Neil	Barra	1813	Barra	Red Point	S: 549, 969; B: 505, 562, 623, 693, 734, 853, 854, 910	ACIH, 29
880	Neil	Hector	1813	Barra	Gillis Point	S: 672, 797	ACIH, 86
881	Neil	John	15/10/1814 / 1817	Rulios / ?William Tell	?Sydney / Big Beach	S: 267, 736	MCI, 64, 140; BPR
882	Neil	Donald	1/9/1808 / 1817	?Borve / ?William Tell	?Sydney / Bras d'Or	S: 304, 627; B: 567, 661, 676	CBLP, 2008; BPR

MACNEIL

ID	Name	Father	D.o.B D.o.E	Origin Ship	Port of Arrival Destination	Relations	References
883	Neil	Alexander	2/2/1817 1817	Brevig ?William Tell	?Sydney Barra Straits	S: 507, 568; B: 915	BPR; CBLP, 2229
884	Neil	Murdoch	1821	Barra Harmony	Sydney Gillis Point		ACIH, 24
885	Neil	Rory	>1822	Barra	Rear Iona	S: 362, 960; B: 501, 536, 576, 630, 747, 788, 839, 906, 974	ACIH, 194-216; BPR
886	Neil	Roderick	29/12/1821 <1827	Bruernish	Big Pond	S: 219, 936; B: 580, 660, 802, 814, 842	ACIH, 115; BPR; CNS, 1871; VM, 29/4/2004
887	Neil		<1827	Barra	Red Islands	H: 543; F: 888	CNS, 1871; RCM; RCML; VM
888	Neil	Neil	c1827 <1827	?Barra	Red Islands	S: 543, 887	CNS, 1871; RCM; RCML; VM
889	Neil	Malcolm	2/6/1822 1828	Sandray	?Cape Breton	S: 792, 844; B: 655, 683	NMD, 13/7/1828; BPR
890	Neil	Ian	<1830	Barra	Washabuck	H: 446; B: 636, 704, 871, 962	ACIH, 115
891	Neil	Peter	24/1/1822 >1830	Sandray	Rear Big Beach	S: 578, 912; B: 520, 699	MCI, 171; BPR
892	Neil		<1840	Barra	Grand Narrows		DW, 8928; HNS, iii, 319
893	Neil	Alex	02/02/1817	Brevig	Goose Pond	S: 498, 564; B: 917	DW2, 7486; SICB, 182; CBLP, 1752; BPR
894	Neil	Michael		Barra	Rear Big Beach	H: 847	MCI, 171
895	Neil 'Ban'			Barra	Christmas Island	F: 896	MCI, 179
896	Neil	Neil		Barra	Christmas Island	S: 895	MCI, 179
897	Neil	Rory		Barra	Cape Breton	S: 965; B: 639, 702, 761, 848	MCI, 180
898	Neil	Alasdair		Barra	MacNeil's Vale	S: 491, 571; B: 510, 512, 654, 763, 807, 862, 918, 975	ACIH, 129
899	Neil	Donald		Barra	Cape George, NS	S: 642; B: 521, 541, 585, 643, 680, 764, 863	DW 8866; HCA,333

MACNEIL

ID	Name	Father	D.o.B	D.o.E	Origin	Ship	Port of Arrival	Destination	Relations	References
900	Neil	Alex			Barra			Mabou	S: 494; B: 495, 544, 546, 644, 777, 780, 849, 864, 942	DW, 8852; MP, 766
901	Neil	James	14/6/1824		Gortien			Big Pond	S: 705, 809; B: 542, 588, 651, 707, 770, 943	ACIH, 115; BPR; CNS, 1871; VM, 29/4/2004
902	Norman		1802		Barra	?Hector	?Pictou	Cape Breton		BCB; ?CBLP, 424
903	Norman	Malcolm	6/8/1806	?1817	Hellisay			Arichat, NS	B: 516, 566, 696	VM, 7/4/2003
904	Patrick	James			Barra		?Pictou		S: 555, 690; B: 526, 616, 721, 822	MCI, 173
905	Paul	Murdoch	1821		Barra	Harmony	Sydney	Gillis Point		ACIH, 24
906	Paul	Rory	>1822		Barra			Rear Iona	S: 362, 960; B: 501, 536, 576, 630, 747, 788, 839, 885, 974	ACIH, 194-216; BPR
907	Paul	John	4/11/1816	1828	Fuday			Irish Cove	S: 350, 752; B: 665, 843	CASKET, 29/8/1901; BPR
908	Paul	John	10/7/1812		Mingulay			Irish Cove	S: 769, 993; B: 596, 650, 659, 774, 851, 979	BPR; NCTC; VM, 29/4/2004
909	Peggie	Donald	1802		Barra	?Hector	?Pictou	Christmas Island	D: 610, 820; Z: 493, 515, 597, 720, 772, 819, 952	MCI, 192
910	Peggy	Barra	1813		Barra			Big Beach	D: 549, 969; Z: 505, 562, 623, 693, 734, 853, 854, 879	ACIH, 29
911	Peggy	John	c1842	1851	?Glen	Admiral	Quebec	Stephen, Ontario	D: 487, 758; Z: 582, 658, 759, 815, 939	SC, 1851; OC, 1861e, 71; BPR
912	Peter		>1830		Pabbay			Rear Big Beach	H: 578; F: 520, 699, 891	MCI, 171; BPR
913	Phil	John	4/11/1816		Barra			Cape North	S: 352, 767; B: 666, 768	BPR; CNS, 1871; VM, 30/4/2004
914	Philip	Donald	1817		Barra	?William Tell	?Sydney	Castle Bay	S: 625; B: 591, 673, 741, 868, 956	MCI, 137; ACIH, 286
915	Rachel	Alexander	10/2/1814	1817	Brevig	?William Tell	?Sydney	Barra Straits	D: 507, 568; Z: 883	BPR; CBLP, 2229
916	Rachel		1822		Brevig		Sydney	Boisdale	W: 511; M: 574, 920, 959	HB, 481; BPR

MACNEIL

ID	Name	Father	D.o.B D.o.E	Origin Ship	Port of Arrival Destination	Relations	References
917	Rachel	Alex	10/02/1814	Brevig	Goose Pond	D: 498, 564; Z: 893	DW2, 7486; SICB, 182; CBLP, 1752; BPR
918	Rachel	Alasdair		Barra	Beaver Cove	D: 491, 571; Z: 510, 512, 654, 763, 807, 862, 898, 975	ACIH, 129
919	Ranald	Murdoch	18/10/1812 >1816	Vaslain	Near Red Islands	S: 142, 866; B: 735, 857	CBLP, 2238; BPR
920	Ranald	Allan	11/2/1808 1822	Allasdale	Boularderie	S: 511, 916; B: 574, 959	HB, 481; BPR
921	Roderick		>1785	Barra	Malignant Cove, NS		MHA, 61-2
922	Roderick 'Og'	Roderick	1777 1801	Brevig Dove	Pictou PEI, Vernon River	S: 923; B: 553, 667, 778, 795	AR, 9, i, 1-20; DW2, 7552
923	Roderick	Gilleonan	c1740 1802	Brevig Hector	Pictou PEI, Vernon River	F: 553, 667, 778, 795, 922	AR, 9, i, 1-20;
924	Roderick	Neil	1802	Barra Hector	Pictou Mabou		DW, 8932; MP, 754
925	Roderick		<1805	Barra	Narrows		DW2, 7536; ICB, 184
926	Roderick		c1787 1805	Barra	N Side, Narrows		SICB, 184; CBLP, 620
927	Roderick		>1809	Barra	S Bras d'Or		CBLP, 513
928	Roderick		c1805 ?1817	?Hellisay	Grand Narrows		VM, 7/4/2003
929	Roderick	Malcolm	12/4/1806 1817	Eoligary ?William Tell	?Sydney Mabou	S: 674, 986; B: 708, 981	CBLP, 2232; CM; BPR
930	Roderick	Hector	31/3/1815 ?1817	Skallary ?William Tell	?Sydney Big Pond	S: 828	VM, 7/4/2003; BPR
931	Roderick		c1789 1817	?Barra ?William Tell	?Sydney Little Bras d'Or		CBLP, 1755
932	Roderick		1824	Barra	S Little Bras d'Or	F: 518	CBLP, 3258
933	Roderick	Neil	c1784 1824	Greian	Cape Breton	S: 35; B: 537, 632, 789, 840	CBLP, 1824; BPR
934	Roderick		28/5/1819 >1824	Greian	Shenacadie	S: 577; B: 538, 633, 790, 841	CBLP, 3073; BPR

MACNEIL

ID	Name	Father	D.o.B D.o.E	Origin Ship	Port of Arrival Destination	Relations	References
935	Roderick 'Jnr'		1771 1826	Barra	NW of Narrows		CBLP, 3149; NMD, 13/7/28; DW, 7539
936	Roderick	Jonathon	c1799 <1827	Bruernish	Big Pond	H: 219; F: 580, 660, 802, 814, 842, 886; B: 705	ACIH, 115; BPR; CNS, 1871; VM, 29/4/2004
937	Roderick	John	22/7/1822 >1848	Berneray	Margaree	B: 709	KMH 25/7/2003; BPR
938	Roderick	John	30/4/1849 1850-51	Tangusdale Lord Nelson	Quebec Brantford, Ontario	S: 756; B: 638, 701, 757, 803, 846	KM, 9/2/2000; BPR
939	Roderick	John	c1842 1851	?Glen Admiral	Quebec Stephen, Ontario	S: 487, 758; B: 582, 658, 759, 815, 911	SC, 1851; OC, 1861e, 71; BPR
940	Roderick		c1817	Barra	Little Bras d'Or		DW, 7537; ICB, 184
941	Roderick		1802	Barra	Lower Washabuck		ICR
942	Roderick	Alex		Barra	Mabou	S: 494, 976; B: 495, 544, 546, 644, 777, 780, 849, 864, 900	DW, 8852; MP, 766
943	Roderick	James	12/7/1812	Mingulay	Big Pond	S: 705, 809; B: 542, 588, 651, 707, 770, 901	ACIH, 115; BPR; CNS, 1871; VM, 29/4/2004
944	Rory 'Breac'		>1785	Barra	Cape George, NS		MHA, 122
945	Rory 'Ban'		>1791	Barra	Malignant Cove, NS		HCA, 61
946	Rory 'Mor'	Donald	1799	Barra	Pictou Iona	S: 606, 794	GALLEY, VI, 25, 15; SCP, 5-6
947	Rory 'Breac'		c1765 >1801	Barra	Christmas Island	F: 504, 523, 601, 607, 719, 836, 948	BPR; EBPR; VM
948	Rory	Rory	c1798 >1801	?Barra		S: 947; B: 504, 523, 601, 607, 719, 836	BPR; EBPR; VM
949	Rory	John 'Piper'	1802	Barra ?Hector	?Pictou Piper's Cove	B: 625, 670, 877	MCI, 118; SRE, 83
950	Rory		1802	Barra ?Hector	Pictou Christmas Island	H: 525	MCI, 163-4
951	Rory		?1802	Fuday	Cape Breton	F: 609, 685	CM, 2001

MACNEIL

ID	Name	Father	D.o.B	D.o.E	Origin	Ship	Port of Arrival	Destination	Relations	References
952	Rory	Donald	1802		Barra	?Hector	?Pictou	Castle Bay	S: 610, 820; B: 493, 515, 597, 720, 772, 819, 909	MCI, 192
953	Rory	Hector	1802		Barra	Hector	Pictou	Piper's Cove	S: 670; B: 527, 557, 617, 722, 784, 796	HB, 474; MCI, 114; BCB
954	Rory	Donald	1813		Barra			Barra Falls	H: 349; F: 547, 561, 622, 686, 733, 787, 823, 955, 973, 978	ACIH, 1
955	Rory	Rory	1813		Barra			Jamesville	S: 349, 954; B: 547, 561, 622, 686, 733, 787, 823, 973, 978	ACIH, 1
956	Rory	Donald	1817		Barra	?William Tell	?Sydney	Castle Bay	S: 625; B: 591, 673, 741, 868, 914	MCI, 137; ACIH, 286
957	Rory	Malcolm		1821-22	Berneray			Shenacadie	H: 1015; F: 508, 628, 629, 832, 869, 958	MCI, 178; BSGN; BPR
958	Rory	Rory	16/9/1819	1821-22	Kentangaval			Shenacadie	S: 957, 1015; B: 508, 628, 629, 832, 869	MCI, 178; BSGN; BPR
959	Rory	Allan	1822		Brevig			Boisdale	H: 15; F: 500; S: 511, 916; B: 574, 920	HB 481; BPR
960	Rory 'Red'			>1822	Vatersay			Iona	H: 362; F: 501, 536, 576, 630, 747, 788, 839, 885, 906, 974	ACIH, 194-216; BPR
961	Rory 'Ban'			<1830	Barra			Antigonish, NS		DW, 8934; HCA, 216, 372
962	Rory	Ian		<1830	Barra			Big Pond	B: 636, 704, 871, 890	BSGN; ACIH, 115
963	Rory			<1830	Barra			PEI, Georgetown		SGSH, 251
964	Rory		c1788		Barra			Christmas Island	F: 753, 781	MCI, 179; BPR
965	Rory 'Big'	Donald		1832-33	Barra			Cape Breton	F: 639, 702, 761, 848, 897	MCI, 180
966	Rory				Barra			Benacadie	H: 540	MCI, 179
967	Rory	Roderick	c1802		Kilbar			Boisdale	B: 548, 641, 980	HB, 515

MACNEIL

ID	Name	Father	D.o.B D.o.E	Origin Ship	Port of Arrival Destination	Relations	References
968	Rory 'Ban'			Barra	Rear Big Pond	H: 184; F: 649, 687, 766, 850	NCTC; BPR; VM, 29/4/2004
969	Sara		1813	Barra	Rear Big Beach	W: 549; M: 505, 562, 623, 693, 734, 853, 854, 879, 910	ACIH, 29
970	Sara	Hector	?1818	?Barra	Mabou	D: 477, 677; Z: 545, 569, 682, 742, 829, 982	DW, 8887; MP, 770; HIC, 557
971	Sara	Alex		Barra	Mabou	D: 62, 496; Z: 586, 648, 703, 765, 808	DW, 8855; MP, 767; HIC, 557; CBC, 1818; BPR
972	Sarah		1802	Barra ?Hector	?Pictou Troy	W: 235	CMC, 29,4,6-11
973	Sarah	Rory	1813	Barra	Barra Glen	D: 349, 954; Z: 547, 561, 622, 686, 733, 787, 823, 955, 978	ACIH, 1
974	Sarah	Rory	>1822	Barra	Gillis Point	D: 362, 960; Z: 501, 536, 576, 630, 747, 788, 839, 885, 906	ACIH, 194-216; BPR
975	Sarah	Alasdair		Barra	Gillis Point	D: 491, 571; Z: 510, 512, 654, 763, 807, 862, 898, 918	ACIH, 129
976	Sarah	Laughlin		Barra		W: 494; M: 546, 777, 780, 864, 942	DW, 8885; MP, 767; HIC, 557; CBC, 1818; BPR
977	Sarah	Malcolm	c1795	Hellisay	Big Pond	W: 607; D: 785	EBPR; VM
978	Stephen	Rory	1813	Barra	Barra Glen	S: 349, 954; B: 547, 561, 622, 686, 733, 787, 823, 955, 973	ACIH, 1
979	Stephen	John	18/12/1822	Mingulay	Irish Cove	S: 769, 993; B: 596, 650, 659, 774, 851, 908	BPR; NCTC; VM, 29/4/2004
980	Thomas	Roderick	c1806	Kilbar	Boisdale	B: 548, 641, 967	HB, 515
981	William	Hector	9/10/1813	Kilbar ?William Tell	?Sydney Mabou	S: 674, 986; B: 708, 929	CBLP, 2232; CM; BPR
982	William	Hector	?1818	?Barra	Mabou	S: 477, 677; B: 545, 569, 682, 742, 829, 970	DW, 8887; MP, 770; HIC, 557

MACPHEE

ID	Name	Father	D.o.B D.o.E	Origin Ship	Port of Arrival Destination	Relations	References
983	Allan			Barra Harmony	Sydney Shenacadie	B: 996, 1000, 1003	MCI, 197-8
984	Angus	John	13/2/1815 1821	Earsary Harmony	Sydney Shenacadie	S: 444, 1000; B: 989, 991, 998, 999, 1009	MCI, 197; BPR
985	Angus	Roderick	14/9/1821	Kentangaval	Boisdale	S: 587, 1011; B: 988	VM, 1/5/2003; BPR
986	Ann		1817	Kilbar ?William Tell	?Pictou Mabou	W: 674; M: 708, 929, 981	CBLP, 2232; CM; BPR
987	Ann	John	1821	Earsary Harmony	Sydney Shenacadie	W: 454; M: 405	MCI, 64, 105; BPR
988	Ann	Roderick	14/11/1819	Kentangaval	Boisdale	D: 587, 1011; Z: 985	VM, 1/5/2003; BPR
989	Anne	John	c1810-12 1821	Earsary Harmony	Sydney Shenacadie	D: 444, 1000; Z: 984, 991, 998, 999, 1009	MCI, 197; BPR
990	Annie			Barra	Washabuck	W: 432; M: 391, 419, 436, 447, 448, 453, 458, 461	SCP, 15; ACIH, 487-8
991	Archibald	John	31/12/1805 1821	Earsary Harmony	Sydney Shenacadie	S: 444, 1000; B: 984, 989, 998, 999, 1009	MCI, 197; BPR
992	Catherine	?Donald	c1786 ?1821	Nask	Christmas Island	M: 294, 307, 320, 358, 374	VM 24/4/2003, 1/5/2003; BPR
993	Catherine			Mingulay	Irish Cove	W: 769; M: 596, 650, 659, 774, 851, 908, 979	BPR; NCTC; VM, 29/4/2004
994	Christian	Rory	1822	Pabbay	Piper's Cove	W: 773; M: 575, 746, 838	MCI, 162; BPR
995	Christian	Malcolm	26/6/1822 <1824	Mingulay	Rear Beaver Cove	D: 465, 1004; Z: 997, 1001, 1002, 1010	MCI, 196; BPR
996	Donald		1821	Barra Harmony	Sydney Shenacadie	B: 983, 1000, 1003	MCI, 197
997	Donald	Malcolm	10/2/1818 <1824	Mingulay	Irish Cove	S: 465, 1004; B: 995, 1001, 1002, 1010	MCI, 196; BPR
998	Ewen	John	10/4/1808 1821	Earsary Harmony	Sydney Shenacadie	S: 444, 1000; B: 984, 989, 991, 999, 1009	MCI, 197; BPR
999	Jane	John	25/11/1809 1821	Earsary Harmony	Sydney Shenacadie	D: 444, 1000; Z: 984, 989, 991, 998, 1009	MCI, 197; BPR

MACPHEE

ID	Name	Father	D.o.B / D.o.E	Origin / Ship	Port of Arrival / Destination	Relations	References
1000	John		1821	Earsary / Harmony	Sydney / Shenacadie	H: 444; F: 984, 989, 991, 998, 999, 1009; B: 983, 996, 1003	MCI, 197; BPR
1001	John	Malcolm	28/8/1819 <1824	Mingulay	Sydney Mines	S: 465, 1004; B: 995, 997, 1002, 1010	MCI, 196; BPR
1002	John	Malcolm	<1824	?Mingulay	Benacadie Glen	S: 465, 1004; B: 995, 997, 1001, 1010	MCI, 196; BPR
1003	Johnathan		1821	Barra / Harmony	Sydney / Shenacadie	B: 983, 996, 1000	MCI, 197
1004	Malcolm 'Binn'	John	<1824	Mingulay	Rear Christmas Island	H: 465; F: 995, 997, 1001, 1002, 1010	MCI, 196; BPR
1005	Margaret	Donald	c1794 1820-21	Kentangaval	Boisdale	W: 13; M: 11	BPR; VCDR; VM
1006	Margaret	Donald		?Kentangaval	Iona		VM, 1/5/2003
1007	Marion		1817	Kilbar / ?William Tell	?Sydney / Barrachois	W: 460; M: 387, 402, 422, 433, 441	HB, 375; CBLP, 2219; SICB, 175;
1008	Mary		1821	Allasdale / Harmony	Sydney / Christmas Island	W: 376; M: 284, 309, 321, 380	MCI, 64; BPR; HB, 335, 351
1009	Mary	John	c1810-12 1821	Earsary / Harmony	Sydney / Shenacadie	D: 444, 1000; Z: 984, 989, 991, 998, 999	MCI, 197; BPR
1010	Niel	Malcolm	14/8/1824 <1824	Mingulay	Shenacadie	S: 465, 1004; B: 995, 997, 1001, 1002	MCI, 196; BPR
1011	Roderick	Donald		Kentangaval	Boisdale	H: 587; F: 985, 988	VM, 1/5/2003; BPR

MACPHERSON

ID	Name	Father	D.o.B / D.o.E	Origin / Ship	Port of Arrival / Destination	Relations	References
1012	Angus	Neil		Barra	Red Islands	B: 1013, 1017, 1018	CNS, 1871; VM 12/10/2004
1013	Christy	Neil	22/11/1814 >1838	Bruernish	Red Islands	Z: 1012, 1017, 1018	CNS, 1871; VM 12/10/2004
1014	Elizabeth		1826	Vatersay	Red Island	W: 244; M: 245, 253, 264, 280	MCI, 84
1015	Marion	Rory	1821-22	Berneray	Shenacadie	W: 957; M: 508, 628, 629, 832, 869, 958	MCI, 178; BSGN; BPR

MACPHERSON

ID	Name	Father	D.o.B D.o.E	Origin Ship	Port of Arrival Destination	Relations	References
1016	Mary	Roderick	1817	Borve William Tell	Pictou Nova Scotia	W: 695; M: 529	NSGP, 7,7; BPR; DW, 7514
1017	Michael	Neil	c1810 >1839	Bruernish	Red Islands	B: 1012, 1013, 1018	CNS, 1871; VM 12/10/2004
1018	Murdoch	Neil	1802 >1832	Bruernish	Red Islands	B: 1012, 1013, 1017	CNS, 1871; VM 12/10/2004

MACSWEEN

ID	Name	Father	D.o.B D.o.E	Origin Ship	Port of Arrival Destination	Relations	References
1019	Catherine	Hugh	16/11/1808 1817	Borve William Tell	Sydney	D: 299, 1021	CBLP, 1766; HB, 541; CM; BPR
1020	Hector		c1797 1817	Barra William Tell	Sydney Boularderie Island		CBLP, 1764
1021	Hugh		c1765 1817	Borve William Tell	Sydney Boularderie Island	H: 299; F: 1019	CBLP, 1766; HB, 541; CM; BPR
1022	James		1792	Barra William Tell	Sydney Boularderie Island		CBLP, 1767

MORRISON

ID	Name	Father	D.o.B D.o.E	Origin Ship	Port of Arrival Destination	Relations	References
1023	Flory		1817	Barra ?William Tell	?Sydney N Mabou Harbour	W: 858; M: 740, 798	CBLP, 2189; BPR
1024	Mary		?1817	Hellisay	Benacadie	W: 516; M: 812, 826	VM 4/4/2003; BPR; CBLP, 1753

MURPHY

ID	Name	Father	D.o.B D.o.E	Origin Ship	Port of Arrival Destination	Relations	References
1025	Donald 'Og'	Joseph		Barra	MacKinnon's Harbour		ACIH, 556

NICHOLSON

ID	Name	Father	D.o.B D.o.E	Origin Ship	Port of Arrival Destination	Relations	References
1026	Alexander	John	1835	Vaslain	Rear Beaver Cove	H: 478; F: 1039; B: 1027	HB, 571; SRE, 69; BPR; MP, 804
1027	Angus	John	?1790	Vaslain	Mabou	H: 167; B: 1026	MP, 418, 804; HIC, 614; BPR; CM
1028	Catherine	Niall	19/11/1819 c1822	Cliad	Boisdale	D: 22, 1042; Z: 1030, 1031, 1034, 1037, 1038, 1040	HB, 577; BPR
1029	Christian	John	28/4/1821 c1821-22	Cliad	Boisdale	D: 534, 1035; Z: 1032, 1033, 1036, 1041, 1043, 1044	HB, 574; BPR

NICHOLSON

ID	Name	Father	D.o.B / D.o.E	Origin / Ship	Port of Arrival / Destination	Relations	References
1030	Christian	Niall	1/3/1815, c1822	Cliad	Boisdale	D: 22, 1042; Z: 1028, 1031, 1034, 1037, 1038, 1040	HB, 577; BPR
1031	Donald	Niall	29/6/1808, c1822	Cliad	Boisdale	S: 22, 1042; B: 1028, 1030, 1034, 1037, 1038, 1040	HB, 577; BPR
1032	Flora	John	c1805, c1821-22	?Cliad	Boisdale	D: 534, 1035; Z: 1029, 1033, 1036, 1041, 1043, 1044	HB, 574; BPR
1033	Ian	John	1802, c1821-22	?Cliad	Boisdale	S: 534, 1035; B: 1029, 1032, 1036, 1041, 1043, 1044	HB, 574; BPR
1034	James	Niall	25/7/1818, c1822	Cliad	Boisdale	S: 22, 1042; B: 1028, 1030, 1031, 1037, 1038, 1040	HB, 577; BPR
1035	John		c1821-22	Cliad	Boisdale	H: 534; F: 1029, 1032, 1033, 1036, 1041, 1043, 1044	HB, 574; BPR
1036	John	John	14/2/1810, c1821-22	?Greian	Boisdale	S: 534, 1035; B: 1029, 1032, 1033, 1041, 1043, 1044	HB, 574; BPR
1037	John	Niall	18/12/1821, c1822	Cliad	Boisdale	S: 22, 1042; B: 1028, 1030, 1031, 1034, 1038, 1040	HB, 577; BPR
1038	John	Niall	6/4/1817, c1822	Cliad	Boisdale	S: 22, 1042; B: 1028, 1030, 1031, 1034, 1037, 1040	HB, 577; BPR
1039	John	Alexander	22/12/1834, 1835	Fuday	Rear Beaver Cove	S: 478, 1026	HB, 571; SRE, 69; BPR; MP, 804
1040	Malcolm	Niall	11/12/1806, c1822	Cliad	Boisdale	S: 22, 1042; B: 1028, 1030, 1031, 1034, 1037, 1038	HB, 577; BPR
1041	Mary	John	3/6/1815, c1821-22	Greian	Boisdale	D: 534, 1035; Z: 1029, 1032, 1033, 1036, 1043, 1044	HB, 574; BPR
1042	Niall		c1822	Cliad	Boisdale	H: 22; F: 1028, 1030, 1031, 1034, 1037, 1038, 1040	HB, 577; BPR
1043	Paul	John	10/11/1818, c1821-22	Cliad	Boisdale	S: 534, 1035; B: 1029, 1032, 1033, 1036, 1041, 1044	HB, 574; BPR
1044	William	John	8/8/1807, c1821-22	Cliad	Boisdale	S: 534, 1035; B: 1029, 1032, 1033, 1036, 1041, 1043	HB, 574; BPR

SHAW

ID	Name	Father	D.o.B / D.o.E	Origin / Ship	Port of Arrival / Destination	Relations	References
1045	Sarah		1817	Balnabodach, ?William Tell	?Sydney, Red Islands	W: 94; M: 87, 88, 90, 95	CCB, 1818; VM, 25/4/03